What stories Joe Nold has to tell! His writings—vivid, heartfelt, elegant—take readers from a hard-times childhood in Canada to adventures around the world, on mountains and boats, and with people so finely drawn, we know them, too.

~ Vicki Meade
Adjunct Professor, writer and editor

Shreds and Patches is a memoir you won't want to miss. Joe Nold has woven the tale of his well-lived life, from his rustic beginnings in rural Canada, to climbing in the shadow of the world's highest summit, to multiple sails across oceans in his small sailboat, Zillah. His writing is skillful, humorous, and honest, and written in a voice best read on a cozy evening by the fire. This is a work of adventure, love, and tragedy, told by a wise and humble story teller.

~ Wendy Sand Eckel
Author, *Death at the Day Lilly Cafe*

Joe's story is a compelling blend: the soul of an adventurer, inspired by an ocean's challenge and a mountain's heights; the heart of a teacher, overflowing with compassion; and the words of a scholar and friend, nestled in gentle humor. His memoir is a joyfull journey, indeed.

~ Denny Kleppick
Author, *Red Sand*

Rarely does one have the great fortune to encounter an adventurer and independent, eloquent, charming writer who weaves a tale worthy of Hemingway but with the dramatic story pacing of Ludlum, and the deeply relevant and revealing descriptions and literary references of T.S. Eliot.

Joe Nold's memoir (and life) contains all the elements of a blockbuster film: a summer bicycle road trip that moves into travels across the United States and then to cargo ships through the Panama Canal and then into his sailing adventures. Gangsters, illegal trafficking, pirates, and mountain climbing combine with delicious descriptions in a story that has the reader breathless while also pondering the elements that made this remarkable man and the significant contributions he made throughout his life journey.

Anyone who reads the first pages will want to read the rest.

~ Mary Bargteil
Author, *Rayleigh Scattering*

"My travels are my home," writes Joe Nold in the Prologue to his compelling book, *Shreds and Patches: A Traveler's Memoir.* A consummate traveler (more than 30 countries on five continents), astute observer, and unflinching reporter of events in his life, Nold's book will appeal to a wide range of readers—adventurers, armchair travelers, social historians, and anyone who appreciates a well-crafted sentence. "A wandering minstrel I," is the book's epigram. While many people wander, very few write about their wanderings as impressively as Nold does.

~ Susan Moger
Author, *Of Better Blood*

An extraordinary life put to pages. Joe takes us on an exhilarating journey; drawing us in to his own joyful soul. We become his new crew, experiencing all the exotic surroundings through his humor, curiosity, bravery and occasionally, the slightest suggestion of naughty.

~ Terese Schlachter
Documentary Producer and Writer

Many may think they have lived an interesting life, but few have been so adventurous as Joe Nold. From climbing some of the highest and technically challenging peaks on four continents, to sailing across oceans, Nold takes us far and wide as he recalls the characters and challenges he embraced along the way of a well-lived life. An ardent observer of the mundane, but fascinating details of daily life, Joe brings a tremendous detail and veracity to his story telling that puts the reader right in the scene. There are moments in time of our shared history, from the Great Depression of the 1930s onward to the present day, that only he has captured with such beautiful prose. An excellent read for adventurers, historians, sailors, climbers, aviators and in fact anybody looking for a great yarn!

~Jon Coile
Author, *Adventures in the Ditch*

Shreds and Patches

Shreds and Patches

A Traveler's Memoir

Joe Nold

To Pat and Noel with great appreciation Joe + Mary

Shreds and Patches
A Traveler's Memoir

Copyright © 2017 by Joe Nold

First Edition

Printed in the United States

Dedicated to Mary and Jennifer

And in Memory of Margaret and Andy

A wandering minstrel I —
A thing of shreds and patches,
Ballads, songs and snatches,
And dreamy lullaby.

~ W.S. Gilbert

Table of Contents

Acknowledgements

I would like to thank those who were instrumental in getting this book published. Vicki Meade, my memoir-writing teacher at St. John's College, introduced me to her writing group. She and the other group members, Mary Bargteil, Jon Coile, Wendy Eckel, Denny Kleppick, Susan Moger, and Teresa Schlacter, supported me with their helpful critiques and unwavering encouragement. Jon and Vicki solved the difficulties of getting the book published, which seemed insurmountable to me, by simply taking over the job. I'd also like to thank those who read my stories and gave me their comments and support over the years, including Jay Shine and Ann Bissell. My wife, Mary, read the stories many times, unlocked some of the mysteries of computer use for me, did lots of copy-editing, and provided time and space for me to write.

From my boyhood years, I acknowledge my parents, Otto Nicholas and Mary Edesse Nold, who gave me life but died too young. Mary Therese Weisgerber nursed and nurtured me when my own mother was unable to do so. My half-brother, Mickey, in spite of being 15 years my senior, was my pal until he left for the Navy. My teachers in Fife Lake, Miss McLeod, Miss Paisley, and Father Beudreau, gave me a love of learning and served as role models for my future career, although none of us realized it at the time. After my father died when I was 13, my foster parents, Harry and Mary Millar, and their sons, Jack and Perry, welcomed me into their family and did more for me than I can tell.

At St. Andrews College, my boarding school near Toronto, I met Don Shaw; he and I have been friends for 75 years and counting. He and his wife, Ursula, and his children, Sabrina, Ramine, Zaria, and Irving, count me as part of their clan. From the St. Andrews years I also remember Gordon Taylor, my English teacher who introduced me to the riches of literature, and Joan Ellis, my first love, who made me wish I had a sister.

From my University of British Columbia years I thank Rod Nixon, fellow traveler and adventurer. What seeds we planted together for our future lives.

During my teaching and travels after graduation, there are so many to remember and acknowledge. At Shirley House School in London, Langley Walter and "Housie" Housemann. At the Eskdale Outward Bound School, Eric Shipton. At Gordonstoun School in Scotland, Henry Brereton, George Campbell, Roy McComish, and the permeating influence of Kurt Hahn, although he had retired from Gordonstoun by the time I taught there. Hahn's philosophy and theories of education were tremendous, lasting influences on me. Andy Clelland, whose death on a mountain still haunts me. I am grateful to and treasure the memory of my first wife and fellow teacher, traveler, and climber, Andrea Lynd Nold. At the Doon School in India, John Martyn, and at the Lawrence School, also in India, Shomi Das. On later summer projects in India, Gulab Ramsanjani was helpful.

How do I begin to thank all those from my years with Outward Bound? Trustees at Colorado Outward Bound School (COBS): Bill Coors, Ruth Brown, Frank Isenhart, Chuck Froelicher, Dr. Ben Eisley, Bob Colwell, and Bill Purdy. Outstanding

COBS instructors and leaders of adaptive programs in schools included George McLeod, Gary Templin, Jed and Perry Williamson, Herb Kincey, Alistaire MacArthur, Jerry Golins, Marlene Manown, Tap Tapley, Terry Burnell, Roy Smith, Paul Sanders, George Sebert, Steve Truitt, Bob Elliot, Emil Zeigler, Junior Weed, Scott Hartl, Reola Phelps, Ron Gager, Bill Forrest, Vic Walsh, Rusty Bailey, John Braman, Andy Arnold, Gordon Mansell, Bob Godfrey, John Evans, and Chris George. Betty Austin-Ware and Maria Weber provided important office leadership. Students too numerous to mention inspired me with their growth in character, leadership, and love of the wilderness. At the Banff Center, John Amatt, Layne Longfellow, Ted Mills, and Jim Gray. With Expeditionary Learning OB, Greg Farrell; with OB USA, Bill Phillips; at Hurricane Island OB, Peter Willauer; OB International, Ian Wade and Derek and Pat Pritchard.

At the United World College in New Mexico, my thanks to Tom Lamberth and Cheryl Burlett, Ted and Lou Lockwood, Howie and Elinor Muir, Andrew and Heather Maclehose, Theresa Beaumont, Neil Hunter, Bruce Ives, Peter Hammer Hodges, Lawrence Tharp, Matt Willen, Hannah Tyson, John Jeffroy, Ann Sawyer, and hundreds of bright, enthusiastic students from countries around the world.

From my sailing years aboard Zillah I'd like to acknowledge the contributions of John Anderson, who converted a boatyard derelict into a beautiful wooden sloop, Helen and Jenny Russell, Roy Hartjen, Brian Sullivan, Jen Nold and Johan Hovelynck, Margaret Nold and Olaf Podehl, Roger Brown, Peter Willauer, Scott Hartl, and my wife and intrepid sailor, Mary Moore. Cruising sailors comprise a far-flung but close community, and I remember many of them fondly: Denise Ward and Frank Hemmert, Marion and Paul Fishman, Michael Comparone, Beryl and Garth Alden, Rob and Jean Stephenson, Mandy and Rob Carpenter and their kids Rachel and Peter, Puck and Chili Rolff, Birgith and Ole Brynildsen, Bronwyn Sims, Toennies Maack and Dennis, and Maria and Peter Korpel. And, of course, Biber and Celia.

I apologize to those who helped to make my life so rich but whose names are lost in nooks and crannies in my brain.

Shreds and Patches

Prologue

I am a part of all that I have met.

~ *Ulysses*, Tennyson.

"Where are you from?" That oft-asked question is hard for me to answer. I don't really have a sense of place, of belonging to any one location. Having grown up in the Dust Bowl of the Canadian prairies during the Great Depression, losing my mother as a child and my father as a teenager, the concept of home does not resonate with me.

I have lived or traveled in more than thirty countries on five continents. I've crossed the Atlantic in a sailboat both ways with my wife Mary, and daughters, Jennifer and Margaret. I've paddled a canoe through the sub-arctic to James Bay, slept in an abandoned Greek monastery at the foot of Mt. Olympus, drunk *Chang* — barley beer — with Buddhist monks in the remote Himalayas. I have lost my way on the Incan Trail in Peru, seen the sun rise on Mt. Kilimanjaro, been followed by Tito's secret police in Yugoslavia. My first sight of the Canadian Rockies was from the top of a freight car, and I've heard loons calling on northern lakes, seen rainbows in the mist flowing into the Grand Canyon. Buried pirate treasure beckoned me to a Pacific island off Central America. I've read Homer's Odyssey while at anchor at Ithaca, listened to Mozart's Requiem in the cathedral in Vienna, basked in the rich glow of the stained glass windows of Chartres cathedral, scorched my bare feet on the sun-baked marble courtyard of the Taj Mahal.

Where's my home?

My travels are my home.

Part One – Prairie Prelude

Chapter 1: A Question of Identity

"Who are you?"

In the fall of 1981 I returned to the prairie village in South Saskatchewan where fifty-two years before, I was born. I entered the Fife Lake Hotel and Cafe and was confronted by a heavy set man, wearing blue denim bib overalls and a green John Deere baseball cap.

Good question, I thought. Wasn't this why I made this journey? But I felt he was less interested in my existential search for identity, than in genealogical fact. I was between careers, between marriages, between travels, and felt life's certainties shifting beneath me. In my early fifties, I felt my best years were past, but still had a few years before me. Could a return to my past inform my deliberations about my future?

I saw him smile.

"Why don't you guess?" I said.

"You from here?" he asked.

"Born here," I said.

"In town or the country?" he said.

"In town."

"You a Beauchamp?" Beauchamp was a pudgy, unsmiling Frenchman, proprietor of one of the grocery stores.

"No."

"A Larson?" I didn't remember who Larson was. He must have been after my time, I thought.

"No," I said.

The men in the back of the restaurant, old men with weathered faces, gathered around us. They were retired farmers, pensioners with time on their hands, living off their Canadian government welfare checks.

"He's a Hostin," one of them said. When my father sold out in 1942, Jules Hostin bought the business.

"Nah. He's not a Hostin," the man in the overalls said.

"Are you a Dufour?" Walter Dufour had been my father's business partner, Nold-Dufour Company Inc., General Store, Hardware, International Harvester dealer, the building next door.

"You're getting close," I said, marveling that the name was still part of living memory.

"You're a Nold!" he declared.

"You're right," I said.

"Hot damn," he chuckled and reached out a broad calloused hand that smothered mine and shook vigorously. "Gotcha. In five tries."

I must be home, I thought. Where else would a stranger know me in five guesses?

Joe as a small boy in Fife Lake, circa 1931.

Chapter 2: To Return To the Beginning

"Window seat or aisle?" the ticket agent asked. I sit by the window. Always do when I have a choice. The aisle seat makes me feel like the prisoner in the tower. I seek out the spectacular view from the window. This is the seat that God would choose had he booked passage on Air Canada. Zeus surveyed the panorama every day as he looked down on the world from Olympus. Except when he was brewing up another thunder storm. For me, looking down on the prairie stirred the sense of return, of coming back. I felt a strong tug.

I was struck by the immensity, an endlessness to the flat prairie stretching so far in the distance that I felt I could see the curvature of the earth. It stirred again that yearning of my childhood, always wondering what was beyond the horizon. And wondering. Would I ever dare to go there?

"Fasten your seat belts." We descended into Regina. At the lower altitude, I realized the geometry of the countryside, roads and property lines running due north-south, unerring east-west. Euclid had prevailed. There was an order, a neatness, a symmetry that was comforting and reassuring. Man bringing order to Nature.

But as a mountaineer I experienced this as a conflict. Symmetry represented control, regimentation, exploitation. Stifling. Certainly the prairies had been exploited. Blake wrote of fearful symmetry. This was the paradox I have struggled with much of my life, the moral dilemma, the tension between freedom and discipline, Give me land, lots of land/ Under prairie skies above/ Don't fence me in, we had sung as children.

Aground. As I walked to the terminal I thought of pilgrims arriving in the Holy Land, kneeling and kissing the tarmac. I didn't feel I had to go that far. Not even for Saskatchewan. But the thought did make me realize that I had come back. But back to what? I was an experienced traveler. But this was different. Here I was a stranger in my own land. This was a journey into another unknown, a journey into the interior, my own. I thought I knew why I had come, but did not know what I expected to find.

I rented a car and drove south on Saskatchewan Highway 2, a straight unswerving line from Moose Jaw. A roadside plaque informed me this was the route of the old cattle drive to Denver in the last century. I'd just come from Denver. At 60 miles an hour on a paved road, the telephone poles flashed by with hypnotic regularity.

The harvest was already in and stubble fields glowed golden bright in the low slanting November sun, just as I remembered late fall. But what I had not remembered was how the landscape was dominated by the sky. If I had painted it, eighty percent of my canvas would be sky. Cloudless sky. This was a dimension of the prairie that went beyond Euclidean geometry. The essence of the prairie was more abstract, something algebraic perhaps, where X was an unknown. Mystical even. It isn't accidental that monotheism was spawned by Semites in the desert. The prairie I knew as a child during the long drought of the thirties had been a desert.

Farms buildings were enclaves that stood out like islands of humanity in the ocean of the Great Plains. More prosperous than I remembered, modern ranch houses were dwarfed by the old traditional high pitched red barns. Next to them were aluminum-sided sheds as large as warehouses that stored immense machines. This was something new. Trees - maple, cottonwoods, elm - stood tall, as stately as sentinels sheltering the settlement. The Saskatchewan of my childhood had been a treeless plain.

Several miles on I stopped at a crossroads, arrested by a cluster of weathered buildings. They stood abandoned, the walls leaning, roofs sagging, the doors and windows boarded up. I felt a stab of recognition, regret. This process had already begun when my father and I fled Saskatchewan in 1942. Saskatchewan was the only province in Canada with fewer people in the eighties than it had in the thirties. Was this what I should expect in Fife Lake?

A road branched, the main road continuing south to Rockglen, the other to Willow Bunch, both villages about twenty miles from Fife Lake. Which do I take? Like Robert Frost, I took the one least traveled by, that led to Willow Bunch. I'm not sure why, but it did make a difference. Willow Bunch was the oldest village in this region, founded in the 1880's, pre-railroad, a French Canadian trading center for Metis, mixed Indian-French-Scots trappers and buffalo hunters. I remembered it being prosperous, by prairie standards, even during the Depression. Situated in a sheltered valley with trees, it had flowing springs even in the big drought. I remembered driving by Willow Bunch with my father on our exodus.

It had survived, thrived. When I saw the neon motel sign, I drove in. I wasn't sure I would find accommodation in Fife Lake. I began to have serious doubts that there would be a Fife Lake. I studied the road map again. It showed a lake marked Fife Lake but not a village.

That evening I strolled about Willow Bunch along the creek under with sagging branches of the tall willow trees. A beautiful village, it seemed vaguely familiar. Eerily so. It never occurred to me to question why. I began to assure myself that this journey was worthwhile, even if I found Fife Lake no longer existed.

In bed that night I reread Pallister's account of his survey of this region for the British Government in 1857. He saw the country as unfit for human habitation, suitable only for buffalo and nomadic savages. That did little to reassure me.

It had been a long day and I began to doze off. It was only then, in my half-sleep that I realized why I felt drawn to Willow Bunch. I knew that my father had been the Saskatchewan Provincial Police constable here, and my mother the primary school teacher. But I had never made the obvious connection. They must have been married here.

Nor had the deeper truth occurred to me. I must have been conceived here, here in Willow Bunch. That woke me up. That wasn't something I could prove. But the evidence seemed overwhelming. Could it be that in their troubled lives they too had known nights of ecstasy? I found this difficult to imagine. I realized that this was taking me further back in my search for roots than I had anticipated. I recalled the lines from T. S. Eliot, "To return to the beginning and to know it for the first time."

My father never spoke to me of Willow Bunch, nor of his days as a policeman. He never spoke of my mother. His past was a closed book. Now I was trying to pry it open.

Chapter 3: A Prairie Pilgrimage

"What the anvil? What the chain?
In what furnace was thy brain?"

Blake again. I slept poorly that night. In the morning I drove on the paved highway south from Willow Bunch. I had known it as a graded dirt track. I was already past the side road when I noticed the sign.

Stop. It was as of I had been summoned. I stopped and turned around. The sign read: Liseux and pointed west. I remembered this as the way we used to go. I headed down on the gravel road toward Liseux.

If I was right, in ten miles I'd come to the Eger farm. That's where I'd turn south to Fife Lake. Sure enough, there it was, the large red barn with John Eger and Sons emblazoned on the high front. Next door was the spacious two-story white house. The Egers were relatively prosperous farmers even in the Depression of the thirties. Occasionally my father, Granny Schneider and I would be invited to Sunday dinner after mass. I remembered dinners there, the refectory table heaped with smoked ham, mashed potatoes, carrots fresh from the garden, hand-churned ice cream, and several sons with voracious appetites.

At the Eger farm I turned south to Fife Lake. A mile down the road, the command again. STOP. What was it this time? Only then I realized that a mile down the road to the west was the Weisgerber farm.

The Weisgerber farm. How could I forget? When I was born, my mother had suffered severe depression, a mental breakdown, later called post partum stress syndrome. She was committed to the Weyburn Mental Hospital where she spent the next two years. I was farmed out to Mrs. Weisgerber. She was a sturdy, loving woman, had given birth to eleven children, eight of whom survived. The same month of my birth, Rosemary Weisgerber was born and shared with me her mother's ample bosom. She nursed me like one of her own for the next two years.

I turned back a second time. The old homestead still stood, now abandoned. The barn roof sagged, grey weathered boards dangled loose. Rusty machinery littered the yard: plows, seed drills, binders, an old threshing machine. Only the farm house was intact, though the doors and windows were boarded up. The family home had been shored up and used as a grain storage bin.

I squinted through the cracks in the boarded up door. Kernels of wheat and mouse droppings littered the floor. Light filtered through the broken shingles, reflecting off motes of suspended dust. Pink wallpaper with a floral design peeled from a bedroom wall. I couldn't hold back my tears. It struck to the core of the feelings of abandonment I carried with me through life.

I had returned to Fife Lake in search of roots. This was deeper than I had anticipated, and as I delved into them, they went deeper yet. How do I unravel the twisted strands of those first two years? In one sense, I'd spent my life doing just that, trying to resolve the contradictions in my life: the need to be nurtured and admired, yet shunning lasting friendships, an ambivalence that began in this house, now-derelict. The past isn't dead, Faulkner wrote, it isn't even past.

I drove slowly back up the road between stubble fields. On the hilltop I noticed out of the corner of my eye, a small fenced-in plot where the buffalo grass grew tall. I passed by and turned south on the road to Fife Lake. Stop! That inner voice again. For the third time, I turned around and went back. I climbed over the barbed wire fence and crossed the field to the fenced-in plot.

I waded through the waist-high grass and came upon five flat granite slabs. One read:

At rest
Our Beloved Mother
Maria Theresa Weisgerber
June 28, 1882-January 29, 1954

She had summoned me from the grave. I had not remembered her having such a commanding voice, but as a mother of eight she knew how to make herself heard. I sensed she just wanted to give me her blessings.

I find many things hard to say. For me this is what prayer and poetry are for, to help bridge the emotional gap. It had been years since I had kneeled in prayer. That morning I prayed. "Hail Mary, full of grace..."

My mother, Mary Edesse Muise, had given me the gift of life. Maria Theresa Weisgerber had kept me alive. Another Mary would nurture me in my aging years.

I took one last look at the abandoned homestead below me. Beyond a patch work quilt of the yellow stubble and brown plowed fields spread to the horizon. Fences lines and telephone poles faded in the distance. The sky was an open vault, a light hazy blue, like a Renaissance painting. The tall grass shimmered in the wind and the fence murmured with a low hum. OMM. What had begun as a journey had become a pilgrimage.

I drove on to Fife Lake, wondering what vestiges of the past would confront me there.

Graveyard where Mary Theresa Weisberger (1882-1954) is buried, which Joe found on his visit to Fife Lake in 1981. She took care of him during his first two years of life.

Chapter 4: Return of a Native

Breathes there a man, with soul so dead,
Who never to himself hath said,
This is my own, my native land!
Whose heart hath ne'er within him burn'd
As home his footsteps he turn'd
From wandering on a foreign strand!

~ Sir Walter Scott

Fife Lake lay in a shallow saucer shaped basin between low lying hills. As I dropped over the brow, the three grain elevators rose into view, stark vertical box cylinders erect against a horizontal landscape, like light houses, beacons of the prairie. Fife Lake was still there, and I was back.

Driving into the village, I felt like the lone cowboy in a Western movie riding up a deserted street in a strange town, uncertain of his welcome. Several buildings were gone, conspicuous by their absence like missing front teeth. I saw that the old boardwalk had been replaced by concrete sidewalk. The two room school house where I attended elementary school was still there, but not the Catholic Church, where I had served as an alter boy.

The railway station house that squatted next to the train tracks was missing. MacLean's grocery store, where the post office had been, was still there, painted a vivid green. Beauchamp's store sign was faintly readable beneath a layer of peeling paint. Newly painted green and yellow bungalows had sprung up between grey weathered buildings, and aluminum-sided mobile homes sat immobilized on concrete blocks. In vacant lots rusting farm machinery was entangled in tall prairie grass and vigorous weeds.

It was the magnificent cottonwoods that presented the most spectacular change. They spread an umbrella of shade across Main Street. I had known only scraggly saplings, their growth stunted by years of drought. I felt we had all been scraggly saplings.

My father had owned the hardware store on the corner. It was still there, smaller and squatter than I remembered, the windows boarded up. Curtains were drawn over the windows in the room above. That's where I was born. If there were any lingering ghosts they remained embedded in the weathered woodwork. At least for now.

I pulled up my rental car next to a white pickup in front of the adjoinin g two-story building. It was the biggest remaining building on the street with the grandiose high false front of a saloon in a Western movie. It had been freshly painted. The plastic Coca Cola sign that glowed above the door announced it to be the Fife Lake Hotel and Restaurant. An obvious place for a wayfarer to stop. I was blasted by country western music as I entered. Molson's Ice flashed in neon above the bar.

Young men in blue jeans, wearing hard hats, Saskatchewan Power and Electric, sat at the bar drinking beer from bottles and munching burgers, engulfed by the pungent smell of frying onions. A cluster of older men huddled in a large booth in the back, nursing cups of coffee. I did not recognize anyone. A stranger in my own land. I had the thought that my father too would have been a stranger in a setting like this.

A no-nonsense waitress in a white blouse and a checkered apron took my order. As a child there had been three grandiose buildings similar to this one. Now only one remained on the street. Which one was it? My father had owned one of them. t Could this be it?

"Has this building always been the Fife Lake Hotel?" I asked the waitress when she brought me beer.

"You'll have to ask Mr. Harkness over there," she replied.

I approached Mr. Harkness, the man in the John Deere cap. "Has this building always been the Fife Lake Hotel?" I asked.

"Who are you?" he said, ignoring my question. In five guesses he blew my cover. He introduced himself as Audrey Harkness, the proprietor. Then he went to the telephone and like the village crier he made the rounds of the community. "Come on down. Julian Nold is back in town." Julian was my middle name, my mother had endowed upon me.

After the crops are in, not too much happens in Fife Lake. The return of a native son was an occasion for celebration.

"Was this the old Fife Lake Hotel?" I asked Harkness again.

Oral history embodies the story of the past among the old people on the prairie.

"No," Harkness said, "Pete Seigo owned the first Fife Lake Hotel and Beer Parlor." I remembered that Peter Seigo had been our next door neighbor when we lived above the hardware store. He was outspoken, pompous, pugnacious. You had to be to run a beer parlor, I figured.

"When Seigo sold out, my father bought up the beer license and tore the building down," Harkness said. "The building we're in now had been George Buie's Chinese Restaurant. You remember George Buie, the old Chinaman." I did. Who could forget him? Chinese coolies had been brought in to build the Canadian Pacific Railroad in the 1880's. When it was completed they were given a free ticket and they scattered across Canada. Today every Canadian town has its Chinese restaurant.

"He was a tremendous eater, could eat a whole chicken for lunch with a huge bowl of fried rice. Flied lice, he called it. Then he'd take a nap. As kids we'd come in to

12

buy a penny candy, and he'd get so mad at being disturbed that he'd just throw it at us. We'd picked up the candy, keep our pennies and run."

"A notorious gambler, you know," Harkness said. "Chinamen are. He had a fabulous memory. Remembered every card on the table. Seldom lost, but no one ever accused him of cheating. A lot of money changed hands. More than some could afford. It was all illegal, of course, but popular, particularly in the winter when men didn't have much to do."

To eat out in Canada in the thirties, was to eat Chinese, but I never at in George

Buie's Restaurant. Ice cream, yes. And candy. Bu not chop suey. Nor flied lice.

"There's a Chinaman in Coronach, (about 25 miles away,) who says that George is still alive," Harkness said. "Lives in Vancouver. Must be 94. Damn, those Chinamen live a long time."

"The cafe had been vacant so my father bought it and combined the two businesses," Harkness said, "the hotel with the bar and restaurant we have today. I took over when my father died."

"You know why they called it a beer parlor?" he asked. "Because you had to sit down. They wouldn't serve you unless you were sitting down. We didn't have a bar in the early days. You had to sit at a table. And the number of tables permitted depended on the number of beds you had in the hotel. That was the law. Still is. That's why we have more hotels per person than any province in Canada."

"And more bars," one the pensioners said.

"Another first for Saskatchewan," Harkness said.

"Jack Dangerfield still alive?" I asked. He was the village drunk, came to town every couple weeks with horse and buggy, collected his mail, bought groceries and then headed for Pete Seigo's beer parlor. A proper gentleman when sober, he was obnoxious when drunk. A foul-mouth, he'd pick a fight with another drunk and Pete Seigo would throw both of them out. They'd continue brawling outside until Jack passed out. Bloody and bruised, his drinking buddies loaded him in his buggy, unhitch the team and the horses took him home.

"What happened to him?" I asked.

"Eventually he went on the wagon," Harkness said. "Dried out. Made a fortune farming during the war when wheat prices were high. Sold his farm for half a million dollars and retired to California. Dead now."

I'd never seen my father enter Pete Siego's beer parlor, even though it was next door. Nor for that matter George Buie's Chinese restaurant. It made me think, Who were my father's friends? Did he have friends?

My closest friend was Glen Cowan. His father was manager of the Pioneer Grain elevator, one of the best jobs in town. "What happened to Glen?" I asked.

"Glen farms north of Regina. We don't see much of him. But we still see Lloyd, his older brother. He bought up land around here, then moved to Kelowna in British Columbia. Better climate. Farms still. He has his own plane. Flies in for two or three weeks each spring to do the maintenance on his machinery, puts in seed, and then flies back to British Columbia. If we get rain, he gets a crop and flies out again to harvest it. Spends the winter in Arizona. He's done well. Farms five sections of land."

I made a rapid mental calculation. One section of land was one square mile, 640 acres. Five sections was more than 3000 acres. Under the Homestead Act settlers were granted 160 acres, the amount of land it was felt that one family could farm with horse drawn implements. This was what modern farming was about, agribusiness.

"His kids aren't interested in farming. Expect Lloyd will sell out sometime too,"

Harkness said.

"What happened to the Red and White Store?" I asked. This had been the largest store in town. My father bought it in 1939, then sold out three years later to Jules Hostin .

"Hostin sold it too. He was more interested in the International Harvester dealership than running a store. Made a lot of money after the war when farm machinery came on the market again and we everybody switched over to combines," Harkness said.

Pity my father lost out on that, I thought

"Frank Weisgerber bought the building," Harkness said. "Tore it down, hauled the lumber to Assinaboia and built himself a new house with it."

"Frank Weisgerber? That's a coincidence," I said. "I found his mother's grave this morning. She raised me as a baby."

He did not respond. Nor did any of the old men who had gathered around us. I sensed they knew about her but didn't want to discuss it. Mental illness was not something one talked about, as if the victim was to blame. I too avoided it and was glad for the evasion.

My return to Fife Lake had become a journey in a foreign land with Harkness my guide.

Fife Lake as seen in 1981. Joe was born on the second floor of the Fife Lake Hardware building.

Chapter 5: The Perfect Spy

Neighbors gathered at the Fife Lake Cafe that night and we continued to disinter more ghosts. But the ghost I most wanted to summon, that of my father, kept lurking in the wood work. I had never seen him enter Pete Seigo's beer parlor, nor George Buie's Chinese restaurant. I did not associate him with an evening like this. Who were his friends? Did he have friends? His name seldom came up in the banter, lubricated with successive rounds of beer. Was it that they knew how he died, and I avoided talking about it?

Perhaps there wasn't much they could talk about. He never talked to me about himself when he was alive. Was there any reason to assume that he shared more with them? He never spoke of growing up in Russia, coming to Canada, becoming a policeman, hen the village merchant.

Before my visit to Fife Lake I did discover a Rosetta stone to his past. Stuffed at the back of an upstairs closet I came across a battered shoe box held together with an old piece of cord that had survived my moves and travels. It contained old letters, photographs, post cards, mementos. There was the skating medal I had won as a seven-year old, an encased bone fragment, the relic of a saint, that must have belonged to my mother, and her rosary. I had not looked at them for more than twenty years. Then I came upon two documents, the Rosetta Stone of my archive. One was an English translation of my father's Certificate of Matriculation from the Gymnasium, a private male college in the town of Pokrovsk, in the province of Samara, issued by the Ministry of Public Education, for the District of Kasan. He went to a private school? A gymnasium? That was a revelation. This was a typical middle class classical college university preparatory education. Over five years, the transcript recorded, he had studied Russian, Latin, Arithmetic, Algebra, Geometry, Geography, History, Natural History, Physics, French and German. Not much different from my prep school education at St. Andrew's College, thirty years later. His grades varied from excellent in two subjects, good in five, satisfactory in three. Not quite as good as my grades, but then his standards may have been higher. His conduct for the six years was reported as excellent. Better than mine.

This was no peasant's education like most of the other German-Russians who had emigrated from the Ukraine. It was the education of sons of businessmen, professionals, government servants. So why had he come to Canada? Fife Lake, of all places?

I looked more closely at the dates on the document. That gave me the clue. The document I held in my hand had been issued on February 28, 1914. It stated that Otto Nicolas Nold had graduated on November 6, 1913. This was less than four months previously. An accompanying letter stated that the document had been sent in response to a request from Canada dated January 30,1914. I didn't have to be Sherlock Holmes to put the clues together. Matriculated in November 6, 1913 in Russia, already in Canada on January 30, 1914, when he requested a copy of his transcript. Elementary Watson, as Holmes could say.

Within three months of matriculating in Russia, he was already in Canada. Why?

Even Holmes could not answer that. He might have pointed out that the early twentieth century was a time of political unrest in Russia. There had been miner's strikes, student riots, deportations to Siberia, several attempts by anarchists to assassinate the Tsar. Was the family in political difficulty? Had my father been involved in student protests? Whatever the reasons, somebody had thought it best to have him out of harm's way. Certainly it was not the promise of cheap land that drew him to Western Canada. Given this education, he had no practical skills that would be of use on the Canadian frontier.

The concluding paragraph of the document gave me the answer: Otto Nold is being issued with this actual certificate...the right to enter without examination into a corresponding grade of a Government Male College, and the rights regarding Military Service Duties, ... laid out in Chapter 67, Statutes respecting Military Service. So he had the choice. Go to college. Or go into the army. He came to Canada to avoid the draft.

How I wished that I had been old enough to have been curious about his past before he died.

Growing up I had always thought of myself as of Russian descent. But Nold is not a Russian name. It was years before I realized that my father was Russian only by nationality, but by ethnicity. Nold is a German name. His family, like many other German Catholics had come from Alsace, a German-speaking enclave of France. After the Franco-Prussian in 1870, they had emigrated to Russia to escape authoritarian Protestant Prussian rule, specifically to evade compulsory military service under Bismarck.

The liberal Tsar Alexander had promised religious freedom, exemption from military service, and for peasant farmers, cheap land. After he was assassinated his successor, the repressive Tsar Nicholas, withdrew these privileges. The Russian Orthodox Church placed restriction on Roman Catholics, the Cossacks waged pogroms against Jews. This was followed by a massive migration of dissidents, liberals, Jews and Catholics from Russia and Eastern Europe to the Canadian and American West in the decade before World War I.

My fater was a part of this wave. His timing was fortuitous. In August,1914, The Great War war broke out, and whatever remaining connections he might have had with Russia were lost in the turmoil of revolution and social upheaval that followed.

My half-brother Michael, ten years older than me, had been much closer to my father, told me the rest of the story. On the Atlantic crossing he met the Schneiders, another German Catholic family from the Ukraine, also emigrating to Canada. They had two sons, about Otto's age, whom I came to know distantly as Uncle Bernie and Uncle Mike. Their daughter Margaret, five years younger, whom my father later married, was Michael's mother. They landed in Halifax, Nova Scotia, traveled together by train, a journey of 2000 miles, west to Saskatchewan.

A Canadian Pacific Railroad land agent had recommended Preeceville a pioneer village on the prairie that promised cheap land and opportunity. My father discovered that the frontier needed farmers, mechanics and laborers, not Latin scholars. He spoke no English, had no practical skills, was totally misplaced. I doubt if he unpacked his bags, but moved on immediately to Regina, the capital, then a small city 50,000. There he found work, went to church and studied English.

In my shoe box archive I found a letter of reference from Father Aug. Sulla OMJ, a Jesuit priest at St. Mary's Church, Regina, dated October 1, 1915. It reads, I have known Mr. Otto Nold for the last two years...the young man merits the best of recommendations. Another from the Royal Grill in Regina, dated December 18, 1916, stated that he had been in their employ for 8 months, and that he was honest, sober, punctual, attentive to his duties. That sounded like my father.

Then he got a break, a real job. I have a copy of a letter written on Sept 8, 1917 by Constable O.N. Nold, RNWMP, in Estevan, Saskatchewan inquiring about correspondence courses in bookkeeping — stenograph and typist, and Good English. Cut off from further education in Russia, he pursued it in Canada. But more significant about the letter is that it is written by a constable in the RNWMP, the Royal North West Mounted Police. That's the forerunner of the Canadian Mounties.

Dishwasher, waiter in 1916. Though it might have been before. A mounted policeman in 1917. Not a conventional career path. What accounts for the rapid upward mobility?

Michael told me the story. Estevan, in southern Saskatchewan, where he was writing from, sits on an extensive lignite coal bed that stretches across much of the southern part of the province and the western United States. In 1917 Canada was at war and coal was essential to the war effort. Production was being threatened by labor unrest, work slow-downs, the possibility of strikes. Many of the miners were recent immigrants from Central Europe, including Germany, some not sympathetic to the war cause. Given the climate of wartime paranoia, even sabotage was suspected.

Otto was recruited by the RNWMP to go into the coal mines in as a plain clothes constable. He was assigned the job of checker to count the coal cars as they came out of the mine, but more important his job was to keep his eyes open and his ear to the ground and listen for hints of subversive talk. Here Otto's broken English with a thick accent, his German-Russian heritage, his knowledge of several languages, were an asset rather than a liability. He had the perfect qualifications and background. He was the perfect spy.

The following year, Michael told me, he was transferred to Preeceville, where he had stepped off the train only five years previously, now a uniformed Mountie. He met Margaret Schneider again, married her, and in 1919, Michael, my half-brother, was born.

The Saskatchewan Provincial Police were organized in 1921 and Otto joined the service. A couple years ago my daughter Jennifer and I were given access to his confidential service file in the Saskatchewan Provincial Archives. His duties were decidedly less glamorous, largely routine. A disgruntled bootlegger whom he had fined, brought charges that his wares had been wrongfully confiscated and consumed at a staff party. Charges were dismissed by the magistrate.

There were also references to his being granted leave to arrange his wife's funeral. Margaret died after five years of marriage. He was also granted medical leave for treatment of his failing hearing.

I had a photograph of him taken by a professional in the 1920's, posed in the full dress uniform of a constable in the Saskatchewan Provincial Police. He wore a long tight fitting jacket that came down over his thighs, riding breeches that billowed out, knee length riding boots like the Mounties, a leather Sam Brown belt across his chest and around his waist, holstered pistol on his hip. This pistol was to be his undoing. With a flamboyant broad brimmed hat, the brim turned up on one side like the Aussies, he stands in a frontal pose, a striking, gallant figure, fully conscious that the apparel oft proclaims the man.

In 1928 the Saskatchewan Provincial Police was disbanded and he did not re-enlist with the newly formed RCMP, Royal Canadian Mounted Police.

I had never seen him in police uniform. That was not the father I knew as a child. There is another picture of him, a snapshot taken 10 years later, in the 1930's. He's wearing poorly pressed trousers, a dark shirt and narrow tie, a sagging loose fitting woolen gray sweater coat. His left hand was in the side pocket, right hand held a cigarette to his mouth. A Humphrey Bogart fedora, fashionable in the 30's, covered his thinning hair. There was none of the High Noon heroics about the Otto, I knew as a child. He was the model of a drab, small town merchant.

Joe's father, Otto Nicholas Nold.

Chapter 6: Nold-Dufour Co. Ltd.

He escapes Russian tyranny, becomes the marshal who brings law and order to the town, and stays on to become its leading citizen, a story plausible only on the frontier, a classical Out West fantasy. That was my father's story as I saw it as an eight-year old.

The decade following The Great War were halcyon years in the Canadian west. There were good rains for successive years that yielded abundant crops. With the reconstruction of Europe there was a market for wheat. Prices were high. The building of a branch line by the CPR in 1927 south from Moose Jaw toward the Montana border, spurred the opening of new land. Villages like Fife Lake founded along the line.

My father was caught up in the euphoria of the times. The Saskatchewan Provincial Police was disbanded in 1928 and he did not re-enlist in the newly formed Royal Canadian Mounted Police. He became a business entrepreneur, married the village school teacher in Willow Bunch, my mother, and started a second family, me.

In partnership with Walter Dufour, he opened a hardware store and an International Harvester Company farm implement dealership in the newly incorporated Fife Lake. It was a village of three grain elevators, a station house, three grandiose commercial buildings with high false fronts, two churches, a two-room school house, and a population of 130. My birth in 1929 represented a population increase of 0.77 percent.

Walter Dufour, as I remember him, was of a tall, lean, handsome man with angular features, long straight nose, ruddy complexion, a full head of wavy greying hair. He had a ready laugh, and the sort of outgoing bonhomie that, I suspect, led him to closing major business deals in the beer parlor. Not that there would have been many major deals in Fife Lake in the 1930's. I now see him as something of a ladies man, Mrs. Dufour, a long suffering, good looking, gracious woman, mother of two sons who were older than me.

They made good business partners, my father with a Germanic thoroughness, Walter a Gallic flamboyance. Between them they could address most customers in their native tongues. When farmers came to town on mail nights twice a week, I heard German and French spoken as often as English in the store. I picked up smatterings of both. There were three grocery stores in Fife Lake. The hardware store filled a promising market niche.

The building squatted on a prime commercial location at the corner of Main Street, and Railroad Avenue, pretentious names I never heard anyone use. It was just called the corner store. An unadorned square box, painted white, it was two stories high, commercial space was at street level, living quarters above. That's where I was born. On the far side of Railway Avenue was open prairie.

They had placed their hopes primarily on the International Harvester Company dealership. IHC was the largest farm implement company in the United States and Canada. Since Cyrus McCormick had invented the horse drawn reaper in 1840, technology had continued to revolutionize agriculture. In the post-war prosperity, farmers began to replace horses with tractors, reapers with binders. As a child I'd been terrified of the steam engine driven threshing machines that looked like smoke belching dinosaurs. Now these were being replaced by diesel engines.

But in the hard years that followed, nobody could afford them. Most horse power was still generated by horses. "It was hard work but a peaceful kind of farming," one of the old farmers told me that night I visited the Fife Lake Cafe. "With horses you had to give them breaks. So you got a break yourself. But today with tractors you can just keep going sixteen to twenty hours a day. Glad I'm retired."

There had been a bumper wheat crop of 1928, but it had not sold. There was a glut on the market and price of wheat plunged from $1.35 to sixty-five cents a bushel. "Not enough to cover the costs of production," Harkness told me. In 1929, the year Nold-Dufour opened its door, there was another good crop, but the grain elevators were overflowing from the previous year's surplus and the price collapsed even further. "That was the year my father turned the cattle out on the fields," an old pensioner told me.

In October the New York stock market crashed and the world economy collapsed. Then in 1931 the prairies were hit by the drought , the worst in Canadian history that would last for seven years. "Just like in the Bible," the old man said. "We began to think maybe we should be raising cattle the way they used to, rather than trying to grow wheat. But there wasn't much of a market for beef either."

"One year the soil was so dry and the rains came so late, we didn't even bother planting," an old fellow said.

"It's only a recession," A.B. Bennet, the newly elected prime minister of Canada and leader of the Conservative Party, assured the country in 1930. "The down-turn is only a temporary thing. No need to panic." The economy would correct itself. The government should not interfere. Even as factories in the east closed down and 200,000 Canadians were put out of work, the government remained in a state of denial. Bread lines formed. Young men and old knocked on the back door, offering to weed the garden or chop wood for a meal.

No one appreciated the devastation of the prairie west. The Bennet Buggy appeared on the front page of the Regina Leader Post. It was the chassis of a Model-T Ford being pulled by a team of horses. "Can't afford gas," the caption read.

By 1931 it was evident that Nold-Dufour Co. Ltd could not support the two partners and their families. One would have to go.

Chapter 7: My Earliest Memories

My earliest memory. A pudgy three-year-old toddler, still in diapers, waddles across a polished hardwood floor. It is winter and the house, like most in Canada, is overheated. Hot air billows from the basement wood-burning furnace that roars like a dragon, and belches heat through a large metal grill set in the floor. I squat, sprawled on the grill like a Christian saint being martyred. Stabbed by pain, my bare legs scorched by the hot metal, I scream and struggle to push myself up, burning my hands. I sit there howling, terrified. I'm burning up. This is my earliest awareness of hell, an insight reinforced by a Roman Catholic upbringing.

I scream again. My mother, recently released from the mental hospital, hears me and stampedes from the kitchen, her face flushed in anger. "Stop that," she shouts. "You know I can't stand that crying," she screams herself. I'm even more terrified. She yanks me off the grill and spanks me on my blistered bottom.

Then she too breaks into tears, and hugs me. "Oh God, what have I done?" she weeps.

This was my first story where the essence of the plot was an ordeal and ever since I have been a teller of tales.

In 1931, my father had moved to Yorkton, a prosperous town of 5000 in central Saskatchewan near the Manitoba border. With the onset of the Great Depression, the hardware business in Fife Lake could not support both partners. He turned the business over to his partner, Walter Dufour, and found a job himself. The Oliver Implement Company hired him as a collector. Farmers bought machinery on credit, and given the collapse of the market for wheat, could not keep up with their payments. The company foreclosed their loans and repossessed their equipment.

He had the right credentials. Just as he had been the perfect spy fifteen years earlier, he was now the ideal collector. His former training as a policeman gave him the right combination of tact and forcefulness. He also knew the territory, having been a police constable in Preeceville, only fifty miles away from Yorkton.

When we moved from Fife Lake, my mother was released from the Weyburn Mental Hospital, paroled to my father. Paroled. I don't like the word choice, but that was what her release document said. A two-year old, I was wrenched from the protective cocoon of the Weisgerber family. We began family life anew. My father traveled most of the week and was often home only on weekends. I was left to the care of this strange woman, my mother.

Another early memory, my terror of the night. Our Yorkton house was on the corner of Halltain Avenue and Water Tower Street, my room on the second floor on that corner. The flashing headlights of passing cars glowed on the walls of my room and I'd wake to beams of light shooting across the ceiling. Lying in my crib with the sides pulled up, I was locked in. The lights darted across my room, struck the different angles of the dormer, dazzling flashes flew off, out into space. I cried out, screamed, even though I knew that my mother did not like me to scream. But nobody came. My father was away. My devout mother was at another church prayer meeting. She had neglected to tell Shirley, the girl next door, my favorite baby sitter, that she would be out. I cried and cried and exhausted, cried myself to sleep.

I wake still at the owl hours of night with anxious thoughts. Thinking back I am reminded of the line from Samuel Coleridge, a night's dismay that saddened and stunned the coming day.

But by day I was resilient. In a yellowing photograph, a child of four, I am standing in the snow on a Canadian winter's day. I wear a snow suit of knitted wool, off-white, a hole in the right knee, already a thing of shreds and patches. A tight-fitting wool cap is pulled down over my ears, woolen mitts are pinned to my sleeves, a ruddy outdoors man prepared to confront the Arctic cold. And there is that chubby face with a round lunar grin, the smile I'd carry through life, my mask to the world. It's the smile that decades later a detractor will call, "Joe Nold's plastic grin."

Inspecting the picture more closely, I notice that I was wearing ice skates. Not just bob skates, the two-bladed skates for beginners, but real single-bladed ice skates. Growing up in Saskatchewan, learning to skate was merely an extension of learning to walk. I can't recall when I could not skate. Already I had begun to define myself through athletic endeavor.

That day my mother took the picture was one of her good days. In the same bundle of fading photographs is one of her, a young woman bundled in a bulky sweater, wearing a heavy wool skirt that came to her ankles. She stood upright on a barren northern lake bordered by white birch trees. She was alone, her body turned at a slight angle, almost regal in her assurance. She was wearing ice skates. My father growing up in Russia didn't know how to skate, so it is to her that I owe this gift.

In another picture, I was standing on a high chair, my half-brother Mickey stood beside me, a dapper young man of fifteen. My head came to his shoulder. We were both clad in sartorial splendor. Michael wore a navy blazer, stylish tight-fitting slacks, a debonair wool cap worn at a jaunty angle like Mickey Rooney in the old movies. I was wearing long pants even though only five, jacket, shirt and tie. It would be nearly a decade before I was suited so elegantly again. She clearly took pride in her boys. Michael boarded at Campion College, educated and disciplined by the Jesuits. He visited on weekends and vacations. When home he was my great buddy. He held me up on my first pair of ice skates, pulled me around the ice rink with a hockey stick, dragged my sled up Water Tower Hill. He often sheltered me from my mother's violent mood swings.

My mother also insisted that Michael learn to play the piano. He had natural talent, took to it eagerly. Her early lessons laid the foundation for his professional career as a musician, a jazz pianist, clarinet soloist, bandmaster in the Canadian Navy. "I have to thank her for making me stick to it," he would tell me in later years.

She was less successful at evoking the musical muse in me. I remember sitting propped up on a stack of books on the piano stool so that I could reach the piano keys. My mother hovered over me.

"Play it again," she commanded, with the strong implication that I better get it right this time. And I fumbled even more. With each mistake my mother became more impatient. "You're just being inattentive. You're being willfully disobedient," she accused, then rapped my knuckles with a ruler. I cowered, the music now blurred by tears, hit more wrong keys and waited for the next blow.

The spontaneous coordination that translates musical notation on a piece of paper to fingertips on a keyboard eluded me. I never did learn to read music or play an instrument. But my mother's efforts were not in vain. I learned that music was important, and have sat many hours in concert halls, trying to know it better. Though I would agree with Mozart that music is the language of the soul, when I listen to the Jupiter Symphony, I mute the kettle drums. They remind me too much of the percussive crack of a ruler.

First Communion is an important coming of age ritual for Catholics, though the age of five is young. My mother had a sense of urgency about it, a burning concern for my spiritual well-being, my soul. Had she known the life I would lead, she would have felt my soul did need saving. So I was inducted into the ranks of the Christian faith with all the pomp of Roman Catholic ceremony. After taking my first communion, I was expected to repeat the sacrament every Sunday, daily during Lent.

From the beginning my relationship to the church was marred. One is not permitted to eat before experiencing the rapture of the holy wafer. So I went to church without breakfast. Rising early, I'd walk several blocks across town to church in a hypoglycemic state, holding my mother's hand, my stomach growling. Light headed I'd make it through the mass as far as the Agnus Dei Peccata Mundi, Lamb of God, Take Away the Sins of the World, when the candle lights would blur, the organ would go off key, and my ears buzzed with the high-pitched whine of a table saw. Then, as if on cue, there would be a resounding thud, like someone beating a base drum, as my head crashed into the wooden pew in front of me. It happened each Sunday. I began to see it as a part of the mystery of communion, as if God had singled me out for special treatment.

Waking in the arms of my father being carried out of church, I was frightened. My father embarrassed. My mother distraught. Even the long suffering priest became annoyed with this weekly display of misplaced piety. After repeat performances, he suggested that I be given a light breakfast before communion. He granted my bowl of Kellogg's corn flakes a pastoral dispensation. As an adult I still need to bring my blood sugar level up before engaging with the day.

The church was the center of my mother's life. A strict Catholic, she was zealous in her devotions. We attended church with scrupulous regularity every Sunday, on feast days, and daily during Lent. She involved herself in church activities, cut flowers for the altar, organized bake sales for the sacristy, was an officer in the Ladies

Aid Society, attended evening prayer meetings, and religious retreats. A forceful woman, she was given to dynamic bursts of energy. There was a driving compulsiveness to her involvement.

Late November that year, 1934, my mother was taken away. She never came back. I never saw her again. She died a month later in the Weyburn Mental Hospital, suffering from visions of persecution, refusing to eat, doing penance for her perceived sins, diagnosed a schizophrenic. I was left with a gnawing doubt that I was to blame. The priest consoled me, saying I would see her in heaven. But I wasn't sure I wanted to go there.

I was five. I did not cry. Not at the time. But thirty years later, as I read Charlotte's Web to my children, I would cry for the death of a spider.

It was the end my infancy.

Joe's mother, Mary Edesse Nold.

Chapter 8: A Prairie Pilgrimage

I was five when my mother died. Granny and Grandpa Schneider came to live with us. They were the parents of my father's first wife, Margaret, the mother of my half-brother Mickey. She too had died young. In their sixties, they were old for their age. Granny did the housekeeping and put in a garden. Grandpa split the wood for the kitchen stove, and in winter shoveled the walk and stoked the furnace. They put up with my spirited naughtiness with a patient indulgence. While not demonstrative, they were caring in their own gruff, no nonsense, Eastern European way. A quiet calm settled over our home.

My father continued to travel for the Oliver Implement Company which required that he be away much of the time, a lonely life. I suspect he was ambivalent about my mother's death, grieved, but also relieved. Their marriage had not been a happy one. A private man, he kept his feelings to himself. I remember a post-bellum tranquility.

Next year I started school. In the eyes of a six year old, Simpson Primary School was a giant's fortress of greying limestone capped with a bell tower. The first grade classroom was a wooden annex, a one story white clapboard addition tacked on to the main building. My teacher was Miss McLeod, a young pert, pretty, cheerful Scottish lass. Warm hearted and nurturing, she was my first love. My mother had taught me the letters of the alphabet, and with Miss McLeod I was introduced to the magic of words, words that told stories. "Run Dick Run," in *Sally, Dick and Jane*. The resolute and independent Little Red Hen. I'll do it myself, she said. And she did. Good girl, I thought, and turned the page to her next adventure.

We had no books at home. Miss McLeod introduced me to the wider world of children's literature, Hans Christian Anderson and the Brothers Grimm. "Fee fo fi fum, I smell the blood of an Englishmun," she read to us. "The better to see you with," the Big Bad Wolf said. The imagined world of terror and triumph, that helped me better understand my own. And The Ugly Duckling, my favorite fairy tale. I have always wanted to be a swan. I began to fill in the void in my own life with fantasy and stories. In time literature became a guide to reality.

I'd do everything I could to be close to my teacher, to get her attention, pushing and shoving so that she would check my spelling book first. I'd clean the blackboard. I was first to earn a gold star for arithmetic sums. I realize I've spent much of my life trying to be first.

"Good morning Miss Mcleod." I'd hurry to school early to greet her with that big smile. I'd stay late until she sent me home. Throughout life, teachers have been my mentors, schools my haven.

A wider door of competitive activity opened, running, jumping and throwing in the spring track meet, ice hockey on the school yard rink. I won my first medal in the city-wide winter ice skating tournament, a bronze. I joined the Boy Scouts as a Wolf Cub, proud of my green beany cap and kerchief and began to earn merit badges. I have spent much of my life accumulating merit badges.

While I began to move out into a widening world, I was always hesitant, quick to close down in the face of any criticism. I harbored my own secrets. I avoided talking about my mother, and later my father too.

I had even a bigger secret. I wet my bed. It drove Granny Schneider furious. I was lazy and dirty, foul, drechlich, she remonstrated in German. Drechlich sounded so much dirtier than dirty in English. Determined to shame me into abstinence she hung my stained yellow sheets on the clothes line as kids passed by our house on their way to school. She pointed to my disgrace, calling out to them to take note. But she spoke poor English and the children only laughed, not at my pissy sheets but at the gibberish of this ranting old woman. Some of them may have wet their beds too. Eventually she desisted and I went on my nightly immersion in the warm tropical seas of my urine.

But the Depression had begun to cast a pervasive pall of gloom. Strangers, young men, some not so young, would knock on the kitchen door. The jobless and the homeless had taken to road. Embarrassed at having to beg, they asked if they could chop wood, or hoe the garden, do anything for a meal. Granny always cooked an extra portion with evening supper for the uninvited guest. Food was not to be taken for granted. I ate what was put before me, thinking of the poor starving Armenians, as Granny had directed, and was thankful for it.

But I remember a deeper sense of threat. That year schools were closed early, a red placard was posted on a neighbor's door and I was confined to my home. She had scarlet fever and other children might have it too. She might die. The following summer swimming pools were closed and yellow placards posted. A little boy had polio and was crippled. That seemed worse than dying.

Grandpa Schneider, never well, began to fade. His complexion became sallow, his skin turned yellow with a waxy tarnish. He was diagnosed with cancer. He left bloody stools in the toilet and forgot to flush, and that winter he died. The priest said we would meet him in heaven. I thought it must be getting pretty crowded up there.

Very early in life I believed that I would not live long either, a belief confounded by my eighty years. I was in no hurry to go there.

I had moved out, moved out into a wider world, whose horizon would continue to move. Not until I had my own family would home be the center of my universe again.

Joe (on chair) next to half-brother Michael, circa 1934.

Chapter 9: The Worst Hard Times

"The top soil just took off and blew into the Atlantic."

~ The Regina Leader Post.

Nineteen thirty seven was the eighth year of drought on the prairies, the worst year in the Dust Bowl. That was the year my father and I, with Granny Schneider, returned to Fife Lake from Yorkton. I was eight years old.

My father's business partner, Walter Dufour, had found a more promising business opportunity operating a service station in downtown Regina, a prime location at the corner of Victoria and Albert. Otto, my father, came back to rescue the struggling hardware store.

Yorkton is in the parkland region of central east Saskatchewan, a country of scattered fields and open meadows among thin birch trees, poplars, and alders, saskatoon and chokecherry bushes, with ponds and small lakes. Heading south to Fife Lake we drove out of the woods onto the treeless plains, the bald prairie. It was mid-summer and what should have been a landscape of green fields of waving wheat, was a burnt umber brown of shriveled stalks and withered weeds. Whirligigs of dust picked up the tumbleweed and piled it on the fences. The ditches were drifted full with a light powdered dirt.

"Driving from Yorkton to Regina in those days was like going from The Garden of Eden to the Dead Sea," John Diefenbacher, later the prime minister of Canada recalled, Pierre Berton wrote in The Great Depression.

"That was the year the lake dried up," Audrey Harness, the proprietor of the Fife Lake Hotel told me the night of my visit. "It turned into a muddy slew. Cattle bogged down, stuck when they came looking for water. When the mud dried it cracked in big chunks, like a gigantic jigsaw puzzle."

Mid-summer that July the temperature registered 115 degrees at the meteorological station in Bengough, the hottest temperature ever recorded in Canadian history, Pierre Berton reported. That wasn't much more than a hundred miles from Fife Lake,

I remembered that the wind seemed always to be blowing that summer, a hot, dry, itchy wind. The sky was gray, a murky gray. Not cloudy. Just murky. The evening sun set in a pale amber glow that felt ominous.

Granny Schneider scolded me for picking your nose so often. In colloquial German she made it sound even more disgusting.

"But you missed the worst of it." The old survivors in the Fife Lake Cafe gathered around to share their memories. "The big blow that year was earlier, in late June," they told me. "A thick black cloud, came out of the west, five miles high. Churning and boiling, it looked as though a volcano had exploded. I was scared."

"Coming closer, it clawed at the ground, chewed the top soil to dust. The sun disappeared. My father tried to round up the cattle and get them in the barn, but they just went crazy. He yelled at my mother. Get the kids in the root cellar.

"We were smothered by a dark gloom. I couldn't see the house anymore. In the cellar it was so dark that I could barely see my little sister across from me. Everything was silent, hushed, as if the air had been sucked out of the room. Then the storm hit."

"It sounded like a freight train passing, thundering down the track, and rumbling past the station. A high-pitched keening overhead became a fluted moan, as the fury of the wind passed high above. The world went dark. Darkness at noon.

"It blew for hours but gradually the wind faded to a low moan, muffled like new falling snow on a dark night, a black blizzard. The sun set in a brilliant orange glow. I thought of what the preacher had told us about Armageddon, and wondered if this was the end of the world.

"When it was done, we couldn't find the seed drill. It was completely buried. Not that we'd have any need for it that year. My father had to round up the horses and dig out the wagon so we could check on the neighbors."

"Tumble weed was stacked half way up the barn wall. Fences completely drifted over. Cattle wandered all over the place."

"They say four inches of top soil blew away."

"Yes. They're sweeping it up in Toronto and Montreal."

"Father Lisieux, our aging asthmatic Catholic priest couldn't preach his sermon the following Sunday. He had almost died of respiratory arrest."

"After the dust storm the grasshoppers came," Harkness said.

"That was later in the summer. I remember that," I said.

"It was ideal grasshopper hatching weather. The larvae were just sitting there in the ground waiting for it to get hot enough. And they emerged as if on schedule."

I had seen them massed high in the sky, cloud banks of grasshoppers, thick enough to shade the sun. It was like looking at an eclipse through smoked glass, my eyes screened by grasshoppers. Swirling in wide overlapping circles, layers of them drifted slowly east with the wind.

Then they came down. Hordes of grasshoppers rained out of the sky. Main Street was carpeted with a crawling mass of insects. They stripped the leaves from the scrawny cottonwood trees that lined the street, and chewed up the tough buffalo grass on the edge of town. In the fields they devoured what remained of the stunted and shriveled wheat, wantonly chewing off the heads. They sang in a high pitched tinnitus of clicking wings and grating jaws.

Driving with my father in the company truck, grasshoppers pelted the windshield with the rattling staccato of a kettle drum. The crushed bodies clogged the radiator and the truck overheated. We stopped regularly to clean the spattered green slime of crushed bodies.

"We turned the chickens and the turkeys out on the fields," an old survivor told me. "Had a lot of fat roosters that year."

"You remember old man Terachuk who had the turkey farm on the edge of town? He just turned them loose on the fields. They came into town, shit all over the place. But we never had better turkeys for Christmas as that year," my friend Harkness said.

The Biblical analogies were too compelling for Father Liseaux to resist. In his Sunday sermon he compared grasshoppers to the locust plagues in the Bible. A believer in the divine justice of God, the good father told us how God had struck down the Egyptians for their wanton, sinful ways. The inference was clear.

The itinerant protestant minister chose Matthew 3:4 for his text: And his meat was locusts and wild honey, and he told the Methodists that God was putting our faith to the test, and foretold better times. And red-winged blackbirds and the meadowlarks, like John the Baptist, appreciated this bounty.

Then in August it rained. Would you believe it? The thunder clouds mounted a mile high, white billowing, boiling and seething, lightning flashed flinging daggers to ground, the low growling of thunder in the distance, heat lightning bursting in a yellow glow across the horizon. Two inches fell in twenty-four hours.

"What didn't blow away that year, washed away," Harkness said. "It was too late to plant again but we did get a lush crop of tumbling mustard and Russian thistle, about the only thing that would grow on a year like that. We cut it when it's still green and fed it to the cattle. It gave us enough fodder to see a couple milk cows through the winter. We'd been thinking of raising cattle, the way the early ranchers had, instead of gambling on wheat. But there wasn't much money in beef either."

With rain came the hail. I could smell it before I saw it, a cold chill in the air, and then I saw a white sheet swooping down like a falling curtain. People talked of hailstones the size of grapefruit. Though I'd never seen it. Hail the size of a pea is big enough to strip a field.

"And you never knew where it was going to hit. I'd seen it come right up the road, flatten everything on one side, not even touch the other," one of the old survivors joined in.

The Regina Leader Post declared 1937 the worst economic disaster in the history of Saskatchewan. I will show you fear in a handful of dust, T. S. Eliot wrote in *The Waste Land*.

But I was eight years old, narcissistic, eternally the romantic, and I was ecstatic. This was real living, living on the edge. I was being initiated into a brotherhood of survivors. It was like adding another merit badge on my Boy Scout jersey, a string of them. Even today as an octogenarian, I feel pride in being a survivor of the Dust Bowl of the Thirties.

30

I see images of vast prairie visas, open skies, the outrageous glory of prairie sunsets, the explosive freshness of rain on a dusty day, ice crystals forming on a window pane in winter as my prairie heritage.

Chapter 10: The Worth of Water

"My soul thirsteth for tee, my flesh longeth for thee in a dry and thirsty land, where no
water is."

~ Psalms 1:3

"When the well's dry, we know the worth of water."
~ Benjamin Franklin, Poor Richard's Almanac.

Fife Lake felt like the real West when we returned in 1937. I knew it all already. I'd seen it in the Gene Autrey western movies on the Saturday matinees in Yorkton. There were the wide main street, the buildings with false fronts, the hitching post in front of the beer parlor. Eight-years old, a child of fantasy, I breathed deeply and took it all in. Though the women were not so pretty as in the movies, and I was disappointed that the men didn't wear their six shooters when they came into my father's hardware store.

In reality life in Fife Lake was like living in another era. It was turning back the clock fifty years. Imagine 1887.

Yorkton, that we had just come from, was an established community, one of the first settlements in Saskatchewan. Founded in 1882, it had a population of nearly 5000 people by 1930. I remembered that Main Street was paved, side streets were graveled and lined with maple trees. There were cement sidewalks, electric lights that turned on with the flick of a switch, water that flowed with the turn of a tap, even toilets that flushed. Milk, bread and ice were delivered to the door. The Hudson Bay Company department store, the Royal Bank of Canada and the Catholic church were built of limestone and brick, as were the convent and the Ukrainian Catholic college. The drug store had three flavors of ice cream, chocolate, vanilla and strawberry. All the amenities of civilization and a movie theatre.

Fife Lake, founded in 1928, had a population of 130 in 1937. It fit into two city blocks. While I was enchanted, I soon learned there was much left unsaid in the movies.

Water was our grand obsession. Who worried about water? I had always taken water for granted, like the air I breather. Not only did the crops depend on it. But so many crucial amenities of domestic life. Gene Autrey never spoke of that.

Shortly after moving to my primitive paradise I was delegated the job of providing the family's drinking and water. Though I the task was onerous, I saw it as something to be proud of. No kid in Yorkton could claim that. I wondered if there was a Boy Scout's merit badge for it.

We had a well in the basement of the hardware store, connected to a hand pump that brought water upstairs to the kitchen, which would have made my job an easy one. But you couldn't drink it. At least you didn't want to. It was murky, a pale nicotine color, and had a faint sulfurous odor. Not totally repulsive. You could drink it. If you had to. Some families in the country with only shallow wells did. But I found it even worse than the cod liver oil my mother had forced down my throat as a young child.

There was a village pump just across the road that tapped deeper springs with cold clear sweet water. I bet even Champion, Gene Autrey's horse, could be led to his water and he would drink. My job was to carry two small buckets-full home each morning before going off to school.

After the kitchen, the bathroom was where we most missed running water most. Though we never had a real bathroom in Fife Lake. The chamber pot was on call at night, the outhouse by day. A cubicle perched on a four-foot by six-foot footing, eight-foot high with a peaked roof, a makeshift latch on the warped plank door, it was parked at the end of the lot. It was the receptacle of all deposits of night soil, as it was called in polite company, whether left there by day of night. I tried to remember whether I had ever seen Gene Autrey flush a toilet.

Outhouses backed on to the back alley. A large ten-gallon bucket was strategically placed under the seat to receive deposits. Each morning my father carried the family commode, an elegant porcelain pot, to the shed and emptied the treasure into the honey bucket. A sanctuary, and meditation center, during the day, I made my own journey there to ruminate, rereading out-of-date comic books left in the paper basket. Toilet paper was a rare luxury. I soon learned that the course newsprint of the Regina Leader Post was a more efficient wipe than Simpson's mail order catalogue with its smoother paper. In winter I did not linger as the metallic bite of cold air ran right up my spine.

Ours was a two-seater, a status symbol perhaps. A novel idea, I thought, but I wondered what would I talk about if Gene Autrey joined me?

In the country the outhouse was enthroned over a six-foot pit until it was topped up. Then a new pit had to be dug. But in the village there was a limitation on how many pits one could dig. Night soil removal, as it was euphemistically called, was a major maneuver, a lively topic of conversation among us children when our parents were not in hearing range. That was before scatology had become fashionable, moved from the back yard into the living room with all those four-letter words. Though Fife Lake had a population of only 130, a hundred and thirty people can generate a lot of night soil.

Once a week, Larry Parks, our village one-man public works department, collected the night soil. He traveled through the back alleys of the village on his horse-

33

drawn honey wagon with immense sloshing barrels that he carted to a coulee well downwind from town.

No bath room? Then how do you take a bath? Not that I thought I needed one. How often did Gene Autrey take a bath? I wondered. Hopefully more often than Father Lesieux, who exuded his own distinct odor, a tinge of camphor from his breathing aid medications, mixed with a unique organic essence of body emissions.

The Saturday night bath was a weekly family ritual. To bathe more often, I was led to believe was self-indulgent, perhaps even unhealthy. Some blamed the flu epidemic of 1918 on excessive bathing. But once a week was a social necessity, even a spiritual necessity before Sunday morning mass. Cleanliness and Godliness went hand in hand to the communion rail.

It was a communal family production. I pumped water from he basement well. Father fired up the kitchen stove. Granny Schneider heated the water in metal buckets. Then she dragged out the oval galvanized iron tub from the closet and placed it on the kitchen floor before the open door of the oven. Father bathed first in the half-filled tub. Another bucket of hot water was added to warm it up, and I bathed. A final bucket and we retreated to the back room while Granny did her ablutions. The faint sulfurous smell of the water was easily dispelled by a good lathering of Lifebuoy soap. Lifebuoy was the product that coined the term "body odor." Lifebuoy really stops B.O., I hummed the radio jingle as I lathered myself.

Though I would never admit it, and didn't want my new friends to know. Bathing once a week was not enough for me. Though eight years old, I still wet-the-bed, mumbled hurriedly as if one word. "You smell like the men's piss-pot in the beer parlor," Granny said in German vernacular. I won't let you go to school like that." She insisted I take a bucket bath each morning with wash cloth and sponge. It was a practice I found useful living on a yacht much later in life.

It wasn't just Saturdays, but Mondays also called for an infusion of water. I was designated Granny's helper. This merited a Boy Scot merit badge. I pumped water from the basement well before going to school. Granny added carbolic softener and bleach, then boiled the laundry in a giant metal cauldron on the kitchen stove before transferring the steaming mass to the washing machine.

I'd never seen such a contraption but soon became intimately familiar with it. This was really turning back the clock fifty years. The washing machine was essentially an old fashioned wooden wash tub that had been mounted on an upright vertical axle. The tub could be rotated back and forth, forth and back, by manpower, pushing and pulling on a wooden lever geared to the side of the tub. The laundry inside sloshed about, propelled by the human agitator. This became my job during holidays, when I didn't have to go to school. After all I was the one who yellowed his sheets. It was laborious, boring, soul destroying. I felt the agony and indignity of a galley slave. Even a Boy Scouts merit badge could not have reconciled me to it.

After half an hour, the longest half hour in history, we wrung the laundry through a contraption appropriately called a wringer, two rubber rollers turned by a hand crank, squeezing out the water.

Then the whole process was repeated with the rinse cycle. Finally everything was hung out on a clothes line to dry. In winter the laundry froze on the line like paper dolls cut out of cardboard, a climactic act of extraordinary beauty. Granny took the rest of the week to do the ironing.

But Granny insisted that I helped, at least during vacation time. I still wet-the-bed, the one who soiled the sheets. She saw it as a form of reform therapy, from the school of thought that the punishment should fit the crime. No truck with progressive notions of positive reinforcement by her.

None of my friends had to do the laundry, so far as I knew. I never talked about it. It became one of my dirty secrets. As I trudged off to school I wondered if Gene Autrey had a Granny to do his laundry?

Chapter 11: Modernity

Technology had not by-passed Fife Lake entirely. Twice a week the CPR passed through and brought mail. Saskatchewan Telephone had wired much of the province in the nineteen twenties. Many people had trucks and some even drove cars, the black Model A Ford. Larry Mack, the CPR station master, a huge man who stood over six feet tall and weighed about 300 pounds, drove a Mack roadster, a chariot of a car that in summer he rode with the top down.

The measure of progress in the twentieth century was electricity. At dusk, nine p.m. in summer and five p.m. in winter, Larry Parks, our public works department, cranked up his diesel generator. It gave a dim flickering light until ten. Eleven on mail nights twice a week when the train came through. Farmers came to town to collect their mail and socialize. Larry gave three warning blinks ten minutes before lights out and I'd hurry to light the Coleman lantern, another of my household duties. More often I'd light a candle to see my way to bed before blowing it out. Like in the movies. You never saw Gene Audrey flick off a light switch.

The radio. We were addicted long before the world became addicted to television. It was the central focus of our living room furniture, a luxury battery powered Philco that stood chest high on me. With luminous dials and somber black speakers encased in mahogany laminate, it endowed the broadcast waves with the prestige and authenticity of modernity. It was our window to the world.

Darkness came early in winter. Late afternoon we crowded on the living room carpet before the radio at the Cowan house and listened to the next daring exploit of the Lone Ranger, racing to the next installment to the rousing rhythm of Rossini's William Tell Overture, Hi Ho-ing Silver. The Green Hornet stung with the frenzied fury of Rimsky Korsakov's Flight of the Bumble Bee. Unwittingly this was my introduction to classical music. It's a bird. It's a plane. It's Superman.

Who knows what evil lurks in the hearts of men? The Shadow knows. I'd hurry home for supper in the dark, fleeing my own shadow.

I saved the box tops of breakfast cereals that sponsored the programs; Wheaties the Breakfast of Champions; Kellogg's Rice Krispies that were shot from cannons, Snap, Crackle, Pop. I'd send them off and wait impatiently for the return mail and my secret decoder ring.

Thoreau would have scoffed at the railroad, as he did in Concord, Massachsetts in 1854, and at electricity and the radio. But as I write I can see him living happily on the edge of town, like old man Tarachuck who raised turkeys. He would have approved of the ethic of scarcity a village like Fife Lake breeds. It guided me through life, as I traveled to remote and primitive places. I have images still of living out west where a hot bath was a luxury worthy of royalty, where the stars out-dazzle electric lights, and the Lone Ranger hi-ho-ing eternally across the open prairie to the galloping rhythm of Rossini's William Tell Overture.

Chapter 12: Games We Played

"Do you remember me?"

People drifted into the cafe after dinner the night I visited Fife Lake. A man of medium height in work overalls and a two-day growth of beard approached me. It looked as if he had just come from doing farm chores without changing his clothes. I noticed the scar on his upper lip.

"Well, you should remember me. I sure as hell remember you," he said. I looked at him earnestly, wondering if he'd give me five chances to guess his name. "I'm Lawrence Lutz. You knocked out my front teeth." I thought of that painting, *The Scream* and cringed.

There weren't enough young children in the village for two teams to play each other in sand-lot softball, even when we let the girls play. But with nine players we could play work-up. We drew lots for positions, batter, catcher, pitcher, basemen and outfielders. Batter was up. When he batter was caught out, he went to left field and everyone advanced one position. When it came my turn to be at bat, Lawrence was the catcher, directly behind me. There was some confusion about the order and Lawrence started walking back from the home plate to the pitcher's box. At the same time Glen, the pitcher, threw the ball. I swung the bat, missed the ball, but hit something soft behind me. The impact resounded with a sickening thud.

I turned around. Lawrence stood there, his face a pale gray, bloody snot streaming from his nose and mouth. He looked as though he was going to faint, then put his hand to his mouth and spit out three teeth. I'd hit him square on the face.

I thought I would faint, then I started to cry, cry and laugh hysterically.

"I still have a broken off tooth up here that gives me trouble at times." Lawrence pointed inside his mouth to his upper jaw, "and this scar."

This is one of my childhood memories that I still recall with shame. The grossness, the insensitivity, laughing in the face of a screaming child as he spit out his teeth and then groveled on the barren ground, picking them up. Forty years later it was a living memory for Lawrence too. It occurred to me that he might want to hit me.

"My god! I apologize Lawrence. Let me buy you a beer," I said.

Lawrence had survived the drought, the depression, but it did not look as though he had prospered. Some few farmers had held out, stayed on, and bought up land as other farmers abandoned the prairie. But some I felt stayed on because they couldn't figure out how to move on. I wondered what other baseball bats he may have walked into during his life.

By 1937 when we moved back to Fife Lake many felt cheated by the promise of cheap land, good crops and a secure old age. But I was protected from the prevailing disillusionment by the cocoon of childhood narcissism. Fife Lake was a glorious place for a child like me. A village of 130 is much like a commune. I was like one of those homeless young men that knocked on the back door begging for a handout, except I did not need to beg. I was invited in by my friend's mothers, eager to nurture a smiling eight-year-old motherless child. I roamed the village as free as an open range chicken, as we all did playing our own games, unhampered by adult supervision, oblivious to the desperation and harshness of the times. Often a loner, rarely in life have I known such a sense of belonging.

Games were serious. Johan Huizinga wrote in Homo Ludens that play was one of the building blocks of society, part of what defines us as human whether it be competitive games of aggression, the roulette of electoral politics, or blowing into a pipe to evoke musical tone, as well as he game of mating. I don't know what he would have to say of our play in Fife Lake.

On the hot dusty days of summer we hid from the sun. There were games of chance, card games like rummy and poker, and dice games like snakes and ladders. I preferred the games of skill, like darts and pick-up-sticks.

Games of Monopoly lasted for hours, sometime days. Take a walk on the Boardwalk. It was the most expensive piece of real estate. What was the big deal? Fife Lake had a boardwalk, although only down one side of Main Street. Had the card said, Take a walk down the concrete sidewalk, I would have understood. Years later I came ashore at Atlantic City from a yacht that foundered off the breakwater. We wrecked directly beneath the Boardwalk and I had the opportunity of taking a walk. It was indeed an expensive piece of real estate.

Village humor was rustic, Chaucerian, centered on the barnyard and the outdoor privy, often cruel. In a rural community animals were valued for their functional value, cats were for ratting and mousing, dogs for guarding and watching. Most dogs were strays that had drifted in from the country in search of food. Bitches in heat were pursued by a Mongolian horde of rapacious males and when they locked we threw stones at them. We'd tie a string of cans to the tail of a dog that wasn't too vicious, then set it loose and laugh when it fled pursued by the clanging cans it could never escape.

Glen Cowan was my only friend who had a dog, a beautiful collie called Laddy. But there was no 'Lassie Come Home' sentimentality when it comes to strays. I've tried to do penance by spoiling a succession of dogs in my more compassionate ears.

The outdoor privy on the back alley side of each lot was always vulnerable to teenage pranksters. We would lie in wait behind an outhouse at the hour for the last going-to-bed pee. When the unsuspecting prey came out to make her deposit—the preference was for a woman, much safer, but also more embarrassing—we'd wait for the first spray, and then giggle, audibly, "Hee, hee, hee!" There'd be a hurried pulling up of bloomers and we'd scatter in the dark.

As far back as Chaucer human waste disposal has been a theme of rustic humor. Years later I taught the Canterbury Tales to English school boys. In the scene

39

where the Wife of Bath emptied her chamber pot out the window accidentally on to the head of her suitor, I'd tell them about my growing up in Saskatchewan, to point out the universality of scatological humor. It was one of my better attended classes.

On Halloween all restraints were set aside. The outdoor biffy was a traditional target. We roved about town in gangs, tipping them over. One year my father woke in the morning to find a weighty two seater parked demurely in the front vestibule of the store. Open for business was pinned to the privy door. Even my father smiled as the retired policeman appraised the scene looking for clues.

There was a wanton recklessness to some of our pranks. We tried to outdo each other in destructive ingenuity. Trick or treat was kid's stuff. One Halloween, Floyd, Glen, Jack and I, the four of us dragged a hay-rake on to the road leading into town. It was a light piece of farm equipment 15-feet wide with curved steel prongs 3-feet long, mounted on two steel rimmed wheels. Used to gather hay, it was easily drawn by two horses, or four boys. We placed it at a blind corner, a little dip at a bend in the road, where an oncoming vehicle would not see it until right on top of it.

The first pickup that came along hit it going 30 miles per hour, knocked it flying off the road in a clatter of sparks and dust, smashing the headlight of the truck and denting the front fender. The pickup narrowly avoided skidding into the ditch. The driver bolted out, shaken, shouting curses. I watched from behind the hedge in the school yard, 100 yards away, aghast. I hadn't expected anything this spectacular. And we fled, terrified of being caught. We decided it was best, to head for home separately, to lay low for the rest of the night and not to be seen together, and establish an alibi.

In later years when I designed adventure programs for court adjudicated youth in Outward Bound, I often reflected on the fine line between a youthful prank and the destructive act of a juvenile delinquent. But my wife, Mary is not so forgiving. "I don't understand why grown men take such pride in telling about their childish pranks? I don't see anything funny."

But Fife Lake had been a sanctuary for me. In the village I felt sheltered from the worst of hardship and despair that ravaged the countryside.

Chapter 13: The Village School

> And then the whining school-boy, with his satchel
> And shining morning face creeping like snail
> Unwilling to school.
>
> ~ Shakespeare, As You Like It ?

Not me. I was no whiner. I ran to school to get there early, eager to be with my friends.

Driving into town the morning of my visit to Fife Lake in 1981, I noticed that the old school house was still there. I expressed my surprise to Harkness. "Yes," he said, "But they've closed in down. Now all the kids are bussed to the consolidated school in Rock Glen," he said.

Rock Glen, though only twenty-five miles away, I remembered as a tortuous journey on a rutted track across the prairie, impassable after rain, blocked by hard packed wind drifts after snow.

"Today on the paved road it takes half an hour," Harkness said. "Now we use the building as a community center. Though we don't have much of a community any more."

In the fall of 1937 I was enrolled in the third grade. It was a two-room school house, grades one through eight in one room, nine through twelve in the other. High windows looked out over the prairie, letting in light from the west. There were rows of desks bolted to the floor, black board behind the teacher's desk, a large display board along another wall.

My teacher, Miss Paisley, was a stoutly mature woman, in her early forties, broad hips and full bosom. A formidable Scot, she wore tartan kilts, knee stockings and Shetland wool sweaters. I remember her being strict but patience, never coddling but affirming, authoritative without being authoritarian, a woman of great dignity. Even the townsfolk addressed her with respect as they might the Mother Superior of a convent. I held her in awe. I image my mother being a teacher like that in her better years.

Miss Paisley drilled us in the basic skills of literacy and numeracy and assigned long passages of memorization. This was the genesis of my love of poetry.

The roar was a ribbon of moonlight

41

Across the dusty moor
The highway man came riding
Up to the inn door...

I revel today at her ability to orchestrate the chaos of the lessons of different grades in one classroom. I always hurried through my assigned lessons, and then would eves-drop on what was being taught in the upper grades. By the fifth grade I had an eighth grade education.

Three principal objectives drove her teaching. First was literacy and numeracy, which she drilled into us. Each year ended in a barrage of competency based tests. This was not a culling process. The school year would be extended two or three days until even the slower students were drilled into competency, brought up to grade level. No child was left behind.

As a second generation immigrant child, Miss Paisley saw it her patriotic duty to indoctrinate us into becoming a loyal British subjects. The school day began with rousing song. In days of yore/ From Britain's shore/ Wolfe the dauntless hero came/ And planted firm Britannia's flag.... Nothing said of the French Canadian defenders. She had us memorize all ten verses of The Maple Leaf forever, in spite of there being no maple trees in Fife Lake, only cottonwoods. Why didn't we sing of cottonwoods forever?

Oh Canada/ Our home and native land...was more direct. We stand on guard for thee. As the threat of war grew in the late thirties, we sang the British national anthem more frequently. God save our gracious King...Send him victorious/ Happy and glorious.

Miss Paisley was hugely successful. Witness the high enlistment rate of local boys in the Canadian armed forces when war broke out in 1939, only two years later.

I also gained my first images of the heroic, particularly early Canadian heroes of Scottish descent. She read us the accounts in Alexander Mackenzie paddling to the Arctic, Simon Frazier man hauling his canoes across the Rockies to be the first to reach the Pacific overland across Canada. Oh how I wished that some day I would paddle northern rivers too.

Miss Paisley never lost sight of the fact that she was teaching the children of farmers, or those of us whose livelihood was dependent on them. By the seventh grade when we from Saskatchewan, I could tell a Hereford from a Black Angus bull, a Holstein cow from a Jersey. I could discourse on the ravages of soil erosion, the need to plow along the contour rather than up and down the fall line, and strip farming, leaving alternate lines of fallow to act as wind breaks,. We planted cottonwood tree along the perimeter of the school yard and watched them wither.

Geography was my favorite subject. In the fourth grade I did a project on Holland where I identified the principal exports as pickled herring, Gouda cheese and Dutch cleanser.

I did well, which pleased my father. Even Granny Schneider was proud of me. With a touch of humor I rarely saw, she called me das kleine brod fresser, the little bread eater, a pun on "the little pro-fessor. I basked in their appreciation and the recognition I got at school.

The school yard broadened our field of play. I pushed girls high on the swing set until they screamed and I could see their skirts billow out. Softball was a boy's game, but Gabrielle was permitted to play. Gibby walked two miles along the railroad tracks to school each day with her two sisters. She could smash a beer bottle with her slingshot better than any of the boys.

In the rooster fight we hopped about on one leg, holding the other behind our back, where the object was to crash into others in order to knock them over. Jousting was more combative still. In pairs, one person, the knight, climbed on the back of his partner, the horse. The knight locked his legs around the waist of his horse then charged another knight, the object being to pull him off his horse. This was the greatest game ever created. Then the girls spoiled it. A couple of the bigger girls enrolled in our knightly lists. At that age they were bigger than me and Glen, and they won all the time. I lost interest and nursed my pride, even then not wanting to be a loser.

School became the center of my universe, as schools would become much of my life, a teacher on three continents, eventually as a teacher of teachers. As a child and as an adult, I found a sense of companionship, community, and identity in schools.

Chapter 14: Catholic Priests

Dominus vobiscum.

My mother would have been proud. When I was nine, Father Lisieux anointed me an altar boy. My black cassock came to my ankles, just like the priest's. My white billowing blouse trimmed with lace flowed over it to my knees. While it was somewhat effeminate by my taste, I reveled in my exalted status. I stood standing center stage before the whole congregation, while they kneeled, swinging the incense pot. When the priest raised the host above his head, the congregation bowed, and I tinkled the tiny hand bell. "Sanctus. Sanctus. Sanctus."

The Catholic church stood on a slight rise on the north side of town, a wooden clapboard building painted white, with gothic shaped windows, comparable in size to Pete Seigo's beer parlor, the other large gathering place in the village that dealt in spirits. We prided ourselves as Catholics in having a resident priest. The thrifty Scots in the Presbyterian Church across town would afford only an itinerant preacher.

Aging, asthmatic, with teeth and fingertips nicotine stained, the good father sucked deeply from his inhaler. But every Sunday I witnessed a miracle, the metamorphosis of this withered fragile little man into the magnificence of a priest, transformed by the starched white cassock with lace trim, the resplendent chasuble of green silk, the black four-cornered hat perched like a coronet squarely on his head. Only his weak voice and the persistent cough gave him away, mortal like the rest of us. The beauty of being a Catholic was that we believed in miracles and as an altar boy I entered into the ceremony, an actor in the celebration of the miracle of the mass.

In those desperate days during the Depression we prayed for miracles, "for those who are hungry...give us this day our daily bread...for the sick that they may be healthy...the souls in purgatory...forgive us our trespasses." Father Lisieux droned on between gasps. Most of all, after seven years without a crop, we prayed for rain. In 1938 our prayers were answered.

The Presbyterians, Glenn my best friend told me, also prayed for the King and the Queen. But in the Catholic Church we observed a strict separation of Church and State. The Church was under the stern grip of Quebecois bishops who still resented the British conquest of Canada in 1760. All our priests were French-Canadians from Quebec seminaries. Tri-lingual, they recited the mass in Latin, and then preached the sermon twice, first in French and then in English. But many in the congregation, older German and Ukrainian first generation immigrants like Granny Schneider, followed the mass by rote, but understood neither sermon.

When I was ten, Father Lisieux prepared me for my confirmation, breathing heavily into his inhaler, as if he was laboring through the smoky depths of Hell himself. He paged through his dog-eared copy of Dante's Inferno, a pictorial edition illustrating in gruesome detail the trials of the damned, the Devil with pitch fork thrusting tortured souls into the burning pit. It was as graphic as any comic book we read and twice as scary.

In the darkened confines of the confessional, "Have you had any impure thoughts?" he asked with an insinuating tone. Impure thoughts? That was a tough one. I was slow to understand that the erotic urges I had begun to have at night were impure. Learning that even my fantasies were sinful, I was well schooled in guilt.

I could recite the Apostle's Creed in Latin by rote, Credo in Domine..,following the priest word for word as he conducted the prayer like a bandmaster. I believe in the holy Catholic Church...the forgiveness of sins....

When Father Liseaux retired to an old age home for priests in Gravelburg, he was succeeded by Father LeMay, a new generation of priests. I was summoned to the rectory with Fernand Girard, the other alter boy, and I stood in awe of this tall robust young man in his thirties, with an athletic build, a man's man as well as a priest. He greeted me with a broad smile and put his hand on my head, something my father rarely did. I felt I was being blessed.

In honor of the new priest, a massive dusting and cleanup of the church was organized by the Catholic ladies of the parish. South Saskatchewan was still covered in dust. The sweeping and scrubbing and painting brightened everyone's spirits. It brought woman to church early and had them staying late. Father LeMay was a new force in the community. Everyone was drawn to him, Catholics and Protestants. Most of all, stocky little Julian Nold, who genuflected before him at the altar every Sunday, and every morning during Lent. My mother's persistence had taken root.

Preparing us for confirmation, he held religious instruction classes once a week . He told us of Moses leading the Jews out of captivity in Egypt, the young David slaying Goliath, and the Crusades. I began to see religion as a robust enterprise, a great heroic pursuit, and envisaged Father LeMay as one of those warrior priests leading Christian soldiers onward.

He told us of Saint Francis of Assizi, his kindness to animals, without a hint of condemnation. I began to question the way we threw stones at the mating dogs locked in heat and tied cans to the tail of strays. In confession I mumbled my contrition. As penance, I saved scraps to feed the strays and prayed that this would shorten my stay in Purgatory.

It was the Jesuits, I believe, who declared that the way to convert the heathen was not to condemn them, but to insinuate yourself among them. Come hockey season, Father LeMay surprised everyone when he turned out with the men's village hockey team. Hockey was the center of village pride in every Saskatchewan village and evidently not proscribed by the Pope. After Sunday mass Father LeMay would often appear at the rink in his black cassock.

A priest in a black cassock on skates? If this wouldn't convert the heathen, what would? What do we make of him, farm boys from neighboring villages

45

wondered? If you were a Catholic would it be a sin to body check him too hard? Just in case, they'd stop in mid-play, "Excuse me Father." And he'd slip by to score.

"Batman," his Protestant team-mates called him. "Our secret weapon. Every team should have a Catholic priest."

I'm not sure that Father LeMay saw this as a conversion opportunity, but it was for me. I knew I had found my calling. I began to see myself as a priest, a high scoring center forward, a paragon of the church militant.

The Christmas of 1939 stands out in memory. Christmas Eve, the climax of the Christian year. It was the first year of the war for Canada. Families flocked to town from farms miles around. Most came in horse drawn sleds that year, for we had snow that December and it was safer since the roads had drifted in. Adeste Fideles. The faithful came.

Waiting for mid-night mass to begin, the men crowded into the beer parlor, women flocked into the Red and White Store, that my father then owned. Mel Parks, our one-man non-denominational village power company, left the electric lights on past the usual ten o'clock, closing down only after the service was over. Seats were full, young children dozing on their parents' laps. The smell of wet wool, mixed with incense and pine needles, permeated the church. Moisture from human breath condensed on the windows and froze in a sparkling glaze. Sprigs of holly and fir branches, shipped in from forests of northern Saskatchewan, decorated the church. The crèche, toy figures of Mary, Joseph and Baby Jesus, were made in Japan.

The faithful gathered in the dim light of the church, whispering, praying, hushed, waiting for the service to begin. The organ murmured soothing fragments of old country hymns. As Father LeMay rose to the altar and the service was about to begin, a hushed silence settled over the church. A child whimpered in the back.

Then the organ burst forth, joyous and heraldic, with the explosive introduction to Bach's Christmas Oratorio. The Catholics had never heard such an outburst of Lutheran exuberance, full bass with foot pedals down, all stops of the soaring trumpets out. What had come over the timid lady organist? Had she raided the communion wine? Startled, I glanced up at Father LeMay. He was focused on my father who was sitting in the front row as he always did, so he could hear better. Father LeMay looked up at the choir loft and smiled. I turned to follow his gaze. The whole congregation turned to see what was causing this magnificent outburst of glory. My father fumbled with his hearing aid. He too turned.

There sat Michael, my half-brother, at the keyboard, smart in his Navy dress blues, with his debonair smile. An accomplished pianist, he had joined the Canadian Navy two years before. Transferred from Esquimalt on the Pacific Coast to join his ship in Halifax on the Atlantic Coast, he had been given ten days leave in transit.

He hadn't told my father that he was coming. It was to be a surprise. He'd arrived on the late afternoon mail train, unexpected and unannounced. Instead of coming to our apartment above the store, he went directly to the priest's house where he rehearsed. Jazz musician transformed to church organist.

My father was not a man to show his emotions but that night tears came. It was probably the happiest Christmas he ever had. And one of mine.

My father later left the church, taking me with him. But the Jesuits claim that if they had a child for his first five years, they would make a believer of him for life. In my case, I became a Jesuitical believer, one who equivocated, had doubts and declared them, one who believed in a Divine Spirit, but there were different paths to realizing Him, or It, or Her, a Spirit that runs through all religions. One who, like a Jesuit questioned the infallibility of the Pope and the Catholic Church's monopoly on the Truth.

But I am still drawn to the Church mass as magnificent theatre, and to the ritual as a poetic statement of certain universal truths. Above all, I have been drawn to the music, the haunting simplicity of the Gregorian chant, the sublimity of Bach's B Minor Mass, even if it was composed by a Lutheran. In later years traveling through Europe I would seek out mediaeval churches, and I have gazed in awe at the soaring nave of Durham Cathedral, and the luminous stained glass windows of Chartres. I will die a recovering Catholic. That should be the end of my ambiguity.

Thirty-nine years later, in 1981, on my return to Fife Lake, I noticed that the church building on the hill was missing. "What happened to the Catholic church?" I asked my friend Harkness.

"The church? Oh, they sold it. George Russell bought it a d moved it to his farm. He turned it into a chicken coop. It's the only chicken coop in Saskatchewan with a hardwood floor."

Chapter 15: An Ode to Cold

> Winter is acummin in
> Lewd sing goddam
> Slideth bus and sloppeth slush
> An ague hath my ham, goddam
>
> ~ E.E. Cummings

Cummings had never experienced winter in Saskatchewan. For me winter was the season of enchantment. If I were ever to experience the rapture I am sure that it would be in winter, on a frozen lake or on a ski slope in deep powder snow.

Growing up in Saskatchewan I cannot remember when I could not skate, anymore than I can remember when I couldn't walk. In the earliest snapshot of myself, with cherub cheeks and beaming smile, I'm in a woolen knit snowsuit, wearing ice skates. In one of the few pictures I have of my mother, before she succumbed to her demons, she stands upright on a northern lake on ice skates. Winter has been ingrained into my Canadian genes.

In Fife Lake the hockey rink was just across the street from the hardware store, virtually in my back yard. Laid out to regulation National Hockey League dimensions, it had four feet high wooden boards on all sides, a small warming hut with a barrel stove at center ice. With the first deep frost, Larry Parks, the village one-man-PWD, attached the fire hose to the village pump. The village elders took turns working through the night, two men pumping, another two spraying, laying down layers of ice.

Glen Cowan's father, the manager of the Saskatchewan Pool Grain Elevator, a strongly built man of medium height, fit and agile, in his mid-forties, was in charge. He was captain of the men's hockey team and played goalie.

Jack Struther's father, manager of the Beaver Lumber Company, supervised the second shift. He was a big, heavy set man in his early fifties, robust, a defense man, "as solid as Gibraltar," the fans said. Young men from the surrounding country came to town to join in. It was a cooperative club effort, the dues they paid to play on the team. As kids, our job was to clean the ice with snow shovels after storms.

My father, not an athlete alas, provided team members with skates and hockey equipment at discounted wholesale prices as his contribution, an act of village boosterism.

After school I'd rush home, grab my skates and hockey stick and dash across the street to be first on the ice. I loved those few moments before the others arrived having the ice to myself, carving my sweeping signature across the silvery surface, fantasizing my opening game at the Maple Leaf Gardens. I played with a demonic fury, dodging in and out among the girls, head down pursuing the black puck in a self-centered game of keep-away. Mr. Cowan came by occasionally to coach us, and I learned that passing was also part of the art of the game. The girls were annoying, cluttering the rink just to be seen by the older boys.

After dinner I'd be out there again, recreational skating under feeble electric lights. Recreation? Who had ever heard of such a thing? A rough house game of tag and crack the whip was our favorite recreational activity.

I remember some nights being so cold my feet went numb. Long after I'd lost feeling I rushed to the warming hut to thaw out around the barrel stove. Feeling returned with a piercing pain, so intense I'd cry. I'd hop about on aching feet, laughing and crying until circulation returned. Then I'd go out again. Is it any wonder that I've had poor circulation ever since, and wear wool socks to bed on many a winter's night?

On weekends the men played surrounding villages, Rock Glen, Coronach, Lisieux, all about twenty-five miles away, a hotly contested prairie bush league. We pee-wees were organized as a team and often the men took us with them, crowded into the back of Cowan's grain truck, sitting on bales of hay, wrapped in blankets, covered a heavy canvas tarpaulin to cut the wind. I'd play in the short exhibition game before the men's game, a transcendent moment of glory as a child.

During the 1930's only the big cities had artificial ice and most of the professional players came from small towns in northern Ontario and Quebec, and the prairie provinces, nurtured by the cold climate and long winters. Like every other boy in Saskatchewan I aspired to becoming a professional hockey player.

The magic of hockey! There's the rough and tumble, the high adrenalin, the competitiveness. Though in those days it was a more gentlemanly sport, not dominated by the brawlers and louts. There was the sheer gracefulness of it, gathering speed in long strides, making a long sweeping turn on one leg like a gull in flight, then with a flip of the ankle gliding backwards, a moment of weightlessness, grounded to earth by only a narrow blade of steel, floating through space over the icy sheen. Rapture.

Chapter 16: Vote Liberal

In 1937 Nold-Dufour Company Ltd. hovered on the brink of bankruptcy, I learned in later years. Two-thirds of the farmers in Saskatchewan were on relief, getting a monthly check that barely covered subsistence. There was some money circulating, most of it spent at the grocery stores. Credit had dried up. Those banks that had survived the crash were not willing to gamble on the wheat crop.

My father sold no new farm machinery that year. No one could afford it. But there was a steady demand for machinery parts to repair their aging equipment. I prided myself in being my father's little helper, and learned to weigh orders for tacks and nails, to count screws and bolts, a steady business bought to repair damaged homes and sheds. Tar paper was in demand. During the grasshopper blight there was a run on insecticide, a mix of arsenic, bran and sawdust that farmers spread to kill off the remaining grasshoppers before they could lay eggs and the nymphs hatched. The provincial government sponsored massive extermination campaigns.

The municipality paid ten cents for a pair of rabbit ears, and two cents for gopher tails and my new friend, Glen Cowan and I stalked them with our sling shots.

More and more of my father's trade reverted to a barter economy. Some farmers paid their bills by providing produce for the family, meat, chickens and eggs, cheese and vegetables. This seemed fair to me as a child, but little did I appreciate that it was an economy of desperation. But that was seasonal and some could not afford even that. One farmer south of town had an outcrop of lignite coal on their land. He mined it with pick and shovel and delivered it to town by the wagon load to pay his bills. Another customer painted the store to pay off his debt. But many debts were simply written off, BAD DEBT stamped across the account book.

A federal government investigating committee was shocked by near-starvation conditions of some families, and recommended that emergency food relief be provided for the needy. That fall boxcar loads of potatoes arrived from Prince Edward Island in the east, apples from the Okanogan Valley in British Columbia, and were distributed to those who were not too proud to accept them.

And there was dried salt cod from Nova Scotia. They couldn't give it away. They begged us to take it, even if we were not on relief. I brought home a huge slab four-feet long, six inches wide, and three inches thick, as hard as weathered boards on a barn door. No one knew how to prepare it. Even after Granny Schneider boiled it for an hour, it was still too tough to chew and too salty to swallow. Had my mother been alive she would have known. She came from Nova Scotia. Granny just threw it out, mumbling something in German about feeding it to das schwein. And that's what most people did, fed it to their pigs. They devoured it, satisfying their appetite both for protein and for salt.

A few families persisted, Catholics who were obliged to eat fish on Friday. They ate it as a form of penance. Father Liseux preached a sermon on the parable of the loaves and the fishes, always a popular theme during depression years. He grew up in Quebec and his house-peeper knew how to prepare it.

Cod stirred political loyalties in the federal elections political campaign that year. Under the cover of night, a partisan party prankster climbed the telephone pole in front of the post office, and nailed a four foot slab of codfish to the top. On it, he painted VOTE LIBERAL, in bright red block letters.

That was my first glimmering of a political consciousness.

The Liberals won the national election based on the eastern Canada vote, but they lost Saskatchewan. We went CCF, Co-operative Commonwealth Federation, the agrarian based socialist party. As early as the mid-thirties the CCF had introduced such radical ideas as workman's compensation, unemployment insurance and universal medical coverage, programs that would take a world war and two decades to be enacted.

It was said of William Lyon Mackenzie King, our eccentric, politically astute and long-lived Prime Minister, that his ass was always in the air, but his ear was to the ground.

The Regina Leader Post reported that 1937 had been the greatest economic disaster in Saskatchewan's history.

This was the time I began to define myself as a dust bowl survivor. I romanticized the experience as an heroic feat. I still have images of vast prairie vistas, open skies, the outrageous glory of prairie sunsets, the explosive freshness of rain on a dusty day, ice crystals forming on a window pane in winter, as my prairie heritage.

But there was no Wordworthian Romantics among those who gathered in my father's hardware store on mail nights when the train came through. They came to town to collect their government relief checks.

Chapter 17: 1938 – A Crop at Last

"It was the best of times. It was the worst of times."

~ Charles Dickens.

There was a succession of blizzards the winter of 1938. Snow fell heavily for the first time in seven years. On my way to school I waded through snow drifts, head down into the wind, fantasizing that I was Scott of the Antarctic, man-hauling my sled to the South Pole as the flag pole in the school yard came into sight.

On mail nights I listened to the farmers gathered in the hardware store commiserating with each other on the bitterness of the winter. The roads were drifted in and they'd come to town in horse drawn sleds.

"Couldn't afford the gas even if the truck could get through."

"Running low on lignite. Have to haul another load."

"Dad gum if the well wasn't frozen over."

"Haven't had a winter like this since twenty-nine."

For all the complaints, there was also quite optimism. "It'll put moisture in the ground."

Come spring there was the great thaw and Main Street turned into a mud wallow, like the rest of south Saskatchewan, prairie gumbo, wet, slick, oozing mud and clay. Weeds sprouted and wild flowers bloomed. Farmers came into the hardware store with muddy boots and I swept up after them with no complaint. Even old Josef Weisgerber, whom I'd rarely seen smile, had a broad grin.

In April the ground dried up enough to be able to plow the weeds under and farmers planted their crops. Light rains persisted through May and the new shoots sprouted a pale fragile green. By June when we burst out of school for the summer vacation, the whole countryside glistened a lush vibrant green. Large strips of land had been left fallow and the patchwork quilt of brown stubble and lush fields stretched to the horizon. Even the meadow larks rejoiced in the sense of fortune.

By late July the summer had heated up. Green wheat stood tall in the fields, shimmering in the sunlight, waving in the breeze. I'd been out on the prairie with Glenn Cowan shooting gophers with our sling shots and saw the clouds build up. They mounted high in the sky, miles high, huge billowing cumulus, boiling and seething, capped in white where they caught the sun. Lower down it darkened to gray and a somber blue. Thunder growled in the distance, daggers of lightning stabbed the ground.   I ran for home. Stumbling over the unplowed field, I prayed I would make it before it rained. Then I saw the hail. I could smell the cold chill then saw the white sheet swooping down. I cowered under the first impact, sheltering under my arms as I was pelted by hail stones, only the size of a pea but still they hurt. Then as fast as it hit, it passed on flattening the field on one side of the fence, and leaving the one on the other side untouched.

We were spared the grasshopper plagues that year, but in mid-summer a brown mould began to appear on some of the crop. "Wheat rust," the farmers called it. "If it ain't one damn thing, it's another." It shriveled the leaves and ate into the stocks and the grain never matured. Those farmers who planted with the common Marquis wheat seed were heavily damaged. But those who could afford to plant with the new strain of Thatcher wheat produced twenty bushels per acre. For the first time in years some farmers had enough of a crop to harvest.

By August the grain stood tall, turning a golden brown, swaying in the wind it looked like an ocean of wheat, though none of us kids had seen an ocean. "All we need now is harvest weather," I heard the farmers say as they came into the hardware store to get machine parts to repair their binders. "Pray for no rain. No early frost." After all the years of praying for rain that seemed strange.

The word was out. There would be a harvest this year.

Chapter 18: A Battle of Titans

There was talk of war in 1938. Saskatchewan had a good crop year, and England was stock-piling wheat in anticipation of conflict. Germany too. Which was good, I gathered, as I listened to farmers talking on nights they came to town to get their mail. "The price of wheat is up again, over a dollar a bushel."

But I watched my father as he listened to the news every evening on the CBC, the Canadian Broadcasting Corporation. He had a worried look. Even though the crops might be good that year, I knew something was not right. A curious nine year old who asked too many questions, I was confused.

The Germans had marched into Austria in March, but the Austrians didn't seem to mind. They cheered. But Nazi storm troopers burned the Jewish synagogues and looted their shops. I didn't know any Jews, but my father had a store and I wouldn't like to see it robbed.

I thought I understand why everyone was so worked up by the Joe Louis-Max Schmelling fight that summer. Fighting was a national sport in rural Canada. On mail nights I often saw the village drunks beating up each other in front of Pete Seigo's beer parlor. But this was more than just another bar-room brawl. Big issues were at stake, and not just the big money. 70,000 people were watching in Madison Square Garden in New York. "It is estimated that 100 million people are listening on radio tonight, world-wide, the largest radio event in history," the announcer said. "In Canada, only the Stanley Cup playoffs of the National Hockey League draws a larger listener audience." Thirty more listeners, mostly men and boys, gathered on the Cowan's front porch around their new Philco radio, the tall one with the big speaker and polished mahogany finish, with the volume turned up. Glen Cowan and I sat out on the lawn, with the other kids.

Joe Louis was the heavy weight champion of the world, a negro. For reasons I did no fully understand, he was our guy. I didn't know any negroes. The only negroes in Saskatchewan were the sleeping car porters who made up the bunks on the CPR mainline. The crowd cheered wildly when Joe stepped into the ring. We cheered too.

But boy, did they ever whistle and boo when the other guy stepped into the ring? Why all the angry shouting. Shouldn't we be cheering for him. Schnelling was a German. I knew lots of Germans. We were Germans, weren't we? Though my father had come from Russia.

"It's because of Hitler and the Jews," my father said. Jews? I didn't know any Jews either, though Father Liseaux spoke about them in catechism classes. The Jews had killed Jesus. But wasn't Jesus a Jew? Granny Schneider seemed like the only person who knew Jews. She had come from the Ukraine twenty-five years before and I gathered in the Ukraine they didn't like them. "Das verdamt Jude," those damned Jews, she muttered as she read Das Bund, her German newspaper. It was all pretty confusing. But one thing was clear. Hitler was a bully. And I never liked a bully.

Was Schmelling a bully too? This fight was a return match. In the earlier fight two years previously, Schmelling had pummeled Louis for twelve rounds before he landed a knockout blow. This was Joe Louis's chance to get even, not only for himself, but for all of us, and the Jews. He was going to stand up to the Germans, even if the politicians didn't. He was our man. Fife Lake was rooting for Joe Louis.

"Somebody's got to stand up to those Nazis," I heard Mr. Cowan say.

Max Schmelling was actually a pretty good looking fellow. I'd seen his picture on the sports page of the Regina Leader Post. Dark hair, somewhat swarthy features, he had a flattened nose, but none of the grudge saw on pictures of Hitler in the magazines.

Over the radio I could hear the frenzy of the crowd in Madison Square Garden. Talking through his nose, the announcer told us the whole Jewish population of New York City had turned out to shout down Schmelling. "They say he's a Nazi and he'll buy another tank for the the German army with his earnings, over a million dollars," he said. The opening bell. Glen was horsing around and I told him to leave me alone so I could listen to the fight. The announcer spoke in a high pitched voice, rapid fire like hail falling on a tin roof, giving a blow by blow account of the fight. They circled each other, Schmelling jabbed at Louis. Louis jabbed back. Once, twice, three times. The crowd had hushed. They shuffling around, circling each other. It appeared as though they didn't want to fight. Then the moment everyone had been waiting for, Louis moved in close with a succession of lefts and rights to the head, to the body. I lost count of the number of left and rights, they came so fast. "Louis has Schmelling on the ropes," the announcer screamed. "He's landed a right to the head. Schmelling's on the ropes. He puts his left arm out to fend Louis off. But Louis unloads a barrage of punches, left and right to the head. Schmelling turns away and Louis lands a body blow. Schmelling's sagging. Louis has him pinned to the ropes. Schmelling drops to his knees. He's down. The referee steps between them and counts. One. Two. Schmelling's up. He wobbles toward Louis with his left arm out. Louis closes with another round of blows. Schmelling is down again. He's on the canvas. The referee,s counting. Three. Four. Five. Schmelling's trainer has thrown in the towel. Joe Louis has done it again. The fight's over."

Over? But it had only just begun. "The greatest boxing match in history, and it's over in only two minutes and four seconds," the announcer screams above the crowd.

Unbelievable. Even the good burghers of Fife Lake clap and cheer. It all seems remote from our prairie village on a hot summer's night, but there is a sense that justice has been done.

Glen Cowan began to punch me, re-enacting the fight. I punched back. We wrestle, rolling in the dusty prairie grass, burning off our pent up excitement.

55

Joe Louis had shown Hitler. But apparently Hitler didn't get the message. That fall German troops marched into Czechoslovakia. A year later it was Poland. Canada was at war.

As a child I'd always seen the Louis-Schmelling fight as the first battle of World War II. And we won.

Chapter 19: Harvest Heroes

The harvest crews began to arrive in late August. I lined up beside the railroad tracks with Glen and Floyd when the first contingent come through on the Monday mail train. They were crowded into the open box cars and many more rode on the roofs lined up like sparrows strung on a telephone line. I'd have given anything to be up there with them. The train stopped for twenty minutes while the freight was unloaded and we climbed the ladders at the ends of the cars, run along the top and down the ladders on the opposite side. I ran into Larry Mack, the station agent, who caught me and boxed my ears.

Most of the men were young with tanned faces and broad smiles. They clearly were enjoying themselves. I know that I would have. But the older men were grave, thin, unwashed, unkempt in worn clothes, weary from the journey.

It has been estimated that 20,000 to 30,000 men came west every year in this vast harvest migration. They came from Ontario and the Maritime Provinces, even the eastern United States, an exodus born of desperation but buoyed by hope. In later years many saw the trip west as one of the great adventure of their lives.

Between thirty and forty men stopped off at Fife Lake that year. This was equal to the adult male population of the village. They headed for the scrub willow grove on the other side of the tracks, south of town and made camp. I followed and offered to help as they strung up ragged canvas tents, unrolled their blanket bed rolls on the ground. Just like the cowboys in the movies. They tore down the CPR snow fence for fire wood and began to heat their billy cans. The station master didn't seem to mind. "It's the least the CPR could do," he said. This was real living, I thought and vowed that some day I too would travel, maybe even ride the freights.

"Where do you get water?" one of them asked me.

"I'll get it for you?" I offered.

"Thanks, but I want to wash up," he said. I took him to the station well and pumped for him. He smiled through the soot from the belching coal burning train. Once he had washed, I was disappointed to see how ordinary he looked. He could have been Glen's older brother.

"Know anyone looking for harvest help?" the men asked at my father's hardware store, the first building on the corner. They were polite but not apologetic as they had been in Yorkton in the early 1930's. Since the Regina riots when the Mounties had been called in to disperse a protest rally, the men had become more assertive. Some were even angry.

They invaded the village, knocking on doors, asking for work in exchange for food. They were thin, unwashed, unkempt and while they evoked pity, there was always vague feelings of threat. The newspapers reported food riots in the cities.

Before the advent of the combine harvester wheat harvesting was a labor intensive activity. It was always a race against time, between the last drying days and the onset of the fall rains. When the kernels of wheat had filled out but still soft, the grain was cut to hasten the ripening process. A standing field was cut by a horse drawn reaper-binder that bundled the two-foot stalks into sheaves, tied together with binder twine, and dumped them onto the field. The bound grain then had to be was stooked by hand, that is, piled upright in stacks, or stooks to ripen. These stood five feet high and were lined up across the fields as far as the horizon like an army massing for a major military assault. It took several men to keep up with the binder.

When the wheat had ripened and the soft kernels were seen to be hard by chewing them, the stooks were gathered in. Horse drawn hay wagons with high wooden ricks came through the fields, and teams of men on the ground hoisted the bundles of grain up on to the wagon, where they were stacked high by another two men. The full load was then driven to the threshing machine, a gigantic machine like a dinosaur, making a deafening roar and spouting fumes and straw dust. It was powered by a power belt running from a large tractor, or sometimes by a steam engine.

The dried sheaves were tossed into the gaping maw of the antediluvian mechanical beast, the straw chewed up and spit out into a mounting straw pile, the precious grain sifted out and deposited in a hopper. The threshing machine could keep up with four or five wagons. It was held up only by the speed with which the bundled stalks could be tossed in. When the hopper was full with grain, prairie gold, it was loaded into a grain truck with a high wooden box and carted to the grain elevators in town along side the railway tracks. My father had a truck and hauled grain, and I used to accompany the hired man when he went out for another load.

On a good year it was often difficult to find enough men to bring in the harvest. There were never enough hands to go around. They worked long hours, were well fed and well payed. But this year only a few transients found work. Many farmers had lost their crop and local boys were out of work. They were first to be hired. The migrant workers realized that many of the farmers were as poor as they.

But during the years of the drought, often there was no harvest worth harvesting. So men would drift in, check us out, find what little work they could, and when they had outlived our frugal charity, would catch the next freight out and move down the line in search of better opportunities.

But I was sorry to see them go. They brought a vision of wider horizons to a child's life. I vowed that some day I'd ride the freights. As a teenager, I did. On a trip across Canada I rode the rods from Banff to Vancouver through the Canadian Rockies when hitch-hiking turned out to be poor.

There was always a sense of relief when they departed. People were ambivalent, wanting to help, but anxious too. People locked their doors. Something they had never done before. Were they blaming the poor for being poor?

Harvest was over and done in two or three weeks. The life of the village returned to a bucolic calm until the next planting season.

The grain elevators had been emptied, so there was a demand for wheat and prices rose. Business began to pick up. Then there was talk of war and the price of wheat futures went higher still.

On my visit to Fife Lake years later, several of the old timers who gathered at the Fife Lake Hotel, spoke of "riding the rods" as one of the great adventures of their lives. When their father's farms had dried up and blown away in the dust storms they too had taken to the road.

One began to sing with a scratchy voice, "Halleluya I'm a bum."

"Halleluya bum again," another joined in.

"Alleluja, give us a hand out/ To revive us again," we all joined in.

Floyd ordered another round of beer.

Chapter 20: Celebrating Christmas

Christmas represented a generational divide, a chasm between my father and me. He had been brought up in Russia where they focused simply on the birth of Christ, not gift giving. That came later on Twelfth Night, the Feast of the Coming of the Three Kings, commemorating the Gift of the Magi. There was a modest exchange of small gifts, none of the commercialism that surrounded a Canadian Christmas.

Even my father couldn't escape the commercialization of Christmas entirely. He bought a Christmas tree, albeit a small one, and decorated it sparsely and displayed it in the hardware store. It was good for business. The line of cheap toys made in Japan sold well. But upstairs, in the apartment above the store where we lived, there wasn't so much as a strand of tinsel.

On Christmas morning I had all the hopes and high expectations of a child. I woke early and bounded out of bed in my flannel pajamas to see my presents. At nine years of age I no longer believed in Santa Claus. But I did believe in my father. There were no gifts. I struggled to hold back my tears, but I could not control my quivering lips. My father saw my dismay and hurried down to the store. He returned with a brand new hockey stick, the kind endorsed by the Toronto Maple Leafs. And a puck. It wasn't the new C.C.M. skates I had hoped for, but my old ones still fit, I figured.

I have never come to terms with Christmas. I suspect I never will. When I had my own children years later in Colorado, we would open our presents on Christmas Eve. On Christmas Day the girls were eager to try out their new skis and we'd rise early and head to Winter Park where there were no lift lines and we had the mountain to ourselves. I had learned to avoid sitting idly on a Christmas Day wrestling with ghosts from my past.

Chapter 21: The Royal Visit

God save our gracious King
Long live our noble King.

Spring rains returned in 1939 and it looked as though the eight-year drought had run its course. There was a feeling of optimism again on the prairie in spite of the storm clouds over Europe. But the threat of war had driven up the price of wheat, so war couldn't be all bad, I thought as a ten year old. But as farmers came to town on mail nights and gathered in the hardware store, I sensed their ambivalence. Many still had family in Europe, particularly those from Poland, the Ukraine and Belgium.

Granny Schneider and my father may have had family in Russia, though they may have disappeared in the Stalinist purges, I would learn in later years. He never spoke of them, at least to me.

In early May Miss Paisley, our primary grades teacher, announced, "The Royal Family are coming to Moose Jaw. Wouldn't it be nice if we could go and see them?"

Was it possible? See the King and the Queen? I was a child addicted to fantasy, but this was too fantastic.

But Miss Paisley, a durable Scot, took her heritage seriously. She saw it her responsibility to shape the hybrid children of European immigrants into loyal British subjects. Particularly those like myself who had French Canadian mothers.

"Wouldn't it be nice Dad?" I told him about it over dinner. To my surprise he didn't scoff at the idea. He smiled. I suspected something was in the air.

This as a low point for the royal family. Only two years before, King George's older brother, the popular former Prince of Wales, debonair Edward VIII, had abdicated the throne. Rather than forego that woman, as the press called her, Mrs. Wallis Simpson, twice divorced, an American no less, as his queen, he chose exile. The constitutional crisis was resolved only when his younger brother, shy, stuttering Freddie, ascended the throne as King George VI.

William Lyon Mackenzie King, the prime minister of Canada, had attended the coronation of King George VI. Feeling slighted by the snobbery of the British aristocracy, he went on to Germany and was greeted warmly by Hitler, whom he congratulated on the state of the German economy, and the prosperity of the German people. "The Germans are more like Canadians that are the English," he told a reporter from the Globe and Mail on his return. A comment he would come to regret.

61

Though the King seemed optimistic that war could be avoided, in spite of the growing belligerence of Hitler, the goodwill tour was important to shore up commonwealth relations. If Britain did go to war, they wanted it understood that Canada would too.

The royal visit became a national celebration. The country was just emerging from the Depression, the drought cycle broken, it was as if Their Royal Highnesses had come to celebrate with us. That spring we had the heaviest rains in a decade. Indeed, rains plagued the royal visit. But on the prairies we saw it as a blessing, the King was called affectionately, "George the Rainmaker." Canadians, who pride ourselves in being unemotional and undemonstrative, lose all sense of control when it comes to royalty. A royalist frenzy swept the country.

God save the King. We sang the national anthem before every major event, hockey games, band concerts, in movie theaters before the feature film. Though it was said audiences in Quebec refused to stand. They preferred, Oh Canada, Our home and native land, sung in French. But to me, my loyalty was to the King.

This was he first time in history that a reigning monarch had visited Canada. The King and Queen arrived in Quebec on the recently constructed Cunard ocean liner, the Queen Mary, the largest, most luxurious ship afloat. A special train took them on their grand tour across Canada, west to Vancouver on the CPR, and back east to Halifax on the CNR, the Canadian National Railroad. They made whistle stops right across the country and thousands flocked to see them in an unsurpassed outburst of patriotism. It wasn't just the Anglo-Scots. Canada, a bilingual and multi-cultural nation, has always had a problem with identity, and the charisma of royalty was an attempt to fill a void. Certainly it embraced me.

Moose Jaw, on the mainline CPR, 150 miles from Fife Lake, was the nearest station where the royal couple would stop. In those days, on the dirt and gravel back country roads, this was a major expedition, like an African safari.

In a chauvinistic burst of patriotism, the village elders rallied. Miss Paisley excused us from school, but gave us a written assignment. We had to record our observations. "This is an historic occasion," she said. "You will remember it the rest of your lives." And I do, though it was less historic than expected.

Pete Seigo, the owner of the beer parlor who had a gift for self-promotion, organized an expedition like a military maneuver. He recruited four grain trucks. Glen Cowan's father, who ran the Saskatchewan Pool Elevator, volunteered his, as did my father. Bales of hay were lined up along the sides for benches. A contingent of forty, men, women and children were signed up, ten in each truck. The day before, in the rain, I helped rig a canvas tarpaulin over the open bed of our truck. Each truck was a self contained unit, with mattresses, blankets, hampers of food, Coleman stoves, pots and kettles, jerry jugs of water were stacked in the back. Half the village turned up to see us load. I felt that another forty would have signed up, if there had been enough trucks.

"It's a once in a lifetime opportunity." Even my father, not a man given to enthusiasm became a Chamber of Commerce promoter. He even gave wholesale discounts on the purchase of flags, both the British ensign and the Union Jack. The maple leaf our emblem dear, The maple leaf forever, had not as yet been adopted as Canada's flag.

I was awake that morning long before my father called me. I'd been awake much of the night listening to the rain tapping on the roof. I didn't even wet my bed. I'd already packed my school bag with my tooth brush, towel and comic books.

In the pale light of pre-dawn the four trucks rallied in front of the Fife Lake Hotel with gentle drizzle filtering down. Pete Seigo called the role and assigned passengers to their vehicle. In the dark I managed to slip into the Cowan truck with Glen, my best buddy, without being noticed.

There was a last minute briefing of the drivers. Jack Struther's father, who managed the Beaver Lumber Company was shaking his head, pointing to the sky, then down the road. But Siego seemed to prevail. His body language made it clear, There's no turning back now.

For years the Catholic priest beseeched the Divine Being, and the Virgin Mary, to bring us rain. After seven years of drought, the fundamentalist Presbyterian minister , not to be out done, chose Genesis 8:18 for his sermon. And the waters prevailed, and were increased greatly upon the earth. In 1939 our prayers were answered and it seemed that for forty days and forty nights it did rain.

The parched ground drank the rain up and the surplus overflowed in the ditches. Glorious, soothing, root penetrating rain, a blessing for all things green. Barnyards turned to quagmires. Main Street turned to a slurry of prairie loam. Our lake, we had forgotten there was an actual Fife Lake, began to fill. As Noah's child I turned my head into it and caught the drops with my tongue, and crawled into the truck behind Glen.

Roads in south Saskatchewan were determined by a surveyor's transit line that led across the open prairie straight and unerring. A highway grader cooped out the prairie loam from a ditch on each side, banked the soil in the center, then graded the crown flat. No gravel. Certainly no pavement. Though bumpy and deeply rutted the roads were passable in the dusty months of summer, and when frozen over in winter, if not blocked by snow drifts. But with rain they turned glutinous like the wheat paste we used to glue pictures into our scrap books at school.

At dawn the convoy moved out, four trucks in convoy, undaunted by the steady drizzle. Send Him victorious, Happy and glorious, we bellowed jubilantly, drowning out the labored roar of the engines. I felt that this was, and would always be, one of the great days of my life. Perhaps it was.

The trucks, whined in low gear, grinding through the mud. Where the wheels struck clay they spun, the tailgates slithered back and forth, the drivers swinging the wheel, a balancing act to stay on the crown of the road. The ruts deepened. No let up of the rain. The convoy powered on, ever more slowly, from fifteen miles per hour, to ten, then barely five, as the trucks lost traction. Then as if preordained, it occurred. The lead truck slipped out of the ruts, the rear wheels spun and it slid through the ooze, slowly, painfully, inevitably into the shallow ditch. It stuck, embedded to the axle.

In three hours we had covered fifteen miles, just over half the distance to Rockglen, the next village 25 miles away. From there the road would be lightly

63

graveled. The rest of the day was spent getting the lead truck out and all the trucks turned around. We followed the ruts back to Fife Lake.

We had packed enough provisions for a banquet and everyone gathered at the great hall in the Presbyterian Church and we shared food and listened to the Canadian Broadcasting Corporation.

The radio was our window to the world announcer rhapsodize on the graciousness of the Queen in her stunning blue satin dress, clapped to the spirited Scottish dancing and bagpipe music in her honor, and stomped to the drum beat of an Indian powwow. We joined the Moose Jaw Church of England choir as they sang, Long may he reign over us, God save the King.

Not four months later, at daybreak on September 1, 1939, without a declaration of war, German tanks rolled across the frontier of Poland, preceded by the blitzkrieg of Stuka dive bombers. Britain and France declared war on Germany forty-eight hours later and Canada was at war.

Chapter 22: The Red and White Store

The crown jewel of Main Street was the Red and White Store, two stories high, with the high false front, popular in frontier villages. It had been painted red, though faded under the prairie sun, but rather than appearing shabby, the building took on the subtle eloquence of a worn oriental carpet. Trimmed in white, with RED AND WHITE STORE emblazoned across the high front. The wide front door was set back in a raised vestibule flanked on either side with wide display windows. It was a general store franchised by a major chain that sold groceries, over the counter drugs, dry goods and miscellany. In 1939 the store came up for sale.

The outbreak of war had driven up the price of wheat. There had been a good crop and many farmers had been able to pay off their back debt. Business was good. My father was able to negotiate a good deal and bought it. He had a new sign painted, Red and White Store, O.N.Nold, Prop. The Red and White Store represented the pinnacle of my father's business enterprise. I thought it was magnificent.

He consolidated the two businesses and moved the stock from the old hardware and implement store on the corner, to the bigger store at the center of Main Street. He expanded the stock with household fixtures such as lamps, and sporting goods, skates, hockey sticks, baseball bats and children's toys, and one battery powered Philco radio, which we kept as a demo in the upstairs apartment. When that one sold he replaced the inventory with another. We now sold everything from tobacco to tractors, darning needles to sledge hammers, from sand paper to toilet paper. The biggest show in town.

On mail nights when farmers came to town, the men gathered in Pete Seigo's beer parlor. The women flocked together in the stores. As the biggest store in town, across the street from the post office, the Red and White store had become an unofficial community center.

I was ten, old enough to tie a bundle securely and make change accurately. I served as a junior clerk, a position of recognition and prestige that I cherished. It made me feel very grown up. I craved recognition. Besides clerking, my father set me up in my own business, a newspaper stand in the back corner of the store. I sold the Regina Leader Post, Tarzan comic books, and learned magazines for adults like True Confessions, Popular Mechanics and Maclean's. I could purchase model airplane kits through the same agency. Most of my profits went into Spitfire, Hurricane, Messerschmitt models

Christmas was joyous that year, in spite of the outbreak of war. My half-brother Mickey had come home on leave from the navy for a couple days and played the organ on Christmas Eve. The stringent years of the Depression seemed over. There was a prevailing sense of prosperity, a feeling of modest affluence. Even my father felt it. For Christmas, I got a new pair of CCM hockey skates, the same brand worn by Syl Apps, star center forward of the Toronto Maple Leafs.

That was the year my father bought the new Speed Queen gas driven washing machine. The tub remained stationary and an internal baffle rotated back and forth inside, agitating the laundry, powered by a two horsepower gasoline motor. Father presented it to Granny for Christmas. She wouldn't touch it. Such a mechanical contraption was more than she was willing to trust. I realized that she saw the old hand cranked tub as enough of a technological improvement over the washboard she had grown up with in Russia.

This was my moment. "Let me help you Granny." Soon I had mastered the mechanics of it. "I'll start it for you before I go to school." The role of laundry apprentice had achieved new prestige. It represented a coming of age experience, a generational transfer of power, that I would appreciate only years later.

With privilege came responsibility. The first week of the New Year we took stock, the annual inventory. Every item in the store had to be counted. "For tax purposes," my father told me. I was put in charge, that's the way he put it, of the hardware department. There was a whole wall of bins, pigeon holes of miscellany, and every pound of nails had to be weighed, every box of screws noted, every loose nut and bolt pulled out and counted. A dirty, dusty, messy job. Mine.

But in actual practice I rather enjoyed the process. I appreciated my father entrusting me with it. There was even something pleasing about the mechanical nature of the task, the counting, the sorting, the organizing of categories, the allusion of creating order out of chaos. Years later I would recall this experience as a shop keeper's son, when I organized the clothing distribution center in a refugee camp outside Vienna, during the Hungarian Uprising.

But there is a worm in every crate of apples. The thing that spoiled it for me was the thought that Glen and Jack and all my buddies were enjoying Christmas vacation, out playing hockey on the newly flooded ice rink.

The war was on every one's mind. Every evening I listened to the Canadian Broadcasting Corporation news with my father. In September Germany invaded Poland in a blitzkrieg with dive bombers and tanks, a new spectacular form of warfare. Britain and France declared war on Germany. Two days later the Canadian Parliament did as well. To everyone's surprise, Russia invaded Poland too, reclaiming parts of eastern Poland, once of part of Russia.

My father was worried about my half-brother Mickey who had been assigned to HMCS Restigouche, on convoy duty on the North Atlantic.

That year one of the best selling item in the toy department was a dart board. On one side was the face of Hitler. On the other Stalin. By the next year it had to be removed from stock. Germany had invaded Russia and Stalin was our ally. It was

66

replaced with a new dart board with a picture of the Japanese Emperor on the opposite side.

There were varied reactions to the war. There was general support, though little enthusiasm. Billy Strang's brother joined the army. The Thomasett boy enlisted in the navy. Far fewer young men came through with the migrant harvest crews. The Catholic priest prayed for peace. The itinerant Protestant prayed for the King.

Granny Schneider was an outspoken war resister. She subscribed to Das Bund, a German language weekly newspaper printed in Milwaukee, sponsored by the American Nazi Party. "Das verdamte jude," those damned Jews, she would rant to her Ukrainian friends on mail nights. And Jews like Roosevelt and Churchill, and the Jewish Wall Street bankers. Within weeks of the onset of war, the paper was banned in Canada, disrupting her flow of invective. My father was clearly relieved. I was confused. Granny could be pretty brusk, but she was also caring. Granny a Nazi?

The Red and White store with its broad display windows was an obvious target for Halloween pranksters. Printing grafitti with soap was to be expected. Tipping outhouses was common practice, ours was enclosed in a large shed abutting the back alley. Invulnerable. I learned that one should not under rate teenage ingenuity.

The front of the store was set back six feet from the boardwalk that in winter was boarded off, making a vestibule where customers could brush snow off their overcoats before entering. The morning after my father came down to open up and there sat a large two seater demurely parked. The door flung wide open, a sign, Open for business, pinned to it. Even my father was amused.

"What happened to the Red and White Store?" I asked Harkness the night I visited Fife Lake in 1981.

"Oh, a few years after Jules Hostin bought the business from your father, he closed the store. Frank Weisgerber bought the building, tore it down, hauled the lumber to Assinaboia (fifty mles away) and built the house he lives in today."

"Frank Weisgerber? His mother nursed me when I was born. I visited the old farm this morning." I felt another ghost was being summoned.

Chapter 23: The Siege of Fife Lake

Rule Britannia, Britannia rules the waves,
Britons never, never, never will be slaves.

The first year of the war did not go well. Hitler's armies had over run most of Western Europe within nine months. France fell in June 1940 and the Nazis occupied Paris. The British Army retreated to Dunkirk and narrowly escaped. The Battle of Britain began in the fall, with nightly air raids on London. German submarines were sinking merchant ships at sea. Ambassador Kennedy, The American ambassador to London doubted, in public, whether the English could hold out and President Roosevelt replaced him.

Miss Paisley had us follow the progress of the war by coloring in each country as it was occupied. But Britain was unconquered, always red, just like the British Empire appeared in red on the world map behind her desk. I learned a lot of geography that year. The German armies advanced from Norway in the north, to Romania in the south-east. I'd never heard anyone talk of Romania. Then the Italians came in the war on the side of Germany and invaded Egypt and Greece.

But we were not to be dismayed, Miss Paisley said. It was important to keep up the moral of the troops. So every day she began the day by teaching us a song. Mademoiselle From Armentieres, Parley Vous, It's a Long Way from Tipperary, Over There, Over There, The Yanks are Coming, but the Yanks weren't coming, mostly World War I marching songs. There didn't seem to be all that marching in World War II. The songs were more sentimental: There'll be Blue Birds Over, The White Cliffs of Dover, Tomorrow when the World is Free, There'll be Love and Laughter and Peace Ever After.... We could really belt out on There'll Always be an England, And England shall be Free, If England Means as Much to You, As England Means to Me. O Canada our Home and Native Land, and The Maple Leaf Forever, sounded pretty wish-washy by comparison.

We had another good wheat harvest. Farmers for the first time in years had money to spend, though there was not much to buy. Factories were turning out tanks and planes rather than tractors and cars. We were encouraged to buy war bonds. I hoarded pennies and bought twenty-five cent saving stamps, my contribution to the war effort.

As an eleven year old, I believed that in the long run the good guys would win. This was reinforced every night as we listen to Superman and the Lone Ranger. But it was hard to deny the threat of the bad guys when my father switched the dial at six o'clock and listened to the CBC evening news.

In spite of the threat, I couldn't help admiring the Germans. Just a little bit. They sure knew how to win a war. There was no getting bogged down in trenches for then. The came in with Stuka dive bombers screaming out of the air and Panzer tanks thundering on the ground. Then in May 1941 they invaded Crete. With paratroopers. That was a novel idea. Even Clark Kent would have a hard time keeping up with them. I had a hard time finding Crete on the map, but wondered, what wouldn't they do next?

That summer, Glen Cowan and I were on a big game safari out on the prairie a mile south of town, shooting gophers with our sling shots. A gentle wind soughed through the prairie grass, when I was startled by series of detonations reverberated over the open prairie. Boom. Thud. Thud. Boom. The sound reverberated form the direction of the village. "D'ya hear that?" I said to Glen. Was Fife Lake being attacked? I didn't see any parachutes in the sky.

"Jeez Glenn, duck." And I dropped into shallow ravine, as terrified as I'd ever been. I fought to keep from panicking. I waved to Glen. "Keep low." The noise continued with sporadic bursts. From what I could tell, Fife Lake seemed to be putting up little resistance. How do I get home? My father had been in the police. I knew he had a gun. But how do we get home without being shot? I crawled back toward town skinning my hands and knees. Between gullies I dashed for cover when whoever they were didn't seem to be looking, keeping my head down.

We crept up to the CPR railroad embankment just south of the village, where I summoned a deep well of courage to put my head up and peer over. Suppose they saw me. How could I sneak close enough to make a dash for the shelter of the hardware store. It was the first building on the corner.

I raised my head slowly, I knew it would be risky but what else could I do? I looked out over the railroad tracks. No paratroopers yet. But the noise was even louder, thunderous, not just small arms fire, heavy artillery, and the revving of a tank engine. It came from over near Larry Parks machine shop on railroad avenue. And then I saw him, the town's diesel mechanic leaning over the engine of an old time-worn tractor that had seen better days. Each time he revved it, the engine backfired. Boom! Thud! Boom! Boom! Loud enough to terrify any paratrooper that would dare assault Fife Lake.

Glen and I stood up and went off in our separate directions without saying a word. I never mentioned it again, to anyone, a day of ignominy, of failed courage at the prospect of battle. I suspect it is the way any soldier might feel in anticipation of combat.

Reports of real casualties began to come back from the war. Doug Schneider, one of Granny's grandsons, a tail gunner in a Lancaster bomber, was shot down over Germany and presumed dead. One of the Thomasett's sons, a local farm boy, was killed on a corvette torpedoed in the Atlantic.

My brother, Michael, who had been on HMCS Restigouche, was transferred to shore duty when the Canadian Navy formed its first band and had recruited musicians from the ranks. Six months later the sister ship of the Restigouche was torpedoed with all crew on board. The war was suddenly much more personal.

That December, 1941, we were invited to Sunday dinner at the Weisgerbers, my surrogate parents at birth, when my mother was taken away. December six, seven years to the day, she had died. The grown-ups turned on the evening news. The Japanese had bombed Pearl Harbor.

It was a bleak, overcast winter day, a dusting of snow on the ground, stubble showing through the brown fields. We drove back to Fife Lake over the frozen ruts of the prairie road.

"Thank God. Now the Americans will have to come into the war," my father had said. But with the sense of relief, was also threat. Now there was a war, not only across the Atlantic, but across the Pacific. Even I could tell by looking at a map that Canada was caught in the middle. This time it wasn't just the goose stepping German paratroopers, but Japanese kamakazi fighters, sneaky Japs, slant eyed little men we would demonize.

The following year the Japanese Emperor Hirohito replaced Stalin on the other side of the dart board.

Bing Crosby and Frank Sinatra now joined the war effort. Don't sit under the apple tree, with anyone else but me...Until I come marching home.

I'll be seeing you, in all the old familiar places, that this heart of mine embraces.

Lovely sentimental songs but no where near belligerent enough to make Miss Paisley's Top of the Hit Parade World War I marching songs.

Chapter 24: Reconnecting – Fife Lake, November 1981

"Frank, come on over. Guess who's here," Harkness called out that night of the Fife Lake reunion. Around nine o'clock the door of the Fife Lake Hotel and Restaurant opened, and a couple entered. They were evidently old customers and had come to join the Friday night party. They leaned into each other unsteadily. I felt this was not the first bar they had patronized that night.

"Do you know him?" Harkness, the hotel proprietor, asked me.

I looked closely. A short man about my height. Ten years older than I. Dark eyes, a sad, almost bewildered look. I did not recognize him, I did feel drawn to him, as I had felt drawn to the hilltop graveyard that morning. Who was he?

"It's Frank Weisgerber," Harkness said, "and Edna."

Weisgerber? Did I hear him right.

I put out my hand. "I'm Julian Nold," I said. "Your mother raised me when I was an infant."

"My God," he said. "My little brother Julian." And he burst into tears. "I used to wheel you and my little sister Rosemary in the baby carriage. You lived with us for two years."

"I found your mother's grave this morning," I said. And I began to cry.

We hugged each other as brothers who were lost and had been found, two grown men sobbing. Beer tears? Real tears? Did it matter?

Edna, His wife, a shriveled little woman, frail, broken by a succession of miscarriages and no children, I learned later, was embarrassed by this outburst of emotion.

"Stop crying, you old fool," she said.

"I'm crying because I'm happy. This is Julian," Frank said. "I never thought I'd see you again in my whole life."

We were saved by the one-man band that had been hired for the night, a Country Western singer who accompanied himself on an electric guitar, playing a harmonica clipped around his neck. An electronic rhythm machine gave a percussive beat amplified by two speakers, the bass dial fortissimo. This wasn't my kind of music, but I recognize All My Rowdy Friends by Hank Williams Jr., popular at the time on AM stations.

The music saved us from further awkwardness. They moved back some tables to make room for a dance floor, the size of a living room carpet. Edna invited me to dance. She was my age, fifty, ten years younger than Frank, I guessed. She clung to me tightly, the way people danced thirty years before, in the fifties. She sang along with the music, Giving It Up For Your Love.

"Remember what we used to do with John Seigo?" she asked in a husky voice.

"Why don't you tell me," I said.

And she blushed. "Across the tracks and in the bushes," she said, to refresh my memory.

I remembered a willow thicket in a dip on the prairie, wolf willows, where the hobos camped, great for shooting gophers. But I couldn't remember what John Seigo and I might have been up to with Edna in the willows. I couldn't even remember Edna as a twelve-year-old, though she clung to me tightly that night.

"I've always loved you," she said.

"You did?

"But Loretta said she would get you," she said, and she sang along with Cheated Me Right Out Of You.

It got crazier every minute. Who the hell was Loretta? The only girl I remembered who stirred my romantic fantasies was Ruth Strange.

Except for Gibby. She was different. Gabrielle Lesbatard, a French family. They lived on a farm three miles out of town, and were poor, very poor. Three girls. But tough. They'd walk to school along the railway tracks every day, through dust storms, hail or blizzards. Gibby was smart, all of us agreed, and pretty, and she could hit a beer bottle with a sling shot better than most boys. We all loved Gibby. Like a sister.

At 1 a.m., mandatory closing time, the musician ended the evening with Willy Nelson's, On The Road Again. Edna helped me finish off the beer that had accumulated on my table, complements of the guests. Standing up to go, she gave me a wet kiss. "My little brother," she said and walked unsteadily to join Frank. The door closed behind them.

Next morning I drove out to the lake, now glistening with a light skim of ice, and wrote long letters to my two daughters, then away from home at college, my half-brother Mickey, whom I had not seen in years, and trying to capture the fullness of that remarkable day and the doors it opened to the past. These letters became the inspiration for this memoir written many years later.

After my last dinner at the Fife Lake Hotel with Audrey Harkness, I started back for Regina. It was a clear star bright night and I stopped several times along the way to jot down notes, recalling my impressions.

You need to get out of the car. The summons came almost as a command. I opened the door and stood by the road side and gazed up. Overhead under the vast vault of the sky the aurora borealis was ablaze, shimmering in a waving curtain of luminous green, the pale green of an unripe apple. Spears of light, purple, green, a faint fiery red, the glowing red of embers, shot up, converging at the zenith, faded, lit up again. I thought I could hear the colors crackle, and then they darted out, disappearing into the universe.

Surely this was as close to the rapture I would experience, at least in this life.

Chapter 25: Exodus

Thirty-nine years previously I had traveled this same road. March, 1942, the year of our exodus. An early spring blizzard raged, driving wet snow, freezing rain, sleet. The unpaved road was churned into deep ruts. Otto, my father, drove our truck, a two-ton blue Chevy with an open bed, overloaded with our furniture. The truck slithered across the slick clay surface from one side of the road to the other as we crept along, wheels spinning. With each swing we came closer to sliding into the ditch and Otto spun the steering wheel back and forth furiously, fighting to keep to the crown on the middle of the road.

I was twelve years old, caught up in the drama, straining to see over the dashboard. I had an imaginative boy's capacity for fantasy, but this was real adventure. I felt both the anxiety, the dread, and delight, that paradox of any true adventure, praying that we not end up in the ditch, but secretly disappointed that we didn't.

Three months before, for Christmas I'd been given diary. In a boy's cryptic fashion, I recorded the events of that day, Said good-bye to Fife Lake. Dad drove to Regina in a blizzard. Took 13 hours. Made it!!!

On a paved highway in 1981, I covered that same 150 miles in three hours.

We were refugees fleeing the dust bowl, fleeing the discouraging years of the Depression and family trauma, part of the farm flight. Industrial Toronto, the promised land, beckoned with its war-time prosperity. Otto too was at a cross-roads.

We drove through North Dakota, caught in a series of spring blizzards that raged from the Rockies to the Great Lakes. For two days we were snowbound in Fargo, in the Elk Horn Hotel, the first time I'd ever stayed in hotel. We followed the snow plows out of town. I turned thirteen as we drove through Chicago in light wet snow. On April the first we drove into Toronto in a steady rain. Like Moses leading the Exodus, we felt we had arrived at the Promised Land.

But Toronto did not work out too well for my father. In fact it did not work out well at all. He had bought a small corner grocery store, the sort that Koreans would run today, a neighborhood convenience store. The store took telephone orders and made home deliveries. He bought me a second-hand Schwinn bicycle with balloon tires and a massive steel carrier basket, my first bicycle. After school I delivered groceries. But the store did not generate the volume of business he had anticipated. Too late, he realized he was competing with a new commercial phenomenon, the supermarket, where customers selected their own goods from open shelves and paid at the cash register on the way out. They liked the choice and the lower prices.

Then that summer there had been a series of burglaries reported in the newspapers. Not a crime wave, but my father detected a pattern, mostly small stores, just like ours. A retired policeman, he could defend himself.

On July 22, 1942, four months after leaving Fife Lake, he took out his service pistol to clean it. Forgetting that when he removed the cartridge clip, there was still one bullet in the breach. He sighted up the barrel and pulled the trigger.

That was the end of my childhood.

Chapter 26: St. Andrew's

I have often thought of my life as a series of dramatic discontinuities, with death acting as the catalyst for change. Going to St. Andrew's was such a change. After the death of my father, in the summer of 1942, that fall I was sent to boarding school.

St. Andrew's College has a venerable tradition, founded in 1899, an independent residential school in the Anglo-Scot public school tradition, for the sons of the wealthy middle class, "the future leaders of Canada," Dr. MacDonald, the founding Headmaster exhorted us in chapel. Vincent Massey, Canada's first native born Governor General, was an illustrious "Old Boy." Located in idyllic isolation, 25 miles north of Toronto, at the edge of Aurora, now suburbia, then a countryside of orchards, woodlots, rolling hills, open meadows and ponds. It sits perched on a low rise overlooking well groomed playing fields, the white lines and goal posts of football fields, a shallow stream meandering through, Shad Creek, picturesque, albeit malodorous with the effluent of a tannery a mile upstream. The elegant tower of a Georgian style chapel rises above wide branching elm trees; the residences, Flavelle House and Memorial House stately in red brick, green slate roofs, dormered windows, border the "Quad," the green carpeted lawn, long enough to run the hundred-yard-dash.

I entered the monumental gates and felt a new world was opening to me, like shipboard immigrants seeing the Statue of Liberty the first time. Barely six months before I had moved from Fife Lake, a primitive village in South Saskatchewan. Dust storms, grasshopper plagues, hail storms, sweeping winter blizzards were living memories. The nearest brick building had been the Rock Glen bank, 25 miles away. Only last March, I had carried the family drinking water each morning from the village well, relieved myself i he outhouse in the back yard. Otto, my father had carried out the "honey bucket." I was thrilled overwhelmed by the elegance. I felt like a castaway washed up on a tropical island, a displaced person, a refugee. Would they really take me in? Would they accept me? I wondered.

From pupa to butterfly, the transition could not have been more dramatic. Could I make the necessary transformation, or would I to remain the grub? I began to re-create myself, from country boy to preppy. "The apparel oft proclaims the man." The training of a gentleman began with grooming. Was this why Mr. Millar had outfitted me in this elaborate wardrobe? I'd never owned a sports coat before and now wore grey flannel trousers and sports coats to class every day, instead of overalls and sweater, and a shirt with tie. I had to learn to tie the tie. On Sundays I wore my new blue suit, a white shirt with the red and white stripped school tie, and black shoes. Brown shoes were for week days only. Sneakers were worn only in the gym. Out of doors and off campus, like all "new boys," I wore my school cap, a red beanie, emblazoned with the cross of St. Andrew, a token of great pride. I felt myself a prince dressed up for a meeting of state or for a funeral of royalty, arrayed in my new wardrobe.

My mother had died when I was five, leaving me with a life-long craving for attention, starved for affection, desperate to be popular, an anxiety I hid behind a wise-guy smirk, that James Cagney smile. Fortunately I was bright enough to do well academically and soon ranked first in a class of twelve. From a one room school house on the prairies to first in my class in an elite Canadian private school, my new family, the Millars were relieved and showed their proud. Teachers marked me as having promise.

But I soon learned that if I was to make it with my peers, the football field was the proving ground. Though small, and somewhat pudgy, I was fast and strong, a recklessly daring tackler. I made the Lower School team and earned my colors, the only eigth-grader to do so.

But the sure-fire way of getting attention and gaining notoriety was to be naughty. "Down to see Mr. Wright." One dark night I was caught by Mr. Ives talking after lights out. He was the master-on-duty and patrolled the halls ferreting out offenders. We called him "Pussy Foot" Ives, because he prowled silently in rubber soled shoes, which we considered an unfair advantage. Talking after lights out was a major transgression, and I was a repeat offender. Mr. Ives, the cop on the beat, booked the charge: Mr. Wright, the house master, was the judge and executioner. I entered Mr. Wright's study. It was in shadow, lit only by a subdued light under a green lamp shade, that cast an inquisitorial gloom. Books lined the walls. There was an aromatic smell of tobacco smoke. Mr. Wright sat behind his desk. I remained standing, beside a large leather arm chair wearing thin pajamas and dressing gown, a recent addition to my wardrobe, and slippers. His voice was soft, sympathetic even. Reasoning sweetly with Jesuitical cunning, he extracted from me my confession, "Yes, I was talking...Sir." My contrition, "Yes, I'm sorry ...Sir." But he never asked me whether I'd ever do it again, knowing that I would, not wanting to compound my disobedience with a lie. There was a note of sadness in his voice, and just when I thought he was going to let me off with "lines," copying out meaningless lines on the blackboard, or "detention," sitting in a classroom on a Saturday afternoon, as he did the last time. But instead, he stood up, walked around the desk and said, "Bend over the chair," in a this-is-going-to-hurt-me-more-than-it-hurt-you tone of voice. Bending awkwardly over the arm of the chair, arse in the air, face down in the seat, smelling the patent leather, I heard the swish of the cane hissing through the air, then felt resounding thwack as it drove home, three well batted swats. My companion in crime, waiting outside the study was next. We scampered up stairs to sit in the bathroom sink, turned the water on cold, and examined our welts. "Sergeant stripes," he said. It was the first of fourteen late night trips Mr. Wright's office. Only one other boy was caned more I that term, Perlman, the only Jew at the Lower School, who never did fit in, and withdrew from the school at

Christmas. But I was a survivor, proud of my record, and went on to popularity, notoriety and boyhood fame.

Homesickness plagued so many of us younger boys but I was immune. Though the Millars had taken me into their family, I had no real sense of home. I always felt like a boarder. I was in a very real sense a displaced person. Like a recent immigrant I was eager to put my past behind me. Though secretly proud of my rugged prairie upbringing, I never talked about it. Nor did I talk about my father who was German and came from Russia and had shot himself. Nor did I mention my mother was a French Canadian, and had died in a mental hospital. This would not have gone over well in the Anglo-Scots culture of St. Andrew's, particularly during the war years.

I had even a bigger secret. I wet my bed. The matron soon got word of it and every day would change my sheets without fanfare or admonition, after we were in class sparing me the shame. I don't know if other boys knew. I suspect not, for we were not a compassionate lot, and though the hazing of younger boys never reached the sadistic proportions of an English public school, there were bullies and I lived in dread of being found out and teased, and held up to ridicule. One thing I could not endure was being ridiculed. Ever.

One of our more common pranks was inter-dormitory gang raids, barging into another dorm and turning over the metal cots, and stripping off the sheets. I felt particularly vulnerable. They'd see the rubber sheet on my bed. I'd be exposed. I fought like fury to defend my corner, and the rough and tumble of my prairie village upbringing stood me in good stead. John Capon was in the bed next to mine. A scrawny kid with big ears, an elongated narrow head, a slight slobbery slur in his speech, he was an easy target. Night after night rowdies would barge in and rip his bed apart. I grew to resent their picking on him, bullying. It was no longer funny, I felt, just mean. So I stood up defiantly beside John, defending his domain and mine. To John's relief and mine that put an end to the hazing. I saw it as an act of protest against social injustice and felt proud.

With all my youthful affection and boyhood loyalty I focused on becoming an Andrean, tried and true. It was a boy's world and I was a boy's boy and fitted in rapidly. The school gave me an ordered life, a predictable environment for the first time in my life, adult discipline and encouragement. I was bright enough to be rewarded by the faculty, enough of a hellion to be popular with my peers. It was a happy boyhood. They were formative years, as happy as I have known.

Our lives gravitated around our peers, but it was the teachers, "masters" we called them, who represented the school as an institution. Many were eccentric. Those were war years and most young men who were fit went off to serve in the armed forces. There was a teacher shortage. The headmaster, Mr. Ketchum, had left for the duration of the war to be director of studies at the newly established Naval Academy at Royal Roads in British Columbia. My first year, in grade 8, "Upper Second" it was called in the English tradition, Mr. Young taught us French. A tall, big robust man, he had a withered left hand that we never saw for he kept it tucked in his jacket pocket. He was clearly impatient with having to teach beginners French. He strutted up and down in front of the black board, drilling us in verb conjugations and pronunciation.

77

He was fixated on us learning proper French nasal intonation.. For the first week we repeatedly practiced, "Ohn, Awhn, Aahn." And the reverse, "Aahn, Awhn, Ohn," like a Buddhist mantra. He became furious with those who could not get it, and he would line us up at the front of the class and give us a swift kick in the rump, to improve our ear. I mastered correct pronunciation readily for my French Canadian mother had endowed me with a nose of the right shape, but I made mistakes deliberately. Who wanted to miss the fun of being kicked at the front of the class and be left sitting alone in his seat?

Canadian History was taught by "Pussy Foot" Ives and though not a particularly dynamic teacher, I delighted in the heroics of the voyages of exploration, the fur trade and the disastrous attempts to find the Northwest Passage. We paddled with Mackenzie to the Arctic, with Fraser to the Pacific. We were shipwrecked with Franklin and debated whether they really reverted to cannibalism. Years later I paddled my own canoe down the Missinabi River to Moose Factory on James Bay, with a copy of "Caesars of the North" in my pack, reliving the fantasies of my boyhood.

Sports were the fast track to popularity. I had never seen a football, yet alone carried one, and though I was a fast runner, I was relegated to the line. There I shunted and groveled in the mud of a rainy Ontario fall, and delighted in the turmoil. I tackled fearlessly and was proud when awarded team colors at the end of the season. But ice hockey was different. Before the days of artificial ice skating rinks, many of the National Hockey League players came from Western Canada, with its long, cold winters, where hockey was supreme. I can't remember when I could not skate, and though small for my age, I was built solidly, was aggressive and fast. I was a peewee star. The team high scorer, I would have been captain of the team, but this was considered inappropriate for a "new boy", only in the eighth grade. But I had my eyes on the prize.

Boxing was compulsory, and we were poorly matched according to weight, but not age or physical strength. I was a chunky kid and in the ring came up against Horwood, who was slim trim, 6 inches taller than I, three years older, an upper classman, weighing only 125 lbs. It was a total mismatch. While he was no great athlete, Horwood's arms were several inches longer than mine and he hammered away at me with a succession of left jabs. I stood my ground, but I could never reach him. Then in the third and final round, he let down his guard, and I landed one well placed blow, straight from my right shoulder to his jaw. Only one blow, but I had carried the family drinking water from the village well since the age of ten, and I had considerable upper arm strength. Horwood was wearing a tooth guard, which I knocked loose, and he choked on it. Coach stopped the fight. Technically it was a knock-out blow, and I thought maybe I had won the bout. Certainly I would have, had it been a free-for-all. But he gave Horwood time to replace his tooth guard, and we fought on the remaining minutes and Horwood was awarded the fight on points. I returned to the Lower School, battered and bruised, proud of my swollen lip and a darkening eye, the hero of my dorm mates. They felt a great fraud had been perpetrated. "You knocked him out," they insisted. But I had enough, and was content with a moral victory.

At Prize Day at the end of the year, I was awarded a book of Cowper's poems, richly bound in red leather, embossed with the St. Andrew's crest, for being first academically in my class. I never read Cowper, but was launched on the trajectory of deceptively easy academic success, collecting beautifully bound, unreadable book prizes each year.

The next year, 1943, I moved up to Flavelle House, the middle school residence. Mr. Tudball, "Tuddy" was our housemaster. A short, robust man, he had an old country charm, a warm smile and wry sense of humor, but when aroused he had a furious temper. On one occasion he became so angry he broke a blood vessel in his right eye, and we would bait him to see if he would do it again. I roomed with football and hockey pal, Bill Howson, a fellow Westerner from Alberta. His father was Chief Justice of the Supreme Court of Alberta. He was a year ahead of me, as were all my closest friends. Horwood, my boxing bete noir, was Head Prefect and I was assigned to him as his fag. I made his bed and swept his room every day. I don't know if he selected me deliberately as his factotum, but he never mentioned our boxing mismatch. I also stopped wetting my bed, miracle of miracles. I had a sense of growing up.

I was now thoroughly inculcated in the achievement ethic of prep school. I took pride in being first in my class each year. In sports I was captain of the junior team, in both football and hockey, games where speed and strength counted. But I never had the hand eye coordination to sink a basketball predictably, or catch a cricket ball bare handed. But I could run, and recall one moment of glory on the football field when I caught the ball on the kick off and ran through the opposing team of peewees, for a touch down. Alas, it was an experience I was never to know again. Boxing also continued to be my nemesis, being short and stocky, I kept coming up against taller boys with longer arms and could never get at them. It was then I got my first pair of skis, wooden boards with cable bindings, on which we would stumble and tumble our way down small hills behind the school. On Sundays I would sometimes take long walks in the countryside, wandering far on back country roads, returning hot and tired for dinner. In the spring track meet I did well in the 100-yard and 200-yard dash, where a quick start seemed to help, but faded to longer limbed boys on the 400-yard and half mile. I was competitive in the long jump, fell behind in the high jump, my stubby legs straining for the bar. .

Those were impressionable years and steeped myself in the heroic. Learning was equated with memorizing and I still declaim lines of poetry I learned over fifty-years ago. Mr. Tudball who taught us English in the Third Form, grade nine, had us memorize long passages of "Horatio at the Bridge," and years later on the banks of the Tiber in Rome, I declaimed:

> *Lars Porsena of Clusium by the nine gods he swore*
> *That the great house of Tarquin should suffer wrong no more.*
> *By the nine gods he swore it, and named a trysting day...*

Less heroically we wiped our dripping fountain pens, before the days of the ball point pen, on Danny, Tuddy's faithful daschund who waddled after him to class every day. Traveling through Belgium, a few years ago I could still recite the moving lines,

> *In Flanders fields the poppies blow,*
> *Between the crosses row on row.*

Tuddy, a World War I veteran had been there and fought in the trenches.

The English syllabus in the following years was replete with heroic sentiment, and the Victorian virtues of duty, persistence, honor and glory. Kipling's poem,

> "If...and what's more you'll be a Man my son."
> "Invictus....I thank whatever gods may be/
> For my indominable soul."
>
> ~ Tennyson's Ulysses

> "My purpose holds to sail beyond the sunset."

British History was taught by Mr. Laidlaw, called "Bobby" for reasons I never knew, in 10th grade, the Fourth Form. On his good days he was wonderful and we relived the Battle of Jutland with Nelson. When told that the signal flag ordered him to break off action, he held the telescope to his blind eye and said, "I don't see any signal." And he sailed into the midst of the Danish fleet to another victory and more glory. Years later I sailed out of Cadiz harbor on the Atlantic coast of Spain in my yacht "Zillah", following in the wake of the French-Spanish fleet in 1805. As we rounded Cape Trafalgar I recounted to my crew Laidlaw's account of how the English fleet was waiting just over the horizon, and a blow by blow account of how they broke the French line and captured or sank half the enemy fleet, and of Nelson's heroic death, shot by a sharpshooter in the rigging. That was Mr. Laidlaw on his good days. On others, he would shuffle into class, head down, hunched over, with a faint odor of alcohol on his breath, and slump into his chair. "Read your book like a novel, boys," he would admonish us, and then proceed to read from the text, having us underline the significant passages in our books.

Scripture too had its heroes. As a Catholic, I never read the Bible. We were spoon fed, or force fed our Christianity from a catechism, a book of moral strictures and dogmatic assertion. The Bible was new to me, and it opened a whole new vista of stories. Moses leading the chosen people to freedom, climbing a mountain to receive the Word, a lesson I took to heart, climbing mountains much of my life in search of higher vision. And David slaying Goliath, was the idol of every small boy growing up, the little guy taking on the big bully; though David did not look all that small when later I looked up at Michelangelo's towering statue in Florence. We would read in the Book of Kings and snicker at David's sexual exploits, delighted but disconcerted. And the Good Samaritan: *A certain man went down from Jerusalem to Jericho, and fell among thieves,* the heroism of the common man. The Beatitudes were heavier going, and Tuddy had us learn them by heart. Learning by heart, sounded so much more evocative than memorizing. But for any lapse of memory we were punished. We were made to stand along the back wall of the classroom, listening to others recite falteringly: *Blessed are the humble and the meek.* And thou shalt be punished if thou dost forget it, I muttered under my breath. I felt the ring of the old English prose in the King James version of the Bible, a new richness in words.

In chapel, every morning before classes, and again on Sunday evening, we chanted psalms; *I will life up mine eyes unto the hills.* And we sang the ancient Crusader's hymn, *Onward Christian soldier/ Marching as to war,* stamping out the rhythm until reprimanded, and for good measure, the school hymn, *Fight the good fight/ With all thy might.* We sang with purpose and conviction, for those were fighting days. We were at war. There was not a pacifist among us. Tattered battle flags from WWI draped from the wall at the back of the chapel. We were imbued with a muscular Christianity.

The trappings of military discipline were instilled most mornings in the spring and fall, weather permitting. Cadet Corps drill was held on the quad, marching to the command of Mr. Wright and the stirring music of the bagpipe band. In the summer term there was an annual cadet corps inspection, in full ceremonial battle colors. Our Cadet Corps was affiliated with the 48th Highlands of Canada, and we wore the dress uniform of a highlander soldier, Gordon tartan kilt with leather sporan, brilliant red tunic with brass buttons, white belt with broad brass buckle, white spats to the calf, over tartan knee socks with red garter tabs, a checkered Glengarry cap perched at a jaunty angle. I felt we were a marvelous spectacle. General Wolf could not have assaulted Quebec with greater pomp and circumstance. It certainly beat the cassock and surplice of an alter boy I'd known as a child in Saskatchewan. I loved the pageantry, the romance of it, the brilliant display of heroics. I learned to march more erect than the next boy, and I polished my brass buttons so carefully that I was awarded the cup as best cadet. The next year a cadet corporal, then sergeant, and lieutenant, and in my last year captain of the corps.

The biggest cadet corps event was the Cadet Corps Ball. It even overshadowed the Armistice Day parade and the annual inspection. It was the great social event of the school year.

Cadet Corps is always associated in my mind with girls. Girls were of course an infinite source of disinformation and erotic fantasy. But in late winter, fantasy took on reality, the Cadet Corps Ball, As fourteen-year-olds in the Lower School we were pressured to attend, for this too was part of the education of a gentleman. It took on the bustle of a military parade. Brass buckles were brassoed, buttons polished, spats and belt whitened, red tunics de-moth-balled, kilts pleated and pressed. But it presented two seemingly insoluble problems. First you needed a girl. And second, you needed to know how to dance! But Mr. Wright, our housemaster and commander of the Corps had thought through every eventuality. The blind date! Shy and pimply girls were conscripted from Branscome Hall and Havergill School, two socially prominent girl schools in Toronto. And we were ordered to appear for dancing lessons parade in the basement hall of Mac Donald House after evening study. Lined up in a row, "by the right," we held our first dancing partner, a hockey stick, at arms length. And to the rhythm of Glenn Miller's "Tuxedo Junction," and "String of Pearls," we marched in place in a small square, "Left, right, left...dip."

Having mastered the mechanics of the fox trot, a week later came the real test of courage, live partners: Mrs. Wright, the house master's wife, Mrs. Grant, the aging Nurse and Matron, the younger Upper School Matron. We moved in tandem terror with a live body held at outstretched arms length. We survived our initiation into the mysterious world of the opposite sex, tongue tied, blushing, stumbling our way through the evening of the ball, our partners trying as hard as ourselves to enjoy themselves, painfully enduring the ordeal. But as the years went by, and we became more debonaire, the girls less giggly and more coy, flirtatious, the ball became a truly gala event. I recall particularly Pipe Major Fraser of the 48th Highlanders, piping us through highland reels, to the swirl of kilts and the flow of evening gowns. It had all the beauty of youthful fantasy, boyhood romance and the sparkle of non-alcoholic champagne.

In the early forties I grew up in the midst of wartime heroics. Movies were always preceded by newsreels, *The Eyes and Ears of the World*, often with Winston Churchill flashing his "V for Victory" at the camera. He scowled angrily with grim determination in the famous photograph by Karsh. We parodied his defiant speech, *We shall fight them on the beaches...we shall fight them in the country lanes... We shall never surrender.*

Early in the war, Buzz Beuhling, a Canadian from Quebec, became the first air ace of the war. Flying with the RAF in the Battle of Malta, he shot down an incredible five enemy aircraft in a Spitfire. I planned to be fighter pilots. Lawrence Olivier's production of Shakespeare's "Henry V" came to Toronto, classes were cancelled for the day and the whole school bused to the show: *Once more into the breach, dear friends, Once more/ Or cover it with our English dead.* A stirring piece of wartime propaganda, in the best sense, one of the first movies to be made in Technicolor. The bloodshed was curiously sanitized, in striking contrast to Kenneth Branaugh's gory post-Vietnam contemporary version. But for us it was an age of heroism, and we believed in the rightness of our cause, and in our heroes, past and present.

After the Battle of El Alamein, the first allied victory in the deserts of Egypt, a turning point in the war, we saw the full length newsreel. Midst the thundering of artillery, the pounding of bombs, sappers lead the advance to clear the mine fields. They were accompanied by the wild, demonic wail of bag pipes. I paraded with a new erectness and pride. "Eyes right!" I commanded my platoon and saluted the larger than life sized statue of St. Andrew, the patron saint of Scotland, at the head of the driveway as we marched by on morning parade.

VE Day, Victory in Europe, came in May, 1945. School was still in session. The Cadet Corps paraded to a memorial service in the Presbyterian Church in Aurora, uniformed in wartime summer khaki. Cars hooted and people cheered us as they passed. Mr. Garret, the acting headmaster during the war years declared a holiday. Many of us deserted and hitchhiked to Toronto in uniform. I sought out Marilyn, the current beauty for whom I pined and we walked hand in hand to see the fireworks and joined in the celebrations. But her mother insisted she not stay out late and we never did get to join in the street dancing. The war was over! But with the egocentricity of an adolescent, I had a sense of disappointment that I would not be able to take part in it. Cadet Corps, which had a purpose until now, became a charade.

VJ Day, Victory in Japan, followed that summer, suddenly, unexpectedly, with the spectacular and awesome impact of two bombs over Hiroshima and Nagasaki, bombs that wiped out whole cities. Bombs created by the force of exploding atoms, a concept I had difficulty understanding, then as now. It was one of those days when time stopped, and you would remember where you were that day for the rest of your life. I had a summer job as a bell-hop at Windermere Lodge, a classy resort hotel on Lake Muskoka, 150 miles north of Toronto. It was a glamorous summer, sunbathing on the dock with the beautiful waitresses, dancing in the evening. There was motor boating. We had free access to the golf course. Too young to buy liquor at the government controlled outlet, the bellhops collected all the empties from the rooms and drained the last drops into a common container. It made a potent brew of scotch, rye whiskey, rum, gin, barely potable even when disguised with orange juice, so there was little temptation to overindulge. But the idea of a celebratory potion was enough for us to commemorate the event with a stomach wrenching toast.

On Armistice Day, November 11 that year, the Cadet Corps was invited by the 48th Highlanders, the regiment to which we were affiliated, to join in a memorial service parade to St. Andrew's Presbyterian Church in Toronto. After opening prayers and the hymn, the congregation remained standing at attention, enveloped by the soaring space of the lofty cathedral. Silent. Then distant and faint, the eerie high pitched wail of a lone bagpipe filtered into the church. It came from behind the alter, clearer now, the piper approached slowly down a narrow hallway, the drone becoming louder. And louder. Standing in the narrow door directly behind the alter, the sound overflowed into the cathedral, the reedy cry of *The Piper's Lament*. Sound echoed off the vaulted ceiling, reverberating through the soaring arches. The bass drones, moaning and groaning their grief for the dying and the dead. The hysterical shrill of the chanter, like the high pitched wail of keening women, mothers and widows, despairing the loss of their men. Barbaric, terrifying music. Then the piper slowly retreated back down the hallway, the sound diminishing eventually to a faint murmur. To empty sound and space. And the loudness of the silence.

In retrospect the war years left me with a world view that imbued my mind set, that created the backdrop for the drama of our lives. I saw the world as in the movies, in black and white. There were forces of good and evil. We felt we stood on the moral higher ground. It was an heroic age. There were just wars, and we grew up believing in our heroes.

But there was an astounding moral gap. It would be years before I, or my generation, became aware of the plight of the Jews. Was awareness of the Holocaust deliberately suppressed, I wondered in later years. For during football season in the fall of 1946, the year after the war when the horrors of Belsen and Auschwitz had been exposed, there was a pep rally in the gym after study hall. We shouted not only school cheers, but lewd limericks and ribald ditties, a couple blatantly racist and anti-Semitic.

Easy, Izey, easy am
We're the boys who eat no ham
Easy Isey, easy ork
We're the boys, who eat no pork
Roast beef rahh.

The cheer leader came from a prominent Toronto family, and went on to become head prefect. But we all laughed and cheered.

There were no Jews, Blacks, or Orientals in the school in my days. The school clearly represented the White-Anglo-Saxon-Celtic, Protestant majority, with a very thin peppering of Catholics, Eastern Europeans and French Canadians like me, who aspired to be like *them*.

So ended the war, at least for us, and the school returned to prewar normalcy, whatever that was. Butter appeared again on the table, more meat, sugar was no longer rationed, nor gas. And we entered the years of post war optimism and reconstruction, and a new found prosperity.

After the war a new lineup of teachers filled the master's common room. Mr. Ketchum, the Headmaster, returned from the Navy and wearing the long black academic gown that all masters wore to class, he strode down the quad each morning, a tall, rather gaunt figure, his gown flapping and streaming behind him. Someone named him, *The Crow,* and the name stuck.

The Romantic poets were introduced to us by one of those marvellous eccentrics, whose name mercifully I cannot remember. He lasted one year and was then I suspect was fired. "We now come to the three sex perverts of English literature, Byron, Keats and Shelley." That got our attention and we learned reams of their poems that have stayed with me. On moonlight passages at sea, I recall Shelley:

That orbed maiden, by white fire laden, that morals call the moom
Glides glimmering o'er thy fleece like floor/ By the midnight breezes strewn.

Every time I fell into love, or thought I had, and out of love again, Byron came to mind; "La belle dame sans merci, hath thee enthrall."

I had greater difficulty with Wordsworth, whom I came to love and later made pilgrimages to Tintern Abbey and his grave in the Lake District. But, "...I saw a host, a crowd of golden daffodils/ Laughing and dancing in the breeze/...Later in a gay and pensive mood," was too much more homophobic youth. The mysticism of "Intimations of Immortality" came later. Coleridge is mesmerizing still, "Alone, alone, all alone, alone on the wide wide sea/ So lonely 'twas that God Himself, scarce seemed there to be." Our teacher was seldom on campus on weekends, and returned on Monday mornings, worn, weary and bedraggled. "How did the lost weekend go, Sir?" I once had the impertinence to ask him. "Nold," he said in a confiding tone, "all I can remember is that she was white." His personal values may have been questionable, but he knew how to teach.

Gordon Taylor was another outstanding teacher, my best. "El Poncho," we called him. Short, squat, narrow shoulders, shaped like a pear, fair round belly and broad buttocks. He taught Shakespeare and brought the Globe theatre of our classroom, a one man show. "Friends, Roman, countrymen, lend me your ear," the harangue of the pagan Mark Anthony rang through the Christian halls of St. Andrew's. I responded to the rising bell each morning quoting Macbeth, "Hear it not Duncan, for tis the knell/ That summons thee to heaven, or to hell." And in my despondent moods: "Tomorrow and tomorrow and tomorrow, creeps on this petty pace/ To the last syllable of recorded time."

But his star performance was Falstaff in Henry IV, Part I, where Falstaff falls off his horse during an attempted highway robbery. Lying prone on the ground, too fat to get up by himself, he called "Poins," his partner in crime, for help. "Poins," El Poncho shouted at the top of his lungs, acting the part, his voice reverberating down the hall. "Poins!" he shouted again, the class bursting out in laughter and cheering. In the midst of the uproar and pandemonium, a face appeared, framed in the small window high on the classroom door, "The Crow," the Headmaster, with a look of, "What the hell's going on?" His office was directly below and sound carried through the heating ducts. We give out another uproarious burst of laughter. Mischevous Taylor read on, picking Falstaff up off the ground, clearly enjoying himself.

There was an air of mystery about Mr. Taylor. Like most of our teachers he had his idiosyncrasies. Commenting on the pantheistic mysticism of Wordsworth's Tintern Abbey, he went on to tell of his own mystical experience of hiking in a wooded glen in Wales during the war. "Under a tree I saw a green fairy," he said and went on to describe the experience in reverential terms. We were hushed, torn between believing him, and feeling that he was putting us on. But he was serious, and though we scoffed, to this day I am not absolutely sure that fairies are not to be seen in Wales. Though I've been there and never saw any.

I knew he spoke fluent Chinese, and with a little probing I learned that he was an ordained Protestant minister who had trained to be a missionary. His mission work had been cut short by the war, but then he was recruited by the Navy as an intelligence officer. "I'm very sad today," he told me one morning in an unusual moment of confidence as we walked together to class. "Three years ago today, five of my colleagues were murdered in Calcutta." El Poncho," the most unlikely suspect for a dangerous career, overweight, unobtrusive, but mentally alert, the perfect spy. Indeed, he did have that pudgy academic appearance of Smiley in a John LeCarre spy novel.

We had an outstanding mathematics teacher in Norman Lane. I was able to comprehend the principles of basic algebra and Euclidean geometry, but the more talented he took on to three dimensional geometry, (or was it four dimensional?) and calculus, not a common high school subject then. He was also an accomplished gymnast, in spite of having a glass eye. Twirling keys and one flew off the ring and struck him in the eye.

But "Normie" was also a hero: not just a school hero, but a national hero. He represented Canada in the first post-war Olympics, and won a bronze medal in canoeing, the only Canadian to win a medal in the games. We felt he should have won the gold. He had trained with Spartan discipline all spring term, leaving school right after classes each day, paddling fifty miles from Toronto to Hamilton and back, returning at night. He would have won the gold, but lost out on a technical decision. He paddled a conventional Canadian canoe with a straight keel. This required the outward thrust of the J-stroke to keep the canoe on course, thereby losing forward power. The Czechs and Germans had developed a canoe with a slight curve to the keel, permitting them to paddle a straight power stroke. The Canadians and Americas filed a grievance, but the Olympic Committee ruled in favor of the Europeans. So Lane paddled third, rather than first, took his disappointment with a true sportsman's grace, resigned himself to being a hero third class.

Latin was a dead language, but taught with a lively flair by an ageing Dr. Robinson. From him I learned what little I know of the structure of the English language, and acquired an early fascination with the derivation of words. Years later I am always pleasantly surprised at how well I could muddle my way through in Spanish in Mexico or Spain, and in Italian, falling back on Latin derivatives. French, though a living language, was taught as if dead, and after six years of uninspired instruction, we were still functionally illiterate. Bilingualism was a non-starter.

Our studies were seldom inspired by the quest for knowledge. In the higher forms, the syllabus was largely examination driven, to jump the high hurdles of the Ontario Senior Matriculation. Physics was taught from a prescribed textbook, the master demonstrating the laws of mechanics for the class, described Archimedes floating in the baths of Syracuse. The course was solidly rooted in Newton, $E=mc2$ not having found its way into the textbook even three years after Hiroshima. Our chemistry teacher was the most successful at grade snatching. The fall term was a hurried survey of the course, the teacher demonstrating the experiments for us, for the chemistry lab was inadequate for students to carry out any but the most basic of experiments. Besides, playing with experiments had nothing to do with passing exams. The second half of the year, we worked our way back through twenty-five years of Ontario Department of Education examination papers, right back to 1922. We learned little chemistry, but we did learn to outwit the examiners.

Culturally Canada was still a colonial backwater, Anglo-Canadians beholden to England, preferably the buoyant optimism of Victorian England, and French-Canadians to France, royalist clerical pre-revolutionary France. A country living in "Two Solitudes," as Bruce McLelland described it. The literature we read was English Literature, Dickens, Hardy, Conrad's "Youth,", not the failed heroism of "Lord Jim." We read no Canadian literature, except for Bliss Carmen's pietistic poem, "Trees," and the humorous short stories of Stephen Leacock. Canadian authors had yet to be gifted by the muse.

There was no Art in the curriculum, though Mr. Ives was an accomplished painter. But the dazzling colors of the Canadian fall, wind swept pines and scudding clouds of painters like Tom Thompson and Lauren Harris, penetrated our consciousness through the framed reprints displayed about the school. But it would be years before I visited my first art gallery.

Music fared somewhat better. We had an outstanding music master in David Ochterlony, who moved on to greater musical prominence. He acquired a music library for the school with a Carnegie Foundation grant, and moving from piano to records opened the door to classical music for us, playing the easily accessible music of Rimsky-Korsakov's "Sheherezade," "The Sorcerer's Apprentice," Mousorsky's "Pictures in a Gallery." Ochterlony, tall, lean, angular, with extended arms and legs he embraced the chapel organ like a huge spider, enticing the racing elegance of a Bach fugue from keyboard, pulling stops, dancing on the foot pedals with a gymnast's agility. The Christmas carol service was the musical highlight of the year, "Jesu Joy of Man's Desiring," in three part harmony, "Adeste Fideles" in Latin, and old English country dance carols, "Ding, Dong Merrily on High." When Mr. Ketchum returned from the war, the Headmast himself conducted. One year I was turned away from the service because I was not wearing my blue suit. Carelessly I had sent it to the cleaners. Standing alone in the window of my room, high up across the quad, the strains of "The First Nowell," snow sifting quietly by the lamplight, I was totally dismayed. Like another Joseph who was turned away from the inn.

Drama received a degree of prominence. We had three very accomplished actors, Don Davis, who went on for a professional career and his own drama company; Mike Magee, later a radio show personality, Mr. Dobbs; and Victor Rodwell. who as a research scientist continued to play amateur roles late in life. They tri-starred in "Arsenic and Old Lace." My role was that of cheer section and audience. I had been in the infirmary with mumps, so missed the school night production. But I was released in time to attend on parent's night. I sat at the back of the theatre, a cavern-like room in the basement of Dunlap Hall, the academic building. I laughed without inhibition, a cheer leading section of one, to the delight of my friends in the cast, but to the annoyance of the audience. It was very funny, and I had just been released from two weeks quarantine. I was merely expressing my joy on both accounts. However, at the end of the show, Mr. Goodman, the chemistry teacher, took me aside. "You remind me Nold of the lines from Goldsmith. He writes of—the empty headed laughter of the village idiot," he admonished. Magee was a good friend. He had come to St. Andrew's on the rebound, not having done well at Appleby School. A born mimic, masterful story teller, I have seen him engage a street corner evangelist in theological debate about the coming apocalypse, quoting non-existing passages from the Bible, baiting and refuting. Brilliant, with incredible verbal recall, fabulous memory, he was the wittiest, most entertaining person I have ever met. But he was totally resistant to academic achievement. We roomed together for part of a year, and he would regale us well into the night, before he was expelled. He was an impossible student, but life lost sparkle when he left. He then went on to follow the races, becoming totally addicted to the track. I spent hours with him in later years, rolling in laughter as he described race after race with breath taking detail, the ups and downs, the fortunes and misfortunes of the life of a gambler at the track.

Girls were an endless source of disinformation and erotic fantasy, as our masculinity heated up. We saw few girls at school, only the kitchen maids. In Aurora, there were the town girls on the streets, at the drug store soda fountain, and in church on Sunday. But these were at-arms-length encounters. We were not permitted weekend leave, but on mid-term break and holidays we began to engage in teenage boy-girl activities, house parties in basement recreation rooms, where we turned the lights low, until mother hostess turned them up again. Movies, where in the semi-dark we risked holding hands. It was the age of the big bands, and we joined the big crowds at Casa Loma, a 19 century "folly," an imitation mediaeval castle on a hilltop in North Toronto. "Swing and sway with Sammy Kaye," was a popular American radio program. "Swing and sweat with Sam Burdett," was our motto for a popular local band. And of course, the Annual Cadet Corps Ball. In spite of the bravado of common room talk, and the fantasies we lived out in the lonely seclusion of our beds, our loves were awkward, often painful, innocent. There were some who bragged about "how far they got," but it was generally discounted. I hadn't got anywhere, and would not know what to do if I did. I desperately wanted to be liked by girls, to be held in warm embracing arms, more a sisterly love. Ian Schofield had a lovely sister, Heather, blond flowing hair, pretty face with a healthy Scottish light skinned complexion, ample breasts, our age. And she went the rounds, several of us dated her, were passionately in love for a time until others caught our eye. She became something of a mascot, a friend and sister surrogate to us all. The sexual urge was strong, but somehow this was confusedly different. I studied the brassier ads in the newspapers, with avid curiosity, wondering what it was really like to penetrate beneath, this long before the day of the fold our pin up nudes of Playboy magazine.

Friendly men with broad smiles and ingratiating greetings lurked about the bus terminal in Toronto, where we returned to school. "Homo," a more worldly wise schoolmate murmured, pointing one out and sniggering. I didn't understand what he was referring to, and still didn't quite comprehend when he tried to explain. I'd heard the term "cock-sucker" back in Fife Lake days, but never associated it with a human act, but thought of it as a worm, or something, like a "blood-sucker." With hindsight, I suspect there was some homosexual activity at school, latent, if not overt, but it was never blatant, as it was apparently in English public schools. If we were blatant about anything, it was our homophobia, a term I learned very much later in my life.

Sex was a lively topic of discussion after lights out in the darkness of our rooms. But it took on a new dimensions with Coach Kendall's lectures on "Sex Education." They were more about morality than biology, more on masturbation than procreation. St. Paul's admonition about casting one's seed. Better to marry than burn. And Coach spelled out in lurid detail the plight of lunatics in an asylum, constrained in straight jackets to prevent them from defiling their bodies, cause and effect somehow reversed. "And this could happen to you," clearly the implication. We listened, and smirked, and for days after, performed a pantomime of an insane inmate delighting in sin, in various postures of physical ecstasy. We were left more confused than ever about the complexity of sexuality, a complexity that has a touch of mystery still.

Cliques formed among the students. There were the Toronto sophisticates, boys from several prominent social families; they called themselves "The Group." Our age cohort responded by banding together and we called ourselves, "de Mob." Several of us, the core, had been together since our first year in MacDonald House, the lower school, Bill Howson, whose father was Chief Justice of the Supreme Court of Alberta, Louis Heit, son of a bank Vice-President, Don Shaw, whose father was President of ICI, Canada Dupont, Ian Scholfield, myself, son of a Saskatchewan village merchant and farm machinery dealer. We prided ourselves in being unconventional, uncouth even. One year Schofield and Howson, forerunners of the skin-heads, shaved their heads. They were gated, providing them with an excuse for not attending the Cadet Corps Ball, which they chose to boycott that year.

"De Mob" had a scoffing rivalry with "The Group," that came to a head around an annual spring softball game. Softball and baseball were not school sports, merely an extra-curricular sport organized by the students, played on Sunday after church. In abeyance to our stuffy pseudo-British tradition, cricket was the gentleman's game.

Sports were king. Soon after the war, St. Andrew's had a burst of athletic prowess. I have often wondered if the scholarship program had something to do with it. A big fellow, Taylor, joined the school for his Senior Matriculation year, a superb athlete, strong physically, well coordinated and fast. He led us to Little Big Four conference championship fame in football. Taylor went on to play college and professional football. There were also two memorable twins, the Middletons, Duff and Mo, short, burly, squat, but fast; poor ball handlers, but once given the ball, they could run.

We celebrated our euphoria with the infamous torch lit snake dance, down Yonge Street, the main highway into Aurora. It was a well coordinated logistics operation, kept a tight secret. Weeks before I crept out at night to cut bull rushes in the swampy fields north of the school, bushels of them and soaked them in kerosene. The night before the big championship game, after study hall, there was a pep rally in the gym. After the customary school yells, the cheer leader Mike Magee sprang the game plan, "Follow me!" he rallied, and half the school did. We scurried across the lower playing fields, with as much stealth as youthful spirits could, and at the narrow footbridge leading to the highway, we handed out cattails, lit them aflame, and four score rollicking, hooting, laughing rowdies debouched on to the highway, blocking traffic, and running charged on the unsuspecting town.

Startling the few people who risked been on the streets at ten o'clock at night, we gathered at the post office, closed ranks, and continued our hilarious celebration, singing ribald songs, "Oh dear, what can the matter be/ Seven old ladies went to the lavat'ry..." and shouting the school yell, "Hoot, hoot mon hoot."

In the midst of the din, a dark blue Chevrolet drove up, nudged at the rear of the crowd, and stopped. An ominous hush. Out stepped Mr. Ketchum, the Headmaster. "Your are all to return to school," he bellowed with an unaccustomed air of authority, something he must have picked up in his Navy days, "IMMEDIATELY," he added for emphasis. Victor Rodwell, one of the conspirators, leapt to the fore. Victor was English, very English. "All right, chaps, let's snake dance back to school," he urged us on. "Rodwell," the ex-navy commander asserted himself again, "you come with me." Ordering him to his side, Rodwell disappeared into the car, like a gangland hostage, and they drove off.

89

Back at school, the Duty Master directed us to the Headmaster's study off Memorial House. I proudly stepped to the head of the line. Ushered behind the closed door, "Nold, what do you think you were up to?" the Head demanded. "I thought it was fun, sir." "Well, let me take a bit of the fun out of it." And I was peremptorily caned, the coup de grace, as were the rest of the miscreants. We shuffled up to our beds, feeling rather superior to the law abiding patsies who missed all the fun. I felt proud too of the Headmaster for his athletic prowess. To cane half the Upper School in just one night had to be something of a school record. Our team went on to victory, another record. But the Head was widely criticized, I learned years later, several of the parents complained, and that righteous act of chauvinism may have led to his early retirement.

"Nothing is so difficult to overcome as the easy won laurels of youth." Is it George Bernard Shaw, or Winston Churchill who said that? My last year at St. Andrew's was the fulfillment of all of a boy's fantasies. Most of my friends were a year ahead of me. They had graduated and I was left, something of a top dog, not a lithe highly strung hunting dog, but a stocky, friendly family dog, a collie, they became inbred. The year was a heady one, and with hindsight was subtly corrupting. I was Captain of Football and Hockey, which gave me a modest hero status among the younger boys, though our teams never achieved great renown. As Head Prefect, came certain perks. I had a private room, the only one in the school, and a fag. Roy McMurtry swept my floor and made my bed. Roy later became Canada's High Commissioner to Great Britain, and then Chief Justice of the Supreme Court of Ontario. Once a week I called a Town Meeting in which I harangued the student body with boyish platitudes, until one day a junior student rose in protest, expressing his resentment with the process. This was John Crosby, who later became Finance Minister in the federal Conservative government. I initiated a more democratic participation in the limited affairs of student government.

I also had the privilege of week-end leave, and after football and hockey games would stay over in Toronto. My social life had taken a dramatic turn for the better. I began to see myself as a social celebrity. I met Joan Ellis at one of our games. She had come with a girl friend. Pretty, blond, with blue-green eyes, trim athletic body, about my height, an infectious laugh and ready smile, I was swept away. I had never known anyone like her. She never knew what she was getting into when she was attracted to me. Joan came from a wealthy Toronto family, went to Havergill, a fashionable girl's school, and had a wide circle of friends. We were invited to parties at prominent homes, the country club, the Granite Club. Joan would send their chauffeur to pick me up, and then present me with the car keys, and we would drive out in the family car. It was enough to turn a poor boy's head. During mid-term break and Christmas holidays we were inseparable, by day, skating, skiing on the golf course, going to the movies. But we also read books together, did our holiday school assignments together. It was my first full and somewhat mature relationship with a girl, the most enduring I was to have for years. In the winter social season as captain of the cadet corps I was invited to the 48th Highlands Ball at the Royal York Hotel ballroom. Joan she was my partner, beautiful in a low cut off the shoulder dress, and we danced highland reels to the tune of bagpipes.

Then my house of cards collapsed, my world came apart and I went into a great funk. In the last week of hockey season I broke my leg. Joan visited me in the school infirmary the next weekend, bringing flowers. I still have difficulty understanding my feelings. I couldn't stand being pitied and resented her sympathy. Was it the flowers she brought? No one had ever brought me flowers. Did I associate them with bereavement, a funeral, death? I wallowed in my own depression and self-pity. I broke off the relationship in a rude and hurtful way, dating one of her classmates later in the year.

I was on crutches for fourteen weeks, striding about on three legs with a leaping stride, soon able to keep up with a rapid walking pace. But the Cadet Corps went on parade without me, and I missed the spring term track meet. Without exercise, I slept poorly, found it difficult to study, and my grades suffered, though I was still able to graduate second in my class, behind Ian Wishart, who went on to be an Anglican bishop.

So that was the way my school life ended, not with a bang but a whimper, to parody T.S. Eliot.

Chapter 27: Algonquin Summer

Two paths diverged in the wood and I was attracted to the one least traveled by.

The first night lost in the woods. I'd arrived after dark and couldn't find the trail. "Just head down to the lake. The cabin is on the shore. You can't miss it," Jack Millar had told me and pointed it out on the carefully sketched map. But I had missed it. So I struck out blindly from the highway, downhill south through the trees. Stumbling over deadfall, jagged limbs snagging on my sweater, I came to the lake, a glistening black sheen, reflecting the light of distant stars No moon. No cabin. Go right? Or left? No need to panic, just wait until morning. How can you be lost if it doesn't really matter where you are?

The ground wasn't flat enough to lie down on so I nested among the pine needles my back to a tree. I sheltered in my Hudson's Bay blanket, folded and pinned to make a bedroll, and waited for dawn. I hadn't counted on the voracious mosquitoes and spent the night in a frenzy, swatting defensively against the onslaught. It was a struggle between snuggling down in the bedroll which was too hot, and coming up for air and being assaulted by the whining drone of the bug. This was living! Just like my French Canadian forbearers, the *coureur de bois,* runners of the woods, the tough, tenacious fur traders who had penetrated the furthest regions of primitive Canada. Here was I, their direct descendent following in their footsteps penetrating the wilderness depths of Algonquin Park. Though only a quarter of a mile from the gravel road, it was night and I had forgot to bring a flashlight.

It was the summer of 1944, the last summer before the end of the war. I was fifteen years old. Harry Millar, my guardian-foster-father had had a serious heart attack and had taken early retirement. He and his wife Mary had moved to Victoria, to be in the more benign climate of the West Coast. What should we do with Joey? Summer camp was a possibility, but expensive.

"Why not let him go up to the cabin?" Jack, their son, had suggested. . As a researcher in medical physiology, he had offered himself as a guinea pig to the Royal Canadian Air Force, to test the outer limits of high altitude flying without oxygen. He had damaged his lungs so seriously that one lung had to be removed, requiring 350 stitches to sew him up again. He had spent the early spring recuperating in the clean, clear, cold fresh air in a cabin on Smoke Lake in Algonquin Park, 180 miles north of Toronto. He had helped build it before the war with university colleagues.

Canada jays, squirrels, chickadees, porcupines visited expecting a hand-out, as well as a lean, scrawny bear hungry the long winter's hibernation. Jack slept on the screened-in front porch. Waking one morning to the rattling of pans, he looked inside at the face of the bear, looking out. The Park Ranger loaned him a rifle, and a couple days later Jack had himself bear steaks and began to salt down and tan a bear rug.

Jack was doing research, completing his doctorate and at the University of Toronto, and he and Hally, his newly pregnant wife, spent their three weeks vacation at the cabin.

The rest of the summer I had it to myself. The canoe was the preferred means of travel. I had been in a canoe once before with another person and had the idea that one person paddled on one side, while the other second paddled on the opposite side. But paddling solo was a different matter. Three strokes on the right, then three on the left, to straighten out, I zig-zagged my way across the lake to visit Louis Heit, a school friend who was a Junior Counsellor at Camp Ahmek, on the Canoe Lake. Louis howled with laughter when he saw me paddle in. I provided great comic relief for the campers, living testimony on how not to do it. The next day a man in his mid-30's appeared at my cabin and introduced himself as a friend of Jack's. It was Bernie Hodgetts, the Program Director of Camp Ahmek. He had seen my stunt the day before, asked Louis who I was, and came over to say hello and to teach me the practical subtleties of the J-stroke, that little twist of the paddle and an outboard push at the end of each stroke, that keeps the canoe back on course.

The canoe had lee boards that clamped on the sides, and a bow stepped mast with a loose fitted gaff rigged sail. And I taught myself to sail. At least downwind, then dropping sail and paddling home at the end of each down lake run. Always pushing the limits, I went out in a storm one afternoon, capsized, and drifted with the canoe for nearly an hour before washing up on the lee shore. I didn't know how to swim, but the canoe floated, there was a buoyant cushion for kneeling, and I just held on. Fortunately, in midsummer the water was warm. It is the cold, hypothermia, that is the killer in the northern Canadian lakes.

Each afternoon I would run up the trail and a mile down the road to the store and post office at the portage, replenish my Spartan larder with canned pork and beans, beef stew and store-white bread, and run back. And for the first time in my life I became addicted to reading, before breakfast by first light and in the evening before it was too dark. The sun was my only clock.

The moon was my celestial lantern on nights when Louis would invite me to parties at Camp Wampanao, their sister camp across the inlet. Too shy to ask a girl to dance, I suffered all the pains of unrequited love yearning to be near a girl, to touch, to hold, to move together in rhythm to the music. It brought out all the childhood feelings of being an outsider.

Late into the night I would return to my cabin in the dark, alone and lonely, to the baleful cry of the loons that darkened my mood. These were waters haunted by the ghost of Tom Thompson, the famous Canadian landscape painter of windblown pines and granite outcrops. Twenty years previously, his body had been found in Canoe Lake, tangled in a snarl of fishing line, foul play suspected, vengeance for an affair over someone else's wife. Between the loons and the legend my imagination worked overtime as the canoe cut line through the flat plane of the turgid waters. With premonitions of something evil I doubled my pace and fled.

Late in the summer Louis got a three day break, and we took a short canoe trip, making a loop of fifty miles, portaging between lakes, trolling for fish, camping on rocky headlands to catch the breeze to escape the tormenting mosquitoes. It was my first "expedition" on land, lake or sea.

I returned to St. Andrew's that fall very fit, tanned and trim, sporting a summer's growth of hair that lasted one day before ordered to have it shorn, and I was back in the routine of prep school.

But the wellspring had been tapped. There was a divergence in my path, and like Robert Frost, whom I did not discover until years later, "I...I took the one least traveled by/ And that made all the difference."

"It was the most formative experience in my boyhood years," I told Jack in later years,"a model for the career I was to pursue in Outward Bound."

Joe canoeing on Smoke Lake in Algonquin Park,
summer 1944.

Chapter 28: Essex Journey

In the mid-twentieth century an old jalopy was the moral equivalent of the raft in Huckleberry Finn, a symbol of striking out on one's own, freedom. In the spring of 1946, the year after World War II ended and gas rationing had been lifted, three of my friends, Don Shaw, Louis Heit and Bill Howson had bought an old 1926 Essex. "De Mobmobile," they called it, and hid it in the apple orchard near school, as we were not allowed to have cars.

Their plan was to drive west that summer on the newly opened trans-Canada highway, a daunting feat on narrow gravel roads. Bill lived in Edmoton, but his father, Chief Justice Howson of he Supreme Court of Alberta sentenced him home immediately after school closed. My adopted family, the Millars, lived in Victoria on the west coast so I took his place. David Roe, who lived north of Toronto, joined us for the first leg. We took off in a great cloud of blue smoke which we should have taken as a warning.

It also became an educational field trip. Louis' father was a vice-president of the Dominion Bank of Canada with a wealth of business connections and provided us letters of introduction. At Kirkland Lake we went deep underground in a gold mine. North of Lake Superior we ate breakfast, steak and eggs at three o'clock in the morning with lumber jacks, the forest being closed at noon because of fire hazard. At the lakehead at Ft.William we climbed high in the towers of the mammoth grain silos, where prairie wheat was trans-shipped on the Great Lakes shipping lanes.

The pavement ended at North Bay and from then on the Trans-Canada Highway, only recently opened, was a gravel road 3000 miles to Vancouver, on the west coast. Our greatest challenge was to keep the old Essex from rattling apart and slowly disintegrating. From the beginning it wouldn't start without being pushed, so we always looked around for a small hill to parks where we could get it rolling, and then jam it into low gear and the car would lurch into motion. At a gas stop a mechanic was curious, looked under the hood, and in two minutes tightened the battery cable to the starter motor, and we were off like a rocket. "Elementary, Watson," Sherlock Holmes would have said. We began to burn oil, some days it seemed to us as much oil as gas; so we collected used oil, which the service stations were happy to be rid of, and recycled it. With the vibration on the rough gravel roads we began to have frequent blowouts. We discovered the nozzles of the inner tubes being sheared off. Again we were baffled. Another mechanic spotted a bolt that secured the outer rim of the tire to the wheel housing worn through. A simple replacement of the bolt stopped the nozzle nipping.   Outside Ft. William at the head of the Great Lakes, 1000 miles from Toronto, and a 1000 miles to anywhere else, the motor began to accelerate though my foot was not on the gas pedal, the gears slipped, and the car lost power. We rolled to a stop in another service station. The clutch had given out. Now what? The Essex, tough a luxury vehicle in its day, had long gone out of business as a car manufacturer. We found an old car in a junk yard, cannibalized it for parts and under the careful tutelage of an amused mechanic learned to replace a clutch.

But it was human error, rather then mechanical failure that nearly put an end to the journey. In the mid-summer heat of the open prairie of Manitoba, the car overheated and it became stifling to ride inside. Don who became an engineer, suggested a novel way of turning on the air conditioning. "Let's ride on the roof." The 1926 vintage Essex had a flat roof. The road was a straight line of Euclidean precision, and we seldom drove more than twenty-five miles per hour. It sounded safe. Why not? "Let's do it." So Don and I mounted the hood and crawled on the roof, converting the car top to a sundeck. Exhilarated and cool we drove on through the prairie expanse of the Great Plains, ecstatic on our private vistadome.

Then without warning, there was crunching thud, the screeching of tires, and Don and I were catapulted off the roof. We landed in a deep dirt ditch, the car stalled, leaning above us on the embankment. I had minor scratches and scars, Don miraculously only a dusting, no serious injury.

"Louis, what the hell?" I didn't know whether to be annoyed or thankful to be alive. He had been reaching down to the floor to pick up the map that had blown off the seat and drove off the road. The car seemed none the worse for its detour, and we climbed back in, seated three abreast, crowded together in spite of the heat, and drove on, like Don Quixote in search of next windmill to tilt.

Only 100 miles from Edmonton where Bill Howson lived, heading for the barn, smoke began to smolder from below. A scorched hole had burned its way through the wooden floor boards. The exhaust pipe beneath was red hot. I jumped out when we had stopped, inspecting the damage from a distance. Once cooled down, the old Essex would not start again. We called Bill and he drove out with the family car and towed us in, an ignominious end to our motorcade. It was with the sense of abandoning a sick horse that we left "De Mobmobile" to be resurrected by Bill. We continued our journey hitch-hiking on to the Canadian Rockies, to Jasper and to Banff.

This was my first sight of mountains, and given the place of mountains in my later life, it should have been an acopolyptic event. But one sees only what one is looking for, which is as true of the natural landscape as it is of art, and the sublimity of the Columbia Icefields, and Athabaska Falls passed with the casualness of looking at a postcard, blurred by the boredom of long hours of standing by the dusty roadside, stultified by the sun, anxiously waiting for the next ride.

In Banff we abandoned the high road, and transferred our patronage to the railroad, the CPR, the Canadian Pacific Railroad. "Riding the freights" was the ultimate adventure, like he harvest crews that got off the trains in Fife Lake during the Depression, a childhood dream being fulfilled. There was the risk, station police with their dogs. We lay in ambush behind the bushes at the end of the freight yard, waiting as the engine approached. My heart beat faster as the train gathered speed, and I felt the sudden urge to pee. Then I dashed up the embankment and lunged for the bottom rung of the ladder on the side of the freight car, yanking my shoulder, then clambered to the top. This was living on the edge. From our vistadome I experienced the full grandeur of mountains for the first time, Mt. Eisenhower, recently renamed for the war hero, Temple Mountain, Yoho, we ticked off the landmarks on our highway map, Horseshoe Tunnel, where the track curved back on itself, one of the masterpieces of railway engineering. But it was cold, at night bitterly cold. We were not prepared, having only light raincoats and sweaters. We welcomed the tunnels which boxed in the warmth of the day, and the hot fumes of the coal burning engine. Take your pick, freeze to death or choke to death, Hobson's choice. But Don noticed that some of the freight cars had large hatches at each end that stood partly open. Raising the lid and looking in we saw there was a large empty space that dropped the depth of the box car. It was a locker where ice was stored to refrigerate the car. The cars carried bananas, that had been shipped from New Orleans with ice, the ice had melted, the space empty, and the cold mountain air now used to keep the bananas cool. We clambered down, crowded in, our own cozy cabin, banana scented, dark and secluded, out of the cold night air. Suppose the hatch closed shut and couldn't be opened from the inside? We slept fitfully.

"Watch out for the station cops in Revelstoke," an old timer told us next night. We saw them standing in the yard as we approached in the dark, next night. Jumping off, before the station lights, we ran for it. I was on one side, Don and Louis on the other. We became separated. I circled widely around the freight yard, waited for them at the other side of town, in vain. So I caught the next freight out, expecting them to be somewhere on it. I found an open door, crawled in, and exhausted, spread out on something lumpy. It turned out be a load of coal. It was uncomfortable, but out of the wind and warm. On the outskirts of Vancouver next morning, I hopped off looking like a miner emerging from the pits. "Where the hell have you been?" Harry Millar roared with laughter when he picked me up opposite the ferry dock in Victoria. I had hid in the rose garden in front of the Empress Hotel, until he drove up. The ring on the bath tub was six inches thick when I emerged, evoking more laughter. Don and Louis arrived two days later. "We've already had breakfast," they demurred. "Just have a piece of toast and a little apple sauce," Mother Mary urged. And they wolfed through a whole bowl and nearly a loaf of bread, while we regaled the Millars with our war stories.

It was another divergent path, a road less traveled by. Don became an inveterate world traveler. The call of the road became irresistible for both of us.

Part Two – First Sabbatical

Chapter 29: UBC – 1948-1949

There is the narrow story we tell about ourselves to give coherence to our lives.
~ David Brooks, The New York Times.

The summer of 1948 I had graduated from St. Andrew's, a small, independent boarding school, with a student body of a hundred and fifty students. I had been showered with honors: head prefect, captain of football and hockey, often at the top of my class academically. Everybody knew everybody, and I had been the proverbial bull frog in the tadpole pond. That fall I drowned in the anonymity of the University of British Columbia, a non-entity on a campus of 8,000 students. It was one of the most depressed periods of my life.

Making the transition more difficult, I chose not to live on campus. Reacting to six years of boarding school life, I shunned the institutional life of campus residence, especially the bleak Quonset huts at Fort Point Grey, a former military base converted to student housing. Union College, once a theology college, where my friend Rod Nixon resided, was more attractive, a grey limestone building of neo-classical design, but it reminded me too much of the colonial splendor of St. Andrew's. So to assert my new independence I found "digs" off campus with a young family who took in student boarders. As the weeks wore on however, I found that I missed the camaraderie and collegiality of boarding school life. I didn't know how to deal with the intimacy of normal domestic living. Without realizing it, I craved a more communal environment, as I would much of my life.

Then there was the weather. I loved winter, the clean air, the snap of the cold, the brilliance of sun on snow. But Vancouver had no winter as I knew it growing up in Saskatchewan and Ontario. In November clouds closed in followed by months of leaking skies. "I've come from dazzle to drizzle," I wrote a former girl friend back east, and thinking of her made me feel even more lonely.

I made a poor choice of courses. It was too late to change when I discovered Economics really was the dismal science, and it required an act of discipline to drag myself to school at eight in the morning to hear Dr. Crum lecture two hundred students in the auditorium. My poor grades were commensurate with the number of classes I skipped. And why had I enrolled in Accounting? I pondered as the term wore on. I found balancing my check book was challenge enough. Ever since winning my first gold star in first grade, I'd prided myself in good grades. Until now. Perhaps I wasn't as smart as I always thought I was, I began to fret. Geography was enhanced by the color slides, a novelty then, and it fed into my fantasies about travel. Growing up in the dust bowl of the prairies during the Great Depression, politics was in the air we breathed, so I found Political History of Canada my favorite course.

A Survey of English Literature, the monumental text nearly two inches thick that encompassed Beowulf to Hardy. Apparently anything written in the twentieth century was not considered literature. It was in English class that I met Rod Nixon. Rod was my first British Columbia friend. A tall broad shouldered fellow, a member of the university swim team, he beamed god humor with a broad smile when he entered a room. He was bright, often the most outspoken student in class. I sought him out and we would meet often to compare notes. When the lecturer recommended we organize ourselves into small seminar discussion groups to discuss our course work, I joined Rod's group.

None of my studies dealt with the Big Issues that I had expected to wrestle with at university. Whatever they were. But I found some of them being addressed outside the classroom. The extra-curricular curriculum. That's where my real education began.

UBC was a vibrant place politically in the fall of 1948. The Cold War was hot. The Russians had blocked rail and road access to Berlin, and the Americans and British were air-lifting coal and potatoes into beleaguered Berliners. A Communists fomented civil war raged in the northern mountains of Greece. Churchill had warned of the iron curtain that closed down on Eastern Europe. President Truman initiated the Marshall Plan for the reconstruction of war torn Western Europe. In Canada the Liberal Party won a hotly contested election, promising an increase in old age pensions and health insurance. We joined NATO as founding members. The world economy was stagnant and tight restrictions were imposed on foreign currency. We heard such weighty issues being hotly debated at the brown bag luncheon circuit on a daily basis.

Many World War II veterans who had returned to university after the war on the G.I. Bill of Rights were still on campus in 1948. They brought life experience, maturity and even notoriety to student affairs. The president of student council, a thirty-five-year- old veteran, kept a bottle of whiskey in his desk drawer. Or so it was rumored.

Another veteran, a third year law student, ran for Parliament that year. With the vocal support of UBC students and the financial assistance of the Longshoreman's Union, he was elected, on the Communist ticket. He returned to campus like a heroic renegade, and Rod and I flocked with the crowd to hear him. There was standing room only. But he was disappointing. Far from being the ranting radical I had expected, and hoped for, he wasn't even eloquent. He spoke with his face buried in his notes. Both Rod and I felt we could have given a better speech. But he said the right things. He accused the Americans of resurrecting the Nazi party in Germany, claimed the Marshall Plan was a Wall Street plot to take over Europe. The Americans were the ones who were being aggressive, surrounding the Soviet Union with missile sites. He denounced the McCarthy witch hunts and this drew loud applause. It was a new slant on international politics that seemed logical and rational. So began my flirtation with communism.

My flirtation became a brief conversion later in the year. The dean of Canterbury Cathedral, a high prelate of the Church of England, an avowed communist, made a speaking tour of Canadian university campuses. "The Red Dean," as the press stigmatized him, addressed a thousand students in the armory, the largest enclosed space on campus. With learned Oxford-accented eloquence, he painted a picture of communists as liberators. "They are agrarian reformers who deliver Eastern Europe out of feudalism. While some of their methods might be seen as too forceful, this is a temporary necessity because of the deeply entrenched reactionary forces. Even Christ threw the money changers out of the temple," he said. "From each according to his ability, to each according to his need. This is fundamental to Christianity." I was converted.

I was eager to tell Perry Millar of the Dean's brilliant speech. Perry was my foster brother war hero who had fought the Nazis in Italy, a mentor. Drawn to him I had enrolled in the University of British Columbia rather than attend the University of Toronto. Perry was member of the first class to graduate from the newly established UBC Law School. He had been prominent in campus politics, defeating communist veterans for control of the campus branch of the Canadian Legion. He listened in silence as I eulogized the communist party line. "Joey, here's something I think you ought to read," he said when I left and he handed me a copy of Arthur Koestler, Darkness at Noon. I read it, the chilling account of Russia in the 1930's, the Stalinist purges and the Moscow show trials, the tools of "liberation." So ended my brief flirtation with communism.

Disillusioned by communism, the next "ism" to invade campus was existentialism. Existentialism enshrined my disillusionment. The Thespians, the university drama club performed Antigone, the modern version written by Jean Anouilh during the German occupation of France. It struck me with a sense of the pervasive power of repression, the futility of politics, of the absurdity of radicalism. About the same time a professional Vancouver theatre group performed Sartre's *No Exit*, a vision of hell where a nymphomaniac, a lesbian and a straight male are imprisoned for eternity, taunting each other in perpetuity. My social life wasn't that convoluted, but often I felt it was equally despairing. I hadn't dated a girl in weeks. Alienation was the fashion of the day and I took to wearing a navy blue beret and smoking a pipe.

In April the sun finally came out and stayed out, two, three days at a time. The daffodils bloomed and rhododendrums blossomed. We looked across the bay to the blue sky above the Douglas fir and snow covered slopes of Grouse Mountain. I acknowledged Vancouver for the beautiful city that it is.

The pace of our English Lit class could not have been more timely. In our seminar one of the girls read Wordsworth's *Daffodils*. "I wandered lonely as a cloud...a crowd, a host of golden daffodils...." We discussed the importance of reflecting on beauty and then Rod read lines from *Tintern Abbey, I have learned to look on nature,...hearing often times/ The still sad voice of humanity....Whose dwelling is the light of the setting sun,/ And the round ocean and the living air, / And the blue sky.* He recited it with dramatic flair as if enchanted. After we broke up that evening, he took me aside. "Joe," he said, "we should visit Tintern Abbey." "Yah," I said. How could I ignore the *still sad voice of humanity?*

A couple days later Rod met me in the campus cafeteria as I was juggling chicken soup and raspberry jello in my tray. "I came across this in the bicycle shop," he said and handed me a thin magazine. It was a back issue of the Youth Hostel Association magazine with an article on cycling in the Lake District in England, Wordsworth country. "This is the way we ought to go," Rod said.

"You're serious about this, aren't you," I said.

"Yes," he said, "aren't you?"

In the next seminar we read Byron's "Childe Harold." Byron too confronted his melancholy through travel, feats of endurance and heroic pursuit. A pilgrimage to Tintern Abbey would be our catalyst.

Rod found another article in the YHA magazine written by a couple who had cycled from Seattle to San Francisco ending up crossing the Golden Gate Bridge. That settled it.

A plan began to take shape. We'd work for the summer. Rod got a good paying job as a fire guard running up and down Grouse Mountain monitoring the Vancouver Water Board catchment basin. My job in construction fell through, so I ended up selling ice cream from a motorized go-cart, a Dickey Dee Ice Cream Man, put-putting around the city ringing a little bell. Then we'd take off the next school year. Leaving in the fall, we'd cycle down the West Coast from Vancouver to Los Angeles.

"It's only 1500 miles," Rod said, when I asked how he intended this to take us to Tintern Abbey. If we were going to do "The Grand Tour," we might as well make it grand. I was to learn that Rod had a knack for grandiosity. Another three or four weeks would take us across the southern states to Miami, where we would work passage on a freighter to Europe. *Voila!* I read back issues of the National Geographic at the library, and fantasized about imbibing bitter ale in English pubs, basking on sunny beaches on the French Riviera, and skiing in the Swiss Alps. We played off each other's fantasies. I shared my thoughts with skeptical friends which was a mistake. I ended up feeling compelled to go, just to save face. "I'm taking a sabbatical," I told the scoffers.

We departed Vancouver in early October on our bicycles, heads down into the driving rain. I didn't feel so much the Byronic hero, as Sancho Panza setting off on a Quixotic quest.

Chapter 30: On the Road

One day in October,1949, I mounted my bicycle and began pedaling from Vancouver to Los Angeles. The rain cascaded in wind-driven squalls, a monsoon deluge descending in pellets that bounced off the pavement. With each gust the headwind struck like a water cannon and I wobbled, nearly blown me off my bike. Head bowed, body bent, I tucked close behind my comrade-in-travel, Rod Nixon, drafting in his wake.

A small sign hung from Rod's rear fender,

To LA
1500 mi.

Traffic slowed to hoot. Some to shout. "Don't you know enough to come out of the rain?" The driver of a passing Ford.

"You're mad. Go home." A battered pickup splashed as he shot by.

That did it. We had encountered many nay-sayers. But it was another thing to be taunted. Didn't they realize that an ordeal was the essence of heroic quest? Even Don Quixote knew that. For Rod these were ideal conditions for a dramatic send-off. I wasn't exactly *Singing in the Rain*, but I was humming. even if it was the *Benedictus*, a funeral dirge. *Blessed are they that go in the name of the Lord*. Rod dismounted and removed the sign.

Rod was fit, very fit, having climbed Grouse Mountain all summer as the fire warden for the Vancouver Water Board, while I rode the Dickie Dee Ice Cream scooter along Kitsilano Beach. Gradually he pulled ahead and before long was a blur on the horizon. My new Rudge touring bike with light weight aluminum frame, narrow Dunlop touring tires and Sturmey Archer five-speed gear shift, was meant to make easy work of hills. But weighed down with heavy paniers, carrying tent, cooking pots, personal belongings and travel library, as the morning wore on, I wore out. No matter which of the five gears I used, I fell farther behind.

Rod was waiting for me at the American frontier. "We've come thirty-two miles," he said, reading the tachometer on his front wheel. "It's taken us three and a half hours. That's about ten miles an hour." He began to play with the math. "Ten miles an hour. 1500 miles to Los Angeles. That would be 150 hours of pedaling. Six days if we did it night and day. That's less than a week," he said. Was he proposing we cycle day and night? I wondered. No. But in later years I would think back to this moment. Was this when long distance solo flying had first occurred to him?

We were waved through Canadian Customs but stopped at United States border. "Where you headed?" the American officer asked.

Do I tell him Tintern Abbey, which was our ultimate goal? I hesitated.

"Los Angeles," Rod said.

The customs officer waved a car through without stopping it. I noticed the British Columbia license. Why was he holding us up? "Where did you say you were going?" he asked a second time.

"Los Angeles," I said.

"That's what I thought you said." He waved us through.

"But sir," I said, "you haven't stamped my passport."

"Oh. You have a passport do you?" he said. "You'll have to go inside for that."

How could he have overlooked that? I thought. This was my first passport. Wasn't the point of having a passport to get it stamped? It was a form of validation. It made me an authentic international traveler. Having secured this stamp of legitimacy, I crossed into the land of the brave and home of the free.

WHAT IS YOUR PLAN FOR ETERNITY?

I was confronted by a massive highway billboard. Sponsored by the Greater Washington Bible Society, it declared. This was like being asked by the parish priest in the confessional, "Have you had any evil thoughts recently?" Eternity? Give us this day our daily bread, and forgive us our trespasses. God, let me make it through today.

The burning issues of the long-distance cyclist could be summed up in three questions. How much farther is it? Where do I spend the night? What's for dinner? Answer these and eternity can take care of itself, I felt.

As the afternoon wore on, I felt I was becoming a beast of burden, an ox, a mindless ox on wheels, like Sisyphus doomed to push his stone eternally uphill. But Camus in his essay of the myth of Sisyphus argued that each of us has his own stone to roll. Struggle wasn't the issue. The existential issue is, what stone do you choose to roll? What does your struggle mean? It is a matter of choice. What was my purpose, the meaning of my riding a bicycle fifteen hundred miles? Did Hobbes have it right "...the life of man is solitary, poor, nasty, brutish and short." Was this the meaning of a day like today, ultimately? Eternally?

I posed the question to Rod when I caught up with him, waiting on the top of a long hill. "You're suffering from hypoglycemia," he said.

"What's that?" I asked. Camus didn't say anything about hypoglycemia.

"Low blood sugar," Rod said.

"Never heard of it," I said.

"It's not widely understood. My swim coach told me about it." Rod swam on the UBC team. "You need to stop for a candy bar. I prescribe Butterfinger for maximum caloric content." So once, often twice a day, I'd stop to have my prescription refilled, at five cents a blood sugar kick.

106

The evangelicals were not the only only ones with an uplifting message. Short perfunctory messages were posted on white fence posts about fifty yards apart along the roadside. *Though super shaved. Listen pard. You'll still get slapped. But not so hard. Burma Shave.* I couldn't remember ever being slapped, except by my mother. Was there something wrong with me? I fantasized being slapped by one of the sorority girls back on campus and pedaled even faster.

According to my tachometer, Bellingham was fifty-five miles from Vancouver. We reached it late afternoon. A commemorative plaque in the city park stated that Bellingham had been the captain on one of George Vancouver's ships when they charted the Straits of Juan de Fuca in 1786. It was a last connecting link with home.

Dusk had settled in. Where do we spend the night? The plan had been to camp. That's why I carried the two-man canvas tent weighing down my pannier, and there was a campground in town. In this rain? "What about the youth hostel?" I asked Rod tentatively. I was reluctant to destroy his enjoyment of an ordeal. "At fifty cents a night it won't break the bank," I said. But I felt he was thinking that we were already breaking it. The Canadian government had imposed stringent currency controls after World War II. We were restricted on the amount of American currency we could take out of the country. But he consented. This time.

"For goodness sake, come in out of the rain." Mrs. Svenson greeted us at the door. The manager of the American Youth Hostel, she had a beaming Scandinavian smile and the rounded fullness of an attractive forty-year old matron. "What a pleasure. I don't get many visitors this time of year," she said. I agreed, it was a pleasure.

The hot shower was pure bliss, soporific. I fell asleep standing up, barely catching myself before collapsing. Revived by a brief nap while Rod showered, and a steaming mug of hot sweet tea, we began the ritual of the evening meal. Who would cook? We drew lots that first night. I won the draw, which gave me the honor of cooking. The first course was chicken soup. "Helps restore your salt imbalance," Rod approved. The main course, Kraft Dinner, macaroni and cheese. "Only one package?" Rod said. I looked at the label. Servings for two, it read. I threw in a second package. Servings for four. "Why not add a can of corned beef," Rod suggested. Of course, we deserved a gourmet dinner our first night.

"On a day like today, you burn at least five thousand calories. You need to replace those carbohydrates," Rod lectured. "Otherwise your body will begin to metabolize protein and you'll lose body mass and muscle." Arcane wisdom poured from him. He'll make a good doctor, I thought. I was glad to be in his care.

Preparation of the meal was only the first step in the dinner ritual. Next came the presentation, like the chef in a French restaurant. It was a ceremony of Solomon sanctity, like first communion or a Jewish seder. The legal principle was divide and choose, the cook divides, the guest chooses. Measuring equal portions with meticulous precision into two mess kits, I held them up to Rod. He inspected each with the scrutiny of a Shylock, then chose. I assumed he would select the portion he considered largest. It was like Justicia, blind folded holding up the scales to dispense equal justice, though here we did it with open eyes. Years later at the dinner table, I still scrutinize each plate as it is served, to see if I'm getting my fair portion, and harboring a twinge of resentment if I feel I'm being short changed.

"Are you sure this is always fair?" I ask Rod. I'd recently read the heroic account of Scott's disastrous expedition to the South Pole. The British team man-hauled their sleds, only to find that Amundson, a Norwegian using dog sleds, had beat them there by a couple weeks. On their return journey, Scott's men were overtaken by a devastating polar blizzard and were confined to their tents. Though only eight miles from their next food cache they slowly starved to death. McGregor, the biggest and strongest man on the team was the first to die. Rigidly enforcing naval protocol, Scott had divided their dwindling food in equal portions. A big man cannot survive on the same ration as a smaller men was the moral of the story.

Now Rod stood five inches taller than me, and weighed twenty pounds more, with no fat, all muscle. "Are you suggesting that I deserve more?" he said.

"I wouldn't go so far as that," I said. "It depends on the meal." With macaroni and cheese it would be acceptable to increase the macaroni, but I hesitated on the cheese.

After our dinner Mrs. Svenson joined us bringing pound cake and apple sauce. Real apple sauce, homemade, like Mother Millar made it. Delicious apples, when Delicious apples were still delicious, with enough tartness to set off the sweetness of the cake. It was a fitting commemoration of the first day of the journey. As long as we burned five thousand calories a day, food became more than a ceremony. It became an obsession.

Day one was an ordeal for me. That was the point of it for Rod. Tintern Abbey remained our distant vision, and I dreamt that night of cycling down an endless road to distant Eternity.

Working as the Dickie Dee ice cream man, with customer, summer 1951.

Chapter 31: Bart – A Fisherman's Hospitality

The sea surf exploded on the beach, surged to the low lying dunes, clawed at the course grass, sighed, then retreated to the tide line. We had cycled 529 miles from Vancouver in nine days and were traveling south on U.S. Highway 101, down the Pacific coast of Oregon. With the wind on my back, I felt weightless, like the seagulls soaring overhead. I stripped off my shirt as I ate my lunch of peanut butter and grape jelly sandwiches. Briefly stretched out on sand I soaked up the warmth of the sun. After five days of headwinds, facing into rain, I felt like I was on summer vacation again, though it was mid-October. My optimism was premature.

At Sea Lion Caves the animals slithered on the rocks, tumbled in the surf, barked and belched, growling in mock battle, warning us to keep away from their harem. Or was it the nursery?

The high dunes began at Florence, immense heaps of sand sixty to eighty feet high, the height of a six story apartment building, great banks that curved and swirled far to the south, disappearing into the sea haze. Dusk settled in early. "A great place to camp," Rod Nixon, my companion-in-travel, said.

I struck up a conversation with a wide-eyed ten-year-old at the boating supplies store. He'd never seen a grown man in short pants before, certainly not riding a bicycle. In 1949 only kids rode bikes and wore short pants in Florence, Oregon. He became our guide, showed us to the trail head and for a dime looked after our bikes. The ridge rose in a wide sweeping curve to the skyline and we trudged up in the loose sand. The camp stove fell our of my pannier and rolled to the bottom. I dropped down to retrieve it and trudged up a second time. When I caught up with Rod he had set up camp and greeted me with an appropriate quote from Shelley, "...boundless and bare/ The lone and level sands stretched far away...I am Ozymandius, look upon my works and despair."

Dark clouds blotted out the remaining light in the western sky. "Looks like more rain," I said. "I don't think Ozy had this in mind," and lit the stove.

"Quick. Put out your light," Rod said and pointed to the river below. The steady glow of a red light was approaching upstream. We waited in silence as a boat emerged out of the dusk. It docked at a jetty downstream from us. When the engine stopped I could still hear the far pounding of the surf.

"What you doing up there?" a man shouted from below.

109

Damn. We've been spotted. Is it the Coast Guard? The Parks Service? The town sheriff? Is it illegal to camp on the dunes? My mind raced. Will it be a fine and jail? Let's opt for jail, I thought, looking at the sheet lightning and clouds gathering.

"Wait here," Rod said and went down to appease or negotiate. He returned with a wide Nixonian grin. "We're invited to spend the night." he said.

"Bart Johanson," a hulking big man in greasy yellow oil- skin overalls, five days growth of grey beard, greeted me and held out a hand the size of a shovel. "Welcome to our humble abode."

Mom, his wife, a bleak little woman wrapped in a faded print cotton dress, stood in the doorway. "DO come in," she greeted us sweetly with a curtsey to her voice.

Humble it was, a house boat, forty feet by sixteen, floated up onto the river bank on an extra high tide and grounded there. The whole house sagged toward the river leaving a two inch gap at the top of the door. It had once been painted white, the roof more recently covered in tar paper. Inside the kitchen-living room took up half the shanty. Two bedrooms opened off that. "The head is up the hill," Bart said. The head? In Saskatchewan we called it "the outhouse."

Humble indeed, but a lucky find. The distant thunder grumbled out to sea. So much for our summer vacation.

"How are the fish running?" I asked. As a prairie boy I thought it humorous that fish could run. I was groping for a topic of conversation the might engage Bart.

"Keeps one in cigarette money," Bart said. But in real life he was a Portland fireman, now retired, he told me, and lived on a meager pension and unemployment insurance.

"I'm going out to take a drift tonight. You want to come along?" he said.

A drift? I wondered. Rod, who grew up in British Columbia knew about drift nets and explained before I made a fool of myself. In spite of my exhaustion from the long day of cycling and hunger, I stoked up on bread and cheese, a hand full of raisons. We put on our rain parkas and joined him. Our supper of wieners and beans would have to wait.

"We need a little warmer-upper before we go," Bard said, and pulled out a bottle of Gallo Chianti from the large cargo pocket of his overalls . He took a swig, passed the bottle around, we each took a swig and Bart finished it off with a long savoring gulp and a final gasp.

"Mom, let's have some of your bottle?" he asked his wife.

"I don't have none," she said. "Besides, you shouldn't have any more."

Mom's comment unleashed a pent up electric charge that shook the house. Bart exploded like a thunder clap with a thesaurus of vulgarity, which was not very original but was hugely expressive. It went on for minutes until he ran out of breathe and collapsed in a fit of coughing.

Threats being ineffective, Bart tried diplomacy, appealing to Mom's sense of fairness. "I gave you half my bottle this afternoon and now you won't even cipricate."

"You drunken ass, you don't even know how to say reciprocate. And you wouldn't know what it meant if you could," Mom said.

"You bitch," Bart cursed and then in another dramatic change of mood, gave Mom a slobbery kiss and stomped out of the door as if to take his vengeance on the fish. "Hurry along. We got to catch the tide."

It was a plywood boat twenty-five feet long, with a covered foredeck and a narrow wheel house big enough to shelter one man from rain and spray. Aft was an open cockpit where a drift net lay in a clump, that reminded me of a manure pile, the iodine smell of sea weed and the stink of rotting fish mixing with the gasoline fumes. We motored into the night. A light rain filtered down, more fog than rain. "The boat's powered by a converted Chevy car engine. Can't beat an old Chevy. An outfit like this costs eight hundred dollars with nets and all," Bart told me over the high whine of the V-8 engine.

A mile upstream he turned back into the incoming tide, threw a lighted buoy overboard in mid-stream, then began spooling out the drift net. Now he motored across the current to shore slowly letting out five hundred feet of net. There we waited as the lighted buoy mid-stream drifted slowly up river. At high slack tide, precisely 9:34 p.m. according to the U.S. Coast Guard tide table, the buoy started to drift down river. Bart started to haul the drift net in. It was a cold, wet, messy job, the sort of work that makes a man age and become arthritic before his years. We offered to help, but Bart would hear nothing of it. He sweat in spite of the cold wind coming off the river. No salmon were caught that night. It would have earned him twelve cents a pound at Columbia River Packers, he told me, but in grocery stores salmon sold for fifty-five cents a pound. "Not much in it for the little guy," he said. He did net a good sized crab and a thirty pound striped bass.

The house was in darkness when we returned. Mom had gone to bed, sleeping off the effects of her secreted bottle of wine. Bart was in greater need than ever for a warmer-upper. "Get the hell out of that sack and get the boys something to eat," he blared, then succumbed to another fit of coughing.

"Bart, be a man," Mom appealed, implying perhaps, "be a gentlemen."

"To hell, you be a woman," he said. "You didn't even cook me any supper before I had to go out fishing." He dragged her out of the bed on to the floor and crawled in himself. "I don't even get fed in my own house," he said.

Mom, disheveled and bedraggled, then appealed to us. "I really don't need to live like this," she said. "I have a house in Seattle that I can return to. But I"m proud. The only reason I stand it is because I love the man."

"Bullshit," Bart shouted from the bedroom.

"I hoped I could make something of this man, but I really doubt it," Mom said.

"Horse shit," reverberated from the bedroom walls, and Bart bounded out of bed, spooned down some warmed over stew from a sauce pan simmering on the stove. "Get me your god damned wine," he said.

"I don't know where it is," Mom said, and began to search in the kitchen cupboards, searching for something she probably didn't want to find.

"You could find the damn thing if you wanted a drink yourself," Bart said. Mom served Rod and I the last of the stew, and we headed for bed.

But Bart was not done yet. "Stick your god damned wine up your ass, and get out of here. Go sleep outside in the rain. That will teach you."

"Bart, this bed is mine," Mom pleaded. "You didn't have a shirt on your back when I came to you."

"I don't give a shit. Get the hell out of here, you lousy bitch," Bart said and cuffed her on the head. And Mom staggered out of the bedroom and curled up in a blanket on the kitchen floor, put her head on her forearm, and was asleep.

I'd never witnessed any thing like this before, except on stage. Erskine Caldwell's Tobacco Road, a raunchy story of Georgia sharecroppers during the depression, had scenes of drunken violence and sexual promiscuity. It had been a sensation until closed down by the Vancouver Police Department. Then I had thought it very funny. Just as I now found Bart and Mom funny. But Mom wasn't having much fun, I began to realize. And this wasn't a play. I wasn't in the audience. I was an actor in this scene, an actor who had lost his part and forgotten his lines. What do I do? Do I just tell Bart to knock it off? But wouldn't he just knock me off? And wouldn't he just take it out on Mom?

Or should I stand up to him? Even though standing tall I might come up to his chin. The only real fight I'd ever been was as a thirteen year old in a dormitory raid at St.Andrew's when I stood up for John Capon. Bigger boys had tried to rip the sheets off his bed and I was mad because they were bullying him. And as an eighteen year old I'd won the trophy for the 155 pound boxing class at St. Andrew's. I'd knocked out my friend Bill Howson in the second round.

Bart was a bully, but he was no 155 pound stripling. He was a gigantic man with a weight lifter's strength, heaving wet fishing nets daily on the turn of the tide. He might be drunk, but I knew he could be a gorilla if aroused. I was scared. No David to confront this Goliath.

Should we just pack up and leave? But heavy rain drumming off the shingle roof, foreclosed on that option. I needed to talk with Rod.

Our bed sloped toward the river like the rest of house. Rod's body weighed down upon me lying on the lower side against the partition. "What should we do?" I whispered.

"I don't know," he whispered back.

"What are you two whispering about?" Bart said from the other side of the thin wall, so close it sounded as if he was in bed with us. I said nothing. Soon I heard him snore, but I was so tired myself I too fell asleep.

I woke in the morning to the sound of rattling pots. Was Bart on the rampage again? But he was in the kitchen washing the dishes. He had put on the coffee. There was the smell of freshly baking bread, and the sizzling of fish and potatoes frying. He was cooking the stripped bass he had caught the night before. Before eating Rod preached a short homily about loaves and fishes. "We thank Thee Lord, and Mom and Bart, for this Thy food."

"Amen."

Last night's theatrics might never have happened.

Rain had turned to hail during the night and the Sahara of our dunescape had been transformed to Siberia, a ghostly white shimmering under the overcast sky. We huddled around the kitchen stove that morning. "Lucky you weren't up on the dunes," Bart said, congenial, cheerful, even the wise old man. "You know lads, you're doing the right thing. You got to get out and see the world," he said philosophically. "Otherwise you end up narrow minded just like the people around here."

I patched the seat of my cycling shorts worn bare by friction as I listened. Rod cornered by Mom, admired her photograph album and listened to the stories of her son who was in the merchant marine. One big happy family. They clearly enjoyed company, the opportunity to talk to young people, and we enjoyed them. They were reluctant to see us go when the hail had melted. Mom pressed a small loaf of freshly baked bread on Rod when we left.

A light mist rose off the wet highway as the tarmac heated up. "What do you think?" Rod said when we had put some distance behind us.

I told him it reminded me of Jack Dangerfield, the village drunk in Fife Lake, who came to town once a month, bought his groceries, headed to the beer parlor, got drunk, picked a fight, got beat up and thrown out. His drinking buddies loaded him into his buggy and his horse took him home. "I thought it very funny as a boy," I said. "But I've never seen a woman knocked around like Mom."

Rod spoke of fishermen in Naniamo coming into a bar where he had a job washing glasses in a beer parlor. "They'd be rowdy but friendly, and two hours later they'd go out on the street and beat each other up. It was like seeing Dr. Jekyll being transformed into Mr. Hyde," he said.

I knew a Mrs. Hyde, my mother, loving, nurturing, the woman who brought me into this world. But I also recalled her demonic changes of mood and didn't want to think about that.

Chapter 32: San Francisco

San Francisco should be approached from the water, the way that Sir Francis Drake would have in 1579 had he not been lost in the fog, the way that the prospectors did in the Gold Rush of 1849, the way Rod and I did riding bicycles from Vancouver to Los Angeles, a hundred years later in October, 1949.

My plan had been a triumphal entrance on the Bay Bridge with photographs of us on our bikes against the San Francisco skyline. "Where you think you're going?" the resolute traffic cop demanded.

" San Francisco," I said. "Sir."

"Not on that you aren't," he said, pointing a demeaning finger at my five-speed touring Rudge.

I was enamored with suspension bridges. Growing up on the prairies I'd never been on one before coming to Vancouver a couple years before. I felt they were the most elegant functional structures created by man. Only the intuitive sense of design of a spider could weave such a web of soaring grace that spanned aerial space, defied gravity. Alas there was no pedestrian lane on the Bay Bridge. There was on the Golden Gate Bridge, but that was nearly a hundred miles around on the other side of the bay. The policeman was not about to grant us access to the busy traffic lanes, so we turned back and boarded the Oakland-Embarcadero ferry.

This was fate. As I stood on the bow, legs outspread balancing with the sway of the boat, I realized that this was the ideal introduction to San Francisco. On our journey south we had hurried through cities, passing through hilly Seattle in an hour and a half, Portland in an hour and a quarter, heads down, pumping hard to catch the next green traffic light. But San Francisco. This was a constellation of a different magnitude, a city of history, of legend, and revered in song, I recalled as I walked by the Clementine Hotel. The Metropolis on the Bay. The City on the Hill. The Doorway to the Gold Rush. The Gateway to the Pacific.

The morning mist filtered through the skyscrapers on Market Street. The Customs House dissolved in a frothy cap of low lying cloud. I breathed in the salty tang of the sea, scanned the expansive panorama, thrilled to the clarion squabbling of the sea gulls, diving for the flotsam trailing the boat. The braying fog horn announced our arrival like the French horns on Handel's royal barge.

We checked in at the YMCA, a real budget buster, a dollar forty per night, each. Had breakfast, ham and eggs, hotcakes and coffee, twenty-five cents each. Still running on empty, we bought a dozen donuts and topped off. Though we had not cycled for the last two days while guests at the Delta Upsilon fraternity house at Berkley, normal portions at the dinner table had seemed frugal. Our bodies still craved five thousand calories a day.

Tourists on the town, we clanged the bell on the Powell Street cable car, climbed Coit Tower and watched the fog roll in from Telegraph Hill. We walked along Sunset Beach and marveled at the wasp-waisted men balancing like ballet dancers on narrow boards riding the Pacific surf.

The sign, outside the Legion Hall of Honor with its magnificent Greek columns, informed me that it was an art gallery. I'd never been in an art gallery. But it was free. Many of the paintings were mid-nineteenth century, carefully crafted European pastoral scenes, sheep grazing on green meadows, the lowing herds of Gray's Elegy, winding slowly o'er the lee, a church steeple in the distance, the gathering clouds. I was reminded of Mark Twain's comment on visiting the Louvre, "I am glad the old masters are dead. I only wish they could have died sooner." Several well crafted nudes in various poses of relaxed boredom caught my interest. I'd never seen a naked woman, so when I felt no one was watching me I examined them studiously. In the room labeled "Impressionists," I liked their use of vibrant color but felt many of the artists should have gone back to drawing school. As for abstract modern art, how to describe "A Purple Square?"

At school Mr. Ives, who was an accomplished artist himself, had hung reproductions of the Canadian "Group of Seven." I admired Tom Thompson and Franklin Carmichael in particular, the way they captured the feel of the north woods of Ontario, where I had spent my summers, the elongated clouds wind blown across stormy skies, the twisted, shorn pines, the dazzle of the Canadian autumn.

But compared to Albert Bierstadt, "The Sierra Nevada in California, 1871-3," Tom Thompson was a poster painter. Bierstadt's painting was huge, as large as a billboard. It covered the whole end wall. Soaring jagged peaks stabbed the sky, the setting sun gleamed through the gathering clouds with dazzling shafts of light, sparkling waterfalls tumbled off the glacial scoured cliffs and fell to a glistening pool where elk grazed andstooped to drink. I just knew that this was great art. If biggest is best, it indisputably was the best. Only in San Francisco.

I've always aspired to see my name in print, and next day when Rod went to visit the Museum of Science and Industry, I summoned the bravado to approach the San Francisco Chronicle, the great Hearst newspaper, to see if I could interest them in a series of articles on our travel exploits. The receptionist referred me to the travel editor. He introduced himself as, "Ed." The name fits the job, I thought, it should be easy to remember. He was a jovial fellow in his forties who enjoyed a good story, and enjoyed telling one himself. "Every young fellow ought to do what you're doing," Ed said. "I did some traveling myself, compliments of Uncle Sam during the war. Those German girls were really something." There was a happy gleam of reminiscence in his eyes.

"You need to do it when you can. You meet any interesting people?" Ed asked. I certainly had not had any encounters with German girls he might have found interesting. But it also made me realize that pedaling a bicycle six to eight hours a day, head down staring at the pavement, you don't meet that many people. It wasn't like hitch-hiking where the forced proximity often led to intimate confiding.

"The day before yesterday I heard Jawharlal Nehru, the prime minister of India," I said. "He spoke in the Greek theatre at Berkeley. But I didn't really meet him."

"Yah, I read about it in the paper," Ed said but didn't ask any questions. I knew I'd have to come up with something better. So I told him about the gas station on Highway 101 outside Tacoma, Washington with the Boeing Flying Fortress bomber on the roof. It perched there like a giant bird of prey. I had stopped to talk with the owner. He had been a tail gunner over Germany during World War II. When he saw a stripped down bomber for sale at a war surplus outlet, he bought it. "You know, I never thought I'd get out alive," he said. "It's the least I can do to remind me to count my blessings." Interesting guy, I felt. Interesting story. Ed nodded. Then I told him about the night we spent with Bart, the drunken Oregon fisherman who beat his wife. That at least got a laugh out of him.

There was another encounter I felt was a good human interest story, a story of loneliness and friendship in a place like San Francisco. But I wasn't sure how Ed would take it.

It had happened the night before. I was settled into one of the over-stuffed arm chairs in the lobby of the YMCA, reading The Chronicle in anticipation of this interview, when a slender mid-sized man in a wrinkled business suit, a nut brown complexion, and a friendly smile introduced himself. "I'm Monghul Singh." In the spirit of Young Man Christian fellowship I introduced myself. Within ten minutes I learned that he had immigrated from India twenty-seven years ago, was an American citizen, operated a tree pruning business in the San Joaquin Valley orchards, and would offer me a job, if I was looking for one. He'd come to hear Nehru, and was delighted to hear that I had heard Nehru too. "A great man," he said. "A great man." Would I like to see something of San Francisco and join him for a beer?

A beer? I wasn't of legal age, but I felt such an evening promised to be more interesting than the night life at the YMCA.

Neighborhoods change suddenly in San Francisco. The Forty-Niners Tavern was just around the corner on the next block. The building looked as if it could have stood there since 1849. A tall man could see over a swinging door. The lights were dim, curtains drawn, saw dust on the floor, the cloying odor of disinfectant that barely stifled the smell of stale beer and a suggestive whiff of urine.

A couple of old fellows sat at a small round table at the back of the room, another with his head down at the bar was being chided by the friendly bar tender, "Now Jack, you know you can't sleep there." It reminded me of how I used to doze off at evening study hall at school to be awakened by Mr. Tudball, the master on duty.

Munghal Singh ordered two beers and nudged me into one of the wooden booths that lined the wall. "What a great place America is, everybody so prosperous, and so friendly. Don't you think so?" He put his hand on my knee and looked me in the eye. Then he leaned over, pinched me on the cheek and tried to implant a curry flavored beer kiss on my lips.

I knocked his hand away. It wasn't as though I'd not encountered a "homo" before, or did we call them "fruits" in that homophobic age? They hung around the Greyhound Bus Terminal in Toronto where we caught the bus back to school. But there it seemed to be more clandestine, not so blatant as here in San Francisco, where such encounters were apparently normal YMCA social behavior.

"Look Singh. You're a great guy. But I'm not that way," I said and pushed him to get up and leave.

"No. No. Don't go. I'm very sorry," he said. "Very sorry." And I believed he was.

The evening was only beginning. The two old fellows who had been sitting in the corner approached us. They stood up unsteadily, staggered across the room and stood at our table. Pop, round Falstaffian face, bulbous veined nose, was swathed in a dark blue overcoat, tightly buttoned to the collar, in spite of the late October heat wave. His hands shook. "Could you lend me fifty cents?" he asked.

"Why should Mr. Singh lend you fifty cents?" I said.

"I need it for a flop," Pop said. He looked at me intently, trying to focus his vision. "I'll tell you," he said, "I'll sell you my overcoat for fifty cents." His coat was scruffy, probably a hand-me-down from the Salvation Army, but clearly worth fifty cents. Singh was not moved. Thinking perhaps that brown-skinned Singh did not understand English, Pop tried to negotiate again, first in Spanish, then Italian, German, languages I could recognize, what sounded like Russian or Polish, that I didn't, and finally Chinese. But not Urdu.

Here was the story I'd been looking for. But where to begin? Where you from Pop? Where did you grow up? Were you in the merchant navy? The more I asked, the more he withdrew, as if suspicious. You the police? Immigration? Or just another do-gooder? he seemed to say with stoney eyes. When I persisted, he became angry. "Lend me fifty cents. I need a flop."

The parks and gardens of San Francisco could have been inspired by Wordsworth, but this was a chapter straight out of Dickens. I decided not tell the editor about my night out in San Francisco.

"Where did you stay?" Ed continued his interview. Of course, as a travel writer he'd want to know that.

I told him of the abandoned farm houses we had found in Oregon. "Some with beds, mattresses, even running water and electric lights, next to unattended orchards, the fruit left hanging on the trees. One farmer let us sleep in the hay loft of his barn, though the cattle objected," I said. "When we were stuck, we could always find dry ground under a highway bridge." I didn't tell him that was my plan for that night when we left San Francisco.

"No five star hotels?" Ed said with a laugh. "I'm afraid that's what our readers are interested in. Let me know when you write your book." Neither of us knew it would be sixty years before I came to that.

Rod and I reclaimed our bicycles late that afternoon and rode south on Highway 82, the route of the old Camino Reale, the Royal Highway of the California missions. We found a grove of trees and camped, not realizing we were in the flight path of the San Francisco airport. Lying awake to the drone of the planes landing and taking off, I remembered seeing displayed in the window of a souvenir shop in Chinatown, a miniature three-masted brigantine in full sail with rigging, anchor at the bow, a diminutive captain standing the helm. Enclosed in a bottle.

San Francisco in a bottle, I wrote in my journal. That sums up the past two days.

Day 24. Mileage 1197. Five hundred miles to Los Angeles.

Chapter 33: Route 66

Coming of age in the post-WW II era, I was lured by the siren call to travel by the weekly radio Top-of-the-Hits Parade with songs like:

California here we come, right back where I started from.
Pardon me boys, is that the Chattanooga choo choo?
I got a gal in Kalamazoo, Zoo zoo zoo.
Out on the plains, down near Santa Fe, I met a cowboy, riding along one day.
And then there was: *Should you decide to go West, Go my way, Take the highway, That's best. Get your kicks, on Route 66.*

To me there was nothing incongruous with the fact that I grew up in Canada and all the destinations were south of the border. I had a sense that it was fated that Thanksgiving Day, November, 1949, when I stood on the shoulder of U.S. Highway Route 66, on the outskirts of Los Angeles heading east, my right arm extended, thumb up, a winning smile. With my companion-in-travel, fellow countryman, university classmate, Rod Nixon, I had bicycled from Vancouver, British Columbia to Los Angeles,1670 miles in thirty days. Confronted with the onset of winter, we had revised our travel plan for the remaining 2759 road miles to Miami, Florida. We would hitch-hike.

"Where you headed?" the driver of the first car to stop asked. He was a stern looking fellow in his thirties, wearing a polyester dark blue businessman's suit, white shirt and tie, his eyes hidden by sun glasses.

To say Miami, I felt, would be stretching my luck. "Los Vegas," I said, hopefully.

"Get in," he said. It sounded more like a command than an invitation. "You drive?" he asked.

"Yes."

"Got a license?"

"Yes."

"You like to earn ten dollars?" he said.

"What you mean?" I said. I thought he was going to charge me ten dollars for the ride.

"I'm looking for a driver to deliver a car to Las Vegas. Interested?" he said.

"Why sure," I said. Ten dollars was a lot of money. In Whittier I'd worked all day pruning trees in the orange groves and was paid only ten dollars, and glad to get it.

"That your friend?" He pointed to Rod, fifty yards down the road. He picked him up.

"You in the car delivery business?" I asked.

"You might say that," he said, then was silent, clearly intending that to be the end of the conversation. My mother had used silence as a form of intimidation and I had that feeling again.

In San Bernardino he turned into the warehouse district and stopped at a used car lot. It was secured by a high chain link fence and guarded by a black Doberman straining at its leash. The watchman, a burly fellow in overalls wearing a NASCAR cap looked up and down the deserted street, unlocked the gate, then retired to his kiosk. He made a phone call, and returned with license plates he attached to two cars and handed the keys Rod and me. I drove a dark grey, recent vintage Chevy Bel Aire, Rod a beige Ford Crown Victoria, both practically new.

"Follow me," Our Man said, and we drove off in convoy.

What kicks. We turned on to Route 66, and I accelerated to catch up.

The highway climbed into the mountains above San Bernardino, through dwarfed juniper and scrubby pinyon trees, scrub oak and mesquite. There were pine forests higher up, blackened and scorched by recent fires. *This sure would be a grind on a bicycle.* I shifted down to take a tight curve at thirty miles an hour, and with a slight tap on the gas pedal accelerated back to fifty. The ecstasy of power.

Cole Porter had it right. *Go my way, take the highway, That's the best. Get your kicks on Route sixty-six.*

Within an hour we came out on to the high desert of Southern California, the Mojave Desert. *On a bicycle it would have taken all day.* Growing up in Saskatchewan during the Great Depression, I'd seen dust storms that left the prairie bare, but never anything like this, a land stripped bare to rock, the glaring yellow light reflected off the sand, a land so stark it had its own kind of beauty. And cactus. At fifty miles an hour the landscape was a blur that flashed by the window. *Not like riding a bike.*

At Barstow there is a major crossroads where the highway intersects with Route 58. Three police cars were parked there, rotating lights flashing. A couple hundred yards before the junction The Man pulled over and stopped. We waited. After several minutes, he rolled down his window, waved us to follow. After a quick U-turn he drove back down the highway. *Strange. What does he know that we don't.* He turned off on *a* side road, and on a series of back streets we by-passed the road block and picked up Highway 66 again east of Barstow.

Baker, California, renowned for having recorded the world's highest temperature, 135 degrees Fahrenheit, was only a moderate ninety degrees that day. We drove past the turn-off to Death Valley, and pulled in at the Big Boy Burger cafe. "What you got that's good today?" The Man asked the pretty waitress, eyeing her bosom bulging from her button down pink gingham uniform.

120

She was young, less than twenty, short cropped blond hair, attractive in a wholesome country way. She blushed profusely, thrust menus at us, and scurried to the kitchen.

A buxom woman wearing a cook's stained apron, came out from the kitchen, if not the owner, clearly the person in charge. To look at her bulk, it was obvious she enjoyed her own cooking. Just as obvious, she did not enjoy our visit. The cook and TheMan, exchanged a few civil words, that seemed to leave more unsaid than what was said, and she returned to the kitchen.

"The hamburgers were delicious," I told the waitress as I got up to go. She gave me a frightened smile. The Man left a generous one dollar tip, then walked out of the cafe without paying the bill. Then I realized, there had been no bill.

Before the Nevada border, we turned off the highway, and crossed the state line on a back road, avoiding the Department of Agriculture inspection station where the California State Police cars were parked. In Las Vegas we drove into another car lot behind a high chain linked fence. This one was much larger than the one in San Bernardino, fifty cars or more, guarded by more dogs, and armed watchmen with tatoos on their forearms, all hiding behind sun glasses. They removed the license plates and one fellow wearing suit and tie took our keys.

The Man dropped us off at the edge of town. He pulled out a wad of money from his pant pocket, held together by a thick rubber band. There were mostly one hundred dollar bills. I'd never seen a hundred dollar bill. In fact I wasn't sure that they printed hundred dollar bills in Canada, certainly not many of them. He fished out two tens, handed one to me, another to Rod. "Be a good idea if you got right out of town," he said. I wasn't sure whether that was a friendly suggestion, or was it a command. He drove off and left us on a parched roadside in the hot dry Nevada sun.

"Not bad for the first day of hitch-hiking," I said to Rod.

"But who was this guy?" Rod said.

We didn't have time to talk. Another car picked us up almost immediately. The driver was an engineer working on Boulder Dam, later called Hoover Dam, thirty five miles south of Las Vegas. "I did a lot of hitch-hiking when I was a student." he said. "How is it going?"

"Boy, have we been lucky," Rod, who sat in the front seat, said. He was still euphoric from driving the new car, and covering five hundred miles in one day. "Sure beats cycling." He told the engineer of our episode.

"But there was something fishy about it, don't you think?" I said from the back seat.

"Fishy, and lucky," the engineer replied. "You were luckier than you realize."

"How's that?" I asked.

"Fishy, because you have just perpetrated a crime. Lucky, because you weren't picked up by the police. It's a widely known stolen car racket. There's a ring organized by the Mob that steal cars in Southern California. They change the plates and smuggle them across the state line to Nevada. They own Las Vegas, control the police. Had you been stopped, he would just driven off and left you to explain. I'm innocent. Just a Canadian college student, driving a stolen car across the state line. Tell that one to the state police. It's a clever way to get cars out of California. If you want to buy a new used car, cheap, Vegas is the place to come."

"The Mob? What do you mean?" I asked. At St. Andrew's I had belonged to a gang that called themselves The Mob, rivals of The Group, the elite Toronto crowd. We played them in non-league sports like softball, soccer and lacrosse.

"The Mafia," he said.

"Don't the Mob, or the Mafia, whatever you call them, ran the crime syndicates in Chicago and New York," I said.

"They do. But they've also moved West. They run the gambling casinos in Los Vegas. You must have noticed the Flamingo when you drove by. It was owned by Bugsy Seigel, the Mafia boss, until two years ago, when he was gunned down in Los Angeles. Probably the same guys that picked you up."

Next morning I stood on U.S. Highway Route 66 again, heading east ...*on to Flagstaff Arizona, Don't forget Winona, Get your kicks....*

Chapter 34: The Deep South

Riding a bicycle to Los Angeles, I felt I was a part of the environment with every hill I climbed, when bucking the wind, drenched by the rain. But hitch-hiking across the southern states, riding in cars, the landscape merely passed by the window. It was the people I met that made that journey so memorable.

After my brush with the Mafia, my first ride was with the engineer, full of facts and figures, who knew the specifications of Boulder Dam, 726 feet high, 1244 feet long, holding back Lake Meade, 115 miles long, a power plant capacity of 1,835,000 horse power, ninety-nine men were killed in the construction. The eternal student, I jotted down the statistics in my journal.

The U.S. Park Service ranger at the Grand Canyon, dropped me off at the top of the South Kaibob Trail, *where you'll get the best 180 degrees view*. Five thousand feet deep, fourteen miles across, I was disappointed, in myself. It was too grand. I was awash in scenery. Couldn't take it in. Where do I find the vocabulary to describe it? Now if I could have hiked down into it, as I would in later years, I might have been able to experience it as environment. But I had slept on the rim and froze, waking to the pale pink glow of early light that generated no warmth, shivering.

But hitch-hiking I found forged a camaraderie of the road. The confinement, the proximity, the restricted space of an automobile, and the hours spent together encouraged conversation, even intimacy, like sitting around a campfire, or Chaucer's *Canterbury Tales.*

There was the traveling salesman who put his hand on my knee, seeking deeper intimacy. "It's a lonely life," he confided. The Methodist minister who preached to his captive congregation of one, a non-believer no less, reminding me of those *numb bum,* Sunday night chapel services at St. Andrew's.

Outside Phoenix a Negro driver stopped for me, Leroy. He was the first black man I'd ever met. Saskatchewan didn't have many Negroes in when I was growing up, if any. But as a boy, I did have two Negro heroes, Jim in *Huckleberry Finn,* and Joe Louis. On a warm summer's night in June, 1938, when I was nine years old, I remember listening to the Louis-Schmeling World Heavy Weight Boxing Championship fight. Half the men in Fife Lake, population 130, and surrounding farmers, had gathered on the Cowan's front lawn to listen to the CBC, the Canadian Broadcasting Corporation, on their new Philco radio. The stakes were high. In the previous fight Schmeling had knocked Louis out in the twelfth round. This was the rematch. The Fight of the Titans. I settled in for a long night.

123

The fight also had enormous political implications. People were listening in on both sides of the Atlantic, and around the world. In 1938 Germany was re-arming. Hitler was threatening Czechoslovakia and he was ranting about the Jews. It was rumored that Schmeling planned to buy a German submarine with his earnings. President Roosevelt had brought Joe Louis to the White House and said he was counting on him. So were we. He had to show Hitler who would fight. And he did.

Opening with a relentless succession of blows to Schmeling's body and head, Joe Louis knocked him out in the first round. The fight lasted two minutes and four seconds. It had hardly begun before it was over.

"I listened to the fight too," Leroy told me. "In Yoakum, Texas the colored folk gathered in the Ebenezar Baptist Church where the pastor brought his radio. "We prayed. And our prayers were answered. You'd have thought it was the Second Coming. there was such jubilation. It was as if Joe Louis was a colored Abraham Lincoln coming to free us again. I was sixteen. Freedom seems to have taken its time."

That ten hours was the most remarkable day of my journey. Leroy was a carpenter. He came from Texas, had moved to Los Angeles during the war to work in the Boeing factory, and stayed. Every year he returned home to visit family. He was a cautious driver, unusually so, I noticed. On the highway he never drove over fifty even when the speed limit was fifty-five. In town he glanced continually in the rear mirror, slowing down to let other cars pass. Seeing a police car, he'd pulled aside and waited for it to drive by.

"Most drivers go five miles faster than the speed limit, rather than slower," I told him.

"That 's all right for them, but it don't do for colored folks." On a previous trip, he told me, he was pulled over for driving thirty miles an hour in a twenty-five mile an hour school zone. The police officer ordered Leroy to follow him to the station and he was fined a hundred dollars. " I said I thought that excessive, and the policeman told me, *Shut your mouth nigger,* and he hitt me with his police truncheon. Then they threw in jail for the night. In the morning I was fined two hundred dollars for speeding in a school zone and obstructing justice." Another car sped by. " I'd like to live to a nice old age, so I drive slow."

In Texas, he turned into an Esso station, pulled up at the pump and waited for the attendant to come out. It was before the day of self-service pumps. " Why you stopping there nigger?"

"I need gas," Leroy said.

"We don't serve niggers at those pumps. Go round the back." There the attendant filled us up at the nigger pump.

"Is it like this everywhere?" I asked, as we drove away.

"Mostly," Leroy said.

I was hungry, hoping he would stop for food. But he kept driving by roadside cafes and restaurants. Outside Pecos he pulled into *Pacos Tacos and Burgers.* "Let's eat," he said.

"Why did you stop here?" I asked.

"Because I'm hungry," he said. "This is the only place along here that will serve colored folk." I started to pay for my hamburger. "Put your money away. You're my guest."

A pickup loaded with bales of hay picked me up outside Dallas. He was genuine Texan, Stetson hat, high heeled boots with pointed toes, string tie and that Texan twang. Outgoing, friendly, he was an incessant talker. I learned about the latest in farming, the increased mechanization since the war, the rotation of cotton with beans and alfalfa, legumes that restored nitrogen in the soil.

Then it was as if Dr. Jekyll had become Mr. Hyde. A Negro was walking along the side of the highway, looking back at the oncoming traffic clearly wanting a ride, but hesitant to raise his arm. I didn't know much about the Civil War, growing up in Canada, but I was pretty sure it was over. Apparently not in Texas. "Look at the ignorant son of a bitch," my friendly farmer exploded. "He's barely one-eigth above an ape. I doubt if one in ten of them is married, yet they breed like flies," and he ranted on. I glanced at the rifle racked by the rear window of the pickup and held my peace.

"You're now leaving the State of Texas and entering the State of Taxes," the next driver said as we crossed into Louisiana. He told me of Huey P. Long, the Kingfisher. "A great governor. He promised us a chicken in every pot, and *gol dang*, he did it. Make sure you stop by the state capital in Baton Rouge." It was not the usual state capital building with the classical baroque dome and Greek columns in front. Huey P. Long's rose majestic, phallic, an assertion of modernity. Bullet holes in the marble had been left there to memorialize his assassination, an idiosyncrasy of American political culture inconceivable in Canada.

In New Orleans I was put up by a Tulane graduate student in political science. We strolled down Basin Street to the lively tempo of Dixieland bands, raucous party goers spilling out on to the streets at three in the morning, negro and white co-mingling in a spirit of joyous festivity. I suspect there was a color bar, but it was not obvious at that hour of night.

Jackson, the state capital of Mississippi, was out of my way, but my friend told me the state assembly was in session. It was great theatre. Sitting in the visitor's gallery was like being on stage. Leaning forward I could almost read the delegates speech notes. Forty percent of the population of Mississsippi were colored, I had read, yet to a man, all the delegates were white, and all male. The speeches were grandiose, sprinkled with statistics, littered with barnyard humor, delivered with an eloquence that enshrined the state highway appropriation bill. One debater was particularly vitriolic, thundering on about potholes, shattered windshields, dangerous highway curves, with impassioned vehemence, arms flailing, face flushed an alarming red. Concluding abruptly, he broke into a broad smile. "How was that?" he said.

The house applauded. He bowed and the vote was tallied on an electronic score board.

"You're not from here," the young woman sitting across from me in the public library that evening said, *sotta voce*. She wore a body clinging wool sweater and pleated skirt, fashionable with college coeds.

"No," I said.

"Where you from?"

"Canada," I said.

"You got to be kidding."

"No kidding," I said. We chatted in the lobby and. I told her of my interest in politics.

"You ought to meet my father," she said and the next evening I sat down to dinner, with Mary Evelyn and her father, Judge Thatcher. He was a corpulent, garrulous man, the successful back-slapping politician, with a sense of humor, who managed to get himself re-elected every four years. He had none of the arms-length aloofness of a wigged and crimson robed Canadian magistrates I knew. He spoke of the changes in the South since World War II when many colored, but white too, went north to work in the munitions factories. "Most never came back, except to visit their poor relatives.

"Things are getting better in the South too, with rural electrification, farmers weaned off cotton and tobacco to grow soya beans and rice. Tax incentives are attracting textile factories driven out by the unions up North."

Not wanting to appear rude, I tried to figure out how to approach him on the issue of race. When he began to talk about the Berlin airlift and President Truman taking a hard line on Communism, I saw my opening. "Sir, I just read that the president had desegregated the military. Sitting in on the state assembly today I noticed there were no colored representatives."

"Oh they're represented," he said. "We represent them. Look at their schools, the country roads, the assistance we give to farmers. They trust us more than their own people not to be corrupt. As colored people become more educated they'll have their own delegates. It has to be a gradual process. President Truman has it right. Start with the military and the federal government. Up North. You can't move too fast. You've noticed, haven't you, there are more riots in Chicago than there are in Mississippi."

In Canada I'd read about the Ku Klux Klan, and thought them a bit of a joke, with their white hoods, and Halloween costumes. In the Jackson library I learned more. The Jackson Clarion Ledger painted them as a force for good, maintaining law and order. But back issues of Time Magazine painted a picture of burning crosses, the lynching of a black man where the known perpetrators were acquitted by a white jury, breaking up a black crowd lining up to vote. And it wasn't just in Birmingham, Alabama, that it happened, but in Jacksonville and Louisville. In Skokie, Illinois, the house of a black family who had just moved into a white neighborhood was fire bombed by Klansmen.

I would have liked to pursue it further but didn't have the courage. Or was it good manners?

"Where are you staying?" Mary Evelyn asked after dinner.

"You can drop me off at the YMCA," I said. When she drove off, I checked out my pack, hiked across town to city park, unrolled my sleeping bag on a park bench in the shadow of a giant Cyprus tree with hanging Spanish moss.

Next day in Alabama, I was picked up by a black man in a well pressed dark blue business suit. He worked for the state, an agriculture extension officer. When I told him of my journey, he said, "You ought to visit Tuskegee," and he took me there. He explained that it was one of the earliest institutions of higher learning for colored people. Founded in 1885, during the days of Reconstruction after the Civil War. Originally a normal school for the training of teachers, it was now a full scale university with graduate schools of medicine, engineering and agriculture. " I have my master's degree in agriculture from here," he said. He took me Alpha Phi Alpha house, his old fraternity, introduced me to the brothers and arranged for me to stay.

The campus was more imposing than I had expected for a Negro university. Traditional stone baronial buildings were laid out around a spacious quad, that made the University of British Columbia campus, littered with temporary Quonset huts, look shabby by comparison. I felt awkward at first, the only white face in a sea of black, but as students they were much like my fraternity brothers at UCLA and Oregon State College, more interested in football team scores than the Senator McCarthy hearings.

I hoped to discuss racial politics, but once again was hesitant. The issues seemed too personal, and at first I found the students reluctant to talk. I felt they felt I didn't belong. Though they may have sensed my hesitance. It was safer to talk about Jackie Robinson who received the National League Most Valuable Player Award that year. "We know all about Canada," they told me. Before coming to the major league he had played for the Montreal Royals.

They told me of the exploits of the Tuskegee Fliers, the all-black fighter squadron, trained right on this campus, that shot down 111 German planes over Italy during World War II. But then could not get jobs on the commercial airlines after the war. I mentioned that President Truman had recently been desegregated the military by presidential decree. What did they think? "Should have happened long ago." I sensed they preferred to dwell on victories rather than whine about abuses.

Next morning at chapel, we clapped joyously to gospel hymns. The chaplain preached patience, restraint. "The day is coming. Trust in the Lord. Don't force destiny. Love thy neighbor."

"Amen," students responded. But they sang, *Go down Moses...Oh Pharoah, Let my people go*, with a militant defiance.

Back in the fraternity house, one of the brothers complained, "The administration talk of patience. That's to please the Rockefeller Foundation. But nothing's happening. They won't take a stand. It can't go on."

Five years later, in 1954 a young black Baptist minister named Martin Luther King Juniior, led the bus boycott in Montgomery, Alabama. A national campaign of non-violent civil disobedience was launched,

And Joe Louis, that earlier generation of fighters? He lost the World Heavy Weight Championship to Lucky Marciano, who apologized for knocking him out. Joe became the greeting doorman at Caesar's in Los Vegas.

Chapter 35: Florida

"Why you going to Miami?" asked Benjamin, a graduate student at the University of Chicago, who picked me up. He was driving to Tampa to spend Chanukah and the Christmas vacation with his parents.

Do I tell him I'm going to Tintern Abbey to read Wordsworth on site? I said, "I'm taking a year off to travel and hope to work passage to Europe on a freighter."

"That won't be too easy," he said. "The unions have those jobs sewn up." I would remember our conversation. "What do you make of the South?" he asked.

"I thought it would be more like California," I told him.

"Well, it is in some ways. People come south for the climate, sun, sand, beaches, like my parents who have retired here.

"But there's a difference in cultures. Both states are invested heavily in agriculture that requires cheap labor. It's he difference between the South and the West. Florida was admitted to the Union in 1845 as a slave state. It was part of the Confederacy during the Civil War. California was admitted about the same time, in 1850, a hundred years ago, but it was always free. Yankees came looking for gold, stayed as entrepreneurs and ranchers. Mexicans provide low cost labor, but by the second generation they too have prospered. In Florida the legacy of past has persisted. Most people come to visit Florida. In California, they come to stay."

He dropped me off in Jacksonville where I had my first encounter with American xenophobia. No sooner had I spread out my sleeping bag behind a hedge in the waterfront park, when a squad car pulled up. He suggested I go to the Seaman's Hostel, as much for my personal safety as for the public safety, and drove me there. Two dollars a night. The first itch was in the middle of my back, between the shoulder blades where it was difficult to reach. Then on my stomach, next my head. Fleas? Bed bugs? I'm getting out. I demanded my two dollars be refunded, to no avail, and stormed out. I found an all-night coffee shop open, and sat at the counter trying to figure out how best to spend the rest of the night. Reaching in my jacket pocket, I found my wallet, and my passport were not there. I'd left them under my pillow. Returning to the hostel, I burst past the night clerk, charged back to my bunk, lifted the pillow. Not there.

"Hey, where do you think you're going?" the night clerk shouted.

"Give me my wallet and passport," I demanded.

"Hold on Buddy. Where do you think you're going. I'm calling the police. You're not even an American."

The same police officer was the same one who had picked me up in the park. I retrieved my wallet, cash intact, and my passport. "Best we can do now is the Salvation Army," he said, and took me there. They gave me a bar of stringent carbolic soap, a hot shower, bed and breakfast at no charge other than the long prayer thanking our Saviour before food was served.

I never did get my refund, but was more than recompensed by the solicitousness of the Jacksonville policeman. And after the tales of police harshness, very surprised. But then, though not American, I was white.

I'd come 1917 road miles from Los Angeles, in six days. On December the first I wrote in my journal: *hitch-hiking is a wonderful institution, not strenuous, fun and cheap. I have covered nearly twice the distance in a quarter of the time, that I would have on my bike, at one-eight the expense, and met twice as many people, which is one of the aims of our trip. In fact the mode of travel is so vastly superior to riding a bike that I could kick myself for not thinking of it sooner.*

Chapter 36: Treasure Hunters

The details were sketchy. "Everything is still very hush hush," Mr. Monroe the shipping agent said, though the next day it was on the front page of the *Kingston Times*. . A British syndicate was organizing and expedition to search for pirate treasure on Cocos Island, which was three hundred miles off the west coast of Panama, belonging to Cost Rica. He had come on board with an important message for Captain Peter. There was the possibility of a charter to carry their equipment, which was warehoused in Kingston. In spite of all the publicity, all transactions were carried on under an imagined cloud of secrecy. It was as if the agent himself did not want to be implicated.

The advance party, we were told, under the leader, an English aristocrat named Cochrane Hervey had gone ahead to Costa Rica, to finalize arrangements there. They needed a small cargo vessel to transport the rest of the equipment to Costa Rica. "All very hush hush." According to Munroe, a vessel like the *Culver* would be ideal. "It sounds pretty far fetched to me," I told Alec.

Facts sifted slowly through the veil of presumed secrecy, though the newspapers were already speculating. Hervey apparently was a direct descendent of Admiral Lord Cochrane, a British naval commander who had fought for the South American colonies during their War of Independence in 1825. From what I gathered from the newspapers, the admiral had come in possession of charts indicating where wealthy Spaniards from Lima had been hidden their treasure, when fled the rebels. These had been passed down through the generations of the family. Hervey had put together a syndicate to retrieve it.

A deal was struck. At least we thought it was a deal. The equipment consisted of four tons of assorted gear, a huge hydraulic pump that fit center ship in the hold, several large curved iron plates, nine feet by three feet, that bolted together made a water tight crib, assorted nozzles and hoses, and five surplus military wooden barges, twenty feet long, six feet wide, three foot draft. These were carried on deck. The excavation plan, so far as I could figure, was to sink the crib over the site, pump out the water, the sand. And with it supposedly, the treasure. It sounded improbable, and with the insistence on secrecy, even a little suspect. But who was I to judge.

The waterline of the *Culver* sank two feet as the load was stowed aboard. When Rafe Brown, my St. Andrew's friend, came down to see us off, he said the boat looked like a floating dry dock.

Though fully loaded, Captain Peter still haggled with Munroe, the agent over the contract. They finally agreed to $500 cash, which wasn't much, another $250 on delivery. Or that's what Peter thought was the deal, though never committed to writing.

We were to meet up with evasive Hervey, the expedition's leader, in Puntarenas, which is on the west coast of Costa Rica. Hervey was finalizing negotiations for permits and customs clearance with the Costa Rican government and recruiting a labor force. Our plan was to drop off their equipment, collect the balance owing in the charter, and sail on to the Galapagos, then cross the South Pacific. Monroe hinted at the possibility, of a four month contract to carry the cargo to Cocos Island itself and a share in the treasure loot dangled before us. Though he could make no promises. Keeping people in doubt seemed to be part of treasure hunting business strategy.

We were ready to leave Jamaica, though Jamaica was not ready to have us leave. The anchor that held us fast was a mighty iron hook, a classic fisherman's anchor, one that weighed nearly 500 pounds. The windlass stood upright on the foredeck, a complex set of big greasy gears that turned small gears, that in turn was turned by two immense cranks, one on either side, manhandled by two men facing each other on opposite sides. "It was designed for Chinese coolies," Alex said as we bent our sweating bodies to the grind, the thick half inch chain coming up slowly, link following link, one link at a time. Then the windlass jammed. Hooked.

Captain Peter at the helm eased the boat forward under power. The boat caught up on the anchor and slowly rotated facing the other way. The anchor chain was still taut. "Try cranking again." Captain's orders. Still hooked. On the third attempt the boat moved sluggishly forward, the chain cranked in slowly, the anchor surfaced with a muddy mess of oily debris, glued to the remains of a rusted out fuel tank that had been discarded and lodged on the bottom. Last call was at the explosives dock on the far side of the harbor where we loaded on 500 pounds of dynamite.

The harbor pilot came on board. I wrote a hurried forlorn letter to Leonie with whom I now felt deeply attached. I felt that had the situation been right we could have become lovers. But I was an innocent still. The harbor pilot agreed to mail it for me, and we headed out the harbor channel to the familiar pounding of the diesel engine.

> *I'm sad to say/ I'm on my way,*
> *Won't be back for many a day...*
> *Had to leave a pretty girl in Kingston town."*

Caribbean Crossing

Panama is 650 miles from Jamaica, a course of 195 degrees, which is slightly west of south, the prevailing winds in April being the north-east trades. "A downhill run," Alec said with a smile. "We've been beating to windward enough for one season."

We sailed from Kingston on the day before Easter, though I think that Peter was not aware of the day, he was so caught up in worry, the cranky engine, the awkward deck load, haggling over the charter with Hervey's agent, Monroe. He just wanted to get away from the hassle, the complexities of life on land, and escape to the freedom of the seas. I was ambivalent. Leonie had invited me to attend Easter Sunday mass with her at the cathedral and dinner with her family.

Once clear of the harbor, we raised sails. The *Culver* , seventy-nine feet long, was a gaff-rigged ketch, a two-masted sailboat, the fore mast, about sixty feet high, being higher then the mizzen, the after mast, about forty feet high. The gaff was a long pole that extended the peak of the sail up and out another fifteen or twenty feet. The advantage of the gaff-rig was that it gave a broader expanse of sail, an advantage running down wind, but it did not point as high going to windward. The boat also carried a jib that ran up the forestay from the bow to the upper cross trees on the foremast, and the flying jib, a staysail that ran from the bowsprit to the top of the foremast.

Alec and I had little difficulty raising the foresail and the mizzen, but raising the main was a different matter. With a sixty-foot mast and a twenty-foot gaff, the combined efforts of all three of us was needed. Peter shut down the engine and joined Alex and I on the foredeck. Had there been six of us we could have broken out in a sea shanty,and pulled in rhythm to *Heave ho and up she rises*. "Save your breath," Peter said. With only the three of us the exercise required an act of gymnastic precision. Peter and I grasped the halyard as high as we could reach. Then in tandem we fell backwards, flat on our backs on to the deck, using the weight or our bodies to pull the halyard down, thereby raising the sail up. At the last instant before hitting the deck, we lunged forward carrying the line to our feet, where we handed it off to Alex who was crouched behind a rack of belaying pins. He took a quick turn around one of the pins, securing the halyard, preventing it from sliding back up. Repeated over and over the leading edge of the mainsail crept up the mast. We couldn't manage to raise the last two feet, and frustrated left it there. They we raised the gaff, and drifted along in a light breeze, under full sail. The sails aloft were a magnificent sight.

But the ship would not hold its course. Even with the helm full down, it headed up into the wind. And the wind was doing peculiar things, coming from the north-west rather than the north-east. A quick glance at the chart showed that if it continued this way we would soon be on the Pedro Banks, navigational hazards off the south coast of Jamaica. So we motored up again.

Once clear of the banks we shut down and drifted in a light breeze. I stood the mid-night to two watch, An Easter moon shimmered over the water. There was little to do at the helm, not enough wind for steerage, sails flogging in the swell. To keep awake I read the book of poetry Leoni had given me and memorized Byron' poem

La Belle Dame Sans Merci....hath thee in thrall.

We drifted for most of the next day, the grey outline of the coast of Jamaica fading into the horizon. Winds were sporadic and light, the boat rolling in an easterly swell. A barge tied on the port deck began to work loose and had to be secured. Peter and I pumped the bilge, another back straining effort as foul smelling oily fluid flushed overboard spreading an iridescent sheen over blue water of the Caribbean. It was a dispiriting day. My stomach began to react to the persistent rolling in the mounting swell. Apple sauce, dry bread and water, was my only food for the day, but I prided myself in holding it down. Peter opened ship's stores and came on deck with a bottle of rum which raised his spirits. *Yo ho ho And a bottle of rum,* I remembered from reading *Treasure Island* and like young Jim, I abstained.

Early morning the third day, the wind shifted to the north east where it ought to be. We did a controlled jibe, shifting the sails from the port side to starboard, an awkward maneuver in a boat this cumbersome. In the process the main sail snagged on the corner of one of the barges on deck, and ripped. We had to drop the main and proceed under shortened sail while Alec mended it. Then the tortuous process of raising the main again.

Once clear of the wind shadow of Jamaica we picked up the full force of the north-east trades. The winds blew steadily day and night, twenty-five to thirty knots, setting the halyards humming. A regular ten-foot wave pattern rolled the boat from beam to beam, an occasional twenty-foot swell heaved the stern high and the bowsprit dug into the surge. Water sprayed over the barges and sluiced down the deck. With water passing by the rudder, the helm responded again and we could steer a steady course, 200 degrees, west of south. Now we were truly on our way to Panama making five knots, covering 120 miles a day.

On night watch I read Tennyson's *Ulysses,* much of which I knew already from memory, having studied it for my Ontario Senior Matriculation exams, only two years before.

Mariners, you and I are off/ Smite the sounding furrows...

The good ship *Culver* was up to the challenge running downwind on a broad reach. But short handed, it was the crew that were being challenged. Two hours on and four hours off was the posted watch schedule. But once Peter had sampled Captain Morgan's distilled spirits, he continued to sample, and the schedule fell apart. The only way I could wake him after my night watch was to sit him upright on his bunk and perch him there with pillows. I was tempted to slap him, but that would have been mutiny. Once he fell out of bed. When he finally did wake up he could not go to sleep again and would stand watch all night. One morning I woke with bladder pressure, went to the rail to relieve myself, and found no one at the helm. The *Culver* was sailing herself. She was nearly on course, a true mistress of the seas.

My challenge was *mal de mer.* It sounds more elegant in French. My stomach sloshed with the interminable rolling of the boat, even before we hit the heavy swell of the trades, light headed, dizzy, a persistent humming in my ears. After two days of apple sauce and dry bread, I graved hot food. How about apple sauce and spaghetti. I'd open a can of tomato sauce for Peter and Alec. The galley was forward on the boat, before the main mast. Poorly lit, dark teak walls, dingy, it reeked of kerosene fumes from the stove, mingled with the smell of cooking food. And in high seas the bow would rise and fall through an arc of six feet or more in the swell. Cooking could be a juggling act as well. I almost lasted the nine minutes it takes to cook spaghetti, when my gorge began to heave. I made it up the galley ladder on to deck, then across to the rail before the heaves came on. When it was satisfied I returned below, finished cooking the spaghetti, served Peter and Alex, brushed my teeth, ate my own dinner and cleaned up after. By the fifth day I had my appetite again and could enjoy regular food.

One week out of Jamaica we picked up the harbor channel and sailed into Panama City.

Off the channel entrance buoy the Harbor Police boarded the *Culver* . They checked the ship's registration, our passports, the cargo manifest. "Five hundred pound of explosives?" the officer asked. He looked at his colleague who took a notebook from his brief case.

"Something to do with a treasure hunting expedition," Peter said.

The officer looked at his colleague again, "Who is this Hervey fellow?" the officer asked.

"Couldn't rightly tell you," Peter said, "never met him." Peter tried not to sound evasive. More note taking.

"Let's see the hold," the officer said. Alex showed him the dynamite, stowed mid-ships, well away from the detonator caps which were stowed in the focsle. Satisfied he said, "Follow us to the explosive's anchorage." And left.

We anchored off, three miles out from the city dock.

It was a Saturday. To avoid paying extra charges for checking in on a week-end, we spent Sunday at anchor, the yellow quarantine flag flying. Sunday, the sabbath, a day of rest, I thought, and after breakfast dug out a book of Somerset Maugham's short stories. But Peter had other ideas. "There's work to be done," he said.

"Isn't there always on an old wooden boat," I said, then wished I hadn't.

The mizzen halyard had to be replaced with the new half inch hemp rope recently bought in Jamaica. Alex tied the new line around his waist and climbed the old line, hand over hand, forty feet up to the cross trees, where he perched as he threaded it through the upper pulley block. I lowered him down. "Want to try it?" he asked. I'd climbed ropes many times in gym class at St. Andrew's, and didn't hesitate. In mock reverence I made the sign of the cross, and kissed the crucifix Leoni had given me, not a smart idea, I started up. As I climbed I realized I was weaker than I thought, and heavier. But all went well until I reached out for the cross-tree, where I could pull myself up and sit. My left hand slipped, and I fell.

The sensation, in after thought, was almost euphoric. It was as if I was outside of my body, watching myself fall, weightlessness, a sense of abandonment as the horizon tipped vertical as the sky poured into the sea. Is this what it is to pass into the next life? And then I hit. But it was a soft landing which confused me. I had hit the gaff that rested on the mizzen sail folded over the mizzen boom. It was like landing on a spring board, absorbing my fall and propelling me up again, before crashing down on the deck six feet below. Lucky that the mizzen sail had broken my fall, unluckily I landed on a large wooden block secured to the deck. I came down on my back, hitting above my right kidney. Glad to be alive I began to laugh hysterically, then as the shock wore off I was sobered by the pain.

Alex and Peter rushed to attend to me, but there was little they could do. They were reluctant to move me fearing a back injury. I hadn't suffered concussion. I had sensation my fingers and toes, mobility in my arms and legs, so they wrote off a broken back. Kidney damage was harder to assess. Broken ribs were a possibility. The least they could do was relieve the pain. Dr. Alex prescribe the old salt's remedy and brought out Peter's bottle of Captain Morgan's rum. I never did get to Somerset Maugham that day but I did write Leoni commenting on the miraculous powers of her crucifix. I continued to take my medicine through the day and my last memory that evening was sitting on deck propped against the cabin, calling for Alex, "More water," I shouted as he bucketed sea water over me to wash off the vomit. Then feeling no pain I passed out for the night.

We were stranded on boat and in the morning waited impatiently for harbor officials. Mid-morning they came, Captain Brown, the port captain, the customs officer, chief of the Canal Zone Fire Department, immigration and another man in plain clothes but clearly an official. They checked our documents, asking probing questions about Hervey and Sorenson. Not only did they search the boat, they pried. In the hold, the focsle, the engine room, lifting the planks to inspect the ballast and the bilge. Questioning each of us separately, the man in the searsucker suit asked us, mainly Peter and Alex, "What do you know about Hervey?" "Very little. Never met him." "What about Sorenson?" "Never heard of him?" "How did you get involved with this charter?" "We were approached by an agent in Kingston, Munroe. Claimed he was Hervey's agent. Payed us in advance. We took the charter." He was so persistent in his questioning that we began to think we were doing something wrong. Something must be up. How were we complicit? I was caught up in the intrigue, saw it as a part of hunting for pirate treasure. But Peter's brow began to furrow, and his face turned red, as it always did when he was stressed. I was relieved when the port captain turned down Peter's offer of a glass of rum.

Captain Brown offered us a ride ashore, saving us the seven dollar water taxi fare. At the dock, the plainclothes man introduced himself, "Jim Cauffie. I'm not busy this morning. Can I drive you around?" We thought this to be rather unusual hospitality, but readily accepted. They dropped me off at a doctor's office, Peter and Alex at the Canal Zone Commissary, where they were able to lay in ship's supplies, American goods at discount prices, for the Pacific crossing. X-rays did not reveal any fractures, but I did have a massive bruise on my back, an ache I'd experience for several weeks.

At the post office there was mail for Peter, news of the Cocos Island Treasure Hunting Expedition that was both confusing and alarming. The elusive Hervey had written enclosing a check for five hundred dollars, "as advanced payment for the first two weeks of a charter to carry the equipment from Puntarenas, Costa Rica to Cocos Island." "What the hell is this?" Peter fumed. "I never agreed to carry the cargo to Cocos Island, certainly not for two hundred and fifty dollars a week. Besides, he still owes me two hundred and fifty dollars to deliver it to Puntarenas." Over lunch in a waterfront hotel, Peter found paper and pen, and wrote Hervey a blistering reply.

Even more baffling was a letter from Mrs. Sorenson. Cauffie had been very curious about what we knew of Mr. Sorenson. Nobody had mentioned the misses. Peter had heard reference to her as an associate of Hervey's but did not know how she fit it. "Sounds like a misfit to me," Alex said, on reading her letter, then passed it on to me. Her letter presumed that we knew much more than we did. The Yacht *Langesund* had deserted the expedition, she wrote, and that "mean, contemptuous, unsportsman husband of hers," had quit. But she was sticking with Hervey, "a good egg." As "god mother of the *Culver*" she wished us well and "please hurry up out to help us out of this jam, you're just the laddies for it." "Well laddies, what do you make of that?" I asked. Peter's sunburn turned a deeper shade of red. Cauffie looked on knowlingly.

Cauffie saw us back to the *Culver* on the port captain's launch and surprised us when he came on board. "I need to talk to you," he said. In the cabin, over a glass of rum he told us," I'm not with the port captain's office. I'm naval intelligence." Every story of pirate treasure is cloaked in mystery, I thought. Cauffie unveiled yet another. He told us that both Hervey and Sorenson had been under surveillance. He felt that the duet, the two of them were up to something. Hervey had been charged in the British court with the illegal sale of arms, to an African country, though it could not be proven because a key witness withdrew his allegation. Sorenson was a Danish citizen who was married to a wealthy American woman. His application for American citizenship had been denied. He was known to hate America and was believed to be in the pay of some foreign hostile rebel group. "When you showed up with five hundred pounds of explosives in the hire of these two notorious characters, it raised eyebrows," he said. "We decided to investigate." He had checked on Peter and Alex records and found them to be trust worthy. But he felt they should be warned. "We think the treasure hunting expedition could be a cover for them to develop contacts for the illegal sale of arms. If you see anything suspicious report it to the American embassy immediately."

"What are we getting ourselves into?" Alex asked. Cauffie boarded the launch. "Have a good transit of the canal," he called and waved farewell.

Transit Ocean To Ocean

"We'll need to be up early," Peter said. Rising at first light he started breakfast while Alex and I began to shorten the anchor chain. With less than thirty feet in we were already sweating. At seven thirty the canal pilot arrived with six burly black deck hands who took over and the anchor rose from the muddy bottom. Peter instructed me in the eccentricities of starting the diesel engine, and by virtue of my handicap, not being able to haul lines because of my back injury, I was appointed assistance engineer for the day. Underway it was my responsibility to keep the engine from stalling out, which it was prone to do when idling.

The Panama Canal is a miracle of human ingenuity, one of the great feats of engineering of the ages. I witnessed it from the confines of the clatter of the engine and the cloying stench of diesel fumes.

Under way by eight we powered up the wide ditch through a tropical swamp, the vibrant green of the jungle contrasting with the red clay of the earthen banks. We entered the steep concrete canyon of the first lock slowly under our own power. "Don't stall," I pleaded with the engine as we powered down. Heavy lines were thrown down from above, nearly eighty feet above, secured fore and aft to the *Culver*, and we were towed through the locks by squat electric cars or tractors, "canal donkeys," the pilot called them. The lines were designed to haul a 15,000 ton freighter, not a fifty ton wooden ketch, and one caught on the guard rail and ripped out a five foot length of planking. Another casualty.

On the long flat fifteen-mile stretch of Gatun Lake we chatted with the pilot, a freckle faced American forty-year old, who grew up near the water in Alabama, wearing tropical khakis and a khaki baseball cap. He was talkative and enjoyed the role of tour guide. "Part of the genius of the Panama Canal was that instead of digging a sea level canal, as the French had tried to do, like they had in the construction of the Suez Canal, the American engineers had built a series of dams, creating this lake that we are floating across." He quoted facts and figures, "The canal cuts off 6000 miles from the 14,000 mile voyage from San Francisco to New York around Cape Horn....took a work force of 39,000 men....27,000 are estimated to have died, the white supervisors as well as the black laborers, mainly from malaria and yellow fever."

By mid-afternoon we had reached the crux of the canal, the Culebra Cut through the Continental Divide, a massive ditch four hundred feet high through unstable rock and porous clay, eighty-five feet above sea level. "Took over 100 huge Bucyrus steam shovels to clear it," the pilot said. Two sets of locks, the Pedro Miguel locks and the Miraflores locks set us down to sea level at Balboa on the Pacific side. Alex came below to spell me so that I could experience the high drama. We entered the lock in high water, the steel gate sixty-five feet high closed behind us. Slowly and gradually we settled into the wall canyon of the lock as the water drained out. On the last lock one of the deck hands threw a line that landed on the binnacle head, a copper cover shaped like a diver's helmet, that protected the compass. It broke the oval glass window, an event I would recall later when we came to repair it. Yet another Panama casualty.

Balboa, on the Pacific side, "actually east of Panama City on the Atlantic side, because of the curvature of the isthmus, " the pilot told us, as he departed with his crew. We motored out to sea. It was a moment for poetry, I said, and recited Keat's poem, "And stout Cortez gazed in wonder on the Pacific/ Silent on a peak in Darien," oblivious to the historic inaccuracies, with the channel markers blinking red and green, the yellow lights of Balboa glimmering to port.

Panama To Puntarenas

"Better come on deck," Alex called out, "there's a ship bearing down on us." All day ships had been passing by us in the canal. Now at night, we were in the middle of one of the world's busiest shipping lanes in the Gulf of Panama leading to the open Pacific. Still more than a mile away, the red starboard running light drawing closer at remarkable speed, we appeared on a collision course. "Sound the fog horn," Peter called to me, urgency in his voice. He shone the bright beam flashlight on the sails, flashing off and on. Still it drew closer, the steady throb of the engines growing louder. At the last moment, Alex swung the helm hard to port, jibing the sails over, and the freighter pounded by as oblivious of our existence as they would have been of our non-existence had they run us down. Nobody seemed to be on the bridge.

We continued south the next day under light variable winds rounding Cape Malo where we picked up the Pacific swell. That night we had another close encounter with a fishing boat, apparently on auto-pilot, the crew unaware of our panic, the mournful bray of our horn, flashing lights. An hour later, I was on watch and spotted another set of running lights in the distance. Changing course from close hauled to a beam reach we steered well clear of his path. But night watch was no longer the relaxed standing the wheel, the *Culver* steering herself while I memorized the rest of Tennyson's *Ulysses*. One was clearly "on watch," eyes constantly straining into the dark for a pin-prick of light on the horizon.

This must be how mutinies begin, I thought. Rounding the cape we had a brisk day of sailing with following winds, west out to the Pacific. Unfortunately the glory of the day was overwhelmed by dissension in the crew. We had changed the order of standing watch so that I woke Alex, and Alex had the difficult task of trying to wake Peter from the soporific effects of rum. I woke to Alex shouting at Peter, and Peter yelling back at Alex, with threats that ranged from kicking Alex's ass, to flattening Peter's nose, and smashing the binoculars on his head. "When we get out to the South Pacific I'm leaving the bloody boat if we can't remain friends." "Oh bugger off." By mid-morning when Peter called me for my watch, the storm seemed to have blown over.

We worked our way north up the west coast of Panama, marking off islands and headlands on the chart, Moro Puercos, Punta Mariati, Isla Jicarita, Isla Monterosa. Work was the operative word. We were constantly raising sails to catch the sporadic winds, then lowering them again to avoid the flogging of the canvas and the banging of the booms. Progress was slow, bucking counter currents and tides. One night of sailing in light balmy winds we lost ten miles drifting with the tide. Reluctantly Peter decided to motor up. For the first time at sea I had the luxury of sleeping through the night. Given the unreliability of the engine, Peter felt that either he or Alex needed to stand watch, though I would be rousted out to help raise sails.

There was a magical splendor to the voyage. The water was clear, a pale jade green near the islands, a deep ink blue in open stretches. I thrilled to the frolicking of dolphins though they soon seemed to be bored with our slow progress. Occasionally we saw giant turtles, with a girth of five feet, sleeping on the surface until startled by our passing. We were always in sight of land, thick deep green coming down to the water's edge, high cliffs on the headlands, mountains 3000 feet high disappearing into a hazy blue haze in the distance. At night the hull lit up with a yellow, purple, green phosphorescent glow. A flow of sparks, like dying embers, trailed off the stern. The new moon rose a fragile sickle that shimmered on the sea like a flickering candle seen through a green bottle.

At night we dodged fishing boats narrowly passing by.

Rain squally passed through, short, violent, tearing at the sails, flattening the waves, heavy drops bouncing off the deck. For a brief half hour we were wrapped in a northern chill.

Some days we drifted for hours, day and night, Peter reluctant to run the engine wanting to avoid the expense, until he too lost patience and we'd move on to the pounding of pistons.

At Matapata Head off the Gulfo Dulce we picked up the coast of Costa Rica. I was awakened at four to an unusual silence. The fuel tank had run dry and would need to be refilled by syphoning diesel oil from one of the fifty gallon barrels on deck. Another night of crisis. We raised sails but in the light breeze only drifted sideways. Even when refueled, the engine would not start and Peter and Alex worked on it well into the morning. I shivered at the helm through a night squall, but by mid-morning under the blazing sun, the decks were so hot I could not walk on them with bare feet.

During the night we passed the headland and motored up the Gulf of Nicoyo, and in the morning, seven days out of Panama, we dropped anchor in the sandy bottom of Puntarenas. I felt our mission had been accomplished but it was not the end, nor was it the beginning of the end, but it was only the end of the beginning, to quote another of my boyhood heroes, Winston Churchill.

Bargaining For Treasure

"Good to see the British flag flying in this part of the world," Hervey said as he stepped aboard the *Culver*.

Mid-morning he appeared with the port captain, a customs officer, Ricardo, his agent, the Mrs. Sorenson, our would-be god-mother, and a Captain Edwards, whom I presumed to be the captain of the *Langesund*. After a week of relative isolation it felt very crowded to have nine people on board, and being uncertain as to how we would be greeted, I felt the air of tension, oppression. Peter was unsmiling, clearly on the defensive.

Hervey, we met for the first time and as the leader of this enterprise, he was a disappointment. A small man, slender with fine bones, a thin build, a receding hairline, he had long wavy light brown hair that turned up at his collar giving him an effeminate look. He wore white cotton slack, recently laundered and ironed, a white shirt, open at the collar, no chest hair showing. Mid-thirties, I guessed. Hardly the criminal type, the international arms dealer, that our friend Cauffie had painted him back in Panama. And the ebullient, talkative, center-of-stage Mrs. Sorenson. She was a tall straight backed woman who stood above Hervey, with greying reddish blond hair, clearly at one time a beauty. A vivacious fifty-year old, she was a non-stop talker, effusive in her enthusiasm to see us arrive. "Now we can get on with this show," she said, ready to conduct. She may have lost her youthful looks but none of her youthful vigor. We were not sure how she got involved in a treasure hunt, and with her incessant chatter, did not have the opportunity to enquire. From the surprising letter we had received from her in Panama, we presumed she was the owner of the *Langesund*, but it was nowhere in sight in the small harbor.

Captain Edwards was a tall dignified Englishman, who looked like an Englishman, ruddy complexion from the tropical sun, stood erect with a military bearing, wearing tropical sand colored khakis, close trimmed hair. Hervey introduced him as the captain of the *Langesund*. "Where's the yacht?" Peter asked. "In the estuary on the other side of town," he said. Otherwise he remained silent, a spectator, like myself I thought. He was the one to be trusted, I felt.

The port officials checked our passports, inspected the cargo on deck and in the hold while the others followed. We expected Hervey to comment on Peter's letter from Panama turning down the terms of Hervey's proposed contract, but no mention was made. We were invited on shore for lunch.

Puntarenas was Costa Rica's main seaport on the Pacific coast. A ramshackle town of about 4000 people, it was the terminus of the railroad that brought coffee down from the highlands, Costa Rico's main export. A long iron wharf ran out into the bay, where ocean going freights took on cargo. It also serviced a major fishing fleet off shore, mainly American tuna boats. The town was laid out on a grid, with two main streets, one along the waterfront, the other at right angles leading to an estuary on the opposite side of town. We met Hervey and his cohort at the Hotel Grand Imperial, a weathered clapboard building with a second story balcony overlooking the harbor.

"Did you receive my letter?" Peter asked. "No. Why?" Hervey asked, the picture of innocence. I could see Peter redden as he asserted that he took the five hundred dollars he had received as the final payment on the delivery of the cargo to Puntarenas, not a down payment for the first two weeks of a charter to carry equipment and a work crew to Cocos Island. "I'm amazed," Hervey said with a dramatic display of disbelief, "that you will not live up to your contract," "I don't have a contract," Peter said. "Furthermore I will not sail for $1000 a month. I demand five hundred dollars a week." "Two thousand a month is out of the question," Hervey said. "There are bigger and better boats here in Puntarenas that we can get for less." "Go right ahead," Peter said. "We've plans for crossing the Pacific and are prepared to do it." "Well, we can still be friends," Hervey said, "even though we fight in court." "Fine by me," Peter said, "but after Thursday, I'll have to start charging you storage." A stroke of genius, I thought. Where did Peter get that idea. "Hurray for Peter," I wrote in my journal.

Mrs. Sorenson came on board the following morning, accompanied by Captain Edwards. She was unsteady and as she stepped from the dinghy I helped her over the rail. There was a faint smell of rum. Peter, not willing to be left unfortified, opened another bottle of rum. Alex cautioned temperance, but that only stoked Peter's impending anger. As the level in the bottle went down, tempers went up and reason went overboard. Insults turned to vulgarity. Then Alex joined in and the madam turned her invective on him. "I can see that Peter is honest in spite of his anger. But you, I don't know about you," she said. "I'm sorry to see friends who I have helped out so much let me down." Indeed she had brought us a pound of coffee and a packet of porridge when she came on board. "I like to take friends at their word," she said and got up to go. Captain Edwards, who had not said a word through the tirade, saw her safely into her dinghy.

Hervey invited Peter to breakfast at eight next morning at the Grand Imperial Hotel, where he had taken up lodging. "Like to come along?" Peter asked me. The Hervey entourage were assembled when we arrived. They had not expected me and had to place another setting at opposite end of the long table. It was clear that they want to exclude me from the bargaining table. I had scrambled eggs, toast and coffee. When was the last time I had an egg? I wondered. After the frugal fare on board the Culver breakfast was a royal banquet.

I sat next to Ivor Brown, a new member of the expedition team, a handsome young black Jamaican, in his mid-twenties. He exuded good cheer and spoke with the accented lilt of the West Indies. It turned out that he had joined the expedition in Jamaica and had come out with Hervey's team on the Langasund. Since not much was happening in Puntarenas, he had taken the opportunity to tour Costa Rica and had just returned. As we chatted I realized he took all the high drama and contrived conflict with a certain skepticism, and like myself was an outsider looking in. He also knew Leonie Samuels, my Jamaica sweetheart. We became good friends, though on opposite teams.

At the other end of the table Hervey and Mrs. Sorenson began to work on Peter. Hervey was in a compliant mood. He agreed to charter the Culver to carry the equipment and crew to Cocos Island for a thousand dollars a month, plus covering such expenses as food and fuel, the cost of repair for any damages to the boat, and as a final concession, "one and a half percent of any treasure found." Would this make me a half percent shareholder in a pirate treasure. That would make a good story to tell my fraternity brothers.

"What do you think?" Peter asked me.

I thought he was stalling for time, feeling that Hervey had some ulterior motivation. "I'd like to think about it," I said.

"Think about it? All you've done is waste time," Mrs. Sorenson said, almost screaming. "You deliberately delayed your passage from Jamaica. Now you're stalling again." A litany of accusations followed.

Peter agreed to the new deal. We returned to the boat to make preparations. Cargo needed to be transferred from the Langesund. It was anchored in the sheltered estuary on the other side of Puntarenas and the Culver, now in the more open harbor, needed to be brought around to it. Captain Edwards, who was to act as our guide, did not want to do it without a pilot, but Mrs. Sorenson insisted. Crossing the entrance bar the Culver ran aground. Coming off with the evening tide, we ran aground again. It was midnight before we had the anchor down. "Another day wasted," Peter said.

The work schedule was regulated by Latin American time, though this would be unfair to the hard working Costa Ricans. Hervey's team slept until ten, breakfasted at eleven, were fully alert by noon, and worked until sunset at six. "It is a masterpiece of disorganization," I wrote in my journal. Paco Rojas, the shipping agent was responsible for hiring local laborers, who would accompany the expedition, a requirement of the government. But Hervey had not arranged accommodation for them so we were never sure who or how many would show up. With each days make shift crew Ivor Brown supervised the transfer of cargo from the Langesund to the Culver, more caissons, lengths of hose, smaller pumps and a generator.

The main cause of ships foundering is faulty sea cocks. Captain Edwards, recently having lost his boat, was not eager to lose another. Those on the Langesund had to be replaced. There was not boatyard where a boat could be hauled. So at high tide he ran the yacht up on the beach and as when the tide ran out, they propped it up with long poles. The poles were braced on the rub rail, a long strip of wood that runs along the top of the hull. The rail was also attached to the deck, a design fault Peter felt, and as the weight shifted on to the poles, the deck began to heave off the hull. Peter and Alex spent most of the night working with Captain Edwards to ease the pressure by shifting ballast. When the boat came off in the morning tide it was easily repaired.

But Mrs. Sorenson was outraged. She accused Captain Edwards of wrecking her yacht, of being careless and incompetent. Why did she have to put up with such a numskull. "It's not enough that you wrecked your own boat. Now you're wrecking mine." Edwards retreated into a silent dignity and said nothing. But Ivor Brown, who had come on board with a work crew, responded. "We've got work to do. Get out of our way with your chatter." I was surprised at his rudeness, but apparently this was a contest that had already been battled out. She retreated into a rum stupor that lasted for three days, until she was finally sedated by the town doctor.

Work continued on the Culver. Rojas's work crew began to show up and we made space for them on the foredeck under the shade of an old sail, on canvas cots. One of the barges had to be off-loaded to make way for a ship's launch that Hervey purchased. Rations were stowed below deck. "Looks like they plan to live on rice and beans," Alex said. He pointed out that they had taken on less food for twenty-five men for one month, than the Culver had for three men to cross the Pacific.

"No problem man," Ivor Brown said, "we'll fish. And there are wild pigs on the island."

A fifty gallon drum of gasoline was lashed on deck, well away from the dynamite stowed in the focsle. "I doubt if that will be enough," Peter told Hervey. The hydraulic pumps, the compressor, the generator, the outboard motor to the ship's launch, all operated on gas. Hervey made no comment.

Peter was summoned to the Langesund to sign the contract. The port captain was there to witness it. Reading it that night, I said to Peter, "So you agreed to accept the five hundred dollars you have already received as a first installment on the Cocos charter."

"What do you mean?" he asked.

"Well, it's right there," I said, and pointed it out. There it was buried in page two where Peter had signed.

"That scheming bastard," Peter said. He turned a flaming red. Without changing out of his work dungarees, which he always did before going ashore, he grabbed the oars of the skiff. Alex and I joined him in a show of force and ship's solidarity. We found Hervey with his team, Mrs. Sorenson, Captain Edwards, Ivor Brown, Paco Rojas, having dinner. I was glad none were carrying guns, or even knives, for there would have been bloodshed.

Hervey, though a small man, who gave the impression of being fragile, but he appeared unperturbed. He seemed perfectly comfortable handling contentions negotiations. He appeared to expect it. I suspected he even enjoyed it. It was his way of controlling others, showing his power and dominance. "Well, if that's the way you want to handle it," Peter told him, "see how you get along without our help. Good luck in getting your cargo ashore. We'll sail the Culver to Cocos Island as agreed to in the charter. And that's it. Period. I should have let the Langesund sink the other night." But it was clear that we were stuck. Hervey had a signed contract witnessed by the port captain, an official who had official power and I felt he could be easily bought.

"I'll think about it," Hervey said.

We were ready to sail. So why the delay? I wondered. It wasn't the Culver holding things back. Then we learned it was the Langesund that was the trouble. She flew the Danish flag. Though owned by Mrs. Sorenson, the Langesund had been registered in the name of her husband, a Danish citizen. Captain Sorenson had abandoned the expedition in Panama but now was pressing a claim against the boat. The Danish government had placed an embargo on the boat. But Hervey had succeeded in having it pigeon-hole, probably by passing money under the table to Costa Rican customs officials. But the repeated delays had given Captain Sorensen time to renew his attack. The Danish government, through its ambassador in Mexico City had sent a formal protest appealing directly to Costa Rican government. The Langesund could not sail without a Danish captain.

Hervey was able to connive a solution. Through his underground network, he was able to track down a Dane, Captain Barney, the first mate on an American shark fishing boat operating in local waters. He had a Danish captain's licence. They were able to contact him by radio and Mrs. Sorenson, Captain Edwards, and make shift crew, took off in hot pursuit.

Captain Barney was a forty-year old of medium height, with a bulging belly, unruly blond hair, and sun-burned face that glowed. Opinionated, loud, he took up a lot of space, both physically and verbally. His papers were sent to the Danish consul in San Jose, but there was a complication. Barney was now an American citizen. The consul would have to check with Copenhagen. We waited.

On shore I ran into Mrs. Sorenson having her mid-morning cheer-me-up with Ricardo, the Costa Rican government liason officer,. From the veranda of the Grand Imperial Hotel, she could monitor harbor activity. She seemed to want company, was was more subdued than usual. For awhile. "Gawd, you always seem so happy," she said. "You must be hiding something. You little bastard." The rum began to fortify. "You're just a bunch of chiselers on the Culver, holding out for an extra five hundred dollars for the charter from Jamaica. But Peter is all right. He's a sincere honest chap," she said. We could unload the treasure hunting gear at any time, as far as she was concerned, if we didn't want to play it straight.

She ordered another rum. "Doble." Double, then turned on Ricardo as the representative of the Costa Rican Government. They, whoever they were, had finally got her angry over the delays in releasing her yacht. "I'm going to show them," she said, and accused Ricardo of blackmail. "I've taken all this guff for four months now. They have nothing on me. Do they think they could get away with it? They better have another think coming." She was a friend of the Astors. And other wealthy New England families. "Who did they think they were treating me this way? These people know me, and they like me. They'd never let me down," she said. A member of her family owned " that damned fruit company" and some financial trust company. "The whole damn thing is perfectly illegal," she said, "and I'm just fed up with it. I don't like to drag my friends into these sorts of things unless I'm really in trouble, but they are always there for me."

I had to leave, but ran into Ivor Brown, the Jamaican mate, next morning. He told me that she went on drinking with Captain Barney and the shark fishermen until five next morning, before the doctor was called to sedate her and put her to bed.

The labor crew moved on board the Culver, twelve local men, farmers, fishermen, craftsmen who hung around the waterfront looking for work. They would do the digging and heavy lifting on Cocos Island. We learned that there was a hierarchy even among workers. Most seemed eager to please, and responded willingly when asked to help shift deck cargo to make more room on the foredeck, except for two men, the one who claimed to be a carpenter, the other an electrician. But now there was little for them to do. They crowded on to the foredeck, stretching out on canvas cots and straw mattresses, sheltering from the sun under canvas tarpaulins stretched from the rigging. "We're looking more like a pirate ship every day," I told Peter. He didn't see that as a compliment.

Another fellow claimed that he had been a cook and was given a promotion with a slight raise in pay. For breakfast he served up spaghetti and rice. For dinner rice, spaghetti and beans. It was a menu that became familiar.

As the week wore on banks of heavy clouds began to build up over the mountains. "It's the beginning of the rainy season," Ivor Brown told me. We had a succession of outrageous sunsets ablaze in fiery reds, glaring yellows, blushing pinks, fading to somber purples that filled the whole sky. In the afternoon we had our first sampling of a tropical squall. I heard it before I saw it, like the galloping horses over the tin roofs, following by the hissing of dragons, as the heavy rain drops beat the water flat. It was like flinging back a refrigerator door as it sucked out the heat of the mid-day. The smell of pungent flowers and suffocating must of decaying vegetation swept from land over the sea. I was struck by the glory of it.

Not the laborers on the foredeck. The meager length of canvas they had been able to scrounge had been inadequate. Peter gave them an old sail. "Make sure we bill Hervey for that," he had said. But they'd had enough. When the clouds began to build up again that evening, enraged by their meager meal of rice and beans, they deserted ship and rowed ashore in force to confront Hervey. He put them up at the hotel, along with the six police contingent who had been assigned to the expedition. I felt the police posed an interesting problem. Were they there to protect us or control us?

I spoke with Don Ricardo, the use of the title "Don" having significance, a recognition of status meriting respect. He was the proprietor of the hotel, a worried, helpful man, always eager to please, I congratulated him on his new found fiscal success. Clearly treasure hunting was good for the hotel business.

Hervey agreed to meet with Peter to renegotiate the terms of the charter. He compromised and was willing to pay two hundred and fifty dollars for the delivery of the equipment from Jamaica. Peter insisted on five hundred, as originally promised by

Hervey's agent in Kingston. "Besides I can't sail with a party this size, unless I am accompanied by the Langesund. I don't have the life saving capacity. It would be worth my captain's license to assume the risk." That was a new card Peter was playing and I admired his conniving with equal cunning.

Then he laid down his joker. "I'll only sail with the consent of the British consul."

I saw Hervey' mouth drop and his jaw muscles tighten. He mumbled something that sounded like, "Black mail."

Hervey eventually agreed to pay the five hundred dollars. But he reduced the share of the treasure from one and a half percent to one percent, but then restored it when Peter agreed to help with all operations, such as loading and off loading, on a consulting basis. It was agreed that the Langesund would stay within hailing distance of the Culver when under way. They closed on that.

Some days leave an indelible impression that last a life time. We had been in Puntarenas twelve days, days of expectation, frustration, dashed hopes and rumor.

The rumor of the day was that we were to sail. Though no one had communicated that to Peter.

Ivor Brown and Captain Barney came on board with a small work crew, eager to transfer the last of the cargo from the Langesund to the Culver. Peter was miffed, feeling he was the last rather than the first to know, and refused to help. "I still don't my a contract," he said, sounding like a staunch union man.Captain Barney blew up. But Peter insisted, "No contract. No work." At noon Hervey sent Ricardo, the liason official, to tell Peter to type up the contract in the way he wanted it worded. So Peter spent the rest of the afternoon tapping away with two fingers, typing up the final draft, in duplicate.

"We sail tonight." The word was out.

"We sail when we're ready to sail," Peter said when he returned on board at six. Peter let it be known there was still work to be done on the Culver before she could sail. And he still did not have a contract.

But the process was set in motion. The pilot came on board, with Peter at the helm, my nurturing the erratic diesel engine, the Langesund in tandem, we crossed the bar at the mouth of the estuary, and motored around the headland and anchored off the town.

The full contingent moved on board, the twelve work crew, six police. Two of the men capsized in the bathtub sized dinghy, beginning their adventure with a baptismal dunking. Peter was summoned to a hurried conference on the Langesund for a last minute council-of-war, and asked Alex and I to join him. We waited an hour before Mrs. Sorensen showed up, followed shortly by Hervey. A fateful delay. Peter and Alex availed themselves of ship board hospitality from the recently restocked liquor locker on the Langesund.

"Why in hell's name aren't you ready to sail?" Mrs. Sorenson asked. She also smelled of rum.

Peter's response was honest, but not very persuasive. The binnacle head is at the hardware store having the glass replace. This had been broken in the Panama Canal. An anchor was at a blacksmith shop having the shaft unbent.

"Why wasn't this done days ago?" she asked.

Peter didn't have a good reply, made even less persuasive by his slurred speech. "I spent the afternoon typing up the contract when I could have done these things. And it still hasn't been signed," he said. "Nor do I have a check for the first month of the charter."

I was assigned to go ashore with Ricardo, the liason official, " to drag Paco Rojas from the clutches of his wife and get that damned binnacle," Mrs. Sorenson stormed. It was well past mid-night. Paco was the expedition's agent. He protested, disagreed, did not see how it could be done before morning. But they found a clerk, who with a small financial incentive agreed to wake the son of the owner who got the key, and I retrieved our binnacle head. Unfortunately it did not last through the night. Peter left it on a diesel drum that was lashed on deck, and in the dark I had kicked it over shattering the glass.

Ricardo had to wake two blacksmiths before we located the anchor in the third one, and we returned with our trophies.

The shipside scene had deteriorated. It was now three thirty in the morning. The Langesund's dingy was tied to the town pier and I took it to row out to the Culver with my loot, when Mrs. Sorenson appeared on deck. "Come back with my dingy," she shouted. I caught up with Peter and Captain Barney were in the bath tub. They had gone back to the Culver to pick up Peter's copy of the contract, that still had not been signed. They passed a bottle of rum between them.

"Bring back my dingy," Mrs. Sorenson hyperventilated. "Captain Edwards, order him to return my dingy. Captain Barney, order him to bring it back. Captain Peter, you order him."

"Give her back her dingy," Captain Barney bellowed, "you little squirt."

I dropped the anchor and the binnacle head on the Culver and joined them on the Langesund. "You little bastard, get off my yacht," Mrs. Sorenson shouted in my face.
"Peter, order him off the boat."

Captain Barney joined the chorus. "Look you grinning ape, when I tell you something is white, it is white." Then he lost his train of thought.

"Are we sailing tonight?" I asked trying to clear the fog rum fumes and ranting.

"I don't know," Captain Barney said. Then he stepped over the rail, dropped into the bath tub and rowed back to shore.

"Where is he going?" I asked. No one knew.

"I won't be insulted on my own yacht," Mrs. Sorenson said, and retired below to the well stocked liquor locker.

"What's holding us up?" I asked Hervey.

"Nothing that I can see," Hervey said. "I have the check. All we need is the contract." Peter had the contract, in duplicate. Having roused the port captain who had been a asleep in the cockpit, they signed, he witnessed. Mrs. Sorenson signed a written statement that the Langesund would stay within hailing distance of the Culver as an emergency safety precaution. They congratulated each other with one last round of rum.

"We'll be ready to sail in an hour," Peter said, though I wasn't sure he'd be capable of rowing the dingy back to the Culver. He wrote a quick note to his wife, enclosed the check and I returned to shore to find Paco Rojas, the agent, to mail it.

Captain Edwards had joined me, coming ashore to find Captain Barney to let him know we were sailing. We found them in one of the bars that fronts for a brothel that was still open at four in the morning.

"I'm not going," Barney said. "I got my papers, but I don't have a contract. The Langesund has not been cleared to sail. I've had enough with that gang of swindlers. I've tried to play ball with them, but they've ignored me all day. Now they want me to go to the slaughter floor for them."

Then he uncovered his conspiracy theory. The Martinoli, a San Pedro tuna fishing boat lay at anchor in the harbor, not a hundred yards off. "Their skiff is out of the water," Barney said. "They're ready to sail. My buddies tell me there are armed customs officials aboard. You might get ten miles off shore, then they'd board you. I don't plan to spend the rest of the jail." When we left, Barney ducked into the back room of the bar where there were others to console him.

The sky was beginning to pale when we reported back to the Langesund. Mrs. Sorenson was not to be dissuaded. "Captain Edwards, prepare my yacht to go to sea."

Turning on me, "You little kike, get those sots moving. We're going to sea."

My sots were indeed besotted, unfit to move themselves, yet alone the boat. I felt it imperative that the Culver sail, otherwise we would be in breach of the contract we had gone to such lengths to negotiate, and re-negotiate, and had signed only an hour before.

Why not? I asked myself.

"Peter, can I have your permission to take the Culver to sea?" I roused him from his stupor.

"What do you want?" he asked. Then he seemed to comprehend. "Yeah," he said, in his broad Australian accent. "Now piss off." And he fell back on his bunk.

I'd little alcohol. I didn't need it that night to get high. Once on the football field I'd caught the ball on the kick-off and ran through the whole opposing team for a touch down. This was another once in a life time experience.

I roused the work crew sheltered on the foredeck, set the foreman in charge of cranking up the anchor. The radio operator spoke a little English so I had him join me in the engine room. I'm not very mechanical, but I had watched Peter and Alex often enough to have memorized the process of starting the engine: open the sea cock, prime the starter motor, open gas cock, close oil valve, open once started, throw the clutch, wait for the high pitched whine as the diesel engine turns over, explodes into a steady pounding rhythm. I couldn't stop the starting motor, but that didn't matter at this moment. I showed the radio operator how to idle the engine without it stalling, then I sprang on deck and went forward.

"Ariba. Ariba." Up. Up. I shouted to the anchor crew, as if I was Henry the Fifth urging the English troops over the barricades at Agincourt. "Once more into the breach my friends,. Once more." I watched as the anchor broke the surface of the slick surface, dripping harbor mud.

Everyone was awake by now. The men were busy keeping out of the way of those working and had begun to pack their gear and tidy the foredeck. All except the six police with their "jefe," the chief. Spectators until now, they became players. While others packed, they unpacked. Out came their rifles, and slowly, casually they began to slip bullets into their magazines. The jefe, a handsome, well groomed young man, clearly of the officer class, proceeded to load his sub-machine gun. He barked an order, and in unison the police pointed their guns, not at me, but at the Langesund along side. Ricardo, the liason officer who spoke good English, was summoned. "They will not allow the Langesund to sail. It does not have port clearance."

"En bajo. En bajo." Put it down, I told the anchor crew. I was relieved to see the police do the same with their guns. I backed up the boat to set the anchor, shut down the engine, sat back on the stern rail and listened to the seagulls roused by the commotion, as the first light of day crept across the harbor. Suddenly I felt very tired.

Hervey was silent but did not seem perturbed when I went on shore with him for breakfast. Was this all just a charade, part of a broader plan? I wondered. If so, who was he putting on the show for? He knew that the Langesund did not have port clearance. Why had he done it then? I thought or Cauffie of U.S. Naval Intelligence in Panama. If the treasure hunt was merely a front for a gun running operation, a reconnaissance, or some form of money laundering, it might make sense. But if not?

Mid-morning, when I returned to the ship I hailed the Langesund for the dingy but was denied its use. By order of the owner.

Interim

The panic of expedition frenzy petered out. The laborers were furloughed and returned to their villages. The police contingent were billeted in the Grand Imperial Hotel. Here they prolonged the sense of crisis. Mario, the handsome young captain, conscious of his exalted position, but easily offended, staggered into the dining room one night, toting his Riesling sub-machine gun. He demanded the return of his revolvers, which Don Ricardo, the proprietor of the hotel had stored in the hotel safe. He refused. Mario, not one to have his dignity so abused, threatened Don Ricardo, making severe insinuations of his mother's fidelity, the legitimacy of his ancestry, while waving his gun in defiance. Fortunately it was unloaded, the bullets also secured in the safe.

Subdued when two burly harbor police appeared, they escorted him to the port captain's office, where all were safely stored.

Mario continued to breach the peace, but fortunately it took on a more amorous turn. In the early hours of the morning he would return to the hotel with a beautiful young woman on his arm, sometimes two, singing Spanish love songs in a rich operatic tenor voice.

As the tempo of the expedition wound down I began to lose the sense that I was part of a treasure hunting expedition. I was played out and did not think about it. There was a sense of unreality about it. I began to see it as a combination of melodrama and farce.

"The expedition will never go," Jose Canas told me. He was a Costa Rican friend who had gone to St. Andrew's. He came down from San Jose for the week-end. "I have friends in the government," he said, "and they tell me people are being payed to see that you don't sail. It's an old trick. When it looks as if the group has something substantial, they force them to sell their maps.

"A couple years ago a party refused and it ended with the death of one of the expedition leaders, a woman."

I told Canas about our encounter with the United States Navy Intelligence officer in Panama, who suspected that Hervey was involved in gun running. "That's possible too," Canas said. "Our last civil war was only two years ago. It left 200 people dead."

But Canas was less interested in revolutionary politics than he was in economic stimulus. The mainstay of Puntarenas's economy was shipping, coffee sent down from the highlands by rail. Next there was fishing, and then the hospitality industry.

When I turned the corner from the Grand Imperial Hotel facing the harbor, and walked down the side street, there were half a dozen bars and restaurants, all of which fronted for brothels. "Prostitutionis a government monopoly," Canas told me. " It is tightly controlled, well regulated. The prettiest young women are recruited in the poor villages, inspected by the local public health doctor, certified to be in good health, disease free and granted work permits. Most come to the capital, but other towns alsos like Puntarenas where they can find work. The brothels are also licensed and government regulated. Once a week all the girls are required to report to the local public health doctor for a medical examination. Since pennacillin has become available things they're pretty safe. It does a good job of knocking out syphilis and gonarea."

The normal contract was for a couple years, I learned, when the women return to their villages, flush with their sizable earnings which is their dowery, a bargaining chip for marriage. Seen in economic terms, prostitution was an effective means of redistributing wealth and a ladder to upward mobility.

Marian introduced herself in the Trocadero and sat down between us. She was a woman of startling beauty. Nineteen years old, already the mother of two, she exuded sensuality. Olive complexion, wavy black hair swept up in coquetish swirl, exposing the curve of her neck. I was reminded of Carmen, the seductress in the tobacco factory in he opera. Her full breasts were pressed against the tight fitting light silk dress, heaving as she laughed at Canas's banter. I had difficulty keeping from looking at the deeply cut neck line. The tightly fitting dress wrapped about her rounded hips and fell well above here knees. Without a hint of provocation she was the most provocative woman I had sat beside. "La belle dame sans merci hath thee inthrall," Byron must have written in such a moment.

Canas danced with her, but when it became obvious that we were not customers, she moved to another table. Business is after all, business.

Why didn't we? I agonized later. It certainly wasn't for lack of desire, nor lack of scruples. Was it merely a failure of nerve? I always found it difficult approaching beautiful women for fear of rejection. But I could not detect an ounce of rejection in Marian. Perhaps it was the economic transaction. I was not in a good position to pay the required five dollars for the service, as reasonable as the tariff might be. But it was more than that. There was a certain fastidiousness about paying for sex. I would have to tend to my own need.

The evening degenerated to a night of drinking. I drank beer regularly in Puntarenas, not for the kick of the alcohol, but to avoid drinking the water. I had little tolerance from rum, though mixed with coconut milk, it was sweetly addictive. I never developed the social skill of sipping my drink. So that night, Canas, whom I had never known very well at school, and I became the best of amigos. We sang the ribald songs we learned in the school bus on the way to football games. "Oh dear, what can the matter be/ Seven old ladies locked in the lavatry...." Canas and the American friend who had come with him, eventually went out to find girls for the night. I returned to the dock where I fell asleep sitting at the top of the ladder, waiting for a boat to take me on board the Culver.

Such nights could have become habit. But Peter and Alex, though both heavy drinkers, were not womanizers. I felt it was the combination that was fatal to the moral decline I saw about me. I was saved, not by evangelical admonition, but by silent example.

We now came ashore for our meals and ate at Hervey's table. One morning a very attractive woman sat beside him, obviously English. She had long blond hair, pale skin with rosy cheeks, straight nose, blue eyes, a small mouth with only the hint of a smile, the sort of classic beauty one saw on an English biscuit tin of expensive tea-time cookies.

"Meet Mrs. Hervey," Hervey said.

Mrs. Hervey? I didn't know he was married. But she was too young to be his mother, so I concluded that she was his wife.

My regard for Hervey went up. I would never have thought him capable of attracting such a beautiful woman. I thought of him as being somewhat effeminite. And I was jealous. It disturbed me to think of her going to bed with him. We became friends. She read poetry and had been to Tintern Abbey. "We have a home in the West Country," she said. "You must come and visit."

That week was a national holiday. It was the first anniversary of the adoption of the new constitution abolishing the standing army, removing the military as the final arbiter of political choice. Not good for Hervey's illegal arms business, if that was his business, I thought. The constitution also enfranchised woman and Blacks. The town's population doubled overnight, people taking the train down from the capital, to stroll through town, lounging on the beach. We were bombarded with fireworks, day and night.

The bull fight was the climax of the celebration. An improvised ring was built on the football field in front of the bleachers seating 500 people, enclosed by a four foot high palisade of cedar planks. I went with the team from the Langesund and managed to slip in beside Mrs. Hervey.

Before the show all the bulls were herded into the ring and milled about to the cheers and the taunts of the crowd. To me they seemed a scrawny lot, a Brahma bull cross mix, with big ears, protruding ribs, bony shoulders, lean rumps, and long horns with the sharp ends clipped. They were underfed and when released their first inclination was to escape, pacifists rather than fighters. They bellowed plaintively, out of fear rather than angry.

The matador, clad in ballet tights and a tight fitting jacket adorned with gold and silver lace, a winged cap that he wore sideways, hair pulled back to a tight bun. He circled the ring, preening himself, waving to the crowd, flashing his red cape. With the fanfare of a trumpet, a signal that the action was to begin, he doffed his hat, made a deep bow before the wife of a public dignitary, and tossed it to her. Mrs. Hervey received the honor from one of the matadors.

The crowd was wound up to a high pitch, the band blared fortissimo, the climactic moment arrived. The gate to the bull pen was thrust opened. But no infuriated beast came charging out. The bull gave a mournful bellow and cowered at the back of the pen. Goaded out by picadors on horses with long prods, he stood center field confused, looking for someone in the crowd to help. He was greeted by taunts.

The matador waved his red cape before his eyes. "Toro," he shouted. The bull, clearly color blind, looked more confused than angry. The matador closed the distance between the two and flicked the cape at his nose. Now totally confused he charged in self-defense. The matador stepped aside, rose to full height on his toes, raised his right arm and plunged a long dart with a ribbon attached into the bull's neck.

"Ole'," the crowd roared.

The bull, smarting from the wasp sting of the dart, turned and charged again. Another dart. Ole'. With each pass the matador drew closer to the bull, and the darts struck higher on the shoulder, the crowd more frantic.

There were a dozen charges by the frightened beast, blood down his shanks, that moment for the final thrust of a fatal sword, but in Costa Rica the climactic killing is prohibited. The bull was released to return to his bellowing brothers. No cutting of the ears presented to the matador for a valiant show. He was given back his hat and presented with a cloth purse weighted with gold coins.

Taunts rather than cheers greeted one matador who had stood too far away from his bull, hesitant to move closer. "No tienne cohones," a man behind me shouted. You don't have balls.

The most aggressive bull of the afternoon came thundering out of the pen and charged. Not at the matador but at the fence. He took out the top two planks, leapt the barrier and ran for the country, followed by boys waving their shirts in matador fashion.

For a grand finale all the bulls were herded into the bull ring and the young men and boys of the town leapt in the join them. It was their opportunity for a moment of glory. "Aren't you going to join them?" Mrs. Hervey asked. I was too dumb to realize she was taunting me, and joined the melee. Big mistake. The first bull that looked at me, was all I needed to duck back to the fence. It was fun running with the crowd behind the bulls through the streets of town.

In Canada we celebrated Queen Victoria's birthday every May 24, with fireworks, a baseball tournament and a track meet for the children. Pretty tame stuff, I felt. Canadians have so little blood lust. No revolutionary spirit.

I had not seen Mrs. Sorenson all week. "She's gone up to the capital, San Jose to negotiate with the government to get the Langesund registered under the Cosa Rican flag," Ivor Brown, the Jamaican mate told me. "The embargo still has not been lifted."

She returned in a fit of recrimination, hostility and self-pity. "You can't do this to me," she screamed at Ricardo, the government liason officer, "I've to friends in the State Department." She raved on and inevitable found oblivion in rum.

Next morning she appeared on the deck of the Langesund in her bathing suit. Unannounced she dove off, swam a few yards toward the pier, then rolled over on her back, floating face up and drifted with the outgoing tide. Those on board thought she had just gone for a swim. Nothing unusual about that. But then a longshoreman on the pier noticed that she just floated under the pier and was drifting out to sea. He sounded the alarm, and George Lee, a new man who had just joined the expedition as an interpreter jumped into the dinghy with one of the work crew and took off in pursuit. They struggled her aboard and rowed back to the Langesund. Now limp, semi-comitose, bathing suit adrift, they had a harder time hoisting her over the rail on board. For days afterwards Lee took great delight in describing the fleshy parts of a woman's anatomy he had groped, how his hands kept slipping over her body, "for a better feel. There was no where to grip. She was like bowls of jelly."

They revived her enough to get her ashore to the hotel, where the doctor came to her beckon.

Captain Barney, who was in the next room, separated only by a thin plank wall, told us of how "the old sea hag moaned like a sick cow all night long."

Neither the Langasund, nor its owner, were ready to go to sea. Hervey decided to go without them. Everyone was to crowd on to the Culver. "We sail in the morning," he announced.

We had the Culver ready. Well as ready as she could be made ready. But again nothing began to move. Fresh food supplies had to be taken on, water and fuel tanks topped up. The work crew rounded up. Who was in charge? Hervey for sure. But to whom was the responsibility delegated? No one was sure. The newly designated Captain Barney would seem to be the logical one. "But nobody told me," he said. Ivor Brown, the Jamaican mate who had been with the expedition since it left Jamaica, stepped in.

The police contingent were dispatched to round up the missing members of the work crew. I found Mario, the amorous captain, walking Harbor Street with two young women, one on either arms. He offered to share Margarita with me. He was interested in Cecilia, the older, more beautiful of the two, "a proper girl,' he assured me, only seen in public with a chaperon. Hence the younger sister. She was a clerk in the book and stationary shop.

I'd been sent to pick up the binnacle head cover that had been repaired again. Returning I met Peter, my captain, Captain Barney, and Eric, another large dairy-fed Dane, a friend of Barney's off the shark fishing boat, the American Clipper. He was joining the expedition, another drunk, but a happy drunk, not a moody one. I was glad that he was joining us. I felt he was the one person who could put a damper on Barney's moods, if not in English, then in Danish.

Next to Eric sat a young naval officer, a second lieutenant in the United States Navy, off the minesweeper anchored in the harbor. He drank Coca Cola, without the rum, and seemed unusually interested in the expedition. He asked probing questions, more probing than casual curiosity. "Who do you think is funding the expedition? What connections does Hervey have on shore? And this Mrs. Sorenson? Who is that Jamaican working for him? And the Costa Rican interpreter?" We were not trying to be evasive, but we did not have good answers to his question.

"Naval intelligence?" I asked Peter when he left.

"Not very," he said.

"What do you mean?" I asked.

"Not very intelligent. Who else would drink Coca Cola without rum?"

Before leaving I stopped at another table to talk with five fishermen off the American Clipper. They said they'd been tracking the expedition for four months now. "We have a vested interest," one of them said, laughing. "Old Captain Sorenson offered to sell us the Langesund for $2500. He showed us the title in his name. It sounded like a good deal even next morning when sober. So we came up with five hundred dollars each, payed the old man who then disappeared. I'm told he went to Panama where he spent most of it on a big drunk. When he was broke the Danish Consul sent him home to Denmark."

"And your title?" I asked.

"Worthless. He didn't own the boat. That American bitch, his wife, does."

"What can you do about it?" I asked.

"Nothing. Wrote it off as a gambling loss. Hah. Hah."

"Sorry fellows, I got to leave." One of the expedition police had come to accompany me back to the boat. We were ready to sail. "I'm so bloody important they've even given me a police escort."

At two thirty in the morning, in a drenching tropical rain, we weighed anchor. I felt it was cold and cleansing, symbolic of washing off the dirt and dismay of the mainland. Or was it a warning, weeping skies foreboding of more grief?

Chapter 37: Cocos Island

On the night we sailed from Puntarenas a deep oily darkness had settled over the bay, black overcast clouds lit up in flashes of sheet lightning. Standing-by at the helm of the Culver, I could feel the electricity in the air and smell the salt tang of the sea, the acrid flotsam of the harbor, of fishing boats and cannery, and the pungent decay of tropical vegetation.

A continent of loyal ladies from the brothels came down to the pier to see us off. As the anchor was cranked up, they cheered, "Buen viaje." Then scattered before the drenching barrage of the rain squall.

Our reality is so shaped by Hollywood. But try as I might, as we motored outward bound for Cocos Island, I could not create a convincing movie scene of the Culver sailing off in quest of pirate treasure. The deck cargo bulged over the top sides like a man with a big gut trying to stuff his shirt front into his trousers. On deck three wooden barges the size of hay wagons, were parked on their sides. The newly acquired eighteen foot ship's launch nestled beside them. Forward were the three Newfoundland fishing dories, one stacked inside the other, our life boats. I felt the old ship had a top heavy uncertainty about it, on the verge of capsizing.

On the foredeck, the twelve workmen and six policemen huddled together like livestock in a railroad yard, milling about in search of shelter from the rain by night, seeking shade from the sun by day. They tumbled over their duffle bags, loose gear, fire arms and into each other.

On the quarter deck aft was the officer class, Hervey and his crew, Captain Edwards and Ivor Brown, off the Langesund; the Costa Ricans, Ricardo, the government liason officer who spoke good English, Mario, the captain of the police, Eduardo, the radio operator also a police officer; Barney and Eric, the two Danes off the American shark fishing boat, who had only recently joined the expedition; and Peter, Alex and myself, crew of the Culver, eleven total. In all, a ship's complement of twenty-nine on an eighty-eight foot motor sailing ketch. If our task had been a simple military objective such as laying land mines on a country road, I felt we could have been an effective force. As treasure hunters, I had my doubts.

"Is this comedy or melodrama?" I asked Ivor Brown.

"Neither," he said. "It's farce."

"How long will it take before we get there?" Hervey asked, impatient even before we had left.

"Cocos is about 350 miles," Barney said. "At five knots we should be there in three days." But Peter, I noticed, did not commit himself. He had miscalculated too often. The voyage from Miami to Haiti should have taken a week. One month later he was still in Cuba waiting for engine parts.

The first two days out of Puntarenas we made good time, picking up katabatic winds that blew off ashore, carrying us south off Punta Judas. A strong current then carried us west past Cabo Blanco. Though the wind dropped, under power we continued on course. Then the engine died. Peter and Alex worked through the night and into the next day to get it running again. And we drifted. Three days out and we were still only half way to Cocos. Hervey was furious. Barney scornful. The men on the foredeck put their heads together and grumbled.

The situation on board had been incendiary from the beginning. I felt it had all the makings of a Hollywood mutiny. Living conditions on he foredeck were appalling. The only shelter was under an old sail Peter had rigged from the shrouds. With each rain squall the men were drenched, and while this was a relief from the heat of the day, at night the men cowered together shivering. A couple men began to cough. Some could shelter in the galley in the focsle, but that became hot, stuffy and claustrophobic, and they retreated before becoming sea sick.

The gentry could retreat into the ship's cabin aft, but that too became oppressive. I found shelter for myself by stretching canvas over the open fisherman's dory. Barney just rolled up in his foul weather gear and slept out in the rain on deck.

With all the rain I felt it was ironic that water became a burning issue. Access to the ship's water tank was from the foredeck. We carried 600 gallons. On the first day 100 gallons had been consumed. Peter was alarmed. *Water water everywhere and all the boards did shrink./ Water water everywhere and not a drop to drink.* Like Coleridge's Ancient Mariner, he had a seaman's dread of critical dehydration. He ordered the pump handle removed and water rationed.

The ship's only head was also forward. After the morning run it was full, blocked and overflowing. Some forceful enthusiast had tried to make it function, and broke off the fitting causing it to spill shit over the focsle floor. I thought that this might be the spark that ignited mutiny. There was a reluctance to clean it up until Mario, the police chief intervened and suppressed any hint of rebellion. Soon it was scrubbed down. The cracked porcelain toilet bowl was committed to the deep and for the rest of the expedition we resorted to buckets. Toilet paper became a dwindling rare luxury item.

Food became a burning issue, not just because of the liberal use of chili peppers. I came to enjoy rice and beans, but when rice and beans were for lunch, and then for dinner beans and rice were for supper, I too felt the cook lacked imagination. When we complained, pancakes enlivened the breakfast menu. Plantain, potatoes, green cabbage and another unidentifiable root vegetable produced an acceptable vegetarian dinner. Fresh meat had been part of provisions but it had to be thrown overboard the second day, crawling with maggots. Perhaps this is what attracted the fish. Barney and Eric caught two tuna the first day, a dolphin the second. Ivor Brown,

155

the Jamaican, shot a middle sized turtle and dove overboard with a line to retrieve it before it sank. Then no fish. Ivor shot a shark but it got away.

Two days of vegetarian fare did not sit well. Barney, who had been most outspoken, became even more obnoxious. " These Costa Ricans may be able live on rice and beans. But not me. I'm no fuggin monkey." Patting his protruding pot belly, he bellowed, "This has cost me ten thousand dollars and I'll be damned if I'm going to let it go to waste on food like this." A disagreeable as he was, service did improve. We not long stood in line on the foredeck, but our food was brought aft in pots. The food was warmer and there was a greater variety of starches.

On the fourth day out we were still only half way to Cocos Island. But then the wind came up, right on the nose. We struggled to make a course of 235 degrees, south-west into the wind, tacking 195 degrees almost due south on the port tack, 270 degrees due west on the starboard tack. But head seas kept pushing us off course, and when Peter took noon sightings the next day, he found we were being pushed off course east by strong currents as well.

On the long, lazy evenings, before the rains came in, we would gather on the after deck and chat. On one occasion I saw the opportunity to ask Hervey, "What do you know about this treasure?"

He shifted his seat and crossed his legs. I sensed his unease. I felt he was wondering what to tell me. Who was this Canadian anyway? What was he doing on the Culver in the first place? A naval intelligence plant? He considered his words. "It goes back to 1821," he said. "That was a time of political upheaval in Latin America, their war of independence from Spain. The British government remained neutral though encouraging the colonists. A weaker Spain was in our interest. Several English sea captains saw the opportunity for personal gain and hired themselves out to both sides, privateers. You might say pirates. A Captain Thompson was one, based in Lima, Peru. The wealthy Spanish were leaving. Eager to get their gold and valuable out of the country they chartered Thompson to carry their belongings to Panama for trans-shipment to Spain. They were accompanied by a small security guard, easily overcome once at sea. The goods were too hot to take right into Panama, so they diverted their course to Cocos Island, a well known watering station. The captain, the mate and two young cabin boys went ashore and hid the valuables. They went on to Panama to arrange for a fence whom they could trust to cash in the stolen goods. Thompson and the mate were recognized, captured and hung. The two cabin boys escaped. It is from them that knowledge of the treasure has been handed down."

Hervey coughed. "Looks like rain," he said. "Think I'll go below."

"Wait," I wanted to say. What happened to the guards? What about the rest of the crew? What knowledge did the cabin boys pass on? What evidence did Hervey have? Maps that X marked the spot? How did he get hold of it? The more I knew the more I didn't know. Hervey must have sensed that, and that I would want to know more, and he didn't want that.

Ivor Brown shed more light on the growing sense of mystery. Ivor, an Afro-Caribbean from Jamaica had been with the expedition four months now, as mate on the Langesund. I asked him what he knew. "Have you noticed that Hervey signs his name—V. Cochrane Hervey. Hervey is a direct descendent of Lord Cochrane, a national hero in many Spanish American countries. He was an English admiral who defeated the Spanish fleet on the west coast of South America during the wars of independence. He was on the sea what Bolivar was on land.

"The story is that the Thompson treasure isn't the only one buried on Cocos Island. Pirates since Morgan in the seventeenth century, and even Drake in the sixteenth century, are known to have stopped there for water. Rumor has it that they also buried treasure, but it was never explained why? There are supposed to be several different treasures in different locations. Lord Cochrane gained possession of charts and sketches that presumably identify their location. Hervey found these in the family archives and has been successful in convincing a number of people come up with the funds to pay for a treasure hunting expedition. And to pay for a number of people such as ourselves to go along with it." He laughed, a deep baritone African laugh. "What do you make of that?"

"So he's not a gun runner after all?" I said. I'd told Ivor of our encounter with Cauffie, U.S. Naval Intelligence, in Panama.

"Oh, I wouldn't say that," Ivor replied.

Eduardo, the radio operator, came on deck with a report that the Langesund might get the Costa Rican flag soon and be cleared to sail with badly needed supplies for the expedition. This set off the rumor, voice *sotta voce*, that should the Langesund show up, Hervey would just take off on it for Panama.

"I don't see why Hervey would even bother going to Cocos Island," Ivor said.

"What do you mean by that?" I asked. He clearly knew something I didn't know. He only smiled.

Rumors have a way of rumors. Eduardo reported that the Costa Rican newspapers had printed a story about the expedition. "The Culver had reached Cocos Island, discharged the work crew who had started operation, and returned to Puntarenas to pick up more laborers. The Culver is now in Puntarenas, they said," he said.

That fed into our own rumor factory. Maybe we should return to Puntarenas. "Before it is too late," Barney said, stoking the growing anxiety. We were running low on diesel fuel. "Do you have enough for the return trip?" Hervey countered by making arrangements by radio to refuel from a fishing boat. The great uncertainty was the foredeck crew who were growing more restive as our diet became more frugal.

"Land ahoy." The fifth day out Ivor spotted it from the deck, a dark object on the horizon. Climbing high in the shrouds he confirmed it. But Peter's noon sighting put us seventy-five miles to the north and further east. Our first false alarm.

We continued to buck into headwinds as we had the previous three days, being set further east by a two knot current. "We aren't moving a foot an hour," Barney said with a low grumble. "If I were running this bloody ship I'd go south of the island, then come north with the wind and the current." But Peter persisted on a course of 270 degrees, heading directly toward the island. The 0800 hours sighting next morning put us thirty miles east of Cocos Island. Visibility was poor. It rained intermittently. Clouds bunched on the horizon and spread across the sky in multiple layers. Peter missed the noon sighting as it was overcast.

Around three he thought he saw something, "Off the lobster pots," which were lashed outboard of the starboard rail. Ivor climbed the starboard shrouds and stood on the cross-tree, "I think I see something to starboard," he said. Barney, not to be outdone by Ivor, climbed the part shrouds but was non-commital.

It was three-thirty, I registered it in the ship's log, when the cloud lifted and through the fog and haze we saw the dull blue confederate gray land mass crouched under a blanket of mist and rain. "Mira, Isla del Cocos," the men burst out singing with loud cheers.

Even Hervey, normally so reserved and controlled was caught up in the spirit of the men. He went below and returned on deck with two bottles of rum. In an uncharacteristic act of good cheer and comraderie sent one to the foredeck, and passed the other around the quarterdeck. The men cheered and sang. The celebration was complete when Barney cast a line off the stern and thirty pound tuna took the bait. They were gourmet rice and beans the cook served up that night.

After supper the men lined with rail with fish hooks and lines, and in half an hour caught half a dozen fish and two baby sharks. Moral ran high, the anxiety about food somewhat dispelled.

Darkness closed in rapidly as it does in the tropics. As we drew closer the island became a hunched brooding hulk against the star lit sky. The chart showed good depth but Peter was anxious approaching in the night. But Captain Edwards guided us safely into the protected anchorage of Chatham Bay on the north-east side. He knew the setting well. I'd heard that he had lost his own yacht on the island the previous year, but did not realize he'd been ship-wrecked for six months before being rescued by a tuna fishing boat that had come in for water. He had returned to Puntarenas where he joined the Hervey expedition with the intention of returning to Cocos to see what he could salvage off the wreck. Only later did I learn that he had been on four previous treasure hunting expeditions led by an American, Forbes.

Captain Edwards had always impressed me as one of the more reliable members of the Hervey party, even honest. He had an erect shoulders back military demeanor, self-effacing, spoke when spoken to, courteous and discrete. But now I began to wonder what was behind that facade. I also learned that he had been to Cocos Island on the four previous American Forbes expeditions. What did he know? What had he done during the six months he was on the island? Had he searched? What had he found? Edwards said little. Was he being evasive or merely reticent?

While Edwards became more mysterious, Hervey became more transparent. I began to see a new side to him. Instead of working behind the scenes in ways that I felt were evasive, even shifty, from that first night he took on the role of expedition leader. After dinner he was eager to go ashore that night. He wanted to see what past expeditions might have left behind by way of building materials that he might use. He had an allusion that the Forbes expedition may have left him a deserted village. I hopped into the skiff with Captain Edwards, Peter, Olsen the Danish fisherman and Hervey and we motored ashore.

As I dropped over the gunwale and pulled the boat up on the beach, I thought of newsreel pictures of General MacArthur wading ashore at Bataan. I felt a kind of assurance that there really is a Cocos Island, that it was not just a figure of fantasy as the last several weeks seemed to be.

Captain Edwards walked over to the wreck of his boat, the hull now battered and filling with sand. The main boom had been propped up to serve as the ridge pole for a tent, an old sail flapping in tatters. He bent his head as if in prayer and I felt his pain. Further up the beach there was the remains of a shanty partly burned that Edwards said they had built when they moved ashore. Flotsam was strewn about, junky odds and ends that Hervey wanted salvaged, a binnacle box, a set of shelves, a portable oven with a broken door, a small cupboard. We filled a ship's water barrel from the fresh water stream flowing off the hillside. I bathed, for the first time in a week, launched the skiff through light rollers and returned to the Culver.

No one could sleep. On board Hervey opened a bottle of rum and proceeded to yarn and chew the fat for a couple hours, I wrote in my journal. He told us more about the Thompson treasure. " The Treasure of Lima, it's called." I noticed that he used the present tense. "When the rebel army under San Martin approached Lima— this would be in 1819, the wealthy citizens banded together a chartered a ship to transport their valuables to the safety of Panama, where it could be trans-shipped to Spain. The English were officially neutral, though some naval officers had offered their services to the rebels." He didn't mention that his great-great grandfather, Lord Admiral Cochrane, was foremost among them. I guessed that if you are of the right pedigree you don't have to brag about it. "But Thompson was a free-booter, the captain of an unarmed merchant ship that offered his services to anyone who would pay. The Spanish gentry were desperate, willing to pay royally. They trusted him, but just to be on the safe side, an armed guard accompanied the treasure.

"There's a fine line between a free-booter and a pirate. Once clear of the Peruvian coast, Thompson conspired with the captain of the guard and they hijacked the loot." As a gun-runner, if he was indeed a gun-runner, I felt Hervey would understand.

"They were then faced with the problem of what to d with it. They'd have to go through Panama to get their money out. But they'd be caught red handed if they went straight in. They'd have to deposit the treasure until things cooled off. With the way the revolution was going that wouldn't be too long. They had the choice of two sets of islands, the Gallipagos, or Cocos, a well-known stop off for ships coming in to replenish their water casks.

"When they got to Cocos we know there was a division of the spoils. Each man got a share, like fishermen getting a share of their catch." Like my half of one percent, I thought. The men went ashore and cached their small fortune in caves, under cliffs and rock formations." Was this why we brought the dynamite? "Half the treasure belonged to the owners, the captain and the mate. This they buried in a large cast iron trunk in ten feet of water in a protected bay." Hervey didn't say which bay. But that must be why we had hauled work barges, hydraulic pumps and hoses, and the heavy metal casings. The reality of a treasure hunt began to seem feasible.

159

"Once unburdened they sailed to Panama to be met by loyal Spanish officials that had been tipped off. Their alibi was truthful. They had encountered pirates, but their explanation was not convincing. Crew and guards were seized, in Spanish fashion tortured and beheaded. Except for the captain, mate and a cabin boy, who would be taken back to the island to identify where the treasure was buried."

"Thompson and his mate were able to bribe his jailers, escaped and managed to get back to England. The Spanish took the cabin boy back to Cocos but he had been terrorized, went insane and was of no use to them. In England Thompson solicited backing for a return expedition, but could find no backers who would trust him. Once a pirate always a pirate," Hervey said.

Hervey enjoyed telling his story. It was well rehearsed. I sensed that he had told it many times before, perhaps when he too was trying to raise money to search for Thomson's treasure. I imagined him standing up in a London club, a half glass of sherry in his hand, telling the story to a group of well dressed potential investors. Clearly he had had some success. He'd got himself to Cocos Island, and all of us. Somebody had to pay the bill. But how much could you believe?

"There have been other possible treasures. We know that a Portugese pirate, Bonati, put in here three hundred years ago. Even the notorious English pirate, Captain Morgan, the King of Belize, is known to have raided along the west coast of South America. He could have put in here," Hervey said.

"Has any treasure actually been found?" Peter asked.

"Why yes. As a matter of fact it has," Hervey said. "In the 1890's a group found treasure valued at a hundred thousand pounds." 1890, I thought, that didn't seem too promising. But a hundred thousand pounds was enough to attract one's attention. A rain squall swept in over the bay, and we scattered for shelter.

Cocos Island, latitude five degrees thirty-three minutes north, longitude eighty-seven degrees three minutes west, is five miles long from Dampier Head on the south west to Colnette point on the north-east, two miles across fro Eaton Head on the west to the east shore. We had made landfall on Chatham Bay, a protected harbor on the north-east side of the island, sheltered from the prevailing south-west winds and Pacific swell, except when the winds shifted unexpectedly, as they did when Captain Edwards lost his yacht. Hervey's base of operation was to be in Wafer Bay on the other side of the island. Early next morning we weighed anchor and motored around to it.

Standing off the north shore I got my first view of the island. The rain had not let up and I saw it only intermittently. Rock faces two hundred feet high plunged into the turgid gray-blue sea. Vibrant green velvety growth was clinging to the hillsides, a maze of ferns, plants with umbrella sized leaves. Vines grew in cracks in the rocks and hung down, tangling in the trees, choking, strangling. Further backs the hills rose to five hundred feet, waterfalls cascading down the sheer slopes. Above and beyond a high ridge, two thousand feet high, capped in fog and churning mist, ran down the center of the island. If there was treasure buried up there, it was going to take a stalwart crew to find it, I felt. So this was the object of our quest? Where would you begin?

160

Rounding the north end of the island, Isla Margarita, a gigantic rock rose out of the sea, a Gibralter-of-the-South Seas. Sea birds rose to challenge us, gulls, terns, frigate birds, fluttering, diving, screaming obscenities, resenting our intrusion, guarding their treasure.

We worked in the rain all that day. "Come the deluge," Ivor Brown threw up his arms to the clouds. "It's like Noah unloading the arc." The scene was chaotic. The work crew were eager to get ashore. The past seven days had been a form of incarceration. Most were peasant farmers, free to wander in the fields, with the feel of dirt between their toes. Had we not snagged two sharks last night, I suspect some would have swum to shore, though we were still half a mile off. There was no organized plan for debarkation, so far as I could see, which contributed to the sense of growing desperation.

Cutting through the confusion, Barney on this occasion was superb. He took over as boss rigger and things began to happen as if by magic. He took off the main sail, ran topping lifts to control the swinging of the boom, rigged block and tackle, and began the discharge the deck cargo. The ship's skiff and the first of the barges were lowered over the side.

Mario, the captain of the police, commandeered the first one, and went ashore to build shelters, for themselves only, it turned out. From the beginning a rigid social structure was imposed. Workers clambered into the next barge, and waited shivering in the rain as their scant belongings were lowered to them. One poor fellow was seasick just from the steady swell in the anchorage. One side of the barge had been stove-in, but defying the laws of stress and strain, the it floated. The rest of "the monkeys," as Barney called them, rowed ashore. "Good riddance," he added. Though creatures more to be pitied than scorned, it did feel relieved to have the ship to ourselves again.

The sense of relief did not last long. To make an early start that morning, the cook had served only a cold breakfast, rice and beans left over from last night. Washed down with a cup of hot sweet coffee it was acceptable, given the circumstances, and there were no complaints. Even from Barney.

While the process of debarkation on board was chaotic, it was even more so on the beach. The cook had gone on shore with the Cost Ricans, toting his pots, pans, charcoal brazier, basic rations, but he was given no help in setting up a kitchen. Everyone clambered to create their own shelter. As a result, lunch did not appear until four in the afternoon, porridge, cold. All the good will, the sense of purpose and excitement generated last night was scuttled in ten feet of water.

Barney went berserk. Reluctant to confront Hervey directly, he took it out on his scape-goat, Ivor Brown, the Jamaican mate. "You dirty black bastard," Barney ranted. "Get him out of my sight. He's just your stool pigeon," he shouted at Hervey. The scene was ugly. Ivor was a big man, young, fit and strong. I feared he would lose his cool. I knew he could look after himself, but it would be messy. The police, unfortunately were all on shore. But that could possible made a confrontation worse. They were armed. Barney persisted like an angry dog that didn't know when to stop barking. Ivor turned his back and proceeded to eat his porridge. Olson, Barney's

Danish comrade maneuvered Barney away until he cooled down, making a dramatic show of throwing his porridge overboard.

The fracas convinced Hervey that he should move ashore. Barney commandeered Hervey's bunk. The ship's complement was now reduced to six, Peter, Alex and myself, Barney and Olson, and to my surprise, Captain Edwards chose to stay on board. I wondered if this was of his own choosing or whether Hervey wanted one of his men go keep an eye on us? Thanks to his resourcefulness, Edwards was able to heat up a charcoal burner, and that night we had our first hot meal of the day, rice and beans, a non-descript vegetable and fish that we caught over the side. We now lived in relative isolation from he rest of the expedition.

I was not looking forward to living on board with Barney, but he redeemed himself. He took over cooking on board, and turned out to be a gourmet chef. He grumbled about the pots, the stove, the damp charcoal, but his meals became an aesthetic experience: red snapper for breakfast, fish chowder for lunch, a banquet of curried rice, fried potatoes and more fish for supper, washed down with coffee. I had not realized the variety of different flavors of fish and Barney blended them like the gourmet he was. After months of Costa Rican cooking we indulged ourselves in a feeding frenzy.

Next morning Ivor rowed out to take me to shore. Barney retreated to the other side of the boat. We had planned to add venison to the expedition diet. We skirted the beach, scanning the tropical undergrowth for the sight of game. I spotted a deer drinking from a stream. Ivor had borrowed Mario's Reisling sub-machine gun. Landing we stalked through the undergrowth until within firing range. Ivor brought it down with a bullet through the neck. It seemed too easy, hardly fair. With our trophy on display we proceeded to camp.

The campsite had been selected by Mario, the police captain. He'd been on Cocos Island on three previous expeditions. Located about seventy-five yards above the beach, it was nestled in at the base of huge broad leafed trees with outspread branches that shaded the area in the heat of the day, and broke the heavy downpour of the tropical squalls, filtering it to a fine drizzle and gauzy mist. The ground was soft and sandy. It was an ideal setting for a family outing or picnic. The men seemed to see it that way, lounging in the shade, waiting for something to happen.

A couple military tents had been erected. These apparently were for the elite, Hervey and Ivor Brown in one, Mario and Lee, the radio operator, in the other. A make-shift lean-to sheltered the galley, food storage bins, a collection of shovels, axes, miscellaneous tools, the cook and as many of those as could crowd in. The rest of the men shifted for themselves with assorted pieces of canvas strung from poles.

"We plan to build a long house," Ivor said, and pointed to six holes that had been dug and the six logs that lay beside them, the projected frame. There were few signs that work was being done. The men seemed to be on holiday, drying wet blankets and clothing, doing their laundry in the stream where the cook drew water. Foraging for food was a game. They fished, gathered mussels at low tide. One fellow climbed the palm trees that hugged the beach and brought down coconuts. The police turned out for targret practice and joined in the sport of seeing how many coconuts they could shoot down. One expert marksman brought down seven with one shot.

On board the Culver we expected to continue the unloading of the cargo, but nobody came out. Hervey did not show his face until four in the afternoon, and then it was with George Lee, the radio operator. "The Langesund has been issued a Costa Rican flag," Harvey told us. "They'll be prepared to sail in a couple days." None too soon, I thought. They were already out of cigarettes, and items like sugar and coffee were in short supply.

"Do you figure Hervey is planning to skip out to Panama on the Langesund?" Barney said around the quarterdeck after supper. "Do you think we could catch them in the Culver?" I was reminded in the idle talk in the small village where I grew up, where not much happened, so we had to make things up.

The next week I had to be reminded that I was on Treasure Island and not on a South Seas luxury cruise. On board the Culver life revolved around Barney's meals. He was a master of creative ingenuity. "Try this one," he'd say, and serve you his latest fish dinner. "This one tastes like chicken, doesn't it?" And it did. A couple days later another fish tasted like pork. We caught baby shark, but out of atavistic revenge would usually kill then and throw them back in. On night Barney cooked one and I was surprised how tasty it was. I'd always thought of fish as just fish, unless you were talking about canned sardines or salt cod. But not Barney. He knew the nouances of eating fish, like some people knew the subtleties of tasting wine. The most prolific fish was a flat black fish, about the size of a dinner plate, with a narrow mouth, that hovered around the boat all day, attracted to any scraps and tidbits thrown overboard, including our crap. We called it crap fish, and though the Costa Ricans claimed it was very tasty, "Muy deliciouso. com porco," we decided to forgo the delicacy.

Even beans. Barney soaked them overnight, and cooked them the next day for six hours on a low simmer with molasses, vinegar and onions. I thought Hervey's mouth was watering when I described the meal to him. Barney served with venison stew.

On shore the work day rarely extended more than a couple hours. The long house slowly took shape with an aluminum roof and siding, a mess hall where the work crew and the police could meet during the day, and the men could shelter from the elements at night. It seemed to be a part of their contract that serious work would not begin until shelter was provided.

Most mornings a crew of four men would usually show up around eleven and with much delay, re-rigging the boom, well coordinated pulling of lines, they'd hoisted another barge overboard, loaded it with gear from the hold, and took it ashore rowing like galley slaves. "Be back in an hour," they said. There was an expedition outboard motor, but it too was temperamental. Hervey seldom showed up.

Peter was frustrated at the slow pace at which the boat was being unloaded. He was particularly eager to get the deck cargo, the barges, off. Sorting through Hervey's equipment in the hold he came upon a chain pulley hoist with a load capacity of four tons. "We can do it ourselves with this," he said. With the greatest of ease and the smoothest operation yet. It was like a pelican launching into flight off fisherman's wharf, as they swung over the bulwarks and dropped overboard. We loaded one with copper piping to clear the port deck, and the Culver began to take on ship-like proportions again. Since no one appeared from shore, we rowed it to an anchored buoy for the night. Unfortunately it began to settle, and by dinner time it had settled one-third into the water. "The pipes will be under water by morning," Peter said. "We'd better row it ashore. Peter and Barney worked the oars, towing one of the ship's dories. I went along to bail.

Approaching shore the four-foot swell broke in a foaming surf, nearly dumping the dory. "Grab a copper pipe," Peter yelled. "Keep us head on to the beach." And we rode up on the crest of the waves, to the cheers of the shore party. We were invited to dinner, but Barney had one of his famous meals simmering and we returned on board.

It was a good day all around. The shore party had netted sixty fish in the small river near camp. The police had shot another deer. On board the Culver we caught twenty fish and six sharks that were killed and thrown back. The lobster pot brought up three crawfish and a moray eel, a fearsome looking creature with a row of razor sharp teeth. The search for pirate gold made little progress.

They were hunched around a low burning ship's lantern and a bottle of rum, when Alex and I went on shore after dinner that night. Mario, the captain of police, was telling Hervey of two previous expeditions to Cocos Island that he had been on. An American-Canadian syndicate, under a professional treasure hunter, Forbes, had made seven attempts, working off the beach on Chatham Bay, on the other side of the island where Captain Edwards boat had dragged, and ran aground.

"Two Canadians, Mike and Harry O'Hara," Mario said. "They come from Vancouver. Perhaps you know them."

"No I don't," I said.

"They split from the main group and set up a separate operation here in Wafer Bay, right where we are sitting. They were looking for gold in caves, hidden behind waterfalls, buried in the mountains," Mario said. "They also drank much rum."

I could attest to that. I'd seen the cache of empty bottles behind the trees when I had been collecting coconuts.

"We were here six weeks. They found nothing. Nada. We were low on food, and had to go. But they were broke. Could not pay the workers or the police. So we seized the yacht," Mario said.

Here his story rambled. Was it the fog of rum? Or was Mario hesitating, wondering how much to say? Returning to Costa Rice, the O'Hara brothers connected with a group of Americans who were involved in smuggling business contraband guns into Panama that was involved in a heated disputed election. It payed well, a profit of twenty thousand colons, four thousand dollars. They were able to pay off their debt, reclaim their yacht, and retired to a luxury hotel to drink the proceeds. The Panamanian government pressured the Costa Rican government, and warrants were placed for their arrest. Harry skipped the country, but Mike spent a token month in prison, where he continued to party with the bribed guards.

Contraband. Gun running. Smuggling. It was difficult to see Harvey's face in the dim light. I recalled our meeting with Lt. Cauffie of United States Navy Intelligence in Panama. He told us he thought that Harvey's treasure hunting expedition was a front for a gun running operation. Mario, as a Costa Rican official must be privy to such information. Was this a cautionary tale?

A holiday mood prevailed at base camp. The work day usually began around eleven, not long before the cook was ready to serve comida. The men ate well, their basic ration of rice and beans supplemented by fish. One night two men netted sixty in the small river that flowed by camp. One of Mario's sharpshooters brought in venison one day, a female hog the next day. They caught a suckling pig that became the camp mascot. The long house was extended and accommodated the work crew, though little thought had been given to the disposal of garbage and human waste.

We lived a separate existence on the board the Culver, anchored a quarter mile off shore. Barney kept surprising us with his culinary creativity. I felt I was in the land of the lotus eaters. It was the full moon of May. In the evening after dinner we'd sit out on the quarterdeck and reminisce. Wide rings circled the moon with a pale rainbow glow.

"Looks like rain," Peter said.

"Not at all," Barney said. "It's just a change of weather fronts."

The argument became more heated with each sip of rum. "Thank God they're not small rings," Olson said. "In Denmark that's a sure sign of snow."

And treasure hunting? "Get serious," Peter said. "He's up to something else."

Then Hervey surprised us. He came out to the boat early, well before eleven. "Eric, I could use your help. Would you mind coming ashore?" Eric disappeared for the day.

"Hervey said he needed someone who knew something about motors and pumps. Apparently he's had a falling out with Brown, so he called on me," Eric said when he returned that night. "On shore he showed me a map. He said it was the map that showed where the thirteenth load of the Thompson treasure had been buried.

The map looked old, yellowing paper, ragged edges, done in great detail of this bay and the river above the camp. It seemed authentic. But I wasn't prepared for his next move. Come with me, Hervey said. He headed up the stream counting off the paces as we climbed. There was path had been cleared by machete that led up a small ridge. At the top I heard the sound of falling water and he headed right to it. We came upon an aread that had been cleared of ferns, vines and the jungle. Behind it was a cave." Eric, the big Danish fisherman, usually so reserved, was enjoying being the center of attention.

"Hervey had brought a flashlight and led the way in. There was two feet of water but it could be drained easily. I was more worried about the lizards spiders. Scorpions. I had to stoop to move. We went in, possibly a hundred feet, though it was hard to tell in the dark. Several arms branched off the main cave. Hervey stopped at a pit that was about four feet deep.

"It looks as if it's been worked over, I told Hervey. Oh yes, he said. A Canadian group worked this cave in 1933. They were mining engineers and skilled technicians; they used mechanical excavation equipment, but found nothing. Though

165

there is always the possibility that they did, and buried it again, and returned later to avoid paying the extortionate fee of the Costa Rican government," Eric said.

I suspect this had occurred to Hervey too.

For the next five days Eric rowed ashore every morning and returned for supper with tales of treasure trove. "The system really works," he said. "In one afternoon of blasting with a water cannon we can move as much gravel and sand as six men digging a week. Whoever designed it was a genius.

"According to Hervey we were looking for a row of steps leading down from the bottom of the cave. So far we haven't found them." Next day Eric announced. "Hervey's calling it off. He's got maps of other caves. We're going to search in them."

"Hervey's not really searching." Peter discounted the whole effort. "He's only going through the motions . He has to impress his investors back in London. Whoever they are."

But Eric's stories of the cave gave treasure hunting a renewed credibility. Just suppose; there might just be something to it. We all had our fantasies of buried treasure. Peter's skepticism did not deter him from planning his own treasure hunt. "Hell, we've come all this way and taken all this crap from Hervey, why don't we search ourselves. Not a quarter of a mile from where the Culver was anchored high cliff ran along the south shore of Wafer Bay. Water gushed over the rim and crashed on boulders below, dissolving into an iridescent spray. Looking at it every day, we soon convinced ourselves that there must to be a cave behind the waterfall. Didn't Hervey say follow the sound of water?

I joined Peter, Alex and Eric when they launched the ship's dory and we rowed ashore. We found a hazardous beach between rocks and timed our landing between surges of the ocean swell. I slipped on wet slimy rocks and clambered over dark granitic boulders, crawling for balance, as I worked our way up the slope, cutting my way through thick vines and chest high lacy ferns. The cacaphony of falling water, a thousand thundering kettle drums grew louder as I drew closer. The water fell into a pool and swirled in large circular eroded bowl at the base of the cliff, poured over the lip and gushed into a second bowl. But where was the cave? I felt hemmed in, entangled in vines, stumbling over fallen trees. The forest was intent on concealing its secrets. If there was a cave there, we didn't find it.

Dampier Head was the southernmost point of the island. It was a barren ghost-like bastion, glowing white plastered in bird droppings. One of the earliest maps to show Cocos Island appeared in Dampier's account of his first circumnavigation, "A New Voyage Round the World" published in 1679. Hervey had an early copy. He speculated that it led to other pirate-privateers visiting the island. He had Eric row him the five miles to explore "other options." However, the surge was high, they were unable to land on the rocky shore, turned back, planning to return another day.

Our illustrious Hervey expedition to Cocos Island was a case study of poor planning, worse execution. We were not ten days on the island when it looked as though it would fall apart. They were dangerously low on food. Hervey's glib comment, "Well, at least they won't starve. There's plenty rice and bean, and spaghetti." As though spaghetti was a luxury item. "And they can always hunt and fish."

They. He seemed to disassociate himself. No bread dear queen. Feed them cake.

Indeed hunting and fishing did sustain us for a week. Then the easy fishing gave out. Ivor Brown tried trolling for tuna. The deer and pigs moved back into hills and the police sharpshooters were unwilling to pursue them. Then the cook ran out of coffee and sugar, as well as seasoning, and even the Costa Rican workers felt rice and beans bleak fare. Cigarette rations were halved, then halved again.

"No coffee. No sugar. No decent food. No work." Hervey had a strike on his hands. In the fashion of Latin American dictatorships, he assigned the management of the work crew to Mario, the captain of police.

Only the promise of immediate relief kept the expedition going. "The Langesund is on its way," Hervey declared. But next day it was still in Puntarenas, preparing to get underway. "It has sailed," Hervey announced the day after. This was verified by Eduardo, the radio operator. "It will be here in five days." Another week went by.

"Langesund ahoy!" It became the punch line of a comic act where the men would scan the horizon every morning. "They've taken off for Panama," Pedro their spokesman, who spoke a little English, said. "Or is it L.A.?"

"We're going back to Puntarenas." The rumor spread rapidly. Neither Hervey nor Mario would deny it.

The negativism was contagious and Peter caught the virus. One evening he went ashore with Eric. Hervey greeted them with a bottle of rum. He should have known better. Peter had not finished his second drink before his neck and face turned a heated red, and he proceeded to provide Hervey with an account of his dubious heritage, his shortcomings of character, and accusations of his dishonesty. "This whole operation is just a front, a cover up, a farce." With that he stomped out, grabbing the half full bottle of run as he went.

The tirade went on for several days and encompassed everyone in contact with him. Barney was the first combatant. Leading off with Australian metaphor, "I'm pissed off," he told Barney to clean up grease, the charcoal soot, on the foredeck where Barney had set up the galley.

"Fluff you," Barney replied, and once the afternoon rain squall had passed through, he rowed ashore. I saw him strolling down the beach in conference with Hervey and in the evening he returned. "I'm moving ashore tomorrow," he said.

Tomorrow, and tomorrow, and tomorrow. It was always going to be tomorrow. They rigged a primitive shelter for him, well away from the crowded conditions and growing stench of base camp. He sat in his smudge until he could tolerate the mosquitoes no longer, and moved back on board. Next day he refused to eat and fasted for a day. I wondered if he planned a hunger strike, an unusually Gandian strategy for a Danish fisherman. Then he resumed cooking, perhaps as a way of redeeming himself. Selfishly, I was delighted for Barney could even make rice and beans with salt pork or bully beef a satisfying meal. But Peter was a bulldog and would not let go of the bone. The battle went on.

Peter seemed enveloped in anger. On now turned on Alex, on me, and even on himself. Cleaning the boat became an obsession as if this was a way of purging himself of the self-hate within him. Alex was assigned the focsle galley where he scrubbed and scraped. I was assigned the engine room lazarette where I grubbed about for three days in a grease pit, wire brushing the rust off spare engine parts and machine nuts and bolts. I hated it. And I my own grudge began to fester. I wasn't being paid. I didn't expect to be paid. Nor did I expect to do this sort of meaningless grunt work. But in fairness to Peter, he was down there grubbing about with me.

The cupboard was bare. Fish weren't biting since our night light had been taken away when the generator was taken ashore. Another day of rice and beans, and Peter agreed to let me go hunting. I'd never shot anything bigger than a twenty-two rifle before , so I felt I was the great white hunter on safari when Mario provided me with an old U.S. Army Enfield 30.30, six bullets, and I stalked off into the jungle. I followed the river above camp, climbing to the ridge on the left bank. A canopy of high trees shaded the area, criss-crossed with game trails, the cry of a solitary bird, the splash of water below.

Half an hour up the hill I came across an opening where the sun through and tall course grass grew tall. There was a faint rustle behind a thicket and I stalked closer. I saw two upright ears, white against brown erect on the alert, and two intense brown eyes. I almost dropped my rifle transferring it from my carrying hand to action station across my chest. I opened the breech, reached for a bullet in my right pocket, began to slide it into the breech when I looked up to see if the deer was still there. The bullet dropped to the ground. I slipped another in, cocked the gun and took aim, cursing myself for breathing so hard. Fired and then opened my eyes. I saw nothing. My leg of venison must have taken flight. Coming around the thicket, there it was, a crumpled heap on the ground. The shot had torn through the neck.

My first kill. I was surprised by my exhilaration, proud of my newly expertise, the sense of conquest I had know in the boxing ring. But when my adrenalin wore off I felt uneasy, a tinge of shame. It seemed too easy, almost unfair. Certainly the deer faced unequal odds.

It was still early in the day and I did not want to return to all the rancor on board. I looked forward to the freedom of the hills, so I strung the deer to a tree and took off to explore the freedom of the hills. Higher up the ridges on both sides of the river converged and I was forced into the ravine. The terrain steepened and I climbed through the muddy eroded slope, clambering up loose rocks and over dead trees.

At breaks between the trees I saw glimpses of the ocean, a thousand feet below. Wasn't it time to turn back? Suppose I injured myself, they'd never find me. I pressed on and eventually reached a point where the land leveled off and opened up to a wide vista. I could see across the whole north-west corner of the island. The ridge swept in a wide horseshoe, I could look down on the bay, Cascara Island off the point and a diminutive Culver bobbing at anchor.

The ridge top was open rolling parkland between widely spaced huge trees, shading the undergrowth, easy walking. There were traces of animals, tracks, turds, ground rooted by pigs. In the distance I heard a cacaphonous roar, the screaming, screeching of raucous seabirds, thousands of gull-like white birds with long beaks, that clung to a grove of trees in squabbling clusters, plastering the trees in swaths of white, feathers, droppings, their young. Boobies, I learned later.

So far no game. Further on I hears a low grunting and stalked toward a swath of tall grass, the grand master of stealth. Then I realized the grunting was behind me. I was being stalked. Waddling on its short stalky legs, snout pointed high, tale erect, confident in not having any natural predators, I was followed by a hog. Now an experienced big game hunter, I felled him with one shot, right behind the eye. It was as if he had walked right into the bullet.

My moment of triumph did not last long. How do I retrieve my trophy? I was several miles from camp, more than a thousand feet below me through treacherous terrain. It weighed at least seventy pounds, though only fifty when gutted. Slung over my back, holding it by its four legs with one hand, clutching my rifle with the other, I followed a ravine down. The slope steepened and I found myself following a water course. Where it was too steep for trees to grow, the sun shone through and the slope was overgrown with thick shrubs, twisted vines, and chest high lacy ferns, where I cut my way through, dragging the carcass behind. An eighty foot waterfall barred my. Do I abandon my prize? I threw it over the edge and cut my way to the bottom, on the seat of my pants, clutching vines to break my fall. It was late afternoon before I emerged from the heart of darkness, collapsed on the beach and rested before rowing back to the boat.

"Why did you take so long?" Peter asked, but he did come back with me to retrieve the deer. It was stiff, began to smell and was coated with millions of fly eggs. But meat was meat, and we gutted it, and Barney produced another of his miraculous venison stews.

"We're going for the mother lode," Ivor Brown said when he came on board with Hervey. I'd been told that the main treasure of the so-called Thompson Treasure was thought to be buried "in nine feet of water" Given the land erosion and the build up of the beach since 1820, that placed it at the low tide line, according to the Hervey's compass coordinates, the precise site, where X marked the spot triangulated with Captain Edwards hand-held British Army field compass. All that we needed to do now was to retrieve it.

Hervey outlined his plan which explained why we had shipped all the heavy equipment, barges, nine foot curved steel casings, pumps, compressors, power nozzles, hoses, most still on board the Culver. It seemed well thought out. The steel casings could be bolted together to form a circular crib ten feet across and four feet down, a second layer extending it to eight feet. This would be sunk over the site, and then water, sand and gold guilders pumped out. It seemed well thought out.

"For once we are ahead of schedule," Hervey said. I had seen no evidence of a schedule three weeks after making landfall on Cocos Island. Now the music was to begin, Hervey waving the baton.

169

Barney was resuscitated from his lethargy and the boss rigger re-rigged the main boom with block and tackle. The last barge was hoisted into the water, loaded with heavy casings and rowed ashore. The only outboard motor on the expedition had jumped its bracket and expired. "Death by drowning," Ivor said. The casings each weighed several hundred pounds and unloading them in the surf was potentially dangerous. They rigged poles Chinese coolie fashion and sweated them to dry land.

Next morning, no one showed. It was another day of rice and beans and no meat. "No coffee. No sugar. No work." Not much could be done about coffee and sugar, but the men took the day off to fish, and the police sharpshooter was dispatched to hunt.

"They have nothing to complain about," Hervey said. "They've been promised a raise in pay and have agreed to a regular eight-hour day. Everything is working smoothly."

It was raining heavily next morning when Hervey showed up with the work crew. This was unprecedented, an affirmation of his resolution. He wore yachtsman's oil skins that reached half way to his ankles, the jacket hung like a sack. His hands dangled like shovels below the short sleeves. With a three-day growth of beard, unkempt hair, thick horn rims to his glasses he looked like a mock pirate captain in a Gilbert and Sullivan comedy opera. But he had mobilized the men into action.

The crux of the offloading was the large extractor pump. It was the biggest and heaviest piece of equipment, firmly placed center-ship in the hold. One of the barges that had been custom cut to accommodate it had been brought along side. It was a precarious operation. Barney and Peter were at logger heads, and could speak to each other only in angry shouts that confused the Costa Ricans. Barney, as boss rigger, shouted orders to haul on the lines, and Peter was worried about damage to his boat. By noon they had man hauled it on to deck, re-rigged the block and tackle, and then lowered it into the barge.

The load looked very top heavy and Barney warned Hervey that there was danger of tipping. "What about lashing two barges together?" Hervey asked. Then he seemed to have a better idea. "Only good swimmers should go in the pump barge." He climbed over rail and dropped into the other barge, and they rowed ashore.

There was a four-foot surf running and if they broached-to, I felt that was where it would capsize. But the crew kept it stern-to and they ran up on the sand. They had missed the high tide, and spent the rest of the afternoon trying to haul the loaded barge up the beach, but managed to move it only twenty feet. Finally they decided to wait for the high tide that evening at ten.

"Why the sudden burst of activity?" Olson asked.

"He's got to show some progress before the Langesund arrives," Peter said, "or before we pack up."

Heavy rollers, the nautical chart for the island indicated for Wafer Bay. The next two days we saw what motivated the cartographer. There was a clear sky, only light winds of the the south-west, no indication of a storm, when the sea began to heavy and the surge rolled in from the Pacific. The Culver lifted, tugging at her anchor, the bow dipping, water breaking over the foredeck. The anchor chain snapped but everything held. On shore the surge broke in a thunderous clap and exploded into foaming spray.

Peter let out more anchor chain posted a night watch. I was on from midnight to four. To stay awake I sang Presbyterian hymns for school chapel at St. Andrew's. "Lord hear us when we pray to thee/ For those in peril on the sea." And recited Tennyson, "Break, break, break, on the cold gray stones Oh sea/ I would that my heart could utter, the thoughts that rise in me."

Scanning the shoreline with binoculars in the morning, I saw the devastation. The steel crib was a torn apart, welded seams split, casings a gnarled heap of twisted metal. Two barges anchored off shore had slipped their moorings and I spotted the wreckage high on the rocks, frames broken, hulls punctured. Most of the cargo carrying capacity of the expedition had been demolished.

"We didn'g have a storm," I said over breakfast. "Where did that swell come from?"

"Hard to say. It could be an earthquake in the middle of the Pacific, or a typhoon in the China Sea," Peter said.

When the surge subsided enough for us to go ashore safely, Mario announced, "We return to Puntarenas."

Hervey objected. "That will be the end of the treasure hunt and we have only just begun. He'd have to negotiate a new contract with the Costa Rican government. But Mario insisted. He feared a rebellion of the workers as food supplies dwindled and there was no sign of the Langesund with relief supplies. It was almost two weeks since it had sailed.

"They've made a deal," Olsen said. "Ivor Brown and Captain Edwards will stay behind on the island with a crew of five workers, the cook and two police, all volunteers," he said. "And all the rifles. They belong to the government, a guarantee that they will get permission to come back. When we return to Puntarenas, Mario is going to recruit a new work crew from his village. When they return he'll be in charge of both the workers and the police."

The next two days saw a flurry of activity. I finished my cleaning job in the engine room and lazarette. Alex re-rigged the ship, dropping the boom and lowering the gaff, bending on the sails. Peter and Eric greased the engine, changed the oil and fuel filters, adjusted the fuel injectors. Barney, mumbling to himself, secured the casings that were left in the hold for ballast, and arranged living space below decks. A work crew from shore ferried water barrels back and forth all day, filling the ship's tanks.

Hervey was impatient "to get on with it. But it's been a revelation to me. I never knew so much needed to be done." But we were still hooked on snags before the anchor could be raised.

The Culver had laid on ship's store for their Pacific crossing at the American commissary, when they passed through the Panama Canal. These had been jealously hoarded. Hervey wanted to purchase some to supplement the rations of the abandoned island party. Alex resisted. "I don't trust Hervey to reimburse us," he said, "and we can't replace many of the items in Puntarenas." Coffee and sugar were no problem, both were abundant in Costa Rica. But he was niggardly when it came to offering biscuit mix, canned Danish butter, and cheese, chocolate and fruit cake. "They'll eat better after we leave than they did before we came," he grumbled as he handed them over. I could see the envy in the worker's eyes. If anything will cause a mutiny, this will, I thought.

The boarding party arrived next morning at eight with unprecedented promptness, bringing three piglets. "Ship's mascots," Olson said. They sheltered in the focsle where there were four coveted bunks, and the rest dropped into the cavernous hold, now transformed from cargo to steerage. Barney supervised a crew to clean it up and settled in with them.

Alberto, the radio operator came on board last with Hervey.

"I need a radio time check so I can adjust my chronometer," Peter told him.

"No possible," Al said. "Batteria dead."

Peter's jaw muscles tightened and he glowed a sunburn red. "Well, I'm not sailing without a time check," he said.

Why the urgency? I wondered. We had sailed from Jamaica and Panama without radio time checks. The Culver didn't have a radio. But Peter was insistent, adamant.

Alberto had a choice. "Either you take the batteries ashore and charge them up, which you should have done before you came on board," and delay departure, which was left unsaid. "Or you bring the generator out and we can sail."

Over Brown's vigorous objection the generator was relinquished. Mid-afternoon we departed. Four men grinding at the windlass made easy work of weighing anchor and raising the sails. The diesel engine responded to Olson's magic touch and we motored out of Wafer Bay. The wind was a steady twenty knots out of the south-west, off the starboard quarter. "We should make good time of it with the wind blowing up our ass," Barney added his optimistic note.

We rounded the north point of the Cocos Island and beyond the bird bespattered cliffs of Madeline Island the ocean stretch a glistening blue to the horizon. After the confines of the island for nearly one month, I delighted in feeling the freedom of the seas once again. I felt a great sense of relief to get our from all the bickering. If financially possible I planned to sign off the ship and leave the expedition.

"Joe, get me the binoculars," Barney said, "I think I see a sail." I saw nothing, but this irascible Dane who had spent his life scanning horizons in search of fish, had spotted another catch.

Just before sunset we came along side the Langesund. Mrs. Sorenson, vibrant in yelllow shorts and tight fitting T-shirt, stood on deck and greeted us. "We need a tow to Cocos," she said. "Our engine broke down off Cape Blanco. We've been in sight of the island for four days but can't any headway with the wind in our teeth."

Turn back to Cocos? Peter would have none of it. "I don't have enough fuel."

Barney was even more determined. "You're not sending me back to that place." He sounded like a convict just released from Alcatraz.

Mrs. Sorenson was not to be deterred. "We've got plenty of fuel." A fifty barrel drum was dropped in the sea, but the lashing slipping of leaving it to float off into the blue Pacific. "Some one get it," she screamed. Brown would have been the logical candidate, but he was back on the island. None of the Costa Ricans seemed willing. They were farmers. Eyes turned to me, the junior member of the crew. I was no great swimmer, but knew how to stay afloat. I tied the end of the line about my waist and dove in. At first I was dismayed to see the Culver drift off, but they circled back picked up the line I had secured the barrel. Barney had rigged a block and tackle and hoist it on deck. It was a minor act of bravado which I rather enjoyed, but was disappointed when Peter passed it off a routine act in the line of duty, expected of any able seaman.

Food was sent across in the dinghy, a stock of bananas, large sack of oranges, limes, that reminded me of Captain Cook's feeding his crews limes to prevent scurvy. This was the first fresh fruit we'd had in a month, except for coconuts. Some of the men had sores on their legs, but these I figured were from unattended cuts. So far no one had lost any teeth. More important for moral, coffee, sugar and cigarettes were in the relief rations. The Langesund drifted away in the darkness.

On board the Culver it could have been a scene from Hamlet. To return to Cocos or not to return. Aye there's the rub. We gathered on the afterdeck. Peter was soft spoken, reasoned, resolved. "We're not towing the Langesund into Cocos."

Barney was equally resolved but less reasoned. He stomped and roared, bellowed at both Hervey and Peter. He had appointed himself spokesman for the down trodden. Those that he had once dismissed as "Indians and Niggers," were now his "Amigos." "We've had nothing to eat all day. Only cold rice and beans cooked on shore this morning. There's no place to cook on board. You've taken away the primus stoves." One stove had in fact been ruined by the men trying to light it, and Peter had removed the other. "Speaking for the men," Barney warned, "there would be trouble if you return to Cocos. You'd better get more stores off the Langesund tomorrow and turn right around for Puntarenas."

"As for you Peter, I'm going to cook your goose when we get back. You're going to end up in jail before I'm done with you." Though outspoken it had the desired effect. Peter brought out extra primus stoves and there was hot coffee for breakfast.

Hervey was very quiet. He remained non-commital. I became aware of how Mrs. Sorenson's demands pressed on him more heavily that any of us had expected. She was bankrolling the enterprise. What can he do if Peter remained uncooperative? And how does he quell Barney's "conspiracy to riot?"

He conferred with Mario, captain of police, then announced, "We'll return to Cocos, unload the casings and the rest of the gear, and carry on the search with the willing helpers and the crew of the Langesund. The malcontents will be shipped back to Puntarenas on the Culver." Mario slept that night with a pistol under his pillow.

At two a.m. we changed tack, started the engine and motored back toward the island. Peter set off flares to attract the Langesund but had no reply.

We lost sight of the Langesund under the cover of darkness. Spotted on the horizon far off to the north east in the morning, she had made little progress to windward since yesterday. We came alongside around noon. "Where have you been?" Mrs. Sorenson demanded. She felt we had come back to give her a tow. Hervey, Mario,

Eric Olson, the Danish fisherman who was a marine engineer, and a policeman, rowed across. They returned an hour later with more fresh rations. "Giving the children their pacifier," Barney said. Eric reported that the Langesund's drive chain had broken. The engine could not be repaired at sea and would have to be worked on in a machine shop.

Hervey was still in a quandry. Mrs. Sorenson was still expecting a tow. He turned to Eric in confidence. "What would it take to get Peter to agree to town the Langesund?"

"If I owned the Culver," Eric reportedly said, "I'd tow, if there was a written guarantee to pay for all damages, accompanied by a check for ten thousand dollars."

Hervey blanched. "That won't be possible," he said. He conferred again with Mario. Both were now obviously worried. Barney continued his rant. All the workers and now the police were set on returning to Puntarenas directly. I noticed that Mario walked about with a holstered pistol.

Late afternoon I rowed Hervey and two Costa Rican laborers back to the Langesund. "Don't be surprised by what you hear," Hervey told me. "My purpose is to go back. I'll do almost anything to achieve that end."

They conferred below, so I didn't hear anything, while I chatted with the skipper, Captain Anderson. He was a tall, well built man, good natured. He seemed pleased to have someone to talk to, but remained discrete in what he said. He was apparently capable, having sailed from Capo Blanco, using his wrist watch for a chronometer, he had found the island. He'd been on Cocos Island fifteen years previously when he was skipper on a tuna fishing boat to fill his water tanks. He knew old Captain Sorenson having met him years ago in the Grand Bahamas.

Orders finally came. "We're going back," Mrs. Sorenson said in a sour voice. I expected her to add, "Damn you."   She doled out additional rations for the Culver's return journey, niggardly portions, I felt. Another barrel of diesel oil was transferred. "You must tow us in from Cape Blanco," she repeated. When I said that this was not possible. "Charity begins at home, you know," she said. "Well, if you won't, have the San Marcos come out and pick us up."

At sunset, Hervey picked up his gear and moved aboard the Langesund. They hoisted sail, and headed down wind to the north-east. It was a week before we saw them again.

On the return passage we jockeyed with a following wind that blew off the stern. It was a delicate balancing act. A slight shift of course, or of the wind direction, and the sails would back wind and the boom would come crashing over in an uncontrolled jib. At times the wind dropped and we just drifted, "as silent as a painted ship, upon a painted ocean." I quoted Coleridge and all the poetry I could remember to keep awake on watch at night. Fortunately the current carried us in the direction we needed to go, north-east back to the mainland. When we thought the wind had picked we rigged the Genoa jib, a massive sail that ran from the fore stay most of the length of the boat. But it would not fill. So we tacked down wind catching the wind off the quarter and made a steady three or four knots.

As a parting gift, Hervey had given me two bottles of rum. "One for Mario and the Costa Rican crew. One for Peter and the Culver's crew."

Peter had been dour since leaving the island, annoyed by the indecision about going back to Puntarenas, or not. "We'd better splice the main brace," he said as soon as the sails had been raised. After his second "short snort" he talked with Eric and expounded on his prospects in the copra trade in the South Pacific. When Eric turned in, he cornered me. By this time his good mood had begun to wear off. "The trouble with you Joe is that you think you know more than you know." There was probably a degree of truth in that. "You always have a wise ass comment to make. Until you're twenty-five you need to have more respect for what older people have to say. You just have to shut up and listen, even if you think they're wrong." I acknowledged that this was not one of my strong points, and drifted off to bed.

An hour later I woke to shouting, thumping on the deck. I jumped into my pants and went above to see Peter down on his back by the engine room sky light, Alex sitting on Peter's chest. Peter was flailing about, cursing, demanding a flare. "Give me the goddam flare, you...." he insisted. I began to humor him, and distracted him by suggesting we dictate a letter to Hervey. This quieted him down and I dragged him to his bed, where he collapsed.

I stood watch from mid-night to four, but early at first light to see Peter probing under Eric's pillow who shared the cabin with me, and pulled out the bottle of rum. Euphoria was followed by brooding morose gloom. By mid-afternoon he had emptied the bottle and Alex and I dragged him to his bunk, muttering, "Never again." He collapsed into a troubled sleep.

In the light following winds the Langesund made better time that the Culver, and it was already in Puntarenas when we arrived. It was a bright, sunny day in late June. Within minutes the dock was lined with cheering women, wives of the workers who had heard of the return of their husbands, mingled with the girls from the brothels soliciting business. In less than a quarter hour, the men had scrambled overboard and headed ashore.

Stage One of the Cocos Island Treasure Expedition of 1950 had put its anchor down.

Stage Two, Hervey was already planning. "You mean scheming," Peter said. He terminated the charter with the Culver and had contracted with a dapper American, Capster, the owner of the San Marco, an idle California tuna boat. Bar talk was rife with rumors. "Who did he sleep with to get the contract? Mrs. Sorenson? Or Mrs. Hervey?"

"Or both?" Barney, our Danish know-it-all, said.

The future of the expedition hung in a balance. Would the Costa Rican government renew the permit. To facilitate that transaction, Hervey and Mario, the well connected captain of police, went up the San Jose, the capital, and Mario was apparently in favor with the party in power, and negotiations went smoothly, according to Capster, who now became my inside source, "Without too much money under the table, though Mario received a generous commission for his efforts."

Money, whether under the table or on the table, continued to be a major impediment. Hervey delayed paying Peter the thousand dollars still owed for the charter of the Culver. This brought on another high volatile confrontation. Peter was worried that he would not be paid since he no longer had the expedition cargo on board that he could place a lien upon. But after several days of haggling and a three day drunk, Hervey came up with a check that cleared with the bank.

Mrs Sorenson had also become disenchanted with Hervey. Back on the bottle she commiserated with anyone she could corner. "I've poured over thirteen thousand dollars in this wild scheme of that phony heir to the Marquis of Bristol," she told me. "And now I have to put up with that intolerable middle class English wife of his."

According to Capster, "Hervey tried to hock his wife's jewelry, but the San Juan jeweler turned him down, claiming they were cheap gems set in iron. Though it is claimed he is worth thirty million pounds. It's merely a cash flow problem." The fate of the expedition seemed to hang in a balance.

As did my own fate. I was undecided as to what I should do. Or what I could do. "I have three options," I told Alex as I unburdened my concerns with him.

"Three choices," he corrected me. "You can have only two options."

"Do I stay with the Culver and cross the Pacific with you?" Alex would have liked that, but applied no pressure. Had he done so I might have made another choice. "Or do I stay with the Cocos Island expedition?" Hervey had extended the invitation. "But what I feel I ought to do is to go home. I've been away for almost a year now and should be getting back and finishing my university degree. But I'm broke and can't afford to do so." I had a bank account in Vancouver, but funds were frozen. There were foreign currency restrictions on American dollars, and I had already spent he annual allowance of two hundred and fifty dollars. "If I could get back to Jamaica, a British colony, it's a sterling area and I could draw funds."

Crossing the Pacific seemed the best option, but I had been sobered by Peter's erratic behavior, and questioned whether I wanted to spend a month with a drunken irascible captain. Besides, how would I get home from the South Pacific. It would mean another year out of university.

I juggled the options, there were only two, for a week, and opted for Hervey. I explained my predicament to him, and he offered to arrange for me to get to Jamaica upon our return from Cocos.

In later years as an old man, I was asked if I had any regrets in my life? And I replied, "I had the opportunity to cross the Pacific under sail, and didn't take it."

I signed off the Culver, and Peter gave me a formal certificate rating me as an able seaman, that is a personal treasure. I moved into the Imperial Hotel at Hervey's expense, and joined in the action of life ashore.

The two Danes, Barney and Eric, "square heads," Peter called them, had preceded me and spent the first week drunk, also on Hervey's tab, shunted from bar to brothel as their credit dried up.

The Fiesta of the Virgin of the Seas fell on July sixteen amidst general skepticism that you could find a virgin in Puntarenas. Overnight the streets were crowded, the Grand Hotel Imperial turned people away. People slept on the beach. The restaurants, bars and brothels thrived, dancing on through the night to dawn. Watered down rum flowed and drinks were cheap. The bar room girls wore their holiday best. Even the proper town young women were gay.

Police intervened to break up a vicious street-side brawl, and when one of the belligerents tried to run away, the policeman shot him. He managed to limp to the ambulance leaving a bloody trail of footprints in his path.

I had met a young school teacher, Senorita Sanchez, who would never dream of being seen in the El Patio, was induced to come in and dance with me. After all it was the Feast of the Virgin. The place was crowded, dozen women of all ages crowded around a short handsome man with a full head of graying hair, in his fifties. "That's President Ulate," Miss Sanchez told me. There did not appear to be any body guard, not great formality. He shook hands with the matrons, kissed the young women with a bachelor's delight. I was told he had two daughters by his mistress.

Was this an act of faith or an act of bravado? I wondered. Only the year before there had been a military coup that had denied him office, then a popular uprising in which two hundred people were killed, to reinstate him. Here he was only a year later, in shirt sleeves, open collar without a tie, hugging the pretty young women. Was he making a statement about the success of the democratic transition in Costa Rican society? Or was it the protective sanctuary of the Virgin. Next morning, he joined the parish priest sprinkling of holy water in the blessing of the fishing boats.

Through some surreptitious process of subterfuge not known to me, Hervey seemed to have come up with the funds to restock the San Marco with supplies for Cocos Island. Mario, the police captain returned from San Jose, the capital, with a smile on his face, a renewal of the treasure hunting permit, permission to sail, and a work crew and security contingent. "We sail tomorrow." Then tomorrow was the day after tomorrow, and then it became the day after than. I wasn't sure if the process of procrastination was Hervey expedition time, or just the pervasive "manana" syndrome of Latin America. I had little enthusiasm for returning to the island, but did want to shake off the lethargy induced by repeated delays.

The Don Aurelio, a 3000 ton coastal freighter, flying the Norweign flag, slipped into harbor and tied up at the town dock. I never gave it a second thought. Coffee is a major export of Costa Rica, and most of it is shipped through Puntarenas. The pier, normally empty, became the center of activity. A stubby shunting engine pushed small freight cars out on to jetty, and a chain gang of stevedors began to hump hundred and ten pounds sacks of coffee beans up a ramp and hold them in the hold. Mildly interested, I watched the operation from the lobby of the hotel, when I saw one Hervey's crew, George Gonzoles, who had been with us on Cocos Island, checking out. "I've signed on the ship," he said, "It's going to Vancouver."

"No, we've got a full crew," the First Officer, told me when I inquired whether they were hiring seamen.

"Go back and speak to the captain," Eric Olson, the Dane who had been on the Cocos expedition, told me. He'd just signed on as the assistant second engineer. Surely I could be second assistant to somebody on a ship this size. I went back and asked for the captain. Captain Fred Thukelson agreed to sign me on as a work-away. This was very different from when we tried to sign on a ship in Miami, or in Haiti. I was returning to my home port and the ship did not assume any liability for me should I sign off the ship. Besides, I learned later, Thukelso was not only the captain, but also a partial owner of the ship, giving him greater discretionary latitude in running his ship. Two days before, I was to sail for Cocos Island, now I was sailing home to Vancouver.

There was not much time for leave taking as the ship left that night. I hailed the Culver from the pier and went on board to bid farewell to Peter and Alex. They had been working on the diesel engine before departing for their Pacific crossing, and were covered in grease, not in a good mood. I sensed resentment in Peter that I was not accompanying them, and was myself ambivalent about missing such an opportunity. With Alex however, I felt a genuine loss and felt of was deserting him. I was losing a real friend. "Keep in touch," he said, and we did for a few years.

Hervey I saw for the last time over dinner at the hotel. Radiant in starched whites, handsome in an effeminate way, charming as always, he gave me his card. "Look me up when you come to England," he said.

"Do come and visit," pretty Mrs. Hervey said. That I would like if it were not for Hervey.

Who was this man anyway? For all his bonhomme, I knew him to be deceitful, a cheat, certainly a schemer. What was his game? Was it a legitimate hunt for a plausible treasure? From what I had seen, the incompetence, the mismanagement that seemed deliberate, I doubted it. More likely it was a scheme to make money, raise funds from wealthy friends perhaps looking for a tax dodge, mobilize an operation for as low cost as possible, dupe the investors and skim off a healthy profit. Probably. Or was the treasure hunt merely a facade?

Cauffie, the United States naval intelligence officer in Panama, had cautioned us that Hervey served prison time for illegal gun running. Was the Cocos Island a ruse, a front for something bigger. Clearly the merchandising of guns was a marketable trade in military junta dominated political Central America. Costa Rica had an armed uprising only the year before. Cauffie may have been concerned about armed unrest next door in Panama.

Three years later I would visit England on my renewed quest to visit Tintern Abbey. I did not visit the Hervey's in spite of her invitation. So I would never know the truth of the man.

Early evening Eric and I went back up the street to the Trocadero for a farewell libation. The beautiful Marian was there, her lovely two young daughters were now with her, installed in the brothel. Negrita joined us, the ravishing mulatto girl from the Caribbean side of Costa Rica. Both women wore tight fitting, body clinging dresses, with short skirts and plunging necklines, dresses designed to display the feminine body rather than clad it. I was young, an innocent most of the time, and I wondered if I would ever be in the company of two such alluring women again. Sixty years later, the image is vivid still, and I don't think I have. They knew we were leaving, and kissed us when we got up to go, with tears in their eyes.

We sailed at midnight. From the afterdeck I watched the lights of Puntarenas recede. I had the sense of turning the page on another chapter in my life, perhaps even closing a book.

Chapter 38: Don Aurelio

The Don Aurelio, a coastal freighter, flying the Norwegian flag, had slipped into harbor during the night. I noticed it tied up at the port pier, but never gave it a second thought. Coffee is the major export of Costa Rica, most of it shipped through Puntarenas. The pier, normally empty, became a bustle of activity. A stubby shunting engine pushed small freight cars out on to jetty, and a chain gang of stevedores humped hundred and ten pounds sacks of coffee beans up a ramp and dropped them into the hold. It looked like an interesting operation so I went out for a closer look. I met a friend, George Gonzoles, who had been with us on Cocos Island, with us coming off the boat. "I've signed on the ship," he said, "It's going to Vancouver."

"Vancouver? Impossible ," I said. "I'm from Vancouver."

"Go and speak to the man," George said.

"No, we've got a full crew," the First Officer, told me when I inquired.

Later I met Eric Olson, the Dane who had been on the *Culver* crew on Cocos Island, and told him of my disappointment. He'd just signed on as the assistant second engineer. "Go back and speak to the captain," he told me. I went back and asked for the captain. Surely they could use another second assistant to somebody on a ship this size. Captain Fred Thukelson agreed to sign me on as a work-away.

There was not much time for leave taking as the ship left that night. I hailed the *Culver* at anchor off the pier and went on board to bid farewell to Peter and Alex. They were doing last minute repairs and tune-up of the ailing diesel engine before departing for their Pacific crossing. Covered in grease, Peter was not in a good mood. I sensed that he resented my deserting them, and I myself was ambivalent, realizing I was missing a once-in-a-lifetime opportunity. With Alex I felt a genuine loss. I was deserting a friend. "Keep in touch," he said, and we did for several years.

Hervey I saw for the last time over dinner at the hotel. Radiant in starched whites, handsome in an effeminate way, charming as always, he gave me his card. "Look me up when you come to England," he said.

"Do come and visit," pretty Mrs. Hervey said. That I would like, I thought, if it were not for Hervey.

Who was this man anyway? For all his bonhomme, I knew him to be deceitful, a cheat, certainly a schemer. What was his game? Was it a legitimate hunt for a plausible treasure? From what I had seen I doubted it. The incompetence, the mismanagement had seemed deliberate, a stall. Was it a scheme to make money, by raising funds from gullible wealthy friends looking for a tax dodge, like Mrs. Sorenson, then mobilize an operation for as low cost as possible, duping the investors and skim off a healthy profit. Or was the whole treasure hunting business merely a charade?

I remembered Cauffie, the United States naval intelligence officer in Panama, cautioning us that Hervey had served prison time for illegal gun running. Was the Cocos Island a ruse, a front for a bigger deal? Clearly the merchandising of guns was a marketable trade in military junta dominated political Central America. Only the year before there had been an armed uprising in Costa Rica. Cauffie may have been concerned about armed unrest next door in Panama.

Three years later I would renew my quest to visit Tintern Abbey and visit England. But I did not visit the Hervey's in spite of her invitation. So I would never know.

Early that evening Eric and I went back up the street to the Trocadero for a farewell libation. The beautiful Marian was there, her lovely two young daughters now installed with her in the brothel. Negrita joined us, the ravishing mulatto girl who came from the Caribbean side of Costa Rica. Both women wore tight fitting, body clinging dresses with short skirts and plunging necklines, dresses designed to display the feminine body rather than clad it. I was young, an innocent most of the time, and I wondered if I would ever be in the company of two such alluring women again. Sixty years later, the image is vivid still, and I don't believe I have. They knew we were leaving and kissed us both when we got up to go, with tears in their eyes.

We sailed at midnight. From the afterdeck I watched the lights of Puntarenas recede. I had the sense of closing a book on one volume of my life.

The *Don Aurelio*, 3000 tons, did the "milk run," in sailor's jargon, on the west coast of North America from Panama to Canada. With a ship's complement of twenty-five or so, there were Panamanians, Ecuadorians, Costa Ricans, a couple Swedes and a Dane on the deck and engineer room crews. Being the only Canadian, I was something of a curiosity and wondered how I would fit in.

But I lucked out again. The purser on a ship is the accountant, book-keeper, the payroll officer of the vessel. Eric knew him. Years before they had been shipmates on a ship out of Hong Kong. Eric told the purser about the young fellow who had hired on as a work-away, a university student, bright guy, Canadian. Next morning I was hailed to the captain's cabin, and promoted assistant purser. I ended up sharing an officer's cabin with him, eating at the officer's mess, instead of chipping paint or cleaning the bilges.

Life on the Don Aurelio is roast beef with gravy, I wrote in my journal. A steward made my bed every morning. The food was better than anything I had in months, since being in the Bahamas six months before. We were served in regal fashion by the mess boy. My companions were a diverse and interesting lot, the captain and two mates, Norweigns; the third mate, Uruguyan; the chief engineer, Dutch; second, a Finn; third, Filipino; fourth, Australian. The ship soon became the center of my universe.

We took on cargo at Corinto in Nicaragua, La Union in El Salvador, Mazatlan in Mexico, was mostly coffee, but also sisal and sesame seed. I went ashore but the towns were dispiriting, hot, dusty, with cobble stone streets, the harbor side bars and brothels run down, poor, even by Puntarenas standards, the bar girls given to weight, swarthy and poorly clad. Mariachi bands serenaded us in the restaurants, but when they danced, it was to a juke box, "Like in America," the bar tender assured us.

When the men came back on board after shore leave, their talk centered on their accomplishments of male virility, and the possible infections acquired in the act, as they lined up to see the ship's medical attendant.

My daily routine was a relaxed one. After taking on cargo, I was busy the next day sorting papers, bills of lading, pecking at a typewriter copying the ship's manifest, running copies on the mimeograph machine. Most days there was rarely more than a couple hours work. The purser retreated to the bar in the officer's mess while I was left to take any messages in his absence.

I felt I had to put up the semblance of work, so I sat at my desk and read. The ship had a modest ship's library a couple hundred books, a good collection of Agatha Christie murder mysteries, and Sherlock Holmes. I also found Joseph Conrad, *Lord Jim*, and was caught up in life at sea in a harsher age. I stood in judgment of Jim, a coward when faced with danger, but wondered how would I have reacted in his situation, abandoning a sinking ship with Moslem pilgrims, only to have the ship towed safely to port by another ship. How would the cast of characters on the Cocos Island treasure hunting expedition reacted?

I found Graham Greene, *The Power and the Glory,* the renegade priest in revolutionary Mexico gave me a more subtle insight into the tension in traditional institutions in the face of social change. Workers of the world arise. Down with the hierarchy. I saw it played out on Cocos Island. Is this what emboldened the laborers to threaten a strike? And Mario, the police officer, to go to bed with his pistol under his pillow.

I was awash in words again and reveled in the world of books. How I delighted in living vicariously again. The last book I had read was Jack London's short stories of men freezing to death in the Arctic, while I sweated in our water front hotel in Port au Prince, Haiti, five months before. I felt I was recovering from a reading deficit syndrome.

But Somerset Maugham, *Of Human Bondage,* touched raw nerve. Philip, the central character, orphaned as a child, sent to boarding school as a boy, dissatisfied with our studies, unsettled about a course of study, undecided on a choice of career, confused about sex, he could have been writing about me.

Do I settle for a respectable, dull profession that holds little interest for me, as Philip did, torn by the urgency of lust and the yearning for love, marry a woman I don't really know to find physical relief and domestic comfort? I return to Vancouver and after ten months the questions are still there. I'm still at sea.

"Have you found yourself?" Ross Johnson, a Delta Upsilon fraternity brother asked. Knowing Ross, I'm not sure whether he is serious or asking in jest.

"I didn't know I was lost," I answered.

Most of my friends asked, "How did it go?"

What could I say? I was stumped. I had neither the vocabulary, the conceptual grasp of the experience, nor the story telling ability. Anyway, how do you describe a treasure hunting expedition in five hundred words or less? Was he interested in the outer journey, moon lit nights on the Caribbean, pretty girls in the brothels? Or the inner journey?

But I found it didn't matter. Most people had an attention span of about two minutes. I had all these fabulous stories. Some of the ribald like the men returning on board the *Don Aurelio* at San Francisco, bragging about getting their shoes shined by a topless shoe shine girl, or their hair cut by a topless barber. But others were deeply felt, passionate, on the passage from Jamaica to Panama on a moonlit night, running down wind in the north-east trade winds in twelve-foot following seas. It was straight out of Masefield. *I must go down to the sea again, to the lonely sea and the sky,/ And all I ask is a tall ship and a star to steer her by,/ And the wheel's kick and the wind's song and the white sail's shaking,/ And a gray mist on the sea's face and a gray dawn breaking.*

I learned to reply in what later would be called sound bites.

With my inner journey, I was more tentative and sparing. Most of discussion was an inner dialogue, walking alone to the sound of the sea along the long sandy beaches of Kitsolano. I had learned little new, mostly what I learned was a reaffirmation, a renewed affirmation of my better self, or what I thought to be my better self. Some of my elders, like Mr. Ketchum my former headmaster, was not so sure. He had greater expectations of me.

Finally, I was reminded by Rod Nixon that I had set out to visit Tintern Abbey and had not made it, so in a sense the journey was not over. Is a journey ever over? There is still so much of life to be experienced. One's journey is never over, until it's over. I knew I would travel again.

Chapter 39: Rod's Epilogue

When does a journey end? When is it over? Is it ever over? In the first of our adventure stories, Odysseus, just home from ten years of wandering, even before he embraces Penelope, is planning his next expedition.

Three years after returning to Vancouver, after three years of study for my LLB, Bachelor of Law degree, I was traveling again. My plan was to spend one year. Five years later I returned, having visited museums and concert halls throughout Europe, climbed mountains in the Alps and Himalayas, and visited Tintern Abbey. I had taught school to finance my travels and was committed to the lifestyle of long vacations. I had found a wife who would share my travels.

The rest of my life would be entwined with climbing mountains, rafting canyon rivers, and sailing on the high seas.

Cocos Island remained a living memory. Ivor Brown wrote me that V. Cochrane Hervey did return to pick up the marooned crew, went through the motions ofsearching for another three weeks, found nothing. He returned to Puntarenas and fled Costa Rica leaving behind an accumulation of debt. *Lay not up for yourselves treasures on earth, where moth and moth doth corrupt, and where thieves break through and steal.* Matthew 6:19-20 had it right. My life investment would be in experience.

The *Culver* did cross the Pacific, in 105 days from Puntarenas to Guam, with stops at the Gallipagos to fish, Alex Bolton wrote me. They had hoped to trade in copra through the South Pacific Islands, but found the market dominated by the native cooperative, established by the American government. They sold the ship to the cooperative. Peter returned to the merchant navy and was the captain of an island freighter. Alex married and came ashore in Hawaii, where he worked in the port captain's office.

Rod Nixon returned to the University of British Columbia and became a doctor, the ideal career for someone with his charm and intelligence. He never did get to visit Tintern Abby, but he never lost his spirit of adventure. As a doctor he learned to fly an airplane, and in his Cesna 180, mounted with pontoons in summer and skis in winter, he was able to make house calls on his rural patients in northern central British Columbia. Always competitive, as he had been insisting on cycling every mile to L.A., because that was what he had set out to do, he began to make solo flights, establishing time and distance flying records. Vancouver to Nome, Alaska. Nome to Los Angles. On his attempt to establish a new solo flight record from Nome to Mexico City, in his reconfigured plane with extra fuel tanks, he plowed into an open field in northern, cause unknown.

Rod was the one who had inspired this journey, My First Sabbatical. To him I dedicate this section of my memoir.

I came like water and into wind I go.

Part Three – Gathering Moss

Chapter 40: Gathering Moss

Two paths diverged in the woods, And I,
I chose the one least travelled by...

~ *Robert Frost*

My life has been a series of dramatic discontinuities. The spring of 1953 was one of those. I was at another cross roads where I could have gone either way. I was about to graduate from law school at the University of British Columbia and I felt the weight of a portcullis clanging down, locking me into a commitment to a career and did not feel ready. I was in no hurry to replace the library in the law school for one in a law office. There was still so much to do and to see and so little time.

I've always had a sense of my own mortality, that the clock was ticking, prompted no doubt by the early death of both of my parents. "Tomorrow and tomorrow and tomorrow, creeps on this petty pace to the last syllable of recorded time," I recalled from gloomy Macbeth. These morbid thoughts were aggravated by the death of a close friend in an ROTC training accident the year before.

So it was with a sense of urgency that I decided to spend a year of travel in Britain and Europe. I was enough of a dreamer to be inspired by the Romantic poets, Wordsworth's musings at Tintern Abbey, the heroics of British military history, Nelson at Trafalgar, Wellington at Waterloo. I grew up in an age of heros, like Churchill. "We shall fight them on the beaches. We shall fight them in the country lanes. We shall never surrender." I would later see the man sitting in the visitor's gallery

I had planned such a journey, journey as pilgrimage, three years before, after my first year of university. But I had been side tracked to bicycling and hitch hiking through the west and south of the United States, and sailing in the Caribbean and off Central America on a cargo carrying 95 foot ketch, in search of pirate treasure.

My plan this time was to work where I could, a work-travel program like the popular travel-study programs, like a "junior year abroad." Or a sabbatical from law studies.

The first leg of my journey was delivering a car from Vancouver to Montreal, at the owner's expense. Then I decided to stay over in Montreal for the summer. I'd never been to Montreal, which at that time was Canada's only "open" city, Canada's New Orleans. You could purchase an alcoholic drink with a restaurant meal. Strip tease bars advertised in neon. Ladies of the night solicited openly on the streets corners. By implication French Catholics went to confession on Saturday. Anglo-Protestants burned in hell, or went back to Toronto.

I found cheap accommodation in a fraternity house off the McGill campus, and studied the "Help Wanted" columns of the Montreal Gazette, the English language paper. What match-up I would I find between the needs of the market place and my wealth of experience and lack of skills?

The Hudson's Bay Company, a large department store, advertised job openings in anticipation of summer sales. I picked up an application form and listed the variety of jobs I'd had during school vacations: a bellhop at Windermere Lodge a fashionable lake resort hotel north of Toronto; a lineman on a survey crew on Highway 17, in far north in Ontario; yardman stacking lumber in a lumber yard at Banff in the Canadian Rockies. I'd washed dishes in a restaurant, much as my father had thirty years earlier as a recent immigrant to Canada. One holiday season I'd humped crates of frozen turkeys in a cold storage locker until laid low by bronchitis and a series of late Christmas parties. As a sleeping car conductor on the Canadian Pacific Railroad the previous summer, I travelled from Vancouver through the Canadian Rockies to Calgary and back once a week.

But my best chance at landing a job, I felt, would be my experience as a salesman. I'd sold ice cream from a motorized scooter with a freezer box, the "Dickie Dee Ice Cream Man," on the wettest summer on record.

The following year, the driest in a decade, I sold agricultural chemicals, weed killers and insecticides. "Looks like you've got a real bad case of peach leaf crawler," I commiserated with one prospect.

"Oh?" he replied, somewhat surprised. "It is an apple tree, you know."

What I had neglected to add to my application was that from the age when I could make accurate change, I had been a store clerk. My father had been the proprietor of a general store and a farm machinery agency in a prairie village in Saskatchewan during the depression. I did no see myself as the son of a shopkeeper. But more important I wanted to avoid any inquiry about my father, or my mother, if the truth be known.

More important, I neglected to add that I had graduated recently from law school. Nor did I mention the elite independent school I had been sent to after my father's death. My application was "the truth," as Huckleberry Finn says of his autobiography, "well mainly the truth, with a few stretchers." What I had left out were the dates so that my application looked like a record of full employment. I felt I had portrayed a young man of great experience, wide interests, and a solid work ethic. The HBC hired me and assigned me to the men's shoe department.

I'd never sold shoes before. In village Saskatchewan people didn't buy their shoes at the general store. They ordered them from the Sears mail order catalogue. I enjoyed the work, the give and take of salesmanship, the direct contact with people.

But selling a shoe is something more, more intimate. The purchase of a shoe is a complex decision making process of matching style with fit, requiring trying on, taking off, trial and error, experimentation. The transaction takes long enough for a connectedness to develop between customer and salesman, a certain bonding as in a helping relationship, commiserating with the multiple problems besetting a foot, tenderness, blisters, cramped toes, corns, bunions, bone spurs. There is also a tactile relationship that is faintly homoerotic, placing a stockinged foot on the steel plate measuring device that marks off length, width, size.

To say nothing of the olfactory phenomenon. I am reminded of proxemics, the study of the social distance between people of different cultures. Some like Italians, for example, like to touch and feel, even to hug. Others like Swedes stand back, keep their distance, remain aloof. Arabs, I am told, when speaking to a person, like to be close enough to smell them. There is something of an Arab in every good shoe salesman.

Montreal was and is traditionally French, with an English minority. After World War II there was an influx of European refugees so our customers had a challenging diversity. But I enjoyed touting the merits of a shoe in my school boy French and using gesticulation when that failed. And if I had a problem, there was always Francois, my floor supervisor, I could turn to. All things considered, I did well as a shoe salesman.

So well in fact, that Francois took me aside one day. A stout little man, thoroughly Gallic in temperament, gracious, matter of fact, nothing slick or pushy about him, as one might expect of a career shoe salesman. He had been selling shoes for ten years or more, all through the war, and before that, during the depression he was happy to have landed a job in the stock room. "Joseph," he spoke to me confidentially, with a French pronunciation, a soft "J" with the accent on the second syllable, "Jo—seff", you sell shoes very good," he said, and paused to let the compliment sink in. "But when a customer asks for a pair of Bata or Clarks shoes (the up-market lines that sold for over twenty dollars), you should send him to me." He said it quietly, with dignity, no sense of threat or condescension.

"Mais pourquoi?" But why? I always tried to speak to him in French. I knew he regarded it as a courtesy regardless of how I butchered his language.

"You see, for all the shoes I sell, I get a commission, and," he paused for dramatic effect, "I have family." It was my first experience in corporate politics and labor solidarity. Twenty dollar shoes were his turf, I willingly conceded and honored the protocol. It actually appealed to the socialist altruism of my quasi-radical youth. "From each according to his work, to each according to his need." After that I never sold a single shoe if I saw Francois standing idle without a customer. I signaled to him. That's why communism failed, I suppose. No competition, no incentive to excel, though this was before the Soviet Union imploded. Besides in Francophone Quebec in the fifties, it was only the Anglo-Scots, the colonial masters, who could afford a $20 shoe. I was only robbing the rich. A modern day Robin Hood, I referred high profile customers to Francois, "our expert."

Francois, on his part, did me a good turn, or what he considered a good turn. As my floor supervisor, he gave me an excellent job report. A couple weeks later I was directed to see the manager, Mr. Smith. Had he checked my job references and discovered that I was a fraud?" I wondered. "Was this my termination summons?" Lester Smith was an Anglo-Scot, as were most personnel at the management level in Quebec at the time, Anglophones French Canadian separatists resented. A confident, pleasant man in his early forties, he projected success in his blue pin striped suit. As a salesmen I wore grey flannel slacks and my blue blazer, just like I had at school.

"Joseph," he said, "I hear good things of you. We (he switched to the royal 'we') are impressed with your deportment, (whatever that was), your conscientiousness, your good work habits." My father had drilled these into me as a boy in Saskatchewan. And Mr. Smith rambled on. Then he dropped the bomb. "We are considering you for management training." I was taken off the floor, and put on the escalator of career success. During the next month I shuffled between the stock room and the purchasing department, was introduced to the intricacies of billing and inventory control, was given "the big picture" of the mass marketing shoes. And I received a pay increase of ten dollars a week.

Three weeks later I submitted my resignation.

Again I was summoned the manager's office. This time I knew why. Lester Smith's demeanor was grave and paternal, the strict father sitting down the wayward son for a serious talk, though he kept me standing. He said that while they were impressed with my work during the last three months, he was chagrined when he reviewed my job history and saw how unfocused my life had been. He cautioned me that I was about to lose a great career opportunity. "Why are you leaving?" he fairly shouted.

"I appreciate this opportunity," I said unconvincingly, "but I don't feel I'm ready to settle down." Though true, I knew how inane that must sound. "I really want to travel." I paused. "Some more," I added. Then realized I should shut up before I made an absolute fool of myself. I was too embarrassed to tell him that this had been my plan from the start. And I felt badly that I had so upset the man.

"Nold, (now on a surname basis) some day you will live to regret this," he said with a Doomsday resonance. "You know," he pronounced with the wisdom of Solomon, "a rolling stone gathers no moss." And so I was terminated.

I walked out of the office with a sense of weightlessness, unburdened by moss. The next week I hitchhiked to Nova Scotia to connect with family roots, then took a bus to New York, and a month later I was on a passenger liner bound for England, now in search of historical roots.

Little did I suspect that my one year sabbatical from law would turn into a five-year Odyssey. It would take me from London to Vienna and Rome, Istanbul and New Delhi; to mountains tops in Scotland and the Alps and on to the Himalayas; from a career in law to a life style of a teacher. Truly a rolling stone.

But it was only in my seventies that I realized how wrong the manager had been. Only when I became my own Sherlock Holmes and sifted through a life time's collection of dog- eared note books, yellow-paged journals, family documents, old letters and photographs, and dredged the muddy waters of memory, that I realized that my life had been in fact a process of gathering moss. Like Ulysses in Tennyson's poem, another rolling stone, "I am a part of all that I have met...."

... And that made all the difference.

Leaving Vancouver in 1953 after law school graduation.

Chapter 41: London – 1954-1955

Through Gabbitas and Thring, a placement agency in London, I found a job at Shirley House School in Watford, a northern suburb at the end of the Bakerloo Line, teaching twelve-year olds. English and British History came easily enough, and to my surprise I enjoyed it. It was reminiscent of my own happy boyhood at St. Andrew's College, a prep school north of Toronto, and I fit in with the masculine camaraderie of boarding school life. I was the rustic colonial among my Empire-centric colleagues.

But more compelling was the cultural scene. It was an hour by train to London and four nights a week I sat in "the gods," the cheap seats at the back of a theatre or concert hall. That year I saw Richard Burton on stage as *Hamlet*, Lawrence Olivier in *Titus Andronicus*, T.S. Eliot read from *Four Quartets*, and Margot Fontaine dance, and heard Furtwangler conduct Beethoven's *Sixth Symphony* in the new London Festival Hall. On Friday afternoons I would rush down to the National Gallery for the free lecture series and was soon able to distinguish a Manet from a Monet.

But the experience that changed my life was a rock climbing course I took at Plasy Brenan in North Wales over Easter. Clinging to a rock buttress by my fingertips was an unexpected experience of high adrenaline, self-revelation and intimations of mortality. During my summer vacation I took a second course in Zermat in the Swiss Alps. Like Keats reading Chapman's Homer, it opened up a whole new world.

After such a year, how could I return to law? I decided to extend my sabbatical. It wasn't a sabbatical really. This was my education. I traveled east to Vienna, still under Soviet occupation in 1954, saw Mozart's *Magic Flute* at the Stats Oper, had a brush with the Yugoslavia KBG in Sarajevo, read *The Odyssey* in a small hotel in Aegina. Art as a visual language spoke to me in Florence. And I was in love with Jackie, a beautiful young Canadian woman. Ski touring in the Otztal, along the Austrian-Italian border, I was nearly carried away by an avalanche. Returning to Britain, my travel budget depleted, I asked myself how could I put off returning to law for yet another year?

Wales, 1953, Joe's introduction to mountain climbing.

Chapter 42: Hitch-hiking

In a less violent age, hitch-hiking was the preferred means of transport for the impecunious. Europe in the 1950's, still recovering from the war, was less affluent, more compassionate. The drivers enjoyed the company. The passengers, the economy. But affluence, drugs, terrorism has all but put an end to its popularity.

During the weeks before Christmas vacation I had survived the lowering gloom of the Scottish winter where the sun set at four in the afternoon and did not rise again until after breakfast at eight by fantasies of flying weightless through knee deep snow in the Otztal Alps. Austria was cheap, very cheap, with the schilling pegged at fifty to the dollar, the Canadian dollar that is, still at par with the American dollar. We were affluent on a pittance. The main expense was getting there. I convinced Jim Lawrence, a fellow Canadian working at a dead end job in London that he could not afford not to join me.

Would there be snow? Checked the snow report at the Austrian Reiseburo, not promising.

Travel for the masses has always been a European tradition. In the Middle Ages it was pilgrimages, such as Chaucer's journey to Canterbury, the French and Spanish to Santiago de Compostello, for greater reward in heaven to Rome. The ultimate benediction Jerusalem, the holy crusade. The modern pilgrims are sun worshipers to the beaches of the Mediterranean, skiers in search of the Holy Grail of snow in winter. We set off in search of snow. Thumbs up!

Like most folk morays there is an art to hitch-hiking. I considered myself a master, having crossed the United States twice. One Christmas a friend, Peter and I had hitched from Vancouver, British Columbia to Mexico City and back, something of a record. It's a matter of how you project yourself. Dress neatly but not too ostentacious, the well groomed mendicant, down and out, but only temporarily. Carry a backpack rather than hand luggage to give you that "Jugendreisse" look, Youth Travel, particularly popular in Germany. The Canadian red maple leaf conspicuously display on our rucksacks conveyed a certain benignity. Nobody hates Canadians.We even found Americans sewing the Canadian flag on their packs. A broad smile helps, even in the rain. If you saw the faintest note of hesitancy on the part of a driver, sometimes a slight bow from the waist, like the maitre d ushering you to your table would do the trick, particularly in France. A friendly wave completed our stage presence.

Strategically where you position yourself makes a big difference. You want to be at the edge of town or city, far enough out to disentangle yourself from the rush and clatter of urban traffic, but not so far out that the traffic has attained highway speed. Tactically it is important to find a place where a driver can conveniently pull over and stop to pick you up with incident. Two people hitch-hiking together can be intimidating, unless one is an attractive woman, like Jackie was when she travelled with me last year. There were alot of girls on the road in those days. There still are today in certain parts of Italy and Eastern Europe, but their purposes are different. Commercial. The monetary flow is reversed. They charge to be picked up. But two men travelling together are better to split up. But we had a strategy that usually worked for us. One stood up front and when offered a ride would tell the driver."Hi, that's my friend (pointing to the guy 400 yards down the road). Do you have room for him?" Providing there was indeed room, it invariably worked.

Standing out on A-10, the London-Dover Road, a country doctor gave us our first ride.

Next morning, Jim Lawrence, another Canadian friend, and I stood out on the A-5, with our thumbs out, hitch-hiking to Dover, the first leg to Austria. We by-passed Canterbury, and like Chaucer revelled in the new sights, new people, the instant intimacy among travelers. A Folkstone doctor gave us a ride and we chatted amiable about Botticelli and the Italian Renaissance masters. "In the room, the women come and go/ Talking of Michelangelo." He laughed, and made a detour to drop us off at the Dover ferry, arriving only minutes before it sailed.

The French social worker in the deux cheveau Citroën.....C'est marche bien

The Dutch have a reputation of being soft spoken, gentle, somewhat lethargic. But don't be fooled. There was a cartoon that was a take-off from Dr. Jeckyl and Mr. Hyde, where the benign Doctor Walker becomes the ferocious demonic Mr Wheeler, one he gets behind the driver's wheel. We met up with him at Ostend.

The next day through Belgium, a kamikazi Dutch driver, averted miles of backed up traffic by driving down the shoulder on the opposite side of the road, outside of the oncoming traffic, then ducking back into line between cars without so much as a glance back, oblivious to the blare of horns, and deposited us safely in Aachen, in Germany after dark.

The Germans invented the autobahn, the world's first thruway system and we sped through the country. Wartime experiences were still fresh in the memory of many and they were eager to tell us. A chubby Dutchman, who had to squeeze into his Volkswagen, told of being conscripted to work in a German aircraft factory, where he was assigned to the payroll office. He attempted sabotage, feeling it was his duty to resist, by falsifying the records, until he was forced to work overtime to correct them. He was reasonable comfortable for the rest of the war, able to use his pay office sinecure to extract extra rations from the kitchen help. His main worry was dodging allied bombs. In the same office, he met a Belgian prisoner and they married. Liberated by the Americans, he offered to work for them and his living memory of the Americans was how well they fed him. He now sold funeral insurance. He too went out of his way to put us on the right road.

"T was the night before Christmas," and the hitch-hiking had been poor. We got only to Koln (Cologne). The Jugendherberge, the Youth Hostel, was closed for the holiday. We tried a Catholic seminary, and the priest referred us to the Bahnhof Bunker, the WW II railway station air raid shelter, that now housed the wayward and the homeless. We entered the huge concrete tunnel to the din of a Christmas party. Six nuns in blue frocks, white kerchiefs, strong, leathery ruddy Germanic features, were giving out Christmas packages of candy, dried fruit and nuts. They sang carols, and the priest told a story of another more bitter winter on the Russian front, competing with the maniacal laughter of an old cynic, who had clearly celebrated on more than candy. A young couple huddled in the shadows were intent on their own pleasure, waiting for the lights to go out. It was a scene out of Hogarth, but we slept, albeit fitfully, grateful for having found room in the inn.

A dubious young German approached us on the streetcar next morning, attracted by the Canadian flag on Jim's pack. He was tall, Aryan, scraggly blond hair, wearing worn blue jeans, filthy shirt and a ragged jacket. It looked as if he had just been released from jail. He had a good opinion of Canadians, who told us in plausible English, because during the war he had been captured by them, imprisoned, and fed well. "Actually I put on weight," he told us, "And nobody stole my wrist watch."

A young construction worker picked us up on the autobahn. He was going to spend Christmas Day with his girl friend. They were recently engaged. "In the villages eighty percent of the marriages are shot gun weddings," he told us. "Not quite so high in the cities. Just since the war." I thought it impolite to ask if that was his predicament.

From Limburg to Frankfurt, we rode with a prosperous looking, well dressed businessman, in a large expensive Mercedes-Benz, a rarity on the roads in the middle fifties. He was untalkative, completely absorbed in his own thoughts, focused on his driving. There was no speed limit on the autobahn, and he drove at a furious rate, 150 kilometers an hour. Assuming that most people like to talk about themselves, out of politeness I tried to engage him in conversation. But every time I asked him a question, he took his foot off the gas pedal and slowed to 100 km/hour before answering. In the interest of making good time I too withdrew into the shell of my own thoughts.

A U.S. Air Force sergeant took us to Heidelberg. He like Germany. "Sure beats Saudi Arabia, my last post," he told us in his soft Alabama drawl. "No booze. No women. We used to fly to Basra with the RAF just to get a drink." He planned to retire in another ten years when he was forty, and buy a ranch in Florida. The next American, also in the USAF, was a Harvard graduate. He was interested in languages, history and culture, and enjoyed Germany. "But the idea that they are hard working is just a myth. The businessmen are energetic. They're doing very well with American aid. But the workers? They're just as capable of leaning on their shovels as anyone else." Curious about the world, he hoped to be transferred to Japan next.

The two young American soldiers who drove us from Karlsruhe to Stuttgart in their middle aged Opel that sounded as if it was on its last legs—or wheels, hated being in Germany and could not wait to get back to Texas. One was a bricklayer. But they did like German beer, "Though it doesn't match Coke and cognac." And German women. "Why the girls around Cologne are as thick as flies around shit, and they cost only five marks ($1.25). My she had a soft ass last night." An American staff sergeant saw Jim's Canadian sign, and backed 400 yards back up the road to pick us up. He was married and his wife couldn't wait to get back to California. She missed the soap operas on English speaking radio stations, the drive-in movies, hamburger stands, and her washing machine.

A German doctor picked us up at dusk. We'd been on the road all day and hadn't eaten, and he fed us bread and honey, and oranges, that were still fairly rare in northern Europe. He drove us to the door of the Jugendherberge, and when we asked him where we could change money, he forced 10 DM on us, and drove off. When I told the herbersmutter, the house mother, that I came from Scotland, she asked me where my skirt was, and whether I could play the "doodlesac," the bagpipes. A friendly girl who joined us for supper, told us there was snow in her village near the Austrian border, which confirmed gloomy weather reports we had heard.

Gibst sow schnee.

Chapter 43: Blumenkohl

Gourmand: One who delights in eating heartily and well.
Usage: A gourmand is one who loves good food and drink and sometimes partakes of them in excess.

~ Webster's II New College Dictionary

"Frommer's Europe on $15 a Day. 1954 Edition." Preposterous! I thought paging through it in W.H.Smith's Booksellers in London.

I lived on $5 a day, given the rate of exchange for the dollar, even the Canadian dollar. I hitch-hiked, stayed at youth hostels for less than a dollar a night, ate bread and cheese twice a day, country apples, and for my big meal pork pie and a pint of ale at a local pub for the equivalent of a $1.50. In North Wales and the Island of Skye in Scotland, where I was rock climbing and could camp, I lived for less, or at least ate better, two pints of ale.

Switzerland, climbing in the Alps was of course more expensive.

I stood before the Rathskeller, the Town Hall Cellar, an eating establishment. A cellar, I thought. Must be cheap. The Austrian equivalent of an English pub? Austria was even more cheap, and Innsbruck seemed a particularly attractive place to put down roots in the Tyrol Mountains. For a week or two at least, long enough for mail to be forwarded.

I scanned the menu posted outside the door, looking primarily at the prices. Several items would blow my budget, but there was a discrete list of items priced in shillings and groshens that I quickly tabulated to cost less than a dollar. I descended steps to the cellar level, pushed open the heavy oak door. Music flowed out into the night.

I looked about and should have known. The four-piece band pumping out oompah music. White tablecloths. Artificial flowers. Candlelight. Clearly not a pub. But it was too late. The waiter, a tall erect Aryan figure looked down at me, discerning, giving me a professional assessment. He eyed my wind jacket with a hood, woolen sweater, baggy corduroys, climbing boots and ushered me to a table in the back corner.

I ordered a beer, not realizing it would cost me half the price of my meal. I studied the menu. "Huhnen leber" was in the bargain column. "Huhnen," I understood as chicken. The next word I had to look up in my pocket dictionary, "leber," liver. Chicken liver. That sounded exotic. I visualized a plate with steaming chicken gravy over mashed potatoes, the tangy taste of liver, perhaps a vegetable, beans, or Brussels sprouts. And all for less than a dollar. I prided myself in experimenting with the local cuisine, particularly the beer and vin de pays, country wine. When in Rome, etc.

The waiter was slow coming to take my order. I have a child's aversion to having to wait for food, a mild genetic hypoglycemic condition. I was getting impatient.

"Was wilst du? What will you have?" he said brusquely using the familiar "du," as if addressing a child or the gardener.

"Huhen leber," I replied, putting on my best "hoch deutsch," high German accent.

"Gibst keine." That took me a moment to figure out. "There isn't any," he was telling me.

I panicked, glanced down at the menu frantically. The next item in the economy column read, "blumenkohl."

"Blumenkohl, bitte," I ordered. "Bitte," is a polite term for please.

"Etwas anderes? Anything else?" he asked with a note of condescension.

"Nein. Nur blumenkohl. No only blumenkohl," I stated emphatically.

He jotted it down slowly, looking over the top of his pad, as if giving me a chance to change my mind. He retreated to the kitchen.

I couldn't find blumenkohl in my dictionary. Blumen, however was flower, which didn't really help. Having been indoctrinated by years of upbringing to eat what was on my plate, I was prepared to eat what I got. So I took a paperback copy of "Catcher in the Rye" out of my jacket pocket and read while I waited, my hypoglycemic index dropping.

The waiter returned in twenty minutes carrying a single plate covered by a dome-shaped lid of highly polished stainless steel. Bowing from the waist, he placed it before me, lifted off the lid with a theatrical gesture, and presented me with my blumenkohl, a large steaming head of cauliflower.

Of course. I should have known. Blumen was flower. And caul would be derived from the Anglo-Saxon for kohl. One of those simple eleven syllable words that came into English usage from the German.

Not exactly what I had expected, but it was all for less than a dollar.

I asked for bread, and looked up to see if the waiter was laughing. Not a smile. He was too professional for that. I looked about the restaurant. Nor was anyone else sniggering. Given the hardships of the war, perhaps many Austrians had been reduced to vegetarianism, I speculated. Fortunately I do like cauliflower and made the most of my gourmandise. But a family sized kilo of cauliflower is indulgent. King John who signed the Magna Carta in 1225 is said to have died of a surfeit of peaches. I didn't have so much as gas from my surfeit of cauliflower.

But I did blow my budget: 85 cents for the main dish, another 10 cents for bread, an exorbitant 50 cents for the glass of beer, plus "service," 15% he added on automatically. Nearly $2. Almost half my daily budget for a plate of cauliflower. I could have done as well by consulting Frommer's, I thought as I put my book back in my pocket and got up from my chair.

I left the small change, a few groschens that amounted to 7 cents, and fled to the door.

Chapter 44: Innocents Abroad in Dalmatia

We crossed the fault line at the frontier. The Austrian border guards were relaxed as they checked our passports, smiling at the two Canadian girls. Dressed in tailored light gray uniforms with green trim, they looked very Austrian, dapper. The side-arms they carried were compact, inconspicuous. The Yugoslav guards flaunted their Kalashnikov high- powered rifles. Their khaki uniforms hung loosely from their bodies, pants baggy. No smiling. Brusquely they asked why we had come to Yugoslavia? Where did we propose to go? Where would we stay? How much money did we carry? They checked our visas suspiciously, then took our passports to be checked again by another official who sat brooding at the end of the coach. The security police? Clearly he was not from the tourist office.

"Are they always like that?" I asked Federenc after we had cleared. He was a Yugoslav art history student I'd met in Vienna and ran into him again on the train.

"It's their job. Security police always think they are surrounded by spies." Federenc spoke good English albeit with a heavy accent and would be our guide and informant the next three days.

I knew little about Yugoslavia. An innocent, I was drawn by the posters in the tourist office, sandy beaches, voluptuous women in bikinis bathing in the sun, Roman ruins, walled medieval cities on the Dalmatian coast. In the fall of 1954 I was on my "Grand Tour." At the Jugendherberge, the Youth Hostel in Vienna I had met the two girls, fellow Canadians, Jackie and Johnnie, "doing Europe." This was still something rare in the early fifties. They were on their way to Greece and though I was travelling alone, when they invited me to join them, I agreed happily.

"Vive Druge Tito," proclaimed the huge red banner across the front of the railway terminal as we got off the train in Rijika. The town still suffered the ravages of war, dock facilities were in ruin, buildings drab, weather worn and unpainted. There were few cars, rusted trucks rattled by belching smoke, outnumbered by horse drawn wagons. Shop shelves were virtually empty, the shop keepers wary as we entered.

"Nobody smiles," I commented to Federenc.

"No. We're still used to tight control. In the past if you were smiling, the police would figure you were up to something," he said with a slight grin, and then soberly said, "but it's more relaxed now since the Russians left." Still he looked over his shoulder as he spoke. We found people were very friendly in private, but still uncertain if it was safe to be seen with foreigners in public.

A platoon of young soldiers, new recruits, marched by singing a jubilant Partisan song, full of camaraderie and triumph, capturing a cheerfulness we seldom saw. If Marx was right that religion was the opiate of the people, in Yugoslavia song was their sparkling wine.

Federenc took the night ferry to Zadar to join a "volunteer" student work party doing archeological restoration. Volunteerism was required. He invited us to join him. In the main salon students gathered around a guitar player. Passing a communal bottle of wine, they sang. The repertoire was varied, melancholy folk songs mourning past defeats, present suffering and unrequited love. Rousing and defiant Partisan marching songs. The empty wine bottle was replaced with a bottle of slivovitz, a throat searing plum brandy, and they sang arias from Italian opera, Che gelida manina, How cold is this little hand, from La Boheme. Then the tempo changed unexpectedly and they began to sing in English in three part harmony, Deep in the Heart of Texas, complete with clapping: The stars at night/ shine deep and bright/ clap clap clap/Deep in the heart of Texas.

"Where did you learn that?" Johnnie asked.

"From Radio Free Europe. Since the split with Russia we are friends with America. They don't jam the station anymore," he said with a smile. Everyone was smiling as they walked the thin line of political correctness.

I was no singer myself, but emboldened by the slivovitz, I joined in. "Do you know this one?" I asked, and began to hum loudly The Song of the Plains, the popular Russian Cossack cavalry song well known since the American tour of the Red Army Choir.

"Not so loud," Federenc hushed me. Embarrassed he said, "Of course we know it. But the police might hear us and they might not understand."

Several of the songs sounded slightly off key to my ear. Federenc explained that the songs came from different parts of Yugoslavia, some were gypsy in origin, others Turkish.

To the casual tourist like myself, Yugoslavia was monolithic, one country, one dominant language, like most European countries. We began to understand something of the variety and the complexity. While nearly all Yugoslavs were Slavs, and although the Serbs and Croats spoke the same language, their written language was printed differently, the Croats using the Roman script, Serbs Cyrillic. Both were Christian, but Serbs were Eastern Orthodox , the Croats Roman Catholic. There was also a large Moslem minority. We were to learn that the frontier was not the only fault line. "Two things unite us," Federenc said, "Tito and our songs."

We found Zadar largely in ruins. It had been bombed heavily by the Americans during the war, and then bombarded again by the Germans when they retreated at the end of the war. The ubiquitous poster of Tito hung above the Lion of St. Mark, the coat of arms of Venice, over the city gate. Six church steeples rose phallically out of the rubble. "In all the air raids not a single church tower fell," Federenc pointed out. "The old people believe it was a miracle."

The students were working on a ninth century church that had been built on top of a fourth century Roman temple, the marble columns incorporated into its walls. Of particular interest were the faded wall paintings, figures of bishops, warriors and saints standing in a row, stern, severe man, bearded, beady eyes, haunting, disapproving, protesting their persecution and martyrdom. Their ghosts, I felt, must be protesting the godless contemporary pagans.

One student working on the site approached me, glaring with the earnestness of a recent convert. "Ich bin ein Communist," he asserted, in good German.

"Vertlich?" Really? I replied haltingly. "Aren't all of you?"

"No, only me," he insisted. He wanted to set the record straight. Only one in eight students were Communists and he was one, I must understand.

"My father is a tailor," he went on. "He's not a Communist," he added disparagingly. "He had a shop before the war but lost it when the Germans came. Now he works again. But he's not permitted to have anyone work for him. That would be exploitation." Clearly he had read his Marx correctly. "He works at home. By himself," he added seeming to admonish his father for persisting in the last vestiges of capitalist entrepreneurship.

The other students were more guarded in their comments. "Tito is a good leader, a good man," one said, adding hesitantly, "But others around him often give him bad advice." This was the closest he came to any political dissent, then rapidly changed the subject. It was much safer to discuss Roman architecture and church art.

We went on to Split, or Spalato, given the more common Italian name, another overnight run on the coastal ferry. Built by the Roman Emperor Diocletian in AD 295 as his summer palace, three thousand people live today within its walls. He was intolerant of political dissent and under his rule hundreds of Christians were thrown to the lions, adding to the galaxy of martyrs and saints. But Christians had their revenge. When Constantine, his successor, converted to Christianity in 313 AD, Diocletian's mausoleum was rededicated as a Catholic cathedral. There it stood, one of the most remarkable cathedrals in Europe, hexagonal in shape, spanning the area of two tennis courts, the dome resplendent in mosaics, the high altar sitting over the Emperor's tomb. Music enveloped us as we entered for Sunday high mass, the slow haunting cadence of a Gregorian chant reverberating through the soaring dome, mystical music from the 9th century, soulful, suffering, enduring.

"Would you like to see the church?" A scruffy little man with a morning stubble of beard came up to us after the service, wearing a thread bare black suit that hung loosely from his frail body, a gray scarf around his neck. He greeted us in German.

"No thank you." I replied abruptly, "I have a guide here," and pointed to the pamphlet they had given me at the tourist bureau. I took him for someone looking for a handout and began to shy away.

"Come, I will show you," he insisted. "I am the priest." Sure enough, beneath the gray scarf was a clergyman's dog collar, though I would never have recognized him as the same grandiose personage, resplendent in the rich green silk chasuble and the gilt edged robe, who had pontificated in Latin poetry from the high altar during the mass. Up there he was transcendent. Standing before us he was the image of oppression.

"Ya, ya. Things aren't what they used to be," he told us. "Before, the church had five priests. Now I am alone. And I am old. No more do we have processions. The young stay away from church." He went on to explain that though religion had not been banned, the wealth and all of the property of the church had been expropriated by the state. "Think of it," he said, "even the robes I wear and the pulpit I preach from belong to them."

Two marble lions crouched by the door, guarding the mausoleum, but even they seemed cowed as we left. Only later did I learn of the forced conversion of Jews, Gypsies, Moslems and Orthodox Serbs in the extermination camps of Croatia before they were executed. Thus their souls were guaranteed a passport to Catholic heaven. An accusation the church denies.

Dubrovnik was the crown jewel of Dalmatia. The wealthiest of the mediaeval Venetian port cities, impregnable for 900 years, its massive yellow sandstone walls rose from the cliff tops above the sea. We walked the ramparts in the evening sunset, the eerie pale yellow light fading to pink, coral, a hushed purple. The past is not dead, Faulkner wrote, nor is it past. Nor is the past dead in Dubrovnik.

"Zimmer privat?" Private room? Bed and breakfast. A wizened little lady with a black shawl drawn tightly over her head pleaded. We bargained and later I felt ashamed. "Three hundred drachmas." That was seventy five cents a night, for the three of us. Twenty five cents apiece for a simple room, unheated. Toilet down the hall, no paper. Coarse linen sheets and plenty of blankets.

And Marissa the daughter. "Sie spreche English," she speaks English, her mother announced proudly. Not only that, she was strikingly beautiful, a tall lithe woman with a full body, firm breasts, wavy black hair that curled around her ears, and fell to her shoulders, Mediterranean olive skin, deep brown eyes, full lips, a long straight nose. Dorian Greeks had settled this coastline in 700 BC. Marissa was a work of art, straight from a classical Grecian urn.

By day she was our guide. "The cathedral here is built on the church that your English King Richard. What did you call him? Couer de Lion like the French. On his way home from the Crusade he was saved by the merchants of Dubrovnik when he was shipwrecked," she lectured us proudly, as if she herself had rowed the rescue boat. Frequently she looked behind and moved on, conducting us through her magnificent city. I was enthralled by both Dubrovnik and Marissa.

We gathered in the kitchen that evening, sipped black Turkish coffee and chatted. She was eager to practice her English. In the privacy of her home after we opened the bottle of light white wine, the conversation turned to politics. We began to learn more of the Byzantine complexity of Yugoslav history and the residual hatred. When the Germans invaded in 1940, there were two resistance movements, the Chetniks, the Royalist party that supported the King, who was in exile. They were mostly Catholic Croats, and the Partisans, Communists trained by the Russians, mostly Serbian Orthodox though Tito was a Croat. Both groups were supplied by the Allies. But as the Partisans became more successful, the Royalists became more concerned about a Communist takeover than the German occupation, and they began to collaborate with the Nazis.

"My father was a Chetnik," Marissa told us gravely, "after liberation they were shot for treason, my father too," she added bitterly.

We in the West had become accustomed to the shifting alliances of war. Russia, originally the enemy became an ally, was now the enemy again. Germany, the former enemy, was being rehabilitated as an ally under the Marshall Plan. Loyalties were relative. But the residual hatred of a civil war goes deeper. Her inheritance was a hatred of Communists. They had shot her father when she was ten years old.

Later, when she was a student at the Gymnasium, she had tried to escape from Yugoslavia. "There were seven of us, four boys and three girls. We bought a small boat. The plan was to sail to Italy. Many people have been able to escape that way. Only Communists can get a passport. If they let all those who want to go, everybody would leave the country," she said in a low voice "We set out one night. Two hours later a police boat picked us up. One of the girls had turned informer." She went to prison for four months. After the split with the Russians Tito declared an amnesty. "Most political prisoners were released at that time."

"But even now that I am free, what do I do? I can't go anywhere without them following me. The only work is with the government. My papers say that I have been in prison. I'm a criminal and they won't hire me. I'm free, but a prisoner in my own country."

But Marissa was not one to be easily deterred. She had another plan. Our last night in Dubrovnik we invited mother and daughter to dinner with us. Mother declined. Marissa chose a small bistro she thought we would enjoy, popular with the young set and catering to tourists who had begun to return to Dalmatia. They were mostly German, but French and British too, not many Americans. We were probably the first Canadians. "They only opened last summer. The food is good. The wine cheap. It won't be expensive," she said. "And you'll like the music."

A lone guitarist played as we entered the Adio Mare. My eyes had to adjust to the candle-light. They seated us next to the pocket sized dance floor, but Marissa asked for a table in the corner and sat with her back to the wall facing the door. Over dinner a chanteuse sang with a husky voice like Marlene Dietrich, a repertoire of Serbo-Croat folk songs, mixed with an international medley, the well known German song Lily Marlene, popular French melodies, songs from South Pacific. Marissa had choreographed the evening well. Over dinner we chatted with two young men at the next table who were interested in Jackie and Johnnie and asked them to dance. Marissa and I were left at the table alone. I was never good at small talk. I always left it to locquacious Johnnie to carry the conversation. I felt awkward sitting opposite this woman. Not only was she bright and very beautiful but I had begun to have romantic fantasies about her as a resistance heroine. The conversation lagged.

Some enchanted evening... the singer crooned.

Marissa broke the silence. Looking me straight in the eye, she asked, "Are you married?"

"Married?" I hesitated," No," I said, looking away.

"Are you in love with one of the girls?" she continued.

What sort of brazen question was that? "No. Not really," I was beginning to feel this was getting complicated, "They're good friends. I met them in Vienna."

You will meet a stranger... the song went on.

There was a long pause, and this time her voice was less certain, "Would you like to marry me?" she asked, her deep brown eyes those of an enchantress.

What can you say to a question like that? I squirmed, uncomfortably. Could she be serious?

"Marry you?" I laughed in my embarrassment, and then felt embarrassed that I had laughed. This was no laughing matter. "Well...I hadn't really thought of it," I answered weakly.

"If you married me they would let me out of Yugoslavia," she went on to explain. "The government gives you a passport if you're married to a foreigner." She was beginning to blush now, which made her even more beautiful. There was a long pause.

"I'd make you a good wife," she promised. My eyes went to her black sweater tight fitting over the swelling curve of her breast. "Or don't you think your mother would like me?"

I assured her my mother would have nothing against her.

"If you don't like me, it doesn't matter. I'll divorce you. It won't cost you anything. I'll pay." She was hesitant but not pleading. It was a business deal, a matchmaker arranging her own marriage.

There was another long heart pounding pause. She was so lovely and yet so terrifying. My hand shook as I poured another glass of wine. She raised her glass and sipped, red wine wet on red lips.

"Would you like to dance?" she asked. Dancing seemed more manageable than marriage. She danced gracefully to the slow strumming of the guitar, her body pressed warmly to mine, two yearning bodies moving as one, the magic of dance. I could have danced all night...

Was this a fairy tale? Would the princess turn into Cinderella at midnight? If so, how could I find her slipper? The music stopped and I stepped back and looked at her in wonder at the mystery of beauty. I grinned, she smiled and tossed her head, her long hair streaming over her shoulder. She knew she was beautiful and was happy to share it. And we danced again, closer, tighter. What did it mean? Could there be a marriage for one night?

Que resta-t-il de nos amours? What remains of our love?

Que rest-t-il de ses bonjours? What remains of those happy days?

The singer broke into the words of longing of the French ballad.

Que resta-t-il do tous cela? dites le mois...What remains of all that? Tell me...

Un souvenir, que me poursuir, sans cesse...A memory that follows me, ...

I slept poorly that night, reliving the evening, fantasizing.

Marissa walked with us down to the ferry next morning and kissed me as I went on board, a chaste, sisterly kiss. The boat pulled out of the harbor, and I watched her grow smaller and smaller as she waved standing beneath the gigantic castle walls of her prison. I had the feeling that my life had become a long succession of departures.

That night over dinner the conversation turned to Marissa. "A remarkable woman," Johnnie said. I was guarded about my feelings but mentioned that she had asked if I would like to marry her, trying to make a joke of it.

"Oh yes," Johnnie laughed, "both men asked us to marry them!"

"And Metnick, my partner even offered to pay me a wedding fee of $500," Jackie chimed in. I suspect neither girl lost much sleep that night.

At Kotor the weather turned cold and we were eager to push on to Greece. "There are two buses to Titograd," the manager at Putnik, the government travel office, told us. "At four o'clock and another at ten."

"In the afternoon? At night?" I asked.

"No. No." he said. "In the morning." He warned us to take the early bus. "There are no reservations. Be there by three."

We arrived to a scene out of Dante's Inferno. Misty rain filtered through the trees. In the murky glow of a single street lamp, an agonized mob of sinners were begging for mercy. "Titograd! Titograd!" they pleaded, thrusting fist-fulls of money at the driver. Two hundred and fifty supplicants vying for sixty seats, another twenty could get on standing up. The driver, like Saint Peter standing at the judgment gate flung up his arms, shook his head. All the tickets were sold. We turned away rejected, dejected. I had images of an eternity of doing penance in Kotor.

"Americani. Americani," I thought I heard the driver call. Sure enough. He was waving at us. We shoved our way aboard the overcrowded bus, the last to get on, and were greeted by the manager of the Putnik office who had warned us to be early. He was making the same trip and had told the bus driver to save three "seats" for us. Jackie and Johnnie each had an arm rest to sit on. I perched on the cover of the diesel engine along with five other men.

The road climbed steeply into the mountains above Kotor, the engine grinding uphill. There was no other traffic on the gravel road, the country-side dark and deserted. People waited at crossroads, standing in the rain, waving frantically and shouting hysterically as the bus splashed by, dumbfounded as we disappeared into the distance. They would wait another six hours for the next bus which would also be overloaded.

In the warmth of the bus the passengers settled down to their breakfast. Out of wicker basket hampers came heavy brown bread wrapped in white cloth, cheese, boiled eggs, sausage and salami rolled in newspaper, all washed down with an earthy red wine that puckered one's mouth. We had failed to provision, but our comrade passengers shared liberally. After all, it was a Communist country. "From each according to his ability, to each according to his need," the Manifesto declared. Cigarettes followed, tobacco fumes blending with diesel exhaust. The bus became warmer still, the air more dense.

Then it hit. A ten-year old girl was first. She vomited explosively on the floor all over the shoes of the man standing in the aisle. Her mother was next, lurching for the window. Spontaneously windows flung open, some people gasping for air, others urgent to vent. Those at the back of the bus caught the spray of those vomiting up front. A window forward was flung open, those behind were slammed shut before the spray blew in. We wallowed in a mire of vaporous fluids like rotting sardines in a fish barrel.

From the depths of purgatory somewhere at the back of the bus, a lone woman began to sing amidst the stench and noxious gloom, a rich contralto, angelic in its clarity. Others joined in, softly, tenderly, the atonal strains of a melancholy Slavic folksong of suffering. Soon the whole bus was singing, drowning out the engine's roar, the metronome of the windshield wipers beating their own rhythm.

As the darkness shaded into dawn, Radio Free Europe came to our rescue and as light streamed over the hilltops the passengers greeted it with "You are my sunshine, My only sunshine," sung fortissimo in four part harmony. "You make me happy, when clouds are gray." The lyrics were Serbian, but the tune unmistakably Americani.

Though we never made it to the enticing beaches promised by the tourist bureau posters, we did have that glorious moment of sunshine, albeit vicariously.

Chapter 45: The Folksinger

"Your tourist visa has expired, the clerk at Putnik, the tourist office, told me."

"Yes, I know. That's why I came here, I told her. How can I get it extended?"

"You'll have to wait. She had a worried look. Come into the next room. And she closed the door."

"Ten minutes later two soldiers arrived, one carrying a Khalishnikov. And they took me off to prison. I was there for six weeks."

We were listening to Jan's story. He had approached our table at the Hotel Titograd, in that far off city in southern Yugoslavia, since renamed. "They told me there were other foreigners in town and I've been looking all over for you," he had begun. "May I join you?" A tall handsome fellow in his early thirties, he had a fair Nordic complexion, his light brown hair spilling over his collar, beard tending to blond. He was simply dressed in khakis, so neatly pressed they looked as if they had been starched.

"Yes. Do sit down," I said pulling up a chair. He was clearly relieved and attracted to the two girls I was travelling with, Jackie and Johnnie, Canadians I had met it Vienna and teamed up with on a tour of Yugoslavia in November, 1954.

"Where you from?" Johnnie asked.

He was hard to place. His English was flawless but accented. "I'm from Holland." That explained the good English. Most Dutchmen are bilingual, often trilingual.

"What brings you to Yugoslavia?" I asked. I suspected a fellow rolling stone.

"Well, I am actually on my way to Israel," he told us over a glass of slivovitz, Yugoslavia's mellow and potent plum brandy. "I plan to work on a kibbutz. So I quit my job and took off."

"What was your work?" I probed.

"An engineer." And he went on with his story. "I left with a sleeping bag and what I could carry in a rucksack. And my guitar. I like to collect folksongs." He had hitch-hiked across Germany and Austria which was easy in 1954. I knew. I had done it myself. "But in Yugoslavia, it's not so easy. There are so few cars and they're always full of people, over full. So I took the ferry down the Dalmatian coast." We had done the same, visiting the marvelous mediaeval walled cities, Split, and Dubrovnik, built by the Venetians on Roman ruins. "I did a lot if hiking, along coast and into the hills. That's what got the Secret Police so curious."

"What are you doing in Yugoslavia? They grilled me," Jan said." I told them I wasn't doing anything in particular. Just looking around. Trying to learn a little Serbian. *Why do you want to learn Serbian?* So I could talk to the people. *Talk to the people? What did you talk about?* Mostly I asked them to teach me their folk songs. They glared at me, accusing me with their eyes. The more I talked the worse it sounded. *Where have you been staying?* The Police questioned me, time and again."

The police keep a record of every foreigner, as they do of their own people, I suspect. We had to check in with them every night. The hotel or guest house where we stayed usually did this for us, taking our passports to the police station. But there was no record of Jan's travels, no paper trail. "If the weather was good I slept outdoors. Or in barns. Sometimes people would invite me into their homes, but I never told the police that."

"Then they searched my pack. They found my journal. *What's this?* Just some notes I've made. *Notes about what?* Mainly the words to folk songs. Folksongs? That really sounded suspicious. Was it in some sort of code? There is no end of protest in a folk song. The more I explained the more absurd it sounded."

They were sure they had caught the master spy red handed. They studied Jan's journal but it was in code—Dutch. Nobody could read it. Even more suspicious. So the incriminating document was sent to Secret Police headquarters in Belgrade to be deciphered and decoded. There was a Dutch consulate in Belgrade but the counter espionage officials were reluctant to show their hand and let the Dutch know they had broken the spy ring. And there was no one in the Yugoslav bureaucracy either who could read Dutch. Yugoslavia did not have a consulate in The Hague. So the journal was sent to Bonn in Germany, where they found someone to translate the Dutch into German, and the German translation was sent back to Belgrade. In the meantime a month had gone by and Jan was still in prison in Titograd.

"At first I felt I'd never get out. I kept thinking of the people who disappeared regularly in the gulags in Russia. Was this my fate? But then you get used to it. They fed me. Nobody beat me. I began to learn more Serbian from my cellmate, though I think he was really there to inform on me. And I had a lot of time to practice my folksongs. The other prisoners like that. So did the guards. They even taught me some of their prison songs. I was probably the most popular prisoner on the block."

In Belgrade the German translation was retranslated into Serbian and that edition was sent on to officials in Titograd. "Yesterday the guards came into my cell smiling," Jan said. No one smiles on duty, or for that matter no one smiles in public in a police state. *Come with us, we're going to take you to the tailor,* they told me in broken German, but I got the gist of it. Was this what they do to spies, dress them up for the public confession before the firing squad? *You're going to have a visitor.* This morning they took me down to the shower. I haven't had a shower in six weeks. Warm water even and a bar of soap. And when I got back to my cell, there was this fresh set of khakis. The ones I have on."

"You're going out to lunch. And they brought me here to the hotel, to the private dining room, none the less," Jan put on airs. "But still under armed guard." He described the scene. White table cloth, flowers, wine glasses, he was kept standing,

212

when in came a tall, dignified gentleman, in a tailored blue suit, a white shirt (something rarely seen in Yugoslavia), a red tie. *Setz dich*, he said in fluent German. Sit down.

"He told me over lunch that he had read my journal. He apologized for the breach of privacy, but said, I am very impressed with the way you interact with the common people. You would make a good comrade, he joked. I enjoyed the folksongs. I know many of them, but some are new. We don't do much singing these days. Not like in the war.

"It took me awhile to appreciate that this wasn't a KGB interrogation. This was an official of a different color. Still a Red—Communist, but his concerns were inspired by a different vision.

"I see you are an engineer," he said after another glass of wine. "Yes." Yugoslavia is very poor you can see. But we are a developing country. We're beginning to industrialise and we need engineers. A person like you with your skill and your understanding of our people could do good things here. Would you consider staying? And he offered me a job!

"Yesterday in prison. Today dinner with the District Commissar. Did I dare refuse? I thought again of the grim, musty prison cell. But the wine was strong, and as diplomatically as I could, I told him, "I have decided to quit engineering. I plan to become a folk singer."

He laughed. Well, come by my office tomorrow and pick up your passport and visa. Stay as long as you like, but be sure to get it renewed before it expires, he told me, and he held his glass up for a final toast. I'd like to hear you sing, he said, but I have a busy schedule. Maybe some other time, when you are famous. We shook hands and he left, followed by the armed guard, and he drove off in the black Mercedes limousine, the only one in town, driven by a comrade chauffeur.

A larger than life size poster of Tito hung from the restaurant wall. We ordered another round of slivovitz and toasted the ubiquitous Comrade. Jan tuned his guitar and after another round of slivovitz, the waiter joined him in singing the defiant and mournful songs of the war ravaged Balkans.

Chapter 46: Crossing to Freedom

"Wenn geght das nachst bus aus Pec?" When does the next bus go to Pec? I inquired at the Putnik office in Titograd.

"Im martz," he replied. In March. Since it was November, I thought the travel agent didn't understand me so I asked him again.

"Ya, ya, im vier monat" he said, in four months. He went on to explain as best as he could in faulty German that Pec was on the other side of the mountains, and there had been heavy snows and the road would be closed until spring.

We had travelled the length of Yugoslavia south down the Dalmatian coast and our plan was to cross the mountains east to Pec, only 60 miles away, and catch the train to Greece.

Titograd was a dead end. In November 1954, it was a muddy, war ravished village with two modern six story buildings of concrete and glass, promise of the reconstruction to come. The Communist regime planned to make it a showplace, in honor of the national hero. "Vive Druge Tito" banners hung from the newly installed electric wires conducting no electricity. The ox carts on the streets outnumbered the lumbering trucks. I saw my first minarets and peasants baggy trousers with tight leggings, a reminder that this had been a part of the Turkish empire until WW I. The majority of the population were still Moslems in this corner of Yugoslavia.

Jackie and Johnnie, the two Canadian girls I had joined up with put our heads together. "There's nothing to keep us here," Johnnie stated emphatically. We decided to catch the midnight train north, a two day detour, backtracking half way up through Yugoslavia.

We jounced all night and into the next day, third class on hard wooden benches. At Sarajevo we changed trains catching sight of the silhouetted asparagus tipped minarets against the dimly lit city sky. as we sprinted to catch the connecting train. It was, people sitting on each other's laps, adults and children alike. Soldiers sprawled in the luggage racks. The only seat vacant was the toilet seat, and that offered only limited time occupancy. We dumped our packs in the corridor, slumped on them and spent the rest of the night trying not to fall off, getting up to let people pass.

"This is one of the greatest feats of railway engineering," said a friendly young railway employee told us. He was a telegrapher and spoke some German. "There are over fifty tunnels in a hundred kilometers." I thought he exaggerated.

Then there was an explosive thud of trapped air, a frenzied rattling of the windows, followed by a furnace blast, a whoosh of smoke that gushed in, yellow, choking, asphyxiating. We had entered the first tunnel. I couldn't see the length of the car.

Is this what it was like to be inside an erupting volcano? I wondered as the sulfurous fumes clogged my lungs. Had Tito invented some secret weapon of mass extermination?

We arrived in Rankovich early next morning, cold, grimy, looking like jaundiced chimney sweeps. The water tap had been turned off in the station WC, but a group of soldiers were washing up under a pump in the station yard. We joined the line. Out of our packs came soap and towels, off jackets, up sleeves, attacking the grit, midst squeals of hilarity and laughter. The soldiers joined in, competing to prime the primitive pump for the girls.

"Look up Jackie." Not able to resist the photo opportunity I snapped a picture.

Pandemonium. It was as if the camera had triggered the fire alarm. There was a brutal shout, and an armed guard came stomping down the station platform, on the double, waving his rifle. The playful soldiers vanished. The guard stood before me pointing at the camera. "Ist verboden!" he shouted,

"Verboden!" he repeated, his face contorted in anger.

"Enshulldigen," excuse me, I said, with an embarrassed smile, fumbling to put my camera away. But this was no smiling matter. One doesn't photograph railways and shipping facilities. Only foreign spies do that. But nobody had seemed to mind along the Dalmatian coast in tourist friendly Croatia. Innocently we had crossed a fault line into Bosnia. I apologized again and retreated to the station house. Later we went into town to find breakfast thinking the matter had blown over.

It was market day in Rankovitch. The muddy street was jammed with horse drawn wagons and ox carts piled top heavy with loads of hay, potatoes and cabbage. That was it, nothing else, potatoes and cabbage, winter survival rations. Swarthy peasants, tanned by wind and weather, were dressed in their best woolens, heavy coarse cloth, grey, brown. The women wore black with faded kerchiefs over their heads.

A proud little man led gigantic black hog a rope leash down the center of the street, followed by a flock of bleating sheep and bellowing cattle, protesting their via dolorosa to the slaughter house. Rows of open air stalls, set up in an open field on the edge of town, were cluttered with crude crockery, metal pots, cheap clothing, the last vestiges of a free market economy. There was nothing frivolous to buy; everything was functional, essential.

One exception was a street vendor, well fortified with slivovitz, the local plum brandy, who sold primitive wooden flutes. He played off key to the amusement of an enchanted audience.

The day threatened rain, yet in spite of the lowering clouds and the muddy drabness, it had a subdued holiday spirit. Hardly the harvest festival of better days, but infused with the joy and bustle of coming together with friends. I thought of farmers gathering in my father's general store in dust bowl Saskatchewan during Depression years, coming not to buy, but just to be with each other.

We wandered through the crowd. Our colorful nylon wind jackets telegraphing, "Touristas." When I took out my camera, they turned their backs.

"You're being watched," Johnnie said. I looked back and saw The Man. Clearly no farmer, he was dressed like the classic sleuth, tan trench coat belted around the waist, a wide brimmed fedora, tilted over one eye Bogart fashion, hands thrust in his pockets, a cigarette in his mouth trailing smoke. He was staring at my camera. Quickly I put it away.

From the market place we headed back to town. Bogart followed. We found a cafe and entered. We were the only ones there. I ordered coffee, but the waitress just shook her head. I thought she didn't understand and repeated the order very slowly, articulating my fractured German clearly.

"Nix. Nix." she told us, clearly perturbed, half angry, but also half afraid. I looked out of the window. There Bogart stood on the sidewalk, casually looking away. We got up and left.

The government hotel, the one modern building, six stories of concrete and glass was down the street. Surely this would be a safe house? We entered the bar and took a table by the window. Bogart appeared across the street, now accompanied by an escort wearing an long leather coat that fell to his shins.

"You don't see many peasants with coats like that," Jackie said.

Leathercoat entered the bar, spoke to the waiter and left.

"Sind sie Deutsch?" Are you German? The waiter came to take our order.

"Nein. Wir sind Canadier. Studenten." No, we're Canadians. Students, I replied. He didn't seem to understand, Perhaps he didn't believe me. He scowled, brought us coffee and left us alone. We sipped our coffee, very slowly. Our honor guard stood outside leaning against the steel lamp post. It had been installed recently but still not connected to electricity. They smoked, chatted, stubbed their cigarette butts with their heels. Then a third comrade joined them, a uniformed policeman, armed. This was it, I thought. We were going to be arrested. Three of them, three of us, the logic was overwhelming. I thought of the Dutchman who spent six weeks in jail before they established his innocence. But they just stood there, three of them now, in a cloud of cigarette smoke.

We ordered another coffee then returned to the railway station. Our escort followed. We still had two hours to wait for our train. To give the appearance of being casual, I took out a deck of cards.

"What would you like to play?" I asked Jackie and Johnnie.

"Patience," Johnnie replied.

I found it difficult to concentrate on the cards, conscious of the three men eyeing us from the station platform. Then the policeman left. Half an hour later he was followed by Leathercoat. I began to breathe more easily. Only Bogart still hovered.

The train arrived only forty minutes late. Unlike Mussolini, Tito was not able to get the trains to run on time. The engine jerked, jolted and slowly we moved out of Rankovitch. Bogart stood on the platform. I was tempted to wave, but thought it would be tempting fate.

216

We were making our get away. It was like the last day of term at prep school. Jackie began to grin, and then both girls began to laugh. Free at last, free at last, Lord God, free at last.

Then the door opened at the other end of the pullman car. A uniformed guard carrying a rifle stepped in, the same guard who had threatened us taking pictures at the station pump that morning. He sat on the last seat and made a studied appearance of not noticing us.

The conductor entered the car. The guard beckoned him. They spoke and the conductor came directly to us.

"Billetes," Tickets, he asked cheerfully. "Deutscher?"

"Nein. Nein. Canadier," I replied.

"Going to Skopje?" he asked in German.

"Ya. And then on to Greece... tomorrow," I replied.

"Passeports, bitte." He looked at them, examined the visas, made notes. "Danke sehr," thank you much, and he returned to the soldier to make his report. It hadn't occured to me before that they still did not know who we were. No one had examined our passports.

"I heard you speaking German," a well dressed young man approached us, speaking much better German than I could muster. He was an engineering student from Slovenia, in northern Yugoslavia, his mother was Austrian, he told us, chatting amiably. Others began to crowd around, attracted to the two young women. A man in a worn tweed jacket began to open a bottle. Then the conductor came up. He tapped the student on the shoulder, leaned forward to speak into his ear, and left. The student looked back hurriedly and saw the armed guard. He blanched, then stood up abruptly, then blushed.

"I must return to my friend," he apologized. His cheek muscles twitched. "He wants me. I must leave," he groped for words. Then he bowed, turned, the train jerked, he stumbled and returned to his seat. Shortly after he moved to another car.

Two stations down the line the guard got off the train and so far as we could tell no one replaced him. We arrived in Skopje late that night. No one seemed to be waiting for us when we got off the train. Nor were we followed as we trudged through the darkened streets looking for the hotel. I kept glancing behind me.

There was only one vacant room at the hotel. The receptionist offered it to the girls. I could share a room with another man, he offered me. I suspected another security informer. But he turned out to be a friendly engineer. With traditional Yugoslav hospitality, he brought our his bottle of slivovitz, and we talked well into the morning. Without urging, he told me of the frustrations of his work. He was working in a steel mill, that operated only at 25% capacity. Another government department had failed to produce enough electric power to operate the plant. "Like so many things in Yugoslavia," he said, "it looks good on paper, makes good propaganda, but doesn't work out." That also explained all the electric light poles we had seen without electricity.

"How lucky you are," he went on, "to be able to travel. I too would like to travel, to study in England, or perhaps in America...but I can't."

"Warum nicht?" Why not, I asked him.

"I'm not a Communist," he replied, "only Communists do they permit to leave the country."

There was a note on my bed when I woke next morning, having slept late. "Mein liber Herr Canadier," it read, my dear Mister Canadian. He wrote how much he enjoyed speaking with "ein gemutlich auslander," a friendly foreigner. He gave me his address, wished me luck in my travels, and bade me farewell.

The Orient Express departed daily from Paris for Istanbul, stopping at Skopje en route. We found seats in a compartment with two other young people who looked like students, a bearded Sikh wearing a turban, and an elderly man who muttered in thickly accented English, possibly a businessman. Though all spoke English there was little conversation, each kept to himself. I recalled the wartime poster, "The wall have ears." The businessman I suspected was another security informer providing surveillance of imagined foreign spies.

At the Greek frontier I left the train to exchange my last Yugoslav drachmas for Greek drachmas. A larger than life size poster of an avuncular Tito was mounted above the barred window labeled "Cambio," exchange. I joined the line.

At the opposite end of the hall customs had a large table. Behind it stood two large men in trench coats. They were questioning a little man with dark curly hair, with Gypsy or Turkish features, their brusque voices rising above the din of the hall.

I looked on, appalled and fascinated not sure whether it was appropriate to be a witness. First they inspected his brief case, then shook everything out on the table. Not finding what they were looking for, they ripped out the lining with a large pocket knife. Then his suitcase. Next they ordered him to take off his heavy woolen overcoat, searched the pockets and ripped out the lining. Then his suit coat.

By now I had reached the cashier's window. When I looked back I saw the little fellow bent down, taking off his shoes, and the henchmen proceeded to rip the heels off, and then the soles. He stood there in his stocking feet, a look of terror on his face, tears welling in his eyes.

I fled, clutching my fist full of small denominational Greek currency, feeling enraged, helpless, cowardly, guilty that I could do nothing to intercede.

Smiling at me from the poster Tito appeared less benign.

"Passports et billets, s'il vous plait," the Greek conductor asked us cheerfully in French. The dour businessman lifted his suitcase down from the rack, and smiled for the first time, his gold capped teeth glistening. He took out a bottle of brandy. "French brandy," he said, and passed around small paper cups. "Join me in a toast to the freedom."

By the second round we knew each others story: the Sihk had just completed his Masters Degree in Agriculture at Michigan State and was returning overland to India overland, something I would do two years later. The young American planned to travel with him and study Sanskrit when there. The English girl was an *au pair*, joining a family in Athens. Jackie and Johnnie told of our encounter. The older man was Greek, a shipping agent and invited us to visit him in Salonika.

Though the sky was still overcast in northern Greece, the light seemed brighter. We had crossed another fault line.

Chapter 47: Olympian Zeus Unpropitiated

What I had hoped for was monastic hospitality. What I found was a monastery in ruins. The monastery walls had collapsed. Charred wooden beams stuck out from the rubble, pointing at the sky in Guernica protest, protesting to Zeus the Thunderer and the gods of Olympus. Or was it the vengeful God of the Apocalypse? More likely Poseidon, I thought on further reflection, for after all he was the god of earthquakes.

On my European pilgrimage in 1954, it was inevitable that I should seek out the holy mountains of Greece, the lofty summit of Homer's Olympus. I'd come on my own to pay homage to Olympian Zeus and climb his mountain, 9,571 feet, the highest point in Greece.

My outdated copy of the Michelin Guide Bleu, French edition, had a footnote on the Monastery of Agios Antonios, nine miles up the valley from Litokhoron, where the train dropped me off. I was low on paraffin, the smelly, slow burning, safe fuel I needed for my Primus stove. In the local bodega I was unable to make my need known, in spit of a brilliant performance of charades. But I did find survival rations, a thick crusted white bread, olives, cheese, a can of anchovies, and a bar of bitter chocolate, tea and sugar, by pointing. That would sustain me for a couple days on the climb.

"Agios Antonios?" I asked the bent over old woman driving her goats, pointing up the road. I wanted to be sure, though no other road led up the narrow valley.

She gave me a toothless grin, shook her head from side to side, said, "Ne," which is "Yes," in Greek, somewhat confusing for the expatriate. Then she began a long discourse with a grave look of warning on her face, which seemed to suggest, "No."

As dusk settled in, I arrived at what must have been the monastery. The day had been overcast, cold and blustery, which intensified the gloom. The scene was one of chaos, like a battle scene in a WWII black and white movie. Later I learned of the widespread devastation in the massive Greek earthquake of 1952, two years earlier.

I poked through the debris. Even in the best of times the monastery would have been a modest one, having perhaps twenty small rooms. A larger building with higher walls could have been the chapel, built on the opposite side of a courtyard the size of a tennis court. Two larger buildings possibly served as kitchen, storeroom and refectory. Along the south facing wall outer wall was a line of monk's cells, room 8 feet by 8 feet square, with domed ceiling of brick and plaster, an open fire place against the outside wall opposite where the door would have been, and a window that let in light and gave a glimpse of the sky. One cell was still somewhat intact, though stripped of all furniture and belongings. Goat dung spoke of recent occupancy.

From the perspective of a mountaineer it was adequate basic shelter. I was happy to accept whatever hospitality the monks, even in absentia, had to offer. In spite of being deserted, the place had the feeling of being lived in, at least in spirit. I pulled aside the ruble, cleared a space before the fireplace, gather wood from the debris and lit a fire.

The Greek tea was pungent and bracing. I spread my ground sheet and unrolled my sleeping bag, and settled in a meal of crusty bread, cheese, bitter black olives as appetizers, like they did in restaurants, followed by the fish course of anchovies. I'd found monastic hospitality after all, I thought, settling back on my rucksack propped against a stone that had fallen out of the masonry wall, and wrote my journal by the light of the fire. I had the sense that I was part of a long tradition of passing solitary nights reading and writing in this room.

I stirred my tea and the spoon clanked against the tin mug. A slight resonance sounded from the dome.

"Doh," I sang out with middle "C", and heard a faint echo, like the delayed sound of the choir in a vaulted mediaeval church. I always loved that tone, where you felt the reverberation in your stomach. I broke out into song.

"Rejoice, rejoice, Emmanuel shall come to thee O Israel." The psalm we had sung in chapel at St. Andrew's as a boy. My evening vespers in a Greek monastery.

I had come to the right place, I felt as I stoked up the fire from the last time

But when I stopped singing, it seemed to be very quiet. It was as if I had been singing to fend off the silence, propitiating something lost in the past. When I turned in I

felt uneasy, restless. There seemed to be something very wrong about the place.

"Of course there is," I said, just to reassure myself. "Just look around." Light from the fire flickered along the crumbling wall.

Was it something more than an earthquake? Some dreadful atrocity of the past? Christian fratricide? Turkish ethnic cleansing? Or a more recent Communist ideological purge? Greek history was uncompromising.

I rolled over to warm my back by the fire and must have fallen asleep.

There was a rustling in the room. I was sure I heard it. What was it? Wide awake now, I didn't move. That would give myself away. It crept closer, cautiously with stealth.

"Keep still," I told myself. "Absolutely still."

Then it tapped me on the head, lightly, almost imperceptibly. My being pounded with consciousness, on the alert, but I had the presence not to move. I feigned sleep. I knew I had to figure out who the intruder was before I made my move. I lie there motionless, every muscle taut, ready to leap.

There was another slight tap on my head. Unmistakable this time. I was lying on my side, left shoulder pressed to the floor. I opened my left eye. Only my left eye. The one closest to the floor, keeping my right eye glued shut. Perhaps I could see my intruder in the dim glow of the dying fire without being seen seeing.

I listened intently. Then I heard a sound I recognized. Scratching. Gnawing. The rustling of paper.

"Get out!" I screamed and bolted upright in time to see a rat, ten inches long, scurry beneath the debris and disappear into the dark.

I built the fire up again, higher this time, speculating that rats were creatures of stealth and dark. I woke every half hour to stoke the flame. It was still dark when I brewed my second cup of tea and treated myself to monastic hospitality, what I had salvaged of my bread and cheese.

Mount Olympus appeared to have a dusting of snow when I had seen it through the clouds the day before when I got off the train. But I hadn't given it much thought for it was quite warm at sea level. A well-marked trail led out from the monastery. I set out at first light. Further up the valley as the terrain steepened there was snow on the ground, but the trail was clearly visible. As I climbed higher the accumulation increased until the snow was ankle deep. More than a dusting, I began to realize.

By noon I was in knee deep snow, and the path, as it zig-zagged up the mountain became more difficult to find. The cloud cover thickened and a light wind began to blow, drifting the newly fallen snow. In the gullies I waded through waist deep. The cloud closed down and I was enveloped in sea of white. There was no trail.

The night before I may have propitiated the Judaic-Christian godhead rejoicing Emmanuel, but evidently the gods of Olympus were unimpressed. I turned back.

> *Never a tremor of wind,*
> *or a splash of rain,*
> *nor errand snowflake comes to stain that heaven*
> *so calm, so vaporless*
> *the world of light.*
> *Here where the gay gods live their days of pleasure.*

So Homer described the heavenly heights of Olympus.

Either Homer was no weatherman, or Zeus had neglected to read the weather report that November day.

There was a night train that took me to Athens. Perhaps the daughter of Zeus, Athena, would be more approachable in her eponymous city.

Chapter 48: The Australian Vorarlberg

I met them on the summit of the Weiskugl, 11,200 feet. That night in the alpine hut, the two brothers introduced themselves with Teutonic decorum. "Mueller," each said, with a brusque handshake. I imagined I could hear the click of their heels. We discussed the next day's climb, the Wildspitze, the highest peak on the Austrian-Italian border, and agreed to go together.

I wanted to be off the mountain before the afternoon sun hit the slopes. But our predawn start was delayed. The younger Meuller woke with a swollen face and badly blistered skin. We sent him down to Wendt with a pillow slip over his head, slits for his eyes, like a Klu Klux Klansman.

The older Mueller brother and I were still climbing to the ridge at noon, a long traverse. The sun beat with summer's intensity, though it was April. Our skis dragged through the softened snow. Then I heard a deep resonating "whoof," like the falling of a gigantic tree. The snow I stood on, a slab three feet thick, began to slide down the mountain. I pointed my skis uphill, ran desperately for the fracture line just above me, and jumped on to the firm snow. Would the rest of the mountain slide? I wondered.

"Meuller!" I shouted, to warn my partner, 100 yards ahead. He turned. Simultaneously, the snow he stood on began to slide. Because he was looking back, he was off balance, fell, and was carried away in the avalanche.

I stood aghast as he disappeared, buried in the churning mass of crumbling snow.

Then a hand emerged, and a ski, his head, another ski, and standing to his waist. While still being carried down by the snow, he worked his way to the edge of the slide path. It was like Lazarus resurrected from the dead.

I skied down to him, and we searched for his lost ski pole and wool cap. We abandoned both, as well as our climb of the Wildspitze, gathered our gear and prepared to retreat to the valley.

As I was putting on my skis, Meuhler approached me. In a German I could not repeat but clearly understood he said, "After what we have been through, we must not stand on formality. We must call each other by our first names." He took my hand in a warm friendly grip. "Ich bin Helmut."

"Ich bin Joseph," I replied.

Chapter 49: Flight of the Maggi

The plane descended on a steep glide path, passed by the control tower 500 feet below, and dipped its wing in salute. It then banked to the right circling over the sparkling sea, and came in for the final landing. David had just throttled back when we heard a horrendous roar as a huge four engine Constellation thundered overhead, a bare 100 feet above us, then pulled up and soared by. A frantic man in uniform burst out of the control tower, waving a black and white checkered flag from the upper balcony, urgently waving us off. We circled again, wide over the Mediterranean, and followed the Constellation as it came in for a landing at the airport at Nice.

We had narrowly avoided a mid-air collision and both of us were badly shaken. What had we done wrong? Our plane, a single engine Gypsy Moth, had no radio, which was not that unusual in 1955. We had followed the accepted procedure, circling low over the tower before landing. No one had flagged us off. "I think we're in for it," David said grimly, taking off his flight helmet. He took the offensive and entered the air control office demanding an explanation. To his relief the Air Traffic Control Officer was apologetic, shrugged his shoulders, and raised his hands palms up with a "C'est la vie" gesture and shook David's hand with a "Welcome to the French Riviera."

This was only my second day in an airplane. The day before, as we came in for a landing at Cannes, gliding smoothly on our final approach, throttled back, the plane took a violent lurch to the left and tipped 90 degrees. The ground suddenly appeared off to the side, as if the earth had tilted, and then it lurched back. Wobbling back and forth, we leveled out and came in for an unsteady landing. The port side engine cowling had become detached from one of its fastenings, flapped out and created an air foil that pulled the nose sharply to the left. Only David's quick reflex action had kept us from crashing. " I've never pulled the stick over so hard," he said as we both climbed out, grateful to have our feet on solid tarmac. I had had near misses mountain climbing, but they were never part of the daily routine.

David and I were old school friends. By chance we had met a couple weeks before, collecting our mail at the American Express office in Paris. We had gone to St. Andrew's College, a Canadian prep school together a couple years apart, were fraternity brothers at university. He came from a wealthy British Columbia family, the Kers, was hard working and bright, academically successful, affable and generous. Though soft spoken, and even a little shy with girls, he had a flamboyant side, flashing bright colored vests under conservative sports coats, driving a yellow Ford convertible with a high decibel diesel truck horn. One of the fraternity brothers called him "Gaylord," and the name seemed appropriate and stuck. When he came to "Do the Grand Tour of Europe," it seemed in character that instead of buying a car, he should pursue his latest hobby, flying, and buy a plane.

The Gypsy Moth was the Model A Ford of pre-war aircraft, mass produced, inexpensive, reliable. Chichester flew one from England to Australia in 1938. In our deluxe touring model, the two seat open cockpit had been enclosed in a plastic hood . Powered by a single engine, with a low wing, it had a top speed of 125 miles per hour, if there was no headwind. It was widely used by the RAF during World War II as a military flight trainer.

I was on my own Grand Tour, hitchhiking my way through Greece and Italy, and was returning to England to find a job teaching. "Would you like to join me on the Air Rally de Paris?" David had asked me. His partner had cancelled at the last minute and the rally fee, already payed, was non-refundable. With little hesitation, I signed on as passenger/observer/part time navigator.

The Rally rallied on June 8, 1955 at Perpignan, a picturesque walled city in southern France, near the Spanish frontier. Planes converged on the small airfield throughout the day, fifty in all. Most were French in their Macchis, and popular American planes Cessna Bonanzas and Navaronnes. There were Piper Cubs and the Pacer; the Piper agent for Europe joined the rally flying the new model Piper Apache, their first twin engine plane. Several Italians joined, including a countess flying a Feroni. There were Brits, and Danes and Swedes, a couple Arabs from Algeria. No Americans and no Germans. Most of the planes were piloted by their owners, businessmen and professionals, doctors, engineers; three were farmers. The two Yugoslavs, clean cut, nattily dressed, clearly military in demeanor, were a center of much discussion. This was meant to be an amateur event. Who in Communist Yugoslavia could afford a private plane? Was it a Tito publicity stunt? The mascot of the Rallee, as the French called it, was Jacqueline, the seventeen-year-old daughter of a French industrialist, who flew with her father, pretty, witty, multilingual, everybody's darling. And there was Annette, a handsome woman in her early thirties, amiable, confident, formidable, the first woman jet pilot in France. The whole affair had a brilliantly casual Gallic quality of graciousness, hospitality, good manners and snobbery. "Magi," our Gypsy Moth, stood out as a beautiful antique; David and I were the only Canadians.

A daunting routine was established from Day One. From Perpignan to Barcelona we had to climb up over the Pyrennees with terraced slopes, like a giant staircase. Clouds gathered on the ridge, deep blue, purple grey, worrying. Approaching the ridge, we were slammed by a down draft and suddenly dropped 500 feet. The camera on my lap shot up, skinning the end of my nose, and rattled on the inside of the plastic cockpit hood. David circled to climb higher and we soared over fields of wheat on the high plateau, green and ripening yellow, then began the long descent to sea level. We followed the Costa de Brava, the sea a deep Mediterranean blue to the south, the sloping fields irregular, unsymmetrical geometric shapes like a Cubist painting to the north. It was here that Picasso as a child first put crayon to paper.

We landed at Barcelona, where a Spanish and a Swiss plane were dueling for priority, a not so friendly competition beginning already. Customs was frustrating, not only because of the bureaucratic paranoia of the officials. Spain was still under dictatorial Franco. But because of the unruly Europeans shoving and barging ahead, no respecters of a "queue", lacking the British sense of politeness and decorum. All of us soon learned the art of elbowing and shoving.

Lunch was served in a hangar, an assortment of rich sandwiches, smoked ham, spiced sausages, and fruit and fresh vegetables. This was a time when it was still difficult to get an orange or a banana in rationed Britain. And two wines, rojo and blanco, extruded from the fine nozzle of a glass carafe shaped like a wine skin, that squirted down my chin and dripped onto my Adam's apple. While we gorged ourselves, folk dancers in traditional costume entertained us, the men in red and white tunics with matching britches, the women in white blouses and full muslim petticoats that flared out under knee- length skirts when they twirled.

We were in the air again at four pm and flew two hours to Valencia for an evening banquet of shrimp and lobster salad, cold cuts with mushroom sauce, two wines and champagne, served in a medieval courtyard with a fountain surrounded by a frog pond and orange trees, the fruit hanging from the branches. It began to feel like an exotic scene out of "A Thousand and One Nights." Gloating over the feast, I grinned at David, "Remenber the macaroni and cheese they used to get at St. Andrew's?"

I chatted with Angus Thom, over dinner. He was a Scottish farmer, ex-RAF. He was also a glider pilot, he told me. "In a glider I fly for the beauty of it," he rhapsodised. "The solitude. It's so quiet. Peaceful. A form of meditation. I only fly power craft when I want to go somewhere. But that's not really flying."

Next morning we were going somewhere. In spite of a poor night's sleep, revelers outside our hotel window until four am, we were the second plane off the ground. David seemed to have untapped energy reserves. He flew. I napped. We followed the coast south, over green irrigated orange groves, and blue- tinted white cottages by the sea, and refueled at a dry grassy airstrip at Carmali. Then began the climb to Grenada, nestled in the foothills of the Sierra Nevada, which were still covered in snow. Buffeted by headwinds, several planes turned back. The rest of us arrived late and the reception at the airport had been cancelled. At dinner served in a grim monastery courtyard the soup and chicken were cold. "Well that's what comes from trying to program the unprogramable," the Scot said. The French were outraged. Grenada is the loveliest of Spanish cities, but we saw little of it. It was here that Queen Isabella of Spain gave sailing orders to Columbus in January of 1492, and the rest is history.

There were delays getting off next morning. We had a frustrating wait for the taxi driver to finish his breakfast. Fueling up at the airport, the attendants spilled gas on the wings, causing further delay as it had to be wiped clean to avoid the risk of fire. David, normally calm and controlled, was furious. Precious time was lost. Planes were hurrying to take off before the day warmed up and strong winds were drawn in from the cool sea. The engine labored as we rose above Grenada. We climbed above the terraced slopes on the mountainside, with their olive groves and pocket sized fields. Long slender lenticulated clouds were forming on the ridge, blowing a sharp narrow spume into the valley. Tossed about in the down draft, David banked and circled again far out in the valley to gain altitude, and took a run at it a second time. The jagged teeth of the rocky ridge loomed up beneath us. We bounced through the air as on an invisible trampoline, down, stomach pressing on ribs, then up, bowels pushing on groin. I clutched for the air sickness bag. It was deafening with the rushing of wind and the roar of the engine. Then we passed over the high plateau with ripening wheat in stone fenced fields. David throttled back, and we began our slow gentle descent to the Mediterranean.

We were among those fortunate to leave Grenada that morning. Waldron, piloting an English plane had left two hour later. He had forgot to secure his seat harness, he told us, and when the plane was hit by a down draft, he shot up when his plane plummeted down, banging his head on the cabin ceiling, along with charts, the veri pistol, and all the cabin clutter." I could just barely keep my hand on the stick," he said, barely maintaining control. Several others planes had to turn back and were grounded until the wind had died down in the late afternoon.

We flew along the Costa del Sol, refueled once near Malaga, circled the gigantic rock of Gibraltar, and crossed over to Tangier. Africa was a new continent for both of us. We followed the beach south along enormous dunes, the grey blue Atlantic to the west, a narrow strip of green cultivated fields to the east. It was a balmy calm evening, a dramatic change from the buffeting we had taken in the mountains that morning. The motor hummed rather than roared. David taught me to handle the controls, and the plane responded with a feeling of lightness, weightlessness in space, and I began to have a sense of the freedom of flight. We put down in Rabat with the setting of the sun, the glaring colors of day mellowing into night. Other planes were lined up alongside the runway as we came in. The ground crew wore greasy overalls and incongruent red fezs. A lone stork stood curiously eyeing us from the grass on the edge of the field.

We were exchanging the day's flight reports with other crews, when Strang-Hansen, an affable Swede, said, "Look, what's happening there?" pointing down the field. The Piper Apache on its maiden flight, the one with the twin engines, was approaching. The Piper agent for France was at the controls and wanted to demonstrate the ability of the plane to land on one engine. This was touted as a remarkable safety feature. But he had miscalculated his glide path and was coming down short of the runway. He accelerated, forgetting that with only one engine operating, the plane would be pulled over. The plane tilted abruptly, rolled to its side, dropped, caught a wing tip, spun sideways, broke the wing in half, collapsed its landing gear, and spun down the runway amidst a spray of gravel and sparks. It narrowly missed twenty planes parked along the runway, then came to a stop. We gasped, failing to grasp the reality of it, and before we could run to their assistance, the owner-pilot stepped out, hastily followed by his lady passenger. They walked away stiffly, almost haughtily as if this was the way Frenchmen always entered Morocco. They had only minor scratches, bruises, but were relatively unscathed.

Rabat, in retrospect, was the high point of the rally, not only because of this spectacular aeronautics display. It was my first time in Africa. The setting was exotic, low flat-roofed mud brick houses painted a glistening white, behind walls, narrow streets and alleys crowded with heavily loaded camels, some pulling two-wheeled carts, men in heavy brown wool loose fitting cloaks in spite of the heat, wearing turbans or the red fez, veiled women in black ankle length gowns.

Dinner was in a Moorish palace, built around a courtyard with a fountain in the center, arcades walled with brilliant ceramic tiles. We left our shoes at the door and sat on low divans, leaning back on bolstered cushions. A quartered sheep was served in a large platter, complete with the head, the eye staring at us reproachfully. Whole chickens came on smaller plates. A bowl was provided for washing hands. No knives or forks, we dug in with bare hands, tearing off chunks and bits. A spiced cornmeal dish mixed with meat, raisins and nuts was passed around, which we compacted it into little balls and popped into our mouths. The meal was a gustatory sensation, not only the savory taste but the tactile delight of feeling and fingering the food like a willful child messing in his plate. There was no alcohol, only water, the Moslem custom. The French felt deprived; what was food without wine? But I was relieved. By custom, the sheep's eyes were reserved for the guest of honor. Who should that be? The Piper Agent won by acclaim. He bravely accepted the dubious honor. Having survived a plane crash, what harm was there in a sheep's eye?

Heading north next morning, we flew at an altitude lower than the tops of the dunes, only 75 feet above the beach. It gave us an exhilarating sensation of speed, with the sand passing so close beneath us. Returning to Europe, we passed Cape Trafalgar where Nelson fought his last naval battle in the Napoleonic War. We landed at Jerez, pronounced "thereth" with a lisp, the name corrupted yet again into English as "sherry." We visited the bottling factories and made up for any alcohol deprivation we may have suffered in Rabat. After a delicious shrimp lunch, another gastronomic delight, we fueled up and flew on to Seville.

"This Rally flies on two types of fuel," Sven, a Swede said before take off, "alcohol for the pilots, gasoline for the planes."

There was a grand reunion at Seville. The planes that did not show at Rabat were already there and we had a great exchange of war stories, tales of air sickness, the closing of the Granada airport. Thom tole of losing his way and putting down at a small airstrip to refuel. There was no wind sock; when landing he came in downwind and was caught by a gust that spun the plane 360 degrees in a ground loop. He told the story with bravado, and I laughed with a slightly hollow feeling. Each day I became more amazed at how little sense men had of their own mortality.

Seville had the mellow, decadent feeling of a beautiful woman, no longer young, but who was still elegant. It had beautifully laid out boulevards, lush overgrown parks, stately trees, weathered villas. There were transportation delays and complaints of cancelled hotel reservations, but after we changed out of flying gear into evening garb in the men's room, dinner made up for the frustration. Succulent steak from Andalusia, the Wild West of Spain, famous for its fighting bulls and where the noncombattants become beef. And wine flowed copiously.

The evening was another chapter from Scheherezade, a Spanish ballet performance by Antonio in the courtyard of the Alcazar, the 14th century palace of the Moors. We approached through fragrant rose gardens and pathways lined with orange trees in blossom. The stage had been erected in front of a stone wall carved in an intricate geometric pattern with the delicacy of lace work. A simple gypsy tune was choreographed into a stunning ballet, the music of a single guitar and the rich voice of a lone tenor that resonated in the confines of the courtyard. The melody rose from melancholy to passionate and defiant, with the atonal disharmonies of Arabic music, the rhythm picked up by castenets, the clapping of hands, the stamping of feet on the wooden platform. The men were in tights and short kilts, white shirts and colored sashes; the women in flaming red, narrow waists, flowing trains down to the knees, long and slender like the elongated figures in an El Greco painting. It captured what some poet has called the loneliness of the Spanish soul.

Columbus would have been entertained in these same halls in 1492, before he set sail from here. It was 2:30 before we were in bed, alarms set for seven.

On the flight to Madrid, 250 miles, we crossed a series of low ridges with high valleys between, like troughs between cresting waves. Olive trees grew in ordered groves and fields of wheat were being harvested. Circling low we saw a donkey pulling a weighed sled round and round on a stone threshing floors, beating the grain from the straw and chaff, a technology as old as the Bible. The landscape had a sameness and it was not always possible to pinpoint where we were on the chart.

Lunch was at the Madrid airport, at the King's Aeroclub with tropical gardens, a swimming pool, stylish women sunbathing on the terrace, soft sofas, nude paintings on the wall. Again several planes did not show up, and at 4 pm we took off headed for France, our last leg in Spain.

Dahl, a Danish farmer, caught up with us at Biarritz. Over dinner he recounted the misadventures of his day. "I lost my way," he said sheepishly. We had told him he shouldn't fly solo. "I was following a railway line that I thought should take me to Madrid. Well, it ended up going to Toledo further south. So I followed another line going north for about 100 kilometers. But still no Madrid. Fortunately there were villages along the way because I was low on fuel. So I put down in a field between the cattle. It must have been the biggest event in the village since the Civil War. I don't think anybody had ever seen an airplane up close. People came on foot, bicycle, on donkey, one old lady on crutches. I don't speak Spanish but they did understand benzine. They brought me gas from the village in buckets, and we strained it through my felt hat. They didn't want to take money. I was their guest, they said. So I gave it to the old lady on crutches and that was OK. The hat I gave to an old man, and he seemed pleased. Madrid? I asked, and they pointed in the direction I had come. I was right all along.

"I got in the plane, warmed up and started to roll. Then I happened to look out of the window, and all the boys were running alongside, and dogs were out front. So I had to stop, turned around, came back. I told them that was dangerous. The old woman boxed their ears. So I tried again. This time the cows were curious and started to come over to see what was going on. You know cows. So I stopped again. The boys took sticks to the cows and drove them off. So I revved up a third time. The field was clear now and I got speed up and was really rolling, bouncing over the grass, when I looked ahead and there was a donkey wandering across the field. It was too late to stop. All I could do was gun it, and pull back on the stick, and hope I'd lift off. Fortunately he saw me coming and took off running. I think I caught some of his tail in my propeller." He paused, refilled his brandy glass, "It makes me thirsty just thinking about it," he said and swallowed.

Crossing into France felt like returning to Europe, the neat patchwork quilt of cultivated fields, trees lining the country lanes, paved roads with the regular traffic of small cars, prosperous villages of white-washed houses, the tri-color French flag prominent. Biarritz, where we luxuriated in a deluxe hotel and banqueted that night, was a popular sea-side resort, the buildings heavy, pompous dating from the era of bourgeois prosperity pre-WWI, with brightly decorated balconies and verandas.

And on to Cognac next morning. "The wine was so bad nobody except the local people would buy it. They didn't know what to do with all the grapes," Eric our English tour guide told us, "so they distilled it. And voila...cognac." And he raised his glass. We made a tour of the Martelli and Hennessy bottling factories the next day. The weather closed in during the afternoon and we were grounded. Accommodations were quickly rearranged.

The sky continued overcast next morning, with alto cumulus, high clouds that caused no delay so long as they stayed high. We flew north to Dinard. Circling St. Malo, across the river, David pointed out that this was where Jacques Cartier had sailed from in 1534 on his voyage to discover Canada. Over lunch the Belgian expressed an interest in buying "Magi," our Gypsy Moth, as a club trainer. He was an engineer and mentioned that he had once considered emigrating to Canada, but decided against it. "I think that people with a professional income in Europe have most of the things a similar person has in America. But people in America don't have many of the things we have in Europe."

"Like the Alcazar and gypsy dancers ?" I asked.

"Yes. And our cathedrals, the art galleries and music. And the different countries that are so easy to get to. Like this Rally." For me, that was a new slant on things. Given the buying power of the dollar at that time, we thought we Canadians and Americans were the ones who had it made.

That afternoon we flew west along the rugged coast of Brittany, over numerous bays with enormous tidal flats, the brilliant blue of the English Channel a striking contrast to the dark weathered rock and green woods and fields. The flight was designed as a time trial though the rules had not been clearly explained, at least not in English. Planes were bunched up at the finishing line over the airport at Brest, some circling, waiting to land at their predesignated times, then landing into the flight path of other planes. It was chaotic, reminiscent of our landing at Nice. Showell, an English pharmacist, and six others refused to land against approaching planes, and were disqualified. The complaints on the ground were heated. An emotional Italian woman pilot mentioned a similar situation six weeks before where two planes collided, killing four of her friends. It was nearing the end of the rally and nerves were strained and tempers frayed.

Dinner was to the accompaniment of bagpipes, the male band dressed in traditional Breton dress, black britches, red jackets, green vests, and wide-brimmed black hats. To the drone of the pipes they perfomed dignified, staid, elegant dances. I thought of the contrast to the flamboyant Gypsy dancers in Seville, and how each embodied national character. Over dinner, as I was biting into a small, tasty grass-fed steak, Dahl, our Danish farmer friend, extolled the merits of grass fed beef over corn fed as in America, "So much more flavor." Then he went on with the woes of the European farmer." Sure, the country eats well. But it's off the farmer's back. We're lucky if we make 4% on our investment."

I leaned over and looked at his bulging waist line with a rude grin, "Yes, you eat well."

"And drink well too," he laughed, filling our wine glasses.

The ground fog lifted early next morning. We followed the coast and passed low over the magnificent Abbey of Mont St. Michelle, a 12th century cathedral rising spectacularly out of the sea. It was built on a rocky mound approached by a long narrow viaduct over tidal mud flats, the soaring Gothic arches and upthrust steeple reaching high into the sky. Ad majoram Dei gloriam. To the greater glory of God.

Following the coast of Normandy up the Cherbourg peninsula, we passed ruined German coastal defenses, now blasted open to the wind and the sand, the site of the D-Day landings in 1944, the greatest invasion from sea in the history of war. The dunes were pock-marked by bomb craters, like the surface of the moon. The sky clouded over, threatening rain, adding to the mood of destruction, ruin and desolation.

At Le Touquet, we came in too fast for a landing, bounced violently almost taking off again, and overshot the runway before stopping. The wheels bogged down in the soft grass, and David was not able to turn the plane around under its own power. We hopped out, pulled the wing around and taxied back to the hangar. David went to bed after the usual festive luncheon. I napped on a sofa in the lobby, then went for a long walk by myself. It was the first exercise I had all week, and I could feel my body begin to unkink from being squeezed in the cockpit seat. The town, a popular seaside resort, had been badly damaged during the war, first by allied bombers invading, then by German artillery retreating. Much of it was still in ruin. But the main street running down to the small fishing harbor was lined with brightly painted fashionable Parisian shops. On the beach, slat fences had been built to keep sand from drifting into town, and sheltering behind them, mothers played with their children. At the edge of town the dunes rose 40 feet high, covered with low shrubs and tough grass. I wandered about exploring the ruins of huge German coastal fortifications, pill boxes and shore batteries, built in reinforced concrete, now mostly buried in drifting sand. "I am Ozymandias," I thought of Keat's poem, "Look upon my works ye mighty and despair." It was a great relief to walk again, to smell the sea rather than gas fumes, to feel the soothing wind on my face, to hear the soft sigh of the wind through the grass, and not the engines roar, and to have two hours of solitude.

231

Dinner was another five course gastronomic delight with three wines, champagne and cognac. But the week of indulgence finally caught up with my digestive tract. We walked through the town in the evening, but I had to retire early and take up my seat on the porcelain throne.

The last leg of the Rally from Le Touquet to Paris was planned so as to arrive at the Paris Air Show, all 50 private planes descending from the skies like homing pigeons, to advertise the allures of private flight. But when we arrived at the Le Tuquet airport at 7:30 am, the cloud cover was down to 500 feet and a gusting wind blew off the English Channel. We were grounded. It was just as well for me, for it gave my intestines respite. I crawled back into the cockpit, out of harms way, and slept from 10am until 2pm. By then the sky had begun to clear, and planes with two way radio were cleared to take off. By four, the rest of us were given the go ahead. Planes crowded the side of the runway, impatiently jockeying for place, and were flagged off one at a time, when the runway had been cleared of incoming traffic. There was a sense of urgency to get to Paris for the final ceremonies.

Flying below 500 feet, we were able to keep beneath the clouds. Bathers waved at us from the beach below. We mistook Le Treport for Dieppe and turned inland. The clouds lowered and we were soon lost. We followed one road and then another road that followed a river, trying desperately to identify villages that should have been south of Dieppe. The weather closed in and we dodged clouds less than 100 feet above the ground, jockeying up and down, anxious to maintain visibility. Then David spotted the junction of two major railway lines that he thought he recognized. We followed south and voila, the overcast lifted, the suburbs of Paris poked through the clouds, and we landed in a gorgeous, warm, sunny evening at Tussous-le-Noble. The journey's official end. There were 70 planes lined up on the edge of the field, but many of our group had not shown up. We had been lucky. Our wrong turn at Le Treport had given us a brief weather window. Others had run into a solid weather front and had to abort their flight in northern France. Quel domage, what a pity, but we were relieved to have wheels and feet on solid ground. The most dangerous part of the day lay still ahead of us, crossing Paris in a taxi.

The closing banquet was at the Aero Club de Paris, the rally sponsor, with the usual gourmet surfeit and alcoholic excess, awards, the so called amateur Yugoslav professionals cleaning house, and speeches. A representative from each country was called upon, and David, from bi-lingual Canada, acquitted himself well. "Nous avons BIEN mange," he said, with dubious pronunciation, to appreciative laughter. An Arab, who had clearly imbibed more than Mohammed would have approved of, suggested the next rally be held in Algeria. Algeria was then in the midst of a bloody revolt against French colonial rule. There were shouts of protest, hooting, hollering, deafening whistles of disapproval until he was cut off by the embarrassed chairman. Several people got up and left shouting lavatory epithets. But the evening was rescued by a plucky little lady in her 70's, a vivacious pioneer aviatrix who charmed everyone with her humor, which I could not follow. "Vive la France," she concluded, to loud applause and I joined in.

Next morning there was a final farewell at the Hotel de Ville, the City Hall, a ponderous Gothic revival building of the late 19th century, like the Parliament Building in Canada, with huge murals of historic battles on the walls. Champagne punch and delicate pastries were passed up, and a line formed for the unadulterated orange juice fruit bowl, as if for a detoxification clinic. It was a moment of farewells, nostalgia and reflection, the war stories subdued. Annette, the attractive jet pilot came by to say, "Au revoir."

"How did your learn to fly?" I asked her.

"I grew up reading Saint-Exupery, *Wind Sand and Stars*. I always wanted to fly." She was a pilot for a French company that manufactured private jets, "Mainly for Middle East oil millionaires," she said." I studied engineering, and took up flying on the side. But flying won out. It would be hard to return to a desk."

Dennis, a thoughtful young Englishman, who flew as a passenger/observer like me, joined the conversation. "This is my first time flying," he said. "Sure, there are moments that are very exciting, and it gives you a great perspective on the world, a bird's eye view. But I never feel I was part of it. You're dependent on so much technology, on so many other people, and so much can go wrong. I'm surprised that no one was killed."

"But isn't that part of the attraction?" Angus Thom, a Scottish sheep farmer cut in." Those of us who flew during the war never...," he paused, "We lived so fully. Every day counted. We survived the war. The question now is how do we survive the peace? With all the boredom, government regulations, bank drafts. We were heroes then. I guess we don't want to let the memory go."

"But not everybody can afford an airplane," Dennis objected.

"But you don't need an airplane," I joined in. "I climb mountains and most of the lads I meet on the cliffs in Wales, or in the Alps, aren't rich. They're mechanics, carpenters, printer's apprentices, teachers like myself. Ask us why they climb. It's great way to feel alive, that's all. No heroics."

Annette walked with us back to the hotel. We passed Notre Dame de Paris, with the graceful flying buttresses supporting the cathedral to soaring heights. "You know it must have been similar in those times. Architects and engineers inventing new ways of building these magnificent cathedrals, developing new skills, creating new visions of beauty. People going off on the Crusades in search of adventure, fame, in the name of God. It's not so different."

Dennis agreed, "Someone wrote that it is human to be curious, and that when Man is not curious, he is not longer Man."

"And Woman too," Annette laughed, and kissed us on both cheeks, a French farewell.

Next morning David and I flew back to England and Blake's "pleasant pastures green."

Chapter 50: Founder's Day At Gordonstoun

The Silver Cloud Rolls Royce limousine purred up the driveway, the elegant old boxy model with high roof, large headlamps mounted on the fenders, rectangular chrome radiator. It came to a stop. But the royal ensign wasn't flying. Was something amiss? The welcoming committee was clustered on the lawn: the Chairman of the Board of Governors and fellow Board Members, the local Member of Parliament, the County Sheriff, the Commanding Admiral of the neighboring Lossiemouth Naval Air Base, headmaster Henry Brereton, housemasters, senior faculty and senior boys.

I was a new teacher who had arrived three days previously. I stood back among the younger faculty hidden in the crowd, seeking anonymity, and wondered what I was doing at an elite school like Gordonstoun.

The Chairman of the Board stepped forward to open the rear door for the honored guest. But no one was there. Looking up front at the passenger's seat, he saw a very embarrassed chauffeur, sitting stiffly in black uniform and driver's cap. On the opposite side behind the steering wheel sat His Royal Highness Prince Philip, the Duke of Edinburgh, handsome, elegant in a charcoal grey Saville Row suit, a broad smile on his face. The dignitaries, their dignity disturbed, scurried around the car to greet His Royal Highness. He was returning to Gordonstoun on Founder's Day to celebrate his old school's coming of age. It was 1955, the twenty-first anniversary of the founding of Gordonstoun School.

Philip was one of the first students to enroll in Gordonstoun, having followed Kurt Hahn from his school in Germany when Hahn, a Jew, fled Nazi Germany in 1933.

The day's program had been choreographed with military precision. The first order of business was to unveil a life-sized portrait of our most famous "Old Boy." This entailed entering Gordonstoun House, the majestic 17th century baronial Renaissance style building, mounting the stairs, unveiling the painting, then retiring to the main hall to be revived by sherry and tea.

But there seemed to be a hitch. The dignitaries conferred briefly by the roadside and instead of entering Gordonstoun House according to plan, the party took off up the hill, behind the shabby wartime Quonset huts that had been converted to workshops and classrooms. Fifteen minutes later they returned chuckling and word filtered through the crowd, "The first thing Philip wanted to see was his pigsty. He raised hogs, you know, when he was here as a boy."

I had arrived at the school only three days before, a new teacher hired at the

234

last moment. But I had not come by limousine. I hitch-hiked, arriving from a week of climbing on the north crags of Ben Nevis only a couple hours away, wearing my climbing boots and carrying my kit in a rucksack. My other belongings had come by railway express, three cases which included forty-two pounds of books, fifty-seven pounds of mountaineering equipment, and eighteen pounds of clothes, according to the bill of lading.

Standing there at the ceremony in my blue blazer and grey flannel trousers, a polyester drip dry shirt with a button down collar, brown shoes instead of regulation black, the best attire I could muster, I felt sartorially naked. The boys were nattily turned out in their school evening uniforms, grey blue short trousers and knee socks, matching jerseys over white shirts with open collar. The faculty and guests were in well tailored navy blue suits with natty pin stripes, the jackets with back slits on each side English fashion, rather than in the center back like mine. And their regimental and college striped ties. I wondered if I too, like HRH, had gotten out of the wrong door.

The day's program resumed slightly behind schedule. A half-mile north of Gordonstoun House the Moray Firth, an open arm of the North Sea, stretched grey and cold. On the cliff top, 200 feet above the breaking surf, a new coast guard watch tower had been constructed. Gordonstoun was famous, not only for its royal patronage, but also for its tradition of sea-going expeditions and the dramatic rescue service training program. The Coast Watchers were the school's elite. Philip officiated at the opening of the new watch tower.

I witnessed the dramatic display of boys raising their instructor Commander Shaw from the rocky beach below. He sat in a "breeches buoy," a device consisting of lines and pulleys that suspended the rescued person seated inside a life ring. The complex operation required skill, coordination and precision of the students, but more compelling was the faith on Shaw's part entrusting himself to their competence. I was impressed as were our honored guests and the press with their dramatic photo opportunity.

Another demonstration didn't come off so well. The Fire Fighters were scheduled to put out a fire in a pile of rotten logs and woods trash piled as high as a crofter's cottage, crackling with resplendent fury, smelling of pine tar and diesel fumes. A student parked the fire truck on the shoulder of the narrow country road, and the crew sprang into action, running out hose, dousing the flames and causing great belching clouds of grey smoke. But the shoulder of the road, weakened by recent rain, gave way gradually. The truck sank into the ditch and slowly rolled over like a lazy St. Bernard wanting its belly rubbed. It was dramatic in its own way, even a photo opportunity, though this was not the point of the exercise. Fortunately, no one was injured. The boy was spared having to explain himself to HRH and next week was put right back in the driver's seat.

"The British have a great sense of theatre," Canadian friend and movie critic Peter Harcourt told me, "the Royal family most of all." I was taken in by the aura of celebrities, the drama of the events. It seemed unbelievable that I was actually here, like Cinderella at the ball.

I had not even heard of Gordonstoun when graduated from law school at the University of British Columbia in June 1953 and in a rash moment decided I wanted to travel for a year before taking articles in a law office. Teaching became a way to finance my travels.

Gabbitas and Thring, "Garb it all and Sting," a placement agency in London found me a job at Shirley House School in Watford, a northern suburb at the end of the Bakerloo Line, teaching twelve-year olds. English grammar and British History came easily and to my surprise I enjoyed it. As in my own happy boyhood at St. Andrew's College, a prep school north of Toronto, I fit in with the masculine camaraderie of boarding school life. Here I was the rustic colonial among my Empire-centric colleagues.

More compelling was the cultural scene. London was an hour away by train and four nights a week I sat in "the gods," the cheap seats at the back of the theatre. I saw Richard Burton on stage as *Hamlet*, Lawrence Olivier in *Titus Andronicus*, T.S. Eliot read from *Four Quartets*, Margot Fontaine dance, and Furtwangler conduct Beethoven's *Sixth Symphony*, On Friday afternoons I would rush down to the National Gallery for the free art lecture. Soon I was able to distinguish a Manet from a Monet.

But the experience that changed my life was a rock climbing course I took at Plas y Brenan in North Wales over Easter vacation in 1954. Clinging to a rock buttress by my fingertips was an unexpected experience of high adrenaline, self-revelation and intimations of mortality. I followed it up with a two-week alpine climbing course that summer in Zermatt at the foot of the Matterhorn. Like Keats reading Chapman's Homer, it opened a whole new world.

After such a year, how could I return to law? I decided to extend my sabbatical another year. More than a sabbatical, it was really my education. I traveled east to Soviet-occupied Vienna, saw Mozart's *Magic Flute* at the Stats Opera, had a brush with the Yugoslavia KBG in Sarajevo, read *The Odyssey* in a small hotel in Aegina, Greece. I came to understand art as a visual language in Florence. Ski touring in the Otztal Alps along the Austrian-Italian border I was nearly carried away by an avalanche. My travel budget depleted, I returned to Britain in early 1955 still ambivalent about being a lawyer. I asked myself how could I postpone my legal career for yet another year? Teach?

"Why don't you try Outward Bound?" a climbing partner suggested. I had never heard of it. "It's a one month adventure course for young men. They climb mountains, plunge into ice cold streams. All in the interests of character building and leadership training. It should be right up your alley." It sounded too militaristic for my taste but I wrote anyway. To my amazement I received a letter from Eric Shipton the warden inviting me to visit the Eskdale Outward Bound Mountain School in the Lake District. A letter from Eric Shipton! He was a legendary figure in mountaineering circles, an icon. I had carried a copy of his book, *Upon That Mountain,* with me through the Alps. Avoiding the self-aggrandizement of heroics, Shipton caught the primitive joy of travel and discovery where the bungling and mishaps were as much a delight as the high achievement. He was the master of the small expedition. "I've never been on an expedition you couldn't plan on the back of an envelope," he had said when introducing one of his slide lectures.

Shipton had led the first reconnaissance on the south side of Everest in the early fifties when Nepal was opened to climbers and he discovered the route that led eventually to the top. But he was passed over when the British came to organize a summit assault in 1953, a massive logistical exercise involving four hundred porters. John Hunt, a prominent mountaineer and major in the army, was appointed leader and the expedition was planned like a military maneuver. Hillary and Tenzing got to the top. Hunt received a knighthood, Shipton a desk job at the Outward Bound School.

Over lunch with Shipton I suggested that a program like Outward Bound should be in schools. "It is," he replied. "The idea of Outward Bound came from a school." And he told me about Gordonstoun, a boy's school in Scotland that took boys mountaineering and sailing as part of the program. "Prince Philip The Duke of Edinburgh went there as a boy," he added.

So I wrote another letter addressed to "The Headmaster" of Gordonstoun School for I didn't know his name. I'd like to visit for a term, I wrote, and would be willing to do anything useful in return for room and board. If they could pay me a small stipend, I'd like to stay for the year. With hindsight the whole proposal seemed audacious. Me at a school for royalty? But the headmaster, Henry Brereton, replied, inviting me to an interview at Brown's Hotel in London. I ironed out the creases in the blue blazer and grey flannels that I had carried in my rucksack the past two years and appeared as well dressed as I could, even wearing a tie, a tartan tie from my days at St.Andrew's, a Canadian prep school with an Anglo-Scots tradition.

Brereton was a tall portly man, slightly stooped from a lifetime of bending to get under the low doorways of Britain's ancient homes. He glowered at me through heavy framed spectacles beneath thickset bushy eyebrows, rather unsettling. He commented on my tie. "The McNold tartan?" he asked with a broad smile. Embarrassed, I felt I was off to a poor start. But he showed a real interest in my travels. We discussed the stained glass windows in Chartres, Michelangelo's unfinished sculptures, *The Slaves*, in Florence, and the Turner exhibit in The Tate. I tried to bring up my one-year teaching experience at Shirley House School, but he didn't seem particularly interested. He questioned me more closely on my mountaineering experience and drew me out about ski touring in Austria. "But are you responsible?" he interrupted. What sort of question was that? I wondered. My first thought was that? I wondered. My first thought was that maybe he saw through me and meant that I should be a responsible lawyer rather than a drifter using teaching as an excuse to travel.

"No, not always," I said hesitantly, but then trying to redeem myself I added, "but I hope to become more responsible." He guffawed and then burst out in hearty laughter and offered to hire me at the magnanimous salary of one hundred pounds for the year, plus room and board. This was my professional apprenticeship, the best hundred pounds I ever earned. Little did I realize that my year at Gordonstoun would be the experience on which I would base the rest of my professional life.

And there I stood on the well groomed lawn as the westering sun cast a yellow afternoon glow on the grass, self-consciously joining the boys in, "Three cheers for Prince Philip! Hip! Hip!..." as His Royal Highness waved and drove off down the driveway, his chauffeur sitting uncomfortably in the passenger seat.

"Quite a Founder's Day," remarked George Campbell, a friendly young teacher who taught geography, as he walked with me off the field. "Too bad Hahn couldn't be here. He would have loved orchestrating an occasion like this. "Only then did it occur to me that something was missing. The Founder was not there for Founder's Day.

Chapter 51: Kurt Hahn Of Gordonstoun

Kurt Hahn, the founder of Gordonstoun School, may not have made it to Founder's Day in September 1955, but as a new teacher I was soon to learn that he was still the guiding spirit of the school. His benign face looked down upon us from the enlarged photograph on the wall as we gathered for assembly each morning in the Great Hall of Gordonstoun House. He was revered by some to a degree that verged on hero worship. Though there were skeptics. But one thing everyone did agree upon was that Hahn made a lasting impression on those who knew him. To me he was a mystery still. Who was Kurt Hahn as a man, as an educator, visionary or wizard?

Henry Brereton, an historian and the headmaster, met with me periodically in the inner sanctum of his book lined study on the second floor of the stately manor house. The meeting did not get off to a good start. I felt his manner cold and preoccupied. "Have you met Nold, the new teacher?" he asked his wife as she came in.

"Well, I did almost meet him," she replied, 'when he looked right through me and saw you," she said is a waspish tone. I felt I was being put in my place. But she left and Brereton became more congenial. He clearly wanted to talk. I felt he wanted to know me better. When I asked him about Kurt Hahn, he responded with alacrity.

Brereton knew Hahn well, having been Hahn's director of studies for nearly twenty years and then succeeding him recently as headmaster.

"He came from a wealthy Jewish family," Brereton told me, "German industrialists." He explained that Hahn was born in Hamburg in 1886 and had studied philosophy in Germany before coming to Oxford. "But he never did finish his degree," he said. "He had a somewhat unorthodox education for an educational reformer." This reassured me about my own lack of academic preparation.

During World War I Hahn had worked for the German Information Bureau interpreting the mood of the British press. At the end of hostilities he became the private secretary of Prince Max von Baden who was the last chancellor of Imperial Germany before the Kaiser was deposed. Prince Max retired from politics and returned to his estate in southern Germany, Schloss Salem, a former Cistercian monastery, It was a large complex of buildings and in one wing he established a school with the idea of educating the next generation of leaders for a democratic Germany and appointed Hahn headmaster.

"With Prince Max's patronage Salem was successful in attracting the children of prominent European families, such as the royal family of Greece and Denmark,

Prince Philip's family," Brereton told me. "They also recruited children from the local community and admitted them on scholarship, like we do at Gordonstoun.

Brereton continued with obvious pride: "But Hahn's defining moment was when he defied the Nazis. It was in 1931 before Hitler came to power. Nazi storm troopers broke into the Communist headquarters in Berlin, destroyed the furniture, burned books, beat up the staff and kicked one of the librarians to death. Hitler praised the act in public. Hahn reacted immediately. He had no sympathy for the Communists, but he condemned the Nazi brutality in a statement to the press that was widely published. Then he sent a letter to all Salem parents demanding that they disassociate themselves from the Nazi party or sever their ties with Salem. It was an act of incredible courage, almost fool-hardy. Many parents objected and told Hahn not to implicate the school in politics. Many saw the Nazis as the lesser of the two evils. But Hahn insisted and he became a marked man.

When Hitler came to power in 1933, Hahn was among the first dissidents. to be rounded up and imprisoned. He was released only because influential Oxford friends intervened on his behalf, but it was on condition that he leave Germany. So Hahn came to Scotland which he knew from his Oxford days.

"Hahn was forty years old, his life was in ruins and he was depressed, but he started over again. Thirty boys, including Philip, followed him from Salem. Friends found Gordonstoun House. And here we are twenty-one years later."

I asked Brereton why Hahn had been at Founder's Day.

"That's an unhappy story," Brereton explained. "As a boy Hahn had a severe bout of sunstroke and it plagued him all his life," Brereton concluded. "Two years ago it took a turn for the worse and required major surgery. So he had to retire. It was a great loss to the school and truly regretable that he couldn't be here forFounder's Day. It should have been his day."

Hahn's life story was an heroic epic in its own way, but it still did not explain tome the deep impression he made on people who knew him. All I knew was second-hand, here say evidence my legal training told me. They spoke of his uncanny intuition, his insight into people, his warmth and deep humanity, his eccentricities, but above all his sense of moral purpose. Over the coming weeks I probed boys and masters alike about the man. Everybody I asked had a Kurt Hahn story.

It was Hahn's eccentricities that the boys remembered most. Powys and Swallow, the two color bearers, prefects, in Duffus House frequently joined me for afternoon tea in my spacious room, cluttered with climbing gear. Powys told me the story of the night that two boys discovered the secret passage in the basement of Gordonstoun House. "There was a narrow tunnel they could barely squeeze through behind some loose stones in the wall. They followed it and climbed a stone stairway in the dark. Two flights up they came to a heavy door. They were able to pry it loose, slowly opened it and there they found themselves face to face with Dr. Hahn. He was sitting in his bathtub bare naked talking to himself. When he saw them he shouted, 'Get out, you rude boys! Can't you see I'm talking on the telephone?'"

I later read the account of the dungeon in Brereton's history of the Gordonstoun estate, "a most nasty dark vault with an iron grate having neither door, window, or chimney, where (the prisoner) lies in a cold and most miserable condition."

"The boys in Gordonstoun House claim they can still hear the moaning and the clinking of the chains on moonlit nights," Powys said with a smile .. I wasn't sure if I was being taken in or not, but I chose not to challenge his veracity. I preferred to live with the mystery. It seemed more in keeping with the man and the place.

But Powys also remembered Hahn with great affection. "He knew every boy in the school and if he saw you on the driveway, he'd always stop and talk."

It was his eccentric appearance that awed Sparrow. "The hat," he said emphatically. "The big floppy hat came down almost to his shoulders like one of those weirdo French artists. And he always wore it out of doors even on rainy days. He had sunstroke, you know, and couldn't stand the sun. His head was huge. And his face was so pale. Shiny-like. You felt it would glow in the dark. Really spooky. Not the sort of man you'd care to meet at night out on the moors."

"The last thing Hahn did every night was to drive out to the watch-tower," Sparrow continued, caught up in the telling of his story. "He used to jog along the trail above the cliffs for half an hour before turning in. I met him one night when I was on coast watch duty. It was really unnerving, this big man coming at me out of the dark. Running." Swallow caught his breath.

"You must have nearly swallowed your tongue, Swallow," I joked emphasizing the "swallows."

He hesitated, then retorted, "A pun, sir: is the lowest form of humor, As an English teacher you should know that, sir," emphasizing the "sir."

"Have another biscuit." I shoved the plate of MacVitie's Hobnobs toward him.

"He was constantly on the move," Roy McComish told me. McComish was a handsome man, insightful and artistically talented, a great cartoonist, and the housemaster of Gordonstoun House. He went on to be a successful headmaster. "You never knew when he would step into a classroom or a dormitory. 'The job of a headmaster is to walk around,' Hahn would day. He had an uncanny ability to sniff out problems and know when someone was in trouble, boys and teachers alike. He was intuitive really. He had a woman's intuition.

"When he was here the school was in a constant state of high alert. 'I'm an old man in a . hurry,' Hahn would say. He traveled a lot, and when he returned you could feel the electricity when he drove through the gate," McComish laughed.

There were varied opinions among the masters. I spoke to Hill, who was something of a polymath, teaching mathematics, French and a section of English. I told him that I was surprised to see how low the academic standards were. "It's all Hahn's fault," he replied. "He hired this bunch of characters, who had great life experience but knew nothing about teaching." I wondered if he included me in his opinionated outburst, and quickly changed the subject.

On another occassion with McComish he told me, "You know the real genius of Hahn was his sense of moral purpose. He had the ability to detect amoral imperative in every activity, and he had the imagination to create activities that demonstrated moral principles. For instance,he banned soccer because he heard that coaches instructed the players to go for the man instead of the ball. It was contrary to the ideal of sportsmanship.

"At one of our track meets with a county school the other boys didn't have track shoes and ran in their bare feet. When Hahn saw this he made the Gordonstoun boys take off their shoes and rerun the meet," McComish explained.

It was the barber in Elgin who summed up Hahn best. "He could read your mind," he told me as I sat in the leather chair having my hair cut. "He could always tell when I was worried and he was the sort of man you could discuss your problems with. And he never forgot a name. Would always ask after my wife and kiddies. If they were sick he'd tell me what I must do for them. A real gentleman he was, sir. You'd never know he was a German." The barber had been wounded in the war and still carried the scars of the harrowing experience.

My colleague Campbell invited me over for a glass of sherry one evening and we discussed Hahn. "Hahn had amazing charisma, the ability to attract the famous and the rich. There was a constant stream of visitors to the school. Royalty, and ex-royalty from former monarchies, wealthy plutocrats, business men and aristocrats, famous authors, well known mountaineers and sailors, the hierarchy of church and state. You never knew who would show up next," and Campbell went on to tell the story of one master who was away for the week-end and returned a day early. He had probably stopped off at the local pub for a last pint. Coming into his room in the dark the master turned on the light and found someone in his bed.

"Hey, you're in my bed," the master told the intruder.

"But I'm a visitor," the uncertain voice replied.

"I don't care if you're the Archishop of Canterbury," the irate master said, "get out of my bed."

The elderly gentleman struggled up in his pajamas and humbly complied. When he stepped into the light the master saw that it was the Archbishop of Canterbury. He had come to visit; and.Hahn had kept him up so late talking after dinner that he asked him to stay over.

"We have plenty of room," Hahn had offered and found him an empty bed.

"Brilliant he was, eccentric for sure, but above all great," Prince Philip said in tribute to his old headmaster.

After a time Hahn's rhetoric, born out of defiance and exile, began to resonate with me. I too began to feel I was being caught up in a moral crusade, a romantic idea that I carried with me into my career in Outward Bound.

But I had yet to see how it would bear up in practice.

Chapter 52: Cairngorms

"What do you see in mountaineering?" Henry Brereton, the headmaster of Gordonstoun School, scrutinized me with a wise owl look, gazing through thick horn-rimmed glasses. The emphasis was on "see." What sort of question was that? As always with the avuncular older man I wondered what was the question behind the question? Was he asking why did I climb mountains? Because they were there? But that sounded too glib. What did he mean by "see?" Looking outward? Or looking inward? English usage left the question a certain ambiguity. I was a young novice teacher who had been hired not on my academic credentials but because I climbed mountains and on most weekends through the fall and early winter of 1955 I had hiked and expeditioned with Gordonstoun boys. Brereton had called me in for an end of term progress review.

The Cairngorms, the rounded, brooding, windswept, cloud enshrouded mountains of northern Scotland were less than fifty miles from the school. It was a drive of an hour and a half on back country roads.

"Would you join us for a day-hike?" Swallow, the Duffus House color bearer invited me. We rose at five, still dark and cooked the breakfast that Mrs. MacIntyre, the house matron, had laid out for us: oatmeal, eggs on toast we fried in bacon grease, jam and tea. Swallow, as a senior boy had permission to drive the school car, a reconditioned London taxi, and we arrived at Glenmore Lodge soon after first light on an early October morning.

The mountains were obscured by the blowing rain as we picked up the path through the forest. The trees had been replanted recently with larch and fir in even rows, a recent reforestation project. They were all the same height; Euclidian symmetry imposed on the random wildness. The summits lost in the mist as we headed up into the Lairig Ghru, a narrow glaciated valley with high granite crags on either side, dour and dark obscured by the storm. It rained with steady Britannic persistence and filtered into my clothes. I cowered further into my anorak which was not waterproof as the label claimed and pulled the hood tighter around my head. I plodded on in silence, in my own world of thought and discomfort.

"This is mountaineering in Scotland for you sir," Swallow muttered. He seemed apologetic for bringing me out on such a day. It was my first Gordonstoun expedition. "But if you waited for good weather, you'd never get out of bed," he added and set a fast pace and we were soon warm. The boys began to chat and laugh. They too seemed to be shaking off the shackles of school routine, joking about the eccentricities of their teachers. Not a word of complaint about the weather. Buoyed by their good spirits, I too began to emerge snail-like from the shell of my damp day despond. Emerging above the tree line an hour later the temperature dropped with the growing force of the north-west gale. But the wind was on our back and we pressed on with no hesitation.

At the Pools of Dee we reached an historical watershed. The main stream ran north away from us down to the River Dee and Aberdeen, "the mouth of the Dee." We left the lush meadow and bracken of the valley and struck up for the ridge, a blurred outline through blown curtains of rain. Armour-Brown led over steep grass and scree. Breathing came harder and the chatter stopped.

Jones and Swallow lagged behind, stopping to catch their breath. Then barged ahead to catch up, breathing hard. I moved up and joined them. "Slow is fast," I told Swallow. "Like the tortoise. Not like a bird, swallow."

"Sir!" he groaned, gasping for breath. "Not that pun again."

"You need to develop a rhythm," I said, "like this." I began to hum and started to plod slowly uphill. Beethoven's Sixth Symphony "The Pastoral" has a joyous passage, the shepherd's song after the thunder storm, that is light and rollicking to the count of three. "Just take a step on every third beat," and I choreographed the dance. He followed in my steps, picked up the rhythm and we waltzed up the hill.

Jones joined the chorus line with a broad grin. "Beethoven in the bracken sir. Fantastic."

Climbing higher the wind intensified, tugging at our clothes. My hands lost their feeling for I had not thought to bring gloves and my anorak had only a single pocket across the chest. It was getting more severe than I had expected, I thought. Linnae, a Norwegian boy, seemed to be the outsider and a loner and had not joined in the banter but he trudged on, the quiet determined stoic. Armour-Brown was in Gordonstoun House and didn't know the other boys very well. He too was silent which was not a good sign, but he too persevered uncomplaining: Do we turn back? I wondered. And when? And who would make the decision? But nobody suggested it and doggedly we went on, our backs still to the wind,

How much further? Higher up it began to hail, small stinging granules that pelted my face when I turned to check on the boys behind, stinging my eyes. And the mist closed in. Visibility now less than a hundred feet Swallow navigated by compass holding it in his bare cold hands. I began to sweat from the exertion inside my gear. What kept the rain out now kept my sweat in, the climbers dilemma. It came as a surprise when the slope leveled and we stood on flat ground by the Summit cairn of Ben McDhuie, a rubble of broken stones covered in lichen. There was not great sense of triumph, merely one of relief. It had taken us four hours from when we left the car.

We turned to face the wind battling our way down the ridge. I staggered to keep my balance hopping over the wet surface of the rocks. A cold mocking sun struggled to emerge through the cloud. Halfway down, we huddled briefly in a Sheppard's stone hut to nibble on cheese, jam sandwiches and chocolate, then moved on rapidly. Only when we had gained the shelter of the trees, were we able to walk the chill out of our shivering bodies. I glanced back at the cloud scudding across the ridge, it seemed so picturesque it was difficult to recall the bitterness of its blast.

"Fair is foul; foul is fouler," Davis said. He played the part of one of the witches in the opening in the opening scene of Macbeth being rehearsed back at school. The boys came alive again, ecstatic, recalling their trying ordeals with the bravado of veterans.

"Did you enjoy it?" I asked Jones back in the car.

"Oh yes sir, except at the time."

Both Swallow and I were planning our next expedition. It was the first time I had been in the mountains with a group of school boys, my introduction to a lifetime profession in adventure education. It also established my reputation at the school. Word got out that, "Nold was keen." And both boys and faculty began to invite me to joint their expeditions, and later to organize and lead expeditions for them. I had come into my own. This was my niche. And it led to a series of spectacular outings that tested the metal, not only of the boys but of myself as well. Like Ishmael in Moby Dick, whenever I felt it was a dark November in my soul, I went on another expedition.

Day dawned in deep russet purple under alto-cumulus, the sky lightening to the red of shepherd's warning, and softening to pastel pink and yellow, the blue sky eventually showing though the dissolving cloud. With early fall, there was a hoar frost veneer on the grass and leaves of birches, chestnuts and oak, turning yellow, orange and brown. The crisp air was clean and cold to taste.

George Campbell, the geography teacher, had organized a field trip for his students the following weekend. On the hike up Glen Feshie he explained the geology. With the broad sweeping gesture of a tour guide he pointed to the high ridges. "Before Europe even emerged from beneath the ocean this was once a mountain range that stretched to Norway. It was as high and as jagged as the Alps." Scoured by millennia of glaciers, the summits had been rounded off, the valleys gouged into a broad U-shape by rock and ice. "Precambrian, some of the oldest rock on earth," Campbell added as he grasped a rough piece of rock and demonstrated the embedded quartz and mica. He compared it to the tighter grains of schist, "Metamorphosed by heat and the pressure of weight." Each of us collected our samples, talismans of past eons. I was entranced not so much by the texture and structure of the rock as by the mystery of time, geological time that transcended not only human time, but the very concept of human time, the thought that my atoms emerged from these atoms, a different vision of creation.

We ascended to the ridge up a modestly steep snow gully. Halfway up, Kennedy, a young thirteen year old looked down at the uninterrupted sweep and froze in his tracks. It was his first time on a high snow field. Acrophobia. I slid down to him, skiing in my boots and stopped at his side. "Don't look down," I held him lightly by the elbow, "and just kick steps hard into the snow." He took a step tentative at first, then another, gradually gaining confidence, he stomped his way up kicking with a storm trooper vengeance and emerged at the top elated. He could have summated Everest.

"Well, it was his Everest in a sense," Campbell commented later. Returning over Meall Dubhag 3268 feet, Kennedy danced down the slope like the other twelve boys. Back at the bus he was eager to know when the next expedition would be. I recalled a passage from Hahn, "Allow a boy to engage in enterprises from which he will fail. Teach him to overcome defeat."

"It's a scientific expedition sir," Powys the helper in Duffus House told me as he invited me to join him and five other boys the following weekend. Field studies projects were required in both A-levels advanced biology and geography. We organized and equipped after classes Friday and didn't get off until six thirty in the evening. We began to hike at dark but put our flashlight away as the moon rose over the mountains to the east. It was the full moon of October. With the light dusting of new snow it cast an unearthly glow and long shadows off the trees. At bends on the trail we walked on each other's shadow. The elk were' rutting, the stags 'bellowing and groaning in their passion, an eerily moaning, an unnerving sound.

Dobson was anxious. "Is it safe to go on?" he questioned. We weren't sure, but there was no turning back. It was midnight before we camped and after a hurried supper of cold corned beef on viscous bakery bread squeezed into wads of compacted dough by the jostling of our packs and a cup of hot sweet tea, we turned in for a night of disturbed dreams.

On Saturday Zaphadoupolos did the cartography, mapping the research area. Wilkinson made weather observations, and took temperature readings. Each boy collected rocks, moss, plant specimens. In the afternoon we crept up the valley. stealthily to count the elk herd, but their spy network was more effective than ours, and they kept moving further afield. Dobson made a very presentable sketch of the valley.

Zaph, wanting to get a better angle for his cartographic sighting, climbed an exposed crag, and freaked out halfway up. But he was ably "rescued" by Powys and Jones who coached him down. Zaph told us later he thought he was going to faint and had visions of falling. I wondered if getting themselves out of difficulties they should not have been in the first place was characteristic of Gordonstoun boys.

We prepared dinner over a Primus stove at four o'clock. I kept a wary eye on the pot, having had my fill of mountaineer's burned macaroni. Meanwhile Dobson nurtured a flickering fire of dry peat which he had dug from the bog beside the lake with his ice axe. We huddled around the fire, primitive ritual, rotating back to front, well roasted on one side, frigid on the other, before turning in for another cold night. The boys sleeping bags were inadequate for early winter conditions.

On Sunday we climbed Loch Einig, post-holing through two feet of new fallen snow along the ridge to reach the summit. We met other Gordonstoun parties, over fifty of our students being out in the mountains this weekend.

On the way out to the car we had to cross a stream to regain the trail. At a bend where it narrowed and deepened, Powys found a heavy plank on the bank that was evidently used to get across. He picked up one end, I the other and we heaved. My timing was off and I slipped, lost my balance and fell in up to waist, much to the hilarity of the boys.

Douglas-Hamilton was not on this expedition, but it was a similar experience that fanned his interest in wildlife study, and he went on to be one of the world's experts on elephants in Kenya. This is what Hahn meant by helping a boy discover his grand passion.

Guy Fawkes Day commemorates a bungled attempt to blow up the houses of Parliament on November 5, 1605. The English celebrate the occasion with fireworks and burring of the culprit in effigy. It was popular with kids, like Halloween in Canada. Campbell had the idea of organizing an expedition for younger boys to celebrate the event and invited me. From the start I sensed difficulties. The students were all new boys coming from different houses. They did not know each other well and had little group cohesion. We were meant to leave early Saturday morning but by the time we had sorted gear and provisioned it was ten thirty before we took off. The drive was a long one, ninety five miles around the Cairngorms to Dewie Lodge. We doddled over lunch, another delay, so it was four thirty before we were on the trail. November is already the season of long nights in Scotland, latitude 57 degrees north, parallel to the southern end of Hudson's Bay.

Following the narrow footpath up the valley of the Dee, night settled on a murky, overcast night, and it was soon so dark we couldn't see the trail. Campbell in the lead had a flashlight, but the rest of us stumbled along, stumbling over stones and catching our knees in deep heather when we lost the trail. Our destination was a bothy, an ancient shepherd's stone cottage, now converted to a backcountry shelter. It was clearly indicated on the map, but Campbell had never been there before. I worried could we find it in the dark? The boys were uneasy. "Are we almost there, sir?" Campbell was noncommittal. Then a faint flicker of light appeared out of the gloom, a mile up the valley. Fortunately there were other visitors or we may never have found it.

But it was on the other side of the river Dee. The map indicated a river crossing. What we found was a cable foot bridge with one line for the feet, another above for hands. The trick was to lean one's weight forward and shuffle sideways. The boys had done this several times on the obstacle course at school but never with thirty pound packs, in the dark. Anderson, a long, lean, lanky lad, who was not very well coordinated, leaned back, his feet shot forward, he catapulted back, and he fell into the flowing stream complete with backpack and full kit. Grabbing hold of the lower cable before being swept away, he waded safely to the opposite shore. Given that cautionary demonstration on how not to do it, the rest of us crossed safely.

Then in our haste to get to the bothy, a boy with the flashlight led off into the dark. "Slow down!" we shouted. Simultaneously Jones tripped and fell flat on his face in a bog, wallowing in six inches of mud, slime, and murky water.

And so we arrived, "Two bods drenched," the boys laughed. They stripped their wet clothes before the stove. The rest of us shared our spare clothes so they could warm up and began the long process of drying out. Canned beef stew and gourmet noodles revived spirit. And I was ready to turn in. But Campbell was irrepressible. He had brought fireworks and they all trucked out to witness the display. I boycotted the event. A poor sport, I turned in early feeling it as all inappropriate expedition behavior.

We were off late the next morning, the boys straggled out as we hiked over the ride, Campbell lagging behind. I was disgruntled, impatient with the delays, the lack of leadership and barged ahead of the group on the excuse that I would prepare tea for them when they returned to the car, which I did.

On later reflection I became aware of that judgmental uncompromising side which would get me into difficulty often in my life.

"What about a Duffus House expedition ?" Godfrey Burkhart, my housemaster asked. I felt his request a vote of confidence. Powys and Sparrow did most of the organizing. My job was to drive the bus. It was a mix of senior and junior boys. Godfrey booked a bothy, a stone cottage in Colymbridge, and after dinner we spent a cheerful evening singing and telling stories cuddled in our sleeping bags around the stove. Once the fire burned down it was cold, the damp seeping out of the stone walls. MacTier, in a lightweight bag, shivered and sighed half the night, until two boys bunched up around him, one on each side sharing their body heat. I thought of Kurt Hahn picking up the Baltic Sea fisherman who had rescued his comrades and warmed them with the heat of their bodies and I, in the morning told the boys the story.

The next day was a great success. I led the junior boys on an easy up Faieill Ridge to the summit of Cairngorm. Baxter, one of the young stalwarts ran the whole way down. The seniors with Brinton, the only American at Gordonstoun, his father an executive with Coca-Cola Europe, and Ian of the Douglas-Hamilton clan, did a long climb over Ben McDhuie, not returning until after dusk. On the way back to school the bus ran out of gas a mile from the gate and they boys hiked the last leg, a joyous singing entrance to Duffus House. I was able to stop a car and get fuel, but then found the battery dead. So the vehicle was picked up next morning by Hunters, the school mechanic and driver.

Gordonstoun prided itself on it intentional diversity. Next week's climbing party was typical. Taylor, a Scot from Glasgow, Horty, whose grandfather has been the pre-war dictator of Hungary, and other "colonials," Powys, Kenyan, Dart, another master from Australia and myself, Canadian. Art was an older man in his fifties, not all that fit, so we walked the old ladies trail to the top of Cairngorm. We chatted amiably as the boys shot ahead. He was visiting from Greelong Grammar School. Australia's elite public school, where he was director of studies. He told me of "Timbertops," their mountain campus, where the sixteen year olds spend the academic year in a program modeled on Gordonstoun. He was a great storyteller, and on the way back in the car he entertained us with his World War II experiences where he was landed on a remote Pacific island with a radio to report on Japanese shipping and airplane movement.

The week before, doing night inspection of a boy's dormitory after dark, a senior boy bumped into him. "You filthy swine," the boy said, "you've been smoking!" and swatted him with an open hand and knocked him onto one of the beds. Realizing who it was too late, he apologized profusely and reported his rude conduct to his housemaster. Proper restitution was made, a long silent walk to the Michal Kirk in the woods, and the boys added another story to their collection of eccentric teachers.

Gordonstoun School was elitist by definition. But Hahn had a missionary's zeal to promote his ideas so they would have a wider following. He saw the need to come up with a program that complemented existing institutions that could be offered by schools, youth clubs, the Boy Scouts. He devised a program that set standard for young people to strive for in four different areas: fitness, an adventurous expedition, a creative project wither cultural or scientific, and service involvement. He called it the Moray Badge Scheme named after the local county. Later HRH Prince Philip would adopt the project and it was renamed, "The Duke of Edinburgh Award Scheme," the Prince's tribute to his old headmaster.

Gordonstoun boys competed for the award. Five boys were ready for their fifteen mile expedition, another international contingent: Kunheim from Munich, Hennessy Junior, English born in India, Maltzahn, an Austrian now living in Paris, Kinwell English, and Mungall a Scot. They needed a driver and knew who to ask. They told me the route over Cairngorm to the Shelter Stone, new country for me and I was intrigued. Their organization was somewhat haphazard, which was often the case when boys came from different houses so we were slow getting off.

We didn't arrive at Glenmore Lodge until well after lunch. I suppressed my misgiving knowing that in mid-November it would be dark by five o'clock. The route to the summit of Cairngorm was straight forward on a well trodden path clearly visible even in the new fallen snow. But beyond that it was not well defined and Kunheim took compass bearings. But even the compass was not that reliable as the rock creates a magnetic variation in some locations. Not confident of themselves or of each other they conferred endlessly finding it difficult to make a group decision. Unwilling to accept Kunheim's lead they went off route.

We traversed the mountain in the dark, the soft snow making for uncertain footing but a faint glow came off the snow and descending we could see enough to be able to skirt the crags which were silhouetted against the mountains. We reached the valley of the Dee safely but the Shelter Stone, our proposed campsite, evaded us. The guidebook described it as a huge granite block that had broken off the crags above and crated a natural cave. We split up, three of us going upstream, three down and searched about among the house-size boulders looking for one with a cellar.

Mungall made the find. "Lucky we brought a Scot along," Kingwell , the Englishman, said.

We crawled in one at a time to inspect. It was about twenty feet long and five feet wide, We crouched under the four foot ceiling. The side facing out had been banked up with rocks and moss. It didn't quite meet the guidebook description but we were out of the wind and so far it had not rained. Disorganized but with the minimum of grumbling we squeezed in and sorted out sleeping spaces. Some previous tenant had had the grace to line the floor with a carpet of moss. "All the comforts of a caveman's home." Maltzan had not lost his sense of humor.

Mungall and Hennessey set the primus stove purring while the rest of us snuggled into our sleeping bags. With soup, canned stew, tea and biscuits life assumed a semblance of domesticity. Through the long evening, the boys told storied, joked, the light of a single candle casting long shadows against the rock. The scene had a haunting, primordial feel, somehow familiar, reminiscent of a cave dwellers past in our ancestral origins, thrilling in its primitive simplicity. Emerging for the last night bladder rituals, the moon broke through the clouds, three quarters full, flashing off the grim crags that stood above us, and the snow slopes above, with beautiful forbidding mysterium tremendum.

Next morning we discovered the true Shelter Stone, a hundred yards down river, spacious by comparison, with standing room. We had lodged in the annex. The boys navigated by compass in the mist to Loc Etchacane, Lock Avon over Ben McDhuie, heavy going with overnight packs. Given the limited visibility, navigation was difficult, further hampered by magnetic disturbance from the rock, causing the compass to waver unpredictably, but they found their way down Corrie Cas, running like young antelope down the sloping meadow.

"Mountaineering in Scotland is essentially an aquatic sport, "Roy McComish, the house master of Gordonstoun House, told me. "If you wait for good weather you'll never climb." I was invited to join their expedition to be followed by their Christmas party.

I knew some of their senior boys from earlier expedition including Hinton, the only American at the school. We left early and drive through sleet, rain and hail, arriving at Glenmore Lodge soon after nine a.m. The boys chose the direct steep Faicill route and set off in the rain, heads down, necks drawn deep in to the hoods of their parka like penitent monks anonymous in their cowls. I had never set off up a mountain willingly on a day like this, but reasoned, this is Gordonstoun. The boys seem to know what they're doing. We looked up at the swirling blizzard along the ridge and barged ahead. There was no rhythm to their pace, a charge of the light brigade and I followed, finding it difficult to keep up. I'd been up late the night before writing Charismas letters and tried to catch up on my sleep dozing on the drive over.

The full force of the gale hit us as we topped the ridge with a blast of granular snow in our faces, like the stabbing of a hundred needles. Covering our faces with our mittens, we leaned into the storm. Hinton in the lead. Walking became laborious. Our wet clothes quickly froze and we were encased in ice, our anoraks like medieval knights in coats of armor. "More like the Tin Man in Oz," Hilton said later. But we were also encased in warmth the wind not penetrating, Visibility was near zero, at the rear of the line I couldn't see Hinton, but the top was not difficult to find as there was no way but up.

But we were not the first to summit that day. Three snow buntings had been caught out in the sudden onslaught and sheltered in the eddy behind the summit cairn. They looked as miserable as I felt in their barren sub-arctic shelter, the snow swirling about them. But not the boys. They were euphoric. Turning our backs to the wind, we were driven along the ridge in a hurried descent, returning to the warmth of the Norwegian hut, a large well constructed log cabin, where we sheltered and partied that night.

What do you make of expeditioning? Henry Brereton asked me at the end of term. I tried to summarize my experiences. I found the boys very fast, I told him, resilient, motivated by the challenges, helpful of each others, the older boys good leaders, competent and compassionate. The expeditions brought out the qualities Kurt Hahn talked about, and I was deeply impressed. I had become a true believer.

But what impressed me most, was something uncanny, something difficult to describe about the mountains themselves. Their age, their durability, their sense of having a past, not only a geological pest but an historic past, and prehistoric. Confident that Brereton would understand, I told him of the rutting elk in the full moon, the circular stone wind shelter built by shepherds on the high ridges, the primitive natural cave of the Shelter Stone. Often I had felt I was walking in the footsteps not only of the boys ahead of me on the trail but in the footsteps of centuries of hunters, shepherds, poachers, and fugitives who had ranged these mountains. I have rarely had such a feeling of being a part of the past.

Brereton nodded in agreement. He got up and brought a book from the high shelf behind him. It was Wordsworth's "Preludes". He turned to a well-worn page and read in a stage voice, "Oh at the time/ When on a perilous ridge I hung alone/ With what strange utterance did the loud dry wind/ Blow through my ears. The sky seemed not a sky/ Of earth, and with what motion moved the clouds…"

"You should read Wordsworth," and he loaned me the book.

Chapter 53: The Dragon's Tooth

The Matterhorn, 4,480 meters high on the Italian-Switzerland border, is the most photographed and one of the most popular mountain climbs in the Alps. I saw it first from Zermatt on the Swiss side in the summer of 1954. The Hornli Ridge curving down to the north is the tourist route, much of it a scramble over rock and scree. On the steep face steel cables have been anchored to provide protection. On a good day over 100 people crowd the summit. My climbing partner and I had looked at it scornfully, not wanting to be trampled in the hordes. We climbed Monte Rosa across the valley, 4 638 meters high instead, a peak we shared with only one other party that day.

The Matterhorn's Zmutt Ridge, however, was a different story. On the west side of the mountain, it is hunched over like a monk in a hooded cloak. The route leads up over a series of gradual steps to a steep wall that soars nearly vertical 300 meters to the summit pyramid, a daunting challenge. When I was invited to join a team to climb it two years later, I accepted with alacrity.

We were all young teachers, still in our twenties, who had taught at varying times at Gordonstoun, the famous boys' school in Scotland. The Zmutt Ridge was Andy Clelland's idea. I was looking forward to meeting him. A tall, lean, angular man, he reminded me of a weathered sheep herder I'd met in the Highlands tending a flock of hundreds with four dogs. He had climbed in the Alps as a Cambridge student and made several impressive ascents. He now taught at Anavrita in Greece, another Kurt Hahn school.

John Ray, the expedition master at Altyre House, an extension of Gordonstoun, was a friend of Andy's and suggested I be invited. He was of true Celt, medium height, thick across the chest, brown eyes, dark hair, perpetually looking as if he needed to shave. It was his first season in the Alps, but he had climbed extensively in Scotland, summer and winter.

I was the least experienced. Two summers previously I'd taken a 10-day mountaineering course in Zermatt, climbed half a dozen modest peaks, and ski toured in the Austrian Tyrol. I was also the smallest man in the group, five feet six inches, 155 pounds. One of my teachers had compared me to a French peasant with my heavy set short build and a Roman nose.

Andy was clearly our leader. I was honored to be invited, happy to follow. But none of us had anticipated the outcome.

We met in Arolla at the head of the Val d'Herens. It was at the end of the bus line, a small village of 35 families, three-story houses of wood and stone, crowded together for mutual protection, a hotel, a store with post office, and a church.

"Bon jour"

"Buon journo."

"Gros Got, God's greetings." We were welcomed at the Mont Collon Hotel as we entered the bar. It was the community center for this mountain outpost in this corner of Switzerland where French, German and Italian came together.

We pitched our tent in the campground above the village on a flat meadow with lush grass and wild flowers, fringed by pine trees, running water from a glacial stream. Across the valley the jagged peak of Dent Perroc, 3655 meters, rose above a row of sharp rock outcrops that looked like dragon's teeth.

By coincidence, the Cambridge University Climbing Club also had set up camp in the valley and Andy went over and introduced himself. With classic understatement the students pointed out the routes they had climbed, emphasizing how friable the rock was, breaking off in large flakes. Andy checked it on the map, already envisaging a climb.

Coming from sea level, we planned to spend the first three days acclimating to 2500 meters. It drizzled much of the time the first two days, but we donned our rain gear stoically and struck out, hiking high in the valley to the foot of the ridges. We returned each evening to dry out at the hotel bar. "Mountaineering is essentially an aquatic sport," Andy joked.

The two-man tent was crowded with three, and soon permeated with the smell of drying boots and sweaty socks. John preferred to sleep outside under the stars, weather permitting. But that last night the three of us were together he was driven inside by a light drizzle, deranging our well-ordered comfort. At 4:30 a.m. when we were jarred awake by the alarm, it was still raining and we all rolled over in unison and slept until 8:00.

At breakfast we sat in silence over our scorched oatmeal, sitting cross legged in the tent like disgruntled Buddhas. John mentioned that he was not feeling too well. His stomach bothered him.

Mist hung over the valley, though Andy, our weather expert as well as our climbing expert, an inveterate optimist, felt that it would clear up.

"It is my duty to be an optimist," I recalled some sage expounding. Dutifully we set off at 10:15 a.m. It was too late for a major ascent but we could reconnoiter the lower approaches to Dent Perroc.

In silence we plodded up a trail zig-zagging through the forest to the upper meadows, breathing hard. Andy set a brisk pace with his long legs. I followed, my heart pounding. John struggled, his stomach pain getting worse.

The sun shone faintly through the mist, and we stopped to take off our parkas.

We threaded our way through large broken boulders, crossed a lateral moraine, headed up a steep couloir and reached the ridge where we stopped for lunch.

Andy and I bolted down bread and cheese, an apple, chocolate and we resumed the climb. John didn't have anything to eat and half an hour later he spoke up.

"Sorry fellows, I've got to turn back."

Andy suggested we all turn back, but John insisted that he would be all right descending alone. I'd been faced with this dilemma before. Was it acceptable to go on? Or wiser to turn back?

"What do you think, Joe?" Andy asked.

I wanted to keep going. "I think it would be O.K. for John to go down by himself ...if he says so." I said.

Andy suggested a compromise that we wait where we were until we saw that John was safely down the couloir, then go on. Agreed.

Half an hour later we saw John at the foot of the couloir and pushed on. Andy led at a fast pace. Too fast I felt, but said nothing. It was now 2 p.m., and I figured it was still two hours to the top. I wondered how far we should go, and began to have second thoughts about turning back with John. Again I said nothing.

The ridge was not particularly steep to climb though it did drop off precipitously on either side. We scrambled, occasionally having to use our hands for balance. But the rock was very loose and broken up in places. One large flat slab tilted slightly when I stepped on it and I scuttled over it hastily like a crab. I wondered if we should rope up. But that would slow us down, I rationalized.

Higher up a stone block 12 feet high towered over the ridge, one of the dragon's teeth we had seen from the valley. Could we climb it directly? Or would we skirt it below? Andy went ahead to explore. He heaved himself up on a rock about the size of a refrigerator for a closer look. Not finding a way up, he backed down. As he did so he stooped and pulled back on the rock he was standing on.

And it gave way in his hands and nudged him off the ridge.

I looked up when I heard the slow grating of rock over rock, as if the mountain were growling.

"Oh Joe," Andy said, with deep sadness. A moment of profound regret and quiet grief. No panic. No screaming. Only despair.

The rock pushed him backwards and he fell. Then bounced. The rock came down on him, and the two continued to bounce, in an avalanche of falling rock, that made a thunderous roar and sent up a cloud of gray dust. He came to rest eventually in a gully 250 meters below and did not move.

I was two meters away, confused, disoriented, dumbfounded. I felt the whole mountain about to go and was surprised that I stood there on solid rock still. My next reaction was unbelief. This couldn't happen to Andy. He was the leader. This didn't happen to leaders.

Then I prayed, pleaded really. Not to God particularly, but to some Divine Presence out there. "Don't let him die." But I knew otherwise and shuddered. Then I pleaded for myself. "How do I get off the mountain alive?"

"Pull yourself together, Nold," I said out loud. My voice gave me equilibrium in a world turned upside down.

A voice called from the valley below, John. I shouted back, "Andy fell!" Several times. But we were too far apart to understand each other and it became a distraction. I needed to focus on my own predicament.

255

I was torn between getting off the mountain myself and a sense of duty to check on Andy. I couldn't just leave him there.

How do I get down to him? The couloir below looked treacherous, lined with loose rock. If triggered it could dislodge another rock avalanche. The initial step, getting off the ridge, was the most difficult. I was carrying the team's climbing rope and set up a rappel and lowered myself safely over the steep edge. Then I worked my way down steep scree, rappelled again off a smooth nearly vertical slab, and slowly descended. At times I lost sight of Andy's body, but a trail of blood and the spattering of what looked like brain tissue, flagged the way. It was a descent into hell.

The limp body lay sprawled horizontally across the slope where it had rolled to a stop.

"Andy!" I shouted, hoping for at least a groan in response. There was none.

When I approached I saw his chest was extended, as if pushed out by broken ribs. I pressed my ear to his body searching for a heart beat. None.

I felt for a pulse on his wrist, again found nothing. Though in my state of agitation I doubt if I could have detected it, even had there been one. I removed his watch. The lens was shattered, the hands stopped at 3:17.

Andy's head was face up, one eye closed, the other staring vacantly into the sky. His nose was pushed to one side, covered in blood. There was a deep gash on his forehead. I pulled a wool sweater from his day pack, a coarse Norwegian knit, a checkered black and white design with a red trim. I draped it lightly over his face, a shroud.

I felt the need to vomit, so I sat down out of sight of the body. A wave of sadness swept over me. I felt I would drown in sadness. It wasn't just for Andy. I had only known him for three days. I grieved also for Pat, a close friend killed in a ROTC training exercise only three years before. But this was different. Here was death staring at me with one eye askew. This was the first time I had confronted death face to face, in the flesh.

The burden of death is cumulative and I was hit by the fact of my own mortality. It wasn't as if I went through life believing that it could never happen to me. I believed it could. Like my parents, I would die young. That was why I was determined to live as fully as I could. Mountaineering was part of that.

Shouts came from the valley and I started down. I met John who waited below and described the accident as best I could. He saw me safely off the mountain. In spite of his stomach pain, he agreed to take over, to make the necessary official arrangements, to contact Andy's family and the school. Cloud settled in the valley and I headed for our tent. I needed to be alone.

Local guides brought Andy's body off the mountain assisted by members of the Cambridge Climbing Club. An undertaker from the lower village made the battered body presentable for a funeral. But I was appalled by the gross distortion of the face in spite of his best efforts. It was unrecognizable as Andy, and when his father arrived the next day I encouraged him not to open the casket.

How to make sense of a son's death to a grieving father? How to make sense of it to myself? I read Dylan Thomas's brave poem, "And death shall have no dominion." But I was not too sure. I lay awake most of the night.

Next morning I walked with Mr. Clelland to the high meadows and looked across at the toothed ridge of Dent Perroc. The black jagged rock looked fierce and threatening, uninviting.

"Why would he want to climb that?" Andy's father asked. I didn't have a good answer and could only explain how the accident happened.

I tried to convey that climbing mountains was more than conquering peaks. We stood atop a rocky outcrop, looking down on the village set among high peaks and glaciers, and I felt he caught the majesty of it, that god-like vision of the world, the sense of awe and oneness.

The alpine flowers were still in bloom in early August, yellow daisies, purple gentians, wine red primulas, blue forget-me-nots and irises. Mr. Clelland was a gardener and collected plants to take back to his garden in Scotland. "They are beautiful," he said, "but poor recompense for the loss of a son."

The village gathered for the funeral, the men in their best woolen britches with knee stockings, grey jackets trimmed with green and silver buttons, peaked alpine hats. The women wore black skirts with a bright floral pattern, white lace kerchiefs on their heads. That morning girls had gone high to the rocky slopes to collect edelweiss and made a wreath which they placed on the coffin. The village priest officiated.

A slim man in a tweed suit stood tall above the crowd with a military erectness and balding head. "Look John, it's Mr. Chew," I said. He was the headmaster of Altyre House, where Andy and John had both taught. Beside him was a short, handsome middle-aged woman. We met her later, Eva Hahn, Kurt Hahn's niece and secretary. They had come to represent the school family.

Six young men from the Cambridge Climbing Club joined John and me as pall bearers. The church bell tolled mournfully, echoing through the valley as we led the procession up the hill to the Protestant cemetery.

"From dust, to dust," the priest intoned as the wooden coffin was lowered into the ground, and he sprinkled a hand full of dirt over the coffin. Then the grave-digger siezed his shovel and hurled gravel and rocks from the dirt pile onto the coffin. It reverberated like thunder as if to awaken the dead and caution the living of the fragility of life. Startled, I heard again the rock avalanche of two days previous and shuddered.

It was the final knell. Our friend was gone.

After the funeral we had lunch with Mr. Chew. He discussed the tragedy factually, asking questions, as if conducting an accident review. But when he got up to catch his bus, he said, "Well, what do you plan to climb next?"

John and I did climb a couple more days, ascended Pigne d'Arolla, crossed over Col Bertol, and descended the Zmutt Glacier looking up at the ridge we had come to climb. But John was drained, physically and spiritually, and at Zermatt we parted.

I never did climb the Matterhorn. But five months later I met a young woman who had. Her name was Andy. And she consented to marry me.

In the Alps, summer 1954, climbing from Zermatt.

Chapter 54: London Cloud

"What are you doing about Art?" the Principal asked, clearing his voice and drawing heavily on his pipe.

"I don't know anything about teaching art," I demurred.

This was my weekly conference with Mr. Selfredge, the Principal Teacher of the Pentonville Street Primary School in the East End of London. Down the street two blocks away was the Pentonville Street Prison that had the dubious distinction of being the last place in England where a man was put to death by hanging.

Teaching was still an avocation for me, rather than a serious profession, a means of immersing myself in a foreign culture and financing my travels. A young Canadian abroad, three years out of law school in 1956, I had taught sixth grade in a small private school in the suburbs of London, and the ninth grade in an elite boarding school on the coast of Scotland, where they valued me more for my mountaineering skills, than my intellectual acumen. I was between jobs, marking time before traveling overland to India to my next teaching post. The London County Council Board of Education, had hired me as a "temp". a I had never taught second grade, certainly not in the slums of London. This was real cultural immersion.

Mr.Selfridge, the Principal, was baffled by me. "What brings a Gordonstoun master to teach here?" I explained my situation, that I planned to move on in a couple months. In the meantime I needed work. "Fair enough," he was satisfied, and seemed genuinely pleased that I had showed up, even if only for two months. I confessed to having no experience teaching second graders.

"Here's what you do." In an English school, I was to learn, the principal is the Principal Teacher, an educational leader who guides and supervises curriculum and instruction, and not merely the one who deals with the politics of the central bureaucracy and the complaints of parents. He took me through the routine protocol of taking attendance, recording students progress, distributing milk at the mid-morning break, a carry over from the post-war Labour government where every child got a half-pint of milk each day.

He became the master teacher. I the willing apprentice.

Arithmetic was straight forward, addition and subtraction, beginning multiplication and division. When it came to problems like: "You buy two candy bars for four pence, a newspaper for your father for a shilling, fish and chips for two shilling and six pence, and pay with a one pound note. How much change do you get?" They figured out the complexities of British currency, twelve pence to a shilling, twenty shillings to the pound, on the abacus of their fingers in an instant. No one was going to "diddle" them. But when it came to the more abstract complexities of the decimal system, carrying the ten to the next column, they would falter.

Each week Mr. Selfridge covered another subject." Writing is important. They need to learn to express themselves. Have them write something every day, just a couple lines in a journal." This was before writing memoirs had become popular. "And they should keep a record of words they can't spell. You spell it for them. Have them write it down in their own private dictionary."

A novel, brilliant idea I thought. No wonder this was the land of Dickens and Shakespeare. And I became a teacher of writing.

"How do you spell skites," Robert asked me one morning.

"Skites Robert? There's no such word as skites."

"Ow, you now sah, like in rowlla-skites." Robert wrote four sentences that day extolling the thrill of his new roller skates.

The children would crowd about my desk, in quest of their word, so tightly it became suffocating. The stench of urine at times overwhelming. But they craved human contact, nudging, touching.. "Ma'am, how do you spell...woops" Betsy giggled, put her hand over her mouth, "I mean sir, Sir."

Occasionally one of the boys would call me "Mom," and be even more embarrassed. I was drawn in by their open love and affection, to my surprise, a child's affection that I was not to know until I had my own children.

A dreary neighborhood of gray stone buildings, smoke stained brick, two, three stories high, slate roofs, the buildings close to each other leaning on each other, windows discreetly curtained off, permitting seeing out, screening out seeing in. Walking the last three blocks each morning from the tube, the London subway, I always had the uncomfortable feeling of being watched. I felt embarrassed when my welcoming party greeted me, seven screaming children who ran down the sidewalk to greet me. They escorted me to school, three holding each hand, another carrying my homework satchel.

The neighborhood may have been drab, but the children, the first post war generation, had spontaneity, joy, cheek, like the Beatles must have been as children, that gave one faith in a brighter day, a zest for living, the indomitableness of the British spirit, Winston Churchill had extolled. Not only would they survive, they would thrive. And I was "Sir", the Canadian school master, whom they had taken to their hearts.

They would spot me each morning as I emerged from the Tube, the London subway, a block away, and come running down the street, my private paparazzi, as if greeting royalty. I felt embarrassed walking through the bleak neighborhood of three story smoke darkened brick row houses, leaning shoulder to shoulder into each other, three steps leading up to the front door, windows discreetly curtained. I always had the feeling of being watched, the curtain slightly parted, drawn aside to peer out, but avoiding being seen by anyone peering in.

England had already begun to experience the wave of post war immigration from the Commonwealth in 1956. Marissa was the prettiest child in the class, a delicate little girl with big brown eyes, curly hair and a Mediterranean olive complexion,

260

recently arrived from Cyprus. She still struggled with English. Indira and Ragiv, both from India, were the brightest, and the best schooled. Roland, from Jamaica, hid behind his West Indian accent by acting the class clown.

But Jeannie was a waif. Thin, pale, gaunt, hair unkempt, clothes she had slept in disheveled. When the kitchen opened, Mrs. Bates would provide her with an unauthorized breakfast before school. Jeannie clung close to my desk, whenever she could, rubbing her arm against mine, craving closeness. One day she arrived at school totally distraught, whimpering, rubbing her eyes, tear streaks down her unwashed cheeks.

"Jeannie, what's wrong?" I put my arm around her shoulders. She felt so frail.

Sobbing, on the verge of hysteria, she said, "Last night Granny was coming out of the pub, and a car knocked her down. And...and they took her away...to the hospital." I held her by the hand and led her down to Mrs. Burkhart, the first grade teacher, a heavy set maternal woman, who knew every child in the school by their first name. She had spent thirty years of her life teaching children in the East End of London. She took Jeannie to her bosom, washed her, fed her, and returned her to my class later in the morning. Jeannie's mother had abandoned her, Mrs. Burkhart told me later. She was being raised by her grandmother, who had her own problems.

At my next in-service training session with Mr. Selfridge, he raised the question of art. "Don't worry," he assured me." They don't need instruction. Just let them express themselves. We have large sheets of art paper, and bright pastel crayons. Just have them draw big. A house or tree should be at least eighteen inches high. People at least a foot tall." Buoyed by these instructions I was launched into a new area of pedagogic expertise.

The children needed little guidance. They had been well coached in the refined techniques of post-modern impressionism by a former teacher, probably Mrs. Burkhart, when they were in the first grade. It took fifteen minutes to distribute the materials, and lower the decibel level in the art room. Once engaged the silence of creative genius prevailed. Intense concentration with occasional burst of excitement, as stick figures kicking footballs, balloons floating off into dazzling skies, the whirling of playground swings filled the paper. Lots of brilliantly colored houses with seaside vistas.

Jeannie had her own set formula, something unique, three big dolls, larger that the requisite twelve inches tall, standing rigidly erect, like wall figures in an Egyptian tomb, except that they were front facing, holding hands, and smiling. An Orphan Annie smile. She did the same drawing every week, varying only the color combination to suit her mood. And she was very good at it, always the first to be done.

Once the children were underway, absorbed in creative endeavor, I dabbled in my own studio piece. Bowls of fruit, mixing reds and yellows, subtle shades of apricot and pink, outlined in black, like a Cezanne; waving trees and storm streaked skies, like Van Gogh. And Jeannie, when she was done would come over and admire my work, a patroness of my creative genius.

One day I attempted a more ambitious mountain scene. A Matterhorn like peak in the top right hand corner, a brown wooden alpine hut lower left, with a curving S shaped trail leading the eye into the master piece. I was working on a deep blue sky, and had left an oval shaped blank space, not yet colored in.

Then Jeannie sidled up. "What's that sir?" she asked, pointing to the oval blank.

"That's going to be a cloud, Jeannie."

"Oh...." There was a thoughtful pause. "What will you colour it sir? Yellow?"

"No Jeannie. It's a cloud. White." I replied.

"White?" she asked. "Are clouds that color in Canada sir?"

Sure enough, when I stepped outside on my way home and looked up at the clouds. Jeannie was right. Clouds in London are yellow. This was a child who had never seen a white cloud.

Chapter 55: Crossing the Theodule Pass

During World War II allied bomber crews shot down over Italy were often picked up by the Resistance partisans and shuttled north to the frontier. From remote mountain villages like Breuil, on the south side of the Matterhorn, they were smuggled across the Theodule Pass to sanctuary in Switzerland.

I was in Breuil late August, 1956.

My plan to spend the summer vacation mountaineering in the Zermatt region, on the north side of the Matterhorn, had been interrupted by the death of a friend and the early departure of my climbing partner for home. I decided to stay on as I had arranged previously for another friend to join me. I was stranded in Zermatt for three days awaiting his arrival.

It was not a good time for me to be alone to brood. I had a friend, Marisa, in Milan only six hours away. We'd met skiing in Austria over Christmas. She was an attractive fair-haired northern Italian, Titian blond, fluent in five languages, conversant in another two, studying to be an interpreter at the University of Milan. She was a good listener, someone to whom I could unburden myself. "Simpatica."

The afternoon local train from Zermatt took me to Brig where I changed to Wagon-lit and arrived in Milan at 11:45 that night. My international ticket gave me squatter's rights to the floor of the second class waiting room where I spread my parka and tried to sleep.

At 8:00 a.m. the next morning I knocked at her family's apartment door. Europe was still rebuilding from the destruction of the war, housing was scarce and expensive, and it was not unusual for adult children to live with their parents. No one answered. I knocked again louder. The door opened across the hall, a neighbor furious at being awakened. Didn't I know it was a national holiday? he bellowed fortissimo. It was the Fiesta of the Assumption of the Virgin Mary, I deciphered without benefit of my interpreter. Or was it the Feast of the Annunciation? The family was not home, he convinced me with fervent gesticulation, a semaphore more expressive than his speech. I fled.

I had parachuted into Italy and missed my partisan rescuer.

There was little to do but play tourist without my interpreter-guide. I found the cathedral, a massive outpouring of Gothic arches and towers, crowded with the faithful. The cardinal officiated, resplendent in a red robe and jewel-bedecked golden crozier, surrounded like a mafia don by a platoon of black-hooded priests. The choir performed the grand opera of a Palestrini mass.

After service over a lunch in a tavern on the plaza, inspired by fettucini and a second glass of Chianti, I plotted my escape.

An afternoon train took me to Chatillon, a railway junction at the foot of the Alps, and a bus up the steep Val Tournache to Breuil. The combined fares came to one third of the cost of returning by train to Zermatt. I congratulated myself on the economy. I would get back by hiking over the Theodule Pass, just like an airman escaping during the war. It was already dusk when I arrived at Breuil. The south face of the Matterhorn glowed a smoky yellow in the moonlight.

Hotels built in the 1930's, fortresses of glass and stone in a style called Mussolini modern, stood sentinel on the mountainside. I tried to find a less expensive pension. "Tutto occupato," the concierge said with genuine regret, arms outstretched, palms upturned, a shrug of the shoulders.

The taverna was crowded but I found a seat at a communal refectory table next to a young man wearing climbing clothes. He was English, as I expected, Thompson, a history teacher at Magellan College School. He'd just hiked over from Zermatt that day. "It's straightforward," he assured me. Dismissively, he mumbled something about Hannibal having crossed the Alps with elephants. "With this moon you could do it at night."

"The road was a ribbon of moonlight," I recited Walter de la Mare's poem as I started up the stony path after midnight. The south face of the Cervino, the Italian name for the Matterhorn, hovered over the valley, glowing in reflected light, so bright I could have read a map. If I'd had a map.

For two hours I trudged along in a moonstruck trance. Then the moon slipped behind the west ridge in a hazy blur and I was in shadow. In another half an hour it was so dark I couldn't see the trail. And lost it. Stumbling through the rubble of fractured rock, I banged my toes, and barked my shins. So I back-tracked and found the trail again feeling the level surface underfoot, like a blind man. Then I lost it again.

Lost? How can you be lost, I thought, when this is where you want to be? Far from being frustrated, I felt it was a unique experience to be staggering about on the dark side of the Matterhorn, a mountain so rich history that it was an icon. Looking up, I could see a red light that was at the top of the ski lift on the pass. With no trail to follow I headed straight for it, stumbling uphill through a landscape of broken rock.

Soon exhausted, I sat down to rest and immediately nodded off. Wakened by the cold, I put on an extra pair of pants and a heavy sweater, and moved on in a game of blind man's buff, groping my way through the mountain's debris. Slowly the red light drew closer.

The black sky took on a hint of gray and the mountains emerged from the darkness. In the half-light I found the trail again and, re-energized, strode on to the pass above.

Dawn in the high mountains is a moment of creation. As in Genesis, the world takes shape out of darkness and void. Every moment is new as light dissolves the shadows and infuses color on the earth. The summit of the Matterhorn caught the first rays of light and flared a deep ruby pink. It turned a brighter apricot and yellow as the sun lighted the steep east face, and glared a blinding white when the sun struck the glacier. There had been a frost overnight and ice crystals glittered like sparks of silver blue.

The Theodule Pass is a great divide, not only between countries, but also between cultures and geographic zones, the worlds of the balmy south and the bracing north. I looked behind me to Italy, the mountain slopes sun-baked and parched with alpine pastures already a ripening brown. Ahead was Switzerland, a world of snow and ice, barren glaciers that clung to the mountainside, in mid-August still covered in perpetual snow. I'd have to cross these glaciers before reaching sanctuary.

The Theodule Hut, a large refuge, is perched on a high outcrop on the Swiss side of the frontier. When I arrived, climbers who had bunked there over night, were getting up. They leaned over the balcony relieving themselves on the rocks a hundred feet below into Italy. Were they making a political statement, I wondered? The sense of smell evokes memory, and for me the odor of the frontier still has the pungence of brewing coffee, frying sausage, warm bread, and a faint whiff of urine. I found a deck chair and dozed again.

Waking, I had a hurried breakfast, McVities oatmeal cookies, Emmentaler cheese, and Tobler chocolate, high energy, compact. I filled my water bottle and started down.

I was worried about crossing the glacier alone. The previous week I was climbing with John on the Pigne d'Arolla. He was in the lead, breaking trail over unbroken snow when his right leg sank through up to his thigh. Fortunately we were roped and I was able to hold him from going farther, and he backed out.

Now alone and unroped, I was in a hurry to get down the glacier before the warmth of the sun softened the snow. A track clearly stamped with boot prints wove a path through the open crevasses. In the early morning the snow was crusted from the night's frost and I descended rapidly over the hard surface.

Crevasses were everywhere. In places I could gape into the maw of the yawning pit and see blue ice thirty feet below. But it was the crevasses one couldn't see that were the greatest worry. They were covered by wind-driven snow that created the essential snow bridges, the only way to cross. But they were also unreliable, potentially dangerous. One never knew when they might give way.

The rising sun beat on my back; I welcomed its comfort and warmth for the first time in hours. But as the morning wore on, I sank in the sun-softened snow.

After two nights without much sleep I began to droop. My eyes closed and I staggered on as if sleepwalking. "Keep your eyes open!" I told myself. I had images of stumbling and falling into a crevasse.

I had read an account of a RAF pilot escaping during the war who fell into a crevasse on this same glacier, the Theodule. He came to rest on a block of ice, 20 feet down, dazed, but not seriously injured. Looked about he saw right next to him a frozen body firmly wedged in the ice, wearing the uniform of the RAF. This gave him added incentive to figure out how to get himself out. It didn't take long for him to figure out that it would be wasted effort to try to climb out vertically up the ice wall without crampons and ice axe. But if he could work his way horizontally along the bottom of the crevasse until he came to the lateral moraine on the edge he could climb out on the rock. Which he did and lived to tell his story and fly again.

It's best not to fall in, my sluggish brain cautioned me.

I could see the lateral moraine, half a mile further down, broken rock and pulverized glacial debris but solidly bedded, terra firma.

The snow was softer now. More dangerous. And I sweated under my extra pants and woolen sweater. My water bottle was empty. The snow was covered in a light dusting of grit blown off the mountain side, so eating snow was out. The moraine drew closer.

Modern man as we know him, the skilled Neolithic craftsman, the reclusive painter of the Lascaux Cave, emerged 25,000 years ago as the glaciers retreated. As I took that final step from the glacier on to the rock of the moraine, I felt I was a survivor of the last ice age.

"Some say the world will end in fire/ Some say in ice." Like Robert Frost I was ambivalent. I descended the rocky trail to the Schwartzee Hotel, stripped to the waist, spread out on the soft grass and basked in the glorious warmth of the sun. After a look back at the Matterhorn, I slept.

When I met my new climbing partner's train that afternoon, I told him of my feat. "Feat or fiasco?" he laughed. "Sounds like Charlie Chaplin crossing the Chilcoot Pass in the Klondike Gold Rush."

Chapter 56: Himalayan Honeymoon

The long curve of the Seri Glacier swept below me. In the far distance to the east, Deo Tibba rose to 20,000 feet along the Himalayan Divide. Around me was a barren waste of snow, rock and ice. In the mid-day sun, the heat waves shimmered on the glaring surface, distorting the jagged peaks, as in a hallucinatory trance. The Kulu valley, from which we had set out three days before, lay below us, lost in the haze. The sky was a chalk blue.

It was a moment when I felt I had witnessed creation, and saw the world resplendent and new, "and it was good."

We were higher than most peaks in the Alps, higher than either of us had ever climbed before. This was why I had come to teach in India.

It was more than a three-day ascent. It was the culmination of three years of climbing. Wales in 1954, Scotland and the Alps in 1955, the Alps again in 1956. And now the Himalayas in 1957. The progression seemed logical, though I knew how little experience I really had. I should have done much more climbing with mountaineers more experienced than me.

Andy had a spectacular day, ascending the Matterhorn in Switzerland the previous year, with a Swiss guide, returning to her hotel in Zermatt that same night. She had never slept in a tent.

We had met as volunteers for a Quaker relief organization in a Hungarian refugee camp outside Vienna, during the Uprising of 1956. When she told me she had climbed, and then agreed to come overland to India and marry me, I felt twice blessed. I had a loving wife and a climbing partner.

She delighted in a climbing husband. "You're a part of the Lynd family tradition," she told me. "My mother and father met on Mt. Washington."

Come summer vacation, we headed to Manaliat the upper end of the Kulu valley at the foot of the Himalayas.

We pitched the tent and collapsed in the mid-day sun. The porters stretched out on their packs and a terrific lassitude set in. The forest green Meade tent absorbed heat and we were driven out. An oppressive hush, disturbed only by the heavy breathing of the porters bore down upon us.

Then the rumble of the first avalanche. It was like a freight train approaching from a distance, passing down the valley in a thunderous roar. A cascade of hardened snow and rock slide below us kicking up a fuming cloud of white dust, a billowing sand storm of snow. It crossed the track we had ascended earlier in the day, and two of the porters would have to descend the same way later in the afternoon.

"It's right on schedule," Andy said. "Just as they said. When the sun hits the slopes at the heat of the day."

We'd been warned about avalanches. On arrival at the Sunshine Orchards Guest House, Major Banon, the local grandee and proprietor, had informed us. "It's been a heavy snow year and a late spring. The high passes to Lahoul and Spiti are still closed. Last week a train of pack mules were carried away with their two drivers."

We also met the straggling members of the 1957 Yorkshire Mountain Club Lahoul Expedition "We didn't get a single peak," Lloyd, the leader told us. "We were aiming to bag a couple 20,000ers that are still unclimbed. But the snow was waist deep and there was huge cornice build upon the ridges." Wind blown snow drifting over the ridges consolidates and just hangs there over space, ready to unload.

"Then the weather turned. It got warm. The snow began to melt and down the cornices came. The avalanches brought down the whole mountainside, down to bare rock. Our base camp was wiped out. Fortunately no one was seriously injured.

"We're packing up, heading home."

There was a long silence, like a solemn moment after prayer.

"Do you think we up for it?" Andy asked later.

I wasn't sure. I'd been in an avalanche ski touring in Austria, but nothing like this.

Banon had suggested the Solang Nal as being more accessible. "We could go take a look at it. We can always turn back," I responded, lamely.

Late afternoon a thin layer of cloud veiled the sky. We watched the two porters descend, their bodies growing smaller with the distance. They crossed the avalanche track safely and disappeared beneath the slope of the glacier.

The low susurrus of a rising wind hissed over the ice, the temperature dropped rapidly and a light dusting of snow began to fall. We put on warm wool sweaters we had bought in Austria, our wind jackets and retreated to the shelter of the tent, Andrea, Wan Gyal, our lead porter and myself.

"We'll need porters," I told Major Banonr when we began to plan the expedition.

Next morning three swarthy men with soft Mongolian features stood in our doorway. "They're Ladakhis," Banon told us, "mountain people from the north. In summer they come down to Kulu to find work.

Two of them, Wan Gyal, who sported an ear ring, and Ang Rup had been on a Japanese expedition the previous summer and inherited climbing boots and wind parkas. The third fellow, a wood carrier, knew the forest trails and would act as guide. He appeared in sandals.

"Those won't do," Banon said and sent him to get boots. He reappeared later in the morning with a battered pair of hand-me-downs, with holes in the soles and down on the heel. Later, on steep snow he took them off and crossed bare foot digging in his toes for better traction.

"They're paid five rupees a day and carry sixty pounds as well as their own food and kit," Banon established the contract.

We'd become particularly impressed with Wan Gyal.

Three of us crowded into a two man tent. It was a deep, cavernous, subterranean green gloom

"It's not as big as our double bed," Andy had said our first night out.

"Tea anyone? Sing a song of Lipton's, Lipton's TEA…" I began to sing as an attempt at bon ami. Tea drinking is a ritual and a celebration in mountains, made elaborate by the need to melt snow, then bring the water to boil (only 180 degrees Fahrenheit at 13,000 feet), and giving the tea time to steep.

While waiting, I began to open a can of powdered milk. The lid was tight and I pried away at it with the screwdriver on my Swiss army knife. I pried harder, then paused, worried that I'd bend the blade. But we must have milk in our tea. I pried once more. And the lid exploded like the cork popping off a champagne bottle. The can detonated in a cloud of fine white powder dusting the inside of the tent in a milky mist..

"Oh, Joe!" Andy gave a suffocated shout from the foggy depths of the tent.

When the air cleared, I glanced at Wan Gyal, this fearless, inexhaustible man. He was terrified. His eyes were ablaze, shining through a fine coating of white powder, like someone caught in the clutches of a creature of Tibetan-Buddhist demonology. I believe he thought we were caught in an avalanche.

Andy sneezed. "Had you let me know I would have brought a powder puff," she said, wiping off.

I laughed, and Wan Gyal saw that it was just the white sahib performing magical tricks. The world was still intact, it was all really just a colossal joke, and he broke out into convulsive laughter.

When the fog cleared enough to see, I inspected the can which I held in my hand, feeling foolish, as if caught holding the smoking gun. "Product of Denmark," it read. Hermetically sealed at the dense atmosphere of sea lever, opened at the rarified atmosphere of 13,000, it was a bomb.

We drank the tea rapidly before it cooled in our aluminum mugs. For dinner that night we had tinned Irish stew.

Food. Our plan had been to live off of what we could buy locally. We didn't have compact dehydrated light weight expedition rations. But the Yorkshire expedition had food left over which they sold to Banon and he offered to sell to us.

"What a windfall, Andy," I said as I examined the cases of British army surplus rations: tinned ham, bacon, cheese and butter, fruitcake and pudding, quantities of Irish stew, dehydrated eggs, and of course, dried milk.

"I've never eaten this well on an Expedition in Scotland or the Alps," I extolled. "It weights a ton, but we will have porters."

We supplemented this with staples from the local market. Sitting cross legged on the floor of a wooden stall, we watched the rotund proprietor measure out sugar, salt, ghur (raw unrefined sugar), and spices, on the hand held balance scale he waved above his head. We needed an extra pot. He weighed that too.

"Food for the month will come to less than 100 rupees," Andy toted up the tally. "That's less than twenty dollars."

"We can afford that," I said, "even on my Indian teacher's salary." Banon was clearly giving us a good deal.

Well fed, crowded but comfortable, I tie off the door flaps and presumed to sleep. It was Andy's third night in a tent. The wind increased, "gale force, buffeting us about." Andy wrote he parents, "flogging the canvas like the frenzied luffing of a sail beating to windward."

She felt claustrophobic and kept waking, sitting upright to make sure the tent did not collapse. I expected her to call, "Pull in the jib," in her confusion.

In fact, at times I did think e were about to levitate. I had everyone move to the windward side of the tent, like shifting ballast on a boat, which at very least gave the illusion of being anchored more securely.

In spite of my exhaustion, I kept waking too. I had anxious dreams and lay there awake in a depressive mood. Were we up for it? I recalled Andy's question. I'd never organized an expedition that took me more than a couple hours from a telephone. What was I doing five days into the Himalayas? What I knew about expedition mountaineering I'd read in books. Was I confusing reality with literary fantasy as I had always done since childhood?

We woke next morning with pounding headaches, the delayed effects of high altitude, dehydration and lack of sleep I felt. The wind had dropped, but when I stuck my head out of the tent, there was a steely over caste haze, a sea of bleakness. And it was cold. Our wet boots under the tent fly were frozen blocks of leather. There was a layer of ice in the cooking pot.

Andy stirred.

"How are you feeling?" I asked.

"Terrible."

It was already seven o'clock. We had missed our early start.

"It might be a good idea to call it a rest day," I said.

"Good thinking," and Andy rolled over and went back to sleep.

We spent the day writing and reading. I updated my journal, Andy wrote letters. I always carried a travel library and Andy dug into Faulkner. I read Herman Hesse's Siddartha. Wan Gyal paged through the Book of English Verse, miming our concentration, not understanding a word, bemused by the penguin on the cover.

The weather cleared and we lunched outside. A fly, caught in an updraft, settled at my feet and struggled in the snow.

"What do you make of that?" I pointed it out to Andy. Deeply immersed in Buddhist mysticism I saw great significance in this omen. All life is suffering, Buddha had said.

"Isn't that just India for you," Andy said. "Flies at 13,000 feet."

We slept well next night and woke at 4:00 a.m. starting breakfast by candle light. It took half an hour to boil tea water, then I fried canned sausages that we ate with chappatis and marmalade.

By 5:30 we were underway in the steel gray light of early dawn, the air stringently cold, the sky clear. We moved rapidly over the frozen snow as the world came into bloom with a somber mauve that lightened to a glowing pink and the glaring yellow of daylight. With the sun on our backs we tread on our shadows as we head up.

Above was an unnamed peak, shown on the map at 15,500 feet, a rounded hump like the mountains in Scotland, nothing technical, not very steep, a walkup mountain, but seemingly endless. No cornice hung above so there was less danger of avalanche.

By mid-morning the snow softened with the gathering heat and we began to sink in. In the lead, breaking trail, with each step I had to lift my knee high, hoisting my boot out of the snow, lean forward and then plunge it in again. Sisyphus condemned to the snow slope.

"How you doing?" I asked Andy.

"Do you want the truth?" she replied.

"No." I paused. "Do you think we should turn back?"

"No," she replied. I was half hoping she'd say, "Yes."

"Let's sit down and think about it," I said, and brought out biscuits, cheese, dried apples and water bottles.

Wan Gyal was the first to get up. He pointed uphill, then to himself. "Should I lead?" he seemed to say. And we took off in his trail.

The summit, 15,500 feet, a rounded dome, dominated by higher, dramatic peaks, was insignificant by Himalayan standards. But we weren't applying Himalayan standards. This was the highest either of us had climbed. We experienced a sense of victory, conquest, not unlike that of a child who pulls herself up on the rungs of a crib, and stands for the first time, seeing the world from a new perspective, an upright stance mastered.

And to be there with Andy, a joint accomplishment, husband and wife, climbing companions.

It was indeed our Himalyan honeymoon.

Chapter 57: Himalayan Pilgrimage

Pilgrimage: 1. A journey, esp. a long one, made to some sacred place, as an act of Devotion

2. any long journey.

On the tenth day we arrived. "Om mani padme hum." Hail to the jewel in the lotus. The prayer flags fluttered in the wind, carrying their message to the world. The stones on the huge cairn at the top of the ridge were carved in the same prayer. We passed to the left, as prescribed for pilgrims, to receive the blessings of the prayer. Below us was the Spiti River with weird rock formations, clay pillars capped with flat stones, multicolored in bands of stratified rock, mud brown, brick red, mustard yellow, somber purple. The colors changed as the clouds passed over the sun. In the thin air I felt as if I was hallucinating. Vegetation was sparse an even the lowly dandelion was a thing of beauty. The glaciers on the mountains above sparkled in the dazzling morning sun.

We looked down on the rooftops of the Buddhist Monastery of Key perched on an aerie like a mediaeval fortress that dominated the valley. A footpath led to it across a narrow ledge, high cliff bands above, a drop of several hundred feet below. The last mile of our pilgrimage.

"Life is suffering," the Buddha said. He must have had Spiti in mind. It is a region of northern India between Kashmir and Tibet. In the rain shadow of the main range of the Himalaya it is dry, desolate and remote. While belonging to India politically, traditionally it had been a part of Tibet and is still Tibetan in language, culture and religion. When the Chinese Communist government annexed Tibet in 1950, they disputed India's claim and relations between the two countries were strained still in 1957, when Andrea, my wife and I visited.

"You can only go as far as the Inner Line," the tall bearded Sikh police inspector had told us. The Inner Line was 50 miles from Tibet. At Kye we had arrived.

It had been a struggle to come so far. We had crossed the main range of the Himalaya by the Rhotang Pass, 13,700 feet, wading through snow knee deep. The ponies carrying our gear had to be dragged through the drifts, one pony walla tugging on the halter, the other hoisting the animal by its tail and heaving forward against its rump.

Three days later at Chenab we had to cross the Chandra River, a raging torrent with the runoff of the summer snow melt. The pony walla refused when he saw a horse belonging to another party swept away in the churning current. The horse swam safely to shore, but he was not deterred and turned back.

We crossed on the "julla," a primitive cable car, a box large enough for one person and baggage, suspended from a thick steel cable that stretched across the river. It could be pulled back and forth by a rope attached to each bank. Wan Gyal, our head porter, went first to pull the rest of us across. Andy next. Prayer flags were waving from cairns that anchored the bridge. Ang Rup, our second porter, said a prayer and followed. I thought of St. Christopher, the patron saint of river crossings, but it was years since I had worn my medallion. I brought up the rear.

On the opposite bank we rearranged out loads. What the two ponies had carried from their backs we now carried on ours and set off to ascend the Kunzum Pass, nearly 15,000 feet high. Physically I found the 80 pound pack as much as I could carry and still walk. But I developed a rhythm that coordinated a slow pace with deep breathe and a steady heart beat. My life took on a sublime simplicity. The only purpose in life was to place one foot in front of the other, and the next, like Sisyphus rolling his stone uphill. My mind assumed a Taoist meditative state. Or was it the dumb resignation of an ox?

Andy, who carried a lighter pack, extolled the beauty of the mountains with rhapsodies of Wordsworthian ecstasy. My vision focused on where I would next place a foot. It took four and a half hours we reached the pass. Standing by the summit cairn carved with mani stones, under the fluttering prayer flags, I felt I had undergone a Buddhist initiation.

We gazed down on two worlds. To the west, the mountains of Lahoul, snow capped and glacial caught in a mauve glow of the slanting afternoon sun. To the east, the dusty haze over the high desert plateau of Spiti, a parched barren wasteland.

We met up with a band of Spiti traders going the opposite way, heading for trans- Himalaya India. They were stocky men with Mongolian features, slanted eyes, round chubby faces, flat noses. The men were dressed in heavy wool gowns, a faded red, knee length felt boots, and red peaked hats with ear flaps that stuck out like wings. The women wore black full length dresses with gray course wool blankets over their shoulders, their hair tied in short pigtails. Most had some item of jewelry, an opaque turquoise stone in their hair, or strung on a necklace.

Their animals were formidable beasts, chaurus, a cross between a yak and a cow. They were mean looking with black hairy coats, horns a foot long. With short legs and deep chests, they were immensely strong, carrying twice the load of a large mule. Unruly, they were led with a ring through their noses.

The lead man was twirling an instrument like a children's toy, about the size of a potato masher with a short handle. It was a hand operated prayer wheel. A small drum inscribed with the mani prayer revolved at the top. With each rotation the prayer was said, a continuous process that reminded me of old women in Spanish churches fingering their rosaries. Repetition seemed to be the path to redemption, prayer flags, prayer wheels, carved stones. It was a process I understood. How often as a child had I received absolution for my innocent sins by having to repeat a hundred "Hail Marys?"

We camped on the meadow below the pass. Wan Gyal brewed tea on sheep's dung. It did little to improve the flavor, but it did conserve our dwindling supply of kerosene.

Descending next day to the village of Losar we came to several small swiftly flowing small streams that we crossed by wading. At each bank, we'd take off our boots and socks, put our boots back on, roll up our trousers and wade in. The water was so cold the pain was excruciating until numbness set in. When the water was higher, we took off our trousers too and braced each other to avoid being swept away.

At one crossing, a party of Indian border police caught up with us A young recruit spoke with Andy. He came from Kerala, the southern most state in India. He'd never seen snow. "Ma'am, would it be warmer," he asked, "if I leave my socks on?"

The day became oppressively hot by noon and stream crossing was a welcome break.

We camped outside Losar, the first village in Spiti, a settlement of 23 houses. Green fields of young barley, and peas, surrounded the village for about 200 yards. There was a single gnarled willow tree. The green was in sharp contrast to the gray gravel and brown wind blown dust of open range.

We left a cache of food with the headwoman of the village, to be picked up on our return journey. She was in charge, her husband being away on a trading trip to Kulu. We were invited into her home, a two storied house. It was built on a stone foundation wall about three feet high. Above a wall of sun dried clay brick rose to a height of 15 feet. It was white washed, with a red decorative fringe along the top. The white, we were told later, kept evil spirits away. Small windows, about 10 inches square, were framed with a black decorative border. The roof was flat, made of a woven mat of willow runners, covered in clay, supported by willow beams. Shrubs were stored on the roof, their winter supply of fuel. We had seen women coming down from the hillsides bearing huge piles of shrubs on their backs. Prayer flags, yellow and white, red and blue, waved on the roof.

I stooped to enter the woven wicker door and banged my head on the low door jamb. During the winter animals were kept on the ground floor providing central heating for the rooms above. It reeked, not unpleasantly, with the acrid pungency of animal droppings. Most of the dung had been hauled out to the front yard where it dried in the sun before being stored for winter fuel.

We climbed a ladder to the living quarters above. It was dimly lit by small windows. The walls were bare, once white washed, now layered with soot. In the center was a clay fire pit that vented through a hole in the roof. The floor was of packed earth smoothed with a cow dung slurry. In one comer, an oil lamp burned in a small shrine with a small statue of Buddha. Blankets and rugs were folded against one wall. We left our supplies in the opposite corner.

We were not invited to tea because the man of the house was not at home, I assumed.

A quarter mile out of town we encountered our first mani wall, a rectangular pile of stones three feet high, about ten feet long, and four feet wide along the side of the trail. It was made of flat stones that had been carved with the sacred prayer and images of the sitting Buddha. The height was perfect to rest our packs, adjust our straps, and by passing it on the left, we acquired blessings for our next incarnation. We found these at each village we entered, a convenient place to rest. I liked the idea of resting as a form of prayer.

We hiked deeper into the vast Spiti valley the next three days. The river cut a deep gorge through gravel banks, then debouched on to flat bottom land, sometimes half a mile across. In places the banks were carved into weird buttresses and pinnacles, tall clay columns and spires, often 100 feet high, capped with flat rocks, perched perilously on top, shaped like a monk's hood, or academic mortar board caps worn at graduation. Above the land was built up in tiers, wide benches and gradual rising slopes where villages were perched amid small patches of green fields. Above the mountains held up the sky.

I had read an Arab proverb. "Three things relieve sorrow: water, green grass and the beauty of woman." Clearly the poet had never been to Spiti. Rivers usually have a life sustaining quality, cooling, soothing, nurturing the earth. Here the opposite was true. The rivers were torrents surging through a wounded land, tearing out great gouges, pulling down rock and silt, draining the land, sucking it dry.

The side streams were too deep to wade, but primitive bridges had been built, simple affairs, two logs stretched between large rocks on opposite banks and stones laid along the top. The logs had been carried by either man or beast ten days from the nearest forest on the other side of the Himalayas.

The wider Spiti River was spanned by a "zampa," a primitive footbridge made with three strands of a steel cable, one for the feet, and two hand rails. Indian government engineers had built it over a gorge where the canyon narrowed and the river roared with a thundering basso. It was the only time I saw Wan Gyal taken aback. Before crossing he paused, looked up at the prayer flags and then threw a hand full of barley flour into the stream to appease the water demons. My pack was top heavy and whenever I leaned on a hand rail for balance, it tipped beneath my weight and the whole bridge swayed. The river hissed and growled only ten feet below, and swirled in a slurry of brown mud.

The original bridge, we were told, had been build of willow runners that were twisted into a crude rope. "The bridge had to be replaced from time to time," an Indian officer said, "when it broke."

At Kibar we approached the Inner Line. A village of forty houses, it clung to the parched brown hillside above green fields of barley, oats, peas and blue poppies.

"Grown for opium?"-Andy asked.

There were signs of development. The village had a school, and the fields were irrigated.

Even weeds seemed more abundant, purple thistles, yellow gorse, stunted wild roses pink and white, sage brush, yellow buttercups, violets, blue poppies, wild onion that had gone to seed. "Many a desert flower are born to blush unseen," Andy wrote in her

275

journal. Women worked in the fields doing the stoop labor, pulling weeds. Men tended the flocks.

Sun and shadows cast changing shades of green, yellow and purple, blending like the soft colors of a Scottish tweed.

We had visitors to our camp, two women with children. A granny with a beautiful wrinkled face carried a tambourine made of sheep's gut stretched over a bent willow frame. Discarded lids of tin cans loosely attached to the rim rattled as she beat a rhythm. The younger woman sang a high, wispy, atonal melody that was lost in the wide valley. They asked for clothing for the children. Regrettably, we had none, and atoned with cigarettes and candy, corrupting influences of civilization.

Later in the afternoon a long caravan of yaks and heavily laden ponies passed. A tall, bearded Sikh in military uniform approached our camp.

"Sub-Inspector Jaswant Singh," he introduced himself formally.

"Will you join us for tea?" I asked.

He eyed Andy. "Love to," he said and sat down.

I wondered how long it had been since he had spoken English, or Hindi, to an attractive young woman. He was clearly eager for conversation. "I'm on my way out after a two- year tour of duty on the frontier," he told us. "What brings you here?" he asked.

Was this going to be an official interrogation? I wondered? But when I told him that I taught at The Doon School, and was doing a holiday trek, he was satisfied.

Inspector Singh was more eager to talk. He had filled the boredom of frontier duty by writing a book on Spiti and he gave us a brief lecture of its history and the recent border conflict with China. But he had little good to day about the people of Spiti. "They're lazy." Or Buddhism. "It's decadent."

"The oldest son inherits the land from the father, and the younger brothers all become monks. They are leaches on society, but it is an effective means of birth control." He was a hard bitten, practical man, but a good soul and eager to get back to the bright lights of the Punjab.

"Be sure to visit the monastery at Kye," he told us as he rode off to catch up to his caravan.

A thick mist obliterated the sky and the mountain ridge next morning. Wan Gyal and Ang Rup stayed in camp while Andy and I went on the visit the monastery. We followed women carrying pyramid shaped wicker hampers on their backs, loaded with barley to be ground at a mill down by the river. Barley flour was their staple diet, baked into flat bread, or roasted and mixed with curds, or in their tea. Fermented and brewed as chang, it became the local beer or whiskey, depending on the potency. Behind them came children with their smaller hampers collecting dung from the police inspector's caravan to supplement the family fuel supply.

A party of Spiti herders were crossing the river. They dragged their horses and mules across and a lead ram, urging them on with threats and shouts. The sheep and goats were thrown in bleating mournfully and forced to swim. I took one step into the river and empathized with the sheep.

We climbed up the steep gravel bank, 700 feet to the prayer cairn where we saw the Kye Monastery for the first time. We followed the narrow trail along the cliff bands and came to a stone gatehouse. I hesitated to enter. Half the door was missing, the other half sagged on its hinges. No one was about. Had it been abandoned? I wondered, then stepped across the threshold.

A long walkway of worn flat stones led up to a tower built into the hillside. We clambered over collapsed mud brick walls and charred beams. It looked as if the monastery had been hit by a disaster. An earthquake? Vandalism? Or military suppression like the Chinese in Tibet? Had the monks been driven out?

"Hello," I shouted at the top. No response. I shouted again. There was a small courtyard ahead. I entered cautiously and shouted once more. My voice reverberated in the enclosed space. Suddenly, I was answered by a huge black mastiff that leapt out of a doorway, growling, snarling and barking. It jerked to a halt as the chain around its neck pulled tight.

Tibetan Buddhism is rich in demonology, fire breathing dragons and ferocious monsters. I was confronted by my first demon. Buddhists, I thought, were pacifists. Someone had neglected to tell the dog.

Guests having been announced, a tall flustered monk with shaven head, wearing a faded red rob appeared, kicked the dog, and with a toothless smile beckoned us to follow. We entered a dark room filled with smoke. There was a small open fire in the center of the floor with an old man and a young boy squatting over it, like the witches in Macbeth. They were frying barley in a flat metal pan. This was the kitchen and evidently we had entered the monastery mistakenly by the back door.

Our guide lead us on through a labyrinth of dark and dusty corridors, up stone steps. We ducked under low doorways and stumbled on the uneven stone flag stones. Eventually we entered a poorly lit room that had the twilight reverential air of an old museum. Dim light filtered in from small windows overlooking the valley. Faded prayer flags, like WWI battle flags hung from the ceiling. It smelled of wax, incense and must.

Candles flickered before a life size statue of the Buddha, cast in burnished bronze. Buddha sat with legs crossed in meditative pose, the right hand raised in blessing, the left hand resting on his knee. The expression was one of renunciation, tranquility, at-oneness, like the enigmatic expression on Leonardo's Mona Lisa. I could envisage the wise and compassionate philosopher who taught The Way, The Tao, the Eight Fold Path: right views, right aspirations, right speech, right conduct, right livelihood, right effect, right mindfulness, right contemplation, a code of morality that pre-dated Christianity by three hundred years.

I was confused. There were tankas, woven silk hangings, draped from the walls with fire breathing dragons, monsters with bared teeth and bulging eyes, fierce, demonic, threatening, like the nightmare scenes from the paintings of Heironymous.Bosch. Where did this fit into a theology of compassion and tranquility?

Our guide was impatient for us to move on. We were led into a small chapel with large golden statue of Buddha at the end. There were three rows of padded benches on each side, a low table between. We were ushered to the table and greeted by three silent monks seated on the opposite side.

"Namaste," I said to break the ice. Then I realized that was the Hindu greeting. Was it appropriate in a Buddhist setting? I pressed my hands together in an attitude of prayer and bowed.

They responded with a Tibetan greeting which I did not understand.

That was the end of the conversation. I spoke neither Tibetan nor Hindi. They spoke no English. We sat staring at each other.

I became conscious of the loudness of the silence. But silence has an important place in Buddhist prayer. Everything grows out of silence and returns to silence. This was the first stage of Buddhist awareness.

Our host monk appeared then and place small round silver cups before us and served us hot tea that tasted salty and had a thin scum of melted butter on top, the Tibetan drink of courtesy. I nodded my head in approval. The monks smiled, grinning through missing teeth. Then our host place a bowl of roasted barley before us. It tasted like popcorn. I would have preferred the salt and butter on my roasted barley, rather than in my tea, I thought. Then I drained my tea cup, which was a mistake. Our host immediately scurried to fill it again from a large blackened copper pot.

We made an attempt to return their hospitality by offering each monk a square of chocolate. They looked at the dark brown substance suspiciously, and nibbled at circumspectly. They ate out of curiosity and courtesy, like Andy and I.

When confronted with unfamiliar situations, one looks for comparisons and metaphors to give meaning to new experience. Was the sharing of food in the sanctity of the chapel like taking communion?

Guest hospitality granted, the monks began to pray. They chanted in a high pitched tone, not unlike a Catholic priest performing high mass. I could not understand the litany any more than I could understand the Latin mass, but I assumed it had something to do with the noble eight fold path of Buddhism. "...right views, right aspirations, right speech, right conduct, right livelihood, right effort, right mindfulness and right contemplation."

The monks gazed about as they chanted in unison. One plucked his scraggly beard with a pair of tweezers. Another monk inspected the light meter Andy was holding. The third peered through the sighting lense of my camera, praying the whole time as if blessing our gear. Occasionally the sing song of their chant was punctuated by the monotone of a long "OM," and they would resume the litany.

Then Andy brought their prayers to a dramatic stop. She unzipped her wind jacket, and the monks reacted in silent amazement. The monks stopped in mid-chant and stared wide eyed in amazement. It was as if she had torn her clothing from chin to waist and was about to expose herself. Then she zipped her jacket up again. The monks looked at each other, broke into laughter, chatted among themselves as if breaking the code, and resumed singing again.

After an hour my hips ached from sitting cross-legged, I finished my tea and turned my cup upside down before it could be filled again. We offered a small gratuity, we excused ourselves with as much courtesy as we could muster, and bowed ourselves out of the hall. Too late, I realized this was a breach of etiquette. I suspect that all the blessings we had accumulated on our pilgrimage were lost by our indiscretion. What sort of pilgrims would take so long to come so far and leave so soon? I thought they must be saying.

On leaving I too was sad. I had been impressed with what I had read about Buddhism and hoped to learn more. But this seemed such a travesty, spiritual insight become meaningless repetition, prayer flags, carved stones, prayer wheels. But spirituality become dogmas was also the difficulty I had with my own religious upbringing.

I recalled my visit, three years previously, to the Orthodox Monastery of Agios Nicolias on Mt. Athos in Greece, a huge monastery that in the 18th century housed a thousand monks. Today a mere dozen remained as caretakers. I expressed my regret to the young novitiate who was my guide. "C'est ne pas l'epogue," he replied. It isn't the epoque. These aren't the times.

A steady drizzle set in as we made our way across the desolate canyon back to our camp.

Three days later we returned over the Kunzum Pass, stopping the summit cairn for our last look back into Spiti. The earthen colors blended in the valley, the mountain peaks probed the sky like temple towers. Prayer flags fluttered in the wind.

I hadn't come seeking enlightenment, I thought, but I had hoped for further insight. The "OM" in particular had fascinated me. It seem simple until I read a passage that explained its significance.

"I can't say I fully understand it," I said, trying to explain it to Andy. "OM really consists of four sounds. The first is 'Aaahhh,' with mouth wide open, resounding from the back of the throat. This represents logic, reasoning, the rationality of the physical." And I demonstrated

"Next is the 'Ooohhh," with mouth partly closed, lips closer together, sound filling the head, representing the dream state, heaven and hell, the god within one.

"And then the Mmmmm," lips closed, sound reverberating deep within, the unconscious, chaos, darkness and void, like the opening in Genesis.

Standing there at 15,000 feet on the mountain pass, probably suffering from anoxia, I found myself repeating the monks' prayer, "Ahhh Ohhh Mmm...."

The effect was mesmerizing, like humming a Gregorian chant in a high vaulted Gothic chapel, or singing a long sustained baritone passage in a Bach cantata, accompanied by a cello.

"This is uncanny, Andy. Try it!" And both of us harmonized one last "OM."

For one moment I thought I understood what the poets and the mystics said about the unity of self and others, as we stood together in the face of the majesty of the desert and the higher peaks. And I realized that climbing every mountain is a quest for deeper insight into the deeper meaning of things. And that every journey is a pilgrimage.

"I can only stand so much reality," I said. "We'd better go down. We've many miles to go before we sleep.

Joe and Andy at the Doon School, India, 1957.

Chapter 58: Chamba – Gourmet Trail Meals

When she got there
The cupboard was bare.

~ Mother Goose.

We were down to the last of our expedition rations. After five weeks trekking in the Himalayas we had opened the last of our cans and would have to live off the land. But in Spiti and Lahoul, bleak regions in the rain shadow north of the divide, it was a mountainous desert, and there was little food to spare. I was hoping to resupply at Kyelang, a large village on the trade route that led from north India to western Tibet.

At the beginning of our journey we had eaten well. In Kulu, where we set out, we had purchased supplies left over by a previous expedition from Major Banon, the local representative of the Himalayan Mountain Club, British army surplus tinned rations which included butter and cheese, powdered milk, dehydrated egg powder, bacon and a surfeit of Irish stew. In the market we bought rice and potatoes, barley flour, lentils, ghur-raw unrefined lump sugar with bits of the cane embedded-and tea, salt and spices, dried apples and apricots, cans of cling peaches.

"Gourmet expedition fare," I told Andrea. We were newly wed, spending the year teaching at The Doon School, an elite school in India.

Kyelang was a sorry village, ramshackle stone buildings with sagging roofs, streets of mud and rocks, covered in horse manure, women doing all the work in the fields, men with the cheerful camaraderie and vacant smile induced by chang, the pungent home brewed barley beer.

The local store stocked barley flour, ghur, tobacco and tea, salt and an assortment of spices. There were dried apples so withered they looked like nuts. Onions and potatoes were the only fresh foods. The trader sent his boy off and he returned fifteen minutes later with six small eggs, befouled with droppings, and a scrawny chicken held by its legs, alive and complaining to attest to its freshness. We had done well considering that some years the valley did not grow enough food in the niggardly soil to feed their own people.

I bought sparingly. We had a long climb ahead of us to get over the Himalayan Divide. "Braumar, on the other side, is only two days away. We can get fresh food there."

Chamba was our objective, about fifty miles away, I figured as I studied the map in the District Commissioner's office. We would catch the bus there. "We can do it easily in four days," I said optimistically.

"Beware of the optimist," a climbing friend used to tell me.

Next day we climbed the steep shale slopes out of the barren river bottom. It was oppressive in the heat of the August sun. The meadows lush grass and alpine flowers in the upper valley were a reprieve. We camped at the foot of the glacier.

Wan Gyal and Ang Rup, our two Ladhaki porters, stewed the scrawny chicken with potatoes and onions and curry. We sucked the last of the flesh off the bones through our teeth and our comrades belched with satisfaction. The curry was too hot for my taste, but it did clear my sinuses and I slept well.

The glacier next morning went easier than expected. The snow had melted off the ice so the crevasses were open and easy to avoid. It wasn't steep, sloping like a long ramp gradually. The surface ice was honey-combed giving good traction. We hid from the sun as best we could beneath floppy hats, coated in white zinc ointment looking like circus clowns, incognito behind sun goggles. We hiked in shirt sleeves like spring skiing in the Alps. Hot head and cold feet, interesting sensation. An interesting metaphor too, I thought.

I remember hearing it before I saw it, a mournful moaning like range cattle complaining, a deep baritone. The bellowing repeated every minute or two. Far up the glacier in the distance, I then saw a lone figure, a black fleck in the mid-day glare. The yeti, was my first thought, the Abominable Snowman. It descended slowly. Drawing closer, the sound was more distinct, a monotone, a single melancholy note blown on a horn.

The creature approached, a young man, dressed in the orange robes of a saddhu, a Hindu holy man. A gray-brown blanket of natural wool was draped over his shoulders. He wore rope sandals and thick woolen socks on his feet. In one hand he carried a wooden staff and a bronze bowl, the other a conch shell that he pressed to his lips and blew a penetrating blast. Then I recognized the sound for what it was, the OM of the Buddhist prayer, "OOOMMM," to fend off the demons that lurked in the remoteness of these sacred but terrifying mountains.

"Namaste. Blesssings," he said, bringing his hands to his forehead and bowing. His long hair was loosely combed, tied in a top-knot on his bare head.

"Namaste," we replied

The porters, awed by the presence of the holy man, said the Buddhist greeting, which he replied.

Then he clutched his conch shell, took a deep breathe, bellowed mightily like the Isrealites before the walls of Jericho, and set off down the mountain, sight and sound fading in the distance. I assumed he was on a pilgrimage to the Buddhist Tandi monastery in the valley, also sacred to Hindus.

It was late afternoon when we reached the pass. We paused for photographs and a last look from the Himalayan Divide. To the north behind us were the bleak brown slopes and the desolate grandeur of the high desert mountains of the Tibetan Plateau, capped in snow. Ahead to the south the magnificent splendor of the monsoon drenched lushness of India with its varied shades of green, pale yellow where the grass poked through the melting snow, lush and vibrant on the meadow, deep and brooding in the forest below.

A huge stone cairn six feet high stood with prayer flags fluttering, broadcasting to eternity the Buddhist prayer "Om mani padme hum. Oh hail to the jewel in the lotus," printed on them. Tridents two feet long of hand forged iron, the trident of Shiva were wedged between the rocks. The trident is demonized in Christianity as Satan's. There was no crucifix as there might have been on a pass in Italy, but otherwise is seemed an ecumenical entreaty for divine protection. Wan Gyal and Ang Rup removed their caps and prayed. We stood in reverential silence. It felt like a holy place.

We made a triumphal entry back into India through patches of snow and high meadows, carpeted in flowers, yellow buttercups, anemones and dandelions, orange lilies, blue forget-me-knots and white narcissus. And there were hundreds of sheep and goats, a thousand or more, tended by a half dozen Gaddis, and an arsenal of ferocious wolf like dogs.

The Gaddis are a hereditary cast of herders who winter in the lower valleys of the Himalayas with their immense flocks, and in the spring drive them up the mountains, following the melting snows in search of pastures. Lean sinewy men, taller than the average Indian, they wore gray and white tunics of tightly woven wool, that came to their hips, were belted tightly around the waist, creating a pouch where they stuffed their personal belongings and even young lambs in need of care. Clamped on their head was a tall circular cap of woven wool.

They were impressive looking men, a lighter complexion than most Indians, some with smoky blue eyes. One legend claims they are descendents of Alexander's soldiers who stayed behind when he retreated from India in 315 B.C.

They recognized our passing in silence, not out of hostility I felt, but out of shyness. I had known the experience of long periods of solitude in the mountains, the loudness of the silence, and the difficulty of the civility of conversation upon my return.

"Namaste," was the extent of our conversation.

We would have reached Brahmaur by dark, had there been a Brahmaur to reach. What we found were four wooden huts, constructed of squared logs, with sloping roofs and flat stones on top to keep the planks from blowing off. They resembled the hay barns I had seen on the alpine meadows in Switzerland, as if designed by the same architect. The same solution to the same problem, continents apart. Only one building was occupied by a single family. The rest were storage sheds for staple food they brought with them in their annual migration, and wool that they took back down. Braumar existed primarily in the imagination of the cartographer of the Government of India Survey, I felt.

There was no trading post, no resupply, but Wan Gyal negotiated the purchase of a chunk of meat. It had to be from the most muscular sheep on the mountainside. We had the last of our potatoes and onions in a mutton stew. I examined our

283

remaining food supply, barley flour, ghur, and tea. That was it, and curry. The cupboard was bare.

"It's only another thirty miles to Chamba," I said. "With light packs and empty stomachs we should make it in two days easily."

Andy didn't see the humor of having an empty stomach.

It rained that night, a solid drenching monsoon rain, rain hard enough that it bounced back up off the ground, not the soggy mist we had experienced in the rain-shadow north of the Himalaya.

The trail down the valley paved with sheep droppings. It ran beside a creek that was the headwaters of the Chamba River. Initially a babbling brook, it was soon a brimming swift stream, and rapidly became a raging torrent. Within a mile it was in full spate tumbling over boulders with a thunderous roar.

In an hour we came to a side stream. It was also in spate. Large rocks had been placed strategically in the stream, as stepping-stones and Wan Gyal boulder hopped across nimbly. Ang Rup followed more cautiously. Andrea hesitated, tightened the waist band on her pack, and crossed one step at a time. I followed, but looking back from the opposite bank realized that I should have gone first.

The valley steepened further down and we entered the forest, large drooping pine trees with damp sagging branches that dripped. We came to another side stream. I was uneasy about crossing this one and considered roping up. But I realized that wouldn't make us any safer. It would be just as easy to drown tethered to the end of a rope if swept away as it would bouncing down a rock strewn ravine.

To give Andy and I the time to consider the options, we stopped for lunch. Food can be reassuring, even if it is only a couple spoons of raw sugar rolled in a cold chappati left over from breakfast.

After lunch the porters prepared to cross. I stopped them and pointed up the steep embankment where a set of tracks led through the tangled growth of rhododendrum bushes. It took us nearly an hour until we came to a place where the stream split around a large rock and we were able to hop across, and almost as long to scramble down the opposite side, slipping and sliding, until we picked up the main trail again. Nearly two hours to cross a mountain stream. It was difficult to estimate how far we covered that day, as there were no recognizable landmarks among the giant trees, deodars, a species of cedar similar to the California redwoods. My best guess was that we had hiked ten miles, mostly uphill and down, and progressed a mere five.

We found a sheltered area to camp on a flat ledge above the river, obviously a campsite used before. It was a comfortable setting, but unnerving, in the literal sense of getting on my nerves. The thrumming of the river was incessant. The sound pulsated in thunderous bursts, then faded, only to surge again. There was the muffled thud of boulders rolling downstream in the current. We had to shout to make ourselves heard. In spite of the spongy moss we lie upon, I slept poorly, waking with a recurring dream of being swept downstream.

We continued downstream on our Via Dolorossa for five days.

For dinner at night and breakfast in the next mornings we had chapattis, ghur and tea. "Half the world subsist on this diet," Andy said. Hunger, we realized, was not just a question of quantity. We had adequate food if you counted only calories.. What we craved was variety. Andy came up with a creative solution to that.

. "Know what I'd like for dinner tonight?" she said one morning. Then coyly , as if ordering dinner at the Algonquin in New York City, where she grew up, said, "I'll start with mushroom soup sprinkled with parsley and just a little sherry in it, dry sherry." And she continued with tenderloin steak done rare, "au jus," sugar snap peas, and creamy mashed potatoes smothered in butter, carrots with hollandaise sauce. "And for desert," she said with a long pause, to give herself time to decide, "lemon meringue pie with just that right combination of tartness and sweetness, and the meringue topping slightly browned."

The ghur and the chappatis never tasted so good.

Next morning she asked, "What are you planning for dinner tonight?"

I'd been brought up on Granny Schneider's German cooking, sauerkraut and sausage and canned peaches in syrup for dessert, followed by six years of boarding school. I never did acquire a taste for gourmet cooking. Eating was simply a biological necessity and full of moral strictures.

"Think of the starving Armenians."

"Thou shalt eat what is upon thy plate," was the Eleventh Commandment.

But I did associate food with certain occasions. When in Vienna the previous year, I had been invited to Thanksgiving Dinner by the wife of the Canadian Consul, who worked with me as a volunteer in the refugee camp during the Hungarian revolt.

"Can I bring a friend?" I had asked. And she invited Andy too. There was browned turkey, sweet potatoes, fresh green beans. A white Austrian wine. Pumpkin pie with whipped cream. After all the goulash we ate in the camp, the meal was from another world. "But I could not keep my eyes off you," I told Andy. " What I remember most is sitting across the table and looking at you between the candle sticks in the soft light."

It rained each day and often at night. The further we descended in the Chamba valley, the wider the side streams became and the higher we had to climb to cross them. The forest was thicker, a rainforest jungle. And it was hot. Even in rain squalls, the mid-day heat was stifling. Improvised bridges of pine logs were also washed away and we had to climb higher to cross. Descending we slithered down muddy tracks and over wet mossy rocks.

Exhausted at the end of each day, we crowded around Wan Gyal and watched him pat the balls of barley dough into a flat circular chappati and slap it on the concave disk to roast over the fire. One at a time. We looked on hungrily.

On the seventh day of creation, God rested. On our seventh day, the trail ended at a bridge. It was a real bridge of squared beams, milled planks, wide enough for a jeep. On the other side was a road with a gravel surface, crowned in the center, with ditches on each side. "Look Dorothy! The Yellow Brick Road!" Andy called out.

Chamba was another eight miles. We were tempted to hike on, but we were already tired. It was overcast, getting dark and threatening to rain. We banqueted on double rations of chappatis and ghur, celebrated with a second cup of tea. Turning in, I instructed Wan Gyal to wake us at "Paunch budgee, five o'clock." That was our code word for first light.

I had just fallen asleep when the tent shook. "Chi sahib. Tea sir." Ang Rup passed a steaming cup through the tent flap. One of the civilized customs of trekking in the Himalayas is that porters wake you each morning with a cup of hot tea. At first I had thought this to be the height of decadence, but after the first morning I was addicted.

"What time is it, Andy?" I asked, holding the flashlight for her.

"Two o'clock," she replied.

I looked outside. A hazy mist hung over the valley illuminated by the eiry glow of the moon above it. Indeed it did look like panch budgee. The porters didn't have a watch, and probably could not have read it, if they had one. Time to them was a function of the circadian rhythm and not a mathematical determinant.

We debated whether to go back to sleep but Wan Gyal was turning chappatis over on the Primus stove, so we got up.

An hour later, the mist had turned to a warm rain and the night into a murky gloom that settled over the valley. In the dark I couldn't see the porters ten feet ahead as we trudged through the night, a firm road under foot. We arrived at the guest house at Chamba in time for breakfast.

Breakfast! Now that was a meal to remember. In the Himalayan valleys, temperate climate fruits are grown successfully, and apples, peaches, apricots, plums, cherries were in season. Tropical fruits were brought in by lorry, mangos, pineapple, bananas. There were omelets, a choice of bread toast or chappatis. We passed on the chappatis. Rich buffalo milk by the glass. Coffee with cream.

After warm showers we dozed in easy chairs overlooking the rose garden, watching guests play lawn croquet. There was chicken tandoori for dinner, salad, cherry pie with home churned ice cream. We had soft beds but my stomach reminded me of King John who died of a surfeit of peaches and I slept poorly.

The bus to Pathankot where we caught the train to Delhi, left early. I looked wistfully at the breakfast buffet, but settled for dry toast and yogurt and Lomotil with my tea.

Part Four – Outward Bound Saga

Chapter 59: C-2

"Sparks are coming off the climbing rope!" I shouted over the sudden rush of wind. Topping the buttress, I saw the approaching storm, black clouds roiling in from the west. Thunder grumbled a deep baritone. Static electricity crackled in the air. I could smell the acrid tang of ozone. Flashes of lightning stabbed the north ridge. The valley faded as shards of mist swept below.

We were nearing the summit of Capital Peak, 14,140 feet, west of Aspen, two Outward Bound instructors, each roped up with three students in tow.

"What do we do?" I called to my climbing partner, Andy Arnold. He was from Colorado. He'd know what action to take.

"Everything I've read says get the hell off the mountain," he shouted back.

"Be off the high ridges by noon," Tapley, the chief instructor had cautioned. But the approach had taken much longer than planned. There we were, mid-afternoon, the summit cairn in sight. Do we push on or turn back?

But it was so close. Only a couple hundred yards. With the steep climbing behind us it was only a walk-up. Still possible. From day one, we had talked about Capital Peak with our students. The last two weeks had been a build up to this moment. This was to be their Everest. It would be an Outward Bound "first ascent" with students, for us instructors a matter of professional pride. We can't turn back now, I felt.

Yet if we're caught in the storm, how do we get off the mountain safely? I went through my mental check list. Move down off the ridge. Get rid of metal: ice axes, pocket knives, and metal canisters, even wrist watches. Crouch in a squatting position, hands on head, elbows tucked on knees. Lightning takes a direct line to ground, bypassing the heart and vital organs. At least that was the theory.

Thunder rumbled over the valley like muffled drums in a military funeral.

Outward Bound was founded in Britain during World War II as merchant seamen survival schools. I was an instructor during the first summer of the Colorado Outward Bound School in 1962.

On the first day of C-2, July 15, Andy Arnold, my co-instructor, and I met our students in Marble, an abandoned quarry town in the Crystal River valley surrounded by aspen forests and high ridges. As they stepped off the bus, students were organized into groups of twelve, named after American frontier heroes, Boone, Bridger, Crockett, Carson, invoking a mountain man archetype.

Our group, Boone patrol, was a diverse lot. "They come from Harvard and they come from Harlem," Outward Bound boasted. Social diversity was seen as an essential component of the Outward Bound experience. I mingled with our boys as we plodded two miles up the dusty jeep road to the school base camp, 800 feet above the valley. It was the first of many miles of hiking we would cover on our way to Capital Peak.

Two boys came from Denver, Louis Garcia, Hispanic, on scholarship, recommended by the guidance counselor at Manual High, an inner city school. And John Cooley, private school, outdoorsman and skier, already familiar with mountains. They came from the Mile-High City, I had little worry about them. Two boys were sponsored by the New York City Boys' Clubs. Daniel Lenihan, a tall lean kid, solid muscle, had a spontaneous sense of delight and wonder at being in mountains. He was white. Arthur Wellington Conquest III was a black Adonis, tall, handsome, muscular. He kept to himself, silent, withdrawn. Two scholarship students from Boston were funded by Outward Bound sponsors back east. The rest came from families that could afford the $350 tuition. They arrived from San Francisco, Chicago, Connecticut.

"No need to rush. Just keep a good steady pace. Develop a rhythm," I told them. That was lesson one, the mountain pace.

The month before I had studied Capital Peak, with map in hand from the summit two miles away. I was eager to climb it. The approach hike would be a long, but a fit group could do it. Jay from Chicago was an athlete. "Yah, I came to Outward Bound to get in shape for football." But could they could work together?

Arriving at the school site, students milled about in front of the imposing three-story A-frame ski chalet style building, the main hall, waiting to draw their camping gear.

"Look out!" A boy shrieked in the middle of the jostling crowd. And everybody scattered. All but one. Standing at the center of an empty circle was Arthur Wellington Conquest III. He had unclasped a six-inch switchblade knife, looked about casually, and then without uttering a word, hurled it high into the air. I gasped and watched as it came down, landing inches from his toes. Arthur stooped and nonchalantly picked up the knife, closed the blade, put it back in his pocket and looked about, silent. Arthur was the only black student on the course. He had made his statement. Everyone knew Arthur was there.

A crisis even before the course began. How do I manage this one? I've never been good at handling conflict. Certainly teaching in elite private schools had not prepared me for this. Do I disarm him? How?

Andy Arnold stepped in. "Arthur," he said calmly. "Why don't you put your knife away while you're in camp. Take it with you when we go into the mountains. You'll want it there."

We continued with equipment issue: backpacks, sleeping bags, mess kits, primus stoves, cooking pots, ice axes, climbing ropes.

And hiking boots that fit. Blisters were our most common medical problem. "My mom always said you never knew another person until you've walked in their shoes," one boy said, "Might as well begin now." New boots were even more unforgiving of tender feet.

That first year, the Colorado program, was modeled closely on the British Outward course. Ralph Clough, "a visiting advisor," came from the Eskdale Outward Bound Mountain School in England. He worked closely with Tapley, the chief instructor, in designing the program and establishing the schedule. We turned to him regularly. As instructors we had as much to learn as our students. The days were tightly structured with a ritual modeled on the military and consecrated by the ecclesiastical.

"Everyone out," the duty instructor shouted at dawn, to the clanging of a triangular steel gong. The day began with the dreaded "run and dip." Stunned into wakefulness, students bolted out of sleeping bags, jogged a mile through the aspen grove in early light and plunged into the melting snow water of Lost Trail Creek. Most American instructors questioned the sanity of the exercise. Even by British Outward Bound standards it was extreme, I learned later. But we took it on faith.

Breakfast in the dining hall was preceded by grace, "We thank thee Lord…." Camp clean-up followed, each group rated on a daily basis, the score tallied as a part of patrol competitions.

At morning assembly Bill Chapman, the school director, led us in prayer and an instructor read an inspirational poem. When my turn, I read from Tennyson, "My purpose holds to sail beyond the sunset…To strive, to seek, to find, and not to yield," a poem I had memorized as a school boy. Outward Bound borrowed for its motto from the passage..

There was basic training in campcraft skills, map and compass, first aid, axemanship, fire suppression with dirt and water, knot tying, rope coiling preparatory to rock climbing. "Never take your brake hand off the rope. You're holding the life of a man in your hands!"

The ropes course was the main challenge, an Outward Bound trademark. Tapley, the chief instructor built one in the aspen grove, probably the first of its kind in North America. There was a vertical climbing rope, the horizontal monkey crawl, the soaring Tarzan swing, walking a high log ten feet off the ground, crossing the Burma bridge 50- feet up between two aspen trees.

Climbing the wall, a smooth fourteen-foot wooden face, required planning, agility and teamwork. Students formed a human pyramid and hoisted Arthur to the top. "Here give me your hand." He hoisted others up. The last man stood below, too far to reach. No one had thought of that. Back to the drawing board. Cooley came up with the plan. Boone patrol was becoming a team.

Leadership training was a key element of the course. Each boy was designated leader for part of a day. At the end of the week they elected their patrol captain. Arthur Conquest, flamboyant and outspoken from the outset, had mellowed. Having a mischievous sense of humor and remarkable charisma, he was popular. John Cooley was thoughtful, confident and very serious. A worrier, he sized things up and thought things through. He was also more experienced in the outdoors. His patrol mates turned to him for advice.

At the end of the first week. I tore a page from my journal and gave each student a secret ballot to elect their patrol captain. Arthur's good humor and growing popularity garnered him five of the twelve votes cast on the first ballot. John Cooley got four. Ben, a good-natured, easy-going kid from California, got three. I was taken by surprise and frankly dismayed. I appreciated Arthur's contribution to the group but questioned whether he could be taken seriously as a patrol captain. We held a run-off. Arthur held on to his grassroots support of five. John picked up three votes and was elected captain with a majority of seven. In later years I acknowledged my own racial bias and wondered how often this happened in life to Arthur.

The second week we went on a three-day expedition into the mountains. Boys stopped frequently to adjust their fifty-pound packs and to check their feet for blisters. They practiced their newly acquired campcraft skills, learning to boil oatmeal for breakfast and cook macaroni in a #10 can without burning them.

On a shoulder of Meadow Mountain, we sat on a high ridge above timberline, the slope below carpeted with alpine flowers, pink Indian paint brush, blue penstamon, purple columbine, yellow asters. We took out our maps and picked out the trail we would follow into the high mountains and Capital Peak on our next expedition.

"You need to dunk them and them dry them," was Outward Bound dogma. We returned to school for more fitness training and low angle rock climbing.

"A certain Samaritan came by and bound up his wounds and had compassion on him..." the director read on the morning we did mountain rescue training.

One night they camped alone in the woods, each boy crouched over his own campfire. It was programmed to be a time for reflection, the forerunner of the Outward Bound solo. "What was meant to happen?" one boy asked when I picked him up in the morning.

"What's for breakfast," another asked.

The 1950's and 1960's were an heroic age in mountaineering, new climbs were being put up in the Alps and Yosemite, the giants of the Himalayas and Andes being summited. In a minor way we saw ourselves in that tradition, putting Capital Peak on the Outward Bound map.

We reorganized our equipment, provisioned for five days and set off on our alpine expedition. On a high traverse around Meadow Mountain we found a steep snow-filled ravine, and learned to use our ice axes, cutting steps and using them as anchors to belay, and practicing the self-arrest. We glissaded down, Cooley, a skier, on his feet. Others sat down and slid on their seats, toboggan fashion. On a steep rock buttress below Snowmass Mountain we spent the day rock climbing.

Late that afternoon we crossed Trail Riders Pass at 12,400 feet as the sun dipped behind the mountain, *terra nova*. We found a flat knoll, a lonely perch, exposed, high above timberline and camped. Five miles to the east the Maroon Bells were aglow in he deep pink of the setting sun. Fifteen hundred feet below, Snowmass Lake

292

sparkled in the last shafts of slanting light, encircled by the somber dark green of the forest.

Our five diminutive tents huddled together in the immensity of the mountains. We gathered water from the trickling snow melt, fired our primus stoves and prepared dinner. There was no wind and in the utter silence, even the boisterous boys spoke in low reverential voices.

Up at first light next morning, after a hurried breakfast we gathered to discuss the plan for the day, the climb of Capital Peak. After my briefing we usually had a reading, or a prayer, before setting off. But today I suggested a short Quaker silence, each to his own thoughts, free to speak as the spirit moved one. Nobody spoke. I got up to go.

"But Joe," Arthur protested, "nobody has said the Lord's Prayer."

"Will you say it, Arthur?" I asked.

And we sat in awe as this child of the ghetto, who had been so tough and threatening that first day, recited in the ringing baritone cadence of a Martin Luther King, "hallowed be Thy name...give us this day our daily bread...the power and the glory...deliver us from evil."

On the map the approach to Capital Peak appeared to be an easy traverse across Snowmass Basin. Skirting a sheer rock buttress, we came to a snow gully too steep to cross with novices. We had to descend over 700 feet to the boulder field below and then climb back up again over loose rock to gain Heckert Pass on the other side. It took longer than expected.

A mile across Pierre Basin, Capital Peak loomed, a massive wall of gray granite, steep, jagged, intimidating. I felt both the threat and thrill, and felt the students were ambivalent.

A steep couloir, a wide gully with loose rock, led to the east ridge of Capital Peak where the serious climbing began. We stopped for a quick snack and water break. Andy and I stepped aside." I didn't realize the ridge would be so long," I said.

"Yes, and exposed too," he said.

"We'll need to rope up, I said.

"But we can't do it with twelve students."

"Three to a rope. We shouldn't take more than that."

It meant splitting the group, leaving half behind, which neither of us liked. It ran counter to everything we had stressed about working as a team.

Do we turn back? But it was only noon. That too ran counter to the whole idea of Outward Bound. We put it to the group.

Ben, the football player from Chicago was clearly relieved. He had not acclimated well, had slept poorly the night before at 12,000 feet. He was exhausted. Frank too, one of the boys from Boston. They welcomed the opportunity to rest up before the long hike back to our campsite. They agreed to wait at the bottom of the mountain until we returned from the climb.

The other ten wanted to push on. "We've come this far. We can't turn back now," Dan, the New York enthusiast, urged. How to decide which six students should go?

"Let's draw lots," John Cooley, the patrol captain suggested, risking his own chance of getting to the summit. Then Arthur, to my surprise, agreed not to go. The rest drew lots.

The crux of the climb was the Knife Edge, a smooth rib that sharpened to a crest, fifty feet across. Looking down it dropped sheer, a dizzying 1500 feet to the boulders below. The other side fell in a series of steep ledges of shattered granite. This was true alpine mountaineering. Once across, the angle of the climb steepened as we moved up the mountain. We threaded our way through huge blocks of fractured granite, keeping to the more solid rock of the ridge. It was slow going, well past noon. We were running out of time.

We skirted the last tower and the final stretch to the summit opened before us. And the heavy dark clouds to the west.

"What do you say?" I asked Andy.

"Let's dash for it."

We stood on the top of our world, nothing higher. A continent of mountains surrounded us, as far as the eye could see. We hurried to sign the summit register, did not stop for a group photo and scuttled down.

Certain experiences are life defining. Outward Bound was one of them for many of us, students and teachers. John Cooley returned to Outward Bound as an instructor, became a successful businessman in outdoor equipment, and at the time of writing was the chairman of the board of the Colorado Outward Bound School.

Arthur Conquest, though he never made it to the summit, found something that deeply touched his inner life, became the first black Outward Bound instructor in the United States. He had a long and successful career with the Hurricane Island Outward Bound School, the New York City Outward Bound Center, before setting up his own organization working with inner city youth. Always a gadfly, in later years he became a relentless critic, the conscience of Outward Bound.

Dan Lenihan studied archeology, took up scuba diving, joined the United States Park Service, where he became the first underwater archeologist ranger.

Andy Arnold completed his forestry degree and then switched to medicine, a profession more people-oriented, and became a country doctor in rural Colorado.

I returned to teaching middle school students social studies in a wealthy suburb of Chicago.

"How did the summer go?" the headmaster asked me.

Sensing that he was interested in more than polite party chitchat, I replied, "Nat, I've learned more about teaching in the last two months at Outward Bound, than I have the last two years at Country Day."

And Outward Bound became my career for the next fifteen years.

Chapter 61: Suspended

I dangled in space, strangled by the constriction of my waist band, gasping for air. "Slack!" I shouted to my belayer above. "You're holding me too tight."

On rappel, I had slid down a single 250 foot rope. It was the longest rappel I had ever done. A separate safety line held me from above. A hundred and fifty feet down, the cliff bulged out in an overhang. Below the bulge I couldn't reach the rock face with my feet and I spun out, back to the wall. There I hung, stuck. At the bottom, another hundred feet below was the boulder field.

"Give me slack." I croaked.

Then I saw it, a ten-foot loop of rope below me, my safety line. It should be taut, holding me from above. Then I realized it was my backpack that had snagged on a rock knob, holding me in a death grip.

"Up rope!" I bellowed with a final desperate burst.

Too late. I came loose and plunged face down in a free fall, like a parachutist leaping into space. Instinctively I clutched at my rappel line. Hang on, I thought. Then dropped until the rope began to tighten. I felt it stretch. The stretch in nylon gives it strength. Hemp rope would have snapped by now. Bouncing up like a yo-yo and then down, until slowly, gently, I came to rest, suspended in space.

This was another Outward Bound challenge, a rappel off the high ridge between Snowmass Mountain and Capital Peak, July, 1964. It was my first year as director of the Colorado Outward Bound School. This was not the first of my summer's challenges.

My career in Outward Bound had experienced a meteoric rise. Instructor in 1962. Mountain program director in 1963. Director in 1964. I was in the right place at the right time. As Woody Allen said, "Eighty percent of life is just showing up."

When I had joined Outward Bound in 1962, I saw it as a logical continuation of my career that combined adventure with education. I'd climbed in Britain, the Alps and the lower Himalayas, taught in Kurt Hahn's school, Gordonstoun in Scotland. Hahn was the founder of Outward Bound. My wife, Andrea Lynd had climbed the Matterhorn. We had climbed in the Tetons and the Canadian Rockies. Two years before Outward Bound was founded in America, we had hiked the Inca Trail in Peru with a group of North Shore Country Day School boys, where I was teaching.

The Colorado Outward Bound School had made a deep impression. Personally it had been a great personal adventure climbing 14,000 foot peaks, being paid to do what I wanted to do. As a teacher I'd seen spectacular growth in students, overcoming fear to develop courage and confidence, inter-racial groups working together, cooperative and caring, leadership emerging. It was for me a transformational professional experience in teaching and learning, that would be life defining.

Invited back after my first summer as the mountain program director, I was impelled into my first experience of leadership as a manager. Since boyhood I'd seem myself as a leader. At prep school, first in my class, captain of football and hockey, head prefect. It left me with more confidence than my abilities warranted. But good leaders aren't necessarily good managers, it took me awhile to learn.

My views of leadership were simplistic. First over the barricades. "Follow me boys." Or a schoolmaster's perception of leadership, standing before a class and hectoring.

But as a manager I had no concept of delegation. Why delegate when I could do it better myself? I dominated staff meetings, talked too much, knit-picked details. Tap Tapley, the chief instructor, who had helped found the school, had developed the program and ran it the first year, was offended by my interference. I undermined his authority, he felt, and responded by boycotting staff meetings. He retreated to the solitude of his house. Both of us were masters of avoidance and neither of us were able to resolve the impasse.

In spite of all, I was invited back in 1964, this time as director.

In many ways 1963-4 was one of transition and turmoil. Andy and I had planned to move on from the North Shore Country Day School in Illinois where we'd been teaching for five years.

I interviewed at the Woodstock School in Vermont that had an active outdoor program. A colleague from my Gordonstoun days had been appointed the director of the International School in Ibadan, Nigeria, and was recruiting staff. The St. Louis Country Day School invited me to interview for the head of their lower school. Vermont? Ibadan? St.Louis?

Outward Bound was not in the picture because at that time it was only a summer job and not a career opportunity. Then in February, Charles Froelicher, chairman of the board, phoned offering me the job of director, a full time position. I'd be based in Denver during the winter, Marble during the summer. So we packed up and moved to Colorado.

My teaching contract had four months to run until the end of the school year. During the interim, the executive committee of the board handled the administration of the school. Most of it devolved on Froelicher. But I was given the responsibility of hiring the instructors.

Froelicher mentioned that he had been approached by Paul Petzoldt, the famous Teton guide and Himalayan climber. I'd read of his attempt on K2 before WWII, where he had set a high altitude record for an American at that time. He was a friend of Tapley's, having been together in the U.S. Army Tenth Mountain Division during the war. He had visited him at Marble at the end of the previous summer, though I had not met him. "He'd make a good chief instructor," Froelicher said.

Paul Petzoldt was a formidable man. He made a trip east that winter with his new wife, a successful Wyoming businesswoman, the owner of the Lander radio station. They came by to visit Andy and me in Winnetka. We met over brunch in a hotel overlooking Lake Michigan, a restaurant more expensive than I would have chosen. Barrel-chested, over six foot tall, he had the ruddy complexion of a man who had spent his life battling the elements, a broad jaw and high forehead. Paul had the longest eyebrows of any person I had ever met, that curled up like the bent bristles of an old tooth brush. People turned their heads when he entered the dining room. He spoke with a voice that would carry across a mountain valley. He was a great raconteur. I forget what we talked about, other than he did most of the talking. I offered him the job of chief instructor. He accepted. Then we reviewed the staff files. He recommended a couple of his friends, Tenth Mountain Division veterans. Paul picked up the tab, asking his wife for her American Express credit card. I left feeling like the rookie junior lieutenant who had been briefed by the veteran master sergeant. I also felt that Petzoldt really wanted to be the director of the school and perhaps already saw himself in that role.

Froelicher had Petzoldt and I fly into Denver for a weekend meeting to plan the summer. A Reader's Digest article from April 1963 continued to generate numerous applications. Froelicher was eager to increase enrollment. With three 28-day courses during the summer months, when students were available, we could accommodate 300. How to handle more? Petzoldt suggested a simple solution, overlap the courses. Since students spent only half their time in camp, the rest on expedition, when the first group went into the field, a new group could begin their course. Groups could shuttle back and forth, one coming in when the other went out, and vice versa. The army did it all the time. Petzoldt sketched out a schedule for the summer. The calculus seemed feasible. At least on paper.

I arrived late for orientation, not able to leave Winnetka until school was out and making the move to Denver. But Paul had organized the school base camp, the equipment and logistics. He had reconnoitered new rock climbing areas, a beginners area on the gentle sloping slab on Sheep Mountain, a high rappel 120 feet above Lizard Lake, an advanced rock climbing camp on the buttress at the base of Snowmass Mountain. The 250-foot high rappel between Snowmass and Capital Peak was his invention.

Snow lay late on the north side of Treasury Ridge. Paul marched students high on the slope kicking steps up, the plunge step down, cutting footholds in the hard snow with an ice axe, glissading down on their feet and the ice axe arrest. As the final test, he sent students down a steep slope head first on their back to execute a self-arrest. Angelo, a Latino boy from New York, crossed himself, said a *"hail Mary,"* seized his ice axe like a drowning man clutching for a piece of driftwood, and shot off downhill in a spray of wet snow.

A great showman, Paul began his evening lecture on hypothermia by walking to the drinking fountain and filling a climbing boot with water. He placed it on the fireplace mantel behind him and left it there. He scorned blue jeans, extolled the merits of wool. "If your feet are cold put on your hat," he said. For years my children thought this was the Outward Bound motto. At the end of the lecture he paused, as if confused. "I feel I've forgotten something."

"The boot!" the boys shouted.

"Oh yes. That reminds me." And he launched into a dissertation on blisters, our number one medical problem. "Soak your boots and wear them around camp to break them in."

The first course went well. But as the summer wore on the complicated schedule clashed and logistics broke down. Capacity was 100 students. On July 22, for example, we had 150 students in the school. One contingent of a hundred scheduled to leave after breakfast were held up by the slow sorting and distribution of field rations. They collided with another fifty students coming in eager for showers and a hot lunch. The logic of our planning had been compelling, the reality growing chaos.

There was the customary attrition of students with minor injuries and those few wanting to drop out. With counseling they could usually be encouraged to succeed. But this took time and became increasingly difficult and students were lost in the shuffle. An instructor twisted his ankle on steep snow slope and had to be evacuated and a relief instructor found. We hadn't planned for relief instructors. They were supposed to be indestructible.

We also had to provide logistics support for two instructors' training courses being run out of Marble by Tapley. This had been overlooked in our planning. When the old school Jeep broke down, students were left without rations in the field until a support vehicle could be found. Some groups were supplied by pack horse.

Then the film crew arrived. The Adolph Coors Company had sponsored the making of a documentary. Paul Petzoldt attached himself to the film crew and organized a separate program for them with equipment, porters to carry heavy equipment, and technical assistance in the high country. Another last minute improvisation.

Instructors complained to the logistics coordinator. An overburdened and an overbearing man, he did not brook criticism well. Tempers flared. He threatened to quit and was not easily mollified.

Then a crisis over food, the most volatile of issues. The cook was a gourmet chef in an upscale restaurant in San Francisco in the winter, where he had season tickets to the opera. Before coming to Outward Bound, he had worked summers in Aspen to attend the music festival there. His cooking was first class, marinated prime roast beef, steamed vegetables, potatoes au gratin. No question of quality, but students complained of the quantity. They were perpetually hungry. They wanted more mashed potatoes and gravy. Peanut butter and jelly on the table. They asked for bread. The chef would have given them cake. He was outraged at the thought of peanut butter and jelly. "Not in my dining room."

I insisted. "I never thought I'd lose sleep over peanut butter and jelly," I told Andrea that night.

But there were deeper issues, or so they seemed at the time. I had "progressive" ideas about Outward Bound stemming from my days at Gordonstoun. I resented the paramilitary trappings. The film, *As Tall as the Mountains,"* captured it all. It opens with the cacophonous clanging of a steel triangle and a photogenic instructor, in real life a polished admissions officer at Dartmouth College, yelling at kids, "Everyone out!" Up at six a.m., we ran a mile and leapt into snow fed Lost Trail Creek. I didn't object to the early rise, the run, or the cold dip. I ran with them. But I felt it could be done with less yelling. Perhaps because I had been yelled at so much as a child by a hyper-tense mother, I always baulked when yelled at. I didn't see why students had to be subjected to it.

I wasn't alone. "No one smiles," a friend commented. I was invited to show the film at a conference convened by Kurt Hahn a couple years later. He expressed concern that we were "fostering a toughness cult."

The final test came at a Chicago suburban high school. At an assembly over 900 students saw the film. Not one enrolled in Outward Bound. The boot camp image of Outward Bound was deeply implanted on the image.

The film featured Petzoldt as "The Old Man of the Mountain." I am filmed reading Thoreau, "I went to the woods to live deliberately...to front only the essential facts of life...and not when I came to die discover that I had not lived."

But I made little headway with the "progressive-ization" of Outward Bound. A schism developed within the staff. There was a military wing, the Tenth Mountain cabal, I called them. I felt they discounted me as a "closet pacifist."

The board of trustees and members of a newly formed national board met at Marble in early August. I presented a report that admitted to the difficulties I'd had, openly and frankly: the stress of expansion, the disorganization, and the conflict of values. Reading between the lines, it was clear there was a clash of egos, mine included.

Paul Petzoldt has asked to make a proposal at the meeting. Given the number of inquiries from the Reader's Digest article, Outward Bound should establish a second school in Wyoming. He offered himself as director. His proposal was tabled for later consideration.

I learned later that after the meeting, Petzoldt, the chef who resented peanut butter and jelly disparaged his culinary art, and the logistic coordinator met with Froelicher, the chairman. They complained of my leadership and threatened to resign if I was reappointed director.

The following week Petzoldt was informed that his proposal had been turned down. Outward Bound's national strategy was to corner-post the country. New schools in Minnesota and Maine were already being planned. The next day, he left. He took with him the office rolodex with the student address lists of recent Outward Bound graduates. From these he recruited the first class at his new school, the National Outdoor Leadership School in Lander, Wyoming. He was immensely successful with his adaptation of Outward Bound. He placed a heavier emphasis on skills development and an adventure ethic.

Petzoldt avoided one of Outward Bound's great errors. We saw the course as a one-time experience, something akin to a conversion experience, being reborn. Kurt

Hahn saw service as the logical follow up to adventure. Paul saw adventure as a succession of experiences. He invited his students to come back year after year, cultivated his alumni and over the years has built a loyal following.

NOLS transformed Paul from the charismatic guide and mountaineer who went through much of his life adrift, to become one of the gurus in adventure education. In NOLS he found a mission. Eventually he had a falling out with NOLS but went on to found the Wilderness Education Association. Paul was never a man at a loss for a new scheme.

My summer had been volatile, contentious. Most of the staff remained outside the fray. Students were positive about their experiences. One commenting in his end-of-course evaluation, wondered if the disorganization wasn't part of the program, intended to test his resourcefulness. I gave a good account of the summer to the board at their fall meeting.

But after presenting my report, I was excused. For nearly an hour I sat in the library before being called back in. "Joe, we've been discussing your performance," John Holden confronted me. He was the director of the Colorado Rocky Mountain School, a trustee whom I admired and turned to for advice. "Can you give us any reason why you shouldn't be fired?" he said.

"Well, I could give you many reasons why I should be fired," I said when I recovered from the blow. "But I can also tell you that no one will be able to run this school so long as the staff feel they can go behind the director's back and take their complaints directly to the board." I felt, perhaps unfairly, that Froelicher had given encouragement to Petzoldt. I thought he wanted my job, if he couldn't have his own school. I defended the decisions I had made and said that I would recommend them again to whoever they chose as the next director.

I was dangling from a high rappel. Suspended.

Joe at Colorado Outward Bound School 1963.

Chapter 62: Exiled

Mist swept across the ridge. Rain dripped off the hood of my green parka and trickled down my neck. The beaten path led through knee high heather, brushing my waterproof pants, soaking my leather boots. I hiked at the end of the line, following ten young Outward Bound students, bodies bent beneath the weight of their water soaked packs. They trod on at a quick pace, breathing hard, eager to reach the meadow where we would camp. *How much longer?* I wondered. Dusk was already settling in, though it was only mid-afternoon. The Lake District in England at 54 degrees north is the same latitude as Hudson's Bay. In November night fell early.

I perspired heavily beneath my waterproof. *Should I unzip my jacket? Which do you prefer?* I asked myself. *Cold and wet from rain? Or hot and wet from sweat?* It was already dark when we camped at four o'clock. I burrowed into our tent, peeled off my wet clothes, put on dry woolies and fired up the primus stove.

I wasn't terminated by the board of the Colorado Outward Bound School in spite of my poor performance in the summer of 1964. Merely sent into exile. "The board have decided to send you to England and see how they run their schools," the chairman told me. So there I was banished to the land of perpetual mists, trudging behind a group of eighteen-year-old factory apprentices over the wind blown ridges of Scafell Pike. After my tumultuous year, I welcomed the raw simplicity of existence, merely having to place one foot in front of the other.

Ralph Clough, the instructor who took me with his group, was an old friend. He'd spent two summers in Colorado as a "visiting Outward Bound advisor." By six p.m. we'd finished our dinner of sausages,(students called them "bangers,") reconstituted dehydrated potatoes, "flap jacks," (a heavy oatmeal biscuit saturated with treacle), capped off with our last cup of tea. I snuffed out the candle and settled in for the long night. For eight hours I slept. Soundly. In the owl hours I woke, lit a candle and read from two a.m. until eight when first light began to gray the sky and Ralph brewed our first cup of tea. After a breakfast of oatmeal and raisins, we slipped out of our dry clothes, folded them carefully in waterproof plastic bags, slithered into yesterday's wet clothes and by ten marched off for another day of character building.

"All pull together/ Through the story weather/ Carry on. Carry on. Carry on," the lead boy broke into the World War II song, and the rest joined in. "Keep on trying/ Keep the old flag flying/ Carry on. Carry on. Carry on."

But the nights. Not a star in the sky, wind flogging the tent, rain pelting the canvas, I luxuriated in my cocoon. To be able to lie in bed for six uninterrupted hours, and read. It seemed like a mountain holiday.

During those nights I reread a thin paperback, *Honest to God*, written by John A.T. Robinson, the bishop of Woolwich. I remember it still forty-five years later. In a modern, scientific and secular era, one needs to demythologize religion, bring it out of the Middle Ages, the good bishop wrote. The stories of the Bible, the creation, Moses parting the Red Sea, Jesus walking on the water, need to be seen as metaphoric constructs, and understood for their symbolic meaning and not as literal truth.

President Kennedy had recently set the goal of placing a man on the moon. Would an astronaut find heaven on the way? No, the bishop reasoned. Heaven was not up there, or out there. "The kingdom of heaven is within you," he quoted from the Gospel of St. John. The idea of a supernatural heaven is the greatest obstacle to intelligent faith, he argued.

This was profound stuff at two o'clock in the morning, by candle light, in a wind-blown tent. Little did I realize that I had stumbled into the greatest theological dispute of the 20th century. Bishop Robinson was declared a heretic and attempts were made to have him defrocked. But the book sold over a million copies. Like Saul on the road to Damascus, I found it raised questions of my own faith and the lack thereof. While not a conversion experience, it set me on the track to probe again for deeper meaning in my own life that led me to the Unitarians. It is the most compelling memory of my exile.

Captain Freddie Fuller put me on to the book. He was the warden of Aberdovey on the west coast of Wales, the first of the Outward Bound schools. A short man, like myself, but broader of girth, he had sparkling blue eyes set off by wrinkles and crows' feet, the bright flushed cheeks of the guardsman on a Beefeater gin bottle. He was in his early sixties.

"How did you come to Outward Bound?" I asked.

"I was sent," he said. *Another exile*, I thought. "During World War II I was in the merchant navy," he told me. " In 1942 over 1500 merchant ships were sunk by German submarines. My ship was torpedoed in the Caribbean. We spent a week in the lifeboats before being picked up by another ship. Two days later we were torpedoed again and spent another ten days in the boats until rescued.

"When I was back to Britain, my boss, Lawrence Holt, the president of the Blue Funnel Line, called me in. He was appalled by the loss of life among young seamen. They were the first to give up, when older men who were less fit held on. Something needed to be done. Then he described the new school he had set up here at Aberdovey. That was the first I had heard of Kurt Hahn and Outward Bound. 'I'd like you to go down there, rest up. Tell them what it takes to survive in the life boats, and let me know what you think,' Holt told me.

"I was impressed with the place, but after a month I was eager to get back to sea. I put in for another ship. Holt wanted me to stay. 'You'll make a greater contribution to the war effort if you do,' he said. Well, the next year I did come back and I've been here ever since."

Freddie had been a seminal figure in the expansion of Outward Bound in following years, four more schools in Britain, and others in former British colonies, Malaysia, Kenya and Nigeria. He had been a consultant to the Peace Corps when they set up a training center in Puerto Rico and to the first American Outward Bound school in Colorado.

"Has the program changed much over the years?" I asked.

"Oh, yes. The early program centered on small boat training, still does. And fitness training, the Olympic events of running, jumping and throwing. We have students compete, not against each other, but against their own best performance in each event. We're not interested in athletic excellence for the gifted athlete, but all round self-improvement for all students.

"During the war that we added mountaineering and rock climbing. The Army trained mountain warfare troops here in Wales and their instructors provided us expertise. We added a three-day expedition to Cader Idris. From commando training we got the ropes course and team problem solving exercises like scaling the wall.

"Training in first aid, sea rescue, fire fighting, mountain rescue and forestry, fosters a Samaritan service ethic.

"From the Peace Corps I learned about drown proofing. When I returned here I had a pool built and now all students do it, bobbing one hour with hands and feet tied. It's an exercise in learning to overcome fear. For some boys its more frightening than the fear of heights in rock climbing.

"Recently I ran a program in Belfast. We brought Catholic and Protestant boys together for three weeks. They camped out in church halls, trained for athletics and played football on local playing fields, rappelled off warehouses, spent their afternoons in service projects renovating homes for the old and the poor. In the evenings they came together to confront religious differences, to discuss the causes of conflict and how to resolve them. And it worked. Young fellows that were throwing paving stones at each other only weeks before, learned to pull together, just like in the life boats.

Could an urban program help us address racial conflict in the United States? I wondered.

I was captivated by Freddie, his creativity, his ecumenical view, Outward Bound adapting to different environments, to different political and social circumstances, to the needs of different people. "Times change. Outward Bound needs to redefine its mission constantly," Freddie said. *What was our mission?* He set me thinking.

"What's the place of religion in Outward Bound?" I asked one evening. I had observed morning prayers, grace said before each meal, and on Sunday boys were permitted to go the church in the village. I'd visited many churches in Britain, most nearly empty.

"There are no atheists in a lifeboat," Freddie said. "Prayer kept many men alive. So we felt it was important to have religious services. Still do. But the church is another matter." Freddie presented me with a copy of Bishop Robinson's book, *Honest to God.* "You ought to read this," he said.

I did read it, and we discussed it late into the night over glasses of port. God, Bishop Robinson wrote,(and here I struggled to understand), was what was ultimate in our lives. It was "the ground of our being," he quoted Tillich, the American existential theologian. God is what gives meaning to our lives and to nature. Whenever we act ethically, lovingly, compassionately toward an-other, we are reaching toward God and embracing ethical values.

"I think that is what Outward Bound is about," Freddie said.

I'd been sent to Britain to learn how they ran their schools. I had difficulty with many of their practices. There was a formality we could never emulate in Colorado. Aberdovey was more hierarchical, quasi-military. Students wore a uniform, neatly pressed navy blue coveralls. They stood for parade each morning for announcements, addressed their instructors as, "Sir."

Other differences struck me as comical, the mid-morning break for tea, "the cup that cheers but does not inebriate," as Lipton's proclaimed. It seemed that time was regulated by cups of tea, like bells in a cloister. In the evening, instructors sauntered down to the local pub to throw darts over a pint.

But there was sense of tradition, the professionalism of a permanent staff, the predictable pace of a year round school that I envied. What a contrast to the frenzied pace of Colorado, where we had to reinvent ourselves each year and cram all our programs into three months of the summer.

Eskdale, the second Outward Bound School was founded in 1950 in the Lake District. I recalled my visit in 1955 when Eric Shipton was warden. It was from him that I learned of Gordonstoun and Kurt Hahn. I felt like a pilgrim returning to the shrine of his patron saint.

Tom Price, then warden, came from that tradition of school masters who were outstanding mountaineers. A lean wiry man of medium height, soft spoken and unassuming, he walked with the light step of a gymnast. As a school boy he had found freedom hiking in these mountains, inevitably he learned to scale its rock faces.

"Initially there were those who had misgivings about whether a mountain school would have the same impact as did the sea school," Tom told me. "In England there is long tradition of the sea to draw upon. But we also have the tradition of the mountains, the Lakeland poets. Wordsworth walked these hills. Keats you know, climbed Ben Nevis. But theirs was a different message, poetry as a window into self, the wilderness as a spiritual quest.

"The programs are different. Instructors will argue which is better. There is a healthy rivalry. It is felt that the crews bond more rapidly at the sea schools and there are more opportunities for service. The mountains are a more personal adventure. The challenge is, how to maintain a balance."

"Programs like this should be in more schools," I said.

"Well, it is," he said, and told me of the outdoor pursuit centers," he said. There were fifty of them throughout Britain, funded by the local county education authorities. Students came with their teachers for a week of adventure activities and field studies. I remembered hiking by Glenmore Lodge in the Cairngorms in Scotland with Gordonston boys years before, but never made the connection. I thought it was a youth hostel. Many of the centers were run by former Outward Bound instructors, Tom told me.

Jack Longland, a pre-war Everest climber, now education officer for Derbyshire, had established the first center. He was a friend of Kurt Hahn's and an Outward Bound trustee. The Hahn influence seemed pervasive. I had meet Jack Longland's son, then a Cambridge student, climbing in the Alps in 1956. The adventure education world seemed very connected. For the first time I began to feel a part of a broader professional fraternity.

Tom Price arranged for me to visit Brathay Hall nearby. Their program combined adventure: mountaineering, rock climbing, kayaking and small boat sailing, with cultural activities: art, music and dance, and field studies projects in natural history. It had the richness of the Gordonstoun curriculum. It was also co-educational. What a difference girls made. It was a place of laughter and joy. By comparison Outward Bound seemed grim and dour.

The Ullswater Outward Bound Mountain School, also in the Lake District had a program similar to Eskdale. The warden, Squadron Leader Lester Davies, had experimented with courses for younger students, fourteen to sixteen years of age. I spoke of the challenge of running these in such severe conditions. "You need to dunk them and dry them," Lester Davies said. It was a chilly day and I moved closer to the open fire.

Was I learning anything about how they run their schools? I'd visited three schools and met three very different wardens. Freddie Fuller was ebullient and full of new ideas. He ran his school as a captain on the bridge, somewhat inaccessible, but there when needed. Tom Price at Eskdale, congenial, the sort of person you'd welcome as a tent mate on a long expedition, ran Eskdale like a professor conducting a graduate seminar, informed, attentive, authoritative without being authoritarian, collegial. Squadron Leader Davies moved through Ullswater, which ran like clock work, with a military stride, attentive to every detail. No instructor would think of calling Captain Fuller, "Freddie." Or Squadron Leader Davies, "Lester." But they did call Tom Price, "Tom." Each marched to a different drummer.

Instructors called me "Joe."

Above all, it was an invaluable recruiting trip. At Eskdale I met Vic Walsh, a 26-year old veteran of the Royal Air Force British special forces unit, who had made several first ascents in the New Zealand Alps, the first ascent of Ronday (20,000 feet) in the Andes. He joined me in Colorado and for the next decade pioneered programs for school groups, delinquents, teachers, corporate managers. He left to become the director of the Pacific Crest Outward Bound School in Oregon and later pursued a successful academic career at Harvard and Portland State College in Oregon.

At Ullswater I met Alistair McArthur, a 23-year old Australian, who after graduating from school, spent two and a half years as a district officer in primitive Borneo. He was on his way to Antarctica. "Colorado is on the way. Why don't you join us?" I said. He spent many productive years in Colorado, became program director and later director of the Canada Outward Bound Wilderness School. Returning to Australia in his middle years, he became an authoritative outdoor programs consultant addressing issues of safety.

At Aberdovey I met Raef Parker. At the time he was also reading *Honest to God*. I recall discussions long into the evening, trying to comprehend the nature of the Divinity, the mystery of the Trinity, the paradox of one God that was as Father, Son and Spirit. Years before on a military training exercise, Raef's parachute failed to open. He landed in a tree and survived. Like Lazarus, he believed in miracles. Raef joined the new Hurricane Island school, founded that year. After a long Outward Bound career, he became president of the Sea Education Association, a tall ships program that offered a semester-at-sea in marine research.

Others followed. Men like them became the bed rock on which the Colorado Outward Bound School, and Outward Bound USA were built. I had tapped a rich talent pool.

At the end of my trip, before flying out of London, I was invited to meet Sir Spencer Summers, the chairman of Outward Bound Trust. A Member of Parliament, successful businessman, he was an imposing man, tall with a long face and prominent aristocratic nose. He was dressed immaculately in a deep blue pin stripe Saville Row tailored suit. In my tweed jacket and gray flannels I felt shabbily clad. He was the corporate power house behind Outward Bound, its chief fund raiser. Every charitable organization needs one.

Sir Spencer and I had a nice talk. I listened and I learned more about the centralized structure of the Outward Bound Trust in Britain. The trust owned all the schools, hired the wardens, approved the programs, raised the capital funds, recruited the students. By contrast, the Colorado Outward Bound School was autonomous. Founded before Outward Bound Inc., the national organization in America, Colorado was responsible for its own fiscal viability. My job as director was different than that of the warden of a British school.

I raised one question with Sir Spencer. Kurt Hahn spoke of the "duty of replication." The outdoor pursuits movement addressed that, I thought. What did he think?

There was an audible, "Harumph. Outward Bound is committed to character training," he said. "You can't do that in one week."

Case dismissed. I would run into the same skepticism again. Historically the fiscal viability of Outward Bound in America was threatened in later years by a similar proliferation of outdoor programs, many run by former Outward Bound staff. Like Britain, the response was to consolidate and centralize.

What did I learn? As I flew home, over Greenland the late afternoon sun cast long shadows of ice bergs, pink, mauve and purple over the blue ice. I reviewed my notes.

Most of all I learned that there was a living dynamic to Outward Bound. It was not cast in a rigid mold. It had evolved over the years, had changed and continued to do so. The Brits had shown that the life enhancing challenge of adventure and the call to service could be adapted to different environments, the sea, mountains, the jungles of Africa and Asia. The Belfast project suggested that it could work in the city too. It worked with different groups, addressed different social need. The British model had served us well. But like Captain Fuller, I believed that Outward Bound had to change with the times.

On the practical side, I learned that my job as a school director was not just to run a program, but to create an institution. That was a daunting challenge, but also intimidating. To do so I needed to attract and hold a professional staff. That meant year round programs to support full time jobs. Where to begin?

I also had a vision, though that overstated my half formed ideas, more an intuitive hunch rather than a rational plan. Fifty outdoor pursuits centers in Britain, many started and staffed by former instructors. Having taught at Gordonstoun I realized that Outward Bound derived from the program of a school. Could we reverse the process? Could Outward Bound in America be the catalyst for the development of an adventure education movement in America?

I would keep to myself. Just like the notion that heaven was not be up there, the idea might be seen as heretical. It would have to unfold in its own time.

And if heaven isn't up there? We need to locate God deep in the human person rather than above and beyond the world, Bishop Robinson wrote. Marrying God with ethics emphasizes this world rather than the next. Without ecclesiastical trappings, wasn't Outward Bound on a similar spiritual quest?

But at that time, Colorado did not need a visionary nor a mystic. It needed a manager. I never did write a report of my exile. Not until now.

Chapter 63: C-13 A Trilogy of Tragedy — Rossetter

Bobby Rossetter, fourteen years old, was last seen ten days before hiking down the path down from Trail Riders Pass in the Snowmass Wilderness Area west of Aspen in Colorado. Over 400 people, including 100 Outward Bound students had combed the mountainsides and the river banks and still had not found the boy. Not a stitch of clothing, none of his backpacking gear, not a foot print. He had disappeared without a trace. We had abandoned the search.

Two days later, Peter Hildt, an instructor with twelve Outward Bound students in Carson patrol, made one last effort. They probed along the banks of Geneva Creek where it flows into the North Fork of the Crystal River, within 400 yards of where the search had begun almost two weeks before.

"Geneva Creek was a virtual waterfall" Peter wrote me later, "tumbling down a 1000 feet over a succession of ledges, swollen by the mid-summer runoff of melting snow. The two streams converged in a steep ravine, forming a dark gray buttress, 80 to 100 feet high, that reminded me of the bow of an inverted ship; two ominous, smooth slopes where the water had eroded the featureless shale, dangerous to descend, or to climb, without being roped up. The Crystal River was only about twenty feet wide but running too deep and fast to cross on foot."

"Further downstream," Peter said, "I came to a log dam of uprooted trees, avalanche debris jammed in a tangled mass, turgid water overflowing gray and opaque, silt laden. Looking down into the whirling mass, I thought I saw a flash as if something metallic. But the afternoon light glinted off the splashing water so it was difficult to be sure. But it was still there. I thought I better have a closer look. So I took off my pack and worked my way down the bank. I stepped out on a log to examine it more closely.

"At first I couldn't find it. Then I got a brief glimpse. It looked like the teeth of a metal zipper reflecting the light. And I recognized the red cloth backing to a zipper. That's all I could see, but I knew that it was the zipper with a red backing, just like the pocket of a Kelty backpack. I had a Kelty backpack, so I knew the zipper.

"Bobby Rosseter had been wearing a Kelty backpack. Could this be his backpack? I couldn't tell, but it was definitely the pocket zipper of a Kelty pack." Peter told me.

Ten days before I was camped with my wife on a high knoll in Bear Basin, below Treasury Ridge at the upper reaches of tree line. Just the two of us.

Snowmass Mountain, 14,092 feet, five miles across the valley, the south ridge curving in an elongated "S", was aglow in the purple late afternoon light. Geneva Lake tucked within the high forest in the glacial bowl at the foot of the mountain. Geneva Falls caught the last flashing threads of silver. Lead King Basin in the valley below nestled in somber shadow. I asked Andy to pose on a rock in the foreground, framing the scene. Her outstretched arms reached to the sky, as if she conducted a choir of angels in the chorale of Beethoven's Ninth symphony. It would make a spectacular promotional photograph, I thought.

I'd smuggled steaks and a demi of Beaujolais in my pack and we luxuriated over a gourmet dinner in the glow of a campfire.

"Hear that?" Andy picked it up first with her sharp hearing. Faint whistle blasts, muffled, indistinct, came from the valley below. There was a minute's pause. Then again. Six blasts in succession. Clearer now.

"That's the international distress signal," I said to Andy. "We'd better pack up." Before leaving school I'd left word where staff could find me. I'd been found.

"Oh no," Andy said. I felt I could hear her thinking, *Sometimes I wonder who you're married to, Outward Bound or me?*

I resented the intrusion but had not choice. I replied with a single long blast on my whistle.

As we descended, the wine and the euphoria wore off. I anticipated some looming disaster. Outward Bound was a high risk endeavor. That was part of its attraction. With the risk came anxiety. What could be amiss?

Half an hour later I met Vic Walsh, trudging up through the aspen forest, blowing vigorously on his whistle. The instructor of Outward Bound Lewis patrol, he was a seasoned international mountaineer, having received his early training in an elite counter-terrorist unit in the British army and gone on to climb in the New Zealand Alps and the Andes. I'd met Vic the previous winter on my visit to the Eskdale Outward Bound Mountain School in the Lake District of England and had invited him to come to Colorado. A soft spoken, unassuming Englishman of Irish descent, he wasted few words, "Ashcrofter have lost a boy and they're asking us to help search for him."

The Ashcrofter School of Mountaineering near Aspen was one of the first summer camps to offer a high adventure program for boys twelve to fifteen. "An Outward Bound for younger kids," is the way Dave Farney, the owner director described it.

We headed down and Vic filled in the details. "Yesterday was the last day of their week long expedition. Coming out from Snowmass Lake, the boys were spaced out on the trail, a quarter of a mile apart. Sort of a solo hike, a time for reflection. They were to rendezvous in Lead King Basin. The lad never showed up."

My first reaction was selfish. *Thank God it's not an Outward Bound student,* I thought.

Kurt Hahn, the German educator who inspired the Outward Bound concept, spoke of Samaritan service, the redemptive power of service, particularly dramatic lifesaving service. Here was our opportunity to put it into practice. On further thought I saw it as a learning opportunity.

It was day seven of a 28-day course, C-13 of the Colorado Outward Bound School, July, 1965. Our students were on their basic training expedition, learning camp craft skills, map reading, route finding, carrying heavy packs for the first time, acclimating to the rarified atmosphere at 11,000 feet.

"How can we turn a training expedition into a rescue operation?" I asked Vic.

He had already discussed it with Paul Sanders, instructor of Outward Bound Crocket Patrol. Sanders was, a member of the elite Los Angeles County Mountain Search and Rescue team, a former US Air Force survival training instructor. A man of medium height, muscular physique, with short cut hair, he had a military bearing. He had a reputation for being attentive to the smallest detail, even to cutting off the handle of his tooth brush to lighten his pack.

Both Walsh's and Sander's patrols were camped in Lead King Basin. By coincidence this was where Bobby Rossetter had been scheduled to rendezvous with his group. end his hike. "We could begin the search there," Vic said. I agreed. In Crystal at the foot of the valley we parted, Vic to rally other Outward Bound patrols were camped nearby. Andy and I returned to Outward Bound base at Marble to organize rescue equipment, transport, and logistics.

Herb Kincey, the instructor of Outward Bound Cody patrol, told me later that they were camped near the Crystal River. Sanders roused them in the middle of the night. "It was pouring rain and we had to pack up and move out. The river was up to its banks, nearly flooding over. We crossed on the sagging cable burma bridge. In the dark you could barely see it, but when the bridge sagged the water almost came up to our boots.

"Is this just another form of Outward Bound harassment?" one student asked.

"Get on with it. It's good character training," another replied.

"Nor was I so sure until I saw the Land Rover at Crystal. A sherpa had been sent to transport us up to Lead King Basin. It was like driving through a boulder field, the old mining road above the canyon was so rough By the time we got there we were convinced that his was no training drill. This was the real thing."

I returned to Lead King Basin early next morning. Six of the eight Outward Bound patrols had gathered there. I met with the instructors and sherpas. Sherpas were outstanding former Outward Bound students who had been invited to return as instructor trainees, fit, motivated, enthusiastic.

"What's the plan?" I asked. Sanders spread out maps and outlined a strategy for the search. Clearly he had done this before and enjoyed the role. "Our first priority is to do a hasty search. We need to run all the trails and over the easy passes, check out the roads, in and around all buildings or cabins in the area. Try to anticipate any wrong turn a disoriented kid could wander off on. The Ashcrofters staff have already done some of this. We'll do it again. If he's alive this has the highest probability of finding him."

If he's alive? This was the first intimation I had that he might not be alive.

There were five obvious routes the boy could have taken. Sanders asked for instructor and sherpa volunteers, and had them select two of their fittest students to accompany them. He assigned them routes and they took off. I expected they'd find him before the day was out.

"The rest of us are the infantry in this campaign, the ground pounders. We'll do a series of line searches" Sanders resumed. "Ten people in a row about 15-to-20 feet apart, we'll search off the trail, behind every rock and under every tree, like a drag net. We'll search in high probability areas, starting at the point last seen."

"His name is Bobbie. Bobbie Rossetter. Fourteen years old and very fit. He's been hiking for the last week, and could wander a long way if lost.

"He was last seen in the thick forest around Geneva Lake." Sanders pointed up the mountainside, a thousand feet above us. "Heavy snow pack has obliterated the trail, but he you might find foot prints in he snow. We'll start there," Sanders said. "We're looking for someone who is alive. He's been missing only since the day before yesterday, so he should be. But he may not be responsive. Call out his name. Look for clues, like clothing, candy wrappers, foot prints.

"We'll also need to search the river banks, but that can wait until later," Sanders said. It was clear by the drop in his voice, that if Bobby was found there. His voice trailed off. Enough said.

For the next three days Outward Bound students and staff were the only searchers. We ran the trails, combed the nearby forest and mountain slopes, scoured the river banks. It was tedious work under the hot July sun, but students stuck with it. I heard little complaining and I was proud of their effort.

We didn't find Bobby Rossetter.

Nor was there any sign of him. As each day dragged on our misgivings grew like an irritant. But no one spoke of it. There was a conspiracy of silence, as if to hint of a fatal outcome would guarantee it happening. To speak of one's own creeping sense of despair would only undermine others resolve. Students muttered among themselves, but said nothing to their instructors. Nor did the instructors voice their growing fatalism. This was a nasty business and we tightened our waist straps and got on with the job. We plodded on like good soldiers, day after day, in what was becoming an exercise in futility.

On the weekend local volunteer search and rescue teams flocked in. Jeeps and four-wheel- drive pickups bristling with radio aerials crowded our one-way traffic mountain road. The air crackled and squawked with walkie-talkies. I had experienced rivalry between relief organizations as a volunteer in a refugee camp during the Hungarian Revolt of 1956, but had not expected it five days into the search for a lost boy in the mountains of Colorado.

By state law the sheriff is responsible for the safety and protection of citizens. The Pitkin County sheriff showed up to assert his authority because the Ashcrofter camp was in his jurisdiction. The next day the Gunnison County sheriff arrived in his 4x4 because Bobby had been lost in his county and most of the search activity was taking place there. We were also on U.S. Government land. The forest ranger made his appearance, prohibited driving motorized vehicles in the wilderness area,but he did grant permission for over flight by helicopter.

Two rescue units were particularly well equipped and professional: the Aspen Search And Rescue Team, and the Rocky Mountain Rescue Group from Boulder. The volunteer groups clearly had more experience in the high mountains than did the sheriff. Who should have precedence?

Until then Outward Bound had dominated the search, only because we'd been asked by the Ashcrofter's director, and because we were there with significant numbers. I sensed that others saw us as intruders on their turf. When the authorities saw that we were willing to perform the menial, boring task of line searching, there was a grudging acceptance of our role. I left it to the sheriffs and the experts to solve their jurisdictional rivalries, only making it clear that I was responsible for the safety and well being of Outward Bound students and staff. All tactical decisions involving them had to have my approval. I was invited to participate in the daily strategy sessions with other team leaders. I offered the Gunnison County deputy sheriff my office at the Outward Bound School as his operational base. It was the nearest telephone. I felt I came out of my first encounter with SAR politics relatively unscathed.

As the search expanded it turned into a quasi-military operation. Technical rock climbers searched the cliff bands and descended the canyon walls of the North Fork of the Crystal River. The State Police scuba team searched the frigid waters of Geneva Lake. The Rossetter family chartered a helicopter, and Paul Sanders scanned the upper alpine meadows as the observer. The Glenwood Springs Sage, the local paper, reported that over 400 persons were involved, one of the biggest mountain searches in the history of Colorado.

The search perimeter was widened, and with it our hopes of finding Bobby alive narrowed. It was still important to find the body, but this no longer had the same sense of urgency. After a week a sense of futility crept in. Students were the first to feel it. Line searching day after day was dull, monotonous, soul-destroying work, and they were worn out. They were slow to get out of their sleeping bags in the morning. They'd argue over whose turn it was to light the primus stove. They complained about the food. The groups split into cliques. They hadn't come to Outward Bound for this. I was slow to appreciate the erosion of morale. Nor did I consider that students were missing several days of technical training.

I was too caught up in the dynamics of a major search, the bravado and the banter among the veteran volunteer teams. It was like a chess game where we were so many pawns and the object was to capture the king. The fact that the king might be dead did not seem to concern them. The morale of Outward Bound students wasn't their problem.

I agreed to one last desperate search around Snowmass Lake where Bobby Rossetter had camped that last night. "Suppose when he was lost, he had turned back," the search coordinator had said. The area was surrounded by a dense forest area that stretched for nine miles to the newly developed ski resort down the valley. Months would be needed to comb the area thoroughly. Two Outward Bound patrols, under

Sander's charge did a hasty line search through the woods, covering a swath a hundred yards wide on each side of the trail for a couple miles below the lake.

Then they were out of food. Fifteen miles from school by mountain trail, they were too far to resupply. I'd have to abandon the search, I told the sheriff.

Like the cavalry of old, the U.S. Army came to the rescue of the rescuers. They sent a high wing military Cessna from Fort Carson, near Colorado Springs. Designed for low altitude reconnaissance with short landing and take off capability, the pilot put it down on the landing strip at Marble, a flattened strip of river gravel in the narrow valley. It came equipped with canisters, shaped like bombs, attached to each wing, that could be deployed with a parachute. We loaded these with emergency rations.

Herb Kincey, the program coordinator, a tall, 190 pound man, volunteered to accompany the pilot as observer-navigator. "The take off was rough, bumpy and turbulent. We barely cleared the aspen grove at the end of the runway. I don't know who was more scared, me or the pilot," Kincey told me later. "We bounced about, like being tossed in a blanket, as we climbed from 6000 feet at Marble to get over Trail Riders Pass at 12,500 feet. My ears popped. It was the closest I've ever come to need an air sickness bag. Then there was a steep glide to Snowmass Lake, 2000 feet below, where my stomach pushed up to my throat."

Early that morning I had hiked out to inform them of the airdrop.. Sanders had the students spread out their parkas and sweaters into a gigantic colorful cross on the meadow above the lake to mark the drop site. When he heard the hum of the plane over the pass, he set off an orange smoke bomb. "Just like the Fourth of July." Students cheered.

The pilot made one pass but dared not come in too low. Tall spruce trees lined the lake shore. Kincey waved out the window with John Wayne bravado. I stood back with students at the end of the meadow.

On the second pass the pilot came in lower and released the two canisters. The parachutes popped and they floated down, slowly coming toward us, drifting with the wind, like the Israelites receiving manna from heaven.

"Look out," one boy screamed. One parachute had collapsed and the canister descended like a rocket. I fled with the boys to the imagined protection of the trees. Sanders stood his ground. The canister hit and exploded in a fine dust of milk powder, spewing oatmeal, macaroni and cocoa mix among the blue forget-me-nots on the meadow.

That night in the dark I hiked out to Aspen to meet Tom and Birdie Rossetter, Bobby's parents. What would I say? The search had to be called off. Members of the volunteer teams were returning to their jobs. Outward Bound had to resume its program.It was hard to tell them that we were abandoning their son, abandoning them too. My mouth felt dry. But I agreed to have Outward Bound groups continue to search the swollen creeks and along the river banks that were on our expedition routes. Without it being said, we were now looking for a body. And I invited the Rossetters to stay with Andy and me at the Outward Bound school, which they accepted.

The ultimate challenge of most Outward Bound courses is the alpine expedition where students climb the 14,000 foot peaks, the Maroon Bells, Snowmass

Mountain, Capitol Peak. Peter Hildt with Carson patrol was on his route to Capitol Peak the next day when he stared down into the turgid waters of the Crystal River and was certain that he had spotted the zipper of a back pack. "It was too dangerous to retrieve it by myself. I'd need help. So I ran back downstream to where my group was camped and told them what I thought I had found," Peter wrote me later.

"I sent two students to Crystal about three miles down the valley. I knew there was no phone, but perhaps they could hitch-hike a ride back to school. I returned to the log jam with two students. After so many days searching for Bobby Rosseter, I did not want to lose sight of that zipper, or whatever else was down there. I was prepared for a midnight vigil if necessary.

"Within the hour, two all-wheel drive vehicles appeared," Peter said, "men with first aid supplies, ropes, chain saws, winches, and many patches on their jackets. My dispatchers had run into members of the Rocky Mountain Rescue Group camped in Crystal. They took charge while I just stood back with my students and observed.

"They uncoiled a rope and lowered a man on belay. It was dangerous work. The steep river bank was slippery. The rushing water was so loud we could barely hear him. They kept a tight rope on him as he moved out on the log. He was sure it was a pack all right. Possibly a Kelty. But was there anything more?

"The team sent down a second rope and he was able to attach it to the pack with a carabiner. We all pulled on the rope but it wouldn't come. It was jammed in the logs.

"He came back up and got the chain saw and began to cut the logs jammed together, holding the pack. Then the whole thing gave away like a dam bursting. We hauled and in came the pack. Attached to it was a blue mountain parka and wet blue jeans. Slumped inside was a limp body secured by the waist belt of the pack.

"I still hold the visual image of the bloated body with flesh as white as snow caused by having been in the frigid water for ten days," Peter told me.

Peter Hildt was one of the younger Outward Bound instructors, a student at the University of Colorado. A strong, big bodied man, with a ready smile, he had been raised in Denver, hiking and climbing in the mountains with his parents since childhood. He had attended the Eskdale Outward Bound Mountain School in the Lake District of England as a teenage boy, and had been an assistant on the first Outward Bound course in Colorado, C-1, the same year I was an instructor. His mother was a founding trustee of the school. But nothing had prepared him for this experience.

"Around the campfire that evening I discussed the events of the past several days with my students," Peter said. "They had become discouraged by the dull plodding repetitiveness of line searching day after day. They had come for an Outward Bound adventure. Not this. There had been a lot of bickering. They felt that Bobby Rossetter had been abandoned by his group leader while lagging behind. Then the discussion turned to how we were all dependent on each other and needed to look out for each other. I mentioned my own feelings and my need of their support.

"Suddenly this lackluster group had a new spirit. They became a cohesive team. I asked if they felt they needed to return to school to recover from the shock of finding the body? Or should we continue on to climb Capitol Peak? They chose to go on. For me, this evening discussion was as uplifting as the discovery of Bobby Rossetter's body was sobering," Peter concluded.

Later I met with the Rocky Mountain Rescue Group to draft a report analyzing the accident and the rescue response. "How do you think it happened?" the search coordinator asked. Geneva Creek, isn't normally very wide or very deep, but this summer it was a raging torrent with the high run off from the melting snow. We speculated that Bobby had tried to wade Geneva Creek and been swept away. Or he may have gone further upstream where he could cross it on a snow bridge. Perhaps he came too close to the edge and the snow collapsed, or he had slipped on the hard snow and been carried down.

Next day I drive the Rossetters to the site where Bobby's body had been recovered. The alpine flowers were in great profusion as they always are in a wet year, yellow daisies, purple asters, golden cinquefoil, red, pink and mauve Indian paint brush, red and purple columbine as delicate as orchids. The vibrancy and beauty were a mocking contrast to the death of a young life, as flowers are in most funerals.

But for the Rossetter family it was the end of uncertainty. I marveled at their composure, buoyed by a Christian faith, an acceptance of the will of God, and even a sense of pride in Bobby their son. He had lived his brief life fully to the end.

I tried to imagine this happening to one of my children, or one of my Outward Bound students. I wondered if I could summon such fortitude. I was to find out sooner than I would have wanted.

Chapter 64: A Trilogy of Tragedy — John McBride

Most mountain accidents occur on the descent, Rick Nehring knew, but he was impatient to get down. The climb had not gone well from the start, he told me later. Since the ten days of drudgery in the Rossetter search, his students had been dispirited. I sensed Nehring had been dispirited himself. Low moral is contagious. Students were difficult to rouse, slow to get moving. They should have set off at first light that morning for a major climb like Snowmass Mountain. Though some students had been up at four, they did not get off until eight.

On the climb, the students' pace dragged. They clearly did not have their hearts in it. What should have been the great event of the course turned into a long tedious trudge uphill. They stopped frequently gasping for breath. Then mid-morning one student complained of a sprained foot, and more time was lost. It was decided that Rich Tuttle, the co-instructor, would return with him to camp. It was not clear to me that Tuttle was happy with this decision.

Both Nehring and Tuttle were young instructors by Outward Bound standards, twenty-two, still in college. Both had been instructors in their college climbing clubs. Nehring from Canon City had led most of the 14,000 foot peaks in the Collegiate Range. Tuttle was the more proficient rock climber having climbed, mostly on the steep faces of limestone quarries with the Iowa Mountaineers. The month before they had completed a four-week Outward Bound instructor training course with "Tap" Tapley.

I didn't feel confident that either were ready to be in charge of a patrol by himself, but that they complemented each other, I thought they would make a good team, and assigned them as co-instructors to Outward Bound Boone patrol. Nehring, a lean young man of medium height, serious to the point of being abrupt, often with a scowl, but he was confident and decisive. Tuttle, somewhat shy, was more relaxed and friendly. Though less experienced in high mountains than Nehring, he was a better rock climber. I had also assigned Gary Randolph to guide the group on the Snowmass Mountain ascent. He was an Outward Bound sherpa, a former student who had been outstanding on his course, and invited back that summer as an instructor trainee. Gary knew the mountain well, having climbed it five times already. He did the route finding, but in other matters, such as the early rise and sending the injured student back, he deferred to Nehring.

It was two p.m. when they reached the summit. The view was spectacular, the dark red sandstone pyramid of the Maroon Bells five miles to the east. The jagged dark gray granite of Capital Peak only two miles to the north. Outward Bound groups were climbing both that day. There were mountains in all directions, as far as the eye could see. There was that moment on the summit when one could feel god-like astride the world. But not today. Someone had forgotten to pack lunch.

They should have been off the mountain by now. Randolph was anxious to start down. Though descending takes less energy than climbing up, it takes more concentration and better balance. Fatigue sets in. There's a greater danger of slipping on the snow, and dislodging loose rocks. And then there was vertigo. A veil of high cirrus cloud moved slowly across the sky, a weather front moving in.

Randolph led down. The south ridge of Snowmass shelves off to the valley to the west. On the east side it drops steeply over rock slabs and snow chutes to a high snow field in a glacial cirque below. Randolph was looking for a safe way off the ridge to the snow basin below. The group moved very slowly. Nehring was growing impatient and felt Randolph was taking too long finding a route off the ridge. He took over the lead.

An hour later they stood at the top of the snow chute leading down the snow basin below. It looked like a quick way off the rocky ridge. Steep. But it will go, Nehring thought. He had descended gullies as steep standing upright, skiing on his boots. Mountaineers called it a standing glissade. The angle was about forty-five degrees, about as steep as a house roof. But it looked a long way down, 500 feet or more. At the bottom there were rocks lightly covered in snow, not obvious from above.

This was the first time his students had made a long descent on snow. They had missed their advanced snow training because of their involvement in the Rossetter search, and had not learned the ice ace arrest, the way to stop themselves should they fall on a steep snow slope.

"Crouch down. Lean forward. Keep your weight over your feet. Balance with your ice axe. And kick steps with your heals," Nehring demonstrated. Then he led down. It looked so easy, funny even, like the Nazi goose step from a squatting position. Students followed in his steps one at a time. Half way down they sat and slid the rest of the way toboggan style. They hooted and laughed, the first fun for the day. Some wanted to climb up and do it again.

All made it safely. All except one.

John McBride stood at the top hesitating. A college student from New York, at twenty-two, he was the oldest in the group, as old as his instructors. But he had never been athletic. "I came to Outward Bound to gain confidence," he admitted without embarrassment in the intimacy of a campfire discussion. He'd been afraid to cross the high log on the ropes course, a horizontal beam ten feet off the ground. Tuttle, the other instructor, had coached him across and his group cheered him on. Now he hesitated again.

"Just look where you place your feet," Nehring repeated. To himself he said, "Just don't look down."

John took a tentative step. Then another. Two more steps. "You're doing great John," Nehring called. Then McBride looked down the slope. He lost his balance, slipped, fell on his back, dropped his ice axe, rolled, tumbled, then slid headlong. He crashed head first into the rocks below. A line of blood trailed in the snow.

Nehring's ran to him, leaping, sliding, at times airborne. He found blood oozing from McBride's head. A flap of skin, the size of a man's hand, was laid open on the top of his head. He had been scalped.

Nehring acted intuitively. He turned McBride around, feet downhill, then placed the flap of skin back on his head, as if it were his baseball cap that had fallen off. He padded it with his wool shirt and tied it in place with the sleeves. That seemed to staunch the flow of blood.

Bleeding. Breathing. Shock. Nehring recalled the mantra of first aid training.

McBride's breathing was shallow, his pallor gray, lips pale. His eyes flickered. He was semi-conscious. mumbling incoherently in a querulous voice. "Quick. Give me your parkas and sweaters," Nehring told his students. "We got to keep him warm." They padded their clothing around McBride as he faded into unconsciousness.

"Please God, don't let him die," his tent mate prayed and burst into tears.

How do I get him to a hospital? Nehring wondered. McBride would need medical treatment if he wasn't to die. His first thought was to summon a rescue party. He scribbled a note explaining the urgency, requesting help and dispatched his fastest runner to return with it to school.

Next how could he move McBride to a safer location. Two weeks earlier in a mountain rescue training class, he had instructed his student in how to construct an improvised litter using their climbing rope, ice axes and parkas, never dreaming they would have to use it so soon. With it they carried McBride down the upper snow basin where the slope was gradual. A quarter of a mile down it dropped off abruptly at the foot of the terminal moraine among boulders the size of upended cars. It was too dangerous for victim and rescuers alike without proper equipment and more manpower.

The sun dropped behind the south ridge at 5:30 p.m., an orange ball in a thickening cloud haze. Shadow stretched across the basin. Suddenly they were cold.

It would be a long night, Nehring worried. He tried to figure out the calculus of triage. He needed to prevent the injury of one student from becoming a multiple tragedy. McBride's injury was obviously life threatening. How long could he survive without professional care? How long could the students survive the less obvious effects of hypothermia. Some wore only cotton T-shirts, having given their protective clothing to McBride. They stomped about to generate body heat, huddled together to preserve warmth. And they waited.

It was about seven o'clock when a boy thought he heard a whistle. Could help be coming so soon? Sure enough, it was six blasts of a whistle from the valley below, the international distress signal. It became louder every minute. Relief was on the way.

Herb Kincey, with Cody patrol, was scheduled to climb Snowmass Mountain the next day and had moved up to the base camp at the foot of the mountain. Nehring's messenger ran into them on his way down. He passed on the gory details of the accident, painting a lurid scene of blood all over the snow. Kincey read Nehring's scribbled note.

"Is he alive or dead?" Kincey asked. The boy wasn't sure and ran on.

Kincey was a big man, tall, flamboyant North Carolinian with a resonating drawl that he held on to with a Southerner's pride. He was affable, gregarious. He'd had extensive experience leading outdoor groups in the southern Appalachians and was a certified Red Cross advanced first aid instructor. The previous winter he'd spent at Outward Bound schools in Britain and Norway. It was his second season instructing in Colorado. I'd asked him to return as program coordinator this summer.

He regularly taught emergency first aid, simulating accidents with lurid quantities of catsup for blood. There'll be no need to fake this one, he thought.

Kincey wrote out a more detailed accident report requesting a Stokes litter, emergency gear, and above all, manpower. He attached a map, indicating the site of the accident and dispatched Gordon Strickler, his assistant, and a student to return to school. He then mobilized his own rescue effort. Three Outward Bound sherpas, who were camped at the nearby rock climbing site at Prospector Springs, were directed to load their packs with climbing ropes and slings. His students brought extra warm clothing, two sleeping bags, waterproof tarps, primus stoves, cook gear, soups and hot drinks. Kincey carried his own oversized first aid kit. Heavy clouds threatening rain were building up as they set off up the mountain.

In a piece of classic Kinceyean theatre, on the first high ridge he fired off six shots from his 22 Magnum revolver, hoping to attract other Outward Bound groups he thought to be in the area. There was no response.

On the glacial moraine, they climbed through boulders the size of houses. Blowing his whistle, six long blasts, Kincey continued up in the growing dusk. On the brow of the moraine, he met two of Nehring's students, who had been sent down to guide them the rest of the way. They arrived shortly after 7.30 p.m. It began to rain.

"How is he?" Kincey asked. Nehring was non-committal. Acknowledging Kincey's seniority, Nehring asked him to take charge. Kincey examined McBride's vital signs. His pulse and breathing were normal, more or less, his face a waxy pale grey-white. "What's your name?" Kincey asked. McBride answered such simple questions of identity, mumbling incoherently between questions. There was no evident of further bleeding so Kincey decided not to change the dressing of the head wound. He left the wool shirt in place, and added several large compress bandages for additional padding, and secured them with roller bandages.

"Help me transfer him to a sleeping bag," Kincey told the students. When they untied the rope litter McBride began to struggle and scream. He kicked and struck out. Four students had to restrain him while they removed his boots and put on dry socks. Woolen mitts were taped to his hands. To keep him from ripping the bandages off his head they tied his arms. He fought them as they worked him into a sleeping bag. "It was terrifying," Kincey said, "for me and for the students." Once secured, McBride was moved to a level snow shelf. An extra sleeping bag was place beneath him. Immediately he was quiet.

Kincey was worried about Nehring's students. They'd had a long day of climbing, and then stood around for several hours in the cold without proper clothing. They'd not had a solid meal since breakfast. He wanted to send them down to their

320

camp at Prospector Springs before it got dark, but felt they'd be needed on the carry out, regardless of how tired they were. They retrieved their sweaters and parkas that had protected John, but still they shivered. A sherpa lit the primus stove and prepared hot soup. In the lee of a huge boulder they huddled out of the wind. With the coming of night light snow flurries filtered down. How long could John McBride hang on? Kincey wondered.

William James, the American philosopher, wrote an essay in 1903, "The Moral Equivalent of War." In it he reasoned that given modern technology, modern wars had become too devastating to be a viable solution to international disputes. But a warlike spirit is in our blood, in the very marrow of our bones, so ingrained in our thinking, he wrote, that war was inevitable unless we found some moral equivalent of the glory attached to war, of the excitement, the drama, the comradeship. He advocated that the young, young men that is, be drafted to work in humanitarian pursuits such as driving ambulances, fighting fires, flood relief, and to dangerous high risk occupations like lumbering, mining and fishing on the high seas. Only then would Man's thirst for the glory of martial pursuits be satisfied. This was President Kennedy's rationale for the Peace Corps. It had inspired Kurt Hahn, the founder of Outward Bound, and was his rationale for adventure pursuits and dramatic rescue training as a part of education. For these Colorado Outward Bound students high on Snowmass Mountain on a cold, blustery night, that was it, the moral equivalent of war.

Back at the Outward Bound school, I was working late when Strickler and two students, burst into my office. "John fell off the mountain and split his head open," the boy blurted out and began to cry. Not another fatality; my first reaction was one of denial. Only the day before I delivered Bobby Rossetter to the mortuary.

Nehring's scribbled note affirmed the urgency. "We need to get him to the hospital." At least he's alive, I thought. It was reassuring that Kincey was on site.

"Round up the base camp sherpas, gas up the Land Rover and load the emergency gear," I told Strickler.

"I'll be out all night," I told Andy, my wife, as I changed my clothes. "A boy's been injured on Snowmass." I kissed her and the children good night, an incongruous moment of normalcy in a world that had turned chaotic.

Eight of us clambered into the long-bed Land Rover. The transmission whined in four wheel drive as we crawled up the steep narrow mining road to Lead King Basin.

The sky was heavily overcast, already dark, when we started up the trail. It was a thousand feet to Geneva Lake. Snowmass Mountain loomed above that. I felt I was acting out an ill fated, inexorable disaster, like in a Greek tragedy and had a depressive sense of foreboding.

The sherpas, however, relieved of their camp chores, were energized by the challenge of being needed. This was much more heroic than scrubbing pots or packaging rations. They were high spirited, eager to push on and I did my best to keep up. As I began to sweat I found relief in the steady plod. The hardest task would have been to sit at home, not knowing what was happening.

We reached the upper basin two hours later. The sky had begun to clear, a faint moon shone through light cloud, glowing on the reflecting snow, ghostly, devoid of color. Scorpio spread her claws high in the sky. Except for the crunch of our boots on the hard snow and the rush of our heavy breathing, there was an eerie silence. It was near midnight when we reached the other groups huddled around a body lay wrapped in sleeping bags, prone on the snow.

"How is he?" I asked, not sure whether this was going to be a rescue or the evacuation of a corpse.

"His pulse is normal," Kincey informed me. "His eyes are dilated. You'd expect that of a head injury. He's responsive, knows who he is. Dozes in and out of sleep. He appears to be comfortable." That was reassuring, but I'd like to have seen more signs of life. When we transferred him to the Stokes litter, McBride groaned, complained at being moved, but then settled down again.

After eight hours of cold and anxiety, relief had come. The students were in high spirits. Their enthusiasm helped shake me out of my mood. I congratulated them on the heroic job they had done. "You've probably saved his life," I was about to say, then thought better of it. I wasn't sure such optimism was justified.

I asked Kincey to stay in charge of the rescue. He organized three teams, twelve in each crew. Rope length by rope length, we picked our way down on steep snow between giant boulders, fighting against gravity to keep the litter under control, like Sisyphus, only in reverse, lowering his rock downhill. Where patches of snow were smooth, we slide the litter, toboggan style.

Teams rotated every 20 minutes. Nehring's students were near the limits of their endurance. After their turn on the litter, they just sit down and immediately fell asleep. They woke with the cold, roused each other and trudged on to catch up to the slow moving funereal procession ahead. McBride, who weighed 180 pounds, grew heavier by the hour. When we came out on to the grass below it was a straight carry over a rocky meadow.

At Prospector Springs we were greeted by Tuttle, Boone patrol's co-instructor. Earlier in the day, now yesterday, he had returned to camp with an injured boy. They had a roaring campfire going and had prepared an Outward Bound cordon bleu meal, macaroni and cheese with tuna fish and hot chocolate. It was the first hot meal Nehring's students had since breakfast, twenty hours before. Some too tired to eat, turned into their sleeping bags fully clothed and fell asleep. For them the worst of the carry was over. "The worst day of my life," one student wrote in his journal.

From here on we were on a trail. We attached a wheel to the litter and sped along at walking pace with little effort. On the steep stretches two anchor men belayed to keep John's chariot from rolling down too fast. The first fiery glow of dawn silhouetted the high ridge to the east, when we reached the Land Rover in Lead King Basin.

I dropped the sherpas off at the Outward Bound school and drove on to the hospital in Glenwood Springs. Alone, with McBride lying on the bed of the Land Rover, I felt I was in a race against time. And time was running out. I was in a hurry, wanting to drive faster, but with every bump on the county road, McBride moaned and I had to slow down.

The slower I drove the faster my mind raced ahead. What would I have to do next? I tried to map out a schedule for my day. I'd read McBride's Outward Bound application. It was signed by his mother. Was there a father? What do your tell a mother? What if he died? God spare me that. I imagined the knock on the door, the ring of the telephone. I'd seen the scene so often on World War II movies. And if he didn't die? She'd have to be told. Who should make the call? Wouldn't it be better to get an Outward Bound trustee like Dr. MacMillan? A surgeon would know what to say.

The attendants were waiting for me at the emergency room entrance. They wheeled John into the operating room. The doctor was in a green gown and invited me to suit up and join him. He was in a somber mood. I felt it was a subtle rebuke, his way of questioning the risks to which I exposed students.

Slowly he peeled the wool shirt from McBride's head. "Who put that shirt on his head?" he asked.

I was expecting a rebuke. "His instructor," I said.

"He did a good job," he said. "It probably saved his life." Then he lifted a flap of skin as big as my hand, off John's head. "Thank goodness the wound is so clean," the doctor said.

Blood and raw flesh. I'd never seen so much human blood. I feared I would faint. Or vomit. But I looked on. There was no way of looking away.

The doctor and the nurse shaved McBride's head, and I watched as he sutured his scalp back in place, his big hands and long fingers, nimble as a sail maker stitching a big patch on thick canvas.

I felt that I was seeing John for the first time. It was the blood that made the difference. Until now he had been the victim, a mere object, 180 pounds of inert mass, a burden. I'd been caught up in the mechanics of the rescue, thinking only of myself, what I needed to do. The rescuer. Duty bound. Heroic.

Only now did I see John as a suffering human being, like myself. One of my own. I was hurt. But I also hurt for him. I wanted him live. To heal. And that he forgive.

Now I could grieve.

"Mr. Nold, you're wanted on the telephone." A nurse summoned me from the operating room. "It's urgent," she said.

Chapter 65: A Trilogy of Tragedy — Lou Covert

The lurid image of John's blood still in mind, I stepped out of the operating room, and picked up the phone.

"Yes?" I said.

"It's Betty," my office manager said at the other end of the line, "George Seffert is here." By the injured tone of her voice I knew something was amiss. Seffert was meant to be leading a group on the climb of South Maroon Peak this morning. "Lou Covert's been badly hurt. George wants a helicopter," Betty said.

"Let me speak to him," I said. There was a scraping of the phone on a metal desk. "What is it George?"

"It's bad," George said. "Lou was hit on the head with a rock. I need to get him to the hospital. Fast."

George, a Bavarian, was not given to overstatement. An instructor with the German Outward Bound school at Baad, in the Austrian Alps, a certified alpine guide, there was no need to second guess him. I had Betty order the helicopter, and I left for Aspen in the school Land Rover, to meet it on arrival.

Only the day before I had delivered Bobby Rosseter's body to the morgue. I'd spent last night carrying John McBride out from Snowmass Mountain and driving him to the Glenwood Hospital. I felt like one of the damned in a Greek tragedy whom the furies were tormenting.

The Maroon Bells are the most photographed mountains in Colorado. They appear on posters nationwide and in travel agencies overseas. For a mountaineer to see them is to want to climb them. Two gigantic pyramids of sandstone, 14,100 feet high, they are deep red, layer on layer of sedimentary rock, fractured, friable, crumbling. I had climbed South Maroon Peak with my patrol in 1962, my first year in Outward Bound when I was an instructor. I remembered an endless succession of horizontal bands, skirting huge stone blocks. There was no distinct ridge, like on Snowmass and Capitol Peak. I picked my route through the rubble never knowing exactly where I was on the mountain. Every rock band looked alike. Only on the summit could I pin point my location. I remembered how I had dreaded the constant danger of loose rock. I'd never climbed Maroon Peak again. But since then several Outward Bound groups had ascended safely.

George Seffert had been assigned to guide Outward Bound patrols on the mountain. He was the paragon of a professional alpine guide.

Bridger Patrol, under the leadership of Lou Covert had been scheduled to climb it that morning. Lou, 28, married with a young son, was a private school teacher at the Eaglebrook School, a boarding school for sixth to ninth grade boys in Deerfield, Massachusetts. Eaglebrook had an active ski and outdoor program the headmaster had expressed interest in incorporating Outward Bound ideas. An enthusiastic outdoors man with years of hiking and camping back East in the Appalachians and Adirondacks, Lou had limited alpine experience. The previous summer he had completed the one month Outward Bound instructors' training course in Colorado under "Tap" Tapley. This was his first season as an instructor.

What Lou lacked in high mountain experience, he more than made up as a teacher with wide interests. His backpack was a mobile library with Peterson's Guide to Western Birds, Craighead's Field Guide to Rocky Mountain Flowers, and his own collection of readings on the wilderness.

The night before the climb, Seffert later told me, Covert's group had bivouacked at 12,500 feet on the meadow above tree line in upper Fravert Basin. The camp was exposed. It had been a cold blustery night with light rain and a dusting of snow flurries, the same weather I had experienced the previous night on Snowmass Mountain, during the McBride rescue. But by morning the sky was clear and Seffert saw to it that they were up early, had breakfast in the dark and made a pre-dawn start, the normal routine in the Alps, second nature for Seffert. He knew the mountain well, having led three other groups successfully to the summit that summer, on a route he had previously reconnoitered. But this time to circumvent a large block perched on a ledge, he decided to take a different route.

A subsequent report written by Willam F. Gerber, M.D., a climbing doctor who chaired a committee that investigated the accident, stated that the 17-man party made its way up the mountain in single file. Seffert was in the lead. Covert was in #5 between two weaker boys. Howard Hoffman, Covert's assistant, brought up the rear. They proceeded in a long diagonal traverse across the south face of the mountain, threading their way through broken boulders, mounting one rock band upon another, steadily ascending. Loose rocks were strewn along the ledges but climbing one behind the other in a diagonal upward line, there is little danger of rock dislodged by those above, falling on the party below.

It was about 7.30 a.m. when they were already a considerable distance up the mountainside, when Seffert found the route blocked by steep tilted boulders that had collapsed on a rocky terrace. They had to reverse their direction. The lead members of the party now crossed back over the rear members of the party, who were about 12 to 18 feet below them. On this switchback, the student in #3 position grabbed hold of a rock for balance, and it came loose. He tried desperately to hold the rock in place, and called out ,"Rock!" As he had been instructed to do. The party below quickly ducked their heads and moved into the face of the mountain, again according to their training and instructions. All except for Lou Covert, the instructor. He looked up. The student managed to hold the rock in place and it did not fall. But the rock next to it was loosened. It dislodged and went hurtling down. Lou Covert was directly below and it struck him on the head. Hoffman, his assistant, estimated the rock to be 12 inches in diameter, weighing about 30 pounds.

As Covert was struck, he immediately went backwards off the ledge, falling about 24 feet, striking a steep terrace of rock and dirt. From there he fell another 40 feet onto broken rocks. Hoffman reached him within a few minutes after the fall. It was apparent that Covert had multiple injuries that were critical. Hoffman did what he could to stop the bleeding, treated him for shock, and when his breathing faltered, gave him mouth to mouth resuscitation. Seffert realized Covert was in grievous condition and needed more help than could be given in the field. He decided to return to school and request a helicopter evacuation. Leaving the group in Hoffman's care, he descended the mountain and took off on the run, ten miles back to school.

On the way down Seffert met Larry Higby, the instructor of Smith patrol camped lower in the valley. They were scheduled to climb South Maroon Peak with Seffert the following day. Seffert informed them of the accident and continued down to the school, arriving about 9.30 a.m. looking for me. Betty Grove, the office manager, reached me in the operating room of the Glenwood Srings hospital. After I had her make arrangements for a helicopter evacuation, Seffert took off on the run to return to the site of the accident.

In the meantime Larry Higby with Outward Bound Smith patrol hurried up to Maroon Peak, prepared to be of help. Higby, a seasoned mountain man from Wyoming, had spent a lifetime ranching and as a hunting guide in the Wind River Range, raising horses and four children. He had worked as a counselor with Indian youth on the Cheyenne reservation for the Bureau of Indian Affairs.

Higby told me later that when he met up with Bridger patrol they were huddled around Lou Covert's body giving him artificial resuscitation. The students had built a low rock barrier to protect him from further rock fall. Higby, who had witnessed death on the battle field during WWII, took Covert's vital signs. He wasn't breathing and there was no pulse, and the body was already cold. Higby pronounced him dead, but the students didn't believe him. "They still gave him mouth to mouth resuscitation," Higby recalled later. "They didn't want to give up. They were reluctant to stop.

He said a few words for the departed dead from the Episcopal Prayer Book, he remembered from the battle front. "We had a moment of silence. Students wept. Then we began to carry Lou's body down off the mountain to the meadow below," Higby said. He despatched two students to run back to school to alert us to Lou's death.

They were on their way down, when the helicopter thudded overhead on its way up the valley. It found a clear space to land on a grassy knoll at the foot of the boulder field. They loaded Lou's body and took off. By the time Seffert returned, Lou's body had been lifted out.

Meanwhile, I drove to Aspen intending to rendezvous with the helicopter and to transport the injured body to the hospital. It wasn't there. I called the school. "Lou's dead," Betty Grove told me. "They've taken his body to the morgue."

Suddenly I felt inexhaustibly tired. I'd not slept the night before, so I was physically tired. But this was exhaustion deeper than sleep deprivation. I felt a draining of the soul. It was one of those moments when I wished that I could pray, share the pain with some Higher Presence. Indeed, blame it on Him, or It. Why? I asked. Why Lou? *Out of the night...black as the pit..,*I recalled fragments of a poem, ... *I thank whatever gods may be, for my unconquerable soul.* Unconquerable? I was not so sure.

After my moment of self pity, I turned the key, started the Land Rover and lumbered up the road to what waited me at the Outward Bound School. I drove back in mental fog, and with every mile the fog bank thickened.

What do I tell Martha, Lou's young wife? She never had seemed very happy at the school, living in a tent with a young son, while her husband was away for days on end. And how could the little boy understand that his father would not be coming back. And what would need to be done with Lou's body?

And there was still John McBride unconscious in the hospital. Someone would have to contact his family.

What was the organizational protocol. This was the first time anything of this magnitude had occurred. There were no precedents. Who should assume responsibility for what? I'd need to notify Chuck Froelicher, the chairman of the board. But didn't he spend his summers at Martha's Vineyard? And the newly established national Outward Bound office? Recently Josh Miner had been appointed president. Should I contact him? I needed to carry out my own investigation with instructors and students.

And the local authorities. Would the Pitkin County sheriff want to investigate? And the press? Given all the recent publicity given to the Rosseter search, I knew the Glenwood Springs Sage would be on it by the end of the day. I would have to prepare a press release. And the insurance company? The financial and legal implications could be disastrous.

And then there was still an Outward Bound course to run. How would I deal with the shock and trauma of students and instructors, those who were directly involved and those who only experienced it vicariously. There was still ten days in course C-13, and in two weeks another course of ninety six students would begin. What program changes were needed?

Martha Covert, now a widow, had been notified of Lou's death when I arrived. Andrea, my wife, Mary Higby and the other instructors' wives had rallied around her and took her infant son under their protective wing. I approached Martha with trepidation, anxious that my own grief not add to hers, which in retrospect was the worst thing to do. What she needed most, I suspect, was others to grieve with her. But I feared that would be seen as weakness. She must have seen it as indifference. How I envied the Homeric heroes who could weep openly for their fallen comrades. The best I could muster was, "I'm dreadfully sorry, Martha." And held back my tears. She glared at me with a look of stony rebuke, angry at me, anger at Outward Bound, and I felt angry at her dead husband for leaving her this way.

There is a small graveyard in the Marble valley below the Outward Bound school, a wind blown, weed strewn prairie wilderness of primitive beauty, with tall grass, stunted pink wild roses and yellow cinquefoil. Martha requested that Lou be buried there among past generations of miners and quarry men. She did not want a minister or priest to preside. A group of volunteers, including Josh Miner the executive director of the Outward Bound national organization, toiled all night digging a grave through six feet of alluvial scree and glacial silt.

It fell to me to lend dignity and solemnity to the occasion. "I will lift mine eyes unto the hills." Howard Hoffman, Lou's assistant intoned the ancient 121st psalm, in rich baritone voice. He would in later years became a rabbi. I read Dylan Thomas, "And Death Shall Have No Dominion," a defiant, obtuse poem. Certainly Outward Bound would prevail, as would the spirit that drew Lou to Outward Bound. Only in retrospect I realized how little consolation this was to Martha. For her, Death had dominion. It had robbed her of her husband, and a caring father for her infant son. Her life had been diminished. Irretrievably so. Without a Christian burial she was deprived further of the comfort of the Christian promise of resurrection.

It was Josh Miner, I believe, who read Carl Sandburg's poem:

> *Now never again come morning*
> *say the tolling bells repeating it,*
> *now on earth in blossom days,*
> *in earthy days and potato planting,*
> *now to the stillness of the earth,*
> *to the music of dust to dust*
> *and the drop of ashes to ashes*
> *he returns and it is the time,*
> *the afternoon time and never come morning,*
> *the voice never again, the face never again.*

The next morning the whole school gathered for morning assembly in the rustic outdoor amphitheater, a semi-circle of horizontal aspen logs, overlooking the Crystal River. Two miles across the valley rose Treasury Ridge, still glistening in midsummer snow. There was a symmetry and a scale to the mountain that was enticing without being intimidating.

What would I say? The uncertainty gnawed at me. What was appropriate? I felt it incumbent on me to honor the dead, both Bobby Rossetter and Lou Covert, as well as acknowledge the injured, John McBride, who was still unconscious three days after his fall. But we also had to move on with the program. During the Civil War they had transformed a hymn "John Brown's Body Lies a Molding in the Grave," into a call to action, The Battle Hymn of the Republic. "And his truth goes marching on." The sentiment was right, but the tone was more chauvinistic than I thought suitable. Then there was Nietzsche's quote,"What doesn't kill you only makes you stronger." That sounded too macabre.

So I spoke of the origins of Outward Bound as merchant seaman survival schools during World War II. It too was a time of death and tragedy, like we had experienced the past week. "Young men, like yourselves, were dying in the life boats when their ships were torpedoed in the Atlantic," I told the students.

"Last November I visited Aberdovey in Wales, the first Outward Bound school, where I met the warden, Captain Freddie Fuller. During World War II he was the captain of a merchant ship that was torpedoed by a German submarine in the Caribbean. They took to the lifeboats and were afloat for a week before being picked up by another ship. Two days later that ship was torpedoed and this time they were adrift for ten days before being rescued again. 'We were cold at night, hot in the daytime,' Captain Fuller told me. 'We ran out of food, and were low on water. Some of the men were sick, others wounded. But we survived.'"

"How?" I asked.

"We prayed," he said. "There were not atheists in the life boats. But more important, we looked after each other. We shared whatever food and water we had. We shared our body warmth with those who were cold. When some were depressed and afraid, we cheered them up, singing songs, telling stories, even jokes, anything to get their mind off the situation we were in.

"But most of all, we were determined to survive. It was a question of will. We still had a war to win. We were determined to prevail, to go on. And we did."

"And now its our turn to move on. There are still ten days of this course before we are done," I told our students. "And we the living owe it to John and Bobby and Lou, the injured and the dead, to take strength from their suffering."

I closed with two minutes of silent prayer.

It wasn't the Gettysburg address but it did feel it helped us begin to comprehend the incomprehensible.

Chapter 66: A Trilogy of Tragedy -- Atonement

A trilogy of tragedy: Bobby Rosseter drowned, John McBride head injury, Lou Covert buried, all within five days. I felt entangled in a web of emotions: shock, dismay, grief, guilt, the demands of duty. And the ghosts of past deaths exhumed from their graves.

At the owl haunting hour, I lie between sleep and awake, listening to the low moaning of the wind through the spruce trees, the rustle of aspen leaves, paranoid about the legal liability, the insurance implications, the bad press. My own fragile career doomed, the captain going down with the ship. I was the one ultimately responsible for the program. I had approved the two disastrous climbs.

Sleep no more. I remembered Lady Macbeth from high school English class, distraught and remorseful. *Macbeth hath murdered sleep.* I thought of the rocky ledge on South Maroon Peak where Lou Covert fell which put an end to my sleep.

But by day there was still an Outward Bound School to run, ninety-five students committed to finishing the course. Another hundred students were enrolled in course C-14 which began in two weeks. "Rationality is the sanctuary of the broken hearted," I was told by a friend. The demands of work pulled me back to reality. It became my therapy.

Now it was imperative that we move on. The solo survival experience began next day, essentially a three day meditation and fast. Given the solemnity of the occasion what would be an appropriate introduction of the experience? The whole school gathered in the outdoor theatre, a mini-amphitheater of aspen logs for benches, looking out to the face of Treasury Ridge, still covered in late summer snow. We gathered in silence and could hear the birds sing.

I told them of the scene in Somerset Maugham's *The Razors Edge*, where Larry, a young fighter pilot in World War I sees his closest friend crash land, burn and die. *"It reminded him of his own mortality,"* Maugham wrote.

"The events of the past week have done that for me, for all of us, I expect, reminded me of my own mortality," I said, and went on to talk of the need to live one's life fully. I closed with my favorite quote from Thoreau, *"I went to the woods because I wanted to live deliberately, to front only the essential facts of life...and not discover when I came to die, that I had not lived."*

After students were placed on their sites, I met with all the instructors and sherpas. We gathered in what we called the library, commemorating Roger Weed, an Outward Bound trustee who had perished on a winter solo hike in the mountains. It was located in the loft above the main hall the imposing three story, A-frame ski chalet style building. High up, under the peak, aspen log beams directly overhead, it was like being in the choir loft of a rustic frontier cathedral, close, crowded, intimate.

"Should we continue to climb the 14,000 foot peaks?" I asked, not implying that we shouldn't. No other Outward Bound school climbed such spectacular mountains. Were we dangerously naive assuming we could climb them safely? The alpine expedition was the essence of the Colorado Outward Bound experience, instructors asserted. It was physically demanding, psychologically challenging and metaphorically compelling. The program would lose its impact if we didn't climb them. Why? Because they were there? No one actually quoted Mallory but the spirit was there. I was assured by the instructors' commitment. The damaged reputation of Outward Bound could still be salvaged by them.

How about South Maroon Peak? No one was willing to lead his group on it. Snowfall the previous winter had been unusually heavy, and it lay still on the northern slopes. The sedimentary layers of sandstone, always unstable were more so than usual, as if the sloping ledges were lubricated by the excessive snow melt. If we were to continue to climb it we would need to reconnoiter a new route, clean it of loose rock, and possibly even flag the route with red paint. Paint the rocks? They did it all the time in Europe. But in the American wilderness? Environmentalism was just becoming fashionable. At any rate, a new reconnaissance would not be feasible that summer. The peak was off limits, at least for this year.

The wisdom of that decision was confirmed a month later when two climbers, scientists at the Los Alamos Atomic Research Center, were killed by rock fall on the opposite side of the mountain. Two years after that I attended the funeral of Ed Hillyard, businessman, renowned environmentalist, Outward Bound trustee, who was killed with his partner on the same face.

Ten years later yet, Barry Corbett, Everest climber, outdoor photographer, was filming skiers on an extreme slope on Maroon Peak, leaning out of a helicopter when it crashed. He broke his back and became a paraplegic for life. Coincidentally Outward Bound had contracted with his company, Summit Films Inc., to make a film incorporating footage of all four schools. He was not able to do any of the filming, but he did the editing. The first film after his partial recovery, with a joyous Cat Stevens sound track, it captured both the exuberance of Outward Bound as well as the indomitable nature of Barry Corbett.

There is a striking elegance in the pyramidical symmetry of the Maroon Bells and I've seen it often on posters in tourist offices from New York to San Francisco, and once in London. It has always brought back for me the inherent ambiguity in mountaineering, the underlying contradiction. I remember my elation, the sense of victory, conquest climbing it as an instructor in 1962. But I also recall my dismay, my defeat, revisiting the site of Lou Covert's fall three years later. The Hindu god Shiva is worshipped as Destroyer and Preserver. I had come to see the Maroon Bells as symbolic of that duality.

Outward Bound has not climbed the Maroon Bells since Lou Covert's death.

Snowmass Mountain was an acceptable risk, as was Capital Peak. The rock on both mountains was granite. Though still friable, it was more stable than sandstone. More important, the routes on these peaks followed the ridges where loose rock was more likely to fall off on either side. Though a decade later I was to learn, it wasn't always so.

"If we continue to climb the high peaks," I asked the instructors, "what do we need to do to be safe?" First we should never attempt major peak ascents until students had basic rock and snow climbing training. This had been missed by several groups because of the time they spent on the Rossetter search. We must make an early start at first light and be off the mountains by mid-afternoon. Each patrol should carry two sleeping bags, tarps, a primus stove, pot and extra food on a summit climb, in case of an emergency. An accident report form should be developed and all emergency communication sent in written form.

Wearing hard hats while rock climbing and on peak ascents was recommended. At that time motorcyclists and construction workers had only just begun using them. Models were being developed for climbers too, but they were hard to find. Bell Toptex in California had developed one for surfers that was bulky but satisfactory for climbers. Then they discontinued the line.

Eventually we found a British model that was lighter and cleverly designed to self destruct on impact, absorbing the shock in the process. The shipment was late in coming and arrived only the day before students set off for Willy's Rock, named for Willy Unsoeld, a famous Everest climber, who later worked for Outward Bound.

The day after the helmets arrived, Nelson Barry, a student wearing one, stood at the bottom of the fifty foot buttress, fumbling to tie into the safety rope which led to his instructor who was seated at a belay site at the top of the cliff. In his nervousness, Nelson tied his knot wrong, which is easy for the novice to do with a bowline. And in his haste, he started up the climb before a fellow student could check his knot, which is the standard procedure. Half way up he slipped, his weight came on the safety rope, but the knot came untied.

Nelson fell.

He came down twenty-five feet, landing on a grassy slope hard enough to suffer a compression fracture of his spine. Then falling backward, he hit his head hard enough to crack the outer plastic shell of the hard hat, and to snap inner suspension of nylon web. The hat was demolished. but Nelson was saved miraculously from serious head injury. He did not suffer so much as a concussion.

Until then there had been some question of how effective climbing helmets would be. So for me it was something akin to a conversion experience. I became an instant believer. For the next ten years as director of the school, I kept Nelson's hat as a memento on my desk, like the crutches, prostheses and votive offerings I'd seen at the Shrine of Our Lady of Lourdes, left by the miraculously cured.

Instructors discussed the need for better headlamps, VHF radios for emergency communication, rescue equipment caches near the rock climbing sites. These recommendations would need to be implemented the following year.

I wrote a brief report summarizing the recommendations and distributed it to all staff and members of the board of trustees. I felt confident that we had experienced a degree of catharsis and had moved through the crisis. But I also realized there was much that was left unsaid. No mention was made of the errors of judgment. Clearly this would need to be addressed. But instructors avoided criticism of their colleagues. For now it was more important to be supportive of each other than it was to find blame.

Two days later the accident investigating committee chaired by Dr. William Gerber, visited the school. He was a neurosurgeon and a climbing doctor, an instructor with the Colorado Mountain Club. Peter Seibert was president of the Vail Ski Corporation, a former member of the 10th Mountain Division; David Michael, an experienced mountaineer and lecturer, an artist living in Aspen; and Asa Ramsay, chairman of the Colorado Rescue Association. A group leader of the Rocky Mountain Rescue Group in Boulder, he had been involved in the Bobby Rossetter search.

I was anxious, expecting to be hauled before an inquisition. But they were less interested in what I had to say than they were in speaking with the instructors and sherpas who had been directly involved.

They addressed what we as staff had avoided. In his written report one member expressed his concern about "a rather cavalier attitude towards the high mountains and their inherent dangers." On Snowmass Mountain route selection should have been the responsibility of the sherpa appointed as guide, and the instructor should not have taken over the lead. McBride should have been belayed on the steep descent. This was the instructor's responsibility, not the students. Dr. Gerber also acknowledged: "McBride owes his life to the care given to prevent shock and undue exposure after his injury."

"The committee got the feeling that some tested routes were not selected because they were no longer interesting to the instructors," they reported. On South Maroon Peak a new route should not have been chosen, and they should not have been climbing "above each other in the fault line."

Though critical of decisions made in the field, the committee endorsed "the ideals and high purpose of this endeavor to help boys grow into men...."

"It is a marvelous and exciting phenomenon at COBS to see the development of inner strength...through competition and the overcoming of obstacles. To test the very limits of one's endurance, courage and imagination allows the boy to see that he is bigger than he thought," Michael David wrote.

Dr. Gerber concluded with a statement from a recent Outward Bound Trust pamphlet: "The aim is to teach that the more adventurous an undertaking is, the more care and prudence it calls for if it is to succeed."

One member, Asa Ramsay, did not concur with the committee findings. He did not submit a written report but at the fall meeting of the Colorado Rescue Association, which I attended, he voiced his reservations. He vehemently criticized both Ashcrofters and Outward Bound for exploiting the wilderness for commercial gain, and subjecting young people to unjustifiable risk, claiming that the high mountains were not a place for the neophyte, particularly in large groups. I was shocked by his outburst, taken by surprise. But remained silent and the accusations died without further comment.

But the point Asa was making did not die. A generation later, as other novices climbed into thin air to their death on Mount Everest, the same accusations were made of their guides and leaders. In a later litigious age and after more fatalities, Outward Bound was to come under further criticism.

The demands of each day's activities helped us through our collective guilt. But the scars of personal guilt took longer to heal, as did the pain of loss. Years later, a friend who had lost students in an avalanche told me, "It took me seven years before I could recall the accident without tears in my eyes, another thirty years before I was comfortable talking about it. It was a process of atonement."

I was concerned about how Nehring and Seiffert would deal with their trauma. This was before we had heard of post trauma stress syndrome. Separately, at the end of the course I called them into my office to discuss the next month's assignment. The sliding aluminum door grated as Nehring entered. I saw him cringe. His face was drawn, unsmiling, jaw muscles tightened, lips dry. He looked like a pariah, waiting to be kicked. I knew he expected to be fired. I had agonized over the appropriate decision, torn between my personal concern for him and my institutional responsibility for safety.

I opened by telling him of the time my climbing partner had been killed in the Alps. We had been a party of three teachers at Gordonstoun, Kurt Hahn's school in Scotland. The headmaster, Bobby Chew, had flown out for the funeral. After the burial, he invited John, the other teacher, and me to tea at the Post Hotel. "Well, what do you plan to climb next?" he had asked us. As a mountaineer in younger days himself, he had felt it crucial that we continued to climb.

"I'd like you to continue too," I told Rich Nehring. He was young, only twenty-two. I assigned him as a co-instructor again, this time with a more experienced man who could be a mentor.

Tears came to his eyes. "I'm not sure I can," he said. "I really need to go home to register for my fall classes. If you can find somebody to cover for me, I'd rather not. But I do thank you for the offer." Clearly he had thought through a face saving way out. The following year, though I had still misgivings, I offered him a contract. The school had continued to expand and I was short of instructors. I felt we had invested a lot in his training and he would have matured from the experience of tragedy. But he did not accept. Though he went on to instruct successfully and safely as an instructor in his college mountaineering club, he never worked for Outward Bound again.

George Seffert was a man in his early thirties, Bavarian with handsome Aryan features, stoic, controlled, mature. He had been criticized by the investigating committee for taking his group on a new route. But he justified his decision because he felt the original route had become less safe. But making the switch back, placing the students in the lead above those following, was an error. He had the confidence to admit his mistake and the maturity to be able to move on. With hindsight it was clear that we should never have had a group that size, seventeen students and instructors, on the mountain. That decision had been mine.

I was never in any doubt of Seffert's competence. The next course he led a patrol successfully with a sherpa as an assistant. But when I offered him a job the following year, he turned me down. He did not return, a pattern I was to see again. Following a serious accident, for which they felt responsible, instructors often did not return.

Howard Hoffman, however, who had been Lou Covert's assistant and had tried to breathe life into his shattered body, and to console the boy who loosened the fatal rock, continued to work for Outward Bound. Later on a spiritual quest studying in Isreal, he developed a wilderness program in the Sinai Desert for troubled youth, modeled on Outward Bound. Returning to America he continued this work, later becoming a distinguished rabbi.

Years later Herb Kincey wrote me, he was driving through Idaho Springs, Colorado, 45 miles west of Denver and stopped at a road side cafe. The young man serving behind the counter looked at him intently, as if he knew him, but Kincey could not place the face.

"He had a drawn, haunted expression on recognizing me," Kincey said. He ordered a cup of coffee.

"Didn't you work for Outward Bound?" the young man asked.

"Yes. Why, did you go to Outward Bound?" Kincey replied.

"I was a student in 1965." The young man paused, struggling for self control. "I was in Lou Covert's patrol. I was the guy that knocked the rock loose," he said. He held back his tears.

They talked, struggling for words to make conversation. "Actually we had a lot to say," Kincey said, "But neither of us could find the words to say it."

As he drove on his way, Kincey brooded, "What brought me to turn off in Idaho Springs, and to drive into that cafe?"

One has to believe there are more forces than we know that bind us in human tragedy. To heighten the mystery, at the time I was writing this, I received an email from Howard Hoffman. I had not heard from him in thirty years. A friend had told me, now a rabbi, he was celebrating his sixtieth birthday. Howard also mentioned " the boy who pushed the rock over on Lou."

"I needn't tell you of psychic connectedness," I emailed Howard.

The Rossetter family turned their grief into an affirmative act. I sensed they had a deep admiration for Bobby. They seemed to respect the fact that he had died engaged in doing something he passionately wanted to do, to hike and live in the mountains. They were proud of him for it. The family provided funds for the U.S. Forest Service to construct a bridge over Geneva Creek, at the crossing where Bobby had been swept away. Built to sturdy government specifications it stands as the Bobby Rossetter Memorial Bridge.

I never heard from Martha Covert again and have never sought her out, negligence I sadly regret. We need an Outward Bound survivors group to help us. And Lou lies moulding in the Marble miners' graveyard.

John McBride spent a week in the Glenwood Hospital before he gained consciousness and was then transferred to the neurological ward of St. Joseph's

Hospital in Denver for further observation before flying home to New York. He recovered fully but it was months before his headaches finally cleared up. Two years later, I had a letter from him. John told me of being on the 8th Avenue subway in New York City during one of the famous brown-outs of the sixties, a power surge that cut off electricity down the east coast from Canada to Florida. It was on a steaming hot summer day with air conditioners working overtime. During rush hour power failed.

The train stopped above 168th Street where it emerged from the tunnel and ran along a high trestle, six stories above the ground. People were exhausted from the day's work in the stifling heat. Now they faced further frustration and delay. Minutes went by. Then an hour. Two hours. Irritation turned to anxiety, children began to whimper. Anxiety began to turn to panic as commuters felt trapped.

"Something had to be done," John wrote. Since no one was doing anything, he decided he had to. He moved down the train until he found a door that would open. Below a narrow plank boardwalk ran along side the rails on top of the railway ties. He dropped down to it, then walked the plank until he came to a ladder. This led twenty feet down to a platform and on to stairs that descended to the street. John retraced his route, climbed back up to the train and proceeded to assist others escape. John's letter concluded: "You know Mr. Nold, I would never have done it, were it not for Outward Bound."

For me personally, I had weathered the deepest crisis of my professional life, with trepidation but without rancor. It had not always been so. I felt that both Outward Bound and I had been strengthened by the adversity. We had been humbled also. I felt a deeper bonding with Outward Bound as an organization, identified with the idea, committed to it as a life journey.

And atonement? At a deeper existential level death has always had a special resonance for me. Essentially I see my life as a series of dramatic discontinuities often prompted by death: both parents when I was still a boy; my best friend at college, my climbing partner in the Alps, other Outward Bound instructors like Lou Covert and colleagues like Ed Hillyard. I have walked in the valley of the shadow of death. Eventually the death of a student for whom I was responsible led to my resignation from Outward Bound. So I *ask not for whom the bell tolls.*

Yet I live my life with enthusiasm and all the exuberance I can bring to it. "Happiness is a form of courage," I recall writing in a boyhood collection of pithy quotations.

With the perspective of seventy years I see my life not unlike a Bach cantata; there is the joyous rapture of violin melody, but always on a lower register, the deep persistent melancholy of the cello counterpoint.

Treasury Ridge in Colorado, June 1974.

Chapter 67: Mobile Courses

The first four years of the Colorado Outward Bound School were pioneering years in which the foundations of an institution were laid. It had been a stormy apprenticeship in leadership for me. But 1966 saw the beginning of a great transition that would change forever the face of Outward Bound: the mobile course, the first contract for service, an exploratory river expedition, our first public school program.

Awareness of Outward Bound had mushroomed and our mail was flooded with student inquiries. The national organization responded to the growing demand by incorporating new schools: Hurricane Island and Minnesota in 1964, North Carolina in 1965.

I was frustrated with having to turn students away and was looking for ways to expand the enrollment of the Colorado school. Overlapping courses had proved disastrous. Could we expand the Marble facility? But I didn't see a capital campaign being feasible at the time. I preferred trustees raising funds for scholarships rather than bricks and mortar. To me it was a matter of pride that half our students were on scholarship. I saw the broad social economic mix of students. as an essential educational ingredient of an Outward Bound course.

How then could we expand student enrollment? We were locked into the British program model centered on a residential facility, the Marble school, from which we ventured out on a succession of expeditions of increasing challenge, returning after each to recoop. "You need to dunk them and then you dry them," Lester Davies, the warden of the Ullswater Outward Bound Mountain Schools said. I knew this to be appropriate, given my own experience of expeditions with Gordonstoun School boys in Scotland ten years previously, where the weather was always a challenge. But was it necessary in summer Colorado?

Perhaps not. In 1962 Paul Petzoldt had run an expedition style course for a group of Peace Corps volunteers going to Nepal, entirely in the field. In 1964 Tap Tapley did the same with instructor trainees. These were special courses, for special groups, with special needs. But why couldn't we design a special course for regular Outward Bound students? Was the notion so heretical?

In 1965 I hired Bill Byrd, a school teacher from Eugene, Oregon, former Teton guide, recently the director of the Peace Corps Outward Bound Training Center in Puerto Rico, to run a satellite program. It operated out of Ruby, an abandoned mining town high in the valley east of Aspen, fifty miles and several mountain ranges from Marble. He directed two courses of thirty-six students in each, without the amenities of a residential base, using only a mobile field kitchen and a pit latrines. Students slept on the ground. Like Thoreau at Walden, they bathed in the pond. Their expedition routes took them through the Ruby and Elk Mountain ranges ending up at the Marble school. On arrival they referred to it condescendingly as "the Outward Bound country club." We had broken the mold. At the time it seemed a radical departure. The mobile course was born.

That summer I had a visitor at Marble, Don Vetterlein, a prominent businessman from Portland, Oregon. "How do you get one of these schools started?" he asked. "One thing you'll need is a director," I said, "and I know just the man for you." We drove to Ruby, and I introduced him to Bill. In 1966 they opened the North West Outward Bound School without a permanent base facility. A mobile school was born.

It was as if America had just discovered backpacking in the sixties and with each year we met more people in the high country. The Snowmass Wilderness Area between Marble and Aspen became more crowded. The U.S. Forest Service imposed a permit system restricting the number of campers. To expand we had to find new areas. The mobile course would make it possible. So when Gary Templin came on board as the new associate director, I saw an opportunity to institutionalize the concept. A friendly critic called it the deinstitutionalization of Outward Bound.

The spring of 1966, Gary Templin and I did an air reconnaissance over the San Juan Mountains of south-west Colorado. Before us spread an ocean of snow, ridge on ridge, like a succession of tsunami waves, one bunched upon the other. As we approached, the skyline was more defined, symmetrical pyramids, flat mesas, humped whale backs, Matterhorn spires, etched against a blue sky.

In the turbulence we were buffeted about, the plane lurching in the updrafts, driving my stomach to my bladder. I regretted not making one last pit stop. Then we dropped in a dead fall and the camera on my lap shot up, clipping the end of my nose, and rattled on the plastic canopy above.

The pilot pointed our Umcompahgre Peak, at 14,309 feet the highest in the San Juans, Vestal and Arrow in the Grenadiers, both over 13,000 feet. We sketched out possible expedition and climbing routes below.

"How you doing, Gary?" I asked. He had just come from sea level in New York City and had a throbbing headache from the altitude. The last time he'd been in a plane like this was in Vietnam a couple years previously.

"Well, at least there are no Viet Cong shooting at us," he said.

Freed from the need for permanent base camp facilities, the new mobility permitted us to develop field operations in other wilderness areas: the Gore Range above Vail, Colorado, the Uinta Mountains and the desert canyons of Utah, eventually going south to Mexico in Baja California.

We began to look into other adventure activities. That summer I rafted the Colorado River on an exploratory Outward Bound expedition. The following year I was on the Yampa and the Green rivers. A couple years later I introduced Sunfish sailing on Lake Powell and Baja California, then desert hiking in Canyonlands; ski mountaineering in the Leadville area, where 10th Mountain Division troops had trained during World War II. Only there did we find it necessary to revert to Lester Davies dunk-them-and-dry-them mandate and built a winterized facility at Leadville. Our catalogue began to look like a prospectus for adventure travel.

These new activities and shorter courses made it possible to respond to a wide range of inquiries. Schools and colleges were interested in incorporating Outward Bound into their programs, as were youth correctional institutions. We developed team building and leadership programs for corporate managers, and offered wilderness adventure trips for trustees and chief executives. With each new program we gained new insight. It was a reciprocal relationship. Often we learned as much from our clients as they learned from us. "Gladly would he learn and gladly teach," Chaucer said of the Oxford scholar.

We began to see Outward Bound not only as a series of structured events, but as a dynamic process that could be tailored to different needs in different locations. Outward Bound was being transformed. Not only was it a program of personal growth and character development but also a catalyst for institutional change that could impact society.

They were heady days of growth and change, hectic and often contentious as were the times, that lasted into the early 1970's. "Given ninety days to plan, we could run a program for anybody, anywhere," I remember telling Gary Templin in a moment of hubris.

Daughters Jen (left) and Margaret in Colorado, 1970s.

340

Chapter 68: Job Corps

Four of us took turns breaking trail in the loose granular snow, zigzagging back and forth, climbing in a series of broad diagonals. On skis I sank to my knees in the unconsolidated snow. After ten minutes in the lead, sweating and panting, I stepped aside and waited for the others to pass then fell in at the end of the line. Chris took over, wearing snow shoes he sank only to his ankles as he trudged ahead, the rest of us following in his track: Vic Walsh, a British Outward Bound instructor with Himalayan experience on skis, Gary Templin, recently hired as associate director of the Colorado school.

We were on the Grand Mesa which rose a mile above the valley of the Colorado River. "The largest flat top mountain in the world" according to the Grand Junction Chamber of Commerce. It topped out at 11,000 feet. The Job Corps Center at Collbran nestled in the northern slope at 7000 feet. We were reconnoitering the area as part of planning an innovative program to adapt Outward Bound to Job Corps.

A tinted straw glow suffused the barren aspen forest, the late afternoon sun of February, already low in the western sky. Spruce trees clustered in compact groves, a somber green, almost black against the dazzling the snow. The slope leveled off at a knoll topped by wind warped trees.

"Let's camp," I breathed heavily. Gary breathed even harder. Only three days previously he'd been walking the streets of New York City. He ran a Harlem youth agency and I wanted to draw upon his experience in developing the program.

Aspirin did not relieve his pain, but he was too proud to complain. He'd been through Green Beret officers training. He knew pain.

At the campsite I stepped out of one ski and sank to my thigh and fell. I couldn't get up until I took off my pack and crawled on it for support. I put my ski back on again.

Together we stomped down a level platform for a campsite compacting the snow, squashing the air out of it as best we could and made preparations for the night. Vic and Chris had brought a small light weight nylon tent that the two of them could squeeze into. In less than five minutes they were settled in comfortably and Vic began to melt snow for tea water.

I had considered bringing my tent, a more spacious A-frame Meade tent made of Egyptian cotton, with sewn in ground sheet. It was state of the art ten years previously. But it weighed fourteen pounds. So I had compromised. Gary and I each had brought just an army poncho, one we spread as a ground sheet, the other we strung from a tarp over us. "That's all we had in Viet Nam," Gary had said.

As soon as our shelter was rigged, Gary had crawled into his sleeping bag exhausted. More aspirin. Headache persisted. "Drink lots of water," I urged, forgetting that water was a scarce commodity. Vic passed him tea in an army surplus aluminum mug that burned his lips. But it revived him enough to stomach macaroni and cheese with tuna, Outward Bound expedition *cordon bleu*.

The other two nestled in their tent, a tight fit, and zipped up the door sheltered in their cocoon. They talked and laughed well after dark. Gary and I listened in silence feigning sleep.

A light wind picked up during the night, a low wistful moan in the spruce forest on the ridge above, as a light dusting of snow drifted relentlessly under the tarp. I suppose I slept, though what I remember was waking regularly to shake it off my bag. Each time Gary too seemed to be awake.

In the morning, lying in his sleeping bag without even getting out of his tent, Vic heated up tea water and cooked oatmeal, a practice he had perfected from years of high altitude mountaineering. Gary shook the snow off his bag, put on his boots and snow shoes and shuffled across to claim our breakfast.

We agreed that nothing further would be gained by heading higher, and given the snow conditions, we were not up for a day of recreational skiing or snow shoeing, so after breakfast we headed down. Chris was exuberant. The snow, a light sugary consistency I would later recognize as depth hoar, had no cohesion and drifted slowly downhill with us. On steeper slopes it could be dangerous, prone to avalanche. Chris plunged into it with a child's abandon as if in a winter fairy land. He began to run downhill, gliding with the snow, like skiing on snow shoes. Then he fell with a headlong dive. He came out of his snow shoes and disappeared in a puff of powder. He surfaced, flailing like someone drowning, spluttering and spiting snow. With our help we eventually got him turned around and upright. He searched for his snow shoes and found one, then dug around looking for the other. He couldn't find it. The three of us joined in the search and dug for over half an hour. We never did find it. Walking on one snowshoe, Chris kept falling. One shoe was more of a hindrance than a help. Finally he gave up and waded through waist deep across to the ridge on the other side of the ravine where wind had exposed the rocks. From there he was able to hop from boulder to boulder the rest of the way down to the valley.

Even at 7000 feet at Collbran, Gary Templin's headache persisted, and still in Denver at 6000 feet. Not until he drank the oxygenated air at sea level in New York City did it abate. It had been a cruel introduction to Outward Bound, baptism by immersion.

The Job Corps contract had been negotiated by me. I saw it as a coup for the Colorado school. I was smugly proud of having pulled it off. On a trip back east the previous November, in New York City I was showing the Coors film *As Tall As The Mountains* to a friend I knew from my year as a graduate student at Columbia. "Job Corps ought to see this," he said. An accomplished outdoors man and the director of a camp on Lake Champlain, he was writing a staff manual for outdoor activities for Job

Corps centers. A friend of his was the program director. Two days later I was in his office in Washington, D.C. It was my first time in the nation's capital, one of those moments when you really believe in America as a land of opportunity and have the sense of being swept up by upward mobility.

Dr. Lou Eigen was a big, assertive fellow, overweight, his shirt buttons pressing. "I don't want to see your film. I know about Outward Bound. What can you do for us?" he said. "Can you work with hard core drop-outs and failures? Could you operate out of a Job Corps center? What could you do in ninety days?" He hammered me with questions. This was, he made me realize, a War on Poverty.

I had entered the meeting thinking I was on a recruiting trip, expecting Job Corps to send students to Outward Bound, like we did with the Juvenile Court of Denver and inner city agencies, like the Boys Clubs of New York City. But Lou Eigen had something totally different in mind. This was entirely new, adapting Outward Bound to the needs of another institution in their setting, a pilot program. A pilot program. I like the idea. It sounded so progressive, cutting edge.

A week later I was meeting with Murray Durst, the director of the Job Corps Center at Collbran, Colorado. As a crow would fly, it was less than forty miles from Marble, but nearly 200 miles to drive around around the mountain to the Grand Mesa. Durst was a man in his forties, slightly overweight but comfortable with himself, easy going, friendly but decisive. Not an outdoors man himself, he got to the point right away. He didn't question the merits of Outward Bound but immediately began to brainstorm how it could be adapted to the center.

"Most of these kids have never been out of the city, and we drop them down here in the boonies. If we did nothing but help them be more comfortable in this environment, the program would be worth it. Our recreation program is limited to basketball in the gym, a pool table in the lounge, and movies. You could help us do better than that."

Then Durst went on to discuss his ideas for a self-governing community. "Could you help us develop a leadership cadre?" Here was a challenge. How transferable was leadership in the mountains back to every day existence in the center?

"Collbran (population 400) is not a red neck community. But they rarely see a black person, other than Sidney Portier in the movies. And here we dump 200 of them in their back yard. It would be good public relations to develop a service corps, a mountain rescue team, train Corpsmen in fire fighting, flood relief," Durst said.

Durst knew how to maneuver through the bureaucratic shoals and within ninety days we had a short term contract for a ninety day pilot program from mid-February to mid-May.

The contract called for me to spend one day a week on site, flying out on the early morning Frontier Airlines flight, returning when I could on the last evening flight. All too often I had to stay over. It was time I could ill afford to spend away from the office. Instructors had to be tracked down. Herb Kincey, who had been program director at Marble the previous summer, was available and Durst hired him in October as a recreational specialist, on the center's payroll. In effect this gave us an extra instructor on the project. I tracked down Vic Walsh when he returned from Britain with Barbara, his new wife. I'd met Vic at the Eskdale Outward Bound Mountain School in the Lake District of England and had invited him to come to Colorado. Chris Patterson, another Brit, I did not know, but he had good credentials as a mountain and was available. In mid-February I'd invited Gary Templin to join us for a week as a consultant program design.

There were over 300 Job Corps centers and I began to have fantasies of Outward Bound in all of them. At the invitation of Job Corps I visited other centers that had expressed an interest in the program. In anticipation of the program expanding I was eager to involve the directors of the other Outward Bound schools. I invited them to visit Colbran, and then to join Vic Walsh and our instructors on a ten day leadership development program for ten selected Corpsmen. We ran it out of Marble.

The ten Corpsmen were a selected group of volunteers, chosen for their leadership potential. Even so we had to revise our assumptions about the learning process. We were prepared for language difficulties with those recently arrived from the Dominican Republic. But they were eager to learn and picked up practical skills such as knot tying, lighting a primus stove, rigging a tent, rapidly. The tent we had them do blind folded.

Vic told us of a boy he was helping learn to read. As if to reciprocate, the boy offered to teach him how to tune his car. He knew his mechanics, but couldn't get a job because he couldn't read the manuals. There are other forms of intelligence.

I tried to help one young man having difficulty with the most basic concepts of map reading. "Place the map down with the top end pointing north," I said.

"North? What's north?" he asked. I learned that north was not a fact, but another abstraction. The sun rises in the east, and sets in the west, but what does that mean if you hadn't noticed either growing up in the inner city.

"How transferable is leadership in the mountains to leadership back in the center?" Durst had asked.

Bob Pieh, the director of the Minnesota Outward Bound School, formerly on the physical education faculty of Antioch College, had an answer. He took charge of the group going over the wall. This was a wooden barrier fourteen feet high, smooth on the outside. The object is to get all ten men over without any physical aids. He let them work it out for themselves. With much milling about and shouting, near fist fights, they began to help each other, organized the order of ascent, realized that the last man was the crux. It needed to be someone small, light and nimble. They tried again and made it, elated by their success.

Then Bob Pieh sat them down and in an interactive dialogue that would have pleased students of Socrates, had them reflect on their experience (John Dewey), analyze and conceptualize their decision making process: defining the problem, assessing their resources, agreeing on a plan of action, testing the plan, evaluating how it went, revising the plan and testing it again.

I stood by taking notes. This was first introduction to group dynamics as a body of knowledge, a process that would become more common as we began to work with other groups, teachers, company managers.

Later in the program, Pieh sat the group down before a flip chart with the decision making process outlined, and they worked on a plan to address the drop-out problem at the center.

My role in the program was primarily administrative and documenting progress. I was able to report subtle but significant in Corpsmen fitness and moral. The drop-out rate for the center dropped from thirty-five percent to five percent. Training in first aid (all Corpsmen took the Red Cross Basic First Aid course) was reflected in the rest of the program. Over 100 Corpsmen participated in a three day camping expedition, which was seen as excellent preparation for them to work out of "spike" camps for back country projects on forestry and conservation.

Outward Bound instructors designed and built a ropes course with Corpsmen and staff, giving them the opportunity to apply their craft skills. This became routine part of fitness training, and an opportunity to develop confidence as well as team work and leadership.

Eight of the ten students who had taken part in Bob Pieh's leadership development program were elected by their peers to the center's leadership council. One went on to a position in the Washington, D.C. headquarters and had a successful career in the agency.

Rock climbing led to mountain rescue training where Corpsmen learned to lower a body in Stokes litter off a cliff face, before the admiring eyes of the camera man from the Grand Junction Sentinel. Then in April a twin engine Aero Commander with six persons on board,in flight from Salt Lake City, Utah to Denver crashed near Meeker, Colorado, 150 miles from Collbran. The Job Corps Center was the largest organized group of manpower in Colorado, west of the Rockies. There were no survivors, but Corpsmen carried out several of the bodies. Overnight Job Corps had a new image in the eyes of the public. It was further enhanced when Corpsmen we called in to suppress a small forest fire. Governor John Love expressed his appreciation on behalf of the people of Colorado.

Sargent Shriver, Director of the Office of Economic Opportunity, wrote: "The next phase of Outward Bound's relationship with Job Corps might therefore be based on translating those relevant techniques to larger numbers of Job Corps staff."

But it never came off. The war in Vietnam took a bad turn. Domestic budgets were cut. Programs were cancelled. Several Job Corps centers closed. In the competition for funds between guns and butter, the butter melted. My fantasy of Outward Bound in 300 Job Corps centers was never fulfilled. Several centers showed copies of "As Tall as the Mountains," and directed their recreation instructors to incorporate outdoor adventure and service into their programs, the vestigial remains of our bold attempt.

Nevertheless it did represent an important transition for Outward Bound. Kurt Hahn, in a stentorian pronouncement, had spoken of "the duty of replication," the need to get the influence to a broader public. The Job Corps project had been a bold effort.

More important, when the position of director of the North Carolina Outward Bound School came open, Murray Durst accepted the job. He represented a new kind of leader in Outward Bound with a different perspective, a different agenda. When Josh Miner resigned as executive director of OBI, the national organization, Murray succeeded him, and saw Outward Bound through a period of transition.

For me, Job Corps opened new vistas. Dealing with Washington bureaucrats appealed to my smoldering ambition. And the romantic in me was stirred by walking the Mall for the first. The Lincoln Memorial is built, partly with marble from Marble, Colorado, where the Colorado school is located. I left a psychic connection, not unlike Wordsworth at Tintern Abbey. Looking up into his sad face and reading again, the words of the Second Inaugural Address, *With malice toward none, with charity for all...let us strive one to finish the work we are in, to bind up the nation's wounds*, I felt Outward Bound more deeply rooted in the American experience. Though a Canadian, I felt very proud.

Not everyone shared the feeling. At the spring meeting of the board of trustees I reported on the progress of the pilot program, my vision of the future, Outward Bound in 300 Job Corps centers. The board's support seemed grudging. Bill Coors saw it as a way of bridging the gap between summer season, a way of building up a permanent staff. Others were more skeptical. With drinks in hand, after the meeting I was cornered by two trustees. "You're selling the soul of Outward Bound for a mess of federal pottage," I was told.

Joe, Jen, and Margaret 1980s.

Chapter 69: Outward Bound at School

"Can you do Outward Bound in a school?" I had shown the Outward Bound film, "As Tall as the Mountains," at a local Rotary Club luncheon. After the presentation Dr. John Stuart, superintendent of schools for a local school district, approached me. This was the opportunity I had been looking for.

"Outward Bound came from a school," I replied. I told him about Gordonstoun, Kurt Hahn's school in Scotland, where I had been a teacher ten years previously. But more relevant to Adams County School District 14, a working class suburb north of Denver, was a project in New Jersey.

Outward Bound school directors at this time began meeting on an annual basis under Josh Miner's coordination. I'd recently met with my colleagues, the directors of Hurricane Island in Maine, Minnesota and North Carolina. We'd been invited to Trenton by Greg Farrell, the director of the community War on Poverty. Farrell had taken an Outward Bound instructor's training course in Colorado, and wanted our opinion and ideas on the feasibility of setting up an Outward Bound type program, adapted to the needs and problems of an inner city high school with a minority student body. We saw difficulties, but were intrigued and supportive of the idea.

"I'd like to start by sending some of our teachers and a group of leadership students to Outward Bound," Farrell said, "and have them come back and set up a program. Perhaps Outward Bound could provide supervision and expertise." Though I didn't realize it at the time, Farrell's formula would become my strategy for program development and institutional change for the next decade. Nor did I appreciate that Greg Farrell would become the most creative and effective agent for change within Outward Bound itself.

Dr. Stuart said that he would be interested in trying something similar in Colorado. Funded by an $85,000 federal grant, the goal of the "Dare to Care" project in Adams City High School was to reduce the drop-out rate in the junior and senior years. Race was not an issue in the school, but delinquency and absenteeism was. Many students came from transient families, with limited income and low expectations. Only twenty percent of the graduates went on to college. Though the wrestling team had won the state championship the year before.

Funding came late, which was not unusual for federal programs. Nor was the project well publicized in the school so we were not able to attract any teachers to attend the Outward Bound course and only a handful of boys. The program began late in the fall with a series of one week "Outward Bound" expeditions in the foothills above Denver. to promote self-esteem, develop team work and leadership skills. Field studies in geology, plant and wildlife identification, local history were incorporated into the program, providing students with hands-on learning experiences. They got English credit for keeping journals. Teachers were encouraged to accompany their students on the expeditions and many did. The bonding between teachers and students was one of the more positive benefits of the program. Teachers were invited to initiate their own courses. A course on human biology incorporated Red Cross first aid. A boy's cooking class in the home economics department was popular.

In the spring term Keith Counts, a science teacher, and another teacher of history proposed a river expedition down the Yampa and Green Rivers in north-west Colorado and eastern Utah. The would combine geology and Western history. Keith was also the leader in the local Eagle Scout troop that had a river running program. They saw it as an opportunity to share the experience with their students. That was the first I'd ever heard of the Yampa River. As project consultant I endorsed it enthusiastically and used the opportunity to attach myself to the expedition .

The trip was a great success. As a consultant to the project I saw it as an ideal integration of teacher initiative, community involvement, a sound academic curriculum. The desert canyons were starkly beautiful, the weather in late May idyllic. The teacher knew his geology and the students traveled with John Wesley Powell's as they read his account of going through Whirlpool Canyon in 1878. Quote.

The students enjoyed themselves, as did I, and we all came back with glorious sun tans. But it wasn't Outward Bound. The oarsman had all the fun. I felt I was merely a passenger. If I did the trip again, I would row my own boat.

The press coverage on the Adams City project from both Denver papers, The Denver Post and the Rocky Mountain News was flattering. I felt they made us sound better than we really were. But not everything went according to plan. The federal funding had been late in being approved so we couldn't start the project until half way through the fall term disrupting class room assignments and schedules. Teachers who had been left out of the project were skeptical of yet another "educational reform."

The principal gave only grudging support. The project had been initiated by the district superintendent and as school principal he saw it as an imposition. The next year he asserted his authority and took personal control of the program in his school. He decided he could run it without Outward Bound. That was an important lesson in school politics for me. I learned that schools were run by principals run with a high degree of autonomy. If Outward Bound was to work in a school it would need the support of the principal.

The next year we found both the man and the school. Bob Colwell was the principal of East Denver High School. East drew students from north-east Denver, a successfully integrated middle class community and the wealthy white neighborhood surrounding the country club. In many ways it was a model integrated urban high school. Mr. Colwell and I worked together on a proposal, and Bill Coors, the chairman of the Outward Bound board of trustees, arranged a meeting with the Lawrence Phipps Foundation. We were granted $25,000 a year for three years. It was my first major grant, a defining moment for the Colorado Outward Bound School and for me.

I read the literature on institutional reform. A Ford Foundation pamphlet spoke of "change agents" and the need for a "critical mass" of support. We'd built into the proposal funding for teachers and boys to attend Outward Bound on scholarship during the summer vacation. Back at school in the fall they would be our leadership cadre.

"Only boys?" Bob Colwell asked. "You know, half the population of the world is female." As the father of two girls that should not have come as a surprise. So East High provided the core for the first Outward Bound course for girls in Colorado, run by Jim Stuckey, a former Denver Public School teacher, a doctoral candidate at Denver University.

Teachers were another challenge. "They need to be young enough to bring stars to their eyes," Kurt Hahn, the guru, himself had said. It was Outward Bound dogma. We had run a course for Peace Corps volunteers. There was Tap Tapley's course for instructor trainees, but it was for skilled mountaineer and outdoors men who wanted to work for Outward Bound. In the past if an adult wanted to learn more about Outward Bound, I would attach him to a student group as a participant observer. But now there were too many inquiries. Outward Bound was becoming popular, particularly in independent schools and agencies. What could we do with the neophyte teacher?

I asked two instructors to come up with a course plan. Austin "Jack" Dempsey, a Canadian who had trained mountain troops in the U.S. Army. A formidable looking man, he was bald headed and looked like Mr. Clean. "I don't get mad. I just get even," he once told an obstreperous group of students. Roy Smith was a Brit, a former safari and mountain guide in Kenya, member of the first expedition to climb Alpamayo in the Peruvian Andes. At the end of their course I de-briefed the Dempsey-Smith team. They were as starry eyed as any adolescent group. We had exploded another myth.

"What did you do with Hussey?" Bob Colwell, the principal, asked when I checked in with East High in the fall. "Why what happened?" I asked, thinking the worst. Hussey was a gentle, self-effacing young man, withdrawn and rather shy. "He's a changed man," Mr. Colwell said, and told me of his transformation, now gregarious, outgoing, interacting with students out in the halls. Outward Bound had worked its magic. East High had provided the impetus for the first teachers' courses.

That fall I assigned Chris George, a British Outward Bound instructor, to East High. He organized after school activities in Denver City Park across the street from the school: orienteering, a timed event following a map and compass course from point to point; leadership games involving team work, group problem solving and decision making; tree climbing using climbing ropes for protection. I was surprised when the program attracted more girls than boys. On weekends he led overnight expeditions out of Bob Colwell's ranch in the foothills west of Denver.

I was eager to have teachers involved but most, particularly married men, worked a second job on weekends, selling tools at Sears, men's clothing at Nordstrom's, some worked as custodians and security guards. "What do you earn?" I asked. Most earned about $100. "Suppose Outward Bound offered you $100 to take students on weekends, would you be interested?" I asked. The response was encouraging. Teachers began to organize their own field trips, such as geology in the Great Sand Dunes of southern Colorado, dentrochronology, a tree ring study of limber pines, some 300 years old, on the high ridges above the forests, and other outings that made the connection between field studies and an academic curriculum. Outward Bound provided logistical and backup support.

At this time a short article in the Rocky Mountain News described a hurricane that struck San Felipe, a poor fishing village on the Gulf of California, not far from the American border. Homes were destroyed, the school nearly demolished. A relief effort was being organized in San Diego. "Would Outward Bound be willing to sponsor a relief expedition over Christmas vacation?" an enterprising teacher asked me. Both Bob Colwell resonated to the idea of a service project. Outward Bound provided the camping equipment, tents and sleeping bags, an instructor to help with the organization of logistics, and a modest stipend for three teachers.

The school committed to raising funds for food and gas, relief supplies such as tools to repair the school, Christmas gifts for the children. Students held bake sales and solicited funds from parents, neighbors and church groups. Chris George organized a mini-marathon, four miles around the perimeter of City Park. It was the first time I'd heard of a race where runners sought sponsors at so much a mile. A private foundation provided funds for the rental of the bus, the most expensive item in the budget.

The Latino Club was made up of a reclusive group of shy kids. One would think they were a secret society, though twenty percent of the student body were Latino. They leapt at the opportunity to help. They sponsored a Mexican fiesta with traditional folk dancing in brilliant costumes, an extravagant spread of hot food, tortillas, quesodilas, enchilladas, *arroz y freholes,* prepared by their mothers, followed by salsa dancing in the gymnasium. It was a huge success. More than any event it galvanized the rest of the school. Not only did they raise more money than any other group. It was a huge boost in self esteem for the Latino students. They sponsored three of their own members to go on the project who assumed a prominent role as interpreters.

"The bus could break down around the corner and it would be worth doing the whole thing again. It has done so much for the school," Bob Colwell told me as the yellow school bus pulled out from the front of the school on the last day of classes, the students singing, "Felize Navidad."

The project was a great success. They dug out four feet of sand that had washed into the school house, replaced doors and windows, and repainted the building inside and out. Good ambassadors they interacted warmly with their Mexican peers. It was a model for adventure through service, the motivation for other field trips that followed. I was impressed by the redemptive power of service. Several students felt it was the greatest experience of their lives. It also opened the border to future expeditions to Mexico for both East High School and Outward Bound.

"Would Outward Bound sponsor a river trip?" In the spring term Elene Franzen, an English teacher, approached me She had been a student at Adams City High School and had run the Yampa River with the Eagle Scout troop, the same group I had accompanied the year before. They were willing to run a trip for East High students she told me. I approved the funding with one stipulation, that Outward Bound could add two of their own rafts to the flotilla, one rowed by me, the other by Roy Muhlberger, the Outward Bound business manager. It was on this trip I had my fated encounter with Warm Springs Rapid. The river program opened a new world of adventure that helped transform the Outward Bound school. A teacher from East High School had pointed the way.

Like Jonah, being spewed forth from the watery depths, for me it had been an epiphany.

Chapter 70: In the Belly of the Whale

The canyon was too high, too wide. A mile up, five miles across. Too steep. The sun too bright. Too hot, a 120 degrees. The persistent drone of the river. The thundering baritone of the rapids. Impossible to absorb it all.

I had grown listless, boxed in, confined, like the twelve Outward Bound students traveling with me. After five days rafting on the Colorado River I was ready to hike out. Five thousand feet up from Phantom Ranch on the river to the south rim of the Grand Canyon.

"We'll leave at two a.m.," Dick McCallum, our boatman river guide said. "We want to beat the heat of the day."

The South Kaibab Trail follows a ridge, a spur that juts out from the main canyon wall. From the crest it was like being suspended in space. A mere sliver of the moon gave just enough light to trick my eyes, scarcely enough light to see the trail. The canyon dropped off into the dark on either side, into a deep, brooding, bottomless gloom. With no wind, the only sound was the crunch of our boots on the loose gravel. I trudged behind the others in silence, retreating into my own thoughts, mesmerized, in a dream state. I feared dozing off while walking, and prodded sluggish thoughts to wakefulness.

The temperature had cooled to 90 degrees and hung there. My pack was light, carrying only a sleeping bag and light summer clothing. Water was the heaviest item, two quarts, four pounds. My bottles dug into my shoulder blades.

McCallum called for a water break every hour. Sweat and drink. Then drove us on. We climbed at the slow pace of a chain gang. With each stop the dark shaded lighter.

The first affirmation of light was an iridescent purple slash flaring across the crest of the North Rim, five miles across the canyon. It glowed to a thin fiery band of red but was too distant. Not real light. But a promise of light. Above us loomed the south rim, still in the dark, a rampart, formidable, impregnable. Our pace quickened.

Abruptly dawn came like a curtain drawn. Looking up I stopped. confused by the spectacle above. A bank of fog was forming on the rim of the canyon directly above us. It was a thick murky grey that illuminated to a glowing white as the light intensified. Fog over the Grand Canyon?

The fog poured over the rim as the day brightened, like a waterfall in slow motion, separating and dividing into tattered tongues of mist, dissolving in a diaphanous flow. Then the sun's rays tipped the canyon rim and exploded. The light refracted into a miniature rainbow. Then another rainbow. A succession, a garland of rainbows like a necklace along the canyon rim, the full spectrum of light from cadmium yellow to indigo.

I felt I was a witness to Creation. A memory I would retell many times over a lifetime.

This expedition had been organized by 1966 Dick McCallum, a professional river guide. In 1966 he had approached me with a proposal to develop an Outward Bound program in the Grand Canyon. McCallum was an impressive man. Over six foot tall, lean, big boned and muscular, bronzed by the sun. Wearing a broad brimmed Stetson hat, he would have been a good stand-in for sheriff of a small Western town. In the wake of John Wesley Powell, he had once rowed the length of the Colorado River from Green River, Wyoming to Lake Mead, Arizona, solo, in an oversized hard shell kayak with a mounted rowing frame, he had designed and built. I was intrigued with the idea of a canyon river Outward Bound program and felt he'd be an ideal man to lead us in this new direction. In 1966 Outward Bound was developing new programs and had expanded into new mountain areas. Why not the Grand Canyon?

I contracted with McCallum to run two groups of twelve Outward Bound students and their instructors, "Jack" Dempsey and Vic Walsh through the canyon. Dempsey's group, whom I accompanied, ran the upper half of the river to Phantom Ranch where they changed over with Walsh's group to run the lower river.

We floated in a thirty foot war surplus inflatable raft, develop by the military in World War II to improvise pontoon bridges to cross the rivers of northern France and western Germany. The "baloney boat," as they were called, had revolutionized river running. From 1868 when John Wesley Powell first ran the Grand Canyon, to 1945, less than 100 people had repeated the feat. Today there are 20,000 a year, in rafts, boats, kayaks, a new recreational industry. Most rafts are motorized. McCallum rowed. I had joined the expedition to do a feasibility study. Could canyon river running be a suitable Outward Bound experience? I appreciated McCallum's muscle powered primitive technology.

But in retrospect while awed by the grandeur of the canyon, I was disappointed by the ergonomics of the experience. It wasn't like climbing a mountain where I felt part of the environment. Sitting on a raft I saw like passing scenery slip by like watching the Grand Canyon on an immense wall to wall, horizon-to-sky, 3-D flat television screen.

The river was immense, but much of the time there was little challenge. Between rapids we drifted in the current over flat water at a steady six miles per hour. By mid-day the heat was soporific and we lounged in a sun-baked stupor, passing the Coppertone until the bottle were empty. Sun burn was our principal medical problem.

We anticipated each set of rapids not so much for the challenge as the relief. "Hang on," McCallum shouted, and we plunged bow first into the froth, stunned by the din of colliding waves and the splash of frigid water, the opportunity to cool off. Then we dried off in the sun, heated up and dozed again.

McCallum did all the work. He had all the fun. We were passengers, not crew. Only the hike out was an authentic Outward Bound experience.

Two years later, I stood on the bank of the Yampa River. The Yampa, a tributary of the Green and Colorado rivers, drains the north west corner of Colorado, the only tributary of the Colorado River system that remained free flowing, undamed, wild. I gazed into the deep hole of Warm Springs Rapid, a gaping maw that sucked into it the full wash of turgid water, flushing over the lip and plunging into a churning brown froth. Then it gushed out like a spouting whale then collapsed.

With the late snow melt run-off in May, 1968, it was a torrent. " Never seen it so high, " Keith Counts, our river guide, shouted over the thundering roar. I knew what Jonah felt like gazing into the mouth of the whale.

Keith Counts, was a resourceful science teacher at Adams City High School, a working class suburb north of Denver. As the leader of the local Explorer Scout Troop he had developed a well equipped river rafting program. As a part of the Dare to Care Program, a federally funded project to incorporate Outward Bound experiential concepts into the curriculum to curb the high student drop-out rate, Keith had proposed a river expedition geology field trip. I went along to evaluate the program.

The students enjoyed themselves, delighted to be freed from a week in the classroom. I was particularly impressed by the rapport between teachers and students, rarely seen in the confines of the school. The canyon was starkly beautiful and a spectacular geology display. But again the boatmen did all the rowing, the students alot of lounging. It was a successful geology field trip, I reported to school authorities. But it was not Outward Bound, I kept to myself. The challenge was missing. I came off the trip envious of the boatmen, frustrated not to have been at the oars.

A year later I was on the river again with Keith Counts and his Explorer Scouts boatmen, this time with a group of East Denver High School students. Outward Bound had received a foundation grant to develop a program to promote racial harmony in the city high school. An English teacher, who had been a student at Adams City High School, proposed a field trip on the Yampa and Green River. I had approved the trip on one condition, that I rowed my own raft, and we contracted with Keith Counts and the Explorer Scout Troop to run the trip. I bought two small war surplus rafts twenty foot inflatable rafts, called "The Green Weeney." Roy Muhlberger, the business manager, the only Outward Bound staff member with river experience, accompanied me on another raft.

As Keith Counts and I stood overlooking Warm Springs Rapid, I said, "I don't remember it being so big."

"It wasn't," Keith replied. Earlier in May there had been a massive rock slide, he explained, that brought down massive boulders and rock debris down the side canyon into the river. Most major rapids are formed this way. Unaware of the change in the river, a couple weeks earlier, a Hatch River Expeditions thirty foot inflatable had hit the hole and capsized with six passengers on board. Fortunately, no one was seriously injured, the incident had been a sobering experience to boatmen like Keith.

"So that's the way you do it," I said to Keith, my heart beating wildly in anticipation.

"Not me," Keith responded resolutely. "I'm going to line the rapid." I could feel my pulse return to near normal, relieved, reprieved, but also slightly disappointed. I walked back upstream with him to help with the lines. He attached a rope to the bow and the stern, and one boat at a time we walked them downstream along the bank. It was a slow tedious process, but on the positive side, it did involve all the students in an exercise involving teamwork.

We had two rafts safely below the rapid, when walking back along the bank, I saw a raft, an assault craft the size as ours, come down around the bend. It was fully loaded with eight boys, four on each side. But there was no one in the center of the raft rowing. They were all paddling. At the rear was the one adult, leaning far out with his paddle to bring the stern about, shouting commands, "Back paddle. Back paddle." With the stern pointed forty five degrees to the right bank, they ferry glided across the current and passed well clear of the hole. Five more boats followed in quick succession, all paddling.

We all stopped to look in admiration and disbelief.

"Who are they?" I asked Keith.

"An Explorer Troop from Salt Lake City," he said. "Their leaders are ex-marines."

If the marines can do it.... "What do you think Roy?" I conferred with my Outward Bound colleague. "Want to try running it?"

Roy Muhlberger was a big man, well over six feet, 200 pounds, fit and athlete. In a previous incarnation he had played college and professional football. Taking early retirement from a large multi-national corporation, he had come to work for Outward Bound as the business manager. As the only person on the Outward Bound staff at the time who had ever rafted a river, he was my in-house expert. I built my career in Outward Bound on other people's expertise.

"Why not?" he replied. After all we were Outward Bound. Then he looked at me, five foot seven inches, 155 pounds. If he had second thoughts, he said nothing.

Muhlberger ran first. I watched with focused attention. He stayed close to the right bank, then on the bend angled 45 degrees to shore, pulling like an Olympic oarsman against the current, he ferry glided across the stream and missed the hole by the width of his raft. A classic text book run.

As I walked back up the river bank to my raft, I was drunk with adrenalin. I shoved off from shore. Looking downstream I was shocked to see how different the river looked from the water. It seemed almost placid, like a flooded paddy field, with no hint of the drop below. Even the noise was subdued as if the river had slowed down. But as I drifted out into the current the right bank moved past at increasing speed. I clung close to shore. Too close. My bow touched a submerged rock, not very hard, but enough to catch the raft and spin the stern out toward the opposite bank, the wrong way. I corrected the angle of the raft pulling hard on the left oar and slowly managed to point the stern to the right bank. But by then I was already past the bend and the blunt stern of my raft was caught in the main force of the current. I pulled hard on the left oar, upstream against the current, like Muhlberger, trying to keep the stern forty five degrees to the right bank. But pull as I might, I was sucked inexorably into the maelstrom.

"Pull. Pull." I heard Keith calling from shore. As in the Book of Jonah, *the men rowed hard to bring it to land; but they could not.* (Jonah 1:13) I pulled. The oars seemed stuck as if I was rowing in mud. The roar of the river drowned out the shouts. Then the bow dropped into the hole. This is it, I thought. Doomed. Joe swallowed by the whale. I was flung from the rowing seat on to the floor of the raft. The raft buckled in the churning pit and then was tossed up, caught by the towering wave on the downstream rim of the hole. I was flushed out. The raft went air born. Looking up helpless, I saw it curve elegantly in an upward curl, almost in slow motion, like an airplane banking.

Submerged, I was tossed about in *the belly of hell* (2:2). Tumbled in the roiling water, I didn't know which way was up, *and the floods compassed me about. (2:3)*. My knees hit rocks that rolled with me along the river bed, and *the depth closed me round about (2:5)*. Then I managed to get my feet under me and was swept downstream in a running motion, like pedaling a bicycle, fending off the rocks.

I opened my eyes to a brown silty froth, a murky glow above. Finding solid footing, I pushed up it with a desperate lunge of a pole vaulter and I emerged into the world of dazzling light and thunderous sound. And air. Spitting out a mouthful of water that tasted of barnyard effluent, I breathed again.

Buoyed up by my bulky Mae West life jacket, I floated on my back, feet first downstream. I did a quick mental check of my vital signs, breathing, no bleeding I could detect, perhaps shock. No apparent broken bones. A bruised knee, but and to my surprise I was relatively unhurt. Vomited from the belly of the whale, I still intact.

But it was a long way to shore. Do I swim for it? "Keep calm," I remember telling myself out loud. "You could be here a long time."

I began a steady back stroke, angling forty-five degrees toward shore, like I had tried to do on the raft. The river current swept me past the eddy where the other rafts had come ashore and I was drawn into another rapid. But by now I was a veteran rapid runner. I took a deep breath and sluiced right through, almost in sport, continuing on down river around the bend, out of sight of the others. Then I felt profoundly alone and hugged my bosommy Mae West life jacket tight to my chest in an attempt to trap my dwindling body warmth.

The river broadened and I was washed into shallows. The footing was slippery, so I rump bumped my way across and came aground on a gravel bar. I staggered on to rocky dry land.

My adrenalin wore off and I began to shiver uncontrollably. In May, snow melt from mountains upstream fed the river. Safe from drowning, would I now perish from the cold? I'd read accounts of survivors from ship wreck found dead floating in their life jackets. I stripped off my clothes and tried to wring out the water, soon realizing that to be an exercise in futility. Naked, I ran up and down, desperate to dry off and generate body heat.

Muhlberger was not long in coming to my rescue and soon had me toweled dry, and warming up in his bulky wool sweater and long johns, many sizes too large.

"Rescue training should be a part of any Outward Bound program," I told him when my teeth stopped chattering.

My raft had taken off down down like a run away horse and was picked up several miles downstream by a group from Ashcrofter's, old friends from a mountain camp near Aspen. My clothing bag which was lashed in survived intact. Though presumably waterproof, everything was soaked, including my sleeping bag. I spent a long night at Echo Park, curled around the campfire, roasting my back while my stomach chilled, then reversing posture, basting myself like a rotisserie chicken. Like Jonah, I *sat in ashes* (3:6).

In the restless hours of that memorable night the vision of a viable Outward Bound program finally came to me. Like Jonah, my immersion was an epiphany. There was almost a haunted quality to the canyon environment inspired a spiritual awareness of human existence, like the mountains had done for me, and the sea. I had scoffed at the lack of challenge in river running, but clearly challenge abounded. Though there were risks but with proper equipment they were manageable. Falling out of a raft wearing a life jacket was not like falling off a mountain wearing a hard hat. From reading the literature I had, I was surprised how rare incidents of death by drowning, or cold water immersion, had been. Those that had drowned had not been wearing life jackets. There was a learning curve that through training and experience could lead to a sense of mastery. And the potential for teamwork.

But most important, I had cracked the code. It was that "Ah ha" moment of the Explorer Scouts from Salt Lake City running Warm Springs Rapid, all eight boys paddling. Crew rather than passengers. That made it an "Outward Bound" experience. By dawn my vision had become a plan.

On our next river expedition Outward Bound would paddle.

Joe on river trip in the 1980s.

Chapter 71: Balarat – Dusk on Bonzai Hill

The world is ordered
      Euclid declared
With squares balanced angular
      On hypotenuse.
And three hundred decades
      The myth prevailed.

Houses row on row
      Concrete boxed on high
Streets consecutive and straight
      First avenue to 108th.

But another order lay
      In gnarl and bend.
A pine root's claw
      Cracking granite
With persistent pry.
      Twisted by mountain gale
Charged with Arctic white.

No Euclid here
      Only forboding and night.

Chapter 72: Language and Educationalese

Meanwhile, back to my mountain-top in Colorado, let me pick up on the theme of the evolution of Experiential Education. By the 1970's Outward Bound was widely known and popular. Several schools, both public and independent, had incorporated Outward Bound activities into their programs. Project Adventure, a widely replicated physical education program, developed by former Outward Bound staff, built ropes courses on playing fields and in gyms, and published as series of "how-to" books. Field studies programs modeled on Powys's scientific expedition were popular. The New York City Outward Bound Center worked with inner city schools, developing experiential programs.

More teachers went through the Teacher's Practicum, but many reported their frustration with the school bureaucracy when they attempted to set up programs. Why not an Outward Bound experience for school administrators. Ed Ad River Trip, a five days seminar for educators, through the canyons of the Green River was born. It is a place of stunning beauty, exhilerating yet safe, an exercise in teamwork, with long evenings of companionship, philosophic discussion and an experience of spiritual renewal. Not surprisingly, it worked. But it was something new at the time. This was the prototype for the river expeditions that have become so popular as a way of attracting potential donors and new trustees to Outward Bound.

In the schools, several programs initiated by teachers never got off the ground because of poor planning. Our next step was to set up a program to educate promising teachers in organizational skills, program design, curriculum development, through a graduate program we co-sponsored with the University of Colorado, a Masters of Education Degree Program in Experiential Education. The name "Experiential Education" comes from the philosopher, John Dewey, the guru of progressive education in America, whose booklet "Experience and Education," was probably the most widely read book on education in the 20th century.

What evolved was a fortunate merger of the analytic, theoretical approach of Dewey, with the passionate, emotive, value oriented approach of Hahn with his sense of urgency. Each illuminates the other.

For example: Dewey wrote,"…if an experience arouses curiosity, strengthens initiative, and sets up desires and purposes that are sufficiently intense to carry a person over dead places in the future ….(it is) a moving force." Hahn in the "The First Law of Salem," wrote: "Give children the opportunity for self discovery. Every child has a *grand passion*…

Dewey had the belief that all genuine education comes about through experience. Hahn wrote that it was our duty to impel youth into value forming experience.

Dewey wrote that democratic social arrangements promote a better quality of human experience. Hahn wrote that above all, development of compassion was the purpose of education.

Hahn's educational manifesto as outlined in "The Seven Laws of Salem" fit neatly with Dewey's process of education. You have a copy of the Seven Law of Salem which I will leave to you to read at your leisure.

The Seven Laws Of Salem

First Law: "Give Children the Opportunity for Self-Discovery"

Every boy and girl has a *grand passion* often hidden and unrealized to the end of life. It can and will be realized by the child coming into close touch with a number of different activities. When a child comes 'into his own,' you will often hear a shout of joy...primitive happiness.

Second Law: "Make the Children Meet with Triumph and Defeat"

It is possible to wait on a child's inclinations and gifts—but you certainly disqualify him for the battle of life. Salem believes you ought to discover a child's weakness as well as his strength. Allow him to engage in enterprises in which he is likely to fail. Teach him to overcome defeat.

Third Law: "Give the Children the Opportunity of Self-Effacement in a Common Cause"

Send the youngsters out to undertake tasks which are of definite use to the community. Tell them from the start: "You are crew, not passengers."

Fourth Law: "Provide Periods of Silence"

Follow the great precedent of the Quakers. Unless the present-day generation acquires early habits of quiet and reflection, it will be speedily and prematurely used up by the nerve-exhausting and distracting civilization of today."

Fifth Law "Train the Imagination"

You must call it into action, otherwise it becomes atrophied like a muscle not in use. Acquire the ability to visualize what you plan and hope and fear for the future. Self-indulgence is in many cases due to the lack of vision.

Sixth Law "Make Games (I.E. Competition) Important But Not Predominant"
Athletes don't suffer by being put in their place.

Seventh Law "Free the Sons of the Wealthy and Powerful From the Enervating Sense of Privilege"
Let them share an enthralling school life with sons and daughters of those who have to struggle for their existence. No school can build up a tradition of joyous endeavor unless at least 30 percent of the children come from homes where life is not only simple but hard.

One wise man illuminated the other and so a new language of Experiential Education began to evolve.

John Dewey's theory of process, the idea of learning as a continuum, one layer of experience building on the last as a means of engaging in the future, led us to examine more closely what we did, and why and how we do it?

Here academics like Tony Richards, who came to CU to do his doctorate, got in the act, jumped on the experiential education train, writing learned theses.

Group development theory led to a better understanding of progressive development with a course.

Decision making process gave us insight into problem solving.

The three day solo experience was examined from the perspective of a primitive vision quest and a Jesuit meditative spiritual retreat.

Outward Bound was seen as an adolescent puberty rite.

Others compared Outward Bound to Joseph Campbell's Journey of the Hero.

The program was examined in the light of Maslow's hierarchy of needs.

In the context of the graduate school seminar we theorerized about Outward Bound ad infinitem and wrote learned papers for the Journal of Experiential Education.

Tony Richards and Jed Williamson, wrote presented workshops yesterday, among them. Both went on to initiate their own graduate programs for teachers, Tony at Dalhousie, Jed at the University of New Hampshire.

"There is nothing so practical as a good theory." I don't know who said that, certainly not Kurt Hahn, but let me give you one example: leadership. It was Bob Pieh, who founded the Minnesota Outward Bound School, now Voyageur, and later the Outdoor Experiential Education program at Queen's University, who put us on to this approach.

Take the wall, ten men or women scaling a smooth fourteen-foot barrier. "Learning is reflecting on experience," to quote John Dewey again. What learning can take place from reflecting on the wall?

After the group had scrambled over, some with bruised elbows and knees, others with bruised egos, Bob asks: Who is the leader? Is it the strong agile fellow, the good athlete who is first over the top and strong enough to hoist others after him? The action leader. "But what about the last person?" one of the women ask. The person who looks ahead, the visionary as leader. Or is it another person who suggests the lightest most agile go last and two strong persons hang over the side the hoist him up? The problem solver as leader. But he's soft spoken and no one hears him. "Hey guys, listen to what Harry has to say. He has a good idea. Let's try it his way." The good listener and team builder as leader. There are competing ideas. The consensus builder emerges as leader.

The discussion can lead to a questioning of what is leadership anyway? The idea of leadership as function and not position. Horizontal leadership rather then vertical leadership. Participatory rather than hierarchical. Emerging leadership. Democratic leadership rather than authoritarian. A discussion of which is most suitable and when? The individual's responsibility for leadership in a democracy. Jim Raffin's idea concept of the crucible of leadership and personal integrity.

So a growing body of knowledge began to develop around Kurt Hahn and Outward Bound. Victor Walsh and Gerald Golins, two bright instructors who went on to be Outward Bound school directors, wrote a defining paper, "The Outward Bound Process." Thomas James, an historian of education, now Vice-Dean of the Graduate School of Education at New York University, wrote a small book, "Education at the Edge," on the first twenty years of the Colorado Outward School. Stephen Bacon wrote, "The Conscious Use of Metaphor in Outward Bound." The AEE, the Association of Experiential Education based in Boulder published a journal and several volumes. Project Adventure has a library of books describing their practices, much inspired by Hahn.

For all that, it must be said there are skeptics. "Come off it Joe. Let the mountains speak for themselves," an outstanding instructor confronted me years ago. And you know what? I believe Kurt Hahn would agree with him. We must not let words be an excuse for action.

By this time, some of the rest of you may feel the same. You have permission to yawn.

At United World College in New Mexico, Joe and dog
Pernod in the 1980s.

Chapter 73: Spring Came to the City

Spring came to the city
With siren's wail
Looming night
Bringing the lonliness of pain
The grief of a million deaths
Instead of promised rest
Relief of needle and pill
To wake to the terror
Of life and facing self.

Yet spring came
to the city.
Three flowering crab apple trees
Easter candles in the rain
Flotsam on the streets
The mighty river flushing
its murk to the sea.
Yes spring came.
Granny toothless and
eighty one
Celebrating the joy
of food and wamth
And being alive, still.
And robot men
Controlling subterranean
decibles
The flow of bodies
Fail safed electronically
Seeking the ultimate meld
Of yesterday today and tomorrow.

When all along the secret lay
In control of breath
A flexible back

365

The throb of heart.

Spring came to the city.

Chapter 74: Millspaugh

The rescue helicopter did not arrive until late morning. I heard the dull rhythmic thudding of the rotating blades as it approached from the valley below, steadily becoming louder until overhead it was deafening.

We stoked up a smoky campfire the pilot an indication of the direction and speed of the wind. Earlier we had laid out a large "X" with sleeping bags to mark a landing site on the open meadow above Geneva Lake.

The machine hovered flattened the grass like in an early winter blizzard, then lowered tentatively as if not trusting, before settling, squatting on the ground, the engine roar turning to a high complaining whine and dropping to a moan as the engine shut down.

The cabin doors had been removed , and a man of medium height dropped out of the passengers side with an athletic spring, ducked beneath the slowly rotating blades and ran toward me. He was the picture of a man of action, wearing a climbers helmet, heavy hiking boots, canvas Patagonia pants with cargo pockets, the flashing badge of the county sheriff over his shirt pocket. He looked familiar, like someone I once knew, but I couldn't place the bushy mustache. It was only when he took off his sunglasses that I recognized Don West, a former Outward Bound instructor. I felt he was an unlikely man to be a sheriff, but an ideal person for an emergency disaster like this.

"I'm so sorry Joe," he said as he enclosed me in a warm generous hug. He had tears in his eyes. I introduced him to the rest of my party, a group of graduate students from the University of Colorado enrolled in a Master of Education Degree Program in Experiential Education, co-sponsored by Outward Bound. The year long program began with a one month Outward Bound course in the mountains west of Aspen. I was the director-instructor-adjunct professor. The twelve graduate students were selected from leaders of programs in schools, youth corrections, community programs that incorporated Outward Bound principles.

The day before, on day twelve of the twenty-one day program, we had set out to climb Snowmass Mountain, 14,198 feet. We roped up in three groups of four. I attached myself to the lead group where I could act as guide but still let a student lead. The other two groups followed behind us but still in sight, 200 to 300 yards apart. Off early, we climbed the south ridge which curves in a graceful sweeping "S" where the rock strata buckles and bends back on itself. It was a clear warm mid-July day, a week after the bi-centennial 1976.

It was mid-morning and we were making good time. John, in the lead, an experienced climber, set a steady rhythmic pace. The summit was in sight 400 yards ahead where the steep ridge flattened out. I was plodding along, breathing hard, caught up in my own thoughts, when my peaceful tranquility was interrupted by a thunderous "Boom!" like a fighter jet breaking the sound barrier. It was followed by the clatter of falling rock. Looking back, I saw a small cloud of dust and shattered rock particles that drifted off in a light breeze. There was a hushed silence followed by the frantic blowing of whistles.

"Just stay here," I told the group I was with, and I bounded off down the mountain, as fast as I dared, conscious of holding myself back, not wanting to complicate a bad situation by injuring myself.

"Don't let it be," I prayed to some undetermined Higher Being, and imagined a variety of worst case scenarios.

Within minutes I was at the site. Marj Millspaugh, a thirty years old biology teacher from Colorado Springs, lie sprawled on the broken rocks, her three team mates crouched over her. Mike McCann was trying to give her mouth to mouth resuscitation, but her face was bloated and blood drained from her nostrils. More blood oozed through her clothes.

"What happened?" I asked.

"I felt we were off route," Tom, a tall, assured Kansan, a Vietnam veteran, the group leader, said. He had in fact gone off route on to the steep side of the ridge. "So I told the group to stay here and I went ahead to reconnoiter. I thought I had found a safe way for them to come up, so I started down to tell them. In the process I dislodged a rock and it hit Marj," he said. I could see the pain on Tom's face, but he was better than most men at controlling his emotions.

The rock he had dislodged was in fact the size of a refrigerator, instantly crushed the life out of Marj, and only narrowly missed killing the other two who stood beside her.

We continued artificial resuscitation on Marj for another hour with no response. We moved to a safer place on the ridge. In the meantime the lead group descended to us, and those behind us came up.

Now what? What do we do with the body? Her team mates did not want to leave her there, and objected. But I pointed out that we were not equipped to carry her out. To do so would only endanger more lives. It would be safer by helicopter. Medical evacuations and body retrievals were standard Vietnam procedures, regularly seen on television. I made the decision to leave Marj on the mountain.

I was more concerned about getting the rest of us safely off the mountain. Dennis was badly shaken. He had narrowly escaped being killed. This was his first experience of death. He was in shock. I assigned two students to look after each of the survivors and led the group back down the ridge.

I had climbed Snowmass on several occasions and knew that the quick way off the mountain was to drop of the ridge down one of the steep gullies that led to the glacial basin to the east. Descending one of these on Outward Bound course C-13 in 1965, John McBride had slipped, fell on rocks at the bottom, suffering major head injuries. Only because of the skillful care of his instructors is he alive. Eleven years later the memory was still fresh.

The main danger, I felt, was not the steepness. We had climbing ropes and could rappel a steep slope. The danger was rock fall. I found a steep sloping rock slab that was reasonably clean of loose rock. and we lowered ourselves safely on a fixed rope, and hiked out over the boulder field that led to the meadow and on to our campsite at Geneva Lake.

Only when I was back at the comfort of our camp did the enormity of the tragedy begin to sink in. This wasn't something that should have happened. Not to me.

What do I do next? Everyone was safe off the mountain. Except for Marj. Do we return to school and call for a helicopter? No one wanted to leave with Marj still on the mountainside. Should I go? But I didn't want to leave the group. Send somebody else. Susan Rogers, one of the team leaders, had been an Outward Bound instructor and course director for girls' courses. She was the logical choice. But she too was reluctant to leave the group. Death had strengthened the bond. I felt it, wanting to be protective and protected in turn.

Susan left in the early evening, after a shared meal, carrying my accident report, explaining the circumstances and requesting a helicopter to retrieve the body.

We sat around the campfire until late. There was little conversation. It would have been a great opportunity to deal with feelings, but I didn't have that skill. Nor did any of the students. Tom kept feeding sticks into the fire, not enough to give off much warmth, but to keep it alight, mesmerized by the flame, as mankind has done to cope with fear, pain and mystery since we lived in caves.

When the helicopter arrived next morning, the sheriff, Don West asked to meet with the group to draft a sheriff's report. Tom retold his account of the accident without apparent emotion, matter fact. I felt he had had to do so before, in Vietnam perhaps, though he never spoke of it.

The helicopter pilot joined us. A small man with a solid build and a ready smile, he walked with a swagger that reminded me of a rodeo rider. We chatted. "What we'll do is this. I need to let the engine cool down and off load the extra fuel I brought to get us home. Don't want the extra weight. 14,000 is about the limit for this bird. Then I'll take the sheriff up and drop him off on the ridge above the victim.

"How will you do that?" I asked. I'd seen air born soldiers rappel from helicopter.

"Just put a pad down on a rock and he can step off. On the first trip I'll drop the sheriff off with a sling and a body bag. He'll hike down and secure the body. Next trip I'll hover over the accident site and lower a hook. The sheriff can attach the body sling to it and we'll fly her down. Then I'll go back for the sheriff." He made it sound so simple.

Between trips the helicopter returned to the meadow, where the engine was turned off and cooled down. The pilot was friendly and eager to chat while he waited for the engine to cool.

"Do you do this sort of thing very often?" I asked.

369

"Yes. Most days," he said. "Not to retrieve bodies. But to carry miners and prospectors to high sites. There's a gold rush on right now. Gold is selling at $650 an ounce and a lot of the old mining claims are being reopened." He explained that he'd fly a work crew high on a mountain, drop them off while they prepared a site for a drill. Then he'd bring them lumber, cement and water, to make a platform for a small drill rig. Next day he'd deliver a small mobile ore drill, that he could nest on to the concrete pad and bolted down.

"I do it all with mirrors mounted in front of the helicopter," he said, "and at the end of the day I pick the crew up and bring them down."

"Where did you learn to fly like that?" I asked.

"Vietnam," he replied.

Through the rest of the morning and into early afternoon, we were glued to the sky, mesmerized by the virtuosity of he man and his machine. The second trip had us aghast. The body bag was suspended head down, secured by the sling around the feet. Though I'm sure that was practical, it did seem irreverent.

Mid-afternoon they fueled up for the last time. Don West, the sheriff, gave me a final hug. I thanked him and the pilot for their mission of mercy, and they took off to deliver Marj Millspaugh to the morgue. We trudged dolefully along the Meadow Mountain traverse to return to school.

It was only when I was in the privacy of my cabin that I felt I could surrender to my grief. I wallowed in self-pity. I had a bottle of red wine in the fridge, but that only made it worse. I wept with abandon, something I had not done in years, since Pat Hannon's death, my closest friend in college, twenty-four years before.

This was only the beginning of the process of disenchantment with Outward Bound.

Chapter 75: The Anatomy of a Mentorship

An eight thousand dollar deficit. It kept me awake much of the night. How do I account for it? I was invited to breakfast by the new chairman of the board of the Colorado Outward Bound School, William C. "Bill" Coors, president of the eponymous brewery. I'd never been summoned to a meeting over breakfast before, certainly not at the Denver Country Club. I didn't know what to expect.

$8,000. Financially the only frame of reference I had was my family bank book that I balanced meticulously every month and never let run a deficit. This sum was astronomic. I ran the figures through my mind, trying to come up with a plausible explanation: there was the unprecedented winter snow fall and the cost of that snow plow we needed to get into the school. The rental of another 4x4 vehicle to re-supply rations to our students in the field during the Rossetter search. John McBride's medical bills which we had not seen the end of yet. And airfare and hotel accommodations for his mother. The list went on. None of these cost over runs had been anticipated or budgeted.

I was still smarting from the fall meeting of the board the year before when one trustee asked why I shouldn't be fired. And I was not certain what the reaction of the board would be to Lou Covert's death, the instructor, and John McBride, the student with head injuries. And now the $8000 deficit. What further evidence did he need of management mismanagement? I passed the balance sheet to Mr. Coors. I felt I was on too thin ice to call him "Bill."

I studied his face as he scanned the document, anticipating a furrowed brow. He flipped to the second page then looked up with a congratulatory smile. "Only an $8,000 deficit? Why that's very good for a start-up organization like Outward Bound," and he handed the report back to me.

Then with a serious tone of concern he said, "What are you doing to groom your successor?"

My successor? I said nothing. So he was thinking of replacing me. Already, at our first meeting.

This was the coup de grace. This was what the elegant country club breakfast was about. The Rocky Ford melon, eggs benedict, served on bone china, English muffins, Brazilian coffee poured from a silver beaker by the attentive waiter who hovered at a discrete distance out of earshot, the starched linen hand towels in the restroom and ice in the urinals to allay noxious odors. A subtle process of termination, cushioned gentility.

"What do you have in mind?" I asked.

"Suppose you drive off Loveland Pass the next time you go skiing. I don't want to be left with an Outward Bound school on my hands. You need an assistant," he said. An $8,000 deficit and now he wants me to hire an assistant. There went my family check book financial planning system out the window.

That was the beginning of a period of creative mentoring. "To be successful," Bill told me (I gradually became comfortable calling him Bill), "you need three things. You need a good idea. You need good men. And you need money. Outward Bound is a good idea," he said. "Your job is to get good men. My job is to get the money." At the end of the year when donations from major donors came in, there was a check for $30,000 from the Adolph Coors Company. I learned about venture capitalism at the non-profit level.

A month later I was in New York City showing the Outward Bound film, "As Tall as the Mountains," to a group of inner city agency heads. There I met Gary Templin. A tall man in his late twenties, with Montana good looks and a college wrestler's build, a thoughtful brooding face that exploded into a warm smile. He was the director of a Harlem street worker program. Having served in Vietnam as an officer in the Green Berets he saw in Outward Bound many of the experiences that had been formative in his life. He was taken by Outward Bound. I was taken by him. As we were leaving I asked in a joking way, "When are you going to come work with us?"

"When are you going to invite me?" he said. At the next meeting of the board of trustees, they approved my hiring Gary, tripling the deficit.

With Bill Coors doing the down field blocking at a board level, and Gary Templin a line backer as assistant director, the Colorado Outward Bound School took on a whole new dimension. As did my career. What had been a program of personal change became a program of social change.

It was the era of President Lyndon Johnson's "War on Poverty." Federal funds were available to get kids out of the inner city in the summer, to fund programs for delinquent youth, basic skill training in Job Corps, school enrichment programs designed to reduce drop out rates. I was excited about a contract I'd been able to negotiate with Job Corps to develop a leadership program in the center in Collbran, near Grand Junction, another in Adams City High School, in a working class suburb north of Denver that had a high drop out rate. Given Gary Templin's experience working with inner city youth and minority populations, and his considerable management skills, I directed the Colorado school in this direction with greater confidence.

Bill Coors, whose political instincts were conservative, nevertheless approved. But several trustees did not. At a cocktail party following a board meeting in Aspen, I was cornered by two of the naysayers. "You're selling the soul of Outward Bound for a mess of federal pottage," one said.

At the next board meeting I gave a report on "Outward Bound in the Mainstream," outreach programs in other institutions. "The only streams I know all run downhill," one of the more conservative trustees interrupted me.

I expressed my doubts to Bill, wondering if the board would approve expanding the Job Corps program to other centers. "Well, if Outward Bound won't do it, let's set up another organization that will." When the project did not get funded, the Adolph Coors Company set up their own program. Gary Templin worked with Coors staff to design "Manpower Challenge," a job training program for young prison parolees. It began with both parolees and Coors floor supervisors going through an Outward Bound course together, followed by several months of coaching, on-the-job training, financial counseling, membership in the credit union, and bus transportation provided from Five Points, the Black community in Denver, to the brewery in Golden, half an hour away.

With a grant of $25,000 a year for three years from the Lawrence Phipps Foundation we were able to initiate a successful program in East Denver High School that drew students from the racially integrated neighborhood of Park Hill, where I lived. When I commented on the generosity and social commitment of the foundation, Bill, who had opened the door, replied, "It was a quid pro quo. I made a similar contribution to their new football stadium." I was beginning to understand the underlying logic of philanthropic giving. Much of it was really a back scratching business. "You give to my favorite charity and I'll give to yours."

The following year Bill arranged a luncheon with the El Pomar Foundation in Colorado Springs. This was the largest foundation in Colorado. It could mean another major grant for a school and community based program. On the way down, Bill driving, I said, "Bill, there are some weeks when I think you spend more time on Outward Bound that you do at the brewery."

He turned to me with a big grin, "You know Joe, you can only get so much psychic reward brewing beer."

Outward Bound found in Bill Coors a benefactor and a visionary, one who saw it as "a good idea" relevant not only to the lives of young people as individuals, but also as a way of addressing the problems of American society in the troubled sixties and seventies.

And I found a mentor who guided me through the minefield of organizational politics; and a friend who shared with me the joy and romance of Outward Bound. We climbed Capital Peak together, Arrow and Vestal in the San Juan Mountains, rafted through Whirlpool Canyon on the Green River, hiked through the desert canyons of Utah in Escalante Canyon.

The year before I resigned from the Colorado Outward Bound School we stood together on the summit of Kilimanjaro. "It sure would be nice to have a can of beer" I said, standing on the equator of Africa.

"It sure would," Bill replied.

"Have one," I said, and reached into my pack and handed him a can of Coors.

Chapter 76: Cataract Canyon – Expeditionary Learning
March 1993

The episode begins with an innocent pee into the mighty Colorado River. The US Park Service regulations mandate that solid waste must be carried out of the canyon, but that you piss in the river rather than on the shore. "The river can absorb the excess minerals more effectively than the land," Bruce Truitt, "Huck," our expedition leader, says with only a suggestion of a smile.

I have known Huck for more that a decade, then a lean, gaunt teen-ager, hired to load and unload the supply vehicles, carrying rafts and rations to and from the put-in and take-out points on river expeditions. Now in the prime of his young manhood, he is in charge of this group of thirty educators. School principals, a couple superintendant, a former private school headmaster, teachers are members of an Expeditionary Learning Outward Bound action centered program planning and team building seminar on the Colorado River. It is early in the season, March, and though the days are warm, the nights are cold, and the murky river, flowing a silty gray, is very cold.

When we beach our rafts on the sandy bar below the Confluence, where the Green River comes down out of Wyoming and joins the Colorado, doubling the river's flow, to study the first major rapid we have encountered, "CJ", a sprightly teacher from Evergreen, Colorado goes down to the river to pee. Hitching up her blue jeans, and the clumsy, heavy duty yellow Helly Hansen waterproof foul weather suit, she lets out a scream. Thirty feet away, a man appears over the sand dune, crawling, arm outstretched to attract attention and collapses. Others gather quickly, Truitt is called urgently to the scene. Further downstream someone notices a tent that has been erected on the shore, the open door flapping in the wind.

Below, at the water's edge, a canoe has been hauled up on the beach, the bow stove in, wrecked. The nurse, who is with the Dubuque, Iowa team is summoned. She is a calming influence, takes the survivor's vital signs: weak pulse, low blood pressure, but temperature normal, otherwise he seems alright. Conscious, though incoherent, he mumbles to himself, disoriented.

Inspecting the tent, newly bought, cheap, they find several knives, a sheath knife, machete, a collapsible army shovel, a 30-30 hunting rifle with a box of ammunition, fishing gear. Fire arms are not permitted in a National Park. His wallet is found in a pack with his driver's licence, Louisiana, and ID—a letter of release from a federal prison. There's a notebook with random comments, dated. Apparently he set

374

out two weeks ago, capsized in the first rapid upstream, losing much of his food, and stove in his canoe. He has recorded each day in increasingly enfeebled writing. Nothing has been written the last three days.

We do not find a Park Service river permit.

"What should we do with him?" Huck gathers the Outward Bound staff around him, Steve Truitt, his older brother, himself a recent river course director, now Director of the Harvard Outward Bound Center: Greg Farrell, Vice-President of Outward Bound USA, coordinator of educational and urban programs. As the former Director of the Colorado Outward Bound School, I am included, and each of the raft instructors. "Do we take him with us? We could carry him our on the supply boat." This is a huge 30 ft inflatable pontoon that is either rowed, or powered by a 75 hp Mercury outboard motor, "baloney boats" the instructors call them. "Students," participants travel in 17ft inflatables, eight to a team, paddling, four on each side, instructor at the stern. "Or do we go for help?" It's a tough call. What is the compassionate response? What is the responsible decision? The debate is both philosophic and practical.

I tell Huck what's on my mind. "Look, you have no idea what sort of a weirdo you're dealing with. He comes down the river alone, with knives, machete, a rifle, in a flimsy canoe, out of season. He has a prison record. You don't know what he'll be like when he gains consciousness. He could be a raving maniac. Your responsibility is to your party. This is a law enforcement problem, and the Park Service ought to handle it."

But how? Moab, where we put on the river two days ago, is 30 miles upstream. Hite Landing 40 miles downstream, through five major rapids. Who can we send for help?

Alan, the river guide who is rowing the baloney boat is the obvious choice. And Peter Baillie, an expert canoeist, instructor with the Voyageur Outward Bound School in Minnesota. "Joe, are you up for it?" I'm a supernumerary, an official stowaway, having talked my way on to the trip, riding passenger on the baloney boat.

Three of us launch out just before dark into the depths of the canyon. The rapids blur together in memory, blank, blank and blank, names bestowed by John Wesley Powell on his famous voyage of exploration in 1885? On the flat stretches of river, we motor, but Alan feels more confident rowing when we come to the rapids, lifting the motor to protect it from submerged rocks. He steers from aft, while Peter and I paddle from either side, my side, grossly underpowered. We work to direct the raft into the tongue of the rapid, where the water is compressed from both sides into a long, smooth, slanting V, lining up the raft at the right angle, taking it head on, and letting the current whip us through. It is an exciting night, glorious, exciting, terrifying. The canyon walls crowd in with the growing darkness. Alan has run Cataract Canyon many times before, but never in the dark. But he knows his position by familiar bends in the river, implanted in memory from previous trips. Peter and I feel growing confidence in his skill and ability, his stewardship.

Kurt Hahn was asked once, what he saw as his greatest accomplishment. He paused, then replied, "The men I hired." We felt Alan deserved a similar compliment that night. When he cut the motor on the approach of a rapid, the mechanical roar of the outboard was followed by a deafening silence, and then the murmur of the rapid downstream that grew louder as we came closer, until we were engulfed in its thunderous roar. The yell, the release as we floated into the calm of the pool below.

Paddling to the river bank, we eddied out, Alan cranked down the outboard and we motor on.

"Last Chance Rapid," just above the flat water of Lake Powell has Alan worried from the start.

"This is the big one."

The full force of the river pours over a five foot ledge that stretches across the full width of the river, tumbling into a hole below, the water cycling back, churning back on itself, tumbling, easily flipping a small raft our size.

There is one place only where the tongue of the river sweeps down and through, carrying one over the drop, and past the holes on either side. But one has to hit it right. We beach on the left bank and climb the high boulders on shore to look this one over. In the dusk I can see where the water drops off into the tumbling maelstrom, and far across, half way to the other side where the main volume of the river flowed in a mighty tongue, drowning out the deep and gaping hole, half the size of the raft.

And directly below, a huge boulder, the size of a cabin, bulging out of the river, water washing half way up its side, then sluicing off.

Visible from the top of the boulders on shore, once back on the raft at river level, all I can see is a smooth line where the water seems to drop placidly over the edge. The tongue could be anywhere in the middle of the river. I pray that Alan is not as disoriented as I am. "Paddle left, HARD!" Alan shouts, and I pull for all that I am worth, but the raft is responsive only to higher forces. The roar is deafening. The raft seems to lift as it went over the edge. The drops. I am left standing on air, then the bow screwed left, the leading edge caught the tongue, and a wall of water five feet high strikes me broadside and I fall into the raft, the wave going over me. Floating upright again, with the buoyancy of the Mae West life jacket, paddle waving in the air, just in time to see the raft slither up the side of cabin boulder, to a 45 degree angle. "Grab on!" Peter on the lower side shouts out. I'm sure we are going to slide right up the rock and tip, when we slither round the rock, washed off by the current and emerge downstream, water in the raft to the brim. Heavily weighted, but still afloat we pull for shore and beach on a gravel bar. Giddy with relief. Grateful for Alan's last minute maneuver. Had we been three feet to the right we would have plunged right into the hole. Thankful to the river gods for their reprieve.

In the deluge our bucket had come detached, and we begin the long and tedious task of bailing out the raft, splashing water out as best we can with paddles, then using a tin cup and the cooking pot we have brought as emergency kit. Drifting downstream, the current slackens as we enter the backed up waters of Lake Powell. Only now do we realize how dark it is, a deep canyon dark. As the adrenalin begins to seep out of our system, we begin to feel the cold. I shiver, and am aware of the symptoms of hypothermia. Alan pulls in to a sandbar on the left bank, a favored lunch spot in better times, we gather driftwood, and light a huge bonfire. Stripping off our clothes, we rig a line to dry them, and run hysterically up and down the sand, stark naked, urging warmth back into our bodies. Standing by the fire we scorch one side and then the other.

Hot tea, soup, cheese and crackers, honey, clothes dry, we re-embark on the river, just as the moon comes over the canyon rim, near the full, brilliantly silver, casting shadows and a silver sheen on the canyon wall. Eerie, zoomorphic shapes haunt my dreams as I doze off to the steady throbbing of the outboard motor.

We reach Hite Crossing soon after midnight. The phone at the end of the dock connects us promptly with the Park Ranger. He immediately jumps into emergency mode. Not too much happens that time of year at his lonely desert outpost. A phone call through to the hospital at Page, Arizona, 150 miles down at the lower end of Lake Powell, alerts the medi-vac helicopter team. "Do you think you can fly tonight?"

"Sure, it's so bright you can see the color of the rocks," the pilot replies over the radio. He is eager to fly. I ask him to stop off at Hite and pick up Alan, who will be needed back upriver.

By 3 am the helicopter is over the rescue site. Huck has a helipad cleared of rocks on a small flat area above the beach, and spotting fires built on each corner. They hear the resonating throb of the helicopter rotors echoing off the canyon walls, light the fires, and by 3:20 am are aloft again, with the victim, whose name I still don't know, on the way to the hospital.

The aftermath is as bizarre as the rescue. Our friend indeed turned out to a parolee from the federal penal system, convicted of a minor drug charge. He was down and out. Just out of prison. His girl friend had recently left him. He lost his job. He was at loose ends, and had decided to get away from it all, and like Huck Finn "to head out to the territory." He had the romantic dream of finding a place as far away as he could get from civilization, build a log cabin and live by hunting and fishing. The archetypal American fantasy. Looking at a map of the United States, Utah seemed to be a place with few roads. Why not try there?

Having wrecked his canoe, he really thought he was going to die. And might well have, had we not come along. Few people raft the river in winter or early spring. It could have been another month before another party came along. At the hospital, he recovered with astonishing rapidity. They kept him overnight for observation, then released him in the morning. The Park Service felt they had done all they could do for him, did not want to complicate his life, nor theirs. So they brought no charges, fed him a hearty meal, gave him a change of clothes, and put him on a bus, ticket courtesy of the US Government, and sent him on his way back to Louisiana.

Expedition Learning Outward Bound is dedicated to helping young people discover the hero within themselves. We all felt pride in our own acts of heroism by end of the expedition. But Meg Campbell was critical. "It's another example of male chauvinism. Why couldn't you have taken a woman with you for the rescue?" My daughters I suspect would agree.

Joe and students at the Wildnerness Leadership
Seminar in Banff, Canada, 1981.

Chapter 77: Islands of Knowing

The slow surge of the sea
I come again to the gray Atlantic shore
Dreams of different lands
Floating on the waves
Under a platinum sky

Eight souls come together
To row the waters of thought
Searching for their inner Truth
And that of the Young.

Seeking connectedness
With each other
Between the islands that separate us
With so much not knowing.

Chapter 78: Return to Geneva Lake

Time present. Overlapped in time past.
Caught in the vortex of time future.

I lie amidst pine needles and kinnikanik
And alpine flowers of a younger age
Pushing through the bare glacial sod
Among spruce bows...
Penstamen, camus, paint brush,
Purple aster and unlikely elephant's head
Glowing colors from my youthful middle years
Shrouded like the shifting mists
Visions of the past
Fading in and out of view.

Visions of glory and friendship
And living on the edge
Early ascents of Maroon, Snowmass, Capital
Arthur reciting the Lord's Prayer from the mountain top.
And tragedy—disappointment, disillusion
And death—Lou, Marj, Arthur
All blurred into the mist
and rain of the past.
And the glow of the sunrise, and the
glare of mid day sun
Glorious fields of flowers stretching
to the skies.
Fields of glory,
Bursts of red and yellow and purple and gold.
Enough to make one believe in God.
Hallelujah!

Encapsulated in an aching body
An overcharged mind.
Seeking for the vision on high

As the curtain is drawn back
And the clouds part

And the path comes into view
A way. The tao.
To mountains beyond mountains,
Ranges beyond the hills
To the last horizon...
The horizon beyond the horizon.

Chapter 79: Outward Bound And The 21st Century—Kurt Hahn Award Address 2002

Heroditus in his History of the Persian Wars, writes of the Persians that they discuss strategy when drunk, and tactics when sober. I assume you have all had enough to drink to bear with me for ten minutes of romantic fantasy about Outward Bound that could be mistaken for strategy. ."

But first let me say how honored I am to be here, albeit somewhat intimidated, and a little confused. Why me? But as Abigail Adams said to John on his being elected President, "it is a flattering and glorious reward." My friends expect me to something pertinent, pith and even prophetic about Outward Bound in the 21st century. But that would be presumptuous. It's over 25 years since I left the Colorado Outward Bound School, and for the past eight years I've been out of the country most of the time, on my own ElderOdyssey, cruising in the Caribbean and the Mediterranean. So it I beg your indulgence. All I can share with you is a few minutes of nostalgia of an old man. TS Eliot put it eloquently, "To return to the beginning and know it for the first time.

Let me return to my beginning. I was in instructor on C-1 and C-2, the first two courses of the Colorado Outward Bound, the first on the North American continent.[Colorado is now up to 999?] The two outstanding students in my patrol on C-2, in July, 1962, were John and Arthur. John Cooley, came from a well-to-do Denver family, was a very serious, rather matter of fact, unsmiling young man, determined, capable, fit. He was already familiar with the mountains, and his patrol mates deferred to his knowledge and elected him their patrol captain. John later returned to the school as a young instructor, had a successful career in business and is now Chairman of the Board of the Colorado Outward Bound School. [If he is at the dinner, have him stand up and be recognized.]

Arthur came from New York City, Arthur Wellington Conquest the Third, a Black from Harlem, sponsored by the New York City Boy's Club .Arthur was also fit, capable, determined and unsmiling. But he had misgivings about the Outward Bound and was not hesitant to let us know. Arriving at the school after a two mile hike up a dusty mountain road, in the middle of a crowd of fifty boys milling around, Arthur whips out a 6 inch switch blade, and flings it mightily into the air. The crowd scatters, the knife lands at Arthur's feet, he picks it up, puts it in his pocket, unsmiling. Not a very propitious beginning, but Arthur is not there to mess around, nor is anyone to mess with him. And beneath the overt aggressiveness he has great charm, sense of humor, and becomes immensely popular. In the election for Patrol Captain, he is the runner up to John.

On our Alpine Expedition, we camped one night on a grassy knoll, high on the mountain side, with a sweeping view over the valley down to Snowmass Lake below. Before breaking camp in the morning we'd gather briefly to discuss the plan for the day, followed by a short reading, and a student would lead us in prayer. This morning I substituted a Quaker silence for the prayer, then got up to go. But Arthur interrupted, "Joe, we haven't said the Lord's Prayer." "Would you lead us, Arthur?" I asked. And in the deep voice of a Pentecostal preacher, Arthur intoned the glorious words," Our Father... for Thine is the kingdom, and the Power and the Glory..." And we set off to climb Capital Peak, 14,021 feet that day, safely. Arthur went on to become the first Black Outward Bound instructor with the Hurricane Island Outward Bound School, the director of a number of programs for disadvantaged inner city youth, and a severe critic of Outward Bound for its lack of opportunity for Blacks, and what he sees as its lack of commitment to the inner city.

We talk of Outward Bound as a life transforming experience. It was for me as much as it was for any of my students. But to return to my fable of Arthur and John, there may be a moral to the story that is may be useful today as Outward Bound goes through the process of defining itself, reinventing itself in the 21st century. Looking back to the past I am struck by how important we felt a social mix was on the program. "They come from Harvard and they come from Harlem," our old friend Josh Miner used to say. We felt that a racial mix was an essential part of the program, part of the quality of the program. The other is the central role of leadership develop as a goal.

Very early there developed a dynamic tension within Outward Bound, between those who saw Outward Bound as a rigidly defined set of activities, lasting a6 days that took place in the wilderness, whose integrity must be jealously guarded, like a corporation that protects its industrial trade secrets, and those who saw Outward Bound being a set of learning principles having broader educational and social ramifications. Murray Durst, an early Executive Director of OBUSA, put the question this way, "Is Outward Bound the guardian of a program, or is it the steward of an idea?"

One of the first to see the potential for Outward Bound as an idea, was Greg Farrell., who is here tonight. His Outward Bound career is instructive, from a strategic perspective. It would make a very good case study of how Outward Bound as program feeds into Outward Bound as an idea. In 1964 we ran an Instructor's Training Course in Colorado. Greg enrolled. A couple years later he was the Director of the War on Poverty Program in Trenton, New Jersey and that fall invited Josh from the national office and the three school to a meeting in Trenton. We visited with school officials, agency heads, and explored ways that Outward Bound concepts could be adapted to an inner city urban setting. While not exactly Outward Bound, it seemed consistent with the ideas of Kurt Hahn, our founder, a German Jew who had stood up to Hitler in the early thirties. It gave Outward Bound a deeper sense of social commitment. Out of the meeting came Trenton Action Bound. The Ford Foundation in those days spoke of "change agents" and "a critical mass for institutional change." The rhetoric harmonized with the dynamism of Outward Bound. Greg sent a cadre of committed teachers, and students who has shown initiative in their schools, and they returned to provide leadership in the program. One of the teachers, Phil Costello, later set up his own program, which is still running in New Jersey.

Trenton Action Bound broke the Outward Bound mold and recast it in a new guise. We begam to see Outward Bound as a catalyst for institutional change. We had a precedent. What followed was a burgeoning of what we called "Outward Bound adaptive programs." In Colorado we initiated programs with Job Corps, the Colorado Division of Youth Services, the "Dare to Care Program" in Adams City High School, a working class suburb north east of Denver, the Senior Seminar in East Denver High School, then were under a court desegregation order. With the University of Northern Colorado, we set up a program for teachers, and later five day river rafting trips on the Green River for school administrators. We reorganized the school to create a Project Center staffed with senior instuctors to provide consulting services, and designed a Master of Education Degree Program in cooperation with the University of Colorado School of Education. One of the assignments of the first class was to organize a conference, and from it came the Association of Experiential Education, that now has taken on a life of its own with over 1000 members. The MEd program graduated three Outward Bound School directors, the directors of numerous other related organizations. Dan Campbell, for example, as Director of the Nature Conservancy in Arizona, received their award for excellence from the first President Bush. Jim Kielsmier, Director of a Denver Urban Outward Bound program went on to head AYLC [American Youth Leadership Program], a service learning program for schools, inspired by the ideas of Kurt Hahn. "Outward Bound needs to reclaim Kurt Hahn," Kielsmier told me at my last meeting with him. But many of these programs withered on the vine through lack of funding, a lack of commitment, and a redefining of the goals of Outward Bound. Outward Bound as program or Outward Bound as idea?

Again it was the wisdom and persistence of Greg Farrell who kept alive the ideal of the Idea. First in his catalytic role in nurturing the founding of the New York City Outward Bound Center, the prototype of other urban centres on Thompson Island, in Boston Harbor, and Baltimore. And second in launching Outward Bound Expeditionary Learning that loops Outward Bound back to its origins in Kurt Hahn's two schools, Gordonstoun School in Scotland, where our distinguished guest, His Royal Highness, the Duke of York, attended as a boy; and Schloss Salem, in the foothills of the Alps in southern Germany.

If Outward Bound is looking for direction, for reinvigoration, it seems to me the direction is clear. Outward Bound as program needs to see itself as more than an adventure school, as important as adventure is. It needs to see itself as more than tough fun for those that can afford it, as more than personal therapy for depressed youth confused by the superabundance of our age. It needs to be more than wilderness therapy for the incorrigible, though it can be all of these.

But from the perspective of a relic from the past, Outward Bound needs to redefine its purpose, to discover the moral equivalent of survival in the lifeboats, out of which OUTWARD BOUND evolved. It needs to redefine its message to project its commitment to leadership and service, an elite if you will committed to more than self fulfillment, committed to facing the challenges of a confusing and often violent age.

In the core of ELOB schools and Outward Bound Urban Centers is a pool of youth talent that ought to be funneled into Outward Bound courses, chosen for their commitment and their talent, and return to their institutions as leaders who inspire by their energy and their commitment, who are both competent and compassionate, who return to lead and to serve. "To serve, to strive and not to yield," to remind us of the Outward Bound motto. The effect would be electrifying, representing an new infusion of talent into the Outward Bound Schools, students and faculty alike. And a strengthening of the Outward Bound back into the participating institutions.

Outward Bound could broaden the pool by recruiting students from two other networks inspired by Kurt Hahn, the United World Colleges in Canada and New Mexico, and the Round Square Conference Schools, modeled on Gordonstoun and Salem.

The effect would be electrifying, representing an new infusion of talent into the Outward Bound Schools, students and faculty alike. And a strengthening of the Outward Bound back into the participating institutions.

Enough, I've only run over my 12 minutes by half an hour. But I have one last Kurt Hahn story, that I'd like to close with. Bruce, you can put the oven timer away. The first time I met Kurt Hahn was a conference on Youth Service at Ditchley, outside Oxford. Prince Philip, the Duke of Edinburgh chaired the conference. In one session, Dr. Flemming DD, the Bishop of Norwich challenged Kurt Hahn, "But Doctor Hahn," he said, "the Good Samaritan never had rescue training!" "Ah yes, ah yes," Hahn replied in his deep gutteral Germanic voice, "ah yes, but if the preacher had rescue training he would not have walked by on the other side!" I trust we do not walk by on the other side.

Joe Nold presented this speech in 2002 at Outward Bound's National Benefit Dinner in New York City, where he was presented the Kurt Hahn Award for outstanding service to Outward Bound's mission.

The paragraph below is reprinted from "Outward Bound's 50th Anniversary in the U.S." website, found at www.OutwardBounds50thAnniversary.Weebly.com.

From 1963 -1972 Joe Nold, a Canadian, was the School Director. Nold started as an instructor at COBS in 1963. He came from an education background; he graduated from the University of British Columbia, and taught at Gordonstoun, one of the schools Hahn founded. Nold strongly felt that Outward Bound was an educational experience, and even from the early days the COBS stated that it was about "character training through adventure." What excited him most was the extent to which Outward Bound spoke to the whole sense of being and meaning and values and purpose of life. It was Joe Nold who forged an important relationship with Bill Coors, president of the board of trustee's for the Adolph Coors Company. Coors strongly believed in the importance of bringing inner city kids to the mountains. He said helping kids like this, who have socially negative attitudes, is what Outward Bound is all about. Through Joe's work to gain key supporters, the school was allowed to continue its growth and innovation. Joe, while in the role of school director, still loved to be in the mountains, and would spend as much time as possible out visiting groups in the field. Joe was also known for reading a quote in the morning that ended with "simplicity, simplicity, simplicity" by Thoreau. Nold was associated with the school from 1962- 1978. The first building as you enter the Marble basecamp is named "Nold House". A peak to the west of Yule Pass is called "Joe Nold" in recognition of the hard work he did as a leader and pioneer with the school.

2015, Margaret, Joe, and Jen in front of Joe Nold House at COBS Marble Base Camp, where Joe and family spent summers during his COBS years.

Part Five – Elder Odyssey, The Saga of Zillah

Chapter 80: Call me Ishmael

Call me Ishmael....Whenever I find myself growing grim around the mouth; whenever it is a damp, drizzly November in my soul; whenever I find myself involuntarily pausing before coffin warehouses, and bringing up the rear of every funeral I meet; ...I account it high time to get to sea.... I quietly take to the ship. There is nothing surprising in this. If they but knew it, almost all men in their degree, some time or another, cherish very nearly the same feelings towards the ocean....

~ Herman Melville, Moby Dick

"Why are you so determined to buy a boat," a friend asked. I had told her about the Atlantic City fiasco. She knew me from my Colorado mountain days and could not make the connection to the sea.

"When I turned sixty," I told her, "I realized I no longer enjoyed carrying a sixty pound pack as much as I used to. If I bought a boat I felt I could extend my life style for another decade." That was my stock response. But it went deeper than that.

As always I was reluctant to talk of my deeper feelings. I recalled Ishmael. And while my thoughts were not suicidal, they were despondent. I was at a low point in my life. Theresa, my young wife, had left me three years before, and I missed her still, dreamt of her regularly, and had not found another abiding companion. As a part of the process of my separation from her, I had also left a comfortable job and a supportive community at the United World College in New Mexico, where I directed the wilderness program. I had returned to my earlier association with Outward Bound, which I had left fifteen years previously, and directed an Outward Bound urban program in San Francisco. When there I had planned to buy a boat and live aboard at Fisherman's Wharf. Living on a boat in downtown San Francisco had great appeal. But the program was closed down, against my urging, and I moved to Cambridge, Massachusetts to work with Expeditionary Learning Outward Bound. It was a temporary assignment, but that didn't work out either, and my contract was not extended. A new breed of younger, brighter people, many of them Harvard educated, were the new generation of creative movers and shakers in Outward Bound. I wasn't sure where to turn. Do I seek another project? Or was this the time to bow out gracefully?

I'd been considering retiring to a boat seriously for at least five years, subscribing to *Cruising World* and reading books on cruising. Tanya Aebi, a seventeen year old girl, had sailed around the world by herself. If a seventeen year old, why not a sixty year old? That obsession had been the main reason Theresa divorced me. "I'm leaving you before you leave me," she told me one day, and she did.

Now I was sixty-four, unattached, with a modest IRA and eligible to draw Social Security. The moment seemed right.

"Decisions and revisions, which a moment will reverse," to quote that gloomy poet, T.S. Eliot. I went back and forth, burdened by the weight of indecision. I felt I was at the end of a long and eventful career, a life that had been useful, but I stood at the edge of a precipice. It was only a short step from indecision to despondency. I began to brood over past failures, I realized that I still had not come to terms with my termination as the president of the Colorado Outward Bound School fifteen years before, and other low points in my subsequent career. It was "a damp, drizzly November in my soul." Like Ishmael I questioned whether it wasn't time to go to sea?

The decisive moment came over lunch with Greg Farrell, a vice-president of Outward Bound USA. He was a friend, one of the wise men in my life. I told him of my dilemma. "I've just come from visiting my mother," Greg told me. "She's in a nursing home and she's not having much fun." That did it. Next day I took out membership in the Charles River Sailing Club, renewed my subscription to *Cruising World* and began to search again for a boat.

Chapter 81: Mayday – A Walk on the Boardwalk

"May Day! May Day! Atlantic City Coast Guard! This is Touch of Gray!" David shouted desperately into the VHF radio. "We're at the harbor entrance. The engine's failed. We're drifting onto the breakwater!"

I scrambled on deck, blinded by the dazzle of shore lights. The boat pitched in the breaking swell. I stumbled as I ran forward to fend off. Cushioned by the backwash, the boat slid by the seawall narrowly missing it by two feet. The yacht drifted into the churning eddy behind the breakwater and slowly turned.

"Drop the anchor!" David commanded from the helm. I fumbled with the slippery rope lashing. The first knot came loose. The second jammed. I cursed myself because I'd secured it so tightly.

"Cut it free," I said to myself, but my knife was buried in an inner pocket beneath layers of foul weather gear. I pried at the knot again until my fingernails pained, and it came free. The CQR plow anchor splashed into the water with a clatter of chain. But it was too late, Touch of Grey was already drifting onto the jetty. I felt the sudden jar of impact, the crunch of fiberglass grinding on rock.

"Get off the boat!" David ordered. In the confusion I hesitated. Surely there was something we could do to save the yacht. But what? I waited for the next surge to lift the boat and stepped across to the large granite block, like boulder hopping over a mountain stream, and I was ashore. It seemed too casual, anti-climactic, a let down.

David ducked below into the cabin and re-emerged with Althea, his tabby gray cat, the ship's mascot. He tossed her to me with a lateral under-hand pass, like a quarterback handing off a football. I caught her. She hissed in protest. Then David stepped over the lifeline and lunged for shore. He slipped on the slimy surface, scraped his knee and scrambled up before the next surge. We stood in stunned silence, two shipwrecked sailors on a rocky shore, survivors with their cat.

Now what? Wasn't that the question I had asked often before? The existential question. I thought of my life as a series of dramatic discontinuities, and there I was at a juncture once again. I had recently retired from Outward Bound and was confronted with the ambiguities of another life transition.

My professional career had been adventurous and fulfilling. That year with Expeditionary Learning Outward Bound, ELOB, a national school reform program based in Cambridge I had rafted down the Colorado River through Cataract Canyon with a team of ELOB planners, rock climbed with a faculty team from the Rocky Mountain ELOB School. My daughter Jennifer and her husband Johann, who work for Outward Bound Belgium, joined me for my last ascent of Snowmass Mountain near Aspen. On the hike in, we identified fifty different species of alpine flowers, including the rare fairy slipper, Jacob's ladder and silky facilia, a symbolic leave-taking to a glamorous career.

My project, however, had not gone well. Three months of work in South Boston High School was aborted, when a fracas between Haitians and Afro-Americans students hit the front page of the tabloid Boston Herald, and flared into race a riot between Black and White students in the Irish community.

I came to realize that Outward Bound was essentially a young person's work, those who were more skilled, with sharper, Harvard-educated minds. At age sixty-four, I decided it would be appropriate to move on. My Outward Bound experience had been largely in the mountains, and now in my sixties, I realized that I no longer enjoyed carrying a sixty-pound pack as much as I had once. If I could learn to sail, I fantasized, I could extend my life style another decade. Like Ishmael in Moby Dick, I knew it was time to go to sea. All I needed was a boat.

Early in my search, I met David Chandler through a yacht broker in Belfast, Maine. David was a tall New Englander with classic Anglo-Scots features, long straight nose, thin lips, a clear skin that any woman would have envied, a full head of wavy hair, flecked with a touch of gray. He had recently taken leave from his job as a sales clerk in a ship's chandlery. His life too was in transition. A failed relationship, the shock of a friend's suicide led to him asking, "What next?" David's answer was a thirty-two-foot, five-ton sloop, which he renamed *Touch of Gray.* He planned to winter in the Bahamas and was looking for crew to sail south. I signed on.

Neither of us had much sailing experience, we discovered. David had operated powerboats in lakes and coastal waters and knew engines. I had no mechanical skill. But I had crewed on a 95-foot cargo-carrying ketch in the Caribbean, years before on a year I took out of college. But I had learned little beyond boxing the compass, sweating heavy gaff-rigged sails and weighing a 500-pound anchor with a manual windlass designed for galley slaves. It did leave me with the conviction that I would return to sea on e day. I had chartered sailboats twice in the protected waters of the British Virgin Islands. But mostly I had sailed small boats, dinghies, Sunfishes and Lasers.

Departing Maine, we safely navigated our way to Cape Cod, down Long Island Sound past New York City, to Sandy Hook, which sticks out like a bent finger on the northernmost New Jersey coast. After two weeks we began to consider ourselves seasoned sailors.

On the fateful day our plan was to sail south, the length of the New Jersey coast, 150 miles to Cape May. The NOAA weather report forecast NE winds 15 to 20 knots, with 3-to 6-foot waves, winds increasing to 20 to 25 knots at night. A small craft warning was in effect. The offshore report mentioned the possibility of a gale later on, a warning we failed to register.

We weighed anchor at first light, 0615 hours. Overhead the sky was clear, and the moon set in an eerie iridescent orange through the lingering mist, like a painting by Turner. There was no wind. "We can make it under power even if we can't sail," David remarked. He was impatient to get to Florida, his departure from Maine having been delayed by his friend's funeral.

By 1000 hours the wind filled in and we raised sails. By noon it picked up to 15 knots. "Oh frabjous day!" I chortled like the Jabberwocky. With the wind out of the north east, we cruised with the sail full out, on a broad reach. The sky was clear, white caps on the waves, a gentle swell, the rigging strained and we made an exhilarating seven knots, hull speed.

The bank of cumulus clouds gathering on the southern horizon seemed benign.

The NOAA weather update at 3:00 p.m. was more ominous. It predicted a storm front approaching the East Coast with gale force winds. I was taken by surprise. Should I be concerned?

"You ever been out in a gale?" I asked David.

"Not in a boat," he replied.

Nor had I. I didn't know what to expect, but it didn't sound good. Should we head for the nearest harbor of refuge? The entire eastern shore of New Jersey is a sandy barrier reef with occasional breaks in the dunes, few safe anchorages. We had already passed Manasquam, the first inlet. Further down the coast there was an entrance at Barnagat Cut but on the chart it looked shallow and would be tricky in a storm swell. Little Egg Inlet, further south still, might do. Atlantic City was only twenty-five miles further, and David Trump had deepened the channel to twenty feet so he could visit the Trump Taj Mahal Casino in his mega-yacht. Cape May was forty miles further.

By 4:00 p.m. the sky had clouded over to a dishwater gray, the wind blew NE 20. With the mainsail swung far out, *Touch of Grey* had a strong weather helm and we could not hold our course. She kept heading up into the wind.

"Take the helm. I'm going forward to reef the main," David said. The reduced sail helped, but in gusts we were still forced to spill wind, with the frantic flapping of canvas, like a flock of startled geese taking to flight.

By 5:00 p.m. dusk had already closed in, the sky a dark battered blue like a deep bruise. Faint lights flickered along the distant shore. These too vanished in a rain-squall. The wind increased to a steady twenty-five knots, gusting to thirty.

"I can't hold the course," David called from the helm.

"Don't worry about your course, David. Sail the wind," I shouted over the rattle of the rigging. "Tack downwind." It was just like dingy sailing, spilling wind to avoid capsizing. But I'd never tried it before with five tons under the sail.

I had second thoughts. I'd read recently about storm tactics in Heavy Weather Sailing and wondered, why not try heaving-to, or lying a-hull, or running downwind under bare poles? It seemed time to do something dramatic. Wouldn't it be safer than approaching an unknown shore in storm conditions? "What d'you think, David?"

Out of the driving rain, a huge ocean-going tug appeared to port with a long barge in tow, passing us well to seaward. We had tacked five miles offshore and were approaching the coast-wise shipping lanes. David's reply was immediate and unequivocal. "I'm not staying out overnight in this. How far is it to Atlantic City?"

I programmed the GPS, the Global Positioning Satellite system. "Eighteen miles to the harbor entrance buoy. We could make it on the next tack," I said.

The gale hit with full force, gusting to thirty-five knots blowing us off course. The seas had now increased to eight feet, lifted the stern and knocked the boat about. I saw another set of running lights less than 400 yards away. A cargo ship, top-heavy with stacked containers, churned by in the dark with a deep growl of engines.

"I don't think he'd see us on a night like this," David cautioned. "Let's go about."

It was too dangerous to jibe. If we lost control of the boom swinging wildly across the stern, it could dismast the boat. So we turned on the engine and powered into the wind, rotating 270 degrees to picked up our next course. Visibility was zero, the dark an opaque rain-driven wall. David steered by compass, the feel of the wind. As we approached shore and the water shoaled, he kept looking at the depth sounder. In fourteen feet of water we went about again. We were four miles north of Atlantic City, the storm unabating.

As we drew closer the city lights became a blurred kaleidoscope of color, the flashing beacon of the Absecon Channel Lighthouse, rotating beams on casino roofs searching the sky, traffic lights changing, red, yellow, green, the red flare of car tail lights, cubist shapes in neon. I had difficulty picking up the flashing green entrance buoy, against the glare. Then I saw the line of channel markers, red, right, returning.

"Should we come in under power, or under sail?" David asked.

I didn't know. We were repeatedly overpowered under sail so I was not confident that would be safe. "Under power. I guess," I replied with a naive faith in technology. David concurred. There was no debate. Both of us forgot the night the engine failed coming into Provincetown, Cape Cod and we made it in with jib alone.

The seas were now on the beam on the run in, and the boat rolled to the rail in the high waves. We staggered to keep balance. The backwash from shore threw up a chop that clashed with the oncoming surge. Waves crashed over the hull, flinging salt spray in our faces. Head up, facing into it I kept wiping my eyes trying to spot the channel markers ahead, spitting out salty brine. Water ran down my neck. With head down, David hunched over the compass until the next set of markers appeared out of the maelstrom. The waves began to crest.

The steady throb of the engine was imperceptible with the din. Then suddenly it raced with an explosive burst of noise, like a Porsch accelerating from a traffic light, and the boat vibrated. Had the transmission gone out? I had a moment of panic. But it was a large wave that had swept under the stern, briefly lifting the propeller out of the water. David reduced power.

The last mile. We were as good as there. We came in along the breakwater that ran parallel to shore only fifty feet to port. It was barely a boat length off. Very close David, I thought.

Looking up, the street lights on the Boardwalk glared above me. Ahead cars crossed on the bridge over the inner harbor. Another 400 yards and we would turn into the marine basin, our harbor of refuge.

Then the engine stopped.

The New Jersey State Marine Police picked up David's May Day call at 8:08 p.m., Saturday, October 30, 1993. They rushed to our rescue from shore, sirens blaring. The Coast Guard cutter arrived fifteen minutes later, but it had a deep draft and could not approach in the shallow water. Uniformed men clambered onto the boat from the jetty. There was great commotion, but little coordination. David and I were shunted aside and stood by passively. I attempted to go back on board to retrieve my wallet and passport, but was ordered off by a State Trooper.

Another Coast Guard vessel arrived, a 25-foot inflatable Zodiak powered by twin 250-horsepower outboard motors. *Touch of Gray* began to take on water, but they attached a line to the bow began to pull her off the jetty. "There's an anchor attached to the other line," I shouted to the young Coastie. They all looked like college freshmen with short cut hair. "You'll need to cut it."

"Yah! Yah!. I'll get it," he shouted back. But in his excitement, he didn't.

The towline went taut and Touch of Gray moved sluggishly toward the basin, still afloat. Then everything came to a stop. She had snagged on the anchor I had dropped earlier. The Coast Guard Zodiac gave a burst of power. Simultaneously the boat was hit by the incoming swell. The bow shot up like a rearing horse bucking the crew on to the deck. In panic they cut the towline and *Touch of Gray* drifted slowly back to shore. She came in under the Boardwalk. The mast snagged on the railing above, began to bend and then snapped with the resounding crack of branches breaking in an ice storm. "Ooohh," a woeful moan went up from the crowd that had gathered. The rigging grated like finger nails scratching on a blackboard.

Meanwhile, the loose towing rope tangled in the propeller of the Coast Guard Zodiac, and SeaTow came to the rescue of the rescuer.

The State Marine Police drove us to headquarters and had us fill out a report. We wondered if we were going to be booked for some marine traffic violation. While I waited for David to fill out an accident report, I had the whimsical thought of playing Monopoly as a child. It was a game based on real estate speculation, right there in Atlantic City. I'd been there before in my imagination. "Go to jail. Go directly to jail. Do not pass GO. Do not collect $200."

But the police were interested only in recording the essential facts. "Gale force winds. Engine failure. Boat wreck on breakwater. No casualties."

"Take a walk on the Boardwalk," was the most dreaded card in the game if it was lined with hotels you didn't own. We crossed the Boardwalk and booked in at The Flagship. "From shipwreck to flagship," I told David as he signed the register, a brave attempt at humor.

The tide was low after midnight and we returned to *Touch of Gray* to see what could be salvaged. She sat wedged among the rocks, half out of the water. "Oh my god," David gasped when we went below. Cushions were afloat, a soggy loaf of bread dripped on the navigation desk, a thin scum of diesel fuel coated the galley. Only in the shattered domesticity of the cabin did he break through his stoic reserve. David found his wallet and bankbook undamaged. My gear was forward, but the cabin door was jammed. Rather than breaking through, I figured I could get it in the morning when a salvage boat would lift the boat off. We retrieved the VHF radio, the inflatable dinghy and the outboard motor. I snagged two bottles of beer and a block of cheese, small consolation for they stank of diesel.

Too tired to sleep that night, I lie awake depressed. I was disappointed at my passivity once I was off the boat. I'd been involved in mountain search and rescue and river rescue for years, and here I had permitted myself to be shunted aside. I was haunted by the possibility of saving *Touch of Gray* had I cut the anchor line. I felt the guilt of a survivor.

David was more resilient. "The boat's insured. No one was hurt. That's the main thing." I knew he was right, and admired his courage in the face of such adversity. Nevertheless it still gnawed at me. Was it courage? Or merely lack of imagination? I brooded.

"Look David! There's no boat!" Next morning we peered below the Boardwalk. A thousand fragments of fiberglass and shattered wood floated in a flotsam sludge where the boat had been. *Touch of Gray* had disappeared.

Clambering down among the rocks along the tideline we found the transom and part of the cockpit washed up. A scavenger, who introduced himself as "Charles" climbed on and ripped out the binnacle for its salvage value. He too had lost his boat, he claimed. An empty fuel can, my down sleeping bag had washed ashore, as well as David's Sebago loafers, one of my Nike sneakers and an unopened bottle of David's very special conditioner shampoo, a treasured commodity. The sea claimed the rest.

We hauled debris above the tide line in a mock environmental clean up, like good Rotarians picking up litter along the highway. The intent was to prevent further pollution in harbor waters, knowing that the main pollutant was the diesel engine lying in the mud on the harbor floor.

There was little of value, but the process was cathartic. There was a note of finality about it, last rites like a funeral. I found myself humming the navy hymn we sang as boys in chapel at St. Andrew's College.

Hear us Lord when we pray to thee/ For those in peril on the sea.

It was my last tribute to Touch of Gray.

Shipwrecked on the Boardwalk. Was it a cautionary tale or a challenge? Was I being warned too of the perils of the sea? Or was it luring me on? I had expected that retirement might be a crisis, but not a catastrophe. But wasn't the archetype of all adventures, *The Odyssey*, a succession of shipwrecks and near escapes, a tale of loss and Man prevailing over hardship and suffering?

What better way to launch an aging man on his "Elder Odyssey?"

Chapter 82: On Buying a Boat

Decisions and revisions, which a moment will reverse.

~ *T.S. Eliot*

"What sort of boat are you're looking for?" the yacht broker asked. I felt I detected a faint note of condescension, but perhaps that was only my uncertainty.

"Nirvana!" I could have answered. Or, "The Holy Grail." For my boat quest was still largely a fantasy. The only thing I knew for sure was that I was looking for a sailboat. Psychologically I was "at sea." At least I could use a nautical metaphor. I was totally bewildered by the choice.

Where to begin? With the size, I suppose. "I'm looking for something large enough to go offshore, but small enough to single hand. Something between thirty and thirty-five feet."

"Rig?" What did I know? I knew the difference between a sloop and a schooner, a ketch and a yawl, but I had no experience with any of them to know defining characteristics. Most small boats I saw were single masted sloops or cutters.

"Keel or center-board?" Centerboard? I thought. My Sunfish and the Lasers I sailed had center-boards, dagger-boards really. I didn't know large boats also had center-boards, but I wouldn't tell him that.

The broker was a tall, well built man, long nose and jutting jaw, wind blown leathery skin, his Shetland wool jersey had the faint odor of lanoline and sweat. He had that know-it-all look of the sportsman who became a businessman, the sort of man who had succeeded in making a business of his sport. Enviable. But he wasn't really interested in helping me find what I needed, when I didn't really know myself. He was interested in selling, selling what he had, convincing me that that was what I needed, what I should buy. I'd run into car salesmen like that. If he knew how little I knew, he'd lose interest, I thought, wouldn't see me as a serious buyer.

"Keel." I said.

"Full keel, or keel with a cutaway forefoot? Or a fin keel?"

Gawd, I didn't know yachts had forefeet. "Full keel," I answered in desperation.

What about construction? I was attracted to the sleek classical lines of wooden boats. But he wasn't interested in that. "Most yachts were now being built in fiberglass. They require less maintenance." Herreshoff, the famous boat designer, called fiberglass boats a molten piece of plastic snot. But I didn't tell him that. And what about steel hulls? They were popular in Europe and I had read you could bounce them off a coral reef? Ferro-concrete boats? That seemed an oxymoron, a contradiction in terms. A boat of concrete, how would it ever float?

This was only the beginning. Then there was the questions of cost. What could I afford? What did a boat cost to maintain, something I had not accounted for. I began to realize that buying a boat was a risky adventure, even before the keel splashed in the water.

I contacted marinas on the East Coast from the Connecticut River to Cape Cod and down east in Maine. Cannell, Payne & Page in Cambden, Maine put me on to a *Southern Cross 31* at anchor in Tenant Harbor. The owner, Mr. Cole, was a slender New Englander, a fit seventy-five year old, spoken, thoughtful man, he reminded me of a university professor, or a retired doctor. He rowed me out to the boat with a strong pull to the oars. I college varsity rower I wondered? Or generations of sea captains in his ancestry? The boat was sloop with white topsides and a pointed canoe stern, a design made popular by the Scotsman, Colin Archer, modeled on the Norwegian sail powered sea rescue boats, reputed to be safer in following seas. Thirty-one feet long, nine feet six inches beam, four feet seven inches draft, a displacement of 13,600 pounds, 4,400 pounds in the lead keel, powered by a twenty two horsepower diesel engine. "Only 500 hours on the engine," Mr. Cole affirmed. There was a working sail area of 450 square feet, with the mainsail, jib and mast head cutter rig, which gave it a cruising speed of seven knots. The construction was double thickness fiberglass, with Airex foam core, which dampened noise and insulated cold, according to the buyer's report I read in *Practical Sailor,* but they questioned its impact resistance, a factor I would reflect upon several months later.

It was comfortably laid up below, a forward V-berth, settees in the main cabin, comfortable for three, a sea-water flushing head, gimbaled stove and a salon table that folded up to the bulkhead. It seemed a perfect match for my needs, at $40,000 a good buy.

Mr. Cole, forever the gentleman invited me for coffee at home, a deceptively simple house with gray weathered shingles and platinum blue shutters outside, but inside pine polished floors, locally crafted rugs, bright shawls over the sofa, and the walls decorated with framed pencil sketches that caught my eye. "If the boat hasn't sold by spring," Mr. Cole told me, "I plan to take it back from the broker and sell it myself for $38,000. That's what I'd get without the broker's fee." I decided to wait.

Getting up to leave, I went up to one of the sketches on the wall to take a closer look. It showed a bright stream of light coming through an open window into a stark empty room. No people. "Isn't this an Andrew Wyeth?" I asked.

"Yes," he smiled. "My wife's a Wyeth." And he showed me the collection and his wife's paintings too. My boat search was becoming a richer quest. Perhaps there was a holy grail to be found.

It was soon after I met David Chandler on *Touch of Gray* that culminated in the Atlantic City adventure and misadventure.

Most the boats on the market were fiberglass, but wooden boats with their elegant beauty continued to have a fatal attraction. On Chesapeake Bay, I looked an old friend, Ray Hartjen, who kept his boat at Soloman's Island. Ray restored old boats and had rebuilt *Sisquit*, a forty foot classic Swedish wooden sloop, Iverson design, ten foot beam and six foot draft, eight tons, powered by a 25 horsepower diesel Volvo engine. Stepping on board, I was struck immediately by the warm glow of the varnished mahogany cockpit, and the snug comfort of the cabin below. Under sail *Sisquit* seemed to lift and cut through the waves with a soothing *whoosh* rather than pound and resonate with a hollow thud, as fiberglass boats often did.

What impressed me even more than the aesthetic functionality of wood, was Ray's range of skills, not just master mariner, but boat carpenter, mechanic, electrician and plumber. I marveled as he maneuvered *Sisquit* into the slip backwards, picking up the spring lines single-handed.

"How did you learn?" I asked that evening over steaks and a bottle of Pinot Noir. He was also a master chef. I chose the wine.

Ray was a well-built man with the ruddy wind-blown face of a Scandinavian, sandy hair, an easy smile and the hardened hands and firm clasp of a man gripping tools. . "My family spent their summers at East Hampton on Long Island Sound," he said. "I was given an eight foot pram when I was six, and my father put a sail on it. I've had boats all my life. I took shop in elementary school and won a prize." At Brooklyn Technical High School he learned mechanics and electronics. In the Army he was picked out of a military police battalion and assigned to General Clark's private fishing yacht in Tokyo Bay. Now, a multi-talented PhD in Learning Psychology, who had invented a teaching machine before the days of the personal computer, he promoted educational reform in public schools for the U.S. Department of Education. Restoring old boats was his hobby.

I contrasted my own background and reflected on my own lack of skill. I grew up in dust bowl of Saskatchewan during the Depression, 2000 miles from the ocean. My early experience of the sea was vicarious, a boy's romantic fantasies spawned by the poetry of Mansfield, *Captains Courageous* and Tennyson's *Ulysses*. Never question the power of childhood fantasy, but I did question the wisdom of a sextagenarian's.

Inspired by the day on *Sisquit* I broadened my search and began to look at wooden boats as well. Those I found, however, were poorly kept with peeling paint, rusty fittings, warped decks, and a musty acrid smell below. Some were clearly derelict. So when I was directed to the Cracker Boy Boatyard, tucked away in a down-in-the-heel neighborhood, just north of exclusive Palm Beach, Florida, I wasn't expecting much.

But *Zillah* was something unique. Blocked up on her seven-foot keel, forty three feet on deck, a narrow nine and a half beam, the slender lines of her bow soared above the cut-away forefoot. She spoke of elegance and speed. Many boats reminded me of sitting ducks, *Zillah* was like a gracious swan.

Peter Baker, the owner, a young looking forty year old Englishman, showed me about. He was a marine engineer who had made a career of restoring classical boats, square riggers and large schooners used in films and television movies, like *Scott to the*

Antarctic. He had similar plans for *Zillah* but had an attractive offer as chief engineer on a research vessel. I assumed he meant marine environmental research, but learned that the stakes were much higher then than. They were looking for ship wrecks with buried treasure.

"*Zillah* was famous in her day," Peter told me, "a Fred Parker design, built by Newman and Sons at Poole, on the south coast of England in 1955. She performed well in several Fastnet Races in the fifties. Made several Atlantic crossings. A stout ocean cruiser, will take you wherever you choose to go."

We borrowed a ladder from the yard and clambered aboard. "The decks will need caulking," Peter pointed out. "But that's a straight forward job. You can easily do that yourself." Forty years before as a seaman on a cargo carrying ketch, the *Culver,* I'd been assigned several days pounding oakum into the deck seams, and sealing them with tar, so the task did not seem too intimidating. "You'll need a new jib. The mainsail is new-used, in good shape. Good solid 5/16th inch rigging. Heavy duty Lewmar 35 winches," he pointed out *Zillah's* stalwart features as we walked the wide decks.

We stepped through the hinged companionway doors of beautifully crafted mahogany and went below. There was standing room for a short man like myself, more mahogany overhead, teak planking along the inside of the hull, drawers and cupboards of light oak around the galley stove and sink, a navigation table and instrument panel opposite. Two settees in the mid-ship cabin, a V-berth forward of the mast where the bow narrows, would sleep four people. There was a head, the nautical term for a toilet but no shower, and hanging closets. I marveled at the ingenuity of the design, the compactness of the space. The cabin glowed with the warm intimacy of an English pub.

Peter lifted the hatch on the step beneath the companionway and showed me the engine, a thirty five horse power Perkins 4-107. It was rusty and greasy but looked functional. Knowing very little about engines, I gave it a casual glance "Does it run?" I asked.

"Sometimes," Peter smiled, "but we'll get it going," he assured me." She's a lot of boat for $20,000. With a little fixing up boats like this sell for $60,000 in England." I too had read the ads in *Yachting World* and that seemed about right. Little did I appreciate that was only the down payment.

I tried not to appear too enthusiastic and arranged to have the boat surveyed before making a final commitment. The surveyor, Al Rhode, was a heavy set, older man, my age, who had difficulty mounting the ladder. His inspection was cursory, but he did comment on how well preserved the boat was… "for its age," he qualified. He suggested a few minor repairs, then certified the boat seaworthy for insurance purposes. So I signed the sales agreement to purchase "as is" in her present condition, assuming responsibility for any defects. Like the marriage contract, for richer or poorer, in sickness or health, I had made a choice.

Proud and overwhelmed both, I was now the owner of a boat, the captain of a ship, the master of my destiny. Or was I? I wondered that night as I moved aboard, and crawled into my sleeping bag, moving inboard a little to avoid the persistent drip from the leaking deck.

Chapter 83: Owning a Boat

> There is nothing—absolutely nothing—half so much worth doing as simply messing about in boats...or with boats....in or out of 'em, it doesn't matter.
> ~ Kenneth Graham, *The Wind and the Willows.*

"Is there life after Outward Bound?" was a question I knew I would have to face, eventually. I'd spent much of my adult life leading expeditions and organizing outdoor programs, mostly in mountains. But upon turning sixty, I realized that carrying a sixty-pound backpack wasn't as much fun as it used to be. Buying and learning to sail a boat when I retired, could extend my active life for another ten years, I reasoned. This was my defining moment.

I had learned about boats, as best I could, by reading. *Cruising Under Sail*, by Eric Hiscock, outlined the basic requirements of a basic cruising yacht. *Practical Sailor* was a consumers' guide on new and used boats and boating equipment. Their reports analyzed sea worthiness, boat performance, durability, structural strengths and weaknesses, owner satisfaction and range of cost.. *Cruising World* articles and stories triggered the overdeveloped romantic aspects of my personality. And I read widely in the literature of sailing adventure, written by adventurers who displayed unique talent for getting themselves out of trouble they should not have been in the first place.

Gradually my fantasy began to take on definition. My boat should be big enough to go offshore safely, yet small enough to be sailed single-handed, something between thirty and thirty-five feet. A sloop rig, with just a single mast and two sails would make for easy handling, and a small auxiliary engine for additional power. A full keel would give greater stability and more protection in the event of grounding. It should have sleeping space for four, and basic live-aboard facilities, galley with stove and sink, indoor toilet, salon table, storage space. The vision became clearer as I read.

Living in San Francisco, I began to visit boat yards and marinas. Later, when I moved to Boston, I resumed my query on the East Coast. From Boston, I probed in remote harbors and bays "down-east" in Maine, later south to Cape Cod, on to Beaufort, North Carolina and eventually to Florida. Over a period of two years, I looked at more than fifty boats. My search for a boat had become like a quest for the Holy Grail.

The variety of boats was overwhelming, the choice confusing. A key issue was construction. Should it be a fiberglass boat or one built of wood? Most boats on the market were fiberglass, and I became convinced that this was the way to go, because of low maintenance, durability, and ease of upkeep.

But two of my friends owned wooden boats. Peter Willauer on *Eight Bells* was founding director of the Hurricane Island Outward Bound School in Maine. Ray Hartjen, an education consultant who sailed on Chesapeake Bay, made a hobby of rebuilding old wooden boats and had restored *Siskiwit* to a beautiful antique. There was something about a wooden boat, I felt, that couldn't be captured in fiberglass: the trim lines, the texture of teak and the warm glow of mahogany, the solid feel as it cuts through the waves. Sitting at the helm of their boats the feeling of tradition and the aesthetic appeal was overwhelming and overpowered my best reasoned judgment.

So I had looked at several wooden boats. But most were badly neglected, run down, and needing extensive repair. A couple were downright derelict, with peeling paint, splitting boards, the acrid smell of rotting wood and bilge water. I marveled that some were still afloat. So when I located the Cracker Boy Boatyard, tucked away on a back street in Riviera Beach, a down-in-the-heel neighborhood just north of exclusive Palm Beach, looking for yet another wooden boat, I wasn't expecting much.

But *Zillah* was in a different class altogether, something unique. She stood tall, regal, blocked up on her seven-foot keel, its cut-away forefoot swooping to the bow twelve feet above us. So many boats I had seen squatted like sitting ducks. With her prominent bow, a narrow beam and tapering stern, *Zillah* was as graceful as a swan. Her lines were sleek and trim, designed for speed, and an eye for elegance. I felt she was one of the most beautiful boats I had ever seen. And she was.

It was love at first sight. One of the great loves of my lifetime. "What other reason is there for buying a boat?" a friend asked.

"Would you like to have a look on board?" Peter Baker, the owner, a young looking forty-year old, an English merchant seaman marine engineer, asked. He had made a career of restoring square riggers and large schooners for motion picture and television. His ships had appeared in films like *Captains Courageous* and *Scott to the Antarctic*. He had similar plans for *Zillah*. But when the Smithsonian made him an offer as chief engineer on their marine research vessel, he accepted.

"*Zillah* was famous in her day," Peter told me, "a Fred Parker design, built by 1955 by Newman and Sons at Poole on the south coast of England." She had raced in the Fastnet and did well. The previous owner had crossed the Atlantic in her several times, the last time solo. "She's a stout ocean cruiser," he assured me. "She'll take you wherever you choose to go."

We borrowed a ladder from the yard and clambered aboard. "The decks will need caulking," Peter pointed out. "But that's a straightforward job." Forty years earlier I'd crewed for six months on a cargo-carrying wooden ketch in the Caribbean, the *Culver*. I'd learned to pound oakum into the deck seams and seal them with tar. So the task did not seem too intimidating, forgetting that hammering several hours a day, on my knees, came easier to a younger, more supple body.

"You'll need a new jib. The mainsail is in good shape. There's good solid 5/16th inch rigging. Those are heavy duty Lewmar 35 winches." He pointed out these features as we walked the wide decks.

We passed through the beautifully crafted mahogany companionway doors and went below. I hit my head on the hatch as we descended, the first time of many. But in the salon there was plenty of head room for those under six-feet tall. I marveled at the ingenuity of design, the functional compactness of space. Galley with gimbaled stove, sink and cupboards to starboard, a navigation table to port. There were settees on each side of the mid-ship salon, with large storage drawers beneath, and book-shelves above. Forward of the mast were a toilet and closets, a V-berth double bunk. Made of oak and teak, the cabin glowed with the warm intimacy of an English pub.

Beneath the companionway Peter showed me the engine, a thirty-five horsepower Perkins 4-107, rusty and greasy but appearing functional. Knowing little about engines, I gave it only a casual glance. An expensive oversight.

"She's a lot of boat for $20,000. With a little fixing up, boats like this sell for $60,000 in England." I too had read the ads in *Yachting World* and that seemed about right. Little did I appreciate that the purchase price of an old boat was merely a down payment.

I felt I should disguise my enthusiasm as best I could until I had the boat surveyed, before making a final commitment. The surveyor, Al Rhode, was an older heavy-set man who had difficulty mounting the ladder. His inspection was cursory. He suggested a few minor repairs and commented on how well preserved the boat was… "for its age." But he certified the boat seaworthy, at least for purposes of insurance. So I signed the sales agreement to purchase "as is," assuming responsibility for all defects. Like a marriage contract, for richer or poorer, in sickness or health, I had made a choice.

Proud and overwhelmed both, I was now the owner of my boat, the captain of my ship, and hopefully the master of my fate.

Or was I? I wondered that night as I moved aboard and crawled into my sleeping bag, shifting inboard to avoid the persistent drip from the leaking deck.

Chapter 84: Restoring Zillah

Owning a boat is also a marriage. "To love, to cherish, in sickness and in health , for richer or poorer. The love never faded, though it soon became apparent that *Zillah* had numerous ailments, and certainly I became poorer rather than richer.

It was also like coming into an inheritance of an encumbered estate. There was the sense of good fortune but also the burden of debt. It didn't take long for me to realized that the purchase price of *Zillah* was merely a down payment. Old wooden boats sell cheap. The real expense comes with the restoration, the need to upgrade equipment, to say nothing of the ongoing maintenance, boat yard and marina fees. Then there were also normal living expenses.

It rained the first three days after I moved aboard, and the leaking decks were a dripping Chinese water torture. But with a professional outdoorsman's ingenuity I rigged a plastic tarp over the berth, and spread out my air mattress and sleeping bag, waiting for the next sunny day to dehydrate. After a couple days of sorting, rooting about, and housekeeping, I luxuriated in the space and facilities, a gimbaled propane stove, oak paneled galley, twin settees, overhead lights, a bookcase over my bunk, where I unpacked Eric Hiscock, Nigel Calder's *Boat Mechanical and Electric Systems* and *Moby Dick*. . I cooked my own meals and ate off the navigation table. "More comfortable than any mountain tent I've ever had," I told Margaret, my daughter in Ottawa, arranging for her to visit.

I woke early my mind awhirl, the first of many sleepless nights. Getting up I began to make a list. (See my journal for Tue Jan11) The next six weeks was an exhausting, often frustrating, yet also exhilarating series of never ending crises. I made lists and lists, and as fast as I checked items off one, I added them to the next.

Caulking the teak deck was the first priority. The old caulk had hardened and cracked and had to be reamed of the seams, than a line of twisted cotton pounded back in and sealed off with a new sealant. It was a primitive skill I had learned forty years before as a seaman on the *Culver,* a ninety-feet cargo carrying ketch, and I proud that this at least was one task where I felt confident. But after a week, prostrate in the form of Moslem prayer, I was dismayed at the slow pace of my progress.

There was no end of free advice and encouragement. I was adopted by the boatyard family of well meaning eccentrics, a fraternity I was to discover that was characteristic of boatyards and marinas. It was one of the great privileges of boat ownership.

For a small country there were a surprising number of Canadians. David Eaton was from Halifax, a retired newspaper man, who was refitting a thirty-five-foot sloop. He was planning to live in the Bahamas with his Japanese mistress. He invited on board for drinks. He talked of his heart condition. "How long do you figure you can live on your boat?" I asked.

"I plan to be carried off the boat in a coffin," he replied and poured another drink.

Another Canadian, Denis, a boat-wright, had contracted to refit a luxury 60-foot cabin cruiser for a wealthy Italian whose plan was to cruise Cuba with a crew of pretty young Cubanas, a private floating brothel.

A tall, thin, overbearing English woman, with a very polished aristocratic accent was supervising the restoration of her luxury classical schooner, which she chartered in the Caribbean to wealthy guests. She'd come in to have the ship repainted and discovered the wooden keel and the rudder stem were honeycombed with teredos. The copper sheathing on the bottom had sprung a leak and they had wormed their way in, reducing the wood to a honeycomb of pulp that had to be cut out and replaced.

Next door at the Riviera Beach Marina, a remarkable, beautiful South African woman lived aboard with her three sons. They had fled their country with their one portable asset, their yacht. They had crossed the South Atlantic without mishap. But the oldest boy, twenty, had just been rescued from a ship lost at sea. He'd been on the delivery crew of an old fashioned 70-foot ketch with high freeboards. Broached by a sudden squall, water was trapped by the freeboards, the wooden railing that runs along the side of some boats. Not able to right itself, it foundered and sank. The crew spent four days in a life-boat before being picked up by a passing Dutch freighter.

A cantankerous Frenchman on the boat next to *Zillah*, who did a lot of shouting at his wife, had been in Cuba when the 100-year-storm of 1993 hit. The boat docked next to him came free of its mooring lines, crashed into him and holed his hull. He came to Florida for major repairs. He saw me attempting to patch a tear in the canvas that sheathed *Zillah's* hull. "Fou!" he snarled. Fool! My French wasn't good enough to understand whether he was referring to me or the boat, or whether he was just offering more unsolicited advice.

It was John Anderson who saved my day. A tall, lean young man with short cropped hair and a radiant pink skin, he had a ready smile and spoke with a broad Midland Liverpool accent. "The home of the Beattles," I said. He was wearing worn blue jeans, leather Topsider slip-on shoes, a tee-shirt that could have used laundering, and had a two-day growth of beard like one of those casual male models featured in fashion magazines.

He was a skilled boat-wright, living next door in the marina, on *Border Law*, a 35-foot Camper-Nicholson yacht that he had bought in Cambden, Maine and rebuilt over the last year and a half. He had come south to escape the winter, with Patty, his wife, an accomplished artist, and Kendall, their demanding three-year old daughter. John was looking for work and offered his service at non-union rates.

In a matter of weeks, rather than months, we caulked the decks, replaced all the water and plumbing hoses, painted the topsides of the hull a glistening polyurethane white, and anti-fouled the bottom. We considered varnishing the cabin top, but this was such a tedious process requiring eight coats with sanding between, that I decided there were higher priorities. Besides, I found the silver gray of faded teak not unattractive.

We gradually worked our way through the boat. I had an electrician rewire the boat and install a shore-power 110-220 volt converter and automatic battery charger. He replaced several cabin lights, rewired the masthead anchor light and put up a white steaming light, half way up the mast. At union rates it was an expensive upgrade.

The mainsail, new used, was in good shape, but the boat had no jib. Mack Sails provided sails for Outward Bound, and he gave me a good price on a 150% genoa.

At the Miami Boat Show dealers had their products for sale at discount prices. I never go shopping. I go buying. But I was carried away. In two days I bought a Profurl roller-furler for the genoa, a small hand operated windlass, a 9-foot Avon inflatable dinghy, a 4-hp outboard motor, night vision binoculars, snorkel gear and swim flippers, and assorted miscellany. Normally parsimonious, a stingy buyer, I became a one day shopoholic, a common addiction in the yachting sub-culture.

Then one day Judy appeared. She drove up in a black Mercedes-Benz. She was an attractive young woman in her thirties, well rounded, a broad smile on an oval face with high Slavic cheekbones, full breasts, slender legs. She climbed the ladder as if she possessed the boat. "I used to be an owner," she said, "with my husband." She was born in Czechoslovakia, raised in New York after her family escaped, she had been married to a Spaniard, an economist-cum- playboy who brought the boat to Florida. He had made several trans-Atlantic crossings, some of them solo. He had hoped to sell the boat, but when he couldn't had financial difficulties that resulted in him losing much of the equipment, such as extra sails, lines and anchors, and having to sell at a give-away price. But Judy had salvaged the oak table that bolted to the salon floor, a beautiful piece of craftsmanship, and she delivered it proudly. I was very appreciative, moved by her continuing affection for *Zillah*. The table was an elegant piece of craftsmanship, and Judy and I became good friends.

John started the engine. In spite of the asthmatic cough and belching smoke, it ran. We were ready to launch.

Hoisted on to the travel lift, *Zillah* soared majestically, swaying in the slings. It was a magic moment of elegance. I looked up at her with pride, pristine, shining like new, something to be remembered. As she was lowered into the slip-way, I held my breath with a child's dread of dropping a precious crystal goblet. John and I stepped aboard and we backed out into the river. The tide caught the stern and we were swept out into the current. *Zillah* had returned to her element, her home. The return of a princess.

Zillah afloat again. *Zillah* restored, reborn. It was a spiritual experience, almost like childbirth. But there was also something whimsical about it, elegant, quaint, something frivolously delightful. It was like Victorians in England during the 1880's building mock castles as country homes, that were called "follies." *Zillah* was my folly, an antique, a gracious replica of romantic past age. I could not have been more delighted. It was one of the great moments of my sailing saga.

Kate, a good friend from Block Island, had come down for the launching and brought a bottle of champagne. Wisely she suggested we drink it rather than smashing it on the bow.

I was ready to sail away. "To sail beyond the sunset, And touch with happy isles," with Tennyson's *Ulysses*. But it was only the beginning of another set of tribulations, the sea trials.

Chapter 85: Sea Trials

trial: *act of trying or testing, or putting to the proof*
an attempt or effort to do something, to try an experiment
subjection to suffering or grievous experience, affliction
an affliction or trouble
a trying, distressing, or annoying thing or person

~ *The American Collegiate Dictionary*

The idea of a sea trial, I had always thought, was a shake-down cruise to put the boat to the test, to work out the kinks, discover the boat's idiosyncrasies, expose its weaknesses. After two months in the boatyard, exposing many weaknesses, I was looking forward to the experience of actually handling the boat at last. What I had not expected was that I would be subjected to so much testing myself, that sea trials would be such an affliction, so trying, annoying and distressing. The authors of the dictionary must have had boats in mind when they came up with their definition.

My daughter, Margaret, an American living in Ottawa, arrived and proudly hoisted the Canadian flag she had brought, to legitimize her father sailing in foreign waters. She was excited with the novelty of a family yacht.

Eager to experience our independence and free ourselves from the ties to shore, Margaret and I nudged *Zillah* away from the marina dock, motored out into Lake Worth, and anchored off the Coast Guard station. The boat swung with the turning of the tide and rocked with the passing of power-boats, and we felt our first time intimations of the freedom of the sea.

Our first sea trial was a short run up the ICW, the Intracoastal Waterway, to give Margaret practice in steering the boat. Cutting across the lake from the anchorage, in what I thought was water deep enough, I ran aground. *Zillah* drew 7 feet 2 inches. The ICW was dredged to 8 feet, though along the edges where the dredger had thrown up debris, it was often less. We were stuck. Annoying, I thought, not realizing it was just a part of a trial. It was my first lesson in the disadvantages of a deep draft boat in shallow waters.

I'd read about "kedging off," in the Annapolis Book of Seamanship.

"A good opportunity to practice," I told Margaret, as if it happened every day. We loaded the fisherman's anchor, with 160 feet of rope and chain, into the dinghy, and I rowed out, abeam of the boat, and dropped the anchor. Margaret attached the anchor line to the windlass, and together we began to crank it in, trying to bring the boat around. Thinking extra power would help, I turned on the engine, and tried to back in reverse. Unfortunately, I let the anchor line go slack, it drifted under the boat, and the rope tangled in the propeller. More trouble.

Though not much of a diver, I put on face mask and snorkel, and looking like some one-horned creature with one round Cyclopean eye, went overboard. To my surprise, the propeller was mounted only about four feet below the waterline, a shallow dive, even for me. With only a dozen attempts, each time surfacing to gasp for air, I untangled the line and emerged triumphantly. My body was painted a celebratory blue, like a South Sea Islander, from the anti-fouling paint on the hull.

"Congratulations. That was quite a Jacques Cousteau act," Margaret said when I climbed back on board. But we were lodged firmly still. Fortunately the bottom was soft mud. We waited for the tide to rise at sunset, when we floated off easily. Margaret had not learned much about steering, but it was a lesson on staying in the center of the channel. For both of us.

"If you ain't been aground, you ain't been around," John Anderson said when I told him my latest misadventure, as if it actually did happen every day.

Two days later was to be our real sea trial. We would take *Zillah* out into open water of the Atlantic. "Fort Lauderdale is a 70-mile run south," I told Margaret. "If we get up early, and we can make it in a day."

It was our first venture alone on the open sea, and both of us were excited. "*Alone, alone, all all alone/ Alone on the wide wide sea,*" I rhapsodized from Coleridge's, *The Ancient Mariner.* The endless expansiveness of wide horizons, which I had first experienced as a child growing up in the open prairies of Saskatchewan, always triggered my whimsy.

"Don't get too carried away, Dad," Margaret said. "Just look behind you," There, just a turn-of-a-neck away on shore, were the loading cranes of the busy commercial port of Riviera Beach, like gigantic praying mantises, pecking at the stacks of railroad-car-sized steel container boxes.

There was little wind, but we were happy to motor. The engine, an aged Perkins 4-107 diesel, the gallant draft-horse of the seas, rattled, tapped and thundered. Ten miles south it coughed, sputtered, revved up again briefly. Then died. This wasn't the trial we had in mind.

We were drifting in the current, a mile off shore on the edge of the Gulf Stream, which flowed north at six knots. We coaxed what little wind we could snare into the sails and worked our way closer to land. When opposite the entrance to Lake Worth we dropped the anchor. And waited.

Do we radio for a tow? That could be expensive. But it wasn't only a matter of money, it was also a question of pride. This was after all, a sea trial. So we waited all afternoon and into the evening.

The tide turned at ten o'clock that night and began to flow in. A light evening breeze came up as the land cooled, blowing off shore. It was enough to make headway and give us steerage. "I think we can sail in, Margaret," I said. It was something I had done many times in a dinghy, beating to windward, returning to shore at the end of a day of sailing. But never with forty-three feet on deck and eleven tons of boat under me.

As we approached the harbor entrance, a darkened boat hovered in mid-channel, a fisherman perhaps, casting in the churning waters. I didn't need a collision on top of engine failure, I thought. "Securite! Securite!" I called the conventional marine safety warning into the radio, loud enough that he could have heard me *viva voce* across the channel. "This is Sailing Vessel *Zillah*. We've lost power and are trying to enter harbor under sail. Would the boat in the entrance please give us right of way."

"Sailing Vessel Zillah," an authoritative voice replied. "This is the United States Coast Guard. Can we help you?"

That brought me up short. It was like blinking headlights at a police car cruising at thirty in a forty-mile-an-hour zone, to move over. "No," I said apologetically. I think we can handle it. Thanks."

"We'll stand by. Call if you need us. Coast Guard out."

The channel was nearly a mile long and about a hundred yards wide, dredged for ocean-going freighters. The tide was flowing in, the wind was blowing out. We beat to windward, pulling in the jib and letting it out repeatedly as we went back and forth on each tack. I tightened down the main so it could handle itself as we went about. But the jib required speed and coordination. With each, "Helms a'lee!" I let off the jib sheet at the critical moment when the jib crossed the bow, and Margaret hauled in the opposite sheet fast and furious.

The inbound flooding tide favored us and we worked our way up the channel, apprehensive each time I came close to the stone embankment on each side. Once in Lake Worth, we let out sails and headed across to the anchorage on a beam reach. Margaret went forward, I turned into the wind, and she dropped the anchor in the same place we had left, with such optimism, 15 hours before.

"So that's what you mean by a sea trial," Margaret said wearily. Was she beginning to question her father's "folly?"

Two weeks later, having had the fuel injectors cleaned, and the fuel filters changed, I took off again. An old friend, Howie Muir, joined me for ten days of cruising. A sexagenarian like myself, he'd had extensive sailing experience. We had done some white-water canoeing together years before. We had contrasting styles of sailing. I was a leisurely sailor, essentially lazy, some would say. When I set the sails, I left them that way, unless there was a compelling reason to change them. Howie, however, was a fiddler as serious sailors are, fidgeting, adjusting, trimming, pulling a sheet taut, letting out a little slack, to get the last ounce of drive out of the wind.

We had a pleasant run from Palm Beach to Fort Lauderdale. An old Florida sailor had told me to stay within a mile of shore, to catch a countercurrent that pushed us south, the eddy off the north-flowing Gulf Stream. I took his advice and sailed the 30-foot depth line and in spite of light winds, we made good time. "Good move," Howie said.

Then we went on to Miami. On this passage, a steady northeast wind, fifteen to twenty knots, gave us an exhilarating run, the sails full, the rigging straining. A legitimate sea trial, I figured. Turning at the harbor entrance buoy we sailed up the big ship channel, giving a wide berth to a 60,000-ton container ship heading out to sea. *Zillah* seemed very small and vulnerable as I looked up at the immense gray wall of its steel hull.

Howie had gone forward as a precaution. Standing look-out at the bow, he held on to the pulpit. "Do you always keep the fore-stay this loose?" he called out and began to tug it back and forth. It should have been rigid.

"I don't think so," I replied from the helm. Then I looked around at the back-stay. It whipped back and forth in rhythm to Howie pulling on the fore stay. Turning about, I saw the back stay grounding plate, a ½-inch thick piece of steel, 6-inches by 4-inches, lift off the deck. Beneath it, corroded screws had pulled loose from the rotten wood.

"My god. You could lose the mast!" Howie sized up the situation immediately. I turned into the wind, and he dropped the main as I furled the jib.

There was a small anchorage off Sunset Island, close to the harbor entrance, that John Anderson had told us about. He planned to be there, visiting an aunt who lived ashore. We maneuvered our way in and found John and Patti at anchor, a rare piece of luck. By next morning, John had located a wood yard that had block teak we would need for the repair, and in two days he had replaced the rotten wood and secured the back stay. "Some day you'll want to replace the transom," he warned.

On the return trip to Riviera Beach, the engine failed again. This had become chronic. "Should I replace the engine?" I asked Roy, the eccentric mechanic at Cracker Boy Boatyard. He had spent four years in the navy on nuclear submarines, an experience that had given him a twisted sense of humor, I felt. Anoxia, perhaps? But he did know engines.

"Do you plan to do any serious sailing?" he asked.

I was reluctant to admit to my exaggerated fantasies. I'd even had visions of circumnavigating, before I knew better. "Well, if I get good enough. Yes." I said.

"Then get a new engine."

Three more weeks in the boatyard, and another $10,000 withdrawn from my pension fund, half the price I had paid originally for the boat, and I had a spotless, shiny sky blue Perkins Prima M-50 diesel engine powering *Zillah*. That should put an end to those trials, I thought, the chronic optimist.

My next trial run I planned to be solo. From the beginning of my Elder-Odyssey, I had anticipated sailing alone when I couldn't find crew. I gloried in the heroics of being master of my ship and dreaded the thought of being a prisoner on my own boat, waiting to find crew to sail with me. In my search for a boat, I had met several sad, lonely men, burdened with derelict boats, holed up in mosquito-infested lagoons. *Zillah* was not going to become an *African Queen*.

My first solo episode was a return to Fort Lauderdale. Canadian friends were anchored there, and it was also an opportunity to visit Judy, the attractive ex-wife of the ex-owner.

I was proud of the way I handled the sails alone. There was little wind and I had to motor most of the way, the glistening new engine thrumming robustly. But when I entered the harbor, unbelievably the engine spluttered to a stop. "Not my new engine!" I threw a tantrum. "Impossible!" Fortunately, I had left the jib up and was able to maneuver safely to anchor in the outer harbor. The second time I had anchored under sail, the first time by myself.

The engine, only one-week-old, was under warranty, so a Perkins mechanic came to my rescue. I didn't realize then that I was initiating a precedent that would be repeated many times, hailing Perkins mechanics in many ports, in many parts of the world. He changed the fuel filter and the engine immediately started up. It was embarrassingly easy. I had not learned yet the pernicious effects of dirty fuel that would often cripple *Zillah,* and the importance of changing the fuel filters regularly. But within two minutes the engine died again.

The mechanic checked the oil. The dipstick came up coated with a milky slime. "That's seawater,"he said. "It could ruin your engine." Water had siphoned from the exhaust outlet back into the engine. We pumped out the contaminated sludge and changed the oil. "You'll need to install a proper exhaust system with a vented loop that's higher than engine," he advised before he left. Malfunctioning vented loops became another recurring theme.

I went back to the boatyard for another week to have a new exhaust venting system installed. Would I ever escape the boatyard? I began to wonder.

Perhaps I should have been prepared for this side of boat owning. My friend Ray, also the owner of a classic wooden boat, delighted in solving such problems. I'd known him to spend three months working on his boat one summer, and only three days sailing. I was slow to learn that it was not enough to have sailed a Laser on the Charles River. Owning a sailboat was more than sailing, more than the romance of the high seas. One had to be also a carpenter, a mechanic, an electrician, a plumber, a navigator, a man with a reckless disregard for comfort, and one with deep pockets.

I also learned that sailing an old boat was an ongoing never-ending sea trial.

Joe with John Anderson in Florida, 1993, undergoing
Zillah's sea trials.

413

Chapter 86: The Charleston Jetty

Come, my friends,....
Push off, ... smite
The sounding furrows....
It may be that the gulfs wash us down....

~ Alfred Lord Tennyson, *Ulysses*

Under a gray, cheerless, pre-dawn sky I followed *Borderlaw* out of Charleston harbor. At the entrance off Fort Sumter it came to a stop. I brought *Zillah* along side.

"Is something wrong?" I asked.

"My GPS is down," John called over the noise of our engines. "I'm not going off shore until I can fix it. I'm taking the Inter Coastal Waterway."

I was conflicted. I felt John expected me to follow. We had agreed to travel together on our way north from Florida to Maine. John, a skilled boatwright, had rebuilt *Zillah* for me and he knew the boat better than I. He had saved me from trouble in the past. Sailing in his wake was a great source of assurance.

This was particularly so now that I would have to sail solo. Margaret, my daughter, had crewed with me from Palm Beach to Charleston, but she had to return to work. Now I was on my own. It wasn't a good time to split from John.

But I had resolved my inner fears, the anxiety of being alone on a 43 foot boat, on the high seas. I was determined not to be a prisoner on my own boat, a captive of every seaport because I could not attract crew. I'd crossed that psychological barrier. I was impatient to go offshore solo. To prove to myself that I could do it.

Besides, two days before I had run aground on the ICW between Beaufort and Charleston, and it had cost me fifty dollars to get SeaTow to pull me off. The stretch ahead was reported to be more shallow still. That did it.

"I'm going offshore," I said.

John didn't argue. I wish he had. We agreed to contact each other by radio every four hours, at noon, four and eight, and rendezvous that night at Georgetown, on the Winyah River, 50-miles down the coast. We parted.

It would be two months before we met again.

There was a gray cheerless pre-dawn sky, as I motored out of the ship channel, a light wind five to ten knots from the north east. Low concrete jetties bordered the channel, which was dredged to a depth of 35-feet, and ran three miles off shore. It was clearly marked by navigation buoys. The jetties protected the channel from silting and surge. Partly submerged, from the low deck of *Zillah*, they were barely visible.

By 8 a.m. I cleared Charleston harbor, raised sails, shut down the engine, and gave an inner cheer. At sea again. I felt like a run-away dog that had slipped its leash.

"Alone, alone, all all alone, Alone on the wide, wide sea…." I rhapsodized Coleridge, when I should have been thinking of GPS coordinates.

My course was forty five degrees, north-east, directly into the wind and waves. I realized I was in for a long tedious day of beating to windward. In the light breeze *Zillah* made poor progress under sail. After the noon radio check with *Borderlaw*, the wind increased, but with it came a 3-foot chop. I motored up. *Zillah* punched into the steep waves making only 4-knots.

At the 4 p.m. radio check I shut the engine down to hear John better. He was nine miles from the Winyah River, he told me. I was still nineteen, I told him. "But I'll make it by dark," I said optimistically.

"We'll have dinner ready for you when you get there," he replied. We signed off. I returned to the cockpit and turned the ignition key.

The engine didn't start.

Trouble shooting engine problems was not one of my strengths. I relied on the fact that the engine was still under warranty, but what good did that do me five miles offshore? I checked the fuel filter, but it did not appear to be very dirty, and cranked over the engine until the battery went low. But still it would not start.

The wind had strengthened. Perhaps I could still make it under sail. So I ran out the genoa and close hauled tacked to windward. But by 6 p.m. I was still well short of the the Winyah River. Do I push on and risk entering a harbor I do not know, in the dark, under sail without engine power? Or should I return a harbor I know? I weighed the options, then turned, let out the sails and ran before the wind back to Charleston.

At 8 p.m. I called *Borderlaw*, but they were out of radio range. So I contacted the Coast Guard and asked them to relay a message to *Borderlaw*, telling them that I had engine problems and was turning back to Charleston.

With evening the sun set with a fierce glow behind gathering purple clouds. Heat lightning flared along the horizon. A twilight haze shrouded the sky, and with dark it began to rain, a light, warm, Carolinian rain.

The wind came up, gusting to twenty knots and following seas began to mount. Waves rose, lifting the stern with a powerful grace, like a male dancer hoisting a ballerina high with each passing swell. Occasionally a large wave surged by with a rushing hiss. The crests began to break.

"It's going to be a long night!" my inner voice spoke out.

Pinpricks of light sparkled from shore, more lights than I had suspected. "Where's Charleston in all that light?" I wondered.

Focused on the lights, I didn't sea the breaking wave until too late. It struck the stern and swung the boat to port. The wind caught the back of the sail and the boom crashed violently from the starboard side to port in an accidental jibe. "That could be dangerous," my inner soliloquy resumed. Fortunately no damage was done.

On the starboard tack I was headed toward shore, though it was still several miles off. The waves piled higher from seven to nine feet high. The last time I'd been in seas like this was off Atlantic City, I thought, with a sense of premonition.

A bright rotating light beamed across the sky. I counted. Two flashes every thirty seconds. Isn't that the lighthouse at the harbor entrance? I checked the GPS which gave me accurate latitude and longitude coordinates. But it was too dark to read the chart. I had left the flashlight in the cabin below. I wasn't able to confirm the coordinates with the chartl. I jibed over, a controlled jibe this time, wanting to keep off the lee shore.

In the dark, land still seemed a long way off. But the water was shoaling, 45-feet the depth sounder read, 35-feet, 25-feet, 18-feet. Then I was sailing in 12-feet of water with cresting seas.

I checked the GPS again. There was a warning beep and the instrument read, "Insufficient satellite data." The batteries would need to be changed.

I tightened the main sail, went onto a beam reach wanting to head further off shore. Running down wind the gust was on my back. But now it was on my cheek and I felt its full force for the first time. I engaged the auto-pilot, and scrambled below out of the rain, to change the GPS batteries. But it did not respond still. My hands were wet and I had to dry everything with paper towel before the signal came up.

The hand-held GPS picked up satellites only when on deck, when free of overhead obstructions. So I came back on deck in the rain, protecting the instrument with a plastic bag. That made it difficult to read in the dark. The harbor entrance buoy was still five miles to the south-east, I figured. Less than an hour at the speed I was going. Possibly forty-five minutes.

And the bright flashing light? I was confused by it. If it was the lighthouse, it seemed too close. I could not locate it on the chart with water streaming down my glasses. I wanted to go below again to check the GPS coordinates against the chart in the shelter of the cabin. But I was reluctant to leave the helm, feeling a false sense of security in grasping the wheel. I began to realize that I didn't know precisely where I was.

But I did know I needed to be in deeper water. So I kept heading across wind in an attempt to take me further offshore. Eighteen-feet, the depth sounder read. But then it shoaled again to 12-feet. Waves were breaking regularly on the stern now, gushing by with the roar of river rapids.

Then I saw them. A line of red and green navigation lights. The harbor channel markers, only four hundred yards ahead, less than a city block away. That's right where they should be, I thought. I turned downwind and headed straight for them. *Zillah* lifted with each surge in the frothing seas and carved her way through.

But what's that? A hundred yards off, a solid white foaming line emerged out of the dark. It was seething, snarling, the crest of a long, continuous breaking wave, parallel to the channel markers. "It shouldn't be there!" But it was too late to turn. So I held my course, desperately hoping that *Zillah* would handle it, the way she did the breaking seas.

THUD. There was the loud resounding impact of lead on concrete, like a demolition ball swung from the crane of a wrecking crew crashing into a stone wall, the shattering noise of two cars colliding. I was flung against the helm. *Zillah* shuddered to an abrupt stop. The boat was pinned, stuck on something relentlessly immovable. Then she twisted agonizingly to port, heeled over to 60-degrees and broached-to. Water poured over the lee deck and into the cockpit. The boom swung out and dipped into the sea. The lower end of the sail began to fill with water.

"You're going to capsize," I told myself, with a calm objectivity. It was as if I was standing behind myself and choreographing the scene for someone else, like a movie director in a high-action ocean storm scene.

Breaking waves beat on the upturned hull, lifting the boat each time and letting her down with a grating thump. "Boats pound themselves to pieces this way," my psychic observer said, with matter-of-fact aloofness.

"Keep your cool. Think. Get to the radio and put out a MAY DAY call," the monologue continued, as it organized my abandon ship strategy. "Then go forward and cut the dinghy loose."

To reach the radio below deck, I had to climb over the helm bulkhead, step on to the topside deck, which was now sloping like a cliff-hanging precipice and then drop into the cockpit. It was an acrobatic vaulting movement at the best of times. I had one foot up ready to leap, when another wave hit, and knocked me down. "Don't get swept overboard!" I waited for a lull. The boat thumped again.

Then the monster surge swept in. I heard it coming with a thundering growl like a waterfall, then I saw the breaking white foam engulf the boat. "In a moment you'll have to abandon ship," the monologue continued with deliberation, like a movie reel winding on when you wish it would stop.

Zillah was about to capsize, the mast laying near horizontal over the water, but then she rose with the wave, and with the grinding crunch of wood scraping on concrete, was swept over.

And floated upright.

Zillah was in the harbor channel, bobbing in calm water. The sails chattered angrily as she turned her bow up into the wind.

The concrete breakwater running parallel to the harbor. Then I remembered seeing it on the chart. At high tide it was submerged under three feet of water. *Zillah* had been swept over the Charleston jetty.

"This isn't over yet," my dramatic persona resumed. "Are you taking on water?" I plunged below into the cabin. It was chaotic, books, crockery, pots, charts, mattresses and cushions strewn about. I tossed the flotsam aside frantically, and pried up the floorboards, checking to see where the water was gushing in. The bilge was half full, but it wasn't rising. I clambered forward through the debris to check the bow, where we had hit. It was dry.

"The prospect of death doth marvellously concentrate the mind," Samuel Johnson wrote. I have survived the worst of it. What do I do now? Do I call the Coast Guard for assistance? I dreaded the confrontation. I saw the matter of fact questions, the nodding heads. It was too embarrassing. So I decided to sneak into harbor alone undetected, unbeknown to the authorities, the wayward dog creeping back to his kennel tail between its legs.

The channel was well marked with lighted navigation buoys, though at times it was difficult to pick them out against the dazzle of city lights. It was a down-wind run, clear sailing. I shortened the jib to reduce my speed. There had been enough excitement for one night.

In *The Odyssey* new challenges relentlessly confront the weary seafarer. I was reminded that this was my *Elder-Odyssey*. Once in the harbor, I had to cross the main big ship channel to head up to the yacht haven. In the dark, a poorly lit freighter blocked my way. I missed the turn and lost my bearings in the maze of city lights. I went below to check the chart but couldn't find a flashlight in the disheveled cabin. A distant red marker glimmered across the bay and I headed to it. Mid-way, the keel touched gently. *Zillah* had run aground. "At least it's mud," I consoled myself. I was too tired to care.

"United States Coast Guard. This is sailing vessel *Zillah*," I radioed, and explained my predicament. I'd been caught. I was going to have to confess my sins and admit to my guilt after all.

"I'll be there shortly," the officer replied. "You must be aground on Middle Ground. It happens all the time. Then *Zillah* bumped. Bumped again and floated off in a rising tide. But the Coast Guard were already on their way.

"Just follow us," the captain said, and led me to the anchorage off the Coast Guard station. I dropped the anchor in 22-feet of water, thankful that it held.

The officer asked permission to come aboard. I was surprised by the courtesy of a request, expecting an angry boarding party. "We need to check that you are in compliance with Coast Guard regulations," he said. Now they'll throw the book at me, I thought. He handed me a form to fill out, in triplicate. "Be sure to press hard on the pen," he instructed. But the form had nothing to do with wreckless behavior, or violations of rules of the road, driving without a license, or sailing on the high seas without a crew. How many life preservers did I have on board? Was there oil in the bilge? Was the no-oil-discharge-sign displayed? Did I have a human waste holding tank, which it didn't. Fire extinguishers, which it did.

Seeing his non-threatening manner, I confessed to going over the jetty. Like the *Ancient Mariner* collaring the wedding guest, I had to tell somebody. "Well, not many boats do that," he said, only mildly interested, as if it happened all the time, like running aground on Middle Ground. After all it was 3 a.m. He was sleepy too.

Then a Coast Guard crewman approached him and mumbled something in his ear.

"I'm going to have to ticket you," the officer said. I should have kept my mouth shut about the jetty, I thought. "You're navigating at night without proper running lights." In going over the jetty the red starboard running light had gone out. With a flourish of power, he filled in a very official document, again in triplicate and handed the original to me. "This a warning." He smiled and bid me good night.

Everybody have their priorities, I thought as I turned below to tidy the chaos of the cabin. I brewed myself a cup of coffee. Decaf. I craved something warm and sweet. But the milk had curdled and I dumped it overboard.

"I shall drink life to the lees," *Ulysses* says in Tennyson's poem. But not tonight.

Chapter 87: Rite of Passage

The prospect of death, doth marvelously concentrate the mind.

~ Samuel Johnson

"Is it wise to be sailing by yourself?" my eldest daughter Jennifer asked when I gave her my embarrassed account of going over the Charleston jetty. She was the sailor in the family, a Hurricane Island Outward Bound School watch officer, Coast Guard licensed. Jennifer had crewed on charter yachts in the Caribbean, and made an ocean passage from San Francisco to Hawaii. Was it a good idea? Was the whole fantasy of retiring to a sailboat a good idea? I had two weeks to consider.

The boatyard where I took *Zillah* for repair was in an isolated location six miles up the Charleston ???River. Several hours a day, between five in the afternoon and eight next morning, the yard was deserted except for Rex, the territorial Alsatian watch dog. I was alone, stranded on a river-bank in the Carolina countryside. I enjoyed the solitude. It was like an Outward Bound "solo," a time to reflect.

Maine fishermen couldn't understand why yachtsmen could willingly tolerate the discomfort of small boat sailing, and apparently enjoy it. Even risk their lives. When they weren't even paid. Why did they do it?

"WHY DO YOU DO IT ?" I wrote in bold cursive on a fresh page, beginning the dialogue between myself and my journal.

"Do you want the 30-second reply or the 30-minute lecture?" I'd replied.

"You could start with a 30-second sound bite," the journal invited.

"It's a great way to feel alive," I scribbled down. "And because it's there," I added.

"I think I've heard that one before," my journal objected. "

"But it does apply to the sea as well, doesn't it?" I insisted.

"And your 30-minute lecture?"

I felt I was on a more solid footing here, for Outward Bound had been founded as merchant seamen survival schools. And wasn't I a recent survivor from the perils of the sea?

During World War II in the Battle of the North Atlantic, British merchant ship owners found that the young seaman died in disproportionate numbers when their ships were torpedoed by German submarines, and they took to the lifeboats. They consulted with Kurt Hahn, a German educator who lived in exile from the Nazis in

Scotland. He had developed a rigorous program of fitness training, expeditioning and crewing on the school's square rigger. The emphasis was on character development, qualities of self-reliance, self-confidence, initiative, endurance, steadfastness in the face of adversity, compassion and moral awareness. Hahn recommended a one month intensive program along these lines and Outward Bound was born.

I'd spent a year teaching at his school and understood the adoption of his regimen to Outward Bound.

The history resonated with me again, a recent survivor of the sea myself.

In Outward Bound we also drew upon the literature of the wilderness to give deeper meaning to the experience like David Henry Thoreau: "I went to the woods because I wanted to live deliberately, to front only the essential facts of life, and not, discover when I came to die, that I had not lived...."

The philosopher, William James saw in dangerous pursuit and strenuous activity, "the moral equivalent of war." Aggression had been drilled into our genes, and was in the marrow of our bones. He advocated conscripting young men to work on fishing boats, in the coal mines, as a substitute for the glory and excitement, the camaraderie and the will to war.

As Outward Bound thinking evolved, we began to see it as a broader educational process, learning as the product of reflecting on experience. So the reflective process took on more importance, and we extended the solo experience from one day of solitude to three. This was interpreted in the light of Joseph Campbell's journey of the hero, an Odyssey, a rite of passage between adolescence and adulthood.

I examined my own experience, in the solitude of the boatyard and began to see my going to sea as a rite of passage, a transition from the demands of a professional life of achievement, to one of sorting out, integration, and acceptance, an Elder-Odyssey.

"Is there life after Outward Bound?" a student once asked Said in jest it had the seriousness that only humor can capture.

I thought back to Ulysses, in Tennyson's poem, asking the same question. Ulysses, a old man, home from his travels, is discontented with the pettiness of domestic life. *"It profits little an idle king....."* What does he do next? And Ulysses resolves to go on, *"...to smite the sounding furrows...."*

The poem had become something of a talisman in my life. The last lines *"...to strive, to seek, to find and not to yield,"* had been adapted by Outward Bound as its motto: To serve, To seek, To find, and not To Yield.

But for me the connection went back further yet. In my senior year at school, the poem had been on the exam syllabus, and I had memorized it. *"As though to breathe were life? Why life piled upon life were all to little, And of one, but little remains to me."* The lines still echoed in my soul. *"I am a part of all that I have met...."* Ulysses says. And I am part of all that I have read as well, I thought.

I was launched on my Elder-Odyssey. *"Perhaps the gulfs shall wash us down."* I had already two close calls. *"Perhaps we shall touch the Happy Isles."*

421

Repairs completed I set sail for Annapolis where Jennifer was to meet me for the passage to the coastal islands of Maine.

Chapter 88: Rounding Cape Fear

"We have nothing to fear but fear itself."

~ FDR

"Right!"

~ JJN

A satellite view of the coast of North Carolina shows three headlands jutting into the Atlantic. The most prominent is Cape Hatteras. 75-miles below that is Cape Lookout, and 70 miles further south west is Cape Fear. In the days of sail, all three were graveyards of the sea, all feared.

Charleston was another 70-miles south west. And I was anxious as I prepared to leave. Only three weeks before I had collided with the harbor entrance jetty and the memory of the near disaster persisted both in my dreams and in my waking thoughts. The damage to the boat had been repaired by the Hasley-Cannon Boatyard in a week. But the damage to my pride and confidence would take longer. The damage to my psyche would stay with me as long as I sailed *Zillah*. I felt I was a damaged soul as I departed Charleston for the second time.

I was anxious. I was alone, sailing solo again. I had tried to recruit friends but none were available on short notice. In the past I had frequently sought solitude, hiking alone, climbing mountains, camping by myself. But I was uneasy sailing offshore alone. *Alone, alone, all all alone/ Alone on the wide wide sea.* Coleridge's lines had a haunting quality. I had read too of solo circumnavigators, and of round the world races for solo sailors. I had listened to Joshua Slocum's voyage on tape. But I wasn't in this class. I questioned whether I wasn't foolhardy, as did some of my friends

But that wasn't the issue. The real issue was whether my boat was a symbol of freedom, or was I a captive of my boat. Samuel Johnson had said that a ship was like a prison, with the added prospect of drowning.

I decided I'd sail.

The thought of sailing at night still haunted me. Mankind has a deep ambivalence about the night that is deeply embedded in the marrow of our bones. It is both a time of mystery and romance, but a time of stealth and duplicity. Even with the romance of moon light, there are lurking shadows. In our primordial past we huddled around fires in the recesses of caves to fend off the dark, and still we stare longingly into the flickering flames of a campfire, and huddle close to our loved ones for warmth and solace. Bring electricity to a primitive village and you cut the birth rate in half, I was told when running a student work camp in India. I decided to avoid the added difficulties of arriving at night, so planned to leave Charleston late in the afternoon, sail overnight and arrive at Winyah Bay, 65 miles north east, my next landfall, by daylight.

I realized too that I must improved my navigating. So I upgraded the GPS. The hand held GPS, when brought on deck to contact satellites, was exposed to the weather. That would not do. So I mounted an all-weather antenna on the stern rail and ran a connection to the monitor mounted above the navigation table. Attaching the instrument to the ship's batteries, I could keep it on all the time, and readily transfer the coordinates to a chart. The day before leaving I spent programming every navigational aid, between Charleston and the Winyah River. As a further precaution, I would also record my position on the chart and in the ship's log every hour.

Mid-afternoon Wednesday I weighed anchor and motored out of Charleston harbor. For luck I wore a tee-shirt a friend had given me in Florida with frolicking porpoises blazoned across my chest. I preferred it to the other shirt she gave me of a killer whale breaching.

And I began to hum, like Pooh Bear when he was nervous, and then began to sing in a low soft reverential tone.

Oh hear us Lord when we pray to thee/ For those in peril on the sea.

Then the psalm: *Rejoice, rejoice, Emanuel shall come to thee/ O Isreal.* Summoning my long neglected Roman Catholic heritage: *Benedictus qui vene in nomine Domine.* Blessed are they that go in the name of the Lord.

And finally, the old Negro spiritual: Go down Moses, way down in Egypt Land/Oh Pharoah, led my people go.

I have never seen myself as a deeply religious man, but that night I thought it best to cover all my spiritual bases.

Once clear of the channel, I raised sails. The wind was light, 10-to-12-knots from the south, a broad reach. Engaging the auto-pilot, *Zillah* steered herself. I went forward to straighten up the deck, securing the anchor, and coiling the anchor line. Lingering at the bow I felt the pulse of the sea rising and falling rhythmically in the quartering waves. I leaned back on the pulpit rail. Looking along the graceful curve to the deck, and up into the billowing sails that soared above, there was a magical fusion between wind and water, sea and sky.

It marveled that I was there, on a boat of my own, heading out to the open waters of the Atlantic. There was a special tang to savoring the experience alone, but I also had the longing to share the moment with those who had nurtured me in my life, male and female, mentors, lovers and daughters. I was on a long journey that had begun with the romantic fantasies of an unruly boy growing up on the prairies of Saskatchewan, 65-years before.

"What a great way to feel alive," I noted in the log.

Then I was brought back to the realities of the sea. This was my first over-night sail solo. How would I deal with fatigue? Caffeine? Or catnaps with an oven timer to wake me on the half-hour? The night was balmy, and with the auto-pilot engaged, I spread a pad on the deck next to the helm, set the timer and dozed.

Through the night the wind shifted east and gradually clocked to the north, then dropped. After trying to coax the dying wind into the sails, I furled in the genoa, tightened down the main and drifted, like they had to do in the days of sail. With the dawn I motored up.

By mid-afternoon Thursday, I picked up the Winyah Bay harbor entrance buoy, "2WB" and dropped anchor in the Winyah River, downstream from Georgetown in early evening.

I lay over at anchor Friday in the Winyah River, catching up on sleep, writing up my journal, and plotting the next passage to Beaufort, North Carolina, 150-miles to the north east. This would take me around the dreaded Cape Fear.

NOAA weather reported "a Bermuda high lingers over the area with variable winds and a buildup of turbulence, severe thunderstorms, moist unstable air to continue through Saturday."

I plotted the next passage, from Winyah Bay to Cape Fear 64-miles at 61 degrees, to the Frying Pan Shoal lighthouse, 72-miles at 64 degrees, another 82-miles to Beaufort. I estimated the time it would take, 15 hours to Frying Pan Shoal at 5-knots, 24 hours at 3-knots if the winds continued light and variable. Winds were backing to the north, which would put it on the nose. If worse came to worse, I could make 5-knots motoring. I checked the fuel consumption, about half a gallon an hour. I would have plenty.

Fishing boats were already heading out to sea rocking the boat with a wake up call at 4 a.m. I had a hurried breakfast, then waited for the tide to turn. With a following wind and an ebbing tide *Zillah* raced down the river at an unprecedented 9.7-knots. The outgoing tide collided with the incoming waves and crossing the harbor entrance bar *Zilllah* crashed into the breaking surf throwing spray over the deck and high into the air. The early morning sun caught the glistening web of mist and we debouched into the open sea through the arch of a rainbow, casting a spectrum of dazzling color over the boat. It was a triumphal beginning of another day, *Zillah* more the breaching whale that a frolicking porpoise.

The wind was from the east most of the day, blowing 10-to-15-knots, which made for good sailing, 6-knots and more. But into the wind it requiring frequent tacking, and at the end of an hour I'd make only 3 ½-knots to windward. In the evening, the sun set with a rich fiery glow and the wind died. I turned on the engine. Even then, heading into choppy seas, I made only 4-knots. The Frying Pan Shoal was still 30-miles east.

I realized that I would not clear Cape Fear in day light. As dark settled in I felt the night angst. I remembered having nightmares as a child, if I was left in my room with the light out and the door closed. Cape Fear was a place to bring out such anxieties.   Was it anxiety or fear? Tillich, the theologian, makes the distinction. Anxiety is a general sense of apprehension, difficult to put one's finger on. Fear is specific. To cope with anxiety, he writes, one must first define it, give it concreteness, turn it into fear, if you will. Fear one can confront. That's what courage is about.

What did I fear?

I went below to study the chart again. There it was clearly defined. From the lighthouse on shore at the mouth of the Cape Fear River a shoal extended east, out to sea for 35-miles. Close in it was shaped round and flat, and then stretched long and and narrow like a handle, the handle of a frying pan, hence the name Frying Pan Shoal. The water was shallow, often less than 10-feet, and the chart indicated, "Breaking Waves." More ominous were the symbols for sinking ships, an upended hull with bare mast tilted at a rakish angle.

I decided to spend the night at the helm. I padded the wooden cockpit seat with life jackets, curled up in a foetal position with one eye focused on the compass, pretended sleep. I set the alarm for twenty minutes, but woke more often to check the compass, my position on the old hand-held GPS, and to scan the horizon for passing ships. There were none. I had Cape Fear to myself that night.

Sheet lightning glowed in e dark far ahead, illuminating banks of billowing cumulus clouds that were building up along the horizon. I tuned into NOAA. They reported "a 60% chance of rain and the possibility of severe thundershowers." I'd not been in a thunderstorm at sea. What was one supposed to do? Drop the mainsail. Disconnect all the electronics. GPS too? What else? I began to hum, "Lord hear us when we pray to Thee/ For those in peril on the sea."

It was a night of stars, lightning flashes, mystery. But mystery was not what I needed tonight. I clung to Euclidean certainty, and prodded myself awake every twenty minutes on my vigil. At 3.30 a.m. I passed the "2 FP" bell buoy, clearing the Frying Pan Shoal. The hand-held GPS read 83 miles to Beaufort in the open waters of Onslow Bay.

No need to fear Cape Fear.

The low rumbling of thunder reverberated through the night. The glare of the lightning made the dark even darker. The clouds mounted ever higher. I felt I was witnessing the opening scene of Genesis, *the earth was without form, and void; and darkness was upon the face of the deep. And the spirit of God moved upon the face of the waters. And God said, Let there be light...* And there was another lightning bolt.

Dawn broke with an awesome splendor. If Jehovah ever chose to speak to me that was the moment. A towering mass of cumulus clouds were stacked one layer upon another, rising a mile into the sky. The first rays of the sun caught the crest and it lit up like a flaring yellow beacon, a torch held mightily high, proclaiming another day in glorious splendor. The sun pierced the lower clouds with beaming rays of light painting broad swaths of deepening colors, fiery tones of orange and red, and toward the bottom darker shades of purple and burgundy. Beneath it all, dark, murky, charcoal gray rain clouds funneled into the sea throwing up a churning froth. Genesis was silent on thunderstorms.

On shore to the west, more clouds were banked up, brooding and gray, devoid of color, waiting to be struck by the golden wand of the sun. A light spattering of rain drifted in a light wind. I motored up and altered course to the west in a futile attempt to outrun the deluge. It was like sailing through a canyon expecting the walls to collapse on me any minute, *walking through the valley of the shadow of death*, in the words of the psalmist.

With sails down and tightly furled, I motored up. A light spattering of rain drifted in the light wind, but I was able to avert the main squall. The cloud bank drifted slowly out to sea, and the cumulus build on shore dissolved in the heat of the day. The sun broke through, the wind dropped and I began my sixth day at sea, adrift, coaxing wind into the sails.

With night the clouds cleared, and the rain washed sky opened to a spectacular display of stars. Overhead, Cygnus, the great swan of the sky flew athwart the spreaders. She seemed to carry *Zillah* with her on her flight. The extended grasping arms of Scorpio, were spread across the southern sky, and I felt I was leaving the bitter sting of my calamity behind. The arc of the Big Dipper swung overhead, and I steered by it as runaway slaves had done to guide them north. "Follow the drinking gourd," they had sung. I too was on a flight to freedom.

By nightfall I was still 20-miles from Beaufort harbor entrance buoy, not wanting to enter in the dark. So I picked up Cape Lookout Lighthouse, 125-feet high, flashing every fifteen seconds, visible 25-miles. It marked Lookout Bight, a small cove sheltered behind a curved sand spit, that beckoned like a bent finger. The channel was deep and marked by a convenient buoy, and I entered. At 4:30 a.m. I dropped the anchor in 20-ft. of sand and went below, turned off the oven timer, and collapsed in sleep.

I was awakened in the morning by the lapping of water on the hull, *Zillah*, swinging at anchor, sun reflected off the white sand beach, seagulls quarreling.

Mission accomplished. My first passage. "I don't feel I've graduated," I wrote in my journal. "But I do feel I've passed the qualifying entrance exam."

Chapter 89: The Waterway Option

"What are your cruising plans?" he asked me, and before I could tell him mine, he told me his.

He took the bowline as I inched my way into the fuel dock, kicking *Zillah* into reverse at the last minute stopping the forward motion. I jumped ashore with the stern line and made fast to the bollard.

Coinjock is a popular fueling station and watering hole on the Inter-coastal Waterway, approximately half way between Beaufort, North Carolina and Norfolk, Virginia. It has the feel of a busy gas station, traffic in and traffic out, the bustle of a steady stream of boats, all in a hurry.

Except for Frank. He wasn't in a hurry. Jovial, with a broad smile, a ruddy flushed face with blue veins on his puffy cheeks, a gin nose. He was in his middle sixties, I guessed. Like me. But I hoped that I didn't look that boozy. I did wish, however, that I could summon his outgoing spontaneity. As a single handed sailor I felt myself becoming a hermit.

He seemed to be on a first name basis with everyone at the marina. "Hon," as in "Honey," he called the attractive young female fuel pump attendant as she unreeled the long diesel hose.

He slipped off his aviator glasses and introduced himself, "Frank." And we had a long talk. He did most of the talking.

"Passed you back along the way.... Beautiful boat.... Sparkman Stevens design? Heading back to Canada?" No waiting for a reply.

"This is my eighth trip up and down the waterway," he told me. "Do it every year since I took early retirement from IBM when they downsized. Best decision I ever made in my life.

"North back home to Connecticut in the summer. South to Florida Keys for the winter. I'd like to cross over to the Bahamas, but the Gulf Stream gets pretty rough, and my wife doesn't like it."

I looked ahead to the 38 foot Bertram Cabin Cruiser on the dock, a boxy boat, designed for comfort, not one of the sleek modern breed of torpedo boats that passed at 25 miles per hour in the six mile per hour zone throwing up a bow wave like a tsunami.

"And what are your plan?"

Plan? I felt he put me on the spot. North in summer. South in winter. That was one option. But I wasn't thinking that far ahead. My plan was to get through the next day safely.

Destination wasn't really the issue as I saw it. I was grappling with the many uncertainties that had crept into my life since owning a boat. Questions of competence and capability. Questions of doing. Do or die, sort of issues.

With an fifty year old boat like *Zillah* there was the question of sea worthiness. I had experienced leaking decks, engine failure, rotting wood. Life on a boat, I'd discovered, had become a continuous sea trial. It was living on the edge, wondering what would malfunction next?

But wasn't the more pertinent issue that of my own competence? A competence seaman, I had come to learn, had to be not only a sailor, but also an engineer, a mechanic, electrician, plumber and wood worker, and I was none of these. Though I felt I was learning by experience and found the process fascinating, I questioned whether my learning curve rose fast enough to avoid another disaster.

It came down to a question of nerve and judgment. I recalled a day of skiing with an Outward Bound colleague. At the end of the day he said to me, "You know Joe, you ski just like you live. Always slightly out of control."

"Yes, I'm heading for Canada," I told Frank. But I didn't give him why.

I kept meeting people who saw the Canadian flag and asked, "Have you come from Canada in THAT?" And I wanted to say that I had.

A touch of Canadian chauvinism. Though we Canadians are the least chauvinistic of people.

So I had plowed my way north through the ICW, frequently touching bottom with deep drafted *Zillah*, drawing seven foot two inches, with little room to spare in an eight foot channel. I was constantly on alert, though rarely in a state of panic. If I ran aground it was only in mud, not the granite breakwaters and jetties of Atlantic City and Charleston, memories that still haunted the owl waking hours of the night.

But on the next leg of journey north, from the Chesapeake to Penobscot Bay in Maine, I felt I need not worry. I'd be with competent hands. .

At Coinjock I phoned my friend Ray Hartjen in Port Tobacco, Maryland, and my daughter, Jennifer, in Belgium to confirm our rendezvous in Annapolis. They were join me for the passage to Boston.

Jennifer was the sailor in the family. I had taught her as a child to sail a Sunfish, but she had gone on to become an instructor at the Hurricane Island Outward Bound School in Maine, and passed her Coast Guard license exam as a certified small boat captain. As a part of her Outward Bound apprenticeship she had sailed from Maine to Florida and knew these waters. To gain experience she had crewed professionally in the Caribbean and made a trans-Pacific passage from San Francisco to Hawaii.

I was proud of her achievement and appreciative of her competence, but somewhat apprehensive of her expertise. This would be a reversal of generational roles, and I was not sure how it would work out. Who would out-boss whom?

Ray, an old friend, was a master mariner in the fullest sense. He had been sailing since the age of eight, when his father rigged a square sail on a small dingy at their summer cottage on Long Island Sound. A skilled craftsman, he had rebuilt several boats, had lured me into my quest for a wooden boat, by taking me sailing in his classical Danish yacht *Siskiwit*, with its swan-like lines and the warm burnish of varnished mahogany wood work. He had made the passage offshore to Maine on several occasions over the years.

With talent like this, what could possibly go wrong?

Chapter 90: Man the Pumps

The boats sinking! My inner alarm went off when Jennifer called out, "Water's coming up over the floor boards."

We were on *Zillah*, a fifty-year-old classic wooden boat, half way between Cape May at the southern end of New Jersey and Cuttyhunk off Cape Cod, 150 miles off shore from Long Island.

I listened for the whirring sound of the automatic battery powered bilge pump but heard nothing. There was a manual switch. I pulled it but still no response. The water continued to rise.

I knew of other old boats that had foundered at sea and began to figure out what we needed to do to save ourselves. My survival gear was limited. There was an aged life raft secured to the fore deck that came with the boat. It had not been inspected in ten years. We could crowd into the inflatable dinghy and attach the outboard motor. But how far could we get on a gallon of gas?

Put out a Mayday appeal! But the boat VHF radio had only a five foot antenna mounted on the stern rail, probably a range of ten miles or less, Ray's hand-held less than that.

Water. But what could we carry it in? Think. Don't panic. Dig out the life jackets.

Jennifer was more focused. "Where's the manual bilge pump?"

I rifled through the bosun's locker aft, and found it buried beneath coils of rope. She began to pump. But the outlet hose was too short to reach the deck.

"I'll need a bucket to relay," she said.

"Check the sea-cocks and thru-hull fittings," was Ray's first response. He went forward to the head, checked it and the galley outlet. Aft, I raised the hatch in the cockpit and I checked the deck drains and the engine. Everything was closed off except for the engine seawater cooling intake and exhaust outlet, and the outlet for the bilge pump.

The bilge pump could be back siphoning. The vented loop could be clogged," Ray said. "Either that or the hull could have sprung a leak somewhere under the water tanks where we can't see it."

Back siphoning? A vented loop? Clogged? I wasn't sure what he meant.

"Try closing the bilge seacock.". I did and all three fell to rotating on pumping and relaying the bucket. We pumped rapidly. The water level receded slowly. When the bilge was drained, Ray said, "Let's check to be sure." I opened the sea cock and water gushed back in. We'd located the problem. I closed it promptly.

So much for diagnosis. What about prognosis? Why wasn't the bilge pump working?

"Probably the electrical connection," Ray said.

To get at that we had to wrestle the pump head out from under the water tanks. It emerged slithery like a snake covered in slime, the head at the end of a five foot length of hose like a cobra. Ray checked for current. There was none. He replaced the corroded wire and the pump purred.

We stood four hour watches, so now at the beginning of each watch we opened the seacock, pumped for thirty seconds using the manual switch, then closed the seacock again.

Head down in the bilge, wrestling the unruly Rule 2000 snake back under the water tanks, Ray reached down and came back with a grease covered steel nut, the size of a walnut.

"What's this?" he asked.

"A nut," I said.

"I know that," he said. "But where's it from?"

He began to probe, checking the nuts that secured the engine mounts to the frame of the boat.

"They're loose," he said, and groped some more under the engine.

"One's missing. The engine must be vibrating itself off the boat frame."

Jennifer looked on silently. I felt the depth of my incompetence.

"You got a large Crescent wrench?" Ray asked. He replaced the missing nut and tightened the rest.

How long had this gone on? What would have happened if Ray had not discovered it? Sometimes consequences are so dreaded one doesn't want to talk about it. We didn't. But we did check the engine mount bolts on a daily basis.

The challenges of the sea were mild compared to the challenges of *Zilllah*. We found our way into Cuttyhunk through the fog which reduced visibility to 100 yards. Stepping ashore I felt I had a charmed life though my boat was bewitched. I would have thought that *Zillah,* the mother of Noah, would have her own magical charms to fend off misfortune.

Two nights later we anchored off Plymouth Rock, where the Pilgrims landed in 1615, feeling thankful for a safe day of sailing.

We arrived in Boston on Sunday, a Sunday in July when the sun shone in all its life affirming brilliance and the light afternoon breeze sent the lapping waves laughing. The whole of Boston seemed to have turned out to celebrate the glory of the day. There were jet skis, water skiers, kayakers and dinghy sailors, cruising yachts, people crowded the ferry boats just to be out on the water. A freighter cautiously inched its way through the milling masses, overhead low flying commercial jets approached Logan Airport across the bay. It was like carnival in Venice.

We maneuvered our way through the traffic, and had a sense of joining in the festivities. People complemented us on the beauty of *Zillah*. It was like a welcoming party.

I furled in the genoa and Ray and Jennifer dropped the main, and we motored for the jetty at the foot of the Customs House, where a Texaco fuel dock was indicated on our cruising guide.

The plan was to dock, refuel and drop Ray off so he could catch a train at South Station, which was within walking distance, to return to Washington. But we couldn't spot the Texaco sign. We hailed another yacht.

"It's been moved up to the Charles River," the skipper told us. We turned back into the harbor, slaloming through the traffic, then...

The engine died.

We'd run out of diesel. I'd not figured we would motor so much and had been reluctant to use the last five gallons in a jerry can tied on deck, in case of an emergency.

"Well, here's your emergency," Jennifer said.

We were in the middle of the harbor, water skiers, jet boats flying by, and no power.

"Run out the jib," Jennifer called out. Ray and I went forward to raise the main. So we too went Sunday afternoon sailing on the bay, like the rest of Boston.

I decanted the last five gallons into the fuel tank. Ray went below and loosened the fuel injectors to bleed the air from the fuel line. "Show me again how to do that," I asked Ray.

The fuel dock was in a narrow cramped space at a back-water marina, the wind blowing us on the pier. Ray brought us safely in. We refueled and motored back to the ferry dock near South Station.

"Well, I guess I earned my passage!" Ray grinned and we hugged farewell.

Jennifer and I motored across the bay and anchored off the Thompson Island Outward Bound Center, where we met old friends.

"Great to see you! Great boat! What are your plans?"

Chapter 91: Down East

"Wind south east five to fifteen miles per hour. Visibility less than a mile in drizzle and patchy fog. Clearing later," NOAA weather reported. Jennifer and I had arrived in Maine.

At anchor in Tenant's Harbor, *Zillah* rocked in the wake of passing boats we could not see, the lobstermen heading out. In the thick air voices carried from shore cut off from bodies. With the fog still thick in pockets our world was bound by the confines of the deck and the mast vanishing in the rigging aloft. We waited.

By mid-morning it began to lift and in the ebbing tide we motored past the rocky headland, high water darkly etched six feet above the flowing current. The wind swept pines above were a deep somber green, almost black in the subdued light.

Standing nervously at the wheel I felt the tug of water on the rudder pushing me subtly out of the channel.

"A little to port," Jennifer instructed.

Out in the open water, Jennifer unfurled the genoa, then went forward to raise the main. The sails filled in the light wind.

"You'll want to head for the Heron Island Lighthouse," she said.

Penobscot Bay was five miles across. All I could see was a shifting haze, perhaps a mile off, opaque, gray, bleak.

"What course do I sail?" I asked.

"There's the chart. Why don't you figure it out?" she replied, not wanting to deprive me of a learning opportunity.

Jennifer took the helm. I bent over the navigation table, ran a line back from Heron Point with the straight edge, subtracted the angle of declination. Or do you add it I wondered? "102 degrees."

"You sure?" Jennifer asked.

"I think I'm sure," I replied.

"Why don't you check it on the GPS?"

That was a whole new set of calculations. Figure out the latitude and the longitude of the lighthouse from the sides of the chart, program it into the computer, then punch, "GO TO HERON LT." And read. "94 degrees. At 4.1 nautical miles. Ground Speed 5.2 knots."

"Which is it?" Jennifer asked.

"94 degrees, I guess."

Jennifer was not satisfied with guess work.

Fortunately the fog cleared and I could set a line of sight course on it. "106 degrees," I said.

There must be something wrong with the compass," Jennifer said. She checked again with a hand held bearing compass. "95 degrees."

The sky cleared to the pale northern blue with wind swept elongated clouds, that swept over the hunched islands. The water was clear and half way across the bay a pair of dolphins cavorted in the bow wave. Sea birds clustered on the far shore, ducks, gannets, and ravenous seagulls, "the rats of the sea." A pair of osprey circled overhead. Lobsters, we were told, were making a dramatic come back and close to shore we dodged the pots. Seals dived in the lush beds of seaweed, then basked on the sun dried ledges.

"This is a whole new world of sailing," I told Jennifer. I was caught up in the richness of the seas, the austere beauty, the ruggedness of the land, a classic Romantic seascape, where harshness was an aesthetic standard.

But Jennifer kept pulling me back to geometry. "What's that point?" she asked, her arm outstretched.

I didn't know.

"You could figure it from the chart," she said, handing me the bearing compass.

"And that one," she pointed to another. This led to figuring out where we were by the convergence of two different back bearings, checking them with the GPS.

I was beginning to learn that sailing in Maine waters was more than trimming the jib, it was also a matter of piloting. The romance of the sea combined with the Euclidean precision of the navigator.

Not to discount the trimming of the jib. We rounded Vinalhaven Island and beat our way up the gut to the town, a working fishing community, increasingly becoming a town of summer vacation homes. The channel was narrow and both the wind and the tide were against us. I was ready to turn on the engine, in spite of the loose mounting bolts.

Not Jennifer. "Sail as close to the wind as you can," she said. She tightened down the main. "I'll handle the jib," she said.

We came what I thought to be perilously close to shore. "Don't turn yet! Give it another boat length.

"Now. Hard to lee," she said, and we went about. This was a passage she had made before. Across the sound was Hurricane Island, where fore several summers after she graduated from Yale, she had been an Outward Bound instructor. She was in her element with her latest student.

Another narrow passage where I thought we would again scrape the rocks brought us back out to Penobscot Bay and we headed back to the mainland, beating into a fifteen knot wind, waves crashing off the bow. Without being told I figured out the course for the Rockland Lighthouse, checked it with the GPS, and two hours later picked it up right where it was meant to be.

"One of the best days of sailing in my life," I told Jennifer as we slipped by the harbor entrance and anchored inside the gigantic sea wall.

Jennifer had to leave, to return to her job and her husband in Belgium.

"If you could only stay another week, you'd make a sailor out of me," I told her as she boarded the bus. There was so much more to say that was not said. I was going to miss her. Not only for the companionship, but also for the slight feeling of dread of sailing solo again.

Rockland was my base for the rest of the summer, my harbor of refuge. It was ideal.. The anchorage was well protected. It was also free. Down wind from the fish cannery, it was not as fashionable as Camden, the yachtsman's haven thirty miles down the coast. It was a working fishermen's harbor, with a well stocked chandlery, a full range of marine services including skilled craftsmen who knew wooden boats. It was the ferry boat terminus that serviced the offshore islands. Rockland had not been "discovered," yet.

Though the process of gentrification had begun. There was an excellent bookstore where you could buy any book on the New York Times Best Seller's list at 25 percent off. An art gallery had an outstanding collection of early American art and Andrew Wyeth paintings. He spent his summers near Tenant's Harbor. There was a movie theatre, where I saw my first movie in months, an Arnold Schwartzenegger production, so bad it was entertaining.

Zillah was in need of care. The process of entropy had taken its toll. The engine, which had vibrated off the frames, had to be remounted, the transom rebuilt, the genoa winches bases reinforced, the compass swung. I made a list of seven major jobs and another twenty-five minor ones. I began with cosmetics, scrubbing off the nicotine colored mustache from the bow, the last memento of the swamps cut through by the ICW.

"Joe, are you there?" The Liverpool accent was unmistakable. I came on deck and John Anderson along side, standing in a dingy. John was the boatwright who had restored *Zillah* earlier in the year. We had started north together in the spring and parted off Charleston, the last time I'd seen him. He was working now in a boatyard in Rockport, twenty miles down the coast, but later in the summer, he told me, he would be free to work on *Zillah*. We went ashore for dinner with Patti, his wife, and daughter, Kendal. It felt like family again.

The circle had been closed. The journey of 1500 miles, Florida to Maine, completed.

Chapter 92: Visiting Crew

I had experienced several extended periods of solitude in my life and valued the experience. At one time I had even fantasized sailing around the world alone. For the last six months I had put it to the test and discovered that I was not suited to the life of a hermit-on-the-sea. It was a moment of self-realization.

With Jennifer's leaving I had a sense of dread in continuing to sail alone.

"I am a lonely monk who walks through the world with a leaky umbrella," a Chinese sage once said. On overcast days with a light drizzle, I began to feel the same.

I needed to re-engage, say hello to the world again.

There was a bank of pay phones at the ferry dock, new phones that worked, and I began to call friends.

"Hi. It's me. Just checking in…" Followed by an optimistic report on the weather. "Ya. It's nice and cool." And more on the rugged beauty of the Maine coast. "By the way, why don't you come sailing."

Most didn't. But several did.

First I had to prepare myself for guests.

On my regular walks to the chandlery I had to pass the barber shop. Twice. Going and coming. I hadn't had a hair cut in six months, since last December when I flew to Belgium for Jennifer and Johan's wedding.

"Pony tail doesn't really suit you, Dad," Jennifer had said before she left.

But once Samson shorn, I looked at myself in the store windows as I passed and felt at a loss. I missed the long tufts that stuck out from my peak cap, like the horns on a Viking helmet. But I was ready to host visiting crew.

Friends from Boston, Helen and Jenny, were first. Helen and I had worked together with Expeditionary Learning Outward Bound (ELOB) in Boston. She was a former course director at HIOBS, knew the area well and loved to teach.

"Every journey begins with a single step, and the first step on any voyage is to plot your course." She picked up where Jennifer left off. Before setting out we wrote down each step of our route, the distance between each way point, the bearing between way points and an estimate of the time it would take, like a check list.

My learning curve shot up and with increased precision I developed the confidence to navigate narrow channels between island and poke into hidden bays and remote coves. In Winter Harbor on Vinalhaven Island we anchored in a deep-water fiord between rocky ledges, less than a boat length from the bare granite shore.

The two women also instituted Outward Bound rituals to life on *Zillah*, an early morning swim with the seals, and a sunset jogging hike on shore.

The sun rose with an ominous orange glow, filtering through the lacey mist.

"Red in morning. Sailors warning." I should have known something was awry the day Joan Welsh, joined me for a day sail. She was an old friend from the Colorado Outward Bound School, now the director of HIOBS, like myself a late comer to deep water sailing.

We were four miles offshore when the wall enveloped us. The wind died. It was like staring at a blank billboard. I strained my eyes staring into the emptiness seeking anything I could see that would give me some assurance. I spotted a line of lobster pots.

"Have you sailed in the fog before?" she asked

In a world deprived of sight we were alerted by sound. Off in the distance there was the low mournful bellow of the Owl Head Lighthouse.

I put my primitive fog horn and blew a feeble blast that left me feeling a bit ridiculous. It was like celebrating New Year's Eve before the alcohol had kicked in.

There was a response, another horn from astern, and the low pounding of a diesel engine as a lobster boat thudded by.

Then I heard the more urgent high pitched challenge of the ferry's horn in the distance.

But how distant?

We were in the path of the island ferry.

"Securite! Securite!" I shouted into the VHF radio. I gave our position, speed and direction, and asked for confirmation that he heard me.

"Yes. We see you on our radar," the ferry replied.

It continued to sound its horn every few minutes. We listened intently as it drew closer. Ten minutes we heard it pass but never did see it.

With GPS we set a course for the Rockland Harbor Lighthouse, and an hour later burst into daylight. Colors never seemed so vivid and vibrant.

"I don't think this is working out for me." Kate was the mother of a young Outward Bound friend. The weather had exceeded he dismal NOAA promise, "Drizzle and patchy fog." It poured. The deck leaked. Her bunk got wet. We had anchored in a narrow cove. I was anxious that we might drag and in the middle of the night had moved the boat to a more secure location, disturbing her more.

I gave her my dry bunk, put on my foul weather gear and slept in her bunk.

"I want you to take me back," Kate said over breakfast. Through rain, fog, gusting winds I got us back safely to Rockland. I took the blame for the weather, apologized for the inadequacies of my boat, and was chagrined at being such a graceless host.

But I was smugly proud of my recently acquired navigation skills.

Canadian friends, Don and Ursula Shaw came for a week. Don and I had attended St. Andrew's College, a prep school, together fifty two years before.

They were world travelers who had sailed off Bora Bora and Tahiti, the coast of Turkey, boated down the Yangste River in China. But *Zillah* was in a different class and were it not for Dramamine it would have been an experience they would have chosen to forget.

Isle au Haut was first mapped by Samuel de Champlain, we Canadians know as the founder of Montreal in 1635. We hiked the towering cliffs that face the North Atlantic where the ocean swell crashes on the shore, cormorants dive and sea gulls scream.

Don claimed that he suffered from a sea food deficiency disorder, which, fortunately, he was able to cure with lobster, negotiated from passing lobster men, three nights out of five.

"I taught you to sail, you know," Andrea, my ex-wife, reminded me. She was suffering from early stages of Alzheimer's disease, but some things she did not forget. As a girl she has spent several summers on the coast of Maine, where her parents had rented a house on Naskeag Point and wrote learned books.

"I want to visit Schoodic Point," she said when she came on board. She couldn't remember what she had for breakfast, or where she had left her tooth brush, but she did remember the dramatic red granite sea cliffs where the deep swell of the Atlantic crashed on the high headland.

In Maine one looks inward, to land, as fishermen do. But at Schoodic one's sight is drawn outward, to the endless expanse of the open ocean.

"I want my ashes scattered here," she said. Six years later we did.

In late August I hauled *Zillah* at the *End of Journey Marina*. The name sounded more like a funeral home than a boat yard, but John Anderson came down from Rockport and remounted the engine of vibrator pads, reinforced the genoa the winches with large blocks of oak under the deck, and rebuilt the transom. Working together we painted the topsides a glistening polyurethane white and added two coats of anti-fouling to the bottom. By Labor Day *Zillah* was resplendent, ready for a party.

"Join us in Long Cove." Peter Willauer had come by to invite us to a get-together. I dropped my anchor. Peter and his wife Betty, came alongside with *Eight Bells* and rafted up. Peter was the founding director of HIOBS, now retired. Other HIOBS veteran came in and by evening five boats were tied together, all hanging on my anchor. I felt they were very trusting, given my history of disasters. But silently I felt proud.

Betty organized a potluck. She managed the pasta. We dug into out liquor lockers, and it was like an Indian potlatch, a great celebration, most of all a celebration of Peter.

He was a survivor of melanoma. They'd given him the full treatment, chemo, surgery, radiation and he'd been told by his doctors, "We've done everything medicine can do for you. The only thing we can hope for now is a miracle."

"Well, we're into miracle," Betty told me. And ten years later Peter still sails, making annual passages between Maine and Bermuda and on to the Caribbean, and crosses the Atlantic in his high performance J-42 that makes seven knots to windward in nine knots of wind.

I felt that the lonely monk had begun to patch his umbrella.

439

Chapter 93: Turning South

It was the end of one voyage, the beginning of another. The GPS read: To Miami, 1307 miles.

The winds were light the next couple of days and we should have had a leisurely sail past Rogue Island, Ship's Stern Island, Cod's Head, Moose Head, Mistake Island, Black Head, names as raw and direct as the Maine coast. But it was far from leisurely. The less the wind, the harder Brian worked to tweek the last puff of push out of it.

"It will pick up off Schoodic," I assured him. And it did, with vengeance.

We were upwind of the gigantic cannery in Prospect Harbor when it began to blow. Before raising the anchor we put the first reef back in the sail. Had we listened to the weather report we might have put in the second reef as well.

The wind was out of the east blowing a steady 10-to-15-knots. Our course was south and we sailed on a reach, making 7.2 knots with the rail down and waves crashing over the bow and blowing off in spray. It was a exhilarating contrast to the variable winds of the previous days.

The wind increased to East 15-to-20. We furled the jib in to the shrouds and with the shortened sail still made 6.8 knots into pounding seas. It was like bouncing down a bumpy country road in an old pick up with stiff springs at 50 miles per hour, on the edge.

In an hour we rounded Schoodic Point. "Give it a wide berth, Brian," I said.

The waves surged high on the granite headland and sluiced back baring long tangles of seaweed that swirled on the slimy rock. We rounded the point and altered course to the south-west running downwind on a broad reach, mainsail swung out, but not so far as to blanket the jib.

The seas began to build up, six-foot waves sweeping in under the helm, tilting the boat forward and giving it a steady shove. But now there was also an intermittent 8-foot ocean swell from the south-east, that rolled it on our beam. I could see it coming and tried to take it on the stern quarter but could not turn too much for fear of back-winding the main and setting up a jibe. The boat heeled 20-degrees with each swell. When the following waves and the beam swell met they collided in an explosion of sea-water that sprayed across the foredeck.

The wind increased to 20-knots with higher gusts and *Zillah* became hard to steer.

"We should have put in a second reef," I said to Brian.

"Do you want me to put it in now?" he replied.

This wasn't something I had done before, under conditions like this, with the boat rolling in the swell, water coming over the deck. It would involve turning into the wind, sailing under the jib, lowering the main leaving the boom free to thrash about. I wasn't about to do it now. I felt we had enough on our hands.

"I think not," I said. "But you could bring the jib in a bit more." That involved my slacking the jib sheet, while steering at the helm, while Brian pulled in on the jib furling line. But that was not significant improvement either.

Then a particularly large swell swept in. I did not see it coming.

"Look out," David called out, and ducked.

I did not see it coming. The swell collided with the following seas and exploded in an explosion of sea-water and sprayed across the deck and into the cockpit. I had been too preoccupied to suit up in my foul weather gear and was drenched. The water off Maine this time of year was about 55-degrees. I was cold, soon shivering.

"I can't stand this for long before hypothermia sets in," I thought. "Brian, would you take the helm?" He'd had the foresight to suit up earlier. Fisherman's genes, I thought.

I went below where I was tossed about as the boat pounded in the waves and heeled in the swell, changed into dry clothes and suited up in foul weather gear, overalls and jacket, well zipped up. I was instantly warm, but began to feel nauseas with the heaving motion in the enclosed space. I rarely got seasick, never on *Zillah* and came on deck gasping for fresh air.

"What's the nearest harbor of refuge?" I asked Brian.

"On this tack we could pick up Long Island," he said. We'd spent a night there on the eastbound journey and knew it to have good protection.

"How far is that?" I asked.

"About twenty-miles."

That would be another three or four hours. I'd be hypothermic by then.

"Nothing closer?" I asked.

"Baker Island is less than ten miles," he said. "But I don't think there's a good anchorage there. From there we could go to the Cranberry Islands."

We sailed on for another hour. It began to rain, visibility reduced to a mile. We steered by compass and GPS, checking one against the other. Our next waypoint was the lighthouse on Baker Island, 105-feet high, flashing every 10 seconds.

"See the island?" I asked Brian.

"What island?"

Gradually a darkened shape emerged out of the mist. The GPS confirmed that it was Baker Island. And there was the lighthouse. I felt the confidence of knowing where I was.

"Precisely where you are," recalling Jennifer's edict.

"I think we ought to head in," I said to Brian. I was still feeling nauseous.

"But there's no anchorage shown on Baker Island," Brian objected.

"No, but we could make for the Cranberry Islands where there's plenty of shelter."

We go about 230-degrees to avoid a jibe, and for an endless moment wallow lifelessly in the trough between 8-and-10-foot waves, and the boat picks up again on a beam reach.

To do so we would have to change course, either jibe or go about.. The fastest way would be to jibe by turning the stern to the wind and letting the sails swing from one side of the boat to the other. But it could also be dangerous. I had capsized on many occasions in dinghies attempting the maneuver. Big boats were known to snap their masts in uncontrolled unintentional jibes when the boom swung wildly across.

To go about when running down wind involved turning back into the wind, pulling in main and jib until the wind had crossed the bow, then letting out again, 270-degrees and picking up the next course downwind on the opposite tack.

"Let's jibe!" Brian said.

He would.

With an experienced crew it was the logical thing to do. I was tempted. But we had never done it before. Did it make sense to practice it under these conditions?

"We'll go about," I said. "You bring the jib across. I can handle the main from the helm."

We skirted the east shore of Baker Island and an hour later rounded up into Gilby Thoroughfare and the wind slowly subsided and the ocean swell was now blocked by the islands. We picked up the harbor channel buoys and anchored among the lobster boats.

"No lobstering today," Brian said as he dropped the anchor. We furled the main. Coiled the sheets. Cooked up bean soup for lunch. And waited for the adrenalin to subside.

We laid over for two days to let the storm pass.

On shore, and I have an eerie flash of recognition. I'd been here before. In the fall of 1958, 36 years before, I had sheltered in this same bay with my friend Ray Hartjen, my wife Andrea and Lane Johnson. We were celebrating the end of a summer season working at a camp in inland Maine with a five day "cruise" in a 19-foot, open deck sail boat, a Lightning, camping on beaches each night. We had come into Cranberry Island before a storm then too. It was one of those moments where I felt that life was a cyclical process, not just chronological or linear, a process of rediscovery, of reinventing myself

Four days later in Rockland, I received a fax from Jennifer. She proposed meeting me with her husband, Johan, in Miami, in early December to spend three weeks cruising in the Bahamas.

A winter strategy was beginning to take shape. I had a plan.

Chapter 94: The Nor'easter

It was the first nor'easter of the season. "The coastal marine forecast from Eastport, Maine to the Merrimac River and out 25 nautical miles. A storm warning is in effect. Monday, winds north-east 30 to 40 miles per hour. More at night, 40 to 50 miles per hour predicted. Seas 12 to 20 feet offshore. Tuesday, wind will shift to the north 15 to 30." We listened again to the NOAA report. I wanted to make sure I heard it right. I'd never been out in 40 knot winds. Do we run for Rockland now to get in before the storm?

"It will be a down-wind run from Pulpit Harbor," Peter said. "Your boat could handle it better than mine." My mentor subtly urged me on. I'm anxious but appreciate the note of confidence.

I look at Scott. He and his wife Hannah have come to sail with me over the Labor Day weekend, but have to be back at work Tuesday. He's a windsurfer and seems eager to experience the storm.

"Pulpit Harbor is a hurricane hole," Peter told me. "You'll be all right there." I threaded my way into the serpentine channel. The sun was setting over the Camden Hills on the mainland, ten miles to the west, a deep outrageous orange, flaming red, alpine glow deep purple, the gathering storm afire. The pine trees on the headland were silhouetted against the glow as we sailed in just before dusk.

"We'll wear life jackets and safety harnesses tomorrow," I told Scott and Hannah, as I foraged for them in the quarter berth. Before it is too dark, we worked together to put a second reef in the mainsail. That reduced its area by half. I'd never sailed with a double reefed main before. Then I ran a safety line along each deck from bow to stern. Should one of us have to go forward on the deck during the storm, we could clip into it with the tether on our harness. It was an added protection against the possibility of being swept over board. I stowed gear safely below, then programmed the GPS.

I was awakened at 2:30 a.m. with the tugging of the boat on the anchor chain. I could hear the wind soughing through the pine trees on the headland, though we were protected in the tight little harbor. Not able to sleep I went on deck, checked the knots on the safety line and the reefing points on the sail. I first light I turned out again and heated water for tea.

The main sail flogged furiously as we raised it when still at anchor. We motored out the narrow channel. The tide created a curious chop and sweeping eddies set us near the rocky ledge. At the entrance we met up with another boat. They seemed to be in difficulty.

"They're turning around," Scott called out. "Heading back in."

Should I do the same? I wondered. The open water of the bay was a maelstrom of churning waves, the tops blown off in a swirling foam. If this were coming on shore, I would turn back, I thought. But its blowing offshore.

We cleared Pulpit Rock with the huge osprey nest perched on top. Even the osprey had fled. I pointed the bow at 268 degrees.

"Let out the main sheet," I called to Hannah, and the sail filled.

"Now pull out the genoa sheet. Gently."

"Scott, keep a tight grip on the furling line. We don't want it to go out too far."

"Shut the engine down."

And *Zillah* merged with the full force of the storm.

The waves rolled down Penobscot Bay, 6-feet high, short inshore waves with a steep front that smacked the boat on the starboard quarter. Occasionally a higher wave would splash over the rail, shove the stern around and then be blown away in spray.

The wind blew a steady 30 knots was my best guess. I had no anemometer. I could hear stronger gusts coming. It was like approaching a waterfall, a low hissing growl, blowing off the tops of the waves. *Zillah* heeled under the strain, and began to nose up into the wind as she was overpowered, luffing wildly as wind spilled from the sails.

"It's like dingy sailing," I told Scott, as I struggled to bring the helm down.

"What course are you steering?" he asked.

"Something between 250 degrees and 290 degrees," I said, taking a quick glance at the compass. Slowly *Zillah* came back on course as the squall blew through.

"See if you can shorten the jib." I explained that Hannah would have to slack the jib sheet without letting it get away from her. Scott would have to have to pull in on the furling line. I wasn't sure it would help. What I really wanted was less main. But there was no way we were going to take another reef under these conditions. We would brave on. Rain was now blowing horizontal across the water. Visibility was less than a quarter of a mile. Were we holding our course? Would Rockland appear out of the gray watery murk?

Half way across the bay we spotted a smaller 30-foot boat, sails down, under engine power bouncing and wallowing in the choppy swell. We altered course to come within hailing distance, but there was no way we could be heard over the basso bellowing of the gale. We passed by feeling slightly embarrassed as we waved.

The lighthouse at the end of the breakwater at the entrance to Rockland harbor emerged through the mist. My navigation was right on. Waves crashed high on the outer wall and spray flew over the top. The wind scooped down over the land but inside the harbor the wave action was only a light chop. We picked up a mooring ball without difficulty and prepared to go ashore.

The dingy became airborne as we raised it off the foredeck, trying to lower it into the water. Wearing life jackets and foul weather gear we motored through the chop to shore.

I returned to the boat to wait out the storm at anchor. The waiting game was almost worse than the challenge of the open water. The halyards eat a furious tattoo on the aluminum mast, no matter how I tightened them. Eventually I tied them with bungee cord to the shrouds. The wind through the rigging gave an owlish hoo, sighing and moaning, with the changing pitch. The buoy from a lobster pot dragged under the hull and thudded sporadically, like someone knocking on a door down a distant hall.

What about the mooring line? *Zillah* tugged vigorously. I went on deck to check for chafe. I noticed another boat nearby tied to two mooring balls. What did he know that I didn't.

I made myself as comfortable as possible. Water dripped through the deck and I rigged a platic tarp over my bunk to keep it dry. I lit the hurricane lantern, for the light and the illusion of warmth. A can of soup and crackers for lunch. Nap. Read another chapter of Moby Dick. Then I began a letter to Jennifer and Margaret who would understand the joys of misery, its spiritual purity.

"A boat is certainly an improvement over a mountain tent," I wrote. "I'm getting a feel for this life. Next year at this time I hope to write you from Europe."

But I haven't been to Canada yet.

Chapter 95: Beyond Schoodic

"Beyond Mt. Desert and Schoodic Point lies a green, lonesome land of ragged islands, rocky reaches, swift Fundy currents, and ever increasing tidal stages,...an exciting, even dangerous coast, ...this is an area for the experienced skipper or the wary neophyte...." Henry Taft wrote in *The Cruising Guide to Maine*. "The best guide book is experience. You'll need practical navigational know-how, a thorough knowledge of your boat and how she acts under all weather conditions."

I knew Taft from when he was the president of Outward Bound USA, and understood him for a man not to exaggerate. I felt myself to be his wary neophyte, and it was with great trepidation that I left Schoodic Point to port, and catching the brisk south-west wind drove on into the unknown, toward Canadian waters.

We were two. Brian Sullivan, a Canadian in his early thirties, taking an extended leave from a career as a computer technician from the University of Ottawa. He was a vigorous, robust man and I was appreciative of the added strength in handling lines. A friend of my daughter Margaret he had responded to my appeal for crew. If things worked out, he would sail with me to Florida.

Though inexperienced as a sailor, he was born in Newfoundland and came with a maritime heritage. He'd grown up around small boats and handled the helm well. Technically competent, he was quick to learn all I could teach him about navigation. He knew more about engines than I did. He read the book on sail trim and soon became the self-proclaimed expert on tightening and letting out jib and main.

We departed from Hurricane Island where we had been invited to a ceremony celebrating the thirtieth anniversary of the founding of the Hurricane Island Outward Bound School in honor of my friend Peter.

"There'll be less fog this time of years," were his words of encouragement as he saw us off. "And no mosquitos."

We left in the rain, which marked it as an authentic Maine sailing experience. But the blue sky broke through the low lying cloud as we beat our way to windward in a

light north-east breeze, and emerged into a sparkling clear fall day.

The open Atlantic swell broke on the rugged rocky shore, but we were blind to its beauty, awed to the point of anxiety, scanning each approaching island warily. There were few navigational aids and we checked and rechecked our bearings as we advanced on the next headland. Petit Manon, Great Wass Island, Cross Island. (Get crusty down east names.) And double checked again.

In the light winds, Brian now our expert on sail trim, said, "Why don't we let out the single reef." I rarely did this as I felt it overpowered the boat and was difficult to handle when the wind came up. It increased the sail area by one third, and we picked up an additional knot. When the wind clocked to the south-west we tried sailing wing-and-wing, the main full out to starboard, the jib to port. It was an interesting exercise, but with the persistent ocean swell the jib would collapse and the main flog. We reverted to tacking downwind at a sober four knots.

It always baffled me that we sailed faster reaching to windward that we did running downwind. Brian explained the physics to me but I was still mystified.

On our third day out we picked up the entrance buoy for Cutler Harbor. But looking toward shore all I saw was an impregnable wall of rock, sixty-feet high topped with stunted pines.

"Watch where the lobster boat goes in," Brian pointed as it ducked behind a headland and disappeared. We entered between solid walls of granite that open up to a village of clapboard houses clinging to the hillside. We anchored at the edge of the working boats. "Be sure to give it plenty of scope," I called to Brian on the bow. "There's a 25-foot tide."

"A Bay of Fundy tide," he replied.

When we left in the morning we were caught bucking a swirling current of the incoming tide that tossed *Zillah* from side to side. At times I thought we'd be swept up on the steep fiord walls. At full throttle we made less than three knots fighting into it.

Once free of the harbor we tacked to windward in a light nor'east 10-knot wind, making 7.6-knots being swept into the Bay of Fundy.

Our destination waypoint was G "1" Fl.G 4 s. off West Quoddy Head. Thirteen miles upwind, it was the north-east point of the United States coast. We rounded the marker at 11:15 a.m. and sailed across the invisible boundary between American and Canadian waters.

"Welcome back to Canada," Brian said, and brought out a bottle of rum, Canadian rum. "I know we don't drink when at sea," he said, not at all apologetic. "But there are certain moments that should be commemorated." I noticed the bottle was half empty. What other commemorations had there been? He poured us each a tot.

The GPS read, To Miami. 1307 nm.

"Let's toast *Zillah*," I said. "To the end of one journey. And the beginning of another.

I turned south and sailed down the coast of Grand Manon Island in Canadian waters.

"Yes. I've sailed from Canada," I should be able to reply, should anyone ask.

Chapter 96: Bahama Passage

"Another day in Paradise," Johann said. We dropped the mooring ball at Warderick Wells Cay at first light and motored out the cut to the deep blue water of Exuma Sound. The sun broke through the cloud on the eastern horizon in long incandescent rays as if announcing the Second Coming.

The wind was light ENE 5-to-10 knots, so we motor sailed south along the Exuma Chain; Hall's Cay, Soldier's Cay, O'Brian Cay, checking them off on the chart. There were no navigational aids, few distinguishing features, the islands low, flat, palm trees etched on the horizon, 60-feet being a distinctive high point. Most were uninhabited. There was a wide expanse of sky with wind blown cumulus cloud, lines of rain squalls caught the morning sun.

"They all look alike," I told Jennifer. I was having difficulty telling where we were by line of sight.

"Yes. But they're beautiful in their own way," she said, taking a sighting with the bearing compass.

Johann spotted the masts of three yachts behind the dune. "That must be Little Bell Cay," he said. We confirmed the location on GPS, jibed over and headed in. We anchored in the small harbor in 18-feet, the water so clear I could see the anchor firmly dug into the sand. The tide raced from the shallow banks that stretch for miles to the deeper channel, flowing at 3-knots. We had learned to set a second anchor down current so when the tide turned the boat did not swing on wide arc of the full anchor rode, ut merely spun on its bow.

The cruising guide identified a sea cave the Johann and Jennifer, both experienced spelunkers, were interested in exploring. This was something new to me. I dreaded caves and found the idea intimidating. I was beyond the age of doing things just because they scared me. "I'll be the designated dinghy driver," I said.

The bluff of coral rock rose the height of a medium sized house straight out of the sea. A 3-foot sea was running and crashed with a 5-foot wave along the foot of the cliff. The entrance to the cave appeared as a dark hole about the size of a wide door. To me it appeared dangerous. But I had spent my life encouraging my children, and other people's children, to take risks. Sensible risks, I reminded myself. I said nothing.

Johann put on face plate, snorkel and fins and slipped overboard. He treaded water as a series of waves came by, then ducked, swimming hard caught a wave and surfed right into the hole.

"It's really quite straight forward," he said minutes later, as he was flushed back out. Jennifer went next and returned to give me a second opinion. The trick was to catch the ingoing swell and not the out flowing drain, and I entered another world.

There was a sense of returning to a gigantic womb. Inside was a domed cavern the size of a small bedroom, lit from a skylight above with a diffused glow. Short dagger length stalagmites hung from the ceiling and in the right light sparkled like stars. There was the astringent smell of sea weed and salt spray, bracing like smelling salts. Our voices were amplified by the dome and the surge of the sea seemed to mutter indecipherable voices. There was a ledge along the sides where we sat, half out of the water.

"I guess you're wondering why I called this meeting?" I said above the gush of the tidal flow. The occasional wave would break all the way to the back of the cave, lifting us in unison, then settling us on the ledge again.

How do I get out without being scraped by the coral? I wondered

Jennifer went first. I hesitated, counting the next series of swells to be sure I got my timing right. I slipped off the ledge as the surge began to flow out, pushed off and kicked like my life depended on it, and like Jonah being vomited from the mouth of the whale, I rode the wave out into the sunlight and the brightness of day.

Johann spotted another cave, a lower entrance, requiring a shallow dive to enter. "It's even more spectacular," he assured me.

"I'm sure it is," I complemented him, but contented myself to snorkeling along the coral reef, and when I got cold to crawl back into the dinghy and warm myself in the sun. I was no Jacques Cousteau, I realized, even though he had endorsed the elegant web footed flippers I wore.

Across the channel a line of "coral pillars" were indicated on the chart. We were not successful locating them, but drifted with the ebbing tide along a coral ledge. It was a self-conducted tour of our private aquatic park, pink fan coral, light brown brain coral, twisted coral stems, basket shapes, hollow pipes, purple, yellow, blue, gray, brown, and multicolored fish, blue fingerlings, parrot fish, brilliant green, spotted yellow and red, nibbling on the coral with their bird beaks, yellow sunfish. I gazed in amazement, the only sound my breathing through the snorkel pipe, a primitive sound in the halls of the deep.

Cold again, for the wind has been blowing from the north east for several days, we climb into the dinghy and soak in the warmth of the sun. Returning to the boat we have a late afternoon lunch, nap, Jennifer studies French, the second official language of Belgium, where she lives. Johann reads Boorsteen, *The Discoverers,* the chapter on Columbus. I drill corroded screws from the broken starboard handrail until I break the bits, then epoxy new screws in, working into the early dark.

"It's too late for a sundowner," I tell the crew, "but perfect timing for a moon-riser." We sip rum and grapefruit juice as the moon rises over the low lying coral ridge to the east, the full moon of December.

We talk of the mystery of life, the wonder at being alive and on a yacht on a tropical night in the Bahamas, the outrageous beauty of it and how fortunate we are. Orion rises over the horizon followed by Sirius, the Dog Star.

We were drawing near the end of our voyage. The next day would bring us 25-miles closer to Georgetown where Jennifer and Johann would catch their plane in four days. That seemed to give enough leeway, even for me with my phobia about missing buses, and trains, and planes.

I was also unresolved about my own plans. Though I had gained great confidence in my sailing competence while in Maine, I'd been shaken by Tropical Storm Gordon, anxious crossing the banks in the Bahamas in shallow water only 8-to-10 feet deep, less than a foot of water under the keel, the water so clear I became fixated with the bottom, coral heads, sand bars. There were few navigational aids, none you could rely on. I had begun to develop a color coded system of assessing the depth of the water, deep blue over 30-feet, turquoise over 15-feet, yellow ten, and brown, turn back if it's not too late.

This was to say nothing of *Zillah's* continuing quirks. There was still water leaking somewhere. The stuffing box? I tightened the screw and greased it liberally. The propeller shaft? I wasn't sure what I could do there? Or was it merely rain water that still worked its way through the deck seams? Wherever it was coming from, every two hours the automatic bilge pump whined into motion. And the bilge pump continued to back siphon.

Georgetown could be a decisive moment. But back in blue water the last couple days, I'd begun to feel more confident.

Little Farmer's Cay was 35-miles from Georgetown. We entered the cut against a strong ebb tide. Four yachts were anchored in the shelter of the coral reef, protected from the NE wind. We headed to the opposite side of the bay, and promptly ran aground. The first of many mishaps.

The tide continued to run for another hour and a half, then turned. By early evening we were afloat again with the tide flowing swiftly in the opposite direction. I motored up to avoid being swept further on to the bar, and moved closer to shore seeking a deeper channel. Johann dropped the 50 pound fisherman's anchor. It didn't hold. I circled back up into the current and tried again. This time it held. We now deployed the second anchor, the 45 pound Danforth. In the dark, the lines fouled and in the process of untangling them the line ran out and fell overboard. With two of us on the foredeck, neither of us had cleated it off.

Johann offered to dive for it, but in the dark with a running current that did not seem like a good idea. So we shackled the 35 pound CQR plow anchor to another line, rowed it out in the dinghy and dropped it down current, hoping it would hold in the turn of the tide.

"Georgetown Harbour is closed." We were listening to the early morning Georgetown amateur radio net with its weather report, local gossip and rumor mill.

"On Sunday an incoming yacht in the east entrance, broached to and was dis-masted in a 15-foot swell. The crew, thrown overboard, were held by their safety harness and washed back on board. There were no serious injuries. Boaters should exercise caution." There followed a heated discussion about whether the harbor was indeed closed. "Winds will increase to 15-to-20 knots out of the NE, with 4-to-6 foot seas. Boats planning to enter should do so two hours before the high tide."

There could be stormy weather, even in paradise.

Gambling on good conditions we decided to move on. Johann retrieved the lost anchor. I needed full throttle, 2200 rpms to buck the incoming tide, beating our way through 6-foot waves, slamming the starboard bow. A half mile off shore in blue water I expected it to subside. It didn't.

"The latest weather report predicts winds to increase, east, 25-to-30. 6-to-9 foot seas," Jennifer had monitored the U.S. Weather Bureau off shore report.

"Jenny, I don't think this is a good idea," I said, as the seas continued to pound on the bow.

"Nor do I," she said. We turned back.

This time we anchored on the east side of the harbor among the four other boats. It was a bit tight, but we were protected from the NE wind. That night the wind backed and blew NW 30 knots, a near gale. We were now being blown on to a lee shore.

In the middle of the night, Tannawaha, a boat with a Canadian family, husband, wife and two children, began to drag down wind from us. Motoring up to reset their anchor they ran afoul of the anchor line of Sheban Gold, a British couple, and wrapped their line around their propeller. They spent the rest of the night diving in the dark to free the propeller.

We had come alongside a 40-foot cabin cruiser, Helen K, but as the boats swung it lay directly ahead, a boat length off the bow, sitting over our anchor. We sat out the night keeping an anchor watch, prepared to motor up should we drag, or should Helen K drag down on us.

Noon the next day, Aura, a sleek aluminum boat from Annapolis with Eric and Mary came in under sail and anchored in mid-bay. They too were in distress. They had blown a gasket and sea water was coming into the diesel engine through the sea water cooling system, and they had lost power.

The storm lasted four days. Jennifer and Johann had to charter an air taxi to catch their plane in Georgetown. Johann cooked up a farewell banquet, snapper and fried potatoes, champagne, a gift sent by his parents, and Christmas cake that I'd bought at Sam's Club in Ft. Lauderdale. Next morning in the blowing rain I saw them to the landing strip, and as they left I felt I was being marooned on a desert island. The last I saw of Jennifer was a face peering from a cabin window, 100-feet in the air, flying away at 100 mph, as the plane gained height and disappeared in a resonant hum into the distance. I wiped rain and tears from my cheeks.

The village of Little Farmer's Cay had one paved street, a row of painted concrete block houses, orange trees planted along the road, symbols of prosperity attributable to the past prosperity of the drug trade. Many houses were only half completed attributable to the DDA and the ensuing economic decline. The people were friendly.

A seafood restaurant was run by a Black Moslem. On the VHF radio he advertised a Christmas Eve festive dinner, lobster, fish served with macaroni and cheese, an island staple and Kalik beer, in spite of religious prohibition. All the cruisers came.

I sat next to Mary, the lady from Annapolis. I was discovering the social side of cruising.

With the first break in the weather boats left for Georgetown. *Aura* and *Zillah* were last. They had not engine. I had no crew.

They planned to leave with the outgoing tide, and I agreed to give them steering by shunting their stern with my rubber dinghy, like a tub boat. They had arranged by VHF to have Annapolis friends, who were already in Georgetown, meet them at the bar and tow them in.

I followed next day, motor sailing in light NW winds. Crossing the notorious bar was anti-climatic. I was anxious following the precise bearings of the narrow entrance channel and watched the depth sounder drop from 10-feet, to eight to seven. But as I made the final turn I motored across to Stocking Island and dropped the anchor in 17-feet of water over sand. The anchor held.

I had arrived. My first voyage off shore. But I was torn with indecision. Was this the end of the line? Or just the beginning? The end of the beginning? Or the beginning of the end?

Chapter 97: Georgetown Harbor

Georgetown is a large harbor, many small harbors in fact, at the southern end of the Exuma chain, 2 miles across, and in places as much as 7 miles long. When I arrived after Christmas, 1994, there were over 150 yachts tucked away in its various coves, boats shifting back and forth depending on the wind direction, but protected from the ocean swell in all directions. Only at the bar at the eastern entrance did waves break. Otherwise it was a land of clear blue turquoise waters, long stretches of sandy beach, scrubby trees. The pleasant laid back town of 500 souls, black, easy going Bahamians, catered to yachties, with low profile restaurants, bars, mini-market with American brand food items, fish market, telephones that worked with an AT&T card, and post office.

They advertised a barbeque twice a week on Volley Ball Beach, and at the Two Turtles Restaurant on Tuesday and Thursday nights. I joined the local lending library for two dollars, and also exchanged paper backs at the book swap section. Every morning on the VHF there was a harbor radio net, that gave a local weather report and analysis, announced daily events and degenerated to harbor gossip.

It was a place where cruisers had to decide. To stop and stay. To turn around and go back. To go on. It was the sort of place I could see, 10 years from now, putting down the anchor and "hanging out," or as one old gaffer said, "hanging on."

It had the reputation of being "chicken harbor," so many cruisers with great plans for going on to the Caribbean getting this far, and turning back. I was there two weeks hesitant about moving on. Did that make me a chicken?

I phoned my dwindling list of sailing friends, but in spite of all the allure of the islands I could entice none. A lady friend did agree to meet me in the British Virgin Islands in March. Maybe. I advertised for crew on the public notice board in town and on the daily radio net, but got no response. Do I continue on solo?

A second boat broached-to coming over the bar and the captain's wife went straight from the yacht to the airport and flew home. The damaged boat was up for sale.

Dinner conversation always turned to, "Where were you during Tropical Storm Gordon?" A Canadian friend on *Coconaut II* was caught in Marsh Harbor in the northern Bahamas and could not get off their boat for five days, praying that their anchor would not drag. Another crew were caught off North Carolina. No one expected Gordon to loop that far north. They lived off granola bars for a week. It was not seem to be a good season to be on the high seas. Not solo. Chicken.

Georgetown was nice. I kept meeting interesting people. A Yukon trapper and hunting guide who had come south to experience the winter and could not wait to get back to the frozen north. His wife was homesick for the isolation of the bush, four hours of sunlight and 40 below weather. I even met attractive women.

But most of my friends had moved on, including Mary and Eric on *Aura*.

But I had an excuse for not joining them. My mail, sent from Boston a month before with instruction to "Hold for Arrival," had not arrived. By mid-January did, having been sent first to Bermuda, in spite of being addressed to the Bahamas. Bermuda? Bahamas? I could imagine the U.S.Postal clerk being in a quandary. How did she know I would find Georgetown so pleasant?

Now I was confronted by my own indecision.

Decisions and revisions, which in a moment I reverse. T.S. Eliot wrote.

There was the anxiety. But deeper than than I began to realize that I needed to work out a viable philosophy that incorporated a concept of cruising and not just passage making. I was always wanting to be going somewhere. Annapolis. Boston. West Quoddy Head. Ft. Lauderdale. And now the Virgin Islands. And on to Trinidad? I'd been task oriented, goal oriented, future oriented, all my life.

I felt guilty just enjoying myself in Georgetown. But guilty because I wasn't doing anything useful or I wasn't going anywhere?

I found it difficult to live in the present...unless I was on the high seas! Then I was all there. And that was the great charm of it.

"Cruising is essentially an escape," I wrote in a letter to Jennifer and Margaret. "An escape to...or and escape from? That's the question. Like Huck and Jim on their raft going down the river."

But there was another escape that caught up with me in Georgetown, the lending library which I joined for two dollars. And I reveled in the escape into the fantasy of literature. I re-read *The Iliad* where Western literature began, and widely from authors like Toni Morrison to Agatha Christie. I hadn't enjoyed reading so much since being sick on returning from Guatemala two years before. It was a joy to be so engrossed, absorbed, relaxed, without being ill.

The waiting game. I came to an acceptance of the fact that whether I turned back or went on, I was not going to find crew. So I began to listen more carefully to the weather, both the U.S. National Weather Service and the local radio net's interpretation. The radio made it sound like a science. The interpretation was clearly an art. The three day forecast predicted a shift to the SE so I topped up with fuel and water, shopped for fresh fruit and vegetables. Another cruiser loaned me maps of the Dominican Republic and Puerto Rico and I ran off copies in town.

As we shot out through the gut *Zillah* seemed to shake off the anxiety of sitting at anchor and the two of us rose to the prospect of blue water and the freedom of the seas.

Chapter 98: The Search for Crew

"I have several friends who would enjoy sailing with you."

"If only I could find somebody like that," I thought as rode my dinghy back to *Zillah*, Georgetown style, throttle full out, standing up as if water skiing, planing through the churning bow wave.

Mary and Henry Eric on *Aura* had had me over to dinner, pasta with pesto, salad, wine, a taste of civilization, a change from the Spartan bachelor fare of *Zillah*. We had talked of travels in Umbria, books. Eric was reading the latest translation of *The Iliad*, Fagel's. We listened to Mozart's 39th Symphony on digital CD disk with a high fidelity Sony sound system.

"How did the two of you meet?" I had asked. And Mary told me of S.O.S., Singles on Sailboats, a sailing club in Annapolis that brought unmarried people together. Henry was a retired engineer, a newcomer to sailing, and Mary a retired commercial real estate broker, an experienced blue water sailor, who had long had the dream of retiring to a sailboat and cruising. She had chartered on several occasion in the Caribbean. They had spent three years searching for a suitable boat, found Sirius, a 40 foot French designed center board sloop, build of aluminum, equipped it for cruising and took off the year before, in time to confront Tropical Storm Gordon in Florida.

When I mentioned that I was looking for crew, preferably female, Mary perked up, "I have several friends who would enjoy sailing with you." The next day she was on the phone to Annapolis.

"Match maker, match maker, make me a match."

I continued to phone friends inviting them to join me, buddies in Maine, Boston, Connecticut, Port Tobacco, Ft. Lauderdale who sailed, and a young woman in Holland, I had met in Guatemala, two years before.

Gladys, a woman I had been introduced to in Cambden, Maine said she would join me in the Virgin Islands. She was a Coast Guard licensed small boat captain, and I was hopeful of a longer tour of duty. "A foot and a half of snow had fallen that week," she said. "It will be great to see the sun again,"

Other friends held out the possibility of joining me later, further down the Caribbean chain.

My cruising friends left Georgetown in convoy, Cursail from Scituate, Massachusetts, the two Canadian boats, *Coconaut II and Uliad*, *Avatar* from San Francisco, among them *Aura*. I was still waiting for mail and once it arrived, I made last minute phone calls, topped up with diesel fuel and water, laid in fresh rations, and hurried to catch up.

Waking at 5:00 a.m., I raised anchor at first light and motored out of the harbor behind *Hugenot*. It was too early to catch the Georgetown radio net weather report, but by my own observations it promised to be a good day of sailing, wind SE 15 knots, seas 3 feet, a steady swell from the east. Close hauled to the wind *Zillah* made 5 knots. If I fell off a little, I made 6-to-7 knots, but this would require an extra tack to make Cape Santa Maria, at the tip of Long Island. My ETA was 1:00 p.m., I figured.

The anxiety of maneuvering my way through the coral heads out of the harbor behind me, the freedom of the seas before me, I was exhilarated to be under sail again. . I raised the main and pulled out the jib. "Benedictus, qui vene in nomine Domine. Blessed is he who goes in the way of the Lord." I sang as I stood the helm and coaxed *Zillah* closer to the wind.

Mid-morning the wind backed and increased to 20 knots. Waves began to break over the bow, pushing me off course. The anchor which had been secured to the pulpit came loose and I had to go forward to secure it, getting soaked in the process. The ocean swell was now 5 feet high, and my speed to windward dropped to 4 knots.

I checked my position on the GPS. I wasn't going to make Cape Santa Maria on this course. Do I go on? The wind was now a steady 20 knots and gusting, white caps everywhere, a 6 foot swell out of the east, right on the bow. I turned back for Georgetown.

Running down wind *Zillah* surged through the waves, the stern lifted high in the swell, the horizon disappearing as I sank in the trough. I searched the horizon for recognizable landmarks, the two houses on the hillside that line up with the channel buoys. Will the waves be breaking over the bar? Three weeks earlier a boat broached-to and was dismasted at the entrance. I turned on the engine as a precaution, letting it idle.

Turning for the harbor channel, the seas were on the beam. A large breaking wave surged in, I turned into it, and *Zillah* slid through. Would it have been better to take it stern-to? But I was already across the bar.

I put the engine in gear, pulled in the main and motor sailed across to my former anchorage, and nestled in behind *Hugenot*, who had already returned.

The wind eventually shifted to the north west and blew a gale with 40-to-45 knot winds for the next three days. I was too late to seek the sheltered side of the harbor, and clung the lee shore of Stocking Island with three anchors down, resetting with each shift of the wind. It was too stormy to cross the wide open bay by dinghy so I spend the next three days ship bound, re-fighting the Trojan war in Eric's copy of *The Iliad*.

Aura meanwhile was caught by the same storm off a lee shore on Rum Cay. The Summer Point Marina offered good protection but the entrance twisted through a narrow channel between reefs. The marina contacted Aura by radio and offered to send a pilot out to bring the boat through. But *Aura's* engine had faltered again, in spite of recent repairs in Georgetown. Eric opted to stay at anchor offshore. The storm intensified and for two days they endured the pitching of the boat into heading seas, and rolling to the ocean swell sweeping down from the north. They put out a second anchor and prayed.

In the same storm, a hundred miles to the south east, *Cursail* with friends Frank and Denise from Siscuite, sheltering off Mayaguez, was struck by lightning, and all their radios and electronic equipment was destroyed.

Eventually we all met up again several days later in Luperon, Dominican Republic. It was the sort of small tropical town by the sea Graham Greene might describe, fish market, taverns and houses of questionable virtue along the main street from the water front. The mood was one of premonition as we exchanged war stories. We did what we could to make physical repairs to the boats and heel the psychic wounds of the crews. Henry was reluctant to speak of his experience.

The village was poor but friendly to cruisers. The markets were well stocked with tropical fruit, bananas, oranges, papayas and an assortment of exotic vegetables. Sue on *Coconaut II* celebrated her birthday. Mary baked a chocolate cake. I too was invited. A local restaurant invited cruisers to a fiesta pig roast, with lively music by a salsa band. I sat next to Mary and Eric. As we left I danced her through the crowd, across the floor to the door. She was a responsive dancer.

Santo Domingo, the capital of DR is on the south coast, a day's journey by local bus. A large contingent of cruisers went together. I wandered alone in the old city much of the time, visiting the cathedral, the art museum that had an interesting collection of classical Spanish paintings, and the beautifully restored former governor's mansion, built by Columbus's son Diego. In the evening we met over dinner.

The course from the Bahamas to the Virgin Islands at the north east corner of the Caribbean was nearly 700 miles, most of it to windward. Once we crossed the Tropic of Cancer, a couple days out of Georgetown, we were in a convergence zone, where the north west winds met the easterly trades. We tried to stage out moves with the following westerlies, or when the trade winds were down. It was pointless to beat into anything over east 15 knot. I joined *Aura* and *Cursail* as we beat our way to windward along the north coast of the Dominican Republic. At night we took advantage of the katabatic effect, wind blowing off the land 5-or-10 miles out to sea, and we made good progress. But by day it was a steady beat into persistent seas, tacking back and forth into waves that kept knocking us back. We also bucked against a one knot equatorial current.

It was a hushed night with bright stars and a thin sliver of the moon when I reached the eastern end of the island, warm and gloomy. I was exhausted from being at the helm for 48 hours, in a semi-hallucinatory state, when I heard deep chested breathing alongside. I could see nothing but heard this rhythmic inhaling and exhaling that pursued me persistently, as if waiting to spring its move. It was a terrifying sound, like being pursued in a dream, running as hard as I could, and not being able to get away. I felt I could feel its breath it was so close. I could smell it, hot and fetid.

Then I realized it was a whale.

But that didn't make me feel any better. I'd heard of whales attacking boats. I'd re-read *Moby Dick* earlier in the year.

"The eastern end of the Dominican Republic off Samana is one of the great breeding grounds for the gray whale," the lady captain of a whale watching boat informed me next day. "In a small boat its best to turn on your engine when they get too close. Just so they know who you are."

The Mona Passage between Puerto Rico and the DR is notorious for stormy crossings. The trade winds funnel through creating breaking waves over shoals. With the winds down, I had an easy crossing, motoring most of the way. Henry and Mary took a sight seeing tour to the rain forest, and crossing two days later, they were pounded. They too tried to motor against the adverse current but again their engine sputtered erratically. They caught up with the rest of us a couple days later, in Boqueron, on the south west corner of Puerto Rico, exhausted and disheartened.

Eric spent the next three days crouched over the engine with a local mechanic, sweating in swim trunks, covered in grease. "I've spent more time in the engine room than I have at the helm," he exaggerated. "Not my idea of cruising."

"Henry's thinking about returning to Annapolis," Mary came across to *Zillah* to tell me. "He's not enjoying the constant worry." I could see the disappointment written on her face. "I'd suggested he replace the engine. But he won't do it."

"The two of us have been planning this trip for three years. It was on my advice that he bought a boat like *Aura*." I listened patiently. What did she want of me? "If he does decide to go home, would you consider taking me on *Zillah*?"

I was stunned. Could she be serious, wanting to move from a modern classy yacht like *Aura* to an old wooden boat like *Zillah* with leaky decks? Mary did not seem like the Outward Bound type. She'd spent the past month trying to recruit one of her S.O.S. friends for me. I was still calling friends .I mentioned that Gladys from Camden was to meet me in Tortola.

"Why sure," I said, somewhat non-committal. Later I regretted my cold response. I did not appreciate that it was February 14, Valentine's Day, 1995. I'd missed my chance.

The next couple of weeks were tortuous days of indecision. Eric was determined to return to Annapolis and sell the boat. Mary was determined to continue cruising, but she did not feel she could abandon Eric before he found crew to take the boat home. I tried to stay out of it, but met up with them as we cruised along the south coast of PR. Then Eric reconsidered, had a change of mind and Mary agreed to stay on. But it was clear that there had been a breach of faith.

I continued to phone my sailing friends.

I left them in Culebra, at the eastern end of Puerto Rico, still not sure what the outcome would be, and sailed on to Tortola, in the British Virgin Islands. I anchored off Beef Island where the airport is located and picked up Gladys. We had a wonderful week of sailing. There was a low pressure ridge off Puerto Rico that deflected the Trade Winds from SE to NE and I was able to sail on a beam reach again. After beating to windward for two months it was like driving on a paved road again, after gravel county roads. *Zillah* cut through the Sir Francis Drake Passage making 7 knots. But Gladys left in a week. She was a large woman and recently had had knee surgery.

The confined quarters on *Zillah* aggravated the injury, she claimed. She was not an Outward Bound type either.

After she left, I sailed around to Road Town, the main city in the BVI to pick up mail, hoping for a letter from Mary. When I motored into the outer harbor, there were several boats on moorings, but only one at anchor. I looked more closely. Gray. Aluminum. Wind generator on the stern. American flag. It was *Aura*.

I crossed over to it in my dinghy and climbed aboard. The greetings were strained. Clearly *Aura* was not a happy ship.

"Will she or won't she? Try to be reasonable," I said to myself. "How could she leave a beautiful boat like this?"

Mary would be a wonderful sailing partner, if she came, an attractive, intelligent worldly woman, a more experienced sailor than I.

But I also liked Eric, admired him; well traveled, cultured, a gracious host.

They had treated me warmly and generously. I was embarrassed to be driving a wedge between them.

"I need to talk to you," Mary said. "Alone."

We took the dinghy back to *Zillah*.

"I've told Eric that I am joining your boat. But I'll stay on *Aura* until he can find crew. He had lots of friends in Annapolis who would be delighted to spend time sailing on his boat."

I'd been searching for crew. What I found was a captain and companion, and I became the deck hand on my own boat.

My boat?

Our boat. For the next eight years.

Joe in the Virgin Islands, 1995.

459

Chapter 99: Visitors

I was embarrassed.

We had spent a couple weeks making *Zillah* more livable. Todd, her son, was coming to sail with us for ten days with his fiancé Taffy.

Mary had insisted on feminine touches like curtains over the cabin windows. We had a foam lined mattress made up for the forward V-berth cabin. The corroded grate over the galley stove burners was replaced, the cupboards scrubbed out and lined with aluminum foil.

It's amazing what a little white paint will do. On a wooden boat the cabin walls are the inside of the hull. *Zillah* was a weathered teak, charming like an English pub, but also dark. Mary, an interior designer in a former life, suggested painting the ceiling and the walls from eye level and above, about one foot, white. The effect was to make the cabin appear twice as big and bright.

Caught up in the boat improvement project, I painted the confined space of the head a brilliant ship's enamel white. The effect was stunning, the Taj Mahal of heads.

As attractive as it was, it did little to improve the quality of the plumbing. A week before our guests arrived the head clogged and could not be made to flush. Not a preferred task, I dismantled it to find that a key valve had collapsed, broken off. Like *Zillah* herself, the head was of vintage heritage, something of an antique. The chandlery in St. Thomas did not have spare parts. Nor could I find a replacement unit.

Had I known Annapolis better I could have suggested they pick up a Henderson pump at West Marine, and bring it with them.

"On the pulling boats at the Hurricane Island Outward Bound School, they just use a bucket," I told Mary.

"Yes. But you keep forgetting Joe that this is not Outward Bound," she replied.

She found a toilet seat that fit over a bucket at a local hardware store and went to the bucket.

"But what about our company?" she asked.

"We'll have to upgrade the system," I said. "Two buckets."

Todd and Taffy took the announcement with resigned humor, too polite to complain.

The Virgin Islands are on of the world's great cruising grounds, fairly predictable trade winds, forty different islands with numerous bays and harbors of refuge, sheltered from the ocean swell of the open Atlantic. Our first day out, beating

460

to windward toward Christmas Island, I asked Todd if he'd like to take the helm. He'd sailed before with his mother and soon had to feel for it.

We were heading toward Blank Rock and I wondered when he would go about, wanting to leave the decision to him.

"Tell me when I should go about," he said.

"When do you think?" I replied, wanting to leave the decision to him.

"Now?" We were getting fairly close and the current was setting us down on the rock.

"Looks good," I said, trying to sound casual, and took hold of the jib sheet prepared to go about.

Nothing happened. We kept getting closer to Blank Rock.

"Todd, turn the helm to the left," I said directly, giving orders now, not making a suggestion.

Todd said nothing. The distance between *Zillah* and the rock drew closer.

"Hard left Todd," I said in a tone that clearly meant it.

"I am," Todd replied.

I jumped aft to the helm, turned the wheel left and it moved limply in my hands. The steering cable had broken.

The emergency tiller, a five foot steel pipe with a fitting that clamps directly on to the rudder head, was stowed in the bosun's locker. I dug it out from beneath ropes and ship's stores. "Must put this in a place where I can get at it easier," I told myself as I searched. Once in place the helm responded and we got back on course without mishap. For the rest of the week we steered by tiller, functional if somewhat more awkward. It was not the first time we had to resort of the emergency tiller.

Todd was apologetic, feeling he had done something wrong and damaged my boat. I was apologetic and more concerned about the impression I was making, what they would think of *Zillah* and the man his mother was entrusting her life to.

The week went well. They basked in the sun. We all snorkeled off the Baths. At night we chose anchorages with restaurants, showers and up-market plumbing. Mary was right. This was not Outward Bound.

But in the future we tried to screen visitors, mindful that sailing on *Zillah* could be an Outward Bound experience, intended or not.

Chapter 100: Creatures of the Deep

"Have you seen the white whale? Captain Ahab."

~ *Moby Dick*

"The *Wreck of the Rhone* is the most popular diving site," Mary said. She had chartered out of the Virgin Islands before and knew the area.

On October 29, 1867, the Royal Mail Steamship *Rhone, 3000* tons was disembarking passengers and unloading cargo off Tortola in the British Virgin Islands, when there was a sudden drop on the barometer, the wind spun rapidly from south-east to north-west. Ominous black churning clouds built up, layer on layer, thousands of feet into the sky, sure signs of an approaching hurricane. Before the day of weather forecasting, this was the first warning the captain had.

The *Rhone*, built in Southampton, England only two years previously was the latest in Industrial Age technology, steel hull, powered both by steam driven engines that turned propellors and sails. It plied between England and South and Central America and the Caribbean.

When the anchor began to drag. the captain hurried to batten down the hatches, stoke the coal burning furnaces and raise storm sails.

It took time to build steam pressure and the ship was sluggish, slow to respond as it moved out. Faltering, it made its way south across the Sir Francis Drake Passage, heading for open water. If only it could have been faster. Just a little faster.

The *Rhone* made it safely past the Pelican and Indians, two rocky outcrops that emerged abruptly from the sea. To have come closer would have been disastrous. It nearly made it around low lying Salt Island, when it was hit by the full blast of the hurricane. Ninety knot winds on the beam drove it inexorably toward the rocky shore. "Only another twenty minutes, another mile and it would have been clear. Then it scraped the bottom, and grounded to a stop. The ship was holed, the boilers burst," survivors said. The *Rhone* went to the bottom with passengers and crew. Few survived.

Today the hull lay on its starboard side, spread over a couple acres, the long sleek bow intact in 70 feet of water, the pointed bowsprit, iron mast, lifeboat davits, signaling canon all visible to the diver. The stern lay in shallows along Black Rock Point, where Mary led me, snorkeling among the Yellow Tail Snappers and striped Sergeant Majors. and a myriad of reef fish.

462

After being under water 130 years, the *Rhone* had become in its after life a natural reef, the prototype of numerous derelict ships and subway cars that are sunk off the east coast of the United States as artificial barrier reef, fish havens and breeding grounds. It is more famous as a wreck than a tramp steamer.

I imagined swimming in an aquarium, dazzled, by the profusion, the variety, darting about in flashes of brilliant colors, red, green, blue, yellow, the full spectrum though I couldn't name any of the fish. It was like trying to describe the shifting images of a kaleidoscope. Yellow fish swam up to me as if expecting to be fed.

"The green ones with the yellow stripes are Parrotfish," Mary pointed.

So began a year long quest, a fish quest, a game of identifying tropical reef fish, as Audubon members identify birds, as I had once identified alpine flowers.

Two summers previously, hiking in Colorado with Jennifer, my daughter, and Johann, her husband, we had counted 55 different species of alpine flowers in a climb of Snowmass Mountain, west of Aspen.

This summer it would be fish.

Mary bought me a copy of Paul Humann's, *Reef Fish Identification*, for my birthday, 422 pages, with detailed descriptions and vivid photographs of over 1000 species. We began to ke compete with each other to be first to identify new ones. A positive identification required that both of us see the fish and agree on its species.

We started with Parrotfish. "But which Parrotfish, Mary?" I asked. Humann listed 17 different specie. There were the ubiquitous green ones with distinctive red or yellow markings, some were gray, others blue, one a deep midnight blue.

It was a major discovery when we both agreed that the brilliant green one we had seen, with a blue tint around its mouth and anal fin, had a yellow crescent shaped tail and a yellow spot behind its eye. "It's a Stop Light Parrotfish!" Mary proclaimed.

Yellowtail Snappers ate out of our hands. There were Blue Tangs, Doctor Fish and Surgeon Fish both with a luminous grey coloring like a shiny polyester, varieties of Grunts with yellow and blue stripes. One of the more spectacular was the Spotted Drum, 9 inches long with a spectacular thin 6 inch dorsal fin curving upward like a waving banner, black and white stripes running the length of its body, white speckles on a black back.

More spectacular still was the Queen Angelfish, disc shaped about the size of a dinner plate, dark blue about its lips and around its head, a greenish blue body with flecks of yellow on its scales, yellow fins and a brilliant yellow tail. It was hard to imagine anything so beautiful, and difficult to describe the elation of our sighting.

Swimming off Monserrat a month later, we spotted our first barracuda. Or he spotted us. Four feet long, with underslung jaw and sharp glistening teeth. I like to think of it as male. Surely the female would not look so rapacious. He had the unnerving habit of following us around. "Mainly out of curiosity," Humann assured us. But only a few months earlier a woman diver in the Bahamas had lost a hand when a barracuda was attracted by her wristwatch.

When under sail we frequently flushed Flyingfish skimming off the crest of waves, soaring great distances. At night they would land on deck.

"Would you like fish for breakfast?" I'd ask Mary when she came on the early morning watch.

Our repertoire of fish stories grew longer and with it our growing enthusiasm. We would regale our friends with the exciting news of our latest identity success, But like most fish stories they become tiresome even when enhanced by the spirited embellishment of Morgan's rum.

"You should have seen the Queen Triggerfish Mary spotted today," I enthused, "a mustard yellow body blending into a purple mauve, lines radiating from the eyes like cosmetic makeup, bright blue mustache strips across its nose, dark blue tail and dorsal fin." And I'd show them the photograph in Humann, fearful that they could not comprehend such exravagent beauty.

Mary, a tea totaller, was quicker than I to pick up on the signs of boredom, and wasn't surprised when they changed the subject to issues dear to a cruiser's heart, their malfunctioning refrigeration, the new Rule 2000 bilge pump, comparisons of the new handheld Magellan GPS to the Garmin 2000.

They seemed unmoved by my sighting of the Banded Butterfly fish the day before, about the size of saucer, oval shaped with a short snout, two broad black bands across its body. And at the same reef, spotting the Four-eye Butterfly fish, so named for the black spot above its tail on a pale blue body!

Eventually this stony response made me founder. What was so fascinating about identifying a fish? Clearly there was something aesthetic. They were truly beautiful, like flowers, particularly seen in the wild, the way Olmstead, the great American landscape architect set flowers off in a natural setting. Take the school of the Rock Beauties we saw at St. Lucia, 8 inches long. oval shaped with a short snout, blue lips, brilliant yellow head and tail, and solid black body, against the background of yellow, orange and purple coral.

"But isn't there something more?" I asked Mary rhetorically. "Isn't it also a question of perception, of seeing, being aware?" I reasoned.

"In the beginning was the Word." I never really understood the passage in the opening of St.John's Gospel. Did it mean that nothing existed until you named it? That by naming it you gave it being?

That was my experience. Tropical fish did not really exist for me until I tried to identify them. Previously they just blurred into the background, or the backwater would be more precise, of the vast omnipresence of Nature. But the closer I looked, the more I saw. The more we saw, Mary and I. It was not just an exciting game. But a new world opened to my awareness.

Or as Sherlock Holmes said of his colleague, "Watson, you see, but you do not observe." Identification had to do with observing, taking the experience in.

Sailing on the sea, we eagerly anticipated new discoveries under the sea.

Before long there became a high degree of repetition, yellow grunts, blue tangs, green wrasses. We kept seeing the same fish over and over again. That added a new dimension to our game. How many different species could we identify in any one location? A fish count as it were, a census. Ile Pigeon off Guadeloupe, where the Jacques Cousteau Marine Park was located, took the record. In two days we identified

45 different species, including 3 new species of Parrotfish, the Yellowhead Wrasse, with broad stripes of green, blue, reddish purple on its body. In all 9 new species and saw many more we could not identify.

"Look at that!" Mary said in horror. We were shopping for fresh vegetables in the market at St. John's, Antigua. A large black woman with a brilliant yellow, green and red kerchief, the colors of a Parrotfish wound about her head and wearing an apron made from a Minneapolis Milling flour sack, squatted on a short stool, cleaning fish with a long steel bladed knife. In the bucket were shiny Blue Tangs, a French Angelfish, and a black Trigger Fish, each of them the size of a dinner plate. I felt betrayed. It was as if someone had lured *Teddy,* my daughter's pet Pekapoo into a trap and was skinning her out for the meat market.

"One man's pet, another man's meat," my unsympathetic friend said that evening after a second glass of rum. "The inexorable laws of the food chain."

This explained the fish traps we had seen at the foot of some of the reefs, and why some bays appeared to be fished out.

Then there were fish that didn't look as if they deserved to be called fish, Needlefish, narrow elongated Pipefish, the Spiny Puffer that would inflate on being threatened. The most spectacular odd bottom dweller was the Flying Gurnard that looked like a giant butterfly over a foot long, with broad spreading fins that looked like wings, that dug for grubs turned up the anchor chain with five fingered claws

The ugliest fish we saw was the Scorpionfish, gnarled like a giant toad that clung to the bottom, so well camouflaged that it looked like a broken chunk of coral rock, with whispy filament appendages growing out of it that looked like sea-weed. It was almost undistinguishable from its surroundings, but for the blink of its eyes. It was our rarest fish. We saw only one in our year of searching, on our last week in Bonaire, before departing the Caribbean.

A rocky headland came down to the water's edge in the bay on Carriacou. Mary and I swam leisurely out to the point on our daily forage. The sea floor dropped suddenly to a deep bottomless blue that made me uneasy. I always felt nervous looking down into the void, fish as far down as the eye could see in the clear water.

I saw it first out of the corner of my eye, something dark and huge coming straight toward me at me at high speed. A shark! Was my instinctive reaction. Pure paranoia. Then it glided by gracefully, effortlessly, vast outspread wings 8 feet across, with a effortless flying motion of an Osprey in search of prey. I saw the enormous gaping mouth, the size of a football, and the two watchful beady eyes. It was on a collision course, then veered off and headed for Mary. I felt tremendous relief, I am ashamed to admit. Then it turned and came back at me. This was it. I had intimations of my own mortality. Then it soared by and swam off.

We hastened back to *Zillah.* For once I was able to keep up with Mary.

"It's a Manta Ray," Mary said, looking it up in Humann. "Feeds on plankton that it filters through the large oval mouth. It's harmless."

"Do you think the Ray has read Harmann?" I asked

I recounted our dramatic encounter our friend Don on Westwind that night. He smirked, "Have you seen the great white whale?" And poured himself another rum.

Mary nudged my foot under the table. I sensed it was time to change the subject. No more fish stories. But this had been one of the great adventures of the Caribbean. We spotted 94 different species of fish that year. That was more than the number of wild flowers I had identified in a lifetime in Colorado.

Spinnaker run off Guadeloupe, 2002.

Chapter 101: Islands that Brush the Clouds

On May 8, 1902 the citizens of St. Pierre, Martinique heard the mountain rumble. Mt. Pelee, 4429 feet high, 5 miles distant above the town, belched smoke and hurled volcanic ash high into the sky.

"There's nothing to fear. Just stay in your houses," officials said, trying to avoid panic. "It will pass, as it always has."

In the early evening the sky darkened and the volcano blew. Thirty five thousand people perished, mostly from the inhalation of noxious gases. One of the few survivors was a petty thief incarcerated in a cell in the basement of the town jail.

The town was utterly destroyed, and because the toxic volcanic ash prevented the growth of plant life, a wide area is still a barren black waste.

On July 19, 1995, sailing in our yacht *Zillah* from Dominica to Martinique in July 1995, winds ESE 15-to-20 knots, 6 foot waves on a beam sea, the rail down, water spraying across the deck, Mary and I had an exhilarating crossing. Glimpses of the conical shape of Mt. Pelee came into view through the light rain and sea mist. On high, heavy clouds scudded across the shoulder of the mountain.

"I'd like to climb it," I said.

"We'll see," Mary said, speaking for herself.

When I'd left to sail in the Caribbean I'd never thought of climbing mountains. I didn't know there were mountains to climb. Only later I learned that the islands were part of a volcanic chain that lay along the tectonic plate separating the Atlantic from the Caribbean. Many are still active. The cruising guide called them, "Islands that brush the clouds."

I'd climbed volcanoes before, Kilimanjaro in Africa, Popocatapetl in Mexico. But to be able to sail up to the foot of a mountain and then climb it was not something I had expected to be able to do.

The EcoTourism Office in St. Pierre provided me with a map and bus schedule. Over drinks on board *Stargazer* I broached Dick and Barbara, the English owners, with the idea of the climb. They were inveterate hill walkers and their enthusiasm convinced Mary.

There was a light drizzle next morning when we met at the boulangerie for coffee and croissant, and a baquette to go with our cheese on the hike. A gentle breeze sent ripples across the bay. We wore our light weight foul weather jackets, though often in the tropics I did not wear mine. I found the coolness of a rain squall bracing, refreshing, a gratuitous fresh water shower that washed off the salt and sweat.

We climbed most of the mountain by bus which took us 5 miles uphill to Marne Rouge, a village at the pass. From there a well marked trail led to the rim. The last 2000 feet of elevation gain would be "au pied", by foot, the receptionist at the tourist office had informed us.

The wind-shield wipers of the bus lashed back and forth in a frenzy when our stop was announced. With a look of disbelief and a slight shrug of his shoulders the driver opened the door and we stepped out into the face of a gale. Blowing rain sluiced down the narrow street.

"Ah! Just like home," Dick shouted over the wind. " In England mountaineering is essentially an aquatic sport. If you waited for the weather to clear you'd never go out," he said, cheering us on. "If it's blowing this hard, it won't last for long." I suggested he lead off up the hill and I fell into my usual position of bringing up the rear, to keep an eye on stragglers. Leading from behind, I called it.

In our foul weather gear I too felt we could brave the elements. But above the village we were exposed to the full force of the blast. Rain pelted down and burrowed into the gap at the neck of my hood and dripped down my chest. Barbara, with a more ample chest than mine soon had a steady stream trickling down her front. In gusts we turned our backs and braced ourselves not to be blown off the trail.

The tile roof tops of the village were still in sight when Mary declared that she was getting chilled. I had images of hypothermia and suggested we turn back. No one argued. It was as if everyone was hoping that someone would say it first.

We huddled in the village café and warmed our hands on steaming cups of hot chocolate, ordered a bottle of wine to go with our baguette and cheese, and caught the next bus back to St. Pierre. From there we climbed Mt. Pelee vicariously, studying the vivid photographs in the museum. Walking through the town we saw the destructive ravages at first hand, many of the half-buried buildings still intact. " Pompey of the Caribbean," the tourist brochure proclaimed.

Undaunted, the next day we set off once more. The mild drizzle at seaside turned into a drenching tempest on mountainside again. We didn't get off the bus, but drove on through the rain forest to the Jardin de Balata, a world famous botanical garden. It was a marvelous feat of landscaping, overlooking a deep ravine with dozens of different species of palm trees, hundreds of exotic blooming and leafing plants. Mary and Barbara, both enthusiastic gardeners had found their magical world.

"If anything were to take me home from sailing," Mary said prophetically, "it would be gardening."

Departing St. Pierre the following day, I looked back at the mountain. The summit was clear.

There had been other excursions into the mountains, guided tours. At St. Kitts Greg's Safari took us in an open bed Land Rover high into the rain forest, where O'Neal, our black guide, identified over 100 species of trees for us, pointing out the medicinal value of many.

"Where did you learn all that?" As a retired teacher I was fascinated by his pratical knowledge.

"I studied forestry at the college," he said. "But my grandmother is a herbalist. The local people come to her for cures. What you would call a witch doctor. She is my real teacher," he added with a note of pride.

Our last stop was the world famous banyan tree. It looked like a thicket of huge tightly packed trees that covered the area of a football field. But it was one phenomenal tree whose tendrils dangled down from branches to the ground and formed new roots and so the tree continued to expand. O'Neal led us through the maze of trunks until we came to large brick building like a factory, a derelict sugar mill with a 60 foot high chimney totally enshrouded by the colossus, embracing the crumbling brick walls like a gigantic octopus in its many entwining arms. "This is the largest tree in the world," O'Neal said. " You can check it out. It's in the Guinness Book of Records."

In Dominica the following week, we took a trip to Victoria Falls where the streams ran hot and cold, hot springs bubbling out of the mountain side.

But I never got to climb to the top.

"What is it about getting to the top?" Mary asked.

Good question. I'd spent much of my adult life worrying the issue. Privately and professionally during 20 years of leading Outward Bound expeditions.

And never did come to a very convincing answer.

Was it merely something physical, the satisfaction of being to the top? Male dominance? Or was it psychological, the feeling of conquest, not so much of the mountain, but rather an inner conquest, conquest of self? Or was it aesthetic? Every view from the top seems a work of art. Or spiritual, the infinity of the horizon that makes so many mountains sacred? Or what combination of these? All of this or none of it, something Beyond. After all, heaven was meant to be somewhere Up There. Or was it Out There? Quantum Physics would place it In There.

"I'll have to think about that Mary," I replied.

Whatever, once one has overcome the fear of height, having learned the measured rhythmic pace, the studied placement of hands and feet, climbing to the top becomes addictive.

On July 29, coasting the western shore of St. Lucia, I spotted the twin Pitons. From several miles away, two gigantic volcanic plugs of solid rock that rose dramatically out of the sea, looked like two breaching whales, leaping out of the water, only they were 2400 feet high.

This was not walk up like the gradual slope of a volcano, I thought. Could it be climbed? The bottom half of the mountain was covered in dense tropical rain forest. The first problem would be to find the foot of the climb. As we drew closer I kept looking up to see if there was a logical approach. The closer we came the further my neck bend back, until we were right beneath this behemoth of rock.

"It's too deep to anchor," Mary said. "We'll have to tie to one of the buoys." Mary had been here four years before on a charter with Henry and S.O.S. (Singles On Sailboats) from Annapolis.

Johnson, a "boat boy", took our line, attached it to the mooring ball, then a stern line ashore and tied it to a coconut tree. Stepping off the boat I was at the foot of the mountain. No avoiding it.

"Can you climb that?" I asked.

"Not me," Johnson replied quickly.

"No. I mean, could I climb it?"

He looked at me skeptically. "You'll need The Man to show you the way," he said, then paused. "It'll cost you a hundred dollars," he added, intending to put me off.

"Where can I find The Man?"

"He over there," he said, and pointed to a tall, muscular fellow lounging beside a tent on the beach, not 50 yards away, a Rastaferian with dreadlocks.

"I know him!" Mary lit ups. "Saja. He led us up to the hot springs when I was cruising here five years ago. I named my cat after him. Saji."

Saja was welcoming, but I wasn't sure he was flattered by having an eponymous pet. He did agree to guide me up the Piton. "Forty dollars," he said.

I didn't bargain. You never bargain with a man to whom you are about to entrust your life.

To beat the heat of the day we set off early morning. It was cool only in a relative sense of not being out in the direct heat of the mid-day sun. I was soon drenched in sweat. we threaded our way through the undergrowth, steadily climbing, following a tangle of animal trails. There was clearly a trail, but not one I could ever have found had I been on my own. Johnson was right. I did need the man.

We climbed on the landward side of the mountain, away from the sea. I could see no further than 10 feet ahead, following in Saja's steps, staying far enough back to avoid the branches winging back in my face. In places we passed through broad leafed plants like hastas, and ferns chest high, damp and claustrophobic. .

Higher up the slope steepened and it became more of a scramble as we moved from tree trunk to trunk. Vines dangled down and I used them to pull myself up. It was more like tree climbing than rock climbing. We maneuvered around cliff bands, the rock covered with thick layers of moss, difficult to gain purchase with my sneakers. I had always climbed in boots. Saja did better with bare feet, digging in his toes.

A steep cliff blocked the way. Saja grasped a vine and pulled himself out over open space scrambling up like on a free hanging cargo net.

"You alright?" he asked.

I looked at the vine dubiously and looked around to see if there was an option. I couldn't see one. "Either this or you turn back," I said to myself. That wasn't an option. Saja reached down a hand but he was out of reach.

A man's reach should be beyond his grasp. I recalled the line from Browning. Or was it the other way around? I shinnied up the vine, like rope climbing in P.E. class, and came out on the cliff top.

We were above the jungle. From there the rounded hump of the mountain top led to the summit, black volcanic rock, deeply rutted and grooved with numerous holds for hands and feet, and we scrambled up, stooping forward for balance, like walking up a steep roof. I was reminded of mounting the steep steps if the Mayan pyramids to the alter on top.

On top we emerged to a view of the open expanse of the Caribbean, a deep ink blue, that stretched to a distant horizon gathering clouds. I looked down upon the canopy of forest green wrapped about the base of the mountain where we had climbed. Directly below *Zillah* lay at her mooring, 2,400 feet down, like a child's toy, tied to her coconut tree.

I waved, hoping to attract Mary's attention. "Look dear, we done it!" But she was engrossed in boat jobs, domesticating *Zillah*.

So I sat and gazed like stout Cortez in Keat's poem, "silent on a peak in Darien."

"What was it like?" I knew Mary would ask. Clearly there was the sheer adolescent animal joy of testing one's strength and nerve in the physical achievement.

"It's a great way to feel alive," Gordon Mansell, an artist mountaineer, one of my Outward Bound colleagues had said.

But there was more. So much more. The sense of perspective, of oneself in the context of the immensity of things. The paradoxical feeling of being separate from it all, unique, and also part of the Universe, the Divine Order of things. As the writer of Genesis said on the seventh day, "That it was good."

I shared my water bottle with Saja who sat there passively. I wondered what the experience meant to him. In Rastiferian cosmology was there a sense of sanctity in high places? Had some black or brown shaman or medicine man sat here in search of wisdom? I asked him, "So Saja, why do you climb the mountain?"

"You pay me forty dollars, Mon."

Two weeks later we listened to the weather radio. "Attention all ships. There is a marine advisory. The volcano on the island of Montserrat has erupted. A thousand people have been evacuated. Ships are advised not to approach within 5 miles and to avoid being downwind of the island."

"That's one volcano you'll not want to climb," Mary said.

Chapter 102: The Weather Outlook

"That's the worst weather report I've ever heard," Mary said.

Radio Antilles opened with a mariner's warning. "The volcano on the island of Monserrat has erupted. I repeat. The volcano on Monserrat has erupted. A thousand people have been evacuated from the island. Ships are advised to avoid the area."

Then it continued with the weather report. Tropical Storm Humberto had passed north of the Leeward Islands and was moving out into the Atlantic toward Bermuda with sustained winds of 65-to-70 knots. Twelve hours behind Humberto, Iris had come ashore at St. Lucia with tropical storm winds of 60 knots and was tracking up the west coast of the Leeward chain of islands bringing heavy rain, mud slides and flood damage. Power lines were down and airline flights was being diverted to other islands.

Stalled a thousand miles offshore, Luis, gaining hurricane strength with maximum sustained winds of 120 knots. was moving west across the south North Atlantic at 7 miles per hour. Another tropical depression is forming off the Cape Verde Islands on the coast of Africa. A tropical disturbance in the Gulf of Mexico had come ashore at Pensicola, Florida with gale force winds and heavy rainfall, causing floods and extensive property damage.

Mary and I on *Zillah* were in Prickly Bay, Grenada, safely south of the hurricane belt. So we thought. It was late August.

Since May we had been sailing down the Caribbean chain, sailing on the protected western coast. The prevailing winds are the easterly trades. Most of the ports and cities are on the sheltered side. Winds were usually in the 15 to 20 knot range. Only between the islands did we get the full force of the Atlantic, 25 knot winds.

When we left the British Virgin Islands in late May, I was attentive to the weather, but had not taken the hurricane threat seriously. Conventional wisdom was that the official hurricane season lasted from June to November, but not much was happened until September.

"The thing is to be south of latitude twelve north by the first of September," Mary said.

But when Hurricane Chantilly blew through in late July, barely missing the Antilles, and Erin struck Honduras a week later. Then Felix a week after that, we began to suspect that this year may be different.

At Wallaballou Bay, St. Vincent, in early August, we had our first experience of what was to come. Radio Antilles reported, "A tropical wave moving through the northern Leewards…could develop convection." Later he spoke of "A tropical disturbance, gale force winds of 35-to-40 miles per hour, with heavy rain…could intensify." There were more tropical waves east of the Caribbean, but he gave no coordinates. "Would that affect us? " I asked Mary. "And if so when? And what do they mean by a tropical wave?"

I was also anxious about the security of our anchorage. The shore dropped off very suddenly and deep. We had all of our chain out, 150 feet and with the help of *Double Trouble*, our beach boy, ('I'm your beach boy,' he told us.) we ran stern lines ashore and lashed them to coconut trees. Not an ideal arrangement, but *Double Trouble* assured us, "No problem."

I woke next morning to the steady rain rattling on the deck, and the low moan of the wind through the shrouds.

We had planned to move on. "I think we'd better wait to see if it blows over," Mary said. By mid-morning both wind and rain had intensified. Off shore the seas grew turbulent, waves began to break, crests blew off in a spume like wind driven smoke.

Feeling uneasy, I went forward with the wind blowing up my back to lengthen the snubber, a 10-foot loop of rope attached to the anchor chain to keep it from jerking so violently. The coconut trees on shore were lashing back and forth in a frantic Dervish dance, spindrift exploded off the churning surface of the water.

Late afternoon another boat entered the bay flying only its jib reefed to the size of a small bed sheet. In spite of the storm. a bevy of boat boys scurried out on their surf boards to handle the lines. "*Double Trouble*" got there first. We watched the drama as they attempted to anchor stern to the wind and to secure their lines to trees on shore. But they could not get the anchor to hold in the steep drop-off close to shore. The wind kept blowing the stern off.

"What do you know about the weather?" A hardy woman, evidently the skipper, rowed across to our boat. She spoke good English with a French accent.

"I think it's a tropical disturbance," I replied. As if that explained anything.

"*Double Trouble*" was more specific. There were hurricane warnings, power lines down, roads washed out. "What cause de wind? It's cause of the coconut trees. It's the trees that bring the wind." He advised her to go to the next bay north where there was better protection. Less coconut trees? I wondered. She pulled up anchor and was last seen rounding the headland to the north, *Double Trouble* on is board in tow, the coconut trees waving a frenzied farewell.

I took a second line to shore and secured it to another coconut tree, trusting it would not bring more wind.

The 6:30 p.m. weather report of Radio Antilles announced, "There has been a weather disturbance over the eastern Caribbean… gale force winds 35 miles an hour gusting higher have damaged telephone lines and radio towers … flooding in lower elevations… plane flights cancelled, diverted to other islands…Upper level conditions favor further developments." Again no coordinates were given. Was it passing through? Was it merely a prelude? Was more to come?

473

Over dinner we turned up the volume of the CD to let Beethoven's *Eroica* symphony drown out the steady moan of the wind through the shrouds. During the night it diminished and the swell subsided.

In the morning I asked Mary, "Do you think that's what they mean by a tropical disturbance?"

On the last leg from Carriacou to Grenada we sailed on the outside, off the eastern shore. We experienced the full sweep of the Atlantic. In the 8 foot waves on a beam sea *Zillah* rolled and the rail was down. Mary came close to being sea sick. We had the feeling of being pushed on to a lee shore and we felt uneasy being on the open sea again.

At Prickly Bay, on the south coast of Grenada, we had to decide. To go on or not to?

Trinidad was 150 miles south across open water, the last link in the Caribbean chain. Mary had booked passage to return to Annapolis for a visit with her family. Her flight was in a week. I would stay and have work done on the boat. While there was not sense of great urgency, we did have to keep moving.

But with Hurricane Iris in the northern Antilles, 200 miles away, we were still anxious. How would affect our region?

We talked with *Southern Cross* anchored beside us, also bound for Trinidad. "What do you think?"

"I'm waiting to hear what Herb has to say." Herb was the omniscient weather guru living in Hamilton, Ontario, who broadcast a daily weather summary for yachtsmen in the North Atlantic each afternoon and evening. Any boat that chose to check in with him could get an individual weather briefing for his region. Among yachtsmen there is a sense of omniscience about Herb that verges on genius.

That evening we listened in as he talked to *Southern Cross*. The big picture was scary as he talked about Tropical Storm Iris in the northern Windward Islands, tracking north up the Leeward Islands bringing torrential rains, flooding and mud slides in Martinique. Conditions in the southern Caribbean would be affected by feeder bands. I wasn't sure what a feeder band was. "Between Grenada and Trinidad, tonight and tomorrow your winds will be north-west, backing to the west and southwest, going to the south and southeast over the weekend."

Southern Cross was focused on the big picture, as was I. And it was very unnerving. "I think we'll play it conservative," our friend on *Southern Cross* told Herb. "We'll wait."

"It will be on your nose if you wait for the weekend." There was a note of insistence in Herb's voice. He never directed you what to do but he did not appreciate his advice not being taken. That was clear.

"What's he waiting for?" Mary said. "That's our weather window." Mary, decisive as always, a former commercial real estate agent, knew an opportunity when she saw it.

I wasn't convinced. I'd have been happy to join *Southern Cross* for a comfortable night at anchor. Mary's enthusiasm was persuasive. Who was I to argue?

At 9:00 p.m. on a dark starless night we thread our way through the dim lights of the boats at anchor in Prickly Bay, and headed out to sea. By mid-night the sky was clear and we sailed south under the outspread claws and the curving tail of Scorpio. The wind was a steady 10-to-15 knots out of the northwest, as Herb had said it would be. We made 6 knots on a broad reach, the auto-pilot steering in a quartering sea.

Lightning flashed ominously to the south. "Probably just heat lightning, It should blow through," I said optimistically.

Before turning in I studied the charts. Tobago was off the north coast of Trinidad, slightly east of our course. The cruising guide extolled the sand beaches, good snorkeling, and a renowned bird sanctuary. "Why don't we spend a couple days there?" I suggested to Mary.

"Wonderful idea," she said and altered course, 150 degrees, SSE.

During the night the wind shifted west, as Herb had predicted. By noon next day we sighted the coast of Tobago. The mountains of Trinidad appeared on the horizon to the southwest. We had drifted east in a setting current and so we motored up to clear the northwest corner of the island.

We had to clear immigration and customs at Scarborough, on the south coast, and it was blowing a steady 15-to-20 knots out of the west when we picked up the harbor entrance markers and motored in, the wind on the stern.

I looked at the anchorage in disbelief. It was open to the west, a narrow breakwater less than 100 yards long provided no shelter. The small harbor was crowded with five other yachts. The swell washed up on a high concrete commercial dock along one side, a death trap for a small boat. A couple hundred yards further back a rusted iron wrecked barge was washed up on shore. The surface of the water had a black demonic sheen under the gray sky.

"Where do we anchor?" Mary asked. No place looked very good. We tried it near the end of the breakwater. The anchor touched in 30 feet of water but in the wind we drifted rapidly toward the yachts.

"We're too close!" I called back to Mary who was at the helm. I began to haul in the chain, hand over hand, sitting on the deck, feet braced against the defunct windlass, pulled with legs and arms, like on a rowing machine.

When the anchor was up, I shouted, "Circle around again." I dropped it a second time further in the harbor. This time it dragged. Back to the Gulag. I raised it again.

"Try it next to the French boat," I called. The chair rattled out and the anchor splashed for the third time.

My experience is that calamities never occur as single events. They compound. The engine stalled. "The anchor just has to hold," I said to myself. I felt it bouncing along the bottom. Then it grabbed and held. Or so it seemed.

"You'd better put out a second anchor," Mary said. So we put the dinghy overboard, attached the outboard motor to it, and lowered the fisherman's into it. Then I looked back. The dreaded concrete dock appeared to be coming closer. I leapt back on deck.

475

"Mary, we're dragging." I turned the engine ignition key. It did not start. "Advance the throttle." It stalled again. Then as if by Divine Intervention it started.

"Do you need help?" The young man on the French yacht had come across to us, sculling with one oar from the back of his dory, continental style.

"Yes!"

He jumped on board. Between us we raised the anchor or the fourth time. It emerged from the harbor depths with an oily lump of mud and offal tangled in fishing line and a large black plastic garbage bag attached to the fluke.

"We've snagged the town dump," the Frenchman said.

We circled, dropped the anchor again, and this time it held. I let out 50 feet more chain, 80 feet, 120, more chain than I had ever led out before. I dreaded the thought of pulling it in. The we set the second anchor.

We were down. Secure. Hopefully. On a boat one has always to live in hope.

"Not much protection from the west, is there?" I chatted with Charles on the Canadian boat we had anchored beside. He spent most of the year in the Caribbean. His wife was an artist who painted bright, attractive representational art, Caribbean scenes, she sold in tourist souvenir shops up and down the islands. A good life. Charles knew his weather.

"It's because of the hurricane," he said. "The prevailing winds are the easterly trades. The harbor is protected from the east. But these are feeder bands being sucked in from the west by the vortex of the hurricane. The harbor, like most in the Caribbean, is protected from the east, vulnerable to the west."

Two days later, there was a spectacular sunrise, high cirrus cloud caught the early morning light, brilliant flaring yellow, then slipped down through lenticulated bands of cumulus, orange, pink, mauve. We passed through the *Boca de Dragon,* named the Dragon's Mouth by Columbus on his fourth voyage of discovery, spectacular cliffs on either side, and entered the Gulf of Paria.

The journey from Nova Scotia to Trinidad completed.

In Trinidad in Chagaramus Bay, also open to the west, numerous boats had dragged and been damaged.

Mary made her flight connection. I scrambled to find a boatyard where *Zillah* could be hauled for reconditioning.

Ten days later Hurricane Luis struck the northern Leeward Islands with devastating force. It was a massive storm, 240 miles across with maximum sustained winds approaching 150 miles per hour. Roofs were blown off, telephone and power lines downed from Antigua to Barbuda. In St. Thomas, hardest hit, 10,000 people were homeless. Yacht sought shelter in the crowded waters of Simpson Bay lagoon. It was reported that of 1500 boats, only a third survived. Miraculously only 17 persons were killed.

Luis blew north into the Atlantic, sparing the rest of the Caribbean. But off the north-east coast, the Queen Elizabeth II bound for New York, was struck by a rogue wave 90 feet high, sustaining only minor damage. Making landfall in Newfoundland, it was the most powerful hurricane on record in Canada.

In the south Caribbean feeder bands swept in from the west again, but this time people were prepared. Those who could sought protective shelter from the west. Others put out extra anchors. I had found an opening in the IMS boatyard and hurried to have *Zillah* hauled the day before the storm hit.

I heard it coming, before I saw it, like an ocean surge seething over the swaying trees. There were screams, more from delight than terror, wild laughter, as the men in the yard ran for shelter. The rain hit like pellets, bouncing off the ground, rattling on the deck with the staccato of a kettle drum.

I strung a blue tarpaulin over the cabin top and a plastic tarp over my bunk, and resigned myself to the vagaries of nature and escaped into the fantasy world of a good book.

Ten days later, Hurricane Marilyn swept across Guadeloupe and the north Caribbean, striking St. Thomas in the U. S. Virgin Islands, leaving another 10,000 people homeless, causing eight deaths, mostly people who went off shore to save their boats.

I was grateful to be south of latitude ten north.

Chapter 103: Atlantic Odyssey

On the third day out of Fajardo, Puerto Rico, the moderate winds shifted to the north-east and we sailed close hauled on a course of 350 degrees toward Bermuda, 300 miles to the north. The wind shift was predicted as we had reached the northern edge of the trade winds. What we hadn't expected were the mounting seas. The five-foot waves increased to twelve and fifteen feet through the morning with no apparent increase in the wind. By mid-afternoon we were surrounded by gigantic ocean swells twenty-five and thirty feet high.

"What's causing this?" Mary asked. My co-captain, she had more cruising experience than I, but neither of us had experienced anything like this. Zillah, our forty-three-foot wooden boat, rose with each swell with rythmic regularity. At the top, as we looked over a succession of rounded hilltops that stretched to the horizon, we caught the wind, then slid down, accelerating in the glide. In the trough we were enveloped in a barren watery wasteland, like being at the bottom of a well. Blanketed from the wind and the sails flogged and the boom lurched. Then up again. And down. Hour after hour.

I scanned the horizon for approaching storm clouds. There had to be a mighty wind to create a swell like that. When would it hit? I took another Dramamine and made a mental check-list of emergency procedures. I realized how ill prepared we were should we be knocked down. But the day was warm, the wind a steady twelve to fifteen knots. It didn't even kick up whitecaps. The sky was thinly overcast with a filtered blue haze, like looking out through a lace curtain on a sunny day.

That evening we listened eagerly for the weather report on the SSB radio. We gave Herb, the weather guru on South Bound II our position and course direction. "As you move north," he told us, "the wind will back and you will experience northwest winds of ten knots. That should carry you the rest of the way to Bermuda."

"But what about the swell?" I asked.

"Oh. It's down that far south?" he replied. "That surprises me. The swell is left over from the storm off Nova Scotia last week. Nothing to worry about. There's no wind behind them."

If this is what could happen with a storm a thousand miles away, what would it be like in the middle of one in the Atlantic? I wondered.

"In ever had any doubt about not going with you, this certainly does it for me," Mary said. "I'll do the rest of my Atlantic crossing in a 747."

Zillah had crossed the Atlantic several times. The previous owner claimed to have done it four times solo. When I bought the boat two years earlier, it was one of the things I aspired to, but would never have told anyone. I was a rank novice, had never owned a boat, had never sailed offshore. What did I know? After two years of sailing from Maine to Venezuela, I felt both Zillah and I were up for it. Besides, I was sixty-six years old and not getting younger.

Mary was supportive of the idea and helped me refit the boat. Zillah was a graceful lady, a racing cruiser built in England in 1955, forty-three feet on deck, narrow beam, deep keel, classic wooden boat lines. She sailed beautifully, was more of a boat that I was a sailor. In Trinidad we did major repairs, "sistered" forty ribs, reinforcing the existing ones to strengthen the hull, replaced the wire rigging and steering cables, recaulked the teak deck, sewed in a third set of reefing points sewn on the main sail, repainted the white topsides and brushed two coats of anti-fouling on the bottom.

Mary insisted I upgrade the safety systems with a six- person Plastimo life-raft, an EPIRB, Emergency Positioning Intermittent Radio Beacon, SSB Single Side Band radio, flares, emergency rations, portable hand-operated water maker, backup battery-powered VHF radio and GPS Global Positioning System. We had a Monitor wind steering vane shipped to Puerto Rico and installed. While there we provisioned at the Sam's Club mega-market. I felt we were "cruising ready." Mary joined me on the first leg of the crossing, the 700-mile passage from Puerto Rico to Bermuda, as we ventured for the first time across the open expanse of the Atlantic.

Bermuda, discovered by a Spanish navigator blown off course in 1515, and settled by shipwrecked English colonists bound for Virginia in 1609, it has been a mariner's transit stop ever since. Quaintly British with narrow winding lanes, pink pastel painted houses with white washed roofs to catch the rain, a climate tempered by the Gulf Stream, it has become popular as a tourist port of call and a haven for offshore banks, as well as yachts.

My crew joined me in Bermuda. Jennifer, my thirty-five year old daughter, was a former Hurricane Island Outward Bound instructor, United States Coast Guard licensed, with past deep water experience in the Caribbean and a Pacific passage from San Francisco to Hawaii. The year I bought Zillah, she had sailed her with me from Annapolis to Maine, and later from Ft. Lauderdale to the Exumas, in the Bahamas. "She's my delivery captain," I said, only half in jest.

Brian Sullivan, black- bearded, rather piratical in appearance with a preference for black clothing, was in his mid-thirties. A mechanical genius who designed computer programs for the University of Ottawa, he had joined me two years previously, and we had sailed from Rockland, Maine to East Quaddy Head, the north-east headland of Maine, and rounded the international boundary buoy, so that I could say that I had sailed the boat from Canada, should anyone ask. And they did. From there we cruised the entire east coast of the United States to Ft. Lauderdale in Florida.

Brian's companion, Samantha, who preferred to be called "Sam," was a water sports enthusiast and a competition swimmer; She had been on a sailboat in the Caribbean, but never crewed.

479

Other than Jennifer, none of us could claim to be experienced ocean sailors, and it showed at times in moments of bluster and anxiety. I recalled an Outward Bound instructor telling me once, after a day of skiing in Colorado, "You know Joe, you ski just like you live. Always slightly out of control." There I was again. I was eager to go, felt up to the challenge in spite of my tension, anxious not so much for myself, but for the others I had encouraged to join me. But I always felt this way before any significant endeavor, that combination of dread and elation.

Not that crossing the Atlantic was a unique experience. We were hardly pace setters or pioneers. With the invention of the GPS even novices like us could find our way across open expanses of water. Between 800 and 1000 small yachts crossed the Atlantic each year, each way. Rarely did your hear of anyone who hadn't made it. But it could happen as we were to learn. The Atlantic is a big ocean.

I have always found lists as a great antidote to anxiety. The bewildering confusion of tasks take on an order. Chaos is defined. You can't confront chaos, but you can check off your list, each item scratched a victory, rewarding you with a glowing sense of satisfaction. Bermuda there was a flurry of activity and last minute refitting. top of the list was replacing the head pump. Jennifer had brought a new Henderson from West Marine and it was the first challenge to Brian's mechanical and plumbing skills. Though I had become comfortable with a squat on the bucket routine, Mary thought it unnecessarily crude, and the new crew were greatly relieved by the upgrade. We had a jiffy reefing system installed, a waterproof cover made for the forward hatch. Jennifer had bought me a new iridescent canary yellow foul weather suit, so I even looked the part of a mariner as I strutted through town on a rainy day. We topped up with diesel fuel and water. My check list of sixty-eight items dwindled to six.

Last trips to shore. Brian had brought a sextant but did not have navigation tables and tried to buy, borrow or copy them from a yacht that had just arrived from Britain. Sam shopped for apples and bananas. Jennifer picked up another roll of duct tape, to coyer leaks in the cabin top and called her husband, Johann, in Belgium. A final weather report from Herb on South Bound II held out the promise of fair weather between cold fronts.

"How do you feel?" Jennifer asked with a broad smile. She was clearly in her element. I was still checking and re-checking my checklists, and my dreams confirmed my lingering apprehensiveness. The night before we sailed I had dreamt I was skiing on the steep roof of a tall church with a group of students and I was afraid we were going to fall off. What would Jung have made of that?

I took the updated crew list to Customs and at twelve noon, May 4, 1996, we weighed anchor and motored out into the Atlantic. Horta, in the Azores, lay 1800 miles to the east.

"Ten years of fantasizing, and two years of planning," I wrote in my journal as we embarked on our voyage.

At 32 degrees North, Bermuda is situated in the horse latitudes, an area of variable winds north of the south-east trades of the tropics, and south of the westerlies coming off the coast of the United States and Canada. For a vessel under sail, the trick is to move far enough north to catch the westerlies, while dodging the North Atlantic gales. Weather forecasting is crucial and we monitored Herb's daily report on closely.

Once clear of the harbor narrows we picked up a gentle wind, WSW 10 knots, and raised the mainsail and unfurled the 150 genoa jib, a flowing sail that stretched from the fore-stay half the length of the boat, the largest sail on the boat. I shut down the engine and a hush fell over the boat for several moments. No one wanted to disturb the silence. Each of us retreated into our own thoughts induced by the mesmerizing lapping of the water on the hull, the land disappearing behind and the open sea ahead. Our diminutive boat was now our universe. It was like a moment of silent prayer.

At the helm I set the Monitor wind steering vane, which we soon treated like a fellow member of the crew and named "Monty." He needed some adjustment, but in the light wind held us on course, ninety degrees, due east. While Monty steered, I used the opportunity to gather the rest of the crew in the cockpit and discuss safety and emergency procedures, something I had overlooked in the confusion and haste of leave taking. In harbor we'd checked all ten thru-hull fittings and sea-cocks. Wooden plugs had been attached to each valve. "Failing thru-hull fittings are one of the major causes of boats foundering," I said somewhat pontifically.

At my sea seminar I pointed out the fire extinguishers, one under the navigation table opposite the galley, another in the starboard cockpit locker above the engine hatch. The same locker also had the backup manual bilge pump, should the automatic pump in the depths of the bilge fail again. The emergency was stowed in the bosun's locker, aft of the helm, should the steering cables break again.

"What do you mean, again?" Sam asked. Jennifer and Brian both laughed. They already the experience of the old boat's susceptibility to equipment failure.

Lifejackets were stowed in the port side cockpit locker. Anyone on deck at night would wear a lifejacket and safety harness and clip into a nylon "jack-line" running from the aft stanchion to the bow-cleat. We'd also wear a battery- powered strobe light slipped onto an upper arm. A Lifesling and horseshoe-shaped life preserver were secured to the rear rail, ready to be tossed should anyone fall overboard.

We worked out an "abandon ship" procedure. Brian and I would launch the Plastimo six-person life raft. Jennifer would activate the EPIRB. She pushed the Test switch. But it failed to light up and beep. This was disconcerting. Mary had tested it the month before when we sailed from Puerto Rico, and again in Bermuda before she flew home. Why did it not work now? Fortunately, there was an emergency radio alarm system on the SSB radio which was monitored by all commercial ships. Jennifer would set that off, then pick up the yellow waterproof buoyant security bag with valuables such as passports and wallets. I'd failed to do this when Touch of Gray was wrecked on the Boardwalk: at Atlantic City. "I don't want to do that again, Sam."

There was a large red emergency grab bag stowed just inside the companionway, with flares, a VHF radio in a water-proof case, batteries, a hand-operated watermaker, fish hooks, a small rubber sling spear gun, emergency food bars and water in cup sized plastic bags. Sam would hoist this on deck.

"No one leaves the boat until water is over the deck," I cautioned. "The boat is probably our best life raft." After the disastrous Fastnet Race off the coast of Ireland, four yachts that had been abandoned, at great risk to crew and rescuers, were found still afloat after the storm.

Later in the afternoon we discussed watch schedules. Some boats prefer regular three-hour watches, day and night. Jennifer suggested four hours by day, and two at night, which gave each crew member four hours of uninterrupted sleep each night, and eight hours off duty during the day. At least in theory. Inevitably there were interruptions, changing sails, pumping the bilge, preparing hot meals. Sam did not feel confident yet to stand watch by herself, so each of us took turns standing watch with her for the first three days. She gained skill and confidence rapidly.

By evening we had run thirty-two miles from Bermuda, the wind had faded to five knots, still from the southwest, our speed dropped to three, then two knots. If we were to escape the Bermuda high, we would clearly have to disturb the sense of nirvana induced by the calm and we motor up. We motored through the night and into the next morning.

The noon-to-noon distance run next day was 128 nm (nautical miles), most of it under power.

"We can't keep that up for long. We don't have the fuel," I discussed the problem with the crew.

"How much we got?" Brian asked.

"About eighty gallons. Two twenty-gallon tanks below deck. Four five-gallon jerry cans tied to the shrouds on deck. We burn three quarts an hour which gives us approximately 100 hours of cruising time," I replied.

"At six knots that's 600 miles," he figured.

"We need to run the engine at least an hour a day just to keep the batteries up and generate enough power for the running lights, the bilge pump and the SSB radio. Transmitting is the big drain."

"One hour a day for twenty days," Brian calculated, "that's fifteen gallons."

"We'll need to reserve some for Horta," Jennifer added. "We could run into an Azores high."

"Fifteen gallons?" I guessed. "That would take us ninety miles."

"Doesn't leave us much," Jennifer said with a long serious face.

"But I always planned to sail. I still do." I tried to sound more optimistic. We discussed ways we could cut down on power, by manually pumping the bilge, limiting talk on the radio, even sailing without running lights on clear nights.

The winds began to fill in the next day, SW 10, increasing to 15 making for beautiful sailing. It was warm, a sunny Gulf Stream-bathed day, the ocean a deep royal blue, a gentle following swell eight feet high, that shoved us along. I was surprised by the size of the seas for so little wind. But Jennifer assured me that this was ocean sailing. It was exhilarating to feel the pulse of the sea again, to gaze at the endless expanse, full of emptiness, the sense of never endingness. The stem lifted and the deck dipped, invigorating on deck, but it was disconcerting below. I had hoped to get by without Dramamine, as I disliked the drowsiness. So I wedged myself into a corner of the cockpit and tried to read, but that didn't last long.

It was a hard course for Monty, the wind steering vane, to hold. The compass wavered between 110 degrees and 130 degrees, before it could correct, nudging us imperceptibly further south of east than we wanted to go.

"Let's put a reef in the main," Jennifer said. "It will balance the sails better." It was her watch. She asked me to take the helm, and Sam to give her a hand. They were suited up with harness on. I switched on the engine and turned into the wind. Jennifer furled in the genoa on the roller furler, and Sam sheeting in the main. They clipped into the safety line and went forward. It was Sam's first time on the fore-deck in a running sea. With eight foot waves the bow heaved and pitched furiously and water sluiced over the deck. They clutched the grab-rails on the cabin top and ducked low as they went forward. The boom was the principal hazard, flinging about in the wind. Should it swing free it could easily knock a person overboard. But they held to the mast, out of harms way, as they lowered the sail to the first reefmg point, secured the luff, the leading edge of the sail, and pulled in the clew, the following end of the sail with the new jiffy reefing system installed in Bermuda.

They were most vulnerable when they had to stand on the cabin top to fold in the excess loose sail and tie it down with reefing points. The wind caught Zillah's high bow, and kept blowing us off. It was only by powering into the waves could I keep Zillah pointed into the wind, the crashing waves spraying over the deck.

Everything secure, they returned to the cockpit, dripping wet, ecstatic with adrenal, laughing. They unfurled the genoa, let out the main, turned off the engine and we resumed our course.

"Well done, Sam. You're now an Able Seawoman," I told her, "if that's the politicallly correct term."

"There has to be a better way of doing this," Jennifer said, as she took over the helm. "It's scary standing on the cabin top with the boom banging about."

The noon-to-noon run was 145 nm, an average of six knots for twenty-four hours, one of Zillah's best days.

The southwest wind continued overnight and into the next day (Tuesday, May 8, Day 4) increasing to SW 20 with gusts to 25 knots. This gave Zillah a strong weather helm. She kept heading up into the wind. The seas increased to ten feet coming over the starboard quarter, which kept catching the stem, throwing us off course. Zillah yawed between 90 and 130 degrees. Occasionally the wind backed the sails and the boom slammed on the shrouds and the jib flogged violently.

There was little sleep during the night. We were flung about in our bunks, held in only by lee cloths stretched from hooks above. Water crashing over the deck sounded like the pounding of a cattle stampede with the bellowing of the wind through the straining rigging. And there was a persistent drip, particularly in the forward cabin.

Brian had the morning watch. The rest of us were trying to catch a pre-lunch nap, when we were called out by a blast of a whistle. "She won't hold her course," Brian shouted, "we need to shorten sail some more."

"I'd like to try something different," Jennifer said as we suited up in our foul weather gear. She explained that if we could take in a reef while under sail, this will give the boat much greater stability, and we won't need to worry about being hit by the swinging boom. I didn't quite understand her tactics but was willing to go along. "Brian, bring her close to the wind and Dad; you pull in the jib sheet." We sailed along close-hauled with the jib and eased the main sheet so there was no pressure on the mainsail. I tightened the preventer to keep the mainsail from flogging. It came down easily to the second reefing point, and we were able to secure the luff and the clew, and tie off the reefing points without the danger of a swinging boom. Within fifteen minutes we were back in the cockpit, adjusted the sails and headed back on course, still making seven or eight knots, our hull speed.

"One person could do that alone, Dad. It would take a little longer, but it would go."

Jennifer assured me as we admired the efficiency and safety of the maneuver. She obviously enjoyed the role of the daughter coaching the father. For years she had been known in Outward Bound circles as Joe Nold's daughter. With her growing reputation, I was having to get used to being introduced as Jennifer Nold's father. But I enjoyed the shift of the spotlight

The noon-to-noon run was a spectacular 166 nm, a record for Zillah.

"This is what an Atlantic crossing should be," Jennifer was elated.

But it was too good to last. In the late afternoon a turgid haze wiped out the brilliant blue sky, turning it to a battle-ship gray. The wind built to twenty-five knots gusting higher. The seas continued to build to twelve feet. It was exhilarating sailing, but being thrown around below decks was almost life threatening. We clung to our bunks. In gusts we made nine knots with a double-reefed main and only a third of the genoa out. Zillah seemed rejuvenated, having found a new youth and vigor as she barreled through the seas, reliving her the hard sailing of her early days when she competed favorably in the Fastnet Race. I could see why she did well. She was more of a boat than I was a sailor. I had the sense of hanging on, and took more Dramamine.

"South Bound II. South Bound II. This isZillah." After dinner, we crouched around the SSB radio. "Our position is North 32.53. West 56.20. Our course 140 degrees." Jennifer reported our weather conditions.

"There's a front lying from 40 degrees north and 54 degrees west to Bermuda, moving in a southeast direction," Herb announced. "It should pass through your area tomorrow. You will experience a wind shift to the northeast (the direction we were heading) gradually clocking to the southeast and back to southwest."

Next afternoon, Jennifer and I were below, reading and napping in our bunks, Sam in the forward cabin, and the sails began to rattle and the blocks to crash on deck as if a jazz drummer in a cocaine frenzy had taken over the kettle drum section in a Carnegie Hall concert: The front had hit, as Herb predicted, with a sudden violent 180 degree shift to the NE 15, with gusts to 20, right on the nose. We brought the sails over, readjusted the sheets and picked up our new course, south-east. It began to rain.

There was little sleep again that night. The wind howled through the rigging. Waves began to build from the north-east, and we tried to sail as close hauled as we could pitching into the waves. We were tossed about in our bunks, held in only by the lee cloths. Water was over the deck dripped below. We tried to keep our sleeping bags dry by rigging plastic tents over our bunks, a desperate move. At 0300 hours the wind clocked to the east and increased to 25 knots, gusting higher. We shortened sail again, furling in the jib even further, but this reduced our speed to five knots.

Gale force winds continued through the next day, blowing 35 knots at times out of the east. Rain came in drenching sheets, narrowing our visibility to less than half a mile. Huge seas built up, often twenty feet high, appearing monstrous under the turgid sky. Gusts with a white spume blew off the tops of the waves and tugged at the sails, heeling the boat down to the rail. In the valleys between swells there was a lull and the sails flogged. But the seas did not curl or break. There was just the persistent heave upwards and sinking down in the mighty swell. Even doped with Dramamine, I felt wretched, like the onset of flu. How much longer could this go on, I wondered.

The noon-to-noon run was down to 127 nm.

We shortened sail again, which slowed us to a sluggish four knots. More lamentable, our course made was only 160 degrees, east of south. We were being pushed further south, south of the latitude of Bermuda, where we didn't want to be.

By dusk on Wednesday, day five, the steely doomsday cap of gray over the sky began to break up, and a thin fragile line of pale blue appeared on the horizon. The wind gave a last gasp, sighed and collapsed. We were virtually becalmed.

The waves gradually subsided and it was steady enough below to put a pot on the stove without risk of its being catapulted off. . Sam lit the burner and prepared dinner, Uncle Ben to the rescue with long grain rice, turkey and peas from cans. Jennifer sliced in a cube of ginger. I objected, not wanting my first good meal in two days to be ruined by some exotic culinary experiment. "No. No." She said, "Ginger is good for sea sickness." She may have been right, for certainly life took on a brighter cast, in spite of the growing darkness.

We took the double reef out of the main and pulled out the full genoa for the first time in two days. But soon the wind collapsed completely and we started the motor. The batteries were very low as the bilge pump had been working overtime during the storm. I decided we should motor through the night without running lights.

At midnight Brian relieved me at the helm. (Thursday, day 6) There was a freighter two miles off the starboard, the first shipping we had seen since leaving Bermuda. Brian questioned sailing without running lights and I agreed to turn them on whenever we saw another vessel. "If one comes close we can always switch on the spreader lights." These are the lights that shine down from the spreaders half-way up the mast. "They'll light up the sails, the whole boat in fact. We also have the man overboard strobe lights. And if they come too close, shoot a flare at them."

We also discussed fuel consumption. We had already used about twenty gallons, the equivalent of one of our tanks.

Through the night gentle zephyrs of wind teased the sails, then shifted further to a SSE 5 to 10 knots. But the seas were confused, tortured waves from one direction clashing with another at each shift of the wind. A rogue wave came out of the gloom, dumping a solid wall of water over the deck as far as the mast and spray back to the helm. Brian had rolled back the tarp tent over his bunk to catch a breath of fresh air and his bag took another drenching.

Stars poked through and by dawn there was a clear sky with a thin layer of cumulus on the horizon. "A day for drying out," Brian announced glumly. He dragged his mattress out and lashed it to the hand-rails on the cabin top. Sleeping bag were tied to the shrouds, damp clothing was looped through the reefing points, and a display of colorful foul weather gear decorated the life lines. We looked like prize-Winning contestants in a Fourth of July pageant sponsored by West Marine. Below decks Brian reconstructed a more serviceable plastic tarp tent over the forward bunks. "This could go on for another couple of weeks," he frowned. Little did he realize how right he was.

"Aahh, the sun!" Jennifer handed me a mug of tea before standing her watch. The day had the warmth of the Caribbean. A scattering of fluffed white cumulus clouds gave body to the deep blue of the sky. "I could stand a week of this," she chuckled, "but it's days like yesterday that help you appreciate it." One of those people who sees her cup half full, I thought. During the last days I'd sometimes seen mine as half empty. I recalled the days in Outward Bound when we considered it a duty to be cheerful.

But by mid-afternoon the wind clocked further to SSW 10 and we were able to sail a course of 115 degrees, but we made only 4.5 knots into the choppy seas. Sailing downwind, the main shadowed the jib which flogged uselessly without drawing. So we dropped the main and sailed under the full genoa, our biggest sail. Monty did not hold a course well with unbalanced sails, constantly turning into the wind It was frustrating Sam at the helm, and she was more comfortable steering herself

The noon-to-noon run was a disappointing 106 run, only 98 on route. We had drifted further south.

Mid-afternoon, I ran the engine to charge the batteries again. With the light wind we could use the boost of power. We felt reassured by the monotonous thrumming of diesel pistons. Half an hour later, I heard was a flat "pop," like a balloon bursting, the battery alarm light glowed red, and the engine stopped. A whiff of smoke came from below. Brian lifted the engine cover and felt the alternator. It was hot, He pushed the Start button. Nothing happened. Again. The engine did not respond. We were without mechanical power.

"At least that don't need to worry about conserving fuel," he mumbled.

Six days out. Distance run from Bermuda 609 nm. To Horta 1250 nm.

Crossing the North Atlantic on the way to Portugal,
1996.

Chapter 104: Only Half Way

An abrupt silence rang out like the one following the climactic ending of a symphony, that instant before the audience coughs and begins to clap. The engine had stopped. I sat upright in my bunk and scrambled for my foul weather gear.

We had been motoring in an attempt to break free of the adverse winds east of Bermuda, to pick up the westerlies that would take us to the Azores, 1000 miles east.

"What's wrong?" I called to Brian at the helm. My first thought was that he had turned the engine off 1 was annoyed.

"Don't know," he replied gruffly. "It just stopped."

"Must be the fuel filter again," I said. I recalled the time off Charleston when the engine stalled with a clogged fuel filter and I almost lost the boat.

"I don't think so." He hesitated. "I've pushed the START button again and it doesn't even turn over." There was a thoughtful pause. "It must be something electrical."

This could be more serious. My first reaction was one of denial. It can't be. The engine was virtually new, bought only two years before, scarcely out of warranty. I didn't have 1000 hours on it. That's like a car that's gone only 6000 miles. How could it be something electrical? I'd gone to all that expense, nearly $10,000 by the time the engine was installed. Diesels were meant to be virtually maintenance-free. What a piece of Perkins junk. 1 raised the engine hood and looked down at the tangle of hoses and wires and warm metal and was confronted with my ignorance. Engine failure was a personal affront.

Brian joined me and we took off the front engine panel. A whiff of smoke rose from the alternator. He touched it and jerked his hand back. "It's hot," he said, "you'd better disconnect the battery."

"I'll need to think about this," Brian concluded and closed the engine hood. Jennifer check our position on the GPS and logged it in. "We're 670 miles from Bermuda, another 1120 miles to Horta." That was our nearest harbor of refuge in the Azores, 700 miles off the coast of Portugal.

"The mark of a good seaman is what he does when he doesn't know what to do," I recalled an old Outward Bound friend telling me. He was a long time instructor at Hurricane Island, the sea school. What do I do now? Do I risk going on? Or turn back? The crew looked to me for some resolution and I debated putting the question to them.

Crowded in the cockpit that evening over dinner, I asked, "What do you think we should do?" We needed a decision. Any decision is better than not decision.

"What are the choices?" Sam asked, right to the point.

"Bermuda is closer than the Azores, we could turn back," I led off "We might be able to pick up the northeasterlies that have been on the nose, and return."

"Another option is to go south and pick up the trade winds. We could make for the Virgin Islands or Puerto Rico and locate a Perkins mechanic." That was a long way about, but it was plausible.

"Or we could go on. That would be my choice," I told them, "but I'm open to other suggestions." I knew the decision was ultimately mine, but I hoped for a consensus.

Silence. Water gurgled along the hull and bubbles disappeared in the wake astern.

Monty, the Monitor wind steering vane, the fifth member of the crew, had made his choice, I felt, and held us true to the course and drove on. Jennifer and Sam waited for Brian to speak.

"People have been crossing this ocean for 500 years," he responded, "under sail. I signed on to cross the Atlantic, -, he added somewhat theatrically, like Churchill defying the German Wehrmacht across the English Channel, "I think we should go on."

"Yes, me too," Jennifer responded. "1 don't trust the mechanical upgrades. The diesel engine, the EPIRB, and the Magellan GPS have already failed. But I do trust *Zillah.*" She added her touch of bravado.

"Certainment," Sam said with a French flare. She grew up in Montreal, bilingual. I felt it a vote of confidence, confidence in themselves primarily. But I felt as if I had screwed up. The captain was after all the one ultimately responsible.

"What emergency procedures do we need to adopt?" Jennifer questioned, ready to move on.

"We'll have to cut back on the use of battery power until I get the engine running," Brian stated. Both Jennifer and I took note of his use of the first person singular "I." Neither of us thought there really much of a chance of getting the engine functioning again. It was another act of Brian bravura. "We'll have to sail at night without running lights. That's the biggest drain," he asserted.

"If a ship approaches, we can warn it off with the strobe lights," Jennifer said.

They were powered by C-cell batteries, and it had been her idea to buy one for each crew member. We wore them when on watch and on deck at night.

"If they come too close, shoot a flare at them." I added, only half in humor.

"We can read the compass with a penlight. It has a red hood so it won't destroy your night vision." It used AA batteries. Fortunately I'd stocked up with Duracell batteries at Sam's Club in Puerto Rico. The bilge would need to be inspected and pumped manually by each of us, first thing when we came on watch. The Sony short-wave radio receiver, run on D-cell batteries, would pick up Herb's daily weather briefing from *South Bound II*. But we could not transmit.

In a life-threatening crisis, however, there was still enough power in the ship's batteries to send out an emergency radio signal. We talked about contacting Brian's father, a retired ship's radio operator in Newfoundland who monitored a HAM frequency. We could also contact passing freighters with the hand-held VHF radio.

The talk was therapeutic. Clearly we didn't see ourselves as victims of our fate but still masters of our souls. "Captain Bligh crossed 2,000 miles of the Pacific in an open boat with 18 men, after the mutiny on the *Bounty,*" Jennifer added. "Surely we're capable of getting a sturdy vessel like *Zillah* to Horta." I suspected she had used the same story to encourage dispirited Outward Bound students in their pulling boats on a rainy day in foggy Maine.

The next five days we needed all the encouragement we could summon. Life aboard became a game of Russian roulette, a gamble on both the weather and technology.

The weather struck first. By noon next day the sky darkened and we were smothered by the gathering heavy clouds, blue, that turned a purplish black like a deep bruise. "We'd better reef down." Jennifer hurried to the foredeck "This looks like a mean one."

The wind shifted suddenly to the NE and we were hit with 35-knot gale force winds. We were enveloped in 6-foot waves as green water crashed over the bow and sluiced down the deck, spray flew as far back as the helm. Seas continued to build, *Zillah* strained up each 10-foot swell like a dray horse pulling up a steep hill, then plunged in a flurry of froth down into the trough. We braced for the next slamming. With a third reef in the main and the jib furled forward of the shrouds, our speed stalled to a mere three and a half knots.

"South Bound II. South Bound II. This is Hannah Ho." We picked up the transmission of another yacht on the Sony receiver that evening. It was positioned 55 miles behind us to the southwest. "When will we get through this mess?" The anxious lady sounded desperate.

"You need to go north," Herb told her in his authoritative voice. "There is a frontal passage," and he gave the details. "You need to get to the north side of it. If you go ESE (which we were doing) you will stay with the front," he admonished, as if she was doing something wrong. "You need to go north," he repeated. It sounded like an order. "Not east. Go NNW if you have to and the wind will diminish and clock. You want to be at 34 degrees north." Our position was 32 degrees 27 minutes north, well over 100 miles south of Herb's way point. "Then when the winds clock you should have SSW winds ten to fifteen knots for the next four days."

We went onto the starboard tack and set a course as close to the wind as we could, 330 degrees, which took us west of north, still into heading seas, a disheartening prospect.

There was little sleep that night. In their forward berth Brian and Sam were catapulted through a six-foot trajectory with the rise of each wave. "It's like sleeping on a trampoline," she moaned.

In my berth mid-ships, I pivoted as though on a rodeo horse, with only the lee-cloth keeping me from being bucked off We cowered in our bunks under the improvised tarp tents that shed the persistent drip from the leaking decks. Sam slept in her foul weather gear.

When we pumped the bilge manually we discovered that the outlet hose was only five feet long. Jennifer pumped into a bucket in the companionway, which I emptied out on the deck, a tedious two-person operation.

"Didn't I see a length of hose in the bosun's locker?" Brian asked when he came on watch. He connected the two lengths of hose, taped the junction, and pumped directly overboard. I was struck by his mechanical ingenuity.

The wind moderated to a steady fifteen knots during the night and Jennifer let out the reefing points when she came on watch. By morning we sailed under full main and Genoa still on a course of 330 degrees. At seven knots it was a rough but exhilarating sail through pitching seas. If only we had been going in the right direction. The noon-to-noon run was only 74 miles on our rhumb line towards the Azores, our worst day yet.

"Do you have a wiring diagram for the engine?" Brian asked next morning. The Perkins Owners Manual didn't include one. But a warranty mechanic had left it two years earlier, in another engine emergency. Brian spent much of the day studying it with the focused concentration of an archeologist unraveling the mystery of the Rosetta stone, deciphering the hieroglyphics of electronic circuitry. From time to time he opened the engine hood and run his hands over the connections, translating the abstractions of the diagram to the concreteness of wires, hoses and steel. He closed it with a long pensive scowl. The rest of us waited for that "Eureka" moment, but none came.

"I've never worked on a diesel engine before," Brian admitted the following day as he bent over the engine. Nevertheless, this creative computer programmer was in his element, scanning the wiring diagram, tracing the circuitry, tightening connections, ferreting out shorts in the system, checking and rechecking leads with the voltmeter. He was like Sherlock Holmes deep in thought, formulating his hypothesis. I was his willing Watson, passing him pliers, wrenches and screwdrivers, reading the voltmeter.

"Let's try the starter motor," he said and connected it directly to the battery, bypassing the alternator. It turned over with a screeching whirr and sparks flew. But there was no response from the engine. It lay silent and dormant like a sleeping giant. "Baffling," he muttered. "The red battery warning light glows red. The alarm buzzer buzzes. But then it stays on even when the ignition key is turned off. It's got to be something in the alternator."

"Elementary old chap," Holmes would have said.

That night we broke through the weather front, and the wind shifted gradually from northeast to east, and by morning it blew lightly from the south and settled in the southwest. Now we could run downwind on our line to Horta 1051 miles east, clear sailing. I felt a great sense of relief as did the rest of the crew. Jennifer brought out clothes and sleeping bags to dry out in the sun and she busied herself with boat tasks, checking the rigging and sails for chafe, whipping the ends of ropes to prevent further fraying. We opened the forward hatch to air out the pungent dank below. Sam read at the helm, monitoring *Monty* who had difficulty keeping a course in the light winds.

But the reprieve was short-lived. It was as if we had been released from the pounding and punishment of the headwinds, only to be snared in an airless vacuum. The wind dropped from ten knots to five, and then we floundered. We lingered five hours in a calm. Dead calm. Not a flat calm, for the ocean continued to heave with the swell, an undulating mirror. With the faintest ripple on the ocean's surface we adjusted sails like chasing ephemeral breezes with a butterfly net.

We were anxious to move on. Jennifer had an Outward Bound staff workshop in Belgium in two weeks. "This isn't one I can miss, Dad. I'm conducting it."

Light winds filled in, but running downwind in *Zillah* had always been problematic. We debated whether to go with jib alone or with both jib and main. I was tempted to put up as much canvas as I could, but then the mainsail blanketed the genoa, which was the largest sail, the workhorse.

"What about wing and wing?" Jennifer suggested, the jib out on port side, the main as far out as we could get it on the starboard side. The difficulty was that in the light winds and large seas, the boom was potentially lethal, a gigantic club that swinging back and forth as *Zillah* rolled in the swells. The boom needed to be secured. But how?

"This is where a spinnaker pole would be helpful," remarked Jennifer. I had carried a 25-foot wooden pole lashed on deck for two years. But it was unwieldy, too heavy for me to handle alone when sailing with Mary as sole crew. I had used it once only, so discarded it when outfitting for the Atlantic Crossing in Puerto Rico. Now I regretted it, for with a crew of four it would have been no problem.

"We could run a preventer line from the end of the boom, forward to a block at the bow, outboard of the shrouds," Jennifer improvised. "And tighten it on the port genoa winch. That would keep it from swinging."

"Makes sense. Let's try it!" The genoa billowed out thirty feet to port, soaring fifty feet to the mast top, the mainsail spread out along the boom to starboard, like a gigantic white moth fluttering out to sea. It was a jubilee moment.

"Not a moth, Dad," Jennifer corrected me. "Pegasus. A winged horse."

Visually impressive. "Awesome!" Sam affirmed from the helm.

But it added little to our speed. With the deep swell left over from the storm the sails collapsed with each undulation and the boat shuddered. Eventually the wind shifted further west, and increased to fifteen knots. We detached our elaborate preventer, went on the port tack and able to make a good six knots. In spite of calms our noon-to-noon distance run was 135 miles, a good day.

When I came on watch at 0400 hours, the darkness had a tangible thickness, mist obliterated the stars. The bow wave sparkled with phosphorescence giving an eerie glow, leaving a long wake astern. We ghosted through the gloom without running lights. "You'll hear a freighter before you see it," Jennifer cautioned me as she turned in.

Morning dawned gray, opaque, the sea and sky merged with a diffused glow like wet slate. The wind died and we were becalmed again, the sails hanging limp, like laundry on the line on a breathless day. But the noon-to-noon run was still a respectable 99 miles. "Horta is 819 miles," Jennifer called from the navigation table, "Bermuda 976 miles. We're over halfway there."

"Only halfway?" Sam asked. Impatience was contagious.

On the fifth day of Creation, *God said, Let the waters bring forth abundantly the moving creatures that have life ... And God created great whales and every creature that moved, which the waters brought forth abundantly.* (Genesis 1 :20-22.) HE must have begun with plankton for the sea turned from a royal blue to a faded hydrangea green, and porpoises followed the smaller fish into the feeding grounds. They leapt about the bow, cavorting in a joyous display of aquabatics, chasing each other back and forth. There was one showman, an extrovert who kept making arching leaps, one after another, as if it was his special trick. Sam went forward to the bow to cheer him on.

The grandmother of turtles collided with the boat with a resounding thud. She was five feet across, with yellow and brown hatched markings, evidently asleep on the surface. Awakened from her mid-ocean siesta, she submerged in a panic. Sharks circled the boat warily before moving on for more vulnerable prey. We came upon one tormented creature who thrashed desperately, rotating frantically as if snagged on a lure it could not disgorge. I never felt pity for a shark before, but I did feel it unnecessary cruelty to leave him that way. However, I was unwilling to risk freeing him.

Jellyfish were prolific, huge Portugese-man-o-war with opaque gelatinous heads, bulbous, volleyball-size, and translucent stringy tentacles three feet long. Jennifer lured one into a bucket and after a hesitant inspection, poured it back. Further on, small ones no larger than peanuts surrounded the boat, millions of them, a jellyfish hatchery. They took God's commandment *to fill the waters a/ the sea,* most seriously.

In a single day we saw more creatures and critters of the sea than we did the rest of the voyage. It also left me with the haunting vision of the Ancient Mariner, *Yea slimy things did crawl with legs/ Upon the slimy sea.*

"Whale ho!" A hundred and fifty years earlier another ship on our course, bound for the Azores, would have been galvanized into action by the look-out's call from the crow's nest aloft. When Jennifer hailed us from the helm, we all scrambled on deck to marvel at these monsters of the deep, one of the largest animals ever to have lived on earth. Even larger than the dinosaurs. Two whales had surfaced four hundred yards to starboard, and cruised along, seemingly without effort at our speed, keeping a beady eye on our boat. I sensed their wary caution of a species that had been hunted for generations.

Yet there was an affinity with these lumbering beasts, in spite of their outrageous size. Something mystical perhaps. I recalled listening to the high-pitched whining, and moaning sounds on the tapes my former wife used to lull her to sleep. Humans were even a related species to whales, both of us mammals, though it was difficult to associate such bulk with conventional mammalian behavior like copulation, or nursing their young.

They kept their distance, maintaining our speed. As curious as I was to have them come closer, I was also apprehensive. Centuries of demonization, from Jonah to Ahab, had imprinted our psyche with a sense of dread. Stories abound of small boats being demolished by whales. Some like Moby Dick attacked out of anger and revenge. Others that had been run down when asleep on the surface, attacked out of self-defense. On other occasions, when we spotted whales off Cape Cod and Samana, on

493

the east coast of the Dominican Republic, I had turned on the motor to signal a truce. But now I had not engine.

Disappointed to see them go, I was also relieved when they sounded, spouting a tall geyser of hot breath that condensed in the cooler air, a mighty belch smelling pungently of undigested seaweed and fish offal, even four hundred yards away. "Next time you want to approach whales to windward," I suggested to Jennifer.

"You say we'll have these light winds all the way to the Azores?" the lady on *Hannah Ho* asked Herb that night.

"No," Herb replied. "You need to get north to 37 degrees north. A front is moving east and you must stay in front of it, or you will have northeast winds again and more calm. Motor if you have to."

"Easy for you to say, Herb." Sam spoke for all of us.

"I know nothing about alternators," Brian had said and he had now spent the last three days filling the gap. We both studied Nigel Calder, *Mechanical and Electrical Boat Maintenance* which was our best source of information. The Perkins Owners Manual didn't cover alternators. It wasn't a Perkins part. Another complaint we noted. "I need to take the alternator off and look at it," Brian announced. The drive belt loosened easily, as did two out of three of the bolts that held it in place. The threads of the last bolt were stripped, something I had done previously by trying to loosen it the wrong way. But I wasn't about to confess that to Brian. We had to saw off the head of the bolt with a bare hacksaw blade painstakingly clenched between our fingers, as the space was too small for the full saw.

"As I suspected, there's a short in the alternator," Brian muttered when we tested it with a voltmeter. He checked the wiring diagram again. "This is what must be shorting out the starter motor."

"Be sure to call me at eight," he said when I relieved him of his watch at midnight. "I need to take the alternator apart tomorrow." As he took each part off, he lined it in a straight row in order on the navigation table, securing each with duct tape, so it wouldn't roll off and fall between the cracks of the floor-boards into the bilge. Meticulously he made a note of each. He explained that the ignition switch turned the starter motor on, but also turned it off once the engine started running and the alternator began to generate power. "I think 1 know how I can by-pass that switch," he affirmed optimistically.

He reassembled the alternator that afternoon, carefully, piece by piece, muttering, as if saying a mantra over each part. He connected a four-foot length of lamp cord with a toggle switch, and attached it to the START button.

The day wore on. The sky had cleared to blue, with scattered cumulus clouds and light fickle winds. We coasted along at a slow nagging three knots. The noon-to-noon run was a mere 75 miles. It was clear that we needed an engine if we were to stay ahead of the approaching front.

It was five o'clock, approaching dusk, when Brian called to me. "Well, let's give it a try," he said with a hopeful smile. I had the feeling of standing at a roulette table with high stakes, gambling on the engine.

"Switch power on," Brian directed.

"On." I flipped the toggle switch.

"Turn the ignition key." The buzzer buzzed. "Push the START button." The engine turned over slowly, grudgingly. Coughed.

"Push it again." And the engine fired with a burst of smoke from the exhaust and a clatter of pistons that picked up to a rhythmic pounding. I waited, still expecting it to die. But it ran on. The eureka moment after four days! The skeptics, myself included, had been proven wrong. Brian grinned through his salt-caked beard. I gave him a huge hug in a rare display of emotion.

"Check the voltmeter. Is the alternator charging?" It wasn't. "A diesel engine doesn't need electricity to run, only to start." Brian had successfully by-passed the automatic turn off switch so that it could continue to run.

We set a course of 100 degrees, our rhumb line to Horta, now 700 miles away and motored off into the gentle swell at a steady 6 knots.

"I never thought I'd delight in the sound and smell of a diesel engine." Jennifer laughed.

Seven hundred miles. How much fuel would we need to motor there? A little over hundred hours at six knots, that would be about 80 gallons. Jennifer figured we had about 60 gallons. "It will get us most of the way."

I turned in early to nap before my night watch. Just as I had reached a semi-conscious state, the engine stopped.

"No, not again! What happened?" I shouted out, reaching for my clothes.

"The engine just stopped," Jennifer replied from the helm, distressed as if she were to blame.

The electrical system, was my first thought. Get Brian. Or could it be the fuel filter? I reconsidered. Sure enough. It was clogged with black snotty diesel slime. Jennifer replaced the filter with a new one, bled the air from the fuel line and-injectors. "Toggle switch on. Turn ignition key. Push START button." We motored on.

"We've made 94 miles in the last 14 hours," Jennifer announced next morning when we turned the engine off. The wind was a light ten knots from the SE. We moved along on a beam reach at four knots under sail. Our noon run was 125 miles. We were out of the doldrums and staying ahead of the front.

Thoughts turned to Horta, only 558 miles away, and warm showers, fresh food, contact with the world beyond, and repairs to the alternator. Or so we hoped.

Chapter 105: Horta

We were not the first to seek out Horta as a harbor of refuge. Eighteen days and eighteen hundred miles from Bermuda, 2000 miles from the East Coast of the United States, another 800 on to Europe, the Azores had been a haven for battered and sea-weary mariners since its discovery by the Portugese in 1351. Columbus has stopped here to refill his water casks on his return in 1493 with the great secret of a New World. The fishing fleets had preceded him returning from the Grand Banks off Newfoundland, though they left no historic record. Few cod fishermen wrote their memoirs.

We were exhausted yet elated, like the completion of a marathon. I felt as though we had achieved something significant, but it was difficult to find words for it, as we rounded the great sea wall that protected the port from the prevailing northwesterly winds that brought us in, and ducked behind the inner breakwater that sheltered the marina. It had finger piers for thirty boats, and another twenty tied to the wall. A hundred boats were crowded together. We cleared custom, officially entering the European Union, and rafted up to another boat, four out from the dock.

We had stayed before the weather front, motoring for three days once Brian got the engine running. We listened on the SSB radio to others behind us battling the nor' easter, urged on by Herb, the weather guru to "Go north. You have to get to the north of the front." We had, and when it caught up with us, we following winds, 20 to 25 knots from the northwest. With sails double reefed we made seven knots with winds on the quarter. Following seas hoisted *Zillah* eight to ten feet high, and we sledded down the waves in a flush of green water and flurry of foam. *Monty,* the Monitor wind steering vane, had difficulty hold the course, as it was difficult to get the right balance of sails and *Zillah* had a strong weather helm in the gusts, and the quartering seas nudged the boat further. It frequently needed a correcting hand at the helm and standing watch demanded vigilance and became tedious.

Life aboard concentrated on the conservation and renewal of energy. We tried to rest as much as we could, but finding it difficult to sleep because of the constant pitching of the boat, but we knew that sleep was an imperative in order to stay awake on watch at night. I never felt really hungry given the motion and it became an act of discipline to prepare meals, and then to eat them, though nobody became seasick. Food was a matter of energy rather then enjoyment. During the day we retreated into our own world, reading or writing, but that too was difficult given the conditions.

Each day became a test of endurance and civility. We became irritated and irritable.

Jennifer had a time table she had to meet, a professional commitment in Belgium in less that two weeks time, and we were still a thousand miles out in the Atlantic. She constantly adjust sails with each change in the wind, trying to drive the boat one knot faster. "I refuse to get up once more in the middle of the night to shorten sails," Brian objected. "We should do it before we turn in." I too felt the strain, preoccupied with how I could get the alternator repaired.

We arrived less than twelve hours before the main force of the storm hit. We were protected by the seawall, but I woke to the wind moaning through the rigging, piping to a high whistle in the gusts. The halyard was clanging on the aluminum mast with the frenzy of a jazz drummer who has snorted cocaine. Jennifer got up to tie it to the shrouds. "So much for our first night without being tossed about by the seas," she said as she nestled back into her sleeping bag and adjusted the plastic tarp to fend off the consistent drip through the leaking deck. Through it all came the incongruous high soprano of Italian opera. A neighboring boat had retreated to their sound system, played fortissimo, to blanket the angry acoustics of the storm.

I lie awake frustrated that this was the first night I had given myself permission to sleep through the night and thinking of the conflicts of transition. There was the relative simplicity of life on the boat, a survival ordeal, and the complexity of life ashore, the entry into an expanding universe.

Horta did not make the transition easier. The weather continued bluster with driving rain, as the front moved through when we went ashore. The town faced the sea, unlike New England fishing ports where the waterfront was lined with sheds and the backdoors of warehouses. The streets were cobbled, buildings a somber granite, stubbornly durable having weathered the ages. Above town, the hillside rose in terraced fields, vinyards and orchards, a husbanded landscape, where cattle grazed.

Shopkeepers were welcoming, the waiters friendly, hospitality a natural grace. But our agenda was pressing, and we were having little success. There was no Perkins representative. We walked the length of town checking with each marine service shop, but could not find an alternator, new or used. "We could order one. It would take five or six days to air freight it from England," we were told. So I called the Perkins distributor in England, and was told they didn't have one in stock. "It is a Lucas part," the service manager said.

"Let's get the batteries charged up," Brian suggested. Like the rest of Europe, the marina had 220 volt power. Our charger was for 110 volt. So we rented one from a service shop, but their electric cord was not long enough to run to the outlet box on the dock. Our cord was long enough, but our plugs wouldn't fit the sockets. All three hardware stores were sold out of the 220 volt plugs. So Brian took off the plugs from the short cord, replaced them on the long cord, and we had power. But half the day was lost in the process. We had a similar quest for diodes that might have helped us repair the alternator. A taxi ride to the electrical shop outside of town turned out go be fruitless. Another day lost. So were right back where we started, an alternator that did not charge, though the batteries were fully charged, which gave us power, so long as the charge would last.

For all the frustration, we welcomed the amenities. Hot water showers. Jennifer found a laundry and we changed from salt encrusted and odoriferous clothing and bedding. The pears at the local market had a spicy Bosque flavor and went well with a local cheese with a slight tang like Stilton. That evening in the restaurant, I couldn't read the menu in Portuguese, but the fish spoke of a thousand years heritage of the sea.

"For all our troubles, we got off easy," I told Jennifer. I'd been talking with the delivery captain of a modem high performance forty-foot Finnish boat that had come in a couple weeks earlier. They'd been caught in a storm that came off Nova Scotia a month earlier, the same one that gave us the 30-foot swells in our passage from Puerto Rico to Bermuda. They'd been knocked down, damaged the rigging, and the rudder broke off at the rudder post and was lost at sea. They'd navigated a thousand miles of the open Atlantic using buckets and drogues off the stem to steer. At sea they had to fend off a seagoing tug that wanted to claim them as salvage, a time honored practice, until close enough to Horta for the Coast Guard to tow them in.

"But they can't fix it here," the captain said. "The owner is having it shipped back to Finland for repairs."

He went on to tell us of another boat in the same storm that was crewed only by the owner and his wife. They were hit by a monstrous wave, the boat broached-to and rolled, injuring both of them. They felt they were unable to handle the boat, put out an emergency call and were picked up by a freighter that came to their rescue. They opened the seacocks, scuttled the boat at sea, so that it would not be a navigational hazard.

"I felt sorry for myself, because 1 had not shoes," 1 recalled an ancient Arab proverb. "Then I saw a man who had not feet."

We refueled, topped up with water and motored out of Horta with a new sense of the meaning of "a harbor of refuge."

Chapter 106: Shipping Lanes

"Security! Security! Security! All ships. This is sailing vessel *Zillah.*" I relayed my position coordinates. "I am proceeding on a course of 100 degrees at seven knots in thick fog. Any ship that has us on their radar, please acknowledge."

We had crossed 2,500 miles of ocean from Bermuda. We were twenty miles off the coast of Portugal traversing one of the busiest shipping lanes in the world and I could not see two hundred yards off the bow. A ship going fifteen knots would close on us in less than two minutes from first being sighted.

Minutes passed. Eyes stared into the colorless void. Shapes emerged through the shifting mist, layers of gray. Then there were no shapes. Except in imagination. The radio was silent.

"I'll sound the fog-horn!" Jennifer, my first mate daughter said. The baleful moan, a song of sadness, is blown away in the wind and swallowed by the fog. Jennifer blows again.

The radio crackles alive. "This is motor ship *Norstrom,*" a mellifluous Scandinavian voice replies. "I have four ships on my radar screen. Which one are you?"

How do I know? I can't see his radar screen, I think. Where are the other three? Sam spells Jennifer blowing on the fog-horn. Why didn't I buy an air-horn?

Minutes later a murky shape emerges off the starboard bow, shades of gray thinning to a pale white as we close the distance between us. It's an ocean going fishing boat, nets hung on outriggers. "Probably on auto-pilot. Doesn't even see us," Jennifer says. Brian at the helm alters course quickly to pass by his stern. "That accounts for one. Where are the others?" We feed on each others anxiety.

Brian, who grew up in fog-bound Newfoundland takes the fog more casually than I do. Too casually I think. He stands the helm with a magazine in his hand, reading. He glances occasionally at the compass. Monty, the wind steering vane keeps the course, needing only periodic adjustments.

I'm intent on the emptiness forward, trying to pierce the opaque wall of dingy gray. Then by chance I glance back. The dark outline of a huge container ship churns by, 400 yards astern, where we had been a scarce two minutes before. It is scarcely visible in the fog, scarcely audible in the wind. With a studied control to my voice, "Brian, would you mind looking behind you?"

Begrudgingly he stops reading in mid-paragraph, slowly turns around and then jerks back. "Holy _____" he shouts, seeing the gray hulk dissolve in the haze.

"Sam, quick. Get on deck." In an instant all hands are on deck, straining to see, to hear, to avoid. It would be the supreme irony to cross 3,000 miles of ocean and crash twenty miles from shore.

The day has been a wild race. At 0000 hours we were 141 miles from Lisbon, still a good days run. After seventy-two hours of motoring, three days to escape the Azores high pressure windless calm, the winds picked up. We entered the Portuguese trades, the steady flow of wind and current down the coast of Europe, blowing a steady north-east twenty knots. With double reefed main and the genoa rolled in to the shrouds, we made a steady seven knots. It became a race to make the coast of Portugal before dark, or at least to cross the shipping lanes before sunset.

Lisbon was a further ten miles up the Tejus (Tagus) River, a busy shipping channel which we preferred to avoid in the dark. But there was a small harbor at the mouth of the river, Cascais, a resort community. It was shallow, but we should be able to nudge in safely, unless the tide was unusually low. The coastal pilot book reported a muddy bottom should we ground out. It would also we well lit from shore lights.

Capo Raso is the westernmost point of Europe and we would have to round it to enter. Jennifer put a waypoint into the GPS one mile offshore. When I came on watch at six p.m. we were only 9.6 miles out on a course of 118 degrees. The winds had continued brisk, sending up heavy seas that made it difficult to hold to the course. The compass swung us twenty degrees off with each big surge before Monty could correct. I believed I could make better time steering by hand, where I could anticipate each swell and head into it before being thrown off course. We made a steady seven knots. Closer to shore in gusts we clocked eight knots, an exhilarating sense of speed.

Another fishing boat emerged from the fog 400 yards off and I altered course to pass 100 yards to his stem, and we surged on into the bleakness. *Zillah* heeled to the rail and water crashed off the port bow. The rigging strained and I said a silent prayer that nothing would give way.

At seven p.m. we were 1.5 miles off Capo Raso and passed it ten minutes later, flying along, seeing nothing but the blanketing gray haze. All crew are in the cockpit on look-out.

"There's a patch of blue sky!" Sam says, pointing up. The mist brightened to a platinum gray.

A long white object forms a blur above water level. "Is it a cruise ship?" Brian asks.

Then the fog lifts. "No it's a building. On shore!" Jennifer says. A large white resort hotel stretching along the rocky headland, came more distinctly into view. The sky cleared to a bright blue, the moon already risen in the east. The sun, brilliant and dazzling shone through the wisp, a brilliant orange ball filtered through the fog bank. Every one laughs, talking, pointing as Europe takes shape.

"Just smell the earth. The warm air. Grass. Flowers," Jennifer said

"I'd cross the Atlantic all over again, just for this moment!" Sam said.

We rounded Cabo Roso and the wind died. We dropped the mainsail, furled the jib and motored into Cascais. An hour later at 8:10 p.m. we dropped anchor, still by daylight.

Brian went below for a bottle of wine, and we drink a toast to our successful Atlantic crossing.

Zillah under sail.

Chapter 106: Coasting

An enormous monument to Prince Henry the Navigator overlooked the Tagus River, a lone figure on the mighty prow of a ship, arm outstretched. Reunited with *Zillah*. Mary and I passed beneath him on our way down the river from Lisbon to the sea. I had the feeling that he pointed the way for us too. We were launched on the next leg of our journey, a cruise along one of the most remarkable coasts of Europe, spectacular in its geography, renowned in history. A new chapter was opening up.

Sines was fifty miles down the coast along an unbroken line of sand hills. Once a fishing village, now a large commercial harbor with oil refineries, it was protected by an enormous seawall. We anchored in sand off the old town, well out of the big ship's channel. By early evening four other yachts came in and anchored nearby.

Cabo Sao Vincente, fifty-six miles further south, is a magnificent landmark, a dramatic headland on the southwest corner of Europe, lands-end, jutting out to the Atlantic, two hundred and fifty feet high. The pounding waves splashed high on the rocks, then crashed at its foot. Swirling currents surged around the base. The chart showed deep water in close, but I was anxious that we would be swept in as Mary approached closer for a better look.

Then we rounded the cape to the calm and quiet in its lee. In the protected Waters of Ensenada da Belixe we found a spot shallow enough to anchor in, close in under the cliff. Above were the lighthouse and a fort that had been restored as a parador, one of a chain of fancy tourist hotels built in historic monuments. Guests negotiated their way down a steep, narrow path to the sea to swim.

At night I found the place eerie, unsettling. The precipice above loomed black in the moonless night. With no wind, the boat circled around the anchor in the eddying current, the chain grated over the rocky bottom. Pebbles rattled on the beach in the ebbing tide, the sound amplified in the dark.

This was a graveyard of ships. Great naval battles had been fought in these waters during the 17th and 18th centuries, and the Napoleonic Wars, for supremacy of the seas. Many a drowned sailors must have washed up on this shore. I felt the presence of the embattled past and couldn't sleep.

Nor was I assured by the remote possibility of Saint Vincent's protection. A ship bearing his remains had been shipwrecked on this point. Miraculously ravens rescued the relics and carried them to Lisbon, where he was enshrined as the patron saint of Portugal.

At two o'clock, always a witching hour for me, a land breeze came up and we swung closer under the cliffs. I decided it was time to move. Guided by the loom of the lighthouse flashing every five seconds, we motored around the next headland to Ensenada da Sagres where the holding was good.

The next morning bathers descended to the beach to soak in the sun. We jumped joyfully off the boat for our first swim in the brisk European waters. I spent the day in the dinghy, scrubbing Lisbon grime from the topsides, enjoyably productive.

But after dark the wind shifted and *Zillah* rolled viciously in the ocean swell now on the beam. "This is like trying to sleep inside a cement mixer," I said, attempting to humor Mary.

"We need to bridle the anchor." She prompted me at first light. I took a line out in the dinghy and lashed it to the anchor chain, about a boat-length ahead of the bow. Mary cranked the line in on the genoa winch, adjusting the angle of the boat so the bow faced into the swell. The rolling ceased. "We should have done it when the rolling began,"

We swam after lunch and then moved a short distance again to Baleeira, and anchored behind a protective seawall among the fishing boats, and several yachts. After two sleepless nights, coasting was beginning to lose its charm.

But we were soon caught up in harbor life. A friendly lady from *Rosebud* rowed over. "I knew Zillah years ago when she sailed off the south coast of England," she said. She and her husband were returning home after a nine-year circumnavigation. "I used to be a reporter for the *Daily Telegraph* and covered ocean racing. She was famous in her day."

Well, 1 think she's still famous, I was about to say, but didn't.

Certain places are hallowed ground though no monuments commemorate them. Certain places are hallowed ground though no monuments commemorate them. The headland above Cabo Sagres was one. After a short walk along the sea cliffs, Mary and I came to the point with a sweeping view west and south out over the Atlantic. This was where Prince Henry the Navigator (1394-1460) built the first naval academy in Europe in1415. A son of King John I, of Portugal, and an English Queen, a Renaissance man, he brought together Mallorcan shipwrights, Genoese and Venetian sea captains, Arab mathematicians; astrologers, Jewish cartographers, who were to change our knowledge and perception of the world. They redrew the earlier Mediterranean-centric maps, that had Jerusalem at the center of the world, to include the Atlantic Coast and the still unexplored Ocean Sea. They recorded the movement of the stars and developed improved navigation instruments that made possible more accurate observations of the sun. They designed and built more seaworthy ships that were lighter, faster and could sail closer to windward.

The buildings had long since been destroyed, but the view encapsulated the vision and the inspiration of this extraordinary man. In what had once been the courtyard, an immense compass rose larger than a tennis court was laid out in black and white pebbled stones, the instrument that still makes it possible for mariners to travel beyond the sight of land.

Hallowed ground indeed, I thought as we walked back. Even the Romans had endowed this furthest point of southwest Europe with mystical significance. They had named it *Promentorium Sacrum*, which was abbreviated to Sagres in Portuguese.

A short run along the Algarve, the southern coast of Portugal, brought us to Lagos. The wind was fickle and we motored much of the way. A gentle swell was running, barely noticeable offshore, but as we approached Lagos, it began to build up. A hundred yards out the seas began to break. Should we change course? I realized I should have checked the chart for depth more closely. But it was too late. We were committed, caught in the surge that swept us forward. Waves crashed on the jetties that guarded the harbor entrance and we rode through the narrow gap in a roar of foamy spray. We held on tightly, expecting to hear the grating, sickening crunch of the keel on the bottom. Then I looked back. The surf was behind us. Eureka. We had cleared the bar. The anchorage was crowded with fishing boats, so we took a berth in the modern marina.

Lagos had been taken over by the holiday crowd, yet the old town kept much of its traditional charm. As in many European cities, the present lives comfortably with the past. It was here that Prince Henry built his ships, the fast moving caravels, and launched them on a series of voyages of discovery that opened the Atlantic. Madeira was discovered in 1419, the Azores in 1427. In 1434 Cape Bojador, then the farthest known point of western Africa was reached and passed. The Portuguese went on to extend the boundaries of the known world. The Cape Verde Islands were discovered in 1456. In 1488 they rounded Cabo da Esparanza (Cape of Good Hope) and Vasco da Gama sailed on to India. Magellan completed the first circumnavigation of the world in 1522.

Enlightened Henry may have been. but this did not preclude an eye for gain. We visited the Mercada do Escava, Europe's first slave market. The early explorations of the African coast had not been very profitable, until in 1444 one of his ships returned with a human cargo of 200 Africans. Later generations rationalized that they did convert them to Christianity. In the elaborate baroque church of Santo Antonio, I wondered how much of the gold ornamentation had come from the sweat of slaves. Did they light candles for their souls too?

Europe was on holiday, so we decided to avoid the vacationing crowds, by-passing the high rise resort communities along the southern Algarve coast. "Just like Miami Beach," Mary said, "only they're built on the cliff-tops." We set a direct course southeast to the large tidal lagoons that lie off Faro.

They were sheltered by a stretch of barrier islands twenty miles long, and we coasted well off shore. We found the entrance at Cabo da Santa Maria and lined up the makers at the end of the protecting sea wall. The pilot book indicated a depth of three meters. *Zillah* drew two and a half, so we knew it would be close with the shifting sand.

"Keep well to the right, Mary," I said, for the channel was indicated on that side. I chose to ignore the cautionary note in the pilot book that the sketch chart was not to be used for purposes of navigation. We could see the breaking swell and headed straight through. The onrushing wave lifted the stem and we gathered speed with the surge. We were in the midst of another exhilarating joy ride. Then the boat almost stopped and lurched wildly to starboard.

"Jeez Mary! Keep it straight!" I shouted over the rumble of rushing water.

"I can't!" She had the helm down hard but the boat would not respond. We're aground, I thought. Then the boat swung just as violently to port. The steering cable broke again, was my next thought. "How do your read the water?" Mary called out.

I looked down and it was swirling in tight whirlpools and spinning off in eddies. It caught the bow, pushing it one way, the stem another. And then back. We were caught between the out flowing tide and the onshore swell.

To add to the confusion, a high-powered red Zodiac inflatable roared out towards us. "Go left!" the skipper shouted, waving frantically, and shot back into the lagoon.

Zillah responded sluggishly making slow headway against the spinning current.

Gradually, painfully, we inched our way upcurrent to the quiet waters of the lagoon. There the channel was clearly buoyed and we moved on to the anchorage and dropped the plow in the middle of a flotilla of yachts and pleasure boats. We felt we had arrived at a true haven.

Life became an unanticipated whirl of social activity. *Bonnie Lass* invited us over for drinks and "chat." We went with them by dinghy to the settlement on the Ilha da Culatra, a quaint village with modest cottages, unpaved sand streets and no cars. It fronted on the beach and we strolled among the sand pipers and dipping birds. Exploring the small islands in the lagoon, we wished we had an Audubon guide to water fowl, for we were on one of the great migratory flight paths from northern Europe to Africa.

It was the sort of anchorage one dreamed about. "Let's stay on a second day," Mary said. Felicity and Mike on *Ten K* hailed us for dinner. The British have the reputation of being aloof and reserved, but the Brits we met cruising defied the norm. If it was a norm. Certainly their capacity for wine, song and their encyclopedic collection of tall tales surpassed my meager repertoire. With a couple glasses of wine I only became garrulous, Mary claimed.

We were rediscovering the charms of coasting. I was reminded of Robert Louis Stevenson who wrote that those who go by train do not travel, they merely arrive. This was even more true today, as people cover vast distances on airplanes, I thought. On *Zillah* Mary and I were true travelers.

Cruising in Europe, coasting, we found combined the adventure of sailing with the convenience of travelling with our home, the interaction with other sailors. and the exposure to a living culture against a background of their rich past. I realized again how privileged we were.

I was struck by the stark contrast between passage making the previous month, and this new adventure of coasting.

"What was crossing the Atlantic like?" one of my landlocked friends had asked.

"It's hard to describe," I'd said. "It's a bit like a marathon." He too was a runner. "You put one foot in front of the other and keep on going until you find the balance between breathing, heart beat and stride. It's mostly rhythm, routine, with few high points. The only climax is the finishing line.

"An ocean passage is also largely routine: eating, sleeping, standing watch and checking gear. One day just follows the next."

"But weren't you afraid?" his wife asked.

How do you answer that without being melodramatic? I could deal with fear in my written memoirs but not in casual conversation. "Not really," I said, "but I did worry a lot." I explained that we listened to the long-range weather forecast each night and worried whether we could stay ahead of the storm systems. Would we run out of fuel, or water? Would the food hold out?

"The crew ate all the cheese, the pre-packaged meals the first two weeks, along with the chocolate and cookies. Nobody wanted the Dinty Moore's canned beef stew," I said. She was an excellent cook and readily identified with that.

"And on an old boat like *Zillah*, I was always worried about what was going to break next?

I admitted that in storms the line between anxiety and fear was often thin.

"How did you sleep? Did you put the anchor down every night?" she asked, and we all laughed.

Yet passage making in fair weather was almost a form of meditation, I tried to explain, the ship became our own universe, a cosmos of our own creation.

If passage making was like a marathon, coasting by contrast, could be compared to a leisurely stroll with the occasional sprint or 100~yard dash. We usually made port each night after a run of fifty to seventy miles. Mary shopped daily for food in the local markets, and on a hot day she rewarded herself with ice cream from a street vendor. In the marina we topped up with fuel and water, and recharged the batteries from shore power, for the alternator was still not functioning. If repairs or spare parts were needed we sought out the nearest boatyard, ship's chandler, or sailmaker. In bad weather, we could layover a day, or even turn back. In a particularly attractive anchorage we lingered for an extra day or two.

The challenges, such as there were, came suddenly and were short lived, a squall, wind gusting off a headland, shoaling water and breaking surf over a harbor bar. The threat was from land more often than from the sea. In a psychological sense, when coasting we never really detached from shore, we were an extension of the land. Mary puzzled over the charts. The river estuaries and coastal harbors further south had shallows at the harbor entrances. After the bars at Lagos and Faro, we were forewarned. So next morning we motored out of the lagoon to the open sea gyrating through the current. With a sense of regret at leaving I took down the red and black courtesy flag of Portugal and hoisted the yellow and orange banner of Spain.

Chapter 107: Ithaca

"...tell me the story...of the wanderer...(who)saw the town lands, and learned the minds of many distant men, and weathered many bitter nights and days...at sea."

~ The Odyssey, Homer

Ithaca, "an island in the running sea", we approach in mid-May over wave tossed seas, SW 20--a brsk, steady wind, rigging humming, ship healing, spay over the bow, making six to seven knots, near hull speed on a close reach, Mary at the helm of "Zillah" broad grin, exhilarating, the best day of sailing this season—all two hours of it before the wind drops, and the "iron genny", a 50 hp diesel engine takes over and we motor up the wide, elongated bay that leads to Vathi, and drop anchor off the town in 10 feet . The wind rising again, we let our all 150 feet of chain, attach the ¾" nylon rope snubber and secure the boat. Another safe passage.

We rent a motor scooter and go in search of Odysseus castle, which we do not find. But my search is a more abstract one. I search of the images that could created a poem, but the muse eludes me. The symbolism of the sea deep Iononian blue, wind tossed waves, rolling seas, the barren rock of an island, white houses clinging to the shore of the sea, clustered high on the protective hill, olive treess clutching, contorted, clinging to the niggard soil, goat mangled hillsides, stripped bare to rock, bed rock, bare.

At home we have no level runs or meadow,/ but highland, goat land," Homer describes Ithaca. "Grasses and pasture land, are hard to come by/ upon the islands tilted in the sea..."

Ithaca was home for Odysseus, and symbolically it is the mythic home of every adventurer. For it is in THE ODYSSEY that Homer gives birth to the ida of adventure, the idea of man struggling, not against fellow man, as in his other great epic, THE ILIAD, but man struggling against the forces of the elements and the mysteries of nature, ever questing, challenging demons and monsters of the deep, but most important of all—challenging himself. That uncertainty, struggle, hardship in itself is noble—is a heroic endeavor. This is the genesis of OUTWARD BOUND and the inspiration, albeit unconscious, of my own journeying to mountain tops and desert canyons, northern Canada rivers and lakes.

"Why are we out here? Why do we go cruising?" the owner captain of yacht "Explorer" asks. He's a retired dentist from Denver."Are we just trying to get away from it all? Or is there something that drives us on?" What is our quest? Odysseus returns to Ithace only to take off again. Tennyson has his Ulysses impatient to be moving on:"How dull it is to pause, to rust unburnished, and not to shine in use, As though to breathe were life? Why life piled on life were all too little..." So is this then the deeper significance of adventure? That life is not a destination but a journey? "And of this life, but little remains to me," Tennyson's Ulysses adds.

"Where's your home?" The Port Captain ask. He lived in Toronto for 15 years.and recognizes the Canadian flag on "Zillah". I point to the boat and shrug my shoulders. "Your travels are your home," Kazanantzakis says of his Odysseus. "What did you do in Toronto?" I ask. "Ran a pizza restaurant." After making a modest nest egg, he returned to Ithaca—home.

We wintered the boat (1996-7) in Sibari, southern Italy. Waiting through April for the weather to clear, in May we crossed to Greece in seas so calm we motor half the way. Dolphins frolick off the bow wave, and in one spectacular show a school of Risso's dolphins, 10-12 feet long, blunt noses, white underbellies, swim so close we see the scars on their bodies, then they breach 8 feet in a spectacular burst straight out of the water like whales. It is as if we witness the fifth day of Creation, when God created all the animals of the earth, fish of the sea and creatures of the deep, mysterious, awesome. Mysterium tremendum.

Landfall at Lakka on Paxoi. Sheltered bay, good holding on a sandy bottom, white washed houses , a fishing village lining the harbor, tavernas on the quay. The waiter takes our painter, the line attached to the dinghy, as we come ashore. "We'd like to have dinner but have not Greek money!" "No problem. Pay tomorrow when the bank opens." Fish out of the sea, Greek salad with goat cheese and black olives, retsina, the pine scented Greek wine, candle light, cats under foot. "Welcome to Greece!" I toast Mary. Paying our bill when we leave next morning, our host shakes our hand, "Come back next year on your way west."

Of f Preveza on the coast of mainland Greece we travel through history. Here Octavius routed the fleet of Anthony and Cleopatra in AD 21 to become the first Roman emperor. Entering the Gulf of Patras, we sail through the waters of the Battle of Lepanto where the combined fleets of Spain, France and the Papal States defeated the Turks in the Battle of Lepanto, and kept Islam at bay and Europe Christian. At Mesolongi we read Byron, who died here of malaria in 1814, a freedom fighter in the Greek War of Independence: "Roll on, thou deep and dark blue Ocean,--roll!/ Ten thousand fleets sweep over thee in vain." Travel in the Mediterranean is a journey not only through space but back through time.

We med-moor at Galixidi, where we catch a bus to Delphi, the most spectacular of archeological sites. Perched high on a mountain side, miles of olive groves, flickering green and silver stretch below to the shimmering sea. Here the ancients came to consult the Oracle and puzzle the riddles of fate. We jostle in the crowd of tourists, busloads of Germans and Japanese, marvel at the cyclopean stone foundations shoring up the Temple of Athena, climb the steep steps of the theatre, built into the natural curve and slope of the hillside, stride the 230 paces of the stadium, where sacred games were held, gaze in wonder at the Charioteer, serene in bronze. I was here forty years ago, I reflect, asking: "Who am I?" Seeking connectedness in antiquity. I return an older man learning to accept who I am.

Passing through the Corinth Canal, a five mile cut through two hundred feet of sandstone, we pay $150 and cut 150 off the sea route around the Peloponesus. At Aegena we compete for space with charter boats that flock in, med-moored three deep, a tangle of lines and anchors like a cat's cradle.

Athens is fourteen miles across the Saronica Gulf, an easy train ride from the Zia Marina to the city centre.

The Acropolis dominant on the skyline, the limestone cliffs resplendent on a rare windy summer day, a rare pollution free Sunday. We mount the processional Sacred Way over marble slabs, polished smooth by pilgrim tourists like ourselves, through the huge gated Propylae to face the Parthenon, magnificent in spite of the uglification of the protective scaffolding, a study of subtle line, balance and proportion, architecture as art form. Pericles masterminded it all in 450 BC, after the Persian War: "Our love of beauty does not lead to extravagence, and our love of things of the mind does not make us soft," he later said at more dire times during the Peloponesus War. From the battlements we look down on the theatre, dedicated to Dionysius, where Sophicles and Euripedes were first performed, the play as dramatic competition. Further west the statium, where excellence in running, jumping and throwing were raised to a religious rite, and warring city states agreed to holy truce. Modern Athens caught up in the hype of playing host to the summer Olympics in 2004.

On another day amble through the Agora, the market place below, and the beautifully restored shopping mall, the Stoa of Attalos, where "all the good things from all over the world flow to us, so that to us it seems just as natural to enjoy foreign goods as our own local goods," Pericles again. Climbing to the Areopagos, Lonely Planet inform us that Saint Paul preached his epistle to the Athenian here. We cross to the Hill of the Pynx, where public assemblies were held: "Our constitutiona is called a democracy because power is in the habds of the people," Pericles said here in 431 BC, "...everyone is equal before the law...No one...is kept in poliical obscurity because of poverty...we obey the law,esecially those which are for the protection of the oppressed."

Athens as a place, an idea, an ideal. "Our city is an education to Greece....Future generations will wonder at us, as present ages wonder now." So Pericles concludes his Funeral Oration for the dead in the grim days during the Peloponesus War, much as Lincoln orated the Gettesburg Address.

We leave earlier than we would have preferred, for the Zia Marina being crowded, dirty and expansive.Mega yachts, charter fleets, local weekend sailors line the harbor. We anchor overnight at Cape Sounion, the southern tip of mainland Greece. Climbing to the Temple of Poseidon on the headland at sunset we pick out the first of the Cyclades (pronounced "kick ladies") to the east, the island chain stretching across the Aegean Sea, the trading route of antiquity, the seaway to the Hellespont and Troy, that we follow the next two months and the following summer.

At Kea, our first harbor of refuge, 10 miles SE, we anchor in a small sparsely inhabited bay, Kavia. Manes rows out to invite us to dinner at his restaurant. He's gregarious, talkative, a gracious host, speaks good English and over retsina talks freely. Born in Egypt of parents born in Cyprus, he left in 1948 with another million foreign nationals, when Nasser nationalised foreign businesses, and came to Greece, the ancestral home. It is a pattern of expropriation, expulsion and emigration that we find common. "Opoughis, ke patris," he says. "Where I travel, there is my country." Greece always poor, was devastated by the war. But with tourism has come some properity, electricity, indoor plumbing and tap water, first world amenities and economic development spured by European Union funds. Manos prospers, but is still pessimistic. Young people leave the islands, first for Athens, but also for the United States, Australia and Canada. Greece's population is declining. The population is declining. Those who stay do not have families. The women work. They prefer to have cars, television and fancy apartments, holidays abroad, to having children. "By the year 2010," he tells us, "there will be more old leople on retirement, than younger people in the work force. Then who will defend the frontierss—Yugoslavia, Albania, Bulgaria and Turkey (emphasis on Turkey) all border on Greece, to say nothing of Egypt, Syria, Levanon, just a short way over the seas." The ancient conflict with Troy begins to take on a contemporary significance.

At Kithnos, a short island hop of 7 miles SE, we enter a small fishing harbor of Loutra, crowded with workiing fishing boats, and squeeze between two at the town dock. The boats reek and nets stacked on the quai crawl with roaches. Only recently have we rid ourselves of our Caribbean colony of roaches that made the trans-Atlantic crossing with us. Out comes the can of RAID and we spray and pray. A fisherman seeing our Canadian flag asks, "You know Vancouver? I spend six months." The extent of his English, but the welcome is clear. At the local mini "super" market Mary buys tomatoes and olives, and the lady shop keeper kisses her on both cheeks. And then kisses me. "Ef caristo," on our evening stroll around the bay we greet an elderly gentleman in a dark city clothes suit. "Good evening," he replies in American accented English. We stop to talk. He's visiting his aged uncle, with whom he lived during the war. "During the German occupation the Allies bombed Pireaus. Food was scarce. People starved in Athens. But in the islands people grew their own food, on these fields," and he pointed to the terraced hillside, now uncultivated, lying fallow, goats grazing among the weeds. "We fed ourselves as well as 300 Italian soldiers and their five German officers."

"Mikanos is the most photographed island in Greece." We are picked up hitch hiking at the bus stop. He turns out to be a tour guide.

Joe and Mary in Paxos, Greece, May 1997.

Chapter 108: Millennium Message

Sibari, Italy December 11, 1999 — Sibari is our winter harbor of refuge after our 3rd summer of cruising in the islands of Greece. We bask in the warmth of the Italian sun 68F/20C, while dazzling lenticular clouds bank up against the mountains above the bay, foretelling the next weather front and storm. It has been another magical year of adventure and misadventures, cultural wonders, historical and political anomolies, and a wealth of new found friends.

Marmaris, where we wintered the last two years in Turkey is a world class marina, 700 boats afloat, another 700 on the hard, professional service facilities, an opportunity to give ageing Zillah a face life, varnishing the cabin top, caulking the deck yet once again and covering with an impermeable polyester compound that scothes 90 % of our leaks and installing a new electiric windlass that comes to the rescue of my aching back. There is a strong sense of community among the cruising "live-aboards", Brits who retire to the Med to escape their miserable winter, Kiwis, Aussies and Americans"on the way around", and Canadians and Americans like myself and Mary, who go only "half way, the other way," as well as Dutch, Germans, Scandinavians, and French. Together we celebrate Thanksgiving American style dinner with Turkey turkey and authentic cranberry sauce; Christmas dinner English style with roast beef and Yorkshire pudding; we join in evenings of games, disco and dancing, bake sales and junk sales to raise money for a Turkish orphanage. It is the closest I have come to belonging to a country club, or a yacht club.

On the broad harbor esplanade overlooking Marmaris Bay stood a heroic statue of Ataturk on rearing horse facing west to Greece. It is taken down and replaced by Ataturk in a schoolmaster's baggy suit and a working man's cap, facing east to Turkey. Inscribed on the base is "Peace at home. Peace in the world."

Departing in May we sail west to Rhodes, with its huge Crusader walled city, and on to Crete steeped in the romance of history. The restorations of Minoan Knossus, a civilization 1000 years older than classical Greece, captures a humanist's delight in nature and the living world, the youthful acrobat in mid flight vaulting a bull, soaring swallows touching beaks. We dock in ancient harbors under massive fortified walls, the military and commercial infrastructure that underpinned the wealth of Venice. Meanwhile the mosques of the much maligned Turks fall to ruin.

On Santorini, the skeleton of a volcano disgorged from the sea , we meet Dionysius and Tonnies on the beach walking our dogs. After sniffing each other, the dogs that is, we introduce ourselves. They learn of Mary's birthday, invite us by for a drink, serve a 5 course meal with champagne. Nikos, their guest is a government official and over dinner they explain passionately Greek support of the Serbs in Kossova, solidarity among Orthodox Christians with a long history of oppression by Turkish and Albanian Moslems. They see freeing North Cyprus as the final act of Greeks gaining independence from the Turks.

Sailing from Skhinousa to Paros we are caught in rising headwinds, Force 7/ 35mph, 9ft seas crashing over the bow, wind driven spray over the deck, rigging straining, the boat heeling, the rail down. We shorten sail. There is less pounding but we make little progress against the heading sea. Mary at the helm has a worried look , "Don't you think we should head off?" Instantly the world changes and running downwind, we race with the seas, surfing through the waves. At 7 knots, nearly our hull speed, we run for Ios and find shelter in a narrow fiord like bay. We bob gently at anchor while above us the wind howls over the cliff tops. The line between an adventure and an ordeal is very thin, the difference often merely a state of mind.

Epidaurus is the best preserved ancient Greek theatre, seating 11,000 people. The acoustics are perfect, a whisper carries to the gods, thirty tiers above. We have tickets for The Birds, a comedy by Aristophanes. Wedon't understand a word, but the combination of slap stick, mime and chorus line conveys the farce about fifth century BC bureaucracy and we are caught up in the laughter of the crowd. Descending the steep time worn steps with a thousand people below me, I have the eerie feeling of being of another age.

Rounding the Peloponnese, Greece's Cape Horn is another bash to windward. We drop anchor in the vast protected Bay of Navaronne. In 1824, the combined fleets of the British, French and Russians came here to the help of the Greeks and destroyed a Turkish fleet. It was a culminating event, leading to the Greeks declaring their independence.

St. Dionysius, a warrior saint, is depicted on a rearing red horse slaying the infidel underfoot. On his feast day we are anchored off the town esplanade in Zakinthos, front row spectators of the celebration as the venerated saint's relics, his bones, are paraded through town, accompanied by chanting priests, the procession led by the garrison military band. Colonel Bogey clashes with Kyrie Eleison. Warrior priests and religious wars, there is no separation of church and state in Greece.

We reread Corelli's Mandolin by Louis de Berniere, a reader's best buy based on war time Cefalonia. If you haven't read it, e-mail amazon.com right now and consider the recommendation my Christmas gift.

The benign winds of the Ionian, after the blustery meltemi of the Aegean, lull us into inattentiveness. In the middle of Preveza Bay, a mile off the town, I tack toward a green channel marker, indicating deep water to starboard (the opposite to American buoys) and run solidly aground. Mary points out the gravel bar is clearly indicated on the chart, but it's not marked by a buoy. The sun sets a flaming orange pink flared across the whole sky. From the dingy I photograph Zillah in sihouette to commemorate the event, our most sensational picture of the year. We spend the night high and dry. "If you haven't been aground, you ain't been around."

Crossing to Sibari on the Boot of Italy we put Zillah to bed for the winter. Sybari was an ancient Greek colony, known for its soft, decadent lifestyle, hence "sybaritic". Suits Mary and me fine.

It's a good life. Yes, there IS life after Outward Bound. Cruising offers a rare combination of the active and the reflective, though at times I still have a twinge of conscience. Should one be enjoying life so much? Shouldn't I be teaching, or preaching, or doing good? What IS the meaning of life? At 70 I'm still hopelessly adolescent, I still ask.

We value our many new friends, but miss our old ones and would like to hear from you.

We listen to the BBC. Turkey has just agreed to preliminary conditions for joining the EU. Greece says it could be an opening for peace in the region. The Isrealis talk with the Palestinians and with the Syrians. So Hark! Can you not hear that Herald Angel singing? Peace on Earth, and Goodwill and Reconciliation. And so Mary and I wish you and yours Peace, Health and Happiness. Lots of Love. And have a Happy New Millenium.

Chapter 109: Travel as Absurdity – To Cyprus and Return

Our Turkish visas expire. We have to leave the country every three months and re-enter with a new visa. "How absurd." But it's the law. "They want tourists to come, but make it difficult for them to stay. Most of us on yachts merely to into Immagration and say we're going, get our passports stamped "Out", return five days later. "I'm back!" And get stamped "In". But if you have a vehicle, that is stamped in your passport and you cannot leave the country without it. The options are expensive. We've already been from Bodrum to Kos last February (another story), 15 miles off shore, $180 round trip. Rhodes, 25 miles last spring and return in the fall, $450 by the time we went back and forth to drop off and pick up our beloved camper van, plus $500 for 5 months storage. Cesme to Khios, 5 miles would be $180, another ripoff. Absurd.

Tascuru to Girne in Cyprus, 50 miles, a bargain, $150 Besides Cyprus could be interesting. The Turkish Republic of Northern Cyprus, broke off from Greek Cyprus in 1976 after 10 years of civil war, a rogue nation recognized only by Turkey,an international trouble spot. The Greeks announced their intention to install Russian medium range missiles. The Turks bluntly replied this would be a hostile act. With 40,000 Turkish troops in north Cyprus, the Greek Cypriots backed down.

On to Cyprus. Beber has her rabies shot and worming pills required to cross an international frontier. We replace windshield wipers on the van, light reflectors for the right hand drive vehicle, inside light fuses, fill the water tank, the spare propane bottle, and gas up. Tuesday is a long days drive, averaging 40 mph we cover 295 miles , most of it over steep and winding mountain roads, south to Fedeye, Antalya, Side, a route we took a week to cover a year ago March, visiting archeological sites. We park on the beach of P?????, the harbor of an ancient Roman city. It is here the Emperor Trajan died. Beber runs unfettered on the beach playing mad dog, snatching up plastic bottles, wind blown bags, snarling and vigorously shaking her head.

The road follows the coast south of Antalya, an endless succession of sharp curves, hairpin bends, steep climbs from narrow coves to rocky headlands, and descents to the next bay. Spectacular views of plunging cliffs, the sea a deep Mediterranean blue."We've never seen it so blue." Mediaval fortresses and castles dominate hilltops. We stop for an hour at Alanya, a magnificent castle vaste, formidable, double walls facing the sea, 30 towers still intact. Beber scampers about exploring nooks and crannies, snapping at tiny liizards sunbathing on the wall. We are invited into the castle mosque by a workman who turns out to be the mullah. young, solidly built, himself formidable, a defender of the faith, and he chants from the Koran for us under the reververating resonance of the arching dome.

We reach Tascuru by mid afternoon, 455 miles from Marmaris, most ot the last 150 miles driven at 20 mph. We park in the town lot 750,000 Turkish lira ($2.50). "That's alot!" Mahmet from the booking agency greets us. We had phoned ahead. Buy our ticket 55,000,000 TL /$150. Beber is very well behaves, tied to the waiting room bench in spite of fellow taunting her. "The ferry leaves at midnight. Be at the dock by 10. I'll help you."

There is already a long line at the control barrier at 10, waiting to get in. I show passports, vehicle registration. "Customs paper. You have?" "No. It's stamped in the passport," I say. The customs officer shrugs, fills in the vehicle registration number in a huge ledger, asks me to initial the entry, and I am passed on. "Seven million, five hundred thousand," the next fellow says. I fork out another twenty dollars. I later learn that is a docking fee. We drive though. Three boats line the dock, one bow-to, with the nose of the ship high above the bow, people and vehicles entering on a ramp. The others stern-to, tail gate lowered. We park and wait.

People mill about the dock, carrying larg bundles, suitcases, duffle, pulling carts and pushing barrows. There's a long line off in a corner."Passport Control" in English, as well as Turkish "Polis" (Police)"We need to get out passports stamped," I say, "that's why we're here!". I wait until the line dwindles, then join. The first hurdle, a fellow behind a window demands 750,000 lira/ $2.50, ($5 for two), fives me two tokens, move along the line to a turnstile, where another fellow drops the token an directs me to the backs of several men clambering at metal grilled wickets, with uniformed police officers behind. I show my passport. Two officers study it. "Visa finish." one tells me, and he flips my passport on the counter and takes the next in line. "No!" I shout. "My visa is good for three months. That's Friday. Today is only Wednesday." "No three months, 90 days." And we argue as to whether three months goes from the 6th of November to the 6th of February, or whether three months is ninety days from November 6, neither of us really understanding each other, my not comprehending his Turkish, he my English. An exercise in futility. Absurdity. Finally to demonstrate, he counts:

November 24 days
December 31 days
January 31 days
Februry 4 days

That's 90 days!!!!!

Passports are stamped. We are legally departed. Almost.

Three ferries line the dock, one bow-to with the front of the boat perched high in the air, passengers and vehicles entering on a ramp. Two are stern to with tailgates down. We are directed to the middle one, the smallest of the three. "I don't want to go on that one, "Mary says, "it doesn't look safe." It's small, deck plates rusted, African

Queenesque run down. Amidst shouts of annoyance we back off, drive to the larger boat, "Girne" neatly printed on the stern, and up the ramp. A clutch of men gather about amidst shouts and hollering. An English speaker is found. "Can I see your ticket? It's for the other boat. This is another line." We back off and angle over to the "Queen".

Passports inspected again, by the ship's officer. "The customs paper for the vehicle." "I don't have it. It's stamped in my passport." I am conducted over to the Customs Office, where I am again queried. "Customs form." They show me a pink sheet that I have a vague memory of once having had. "I don't have it. But it's stamped in my passport." There they show me the number of the form. That's what I need. The pink sheet. I throw up my hands, shake my head. No one speaks English, but I get the gist. Ushered up to the customs administrative office, heated, plush chairs, cups of tea, cigarette smoke, Ataturk frowning on the wall, I'm informed by an authoritative gentleman in a business suit. "You can't go tonight. We'll call Marmaris (where I entered with the vehicle in November) and get them to fax a copy of your permit." "But my visa exlpires today. The police will give me trouble." "No problem!" "No problem for you. A problem for me!" "No. We talk to police."

"You won't believe what I've been through," I tell Mary when I return to the van. "They won't let us go." "Why not?" "I don't have the pink customs sheet." "Have you looked in the green file?" she asks. "Yes. It's not there." "How about the pink folder?" I dig in the remote corners aloft in the van, retrieve it, out pops an brown manila folder labelled "Van Registration and Insurance, and inside...the PINK SHEET!!! Back to the customs office and in 15 minutes we drive on to the ferry.

Vehicles load by the stern ramp, then are lowered into the hold on a lift. The van is too tall to fit on the lift. We back off, another vehicle with trailer backs in, we follow and park on the stern deck. "What an absurd night. Thank gawd it's over." We make up the van bunks and collapse into bed. I lie awake, waiting for the adrenalin to subside. Try to sleep as the ship rolls in the swell of the open sea. Little do I realize, it's not over yet.

Last on, first off. Debarking at Girne early next morning, I feel like a refugee. Mountains rise abruptly above the town. Passengers from other boats flock to Passport Control. We wait for the crowd to thin, chatting with two Turks who consoled Mary last night. "Just stay with me, the burly, swarthy, unshaven fellow says. He's driven from London in a cargo van hauling a huge heavily loaded trailer, through winter conditions in Eastern Europe, Hungary, Romania, Bulgaria, a trip he does regularly carrying family belongings, childrens toys, mattresses on the roof. "Looks like a casual form of smuggling to me." We chat. He points to a mediaeval castle perched dramatically on a high rocky outcrop, miles away and at least 1500 feet high. "I was stationed up there for seven years when I was in the army," he says with pride."The Greeks came with a gun boat. But we bombed tham and they went away. Not to come back." "We had eight years of civil war killing each other," Raiffe, his older companion says."Then the Turkish army came in, and there has been no more killing." They have driven from England in tandem. But Cyprus is di vided, Greek in the south, The Turkish Republic of Northern Cyprus in the north, a United Nations Peace Keeping force between. "The Americans are our friends," he adds, perhaps for Mary's benefit, "We are safe with them. The Americans look after us."

"We plan to go to Greece later this summer. Please do not stamp our passports." The Passport Control Officer gives us an official slip of paper, with appropriate stamps instead. "Do not lost," he cautions. We need car insurance. Our Turkish smuggler says we can get it cheaper on the boat than in town. Thirteen million Turkish lira/ $35. Then customs.for the vehicle permit TL 7.5 million/ $20. And we have all the paper work. Almost.

Drive up to the barrier, for the customs inspection. "You have a dog," a polite, mustached, handsome Customs Officer addresses us. "Yes," I reply, thinking I have found another dog lover.. "It must stay here.You pick it up when you leave." No!" I almost shout in outrage. He directs me out of the line of traffic to park on the side. Only in Britain do they still quarantine animals on entry. For 6 months. Now we learn Cyprus too, a hang over from British rule (1967). "We'll leave. Go back to Turkey." I pout. "All right," he replies. "It's not all right, but I will not leave the dog." One of the reasons we chose to come to Turkish Cyprus was that we were told we could bring pets in. "No, dogs, cats, parrots, all pets are quaranteened."

We begin the whole process in reverse. The ferry captain escorts me to the booking office. Refunds ten million lira of the insurance, the other 3M was administrative charges. We rebook on the noon ferry for Turkey, pay another 7.5M/$20 harbor fees. At passport control there is poster: "The women of Turkish Cyprus seek solidarity with the women of the world and protection from the atrocities of the Greeks." I envisage an animal rights poster next to it. Clear passport control departing. Papers stamped by customs. Checked by police control on the dock. We board the ferry, depart half an hour early and return to Turkey.

Twelve hours spend in the Kafkian world of the absurd.

The skies cloud over. It is raining when we dock in Turunc. Like viewing a film being rewound, we go through the reverse process. At passport control we pay 750,000 TL/ $2.50 for a token, that is dropped into a turnstile by a second guard. My Canadian passport is stamped by a third uniformed police officer, a woman. Mary is directed to another office for an American visa, $45. We pay another 250,000 TL/ 75 cents I'm not sure for what, and we have passed immigration. Now for customs. The infamous pink sheet is filled in quadruplicate. I still have three months or 90 days on my former vehicle permit, but the customs officer only gives me 70 days. He begins to count up the number of days I've already been in Turkey, from when I arrived by airlines from New York, 110 days. Not when we arrived with the van by car ferry, 90 days. Apparently I am permitted to be in Turkey only 180 days. This is news to me, and to most people at the marina in Marmaris, though Mary has heard reference to it as a regulation not being enforce. Subtract 110 from 180 leaves me 70 days. I argue again that my previous permit was good for 90 days. But no. 70 days. Another TL 5 million, $15, and we walk our with pink sheet in hand. It is now dark, raining still. Another half hour out of the murky gloom another uniformed officer, customs control shows up. He checks passports and customs vehicle permit pink sheet. The wants to see the chassis registration number. Where the hell's that? We look in the door jambs, on the dashboard by the windshield. "Try under the hood," Mary suggests. We grope in the dark find the plaque, he flashes his light on it, beckons us on. Drive another 100 yards, past a line of cargo trucks pulled off to one side, stop at the metal barrier. Wait another half hour a guard to show up. Another inspection of passports, the pink sheet, and the gate rolls back and we are released into Turkey. "It doesn't really make you feel as if you are wanted in Turkey, does it?" We discusss the contradictions. "They want tourists, but create incredible difficulties." "It will be awhile before they get into the European Union with practices like this."

To decompress we rent a room in a clean, warm pension, space heater, warm shower. Rain continues and next day we read abd gaze out at the grey Mediterranean, through rain pelting on the picuture window, and I write up my impressions. Plutarch wrote of ancient Turunc:"From this haven in former times, has come forth a powerful army of pirates..." So what is new under the sun?

To put it in perspective, I call Jennifer a couple days later. "When we were leaving JFK on one or out trips back to Belgium, they took Johann out of line and put him in a room with two other men whose hands were handcuffed to the legs of a chair. Immigration and customs officials are a breed of mankind unto themselves."

Chapter 110: Crete

One of the attractions of Crete is the contrast and the variety. A spectacular coastline of contorted volcanic seacliffs, high mountains to 6000ft arrayed ibe rudge beyond the next, fading into the distant blue. Steep canyon ravines, choked with red and purple oleander. Hillsides planted row on row in olive groves, mile upon mile up the slopes.High mountain plateaus and valleys, the wheat or barley already russet brown for harvesting. White washed Greek Orthodox chapels on hilltops. Ruins of the lost Minoan civilization 1500 BC dotted over the countryside, those at Knossos restored in archaic splendour. Museums. We take it all in.

Hania, or Xania, or Chania—take your pick, westernmost of a string of harbors, guarded by Venetian forts and seawalls,narrow twisting alleys, a maze, every street a defensive redoubt, the waterfront esplanade a cavalcade of tavernas, cafes, discotiques, gift shops, jewellers, leather jackets and fur coats, vieing for space with ice cream stands, balloon vendors, cashew and pistachio nut carts, thronged with torched northern euros in search of sun.

We tie up in the midst of the scene at the town dock and rent a car to explore the hinterland. I had made an earlier attempt to climb Mt Ida, 6000 ft, but took a wrong turn at the pass, ended up on the wrong ridge to find myself blown off my feet in 50knot winds and still 2 miles from the summit. "The only car they have left is three years old but they day its in good shape," Mary reports, "and the price is right. Less than $20 a day." We go to pick it up a 9am. "Be ready in half an hour." At 10. "Be ready at 10.30" They show up with a diminutive Fiat Panda, not particularly beat up, an undusted white.Certainly 3 years old. From the start I should have been wary. I go to put the lunch, water bottles, hiking boots, wind shirts in the trunk. Doesnt open. No right rear view mirror. The windshield wiper (one only) mounted so it stops in arrest position in mid window, face front to Mary in the navigators cockpit. A touchy clutch, gas pedal sticks. So that each start up and gear shift is a stall out, or roaring revs, until I master the precise synchronized touch. But by 11 oclock it is already hot, the morning is shot, and we are eager to climb to the cool of the hills. We climb, the road south zig-zagging, cork screwing, switch backing into the hills, above the orange groves and their protective cane rush windbreaks, to the open range olive trees. Above to rock and thorny, weathered maquis shrub, with fragrant herbs and purple thyme like heather. But today he only breeze is that generated by the overheated car and its four gears as we snail our way up the steep inclines, the sun beating on lap and chest, no air coming through the non functioning vents. The hills too have long since lost their morning cool.

Our quest is five Byzantine chapels with 14-15 century frescoes, high in the hills that have escaped the ravages of the Turks and later invaders. Kandanos, where we stop to buy apples and cheese, and succulent peaches, was demolished in WW2 by the Germans, reprisal for the killing of 25 soldiers by the Resistance. We find Agia Anna, 1460, the chapel of the mother of Mary,nestled in a grove of ancient olive trees, contorted trunks, some 5 to 7 feet through,hundreds of years old.. But the Turks have been here first. They eyes of the saints have been gouged out. But several of the frescoes are delightful, particularly the touching scene of Joachim kissing Anna. They are an old couple, childless, and she announces she is with child, the future Mary.

St. George, the dragon slayer, along with St. Demetrias, the patron saint of Greece, mounted on rearing horse spearing the infidel (a Turk?) underfoot, are favorites. In his chapel 1410 the frescoes are robust, dynamic, fierce even, "Onward Christian soldiers" kind of thing. But a smaller tableau 19th century of the same theme has George a pretty young lad with curly hair, blush cheeks, his horse could be from a circus merry go round, the dragon a fawning pleading wimp, a young child (where does he come in? a symbolic Christ perhaps?) riding pillion. The afternoon heat is now cooking. Mary stays in the car in the shade ofl a gigantic olive tree, surely as old as the chapel of Agia Panagia, 1450. Here the Christ Pancreator (creator of all things) has been well preserved, eyes and all, the face and shoulders of Christ in the vaulted ceiling of the apse at the head of the church. Christ, forceful, dynamic, deep sad but determined eyes, the firm jaw of a Cretan resistance leader. None of the compassionate tenderness of an Italian Rennaissance Christ. Haunting in its power. Mysterium tremendum.

But we've had as much heat as we can take and drive on, down to the south coast, the Libyan Sea hat stretches a mere 250 mi south to Egypt, and bathe on the beach at Paleochora. Relief! After bathing Beber and I walk west along a rocky shoreline, flat sedementary layers that shelve out to sea. Circular holes are ground into the flat rock, 2ft, 5ft in diameter, quarried for millstones we speculate. To shore the cliffbands are eroded out creating a natural bridge. Mysteries of nature.

More to follow. !!!! Joe

"Lets take another route back." The map showed a good road through Temania.But first to call the rental agency. Fed up with the clutch and stalling out. Mary fed up with the windshield wiper slashed across her view. Not only does the trunk not open, the right door does not lock. Tell them the car is unsatisfactory. Return it tonight. Demand a new one tomorrow. A prophetic summons. The road sign to Temania didnt quite match the map, but the surface is good, recently paved, and climbing steadily into the mountains. Rental cars pass us, others coming down, a well travelled route. But above Azogires the pavement stops. We proceed on rocky gravel and loose rocks. Then something hits, or snaps, and there's a high pitch whine, shreiking, mechanical whirr.Stop! The screech continues, the cooling fan still whirring. Turn the key again. It stops. The loudness of the silence. "Now what?" We risk running the car again, enough to turn around and coast back downhill 2 km to

Azogires, a widening in the road, two houses and a taverna with a sign advertising "Rooms." We stop smoke seeping out under the hood. A series of telephone calls establish where we are, that we are not driving the car any further. That they will pick us up. It is 7 pm. "This could be an interesting evening."

The tavern keeper, a wiry, agile old man in his 70s, a wizened severe face, full head of dark hair, flecked with grey. Speaks no English. "Greek salad. Two, Bread. Wine, vino. Water." we manage to get across. Eventually between phone calls it appears, served by a young fellow, 14 or so, who appears from a house across the road. A handsome looking kid with classical Cretan features, a wave to his hair that falls over his forehead, speaking English with an American accent. "Where did you learn your English?" "In the United States."Like many Greeks after the devestation of WW2 and the bitterness of the civil war that followed, Eftides father left, went to sea, jumped ship in NY, washed dishes in a Greek restaurant, ended up owning string of restaurants in Des Plaines, Illinois. Came home to acquire a wife, raised his family at home, then brought them out to the States. Eftides had spent 6 years abroad, and now returned, "To help grandfather" and become a Cretan. Out of school this past year "To improve my Greek", working with old Eftides, his grandfather fencing in sheep and goats on the mountainside, planting olive trees: "We use the wild olive to root, they are more hardy, then graft domestic olives that bear better fruit." He left us to bring in the chickens that range in the yard, "Otherwise the martins will get them." "Do you plan to go to university?" "Oh yes". "What will you study?" "Computers." He doesnt seem torn between two world, but confidently lives with one foot in each. Transcending Thoreau.

Nine oclock they phone us, they're on the way. Another car drives up, a rental car, but not our company. A frazzles and sun fried blond woman of middlish age steps out. She looks exhausted, disoriented, confused, anxious. She speaks plausible English with a French accent. She's looking for a hotel where there's a boat captain who takes people out to see the dolphins. "Is this it?" Young Eftides translates for Grandfather Eftides and he bursts out laughing, the first sign of levity we have seen in the old man. We all laugh. "There are not dolphins here in the mountains." "Do you have food?" And Eftides rattles off a menu that includes salads, soups, sandwiches. He could be back in Des Plaines. She orders a grilled cheese sandwich and house wine. "From the barrel, we make it right here from our own grapes," pointing to the arbor overhead stretching to the house across the road. I join here with wine. She's Belgian, here in Greece for a retreat. "No, its not exactly a retreat. There are places in the world where there is a strong spiritual aura, near Ierapetra (an ancient minoan city on the S coast of Crete), Monte Saint Michele (coast of Brittany in France, Peru . We meet with a medium, a Canadian from Quebec, and through him we are able to reach St. Michael. The vibrations are very powerful." But now she is tired. She has been driving since 11am. "Do you have a room?" Eftides is apologetic. "The room is being retiles. Will not be ready for another week, and then it is booked by an English couple." "Then I'll sleep in the car," Madame says.

With the stabbing glare of a flashing yellow light a heavy duty flat bed truck roars up the hill and stops.Our rescue vehicle arrives. Eleven oclock. The driver gets out, inquires in Greek, that I dont understand. "Do you speak English?" "No. Do you speak Greek?" I'm put in my place. I try to explain. "Water OK. Oil OK. Run engine—smoke." "Where smoke?" I point vaguely under the engine block. So much for diagnosis. He closes the hood, moves the truck up the road, backs down to the Panda, lowers the tail gate ramp, winches up the car. And in 5 minutes we have payed our bill, thanked Grandfather, bid farewell to Eftides and St. Michael's acolyte, the driver has a parting glass of raki, "One for the road," and by 11pm are hurtling down the road and over the mountain to Hania. He drives to the sound of traditional Greek music, the wild demonic rhythm, high pitch violin, sorrowful, defiant singing, more like wailing off key to the untuned western ear. The faster the music, the faster he drives. Raki power. I"m fascinated. "You would be. You've had three tumblers of wine,"Mary says, sitting beside me cold sober, clutching the door on every curve. "I imagine the car flying off the trailer and poor Beber in it." We are back on the boat by 1am and board Zillah, the din of the shoreside disco beating out yet other rhythm.

"We have three options," the beautiful young woman at the car rental agency tells me next morning. "We can refund your money, or give you another car. Or tomorrow we can upgrade your car at no extra cost. We are very sorry this happened to you." I feign extreme annoyance and accept the refund with great gravity. Little does she know it is one of our more hilarious days in Crete. Two days later we sail. Five days later we arrive in Santorini.

Chapter 111: St Dionysius Festival

We have the feeling of returning to the world, the Ionian Islands are forested, rounded contorted leafy olive trees with silver grey and green leaves, tall spiky dark green cyprus, standing erect like sentinels. It all appears lush compared to the barren, eroded goat devastated islands of the Aegean, earlier in the summer. Yesterday we had our first full day of sailing in a month, since forcing our way to windward around the bottom end of the Peloponesus, either motoring in flat calm, or pounding into choppy head seas. And rain, a full hour of steady drizzle, the first rain since April, back in Turkey. A day remeniscent of sailing in Maine, with the Camden Hills or Mt Desert shrouded in mist. A delightful change from the hazy and blazing sun of the past several weeks. Tow head waves with temperatures of 105 F.

Cruising north up the Ionian Islands, Zakinthos with dramatic sea cliffs and deep caves, we take an excursion boat to get in closer, a busmans holiday. Anchored 100 yards off the main town on the festival of St Dionysius, the patron saint of the island, we have ringside seats, or waterfront view, of the procession where they parade the saints relics (bones in a gold chasule) a mile down the waterfront street, to the chanting of the priests, the trumpets and drums of the military band, 5000 people along the quay burning incense, lit candles, fire works spiraling off into the sky, the thunderous boom of roman candles. The blue and white flags of Greece, intertwined with the double headed eagle of Constantinople, gunpowder mixed with incense, Colonel Bogey with Kyrie Eleison. No seperation of church and state here. Greek nationalism preached from the pulpit. Militant saints, St George slaying the dragon, St Demetrios slaying the infidel (A Turk?), role models for militant monks and priests. The war of liberation still being waged, so long as Turks continue to occupy Northern Cyprus, the last of the Crusades. New insights into the fierce hatred aroused by nationalism, wedded to religous fanatacism.

Priests were a part of the Resistance to the Germans in WW2. In a monstery in Crete there is a memorial to a priest caught transmitting information on troop and ship movements to the British, the bulky field radio still on display. We speculate whether in 500 years it too will become a relic.

All an interesting adjunct to cruising. We are well. Its good to be among islands again. The last couple of days we run into people we knew in Marmaris, and have wonderful taverna evenings ashore swapping war stories that get more outragous with each glass of raw retsina. The winds are a good deal lighter here in the Ionian, out of the range of the meltemi, the fierce winds that sweep down from the Balkans to the eastern Mediterrarean. We idle our way north, motoring much of the time, and in 2 or 3 weeks will pick a weather window and cross over to Italy. The sense of bringing a 3 year Odyssey to an end.

Chapter 112: Margaret's Birthday Storm

We celebrated Margaret's birthday Sunday with a magnificent pyrotechnic display of lightning, thunder rumbling off on the southern horizon, a rising swell of rushing waves, the boats at anchor rolling and pitching in the gathering storm. We crossed from Greece to Italy Saturday, motoring the whole way, 40 some miles from the last Greek island, a 3 ft swell right on the beam, 5 ft with each passing freighter on the horizon, uneventful, but uncomfortable. Ste Maria de Leuca is at the southern tip of the heel of the boot of Italy, a well protected little harbor, behind a gigantic 50 ft seawall. Somebody had connections with the cement industry, classical Italian overkill. But the marina cost $30 for the night, no head, showers or facilities. Rip off. And we were used to free docking and anchoring all through Greece with a couple exceptions, where we payed $5 or 10. Besides we had no Italian money, the local money machince rejecting my Mastercard. And I jealously held on to my limited horde of American greenbacks. So we cast off and motor out to anchor off the harbor, tucked behind the seawall, protected from the SE, with two other boats. Rolling seas, but a gentle NW wind steadying the boat. Since we didnt have enough money to buy wine, I didnt wake at 2am to pee, and slept the sleep of the innocent.

Mary woke at 5am to the rolling and pitching of the boat, Beber scambling on the deck looking for safe refuge under her cockpit seat kennel. The wind had shifted to SW so the seawall provided no protection, dark menacing clouds scudded across the sky amidst sheet lightning and glaring flashes. Temperales is the Italian for thunderstorms, oft repeated this time of year on the radio weather report. I woke more slowly and stood gazing at the spectacle from the doghouse window, the companion way doors closed against the rain. And stood for maybe 10 minutes, marvelling in the spectacle. Then I thought, maybe it would be a good idea to put clothes on, and a foul weather jacket. On deck I saw the boats had swung, so that the French ketch that lay alongside was now only a boat length ahead of us. We were not in a good place should she drag. Astern was a projection of the sea wall perhaps three boat lengths away. We were not in a good place should we drag. So there I sat. Still not fully awake. Certainly not alert. One of those moments where you wonder, What am I doing here? Am I having fun yet? And I wasnt in the cockpit more than 10 minutes, huddled against the wind, when. Thunk. Thunk. Thunk. Mary, we're touching bottom. I turn the engine key, rev up. Jump to the helm. Will we move off or not? Mary scambles up into the cockpit, pulling the drawstrings on her sweat pants. Take the helm. Full throttle forward. I stumble forward in the flashing light and start to wind in the anchor. Step on the windless control button. Nothing happens. Back to the cabin to close the circuit breaker. The windlass slowly turns over, the the anchor painstakingly comes up. We are a dingy length away from the ketch. But afloat. Whats happening? Mary calls out urgently. The anchors up. Motor back in. I shout over the wind and crashing waves. Within minutes we are back in the protection of the harbor, grateful that the Italians have been so generous in their expenditures on concrete and tie up at the townd dock, opposite the marina. A Customs boat that just came in from the storm, out prowling for smugglers perhaps, has docked ahead of us, and their crew take our lines. We tie up. Brew a cup of herbal tea, no caffeine. We dont need the adrenalin boost. Welcome to Italy. We recall the gales off Sardinia and Sicily three years ago.

Chapter 113: Biber – Canine Crew

"Is she a Border Collie?" the asked. For she was about that size and shape, nose coming to a point, lean muscular body. A beautiful dog, white peppered with black, and a long, sweeping flamboyant tail like an ostrich plume. "Biber" we named her, the Turkish for pepper.

"Well, yes," I replied, "sort of. We picked her up at Marmaris on the coast of Turkey. That's twenty five miles from Rhodes in Greece. Almost the border."

Mary and I had been sailing in the Eastern Mediterranean and Biber appeared one morning, a marina dog, a stray, perky ears erect, not pleading, but confident and curious. "You sure you wouldn't like to feed me?" she seemed to say, head bent to one side. "You could even adopt me, if you wanted to." And Mary who was pet-deprived, could not resist and we added Biber to the crew list.

In Greece she was a great hit, until we confessed that she was a Turkish stray, and canine-philia instantly turned to xenophobia, with the Greeks instant aversion to anything Turkish. She was a great pet, "The cleverest dog I've ever had," Mary said.

"You have to be clever to survive on the waterfront," I agreed.

After three years cruising among the Greek Islands in the Aegean and Ionian Seas, we began our journey west on the long journey home. We wintered in Sibari, a well protected marina in the south of Italy. That final Sunday, we walked the beach, Beber and I, one of those clear crisp days the Italians boast of, waves lapping on the golden sand, the mountains to the north, crystal clear, peaked with snow.

Biber, as soon as she spotted the sand, ran her game of circles and figure eights, attacking plastic bottles with demonic fury and then charging off down the distant beach in pursuit of an immense flock of seagulls sitting on the sand huddled like cobble stones. They burst into the air, circled and settled 100 yards off shore, safely at sea. Only two wise old crows stayed to taunt Beber, lifting casually as she sprinted at them, gliding just far enough to be out of range and landing thirty feet away.

Mary, who had flown home to Washington to visit family, returned that Monday. Biber and I drove north in our camper van to Naples, five hours by autostrada, to pick her up. Biber perched in the front passenger seat, copilot and observer. We camped in a service plaza outside Sorrento, resumed the journey next morning predawn. We arrived at the airport several hours early, had breakfast, napped, Biber doing her morning business on the grassy verge beside the roadside parking. We were on stage for Mary's arrival at 11am, Italian Airlines only half an hour late.

Biber greeted Mary with her customary hyperactive enthusiasm and doting love. While I loaded the book-weighted duffle bags into the van they walked the grass patch again. This is when it must have happened.

Back in the van, Biber began to cough, a rasping cough, periodic, subsiding only to recur again. Mary was exhausted by the overnight flight and still recovering from flu, so I set up the port bunk in the van and she rested, reclining on the way back south to Sibari. Biber's cough continued and on into the night.

We slept poorly that night, Beber continuing to cough and in the morning we were concerned enough to call a vet. Lucia, the marina receptionist made the call and by eleven Dr. T showed up. He spoke only Italian, I spoke none. We had a discussion about the symptoms, Lucia interpreting. Beber was coughing up a good deal of mucus now, the occasional solid blob, and thin traces of blood, and was gasping more frequently with a rasping sound.

The vet said he thought she had swallowed a chicken bone. But I said I thought that highly unlikely and suggested it was in the chest, bronchial. Taking her temperature and listening to her lungs with a stethoscope, he agreed with the bronchial diagnosis, gave her an antibiotic shot and left, scheduling a return call next day at the same time.

By late afternoon Biber was clearly worse, coughing up more blood in her sputum. We had Lucia call the vet again, saying that we wanted to bring her in for further care. But he refused, said he'd come again in the morning.

The night was terrible, Biber repeatedly gasping for air, spitting up more blood. She spent much of the night standing over her bowl, it being less painful than lying down it seemed. This wasn't just bronchitis, we felt. By morning we began to suspect it was poison.

Mary was frantic. "We need to find another vet," she insisted.

Ingrid and Gerhardt, fellow cruisers, a German couple, had a large beautiful Schnauser. We saw them as they came to work in the yard at nine o'clock. Ingrid recommended their vet, Dr. Romanelli. He drove right over—half an hour away. His diagnosis was immediate—rat poison. "The poison works by breaking down the blood vessels," he said. We cancelled Dr.T, over Lucia's objection and drove Biber to the vet's office. He went into emergency mode, oxygen, multiple antitoxin injections, H2O drip for dehydration, plasma drip to replace blood cells.

But by now Beber was prostrate, breathing heavily, her whole body heaving. "It may be too late," the vet said, in Italian, then in French. Ingrid translated for us. She had accompanied us the whole way and having had some medical training she assisted the vet. We get more antitoxin from the local pharmacy. The saline and the plasma dripped as regularly as the second hand on the clock, but Biber's breathing came heavier. She fought bravely, her eyes clear and searching as if wondering what she had done wrong. Mary tried to calm her, to soothe her. The minutes ticked by, an hour, but her breathing became shallower and then blood began to hemorrhage from her mouth. The vet nodded his head, resigned. "Please give her a shot to put her out of her suffering," Mary said tearfully.

And that was the end.

We wrapped Biber in the blue and green beach towel she had slept on. I found a plastic crate on the boat and curled her still pliable body into it, and carried her out to the beach she loved with such carefree abandon. We dug a 3-ft hole just behind the bushes, covered her over with sand and rocks, a good Moslem burial appropriate for a Turkish marina dog. Mary put her bowl and half a box of "Markies," her favorite dog treats in her coffin crate, just in case her spirit needed nurterance on the journey to the next doggie world. And, in case that world was a playground paradise, Mary plunked an empty plasticwater bottle on the mound, Biber's favorite play toy.

If dogs have ghosts, Beber's will romp and range on her favorite beach for dog's eternity.

We were hushed, crushed, astounded, dismayed. Confronted by the mystery of death, recalling other recent and not so recent deaths. But that is another message. Ask not for whom the bell tolls.....

An epilogue. As I wrote something uncanny occurred. There was another dog in the marina complex that was an almost identical look-alike to Biber. Another stray, similar size, just a little heavier, the same black and white coloration, though his face was all black rather than with the splash of white Biber had, curly hair, the long bushy tail, half the length of the dog himself. Most people mistook them for each other. A few minutes after our return from the beach he came by the van. We had some of Biber's food left, and Mary went out to feed him. He ate a little, then laid his head on Mary's lap. When she returned into the van, he stood outside and howled, then went on doing his rounds.

The reverence and solidarity of strays. Aren't we all strays?

Joe and Mary aboard Zillah with beloved ship's dog,
Biber.

Chapter 114: West Med 2000

We winter in Sibari, located on the instep of the boot of Italy. The entrance channel choked with sand that keeps the dredge operating year round, entered by a wavering channel parallel to the beach, inside the bar. Contact Lucia at the office on VHF and Guitano, the dockmaster comes out to guide us in. The marina has seen better days, but it is protected from the rough winter gales—Mediterranean winters are windy and wet, a storm barrier protects the inner harbor against storm surge, the boatyard have craftsmen and facilities for all manner of maintainance and repairs. There are hot showers, a coin operated laundromat, e-mail access by phone, a skippers lounge with Italian TV and fridge. The staff are welcoming and accomodating. Markets are five miles away, the marina provide transportation a couple times a week. We have our trusty Talbot/Peugot camper van and we explore many of the villages about, Mary acquiring linguistic proficiency in survival Italian.

There's a transient community of cruisers, German, Swiss, Austrian, Brits, some who return year after year, and one American. Yvonne and Erik, a Swiss builder and contractor, who circumnavigated several years back, old timers at Sibari, are here only for a couple weeks over Easter, to escape the bleakness of the alpine spring; they invite us to dinner, mittdag essen, the noon meal, meat balls with gravy, shredded potatoes fried, no vegetable, typical heavy European fare, and a red wine with an earthy bite. Rhea on the big, near derelict old style motor yacht down the dock, invites us over for a birthday drink and goodies, they're Dutch and have parked their great white whale in Sibari—"In Holland we have 3 weeks of sunshine a year," her husband, Tim says, "if you're lucky. Here we have forty." We share Christmas and New Years with convivial friends, fellow nomads of the sea.

We take trips, north through France to Denmark in the fall; Venice, Florence, Tuscany in the spring. Mary returns home for a couple months, I visit Isreal. So when we return to Zillah we enjoy the quiet time.

The weather swings dramatically from sunny skies, warm in the 70's/ 20C, lenticulated clouds stacked in layers against the mountains that surround the bay. Some days a soft, mellow, quiet drizzle. Evenings we walk a beautiful sand beach, with a dramtic view down the coast and around the bay to the mountains. The lights of hill villages flicker on, high up on the slopes, as dusk crowds out the light of day. Beber, our little Turkish street dog, vents all the pent up energy of the day, chasing sea gulls back and forth along the beach.

ON THRUHULLS AND SEACOCKS: SIBARI BOATYARD—APRIL

Zillah has to be hauled for maintainace and her perennial face lift. When we pull the boat, the bottom looked like a coral reef there was so much growth, animal and vegetable, barnacles, a spagetti like worm, another translucent creature about the size of a cocktail sausage. Fascinating like a Jackson Pollock painting. .

A major retrofit is also needed. When I went to turn off the head thruhull outlet seacock last fall, it stuck. So I tapped the handle lightly with a hammer and it came off in my hand, and a geyser of water gushed into the boat. Easily stopped off with a wooden bunge, I checked others. When I went to loosen the bolts on the thruhull fitting that drains the deck scuppers, the head of the bolt came off in the wrench. Time to replace the seacocks and through hull fittings which were probably installed in 1955 when the boat was built. I've had all eight pulled and replaced with new ones—ball valves, made of plastic, no corrosion. I shuddered to think of the cost. The yard would not give me an estimate as work on an old boat is difficult to assess the time things take. So I pay for labor, by the hour, plus parts. Labor as you can imagine in Italy is as much a social event as it is work, and the job crept along as the cost galloped ahead.

But it had to be done, and I had neither the tools nor the skill do it myself. More important my stiffening body can't be twisted and contorted into the cramped confines of Zillah's depths. The last time I stuck my head down the cockpit bilge I couldnt get back out. There I was de profundis. Mary had to come to my rescue, a tug of war pulling my legs while I struggled below pushing up with my arms. Each day a work crew came by, 2 or 3 men. The first day to extract the old fittings, grinding off the heads of the bolts outboard and bashing them inboard. Next day another team to cut and fit hardwood backing plates over the open holes, many trips up and down the ladder to the trim saw in the shed. Third day to centre the backing plates and epoxy them into place. The next two days, wait for the epoxy to set up. Next they drill through the backing plates and install new fittings. A final connecting of hoses and the job is done. Should Zillah sink at least it will not be from failure of a thruhull fitting, a major cause of boats foundering.

They pulled the propellor and the propellor shaft and replaced the cutlass bearing. The topsides were spray painted a glistening white, and the bottom painted with a bright Mediterranean blue anti-fouling, and Zillah was launched looking like new.

LETTER APRIL 28, 2000 FROM SIBARI

The sun shines through a high cirrus haze, a light breeze off the sea, a slight chill in the air, reminiscent of San Francisco weather, too cold to risk varnishing. We're getting ready for a big year—the Western Med, Gibralter, Canaries, an Atlantic Crossing, and warm water and snorkeling in the Caribbean—Ahhh. Lots of anticipation, and the gnawing uncertainty and anxiety that is a part of all big dreams. We work through the long list of tasks needed before we sail. Varnish on sunny days, and it goes well. Last year we put 8 coats on, and the vertical side surfaces have held up and need only to be lightly scuffed with sandpaper and varnished. Top horizontal surfaces have peeled in places, like the toe rail and cabin top, but I find the old stuff can be removed easily with a heat gun, a glorified blow drier, sanded and then revarnished. Quite a different job to the massive task of last year, and Mary and I poke away at it in a leisurely fashion. Below decks on overcast days we sort and reorganize gear, clothes, books, discarding those treasures we have carted around for five years and never used, old clothes go to Caritas, the Catholic relief organization like the Salvation Army.

But books are the hardest. We give some away to an English couple down the dock, another packrat. Keep a small bundle to trade. But its like pulling teeth to let go of such old favorites as Huckleberry Finn and Charlotte's Web. To say nothing of Thucidides and Manchester's biography of Churchill or McCoullough's Truman. In the old days they used to ballast boats with bricks. We could do the same with books, if we could figure out how to keep them dry in the bilge. But we need the space. Where will we put the extra food and water we'll need for the Atlantic Crossing? The duffle for the extra crew? And the crew itself—the foot of the port bunk tucks under a little nook by the mast, now the locker for computer, personal documents and papers, the backup Sony shortwave radio. Where will they go when we have four people on board? So we sort and store—stuff to ship back to the States, (we consider finding a shipping line out of Naples, but how do you handle customs?), stuff we'll want on the crossing like extra foul weather gear, and a bundle for the Caribbean with extra snorkel gear. And we stuff it into the quarter births, trying to create some logical order to the packing, like packing a backpack.

But the pace is relaxed. We have two weeks still. We chat with boats along the dock. Brian and Bud, two Irishmen across the way polish up their fibreglass hull to a sheen, and rig sails; they're bound for Crete next week. Every week more boats are launched, having been stored on the hard for winter. There's a hum and a bustle in the air, a sense of expectation. Several boats are paid up until the end of the month, and this weekend we expect a big exodus. We have become a bit leery of late spring and early fall gales, and give the weather gods another two weeks to blow themselves out.

And we enjoy being back on Zillah. She is looking very pretty with the new paint job on the hull, and now the varnished cabin top. And she is our home. Mary found a radio shop in Corigliano that was able to revive our CD player so we enjoy Mozart and Bach with our evening meals again.

We talk about how fortunate we are to be living this life. What a priveleged moment in history we live in. In what other era would a poorly paid school teacher afford a boat, have the leisure time and resources to cruise the seven seas and explore the wonders of the world? How fortunate we are to be white in an unfair world where the distribution of wealth is so disproportionate to need. And to have grown up on a continent that has been relatively immune to wars. What a great year this will be.

THE PASSAGE FROM SOUTH ITALY—SIBARI TO SICILY

Mary is at the helm. We cross from Rocello Ionico on the toe of Italy to Siracusa (Syracuse) on the east coast of Sicily, 93 nautical miles on a course of 215 degrees southwest. A day of motoring, leisurely reading as we slip along the shoreline, backed by the Calabrian mountains. Entering the gap between the mainland and the island, a swell from the NW lifts and rocks the boat. At dinner we turn south, waves on the stern, a gentle hoist and heave to the boat.

"Before dark I'd like to raise the mainsail." "How so?"Mary asks. There is very little wind. "Well for one, it makes us more visible. There'll be a moon tonight." We've seen freighters passing in the distance all day.

"Second, if there is wind I'd prefer not be go on deck in the dark." There have been light katabatic winds, the cool mountain breezes blowing out to sea at night." "OK." Up main, close hauled and tightly cleated, and the sail fills with the forward motion of the boat, 6.5 knots motoring at 2200 rpm. "A Perkins breeze," Mary calls it. We are powered by a 55hp Perkins diesel engine.

We are six days out of Sibari, on the first leg of our ElderOdyssey 2000 that will take us to the Caribbean by New Years, wind gods willing. "ElderOdyssey. I don't like the name," Mary says, "I don't feel that old." But at 71 I take a certain pride in having weathered the years so well.

The first four days we had virtually no wind, glassy seas, mere riffles on the water. We motor leisurely, relaxed; it's been idyllic, scenic. We pass fishing villages along the coast, olive groves clustered on the hillsides, the symetrical rows of orange groves on the lower slopes, wheat fields a honey ripe. Hilltop villages dating from the Middle Ages, well back from the sea, each a fortress against marauding seafaring pirates. We stopped at Crotone founded by the Greeks in the 6C BC. "I'm getting hooked on this motoring," I told Mary, "I don't know what we'll do if we ever have to sail." We catch up on our reading. I struggle to understand "The Education of Henry Adams."

The wind catches up with us at Le Castella, along the south coast, SW 25 knots, on the nose, a five foot chop, so we sat tight for a day and explored the town and the castle. Built by the Spanish in the 16C on ancient foundations it is being beautifully restored by the Italians. They are big on restoration, keeping traditional skills alive, the labor intensive work providing badly needed jobs in the depressed south. Jobs are good politics. We sat out a second day to let the seas settle. Then on to Rocello Ionico 47 miles at 225 degrees, winds 15 knots, shifting from south to west and all points between, so we sailed the wind, changing course to give us our first day of sailing. No pounding of the engine, the sound of water gurgling along the hull, the peace and serenity of the sea. We motor in the last 10 miles against headwinds and rising seas. There were six yachts in the fishing harbor and all the crews poured out of their boats to help us with our docking lines, amidst a confusion of German, Scandinavian, Swiss, Dutch, and one fellow Canadian, in a babble of English and conflicting directions.

On the final run, 50 miles now to Siracusa , Mary stands watch. There is a suggestion of wind. We run out the genoa and immediately it fills. But the wind gods taunt us. With Mediterranean duplicity it hits suddenly, rises rapidly and in 15 minutes we go from near calm to near gale. Zillah heels, the rail goes down and like a race horse out of the starting gate, "We're off!" Experience has taught us to anticipate squalls so we sail with the main double reefed permanently. Now we take a double reef in the genoa, furling it back in, reducing the sail by half. Checking our speed on the GPS (Global Positioning System) we are still making 7.2 knots, near hull speed even with shortened sails. On a beam reach, the boat heels with the gusts, is thrown about in the trough between eight foot seas, waves crash over the bow. It's going to be a long night. Mary has the helm under control. I curl up on the cockpit cushions and try to doze. But random waves break over the cockpit combing and douse my face. Refreshing but hardly soporific. At 2300 hours Mary asks me to relieve her watch.

At the helm, my world centers on the red glow of the binnacle light above the compass. The light is damaged and I have jury rigged a red bulb that glows too brightly. While lighting the compass it also destroys my night vision. So my sole point of reference is the gyrating needle of the compass, waving back and forth 20 degrees either side of the course of 220 degrees. It is a wild night to remember, wind gusting to 35 knots, boat heeling to 35 degrees, rolling in 8 to 10 foot seas. Occasionally there is a roar out of the dark, like approaching rapids in a river canyon, a breaking wave rushing by, heard more than seen. I turn the stern quarter to where I imagine the wave to be and Zillah lifts gently and the wave roars past,the boat heeling and heaving, bobbing and weaving. I'm always anxious the first night out at sea. I'd be a fool not to be. But with each hour I regain confidence in myself and Zillah. For greater confidence I sing to myself the old sailors' hymn, "Lord hear us when we pray to Thee/ For those in peril on the sea." Just in case.

The moon rises over the eastern horizon soon after midnight, and disappears into a low hanging bank of cloud, to appear again higher, back lighting a gloomy, haunting sky, evoking lines from Shelley, "that orbed maiden/ By white fire laden...glides glimmering o'er thy fleece like floor/ By the midnight breezes strewn." Shelley and the navy hymn all in one night—too much.

The wind subsides but the seas still run high. The aftermath is worse than the storm. The genoa flogs and the boom swings violently back and forth as we wallow in the trough. One hand on the helm, the other on the main sheet, I try to brake the wild swinging action. Mary cannot sleep with the banging and the racket, comes up at 0200 hours and we furl in the genoa, pull in the main, secure it midships and continue on by engine pounding at 1800 rpm, bashing through the chop.

Siracusa 11.9 miles at 220 degrees, the GPS reads. We scan the shore lights off the starboard bow with binoculars searching for the navigation lights marking the harbor entrance; lights pop up out of the dark, small fishing boats moving between their traps and nets, then disappear again. "There it is, Mary. Flashing green." At 0400 hours we pass beneath the sombre fortress on the rocky headland, the offshore swell crashing on the seawall in a seething spray, and enter the quiet waters of a magnificent oval shaped bay. I've been reading Thucydides and I have an uncanny feeling. It is here the Athenian fleet was trapped and destroyed in 413 BC, the army captured and 7000 prisoners condemned to life of hard labor in the quarries, the beginning of the end of

Athen's defeat in the Peloponnesus War. It is a damning commentary on the divisiveness of democratic politics and military arrogance. Is there a moral for today?

"Depth of twenty feet," Mary calls. We drop the anchor in the bay across from town, but it doesn't hold. "Try fifteen." It still doesn't hold. "Let's just let out all the chain. There's no wind. We won't drag," I call back. "I'll keep anchor watch, sleep in the cockpit." The adrenalin drains out. I brew a cup of tea—herbal tea no caffeine, roll up in the canvas sail cover and before the tea cools, I'm asleep.

A region of convergence, the southwest corner of Italy, the northeast corner of Sicily, along a volcanic faultline—Vesuvius, Stromboli, Etna; an epicentre of weather systems, the Aeoleian Triangle, like the Bermuda Triangle, of fickle winds and sudden storms, ship disasters; the convergence of races and civilizations, the path of invaders and conquerors, a history crowded with plunder, rapine and conquest; a land shrouded in Western Man's earliest myth, the travels of Odysseus, blown off course when his men inadvertently open his bags, believing him to be hoarding gold, they release the forbidden winds and are driven to these islands, islands of contorted forms, sulphurous fumes, inhabited by demons and monsters. We journey through the Straits of Messina on our own contemporary Odyssey.

At Syracuse, we wait out the weather front in the shelter of the bay, winds outside NE 25 with an 8 ft swell. We visit the archeological ruins, a Roman theatre carved out of the walls of the marble quarry, and walk the shadowy alleys of the old town, narrow streets with leaning walls, laundry hanging from the balconies, slowly being restored, gentrified, crumbling mansions, overlooking expansive views of the sea above the high sea wall; the cathedral built on the site of the Temple of Athena, eight huge Doric pillars still intact, built into the walls. But the post war prosperity that has rejuvenated most of Europe, has passed Sicily by. There have been too many Mafia payoffs.

With the first break in the weather, we motor north to Catania. No wind. Then on to Taormina where the full fetch of a nor'easter blowing down the Straits of Messina buffet us head on with 6 ft seas. We turn back and find refuge behind the sheltering rocky outcrops of Acitrezza, the rocks flung in Homeric legend, by Polyphemous, the one-eyed Cyclops blinded by Odysseus as he fled the cave.

We motor out before dawn the following day, Mt. Etna looming above us fuming and resplendent on a rare day when the haze has blown off the summit, leaving a thin film of volcanic ash sprinkled over the town, and on Zillah's deck. Off Taormina we hit the windline again, and are slowed from 7 knots to 4, but the seas have not had time to build up, and we motor on. At Messina, we wait for the tide to turn and catch the northward flow through the narrow straits. At slack tide the whirlpool of Charybdis that nearly engulfed Odysseus is flat and benign, small fishing boats clustered in the centre where the fish feed in the churned up waters. The ferry boats shuttling freight trains and 16 wheeler cargo trucks across from the mainland are a principal navigational hazard. We avoid Scilla perched on a cliff on the Italian shore where the eight armed serpent plucked Odysseus's seamen off the deck and devoured them. In the straits, swordfishing boats stalk their prey, 35 ft boats with a tremendous long bowsprit, 50 ft., longer than the boat itself, and a tall, outsized mast, 50 ft up, two men scanning the waters from the crow's-nest.

We find good shelter at Milasso, diesel, camper gas, a fresh fruit and vegetable market, and next day cross to Isolata Volcan, motoring again into winds NW 10 knots. We anchor offshore in bubbling murky waters, smelling of sulphur. On shore holiday makers wallow in the grey-brown mud, and stew in the steaming muck, a scene from Dante, with young and old, fat and thin, twisting and writhing in the primordial ooze, "taking the cures." We climb the volcano, 1500 ft in the early morning, before the heat of the day, in a long procession of hilltop pilgrims, seeking a perspective on life from high places. Mary's first mountain ascent, a memorable day.

CROSSING TO AMALFI

We consult Aeolis, the weather god on VHF 68. Winds NE Force 3. Light but on the nose. We motor most of the way, Otto, our auto-pilot steering. Amalfi, Italy's first republic, a maritime city state that cashed in on the Crusades, transporting warring Christians to the East, hauling back their loot. But it was the sack of Constantinople, robbing other Christians, the heretical Greeks, that brought real prosperity. Villas were built into the steep hillside, with connecting alleys and tunnels under six story apartment blocks. In the waterfront piazza, a statue to Flavio Giorja, 14 C, who recognized the merits of a magnetised needle in a bowl of water, a Chinese idea, and comes down to us as the "inventor" of the compass.

On the steep and winding road to the hilltop villages, there is only one wrecked car on the narrow road, in spite of the blind curves, hairpin bends, places where two cars cannot pass, barely wide enough for the bus; the driver stands beside his car, the front grill and bumper lying on the shoulder, a frightened, pleading, anxious look on his face, almost in tears. "Let me shake your hand," the Italian lady says to the bus driver when we reach the top, complimenting him on his cautious driving. . From the gardens of the Belvedere, among acres of roses, hydrangeas, fuschias, we gaze down to the red roofs of Amalfi and the glistening sea beyond. In the cathedral, Jonah has an alarmed look on his face, as he disappears into the mouth of the whale, on the carved ivory plaque under the pulpit, a compelling symbol for a maritime people.

Capri, 25 miles off shore, 1000 ft cliffs rising out of the sea, caves high up, a myriad seabirds, circling like swarming bees above the rookery; not the gracefull patient soaring of hunting birds, but agitated, quarrellous, arguing for space, competing for mates, a shrill cacaphony of shreiking cries. Far cry from the Capri of romantic ballad. We anchor off the rocky lee shore. In the evening it clouds over, faint rumblings of thunder to the east over the mainland. We are sheltered from the light 10 knot wind from the north, but during the night the swell builds up and wraps around the island, nudging us to shore. It is here that Sirens beckoned unsuspecting sailors close to the rugged shore, luring them to their rack and ruin and Odysseus plugged the ears of his crew with wax, and had them tie him to the mast. I take it as a warning and at first light, turn on the engine, pull up the anchor and motor out.

We by-pass Naples and move from the mythical to the classical. Ventoteni is an ancient Roman galley harbor, 200 yards long, 100 yards wide, about as large as two football fields, carved out of the rock, a soft volcanic tuffa. Boat sheds were carved into the cliffband where PADI shops now rent air tanks and diving gear. Small boats crowd the harbor. We anchor in the larger Puerto Novo. In the village, there's a memorial in the piazza with the names of those killed in the "Guerra Grande." On the back is a plaque dedicated on "22 May, the 11th year of Fascism." I'm surprised because we seldom see references to fascism, or to Mussolini on the prolific public monuments he ordered built to the greater glory of himself and Italy. In many places they have been obviously erased. We are reminded that during Mussolini's regime this island was a prison for the political prisoners and ponder. Have all the political prisoners left, leaving behind only the fascist prison guards and their monuments?

We poke into the small church, almost a full crowd on Pentacost Sunday. This is the feast where the Holy Ghost appears to the disciples who are frightened and dismayed, bewildered after the death of Christ and He consols them and encourages them to go out and preach the Good Word to all lands, and gives them the gift of tongues. The priest is Black! We knew there was a shortage of priests in Italy. Like most Christian countries there has been a great falling off. Though a Catholic country and the Pope is revered like a celebrity, less than 15% go to church regularly. But we had not imagined they were recruiting priests from Africa. Somolia, Eritrea and Ethiopia were occupied by the Italians in the 1930's, and still have an Italian presence. The priest is clearly a man of many tongues but he preaches in Italian. Disappointing.

And on to Ponza, bleak and barren, volcanic, the cliffs layered bands of sulphur yellow, browns and buffs, gray patina, and black basalt, bent from the horizontal and warped to the vertical. But the village is the prettiest we have seen, houses pastel cubes, stacked on the hillside, a blaze of colors, pinks, corals, pale yellows and forget-me-not blues, interspersed with white, dramatically topped by a white phallic lighthouse on the headland. It is a seaside weekend holiday resort, crowded with Italians. We anchor in the bay between two other yachts flying American flags. Sunday the fishing fleet is in, at least 50 boats rafted up, three deep in the crowded harbor. Front street along the quay has fish stalls, dockside restaurants, bars and gelaterias, ice cream parlors. High street above is lined with souvenir shops, boutiques, and numerous shoe stores. We marvel at how many pairs of shoes every Italian must have to keep so many in business. A loudspeaker from the church belfry blares a congregational hymn. Outside the church, a woman and two men, emerging from Pentacost vespers block the sidewalk. They stand three feet apart, shouting at each other, all three at once, gesticulating, arms flailing, eyes glaring, nostrils flaring, intent. But nobody strikes anyone. And no one seems to mind, the crowd move politely around them and walk on. The trio continue to rant, exercising their God given gift of tongues.

We motor back on the mainland and find a berth in the marina at Nettuno. It is 35 miles with no wind and a 3 to 5 ft swell that rocks and rolls the boat back and forth uncomfortably. This is becoming tiresome. We've motored over 100 hours since leaving Sibari 3 weeks before. At 6 mph that's 600 miles! And still not a solid day of good sailing. But life is good, and we read "The Wind and the Willows," and agree with Rat, "There's nothing, absolutely nothing like messing about in boats."

Isle of Capri, Italy, 2000.

FIUMICINO AND ROME

We cross the bar at the entrance, motor against the current up the canal, pass under the drawbridge, open 7.30 am, 2.30 pm and again at 4.30, and tie to the stone quay. Fishing boats line the opposite wall. It's like camping in Central Park, planes landing at Fiumicino Airport, Rome's terminal one mile away, boats passing in and out, cars and trucks a steady stream of traffic on either side of the canal, people walking on the esplanade above, fishermen leaning on their rods on the seawall. But its the ideal place to visit Rome from a yacht, providing you can tolerate the noise and the bustle, and the flotsam and jettsom that drifts down the Tiber Canal, an open storm sewer, 15 miles downstream from Rome. Michael and Susan, cruising friends on "Trilogy" have wintered here.

A short ride on a bus takes us to the Metro, and within an hour we get off at the Coliseum, where the roar of lions is supplanted by the growling of motorcycles. We imbibe Rome is small doses. There is so much to see, it is hard to take it all in, a struggle not to be overwhelmed. Our best day in the city was three years before, on a Sunday when they ran the Rome Marathon. Traffic was blocked off, the centre of the city a connected pedestrian mall, the way the city was meant to be seen before being traumatized by the automobile. We ambled from Constantin's Triumphal Arch, past the Forum up to the Pantheon, to the Spanish steps and the fountains, amidst a relaxed, cheering, leisurely crowd, dodging the panting runners.

We are impressed by a huge series of maps on an outside wall of the Forum, showing the expansion of the Roman Empire through the centuries. By 200 AD it stretched from Hadrian's Wall on the border of Scotland to the Persian Gulf, from Spain to the Black Sea, and trade routes on to the Caspian, fleets that sailed to India. And this before mechanization, radio or e-mail, when the world moved at the pace we do on Zillah, 6 mph at sea, 15 miles a day by land. Returning at rush hour, the Metro is packed, a pretty young gypsy woman, nursing child at her breast, a diverting decoy, crowds against my hip, a quick flick of her hand into my pocket which disappointingly is empty.

We negotiate with Kelly Maria, an American yacht alongside, for the sale of our campervan, and Mary takes a trip back to Sibari with them for a test drive. Given the marvels of instant international e-mail communications and electronic money transfers, the deal is done.

A long days motor sail up the coast to Ponza, where we anchor overnight and push on to Elba.

LETTER FROM ELBA JUNE 22, 2000

Our first full day of sailing, gentle NE winds, 10-15 knots and we are delighted to coast along at 4.5 knots without the incessant hammering of the diesel engine. Later to discover a chunk of black plastic wrapped around the prop. That probable slowed us a knot.

Elba, rugged granitic mountains covered in maquis, tough thorny bushes. Fishing villages now holiday resorts along the coast, the beaches already crowded. Particularly popular with Germans, as it is only a short hop over the Alps, ninety miles an hour on the autostrada. Here Napolean took a more leisurely vacation during his eight month exile, before he escaped for one last campaign and final defeat at Waterloo.

We motor ashore and return to find one tube of the dingy collapsed. The valve is stuck so there is no way of reinflating it. "Dingy ist kaput, non functionare," I tell them at the chandlery in my best international boat-speak. I tell Mary about Roy Smith, an Outward Bound instructor, who led a National Geographic expedition down the Omo River, a tributary of the Nile, in rubber rafts and was attacked by a crocodile biting through one tube. We look for the monster in Portoferio harbor, but if he is there he eludes us. At Marina Campo, 4 hours around the other side of the island we find Sandro, the only repair man of inflatibles on the island.

A WEEKEND IN CORSICA—FRIDAY TO MONDAY JUNE 23-26

We had read up on Corsica. A part of France, though fiercely independent, a rugged island with a rocky coastline, forbidding seacliffs, deep fiord like bays, a mountainous interior with isolated villages, all within a couple hours of the sea. If we can find a place to leave Zillah secure, we planned to tour inland. But it also makes its own weather. The Mediterranean Waters Pilot warns of fierce and unpredictable winds, "Always get a good weather report before passage making." The crossing, 38 miles west from Elba is much the same as we have experienced the past month, light winds on the nose; we motor sail. Anchoring off Macinaggio, the harbor on the NE corner, we swim in clear water, that is warm enough, for the first time this summer, for our stiffening bodies. I scrub the hull of Fiumicino detritus.

We can't pick up the French weather report on the radio, so we dingy to shore and check the printed report on the Port Captain's bulletin board. "Winds force 3 and 4 (15-20 mph) along the NW coast, but Force 7 (35mph) locally." What does that mean.? "And Force 7 and 8 on the extremities." Another ambiguous statement. "Force 7 off Cape Formentero." That's on the southern end of the island, on the narrow straits between Corsica and Sardinia, notorious for bad weather. Makes sense.

We're eager to get around to Calvi, on the west coast, because this is where one of the few protected anchorages is located. Next morning, Mary, an iconoclast when it comes to believing weather reports says, "Let's go out and see what it looks like." We motor out, not enough wind to sail, but an hour later off Cap Grosso, at the north "extremity", high cliffs coming down to the sea, we run into the full force of a gale, 30 knot winds, 8 ft seas, and turn back. Again the wind drops and we motor into our anchorage.

We planned to go ashore to phone and sample French cuisine, but by mid-afternoon, the wind picks up SW 20 with choppy seas. So we sit tight. An omelette for dinner, the last of the bread, with Italian wine. All Saturday night, it blows, 25-30 knots. I keep anchor watch, sleeping fitfully, in the starboard berth in the main cabin. I have a frightening dream. I'm a passenger in a car that is going too fast, and want to get out. I know we're going too fast, but if I tuck and roll I won't hurt myself too much. Out I go. And wake up on the floor in pain. I've fallen out of the settee, banged my knee and elbow on the cabin table, scraping the skin off my big toe. I had a similar dream five years before, lying at anchor in Ft. Lauderdale as Hurricane Gordon blew through. That time I hit my nose and required five stitches.

Sunday, the wind increased to gale force. A dingy, tethered to the stern of a yacht anchored near us, flips and rotates in the wind, like an unruly kite. We read, write letters and journals, keep a weather eye on the wind, check the anchor. I tinker with the vented loop on the head. Anything to fend off cabin fever. The weather outlook, "Winds NW 5, decreasing." During the night the wind drops.

Monday 0525 hours. Anchor up, no wind, we motor out in flat seas. Fifteen minutes off shore we raise the sail, and set our course for Spezzia, back on the coast of Italy. Off shore the winds are light, the seas huge 10-12 ft swells left over from yesterday's gale. We motor much of the way and have a beautiful breeze to sail into the harbor. Walking the esplanade that night we feel the pavement heaving beneath our feet, as we regain our land legs. So much for our weekend in Corsica.

From Spezzia we motor sail along the rocky coast of the Cinque Terra, the five isolated villages clinging to the mountainside. We had hiked the precipitous trail that snakes its way along the coastline, the previous year. We tie up at the town dock at Santa Margherita in a light rain, and next day motor slowly around Portofino headland on a glassy sea. Crossing the Bay of Genoa, Columbus birth place, by-passing the huge meglopolis, we anchor off the harbor entrance at Varazzi. In the evening, hoots, whistles, cat calls and blaring car horns proclaim Italy's last minute penalty short goal and victory over Holland, for the World Cup semi-finals. In the marina at Alissio, we are rammed by a British yacht coming into dock, slightly out of control, bending one of the stanchions and putting a sag in the life line, plus pushing us onto the concrete dock, flaking 6 inches off our new paint job. We settled amicably for 150 English pounds over gin and tonic. We speculated how much he had imbibed before docking.

Canada Day—July the First—Mary's Birthday, we celebrate at San Remo, on the Italian Riviera. A mock "surprise" party, I package the presents she has already seen, in colorful gift bags we stow just for such occasions; purple Benetton slack suit with white vest, she looks very chic in; an opaque butterfly cut from a geode, with silver antenna and legs. We dress up and go out to dinner at Los Tres Pinos, under the pines along the waterfront, order a pasta flavored with zuccini blossoms, sword fish filette in a tomato sauce, a small carafe of Soave, and a cherry in Mary's glass of agua mineral sin gaz, her cocktail.

JOUSTING THE MISTRAL

It has been a summer of motoring, 200 hours, 1200 miles since putting to sea in mid-May and finally at San Remo, the last port of call on the Italian Riviera we catch up with the wind. We sit out a day as a nor'easter blows through, then put out in NE 25 knots and run down wind in 6 to 8 ft seas, a real "Yahoo!" day, making 6 knots with only the double reefed genoa up, high flying for us; past Menton, first harbor of refuge in France; past Monte Carlo a square mile Manhattan transplant on the Riviera Coast. A spectacular day, sparkling seas, mountain range rising above the coastal strip, Zillah soaring in the following swell, Mary jubilant at the helm. I'm anxious about entering harbor with a breaking swell over the entrance, forwarned by the French Coast Mariners Pilot, so we sail on. Cap Ferrat, a spur jutting south from the coastal mountains gives protection from easterlies and westerlies, but is open to the south. So we duck in and anchor off Villefranche, a suburb of Nice, below palaces and villas of the famous and the rich. We meet up with "Navarra," Rob and Mandy and their two children, Peter 5 and Rachel 7, Kiwi circumnavigators we met in Marmaris, Turkey two years ago. Going ashore to admire the gardens and real estate, we walk the narrow lane leading to the headland, but see only high hedges, boarded fences, warnings to keep out, security guards and watch dogs. Welcome to the Riviera.

Mandy give us directions where to find the open street market, supermarket, post office and most important, a laundromat that charges by the kilo rather than by the article, and telephone boxes where we can e-mail, all within a 15 minute walk on shore. In clear, clean water, we enjoy the swimming. The wind shifts to the SW in the night and a gentle swell rolls into the bay. When the wind drops Zillah rolls back and forth demonically, then temporarily abating, only to start up again. At 1am Mary insists we put out a stern anchor to put us bow to the swell. In the morning we motor around to the east side of the Cap Ferrat and find a patch of sand among the weeds and rocks and put down the anchor off Beaulieu. Good holding. A spectacular stretch of coast, mountains rise 2000 feet above the sea. A beautiful seaside resort, the Grande Hotel Royale with a rococo flamboyance, buildings in Palladian Renasissance, a reconstruction of a Greek villa in the classical style, an austere monument to the Resistance. A South African couple, Nick and Marina, apple growers, who are on "La Rose", come by and we walk together along the promenade. It goes for miles out to the lighthouse on the cape. Someone had the foresight to establish an easement across the waterfront of the estates. It's the sort of place that makes you want to stay and visit again.

But even the roses in paradise have thorns. I wake at 0500 hours to pee, check the bilge, and find water within 6 inches of the cabin floor boards. Why doesn't the automatic bilge pump kick in? The wind shifts back to the SE so we motor around to Villefranche again.

Another wind shift the following day, SW 10-15. Building through the day, boats begin to pull out. Next to us, a towering 70 ft ketch begins to drag. It is a classic design with masts that reach to the sky, high bulwarks, an extended overhanging bow,"Tika" lettered on the stern, Australian flag. There's only one person on board and he wrestles to tie the dingy down on deck in the rising wind. He races frantically for the bow, high out on the bowsprit to let out more anchor chain. Still the boat drags. He dashes back to the helm to start the motor. "Looks like he's in trouble," Mary says. "I'd better give him a hand," I reply and charge over in our dingy.

"Tell me what do to to help." "Take the helm and motor up slowly." He tries to set the anchor again, but still we drag, this time down on to Zillah. Motoring slowly into the wind we finally get the anchor up. John comes back to thank me, I return to Zillah in my dingy, "Tika," motors out of the bay.

Back on Zillah, Mary and I debate whether to ride it out, or to move back around to Beaulieu again. "Navarra" and "La Rose" have already pulled out. The decision is made for us. We begin to drag. The dingy is still down, and in the blustery wind there is no way to raise it on deck; it is a lightweight inflatable and would take off like a balloon. But I am reluctant to leave the outboard motor on the dingy in the open sea around Cap Ferrat, fearing it could flip. Standing in the dingy, holding the motor in my arms, I try hoisting it up to Mary on the stern pulpit. A 3 ft wave lifts the dingy, catches me off balance and throws me down on my back into the dingy bilge, pinned to the floor, the motor on my chest. A brief wrestling match with the motor, a mighty hoist by Mary and I'm off the mat, the motor is hoisted aboard. Securely bolted to the pushpit, we motor out and shelter off Beaulieu once again.

But there is always the nagging urge to move on. We try to get a fix on the weather. The French report on the radio comes across too fast, and while there is an English report from Radio Monaco VHF 23 the English is so accented it is more difficult to understand than the French. We do get a report though that there have been thunderstorms in northern France, in the Ardenne, a woman struck dead while picking lettuce. "Do we have any lettuce on board?" I ask Mary. We raise anchor and sail on.

At Antibe, we anchor off the old City Wall, amidst windsurfers, a group of well tanned teenagers flitting about the bay on a fleet of Lazers, boys and girls, amazingly skilled and expert. Picasso spent time here, and we visit the museum, delighting in his nymph and satyr and rapacious bulls phase of painting.

A gentle afternoon sail, wind S 10-15, takes us to Rada de Agay, the next bay giving protection from east and west, but open to the south. We meet up with Ekhart and Gisela, a German journalist, with a warm spot in his heart for Americans, having spent an enjoyable 10 years in New York as a foreign correspondent. Checking their ship's log, they discover that it is a year ago almost to the day, that we met on the island of Ios, in Greece. Cocktail hour is interrupted when the wind shifts to the west, and blows up to 20 knots and they have to scramble to secure their boat. Caught in building seas, at 11pm we raise anchor and motor across the bay, and anchor again under the protection of the headland. The automatic bilge pump is still not working and it takes 10 minutes and 200 strokes by hand to pump dry. A swell sweeps around the headland into the bay, and we have another night of interrupted sleep.

The mistral, winds that blow with gale force come down the valley of the Rhone in south-central France and out over the coastal Mediterranean can last several days. We are windlocked in Rada de Agay for the rest of the week. Mary takes the opportunity to visit with Puck and Chieli Rolf, a Dutch couple we met at Marmaris in Turkey, who have retired to southern France. I boat watch and tend to badly needed repairs, the float valve on the automatic bilge pump, the vented loop on the head pump outlet hose, the sag on the damaged lifeline. With a shift in the wind I have to motor across the bay again and re-anchor. On shore I hike to the summit of Roche Rouge, the rocky ridge above the bay. I read John Julian Norwich's beautifully written "History of Venice," and relive their perilous glory. On the eve of Bastille Day, July 13, harbor authorities have me move across the bay again, to avoid the fallout of the fireworks display.

The wind is down when Mary returns next morning. Within an hour, we are underway motoring with a gentle following SE wind, not enough to raise the mainsail. Then the wind drops completely and shifts to the NW. Within 15 minutes it is blowing 25 knots on the nose. We batten down and scurry for the protected marina of Frejus, the mistral blowing the tops off the white capped waves.

Frejus is everything Zillah isn't. Up market, modern, chic, noisy, a jet set resort, luxury condos rising above the marina, sparkling in reflected glass, boutiques, ship's chandler selling bikinis, yacht brokers, crowds. A restaurant 100 ft from our boat dock playing classical jazz, live on synthesizer, mobile market stalls are lined up for a mile along the esplanade, wind blown sand lifting off the beach. We wait out a weather front in the shelter of the marina to the furious flapping of flags and a high pitched whine through the rigging.

Bastile Day celebrations in the inner harbor, a water jousting event draws a cheering crowd. Two boats with high 6 ft prows, topped by a small platform, 2ft x 2ft mounted above the bow, face off. Each boat is powered by a 12 man rowing crew. A

544

big hunk of a man mounts the platform aloft on each boat. They are helmeted, wearing big padded gloves like an ice hocky goalie, chest pads like a home base umpire, and carry a 12 ft jousting pole capped by a boxing glove. Heraldic regalia. Rowers bend to their oars, they gain forward momentum and the two boats charge bow on, port to port. The two jousters raise their poles, square off, aim at the opponents chest pad, and brace for the collision. The object is to knock their opponent off his perch. The crowd cheers, others groan as their champion goes down in a resounding splash. And another set of combatants suit up. It is a game that could be as old as the gladiatoral contests in the ruined Roman ampitheater behind the modern condos. It occurs to me that jousting is a good metaphor for cruising the mistral battered coast of southern France—wind jousting. We lay over for another day waiting for the weather front to blow through.

The weather report on the Port Captain's bulletin board, which we laboriously translate from French, indicates a break in the weather for the next three days. "Let's go for it!" Checking the charts for the next harbor of refuge, we free the mooring lines, tangle with the boat in the next slip, and motor out of the harbor. It turns out to be a glorious day of sailing. Gentle SW 15 knot winds, along a beautiful coastline, we make one long tack out to sea for two hours to clear the headland jutting down from St. Tropez. We have friends there, and had hoped to visit with Annie and Claude, but they are off autocamping in Norway. In early evening we motor into Lavandou, and pick up a berth at a finger pier.

CROSSING TO THE BALEARICS

The Balearics, an archipelago of three major islands, lie between Africa and Spain in the western Mediterranean. Next morning the weather report is favorable for the big crossing--210 miles on a course of 210 degrees, SSW, an overnight passage. We are prepared for the worst when we motor out, with clear skies, a sea haze and light cumulous, not enough wind to sail, passing motor yachts creating a swell. Occassionally the wind came up W 15-20 and we'd get a couple hours of sailing, but then back to motoring. Dolphins accompanied us part of the way, a school of young ones, 3 to 5 ft long, frolicking off the bow wave, practicing the high jump off the beam. The first of the summer, a good omen. At sunset there was an extraordinary display of weather systems, layers of cloud, thin, hazy, diaphonous overlaying each other, passing in different directions, catching the low slanting light in a rage of color, watery, pastel pinks, corals and yellows, before the sun dipped below the horizon in an egg yolk yellow. A bizarre spectacular Turner sky. The wind dropped, the moon rose a humpty dumpty orange smiling glow. We motor, and motor-sail through the night and next day, faithful "Otto," the autopilot doing most of the work, while I journey to the Levant with Norwich's "History of Venice."

Prepared for the worst, did I say? Late afternoon on the second day out, Mary detects water in the bilge, up to the floor boards. Man the pumps! The manual switch activates the Rule 2000 electric bilge pump, and assisted by hand pumping it is quickly cleared. I check the float valve again. Non functionare, though I had repaired it only a few days ago. A couple hours later the battery light on the control panel glows red, and the rpm needle drops alarmingly to 1200 rpms, yet the battery continues to charge, and we maintain boat speed. Never did figure out that one. A mystery of the occult art of electronics.

Land ho! Menorca comes into sight just as night settles in. The wind drops and we begin to scan the horizon with binoculars, trying to pick out the harbor lights of Fornells. Going below, to check our position on the GPS, I detect bilge water has backed up to the floor boards yet again. Real panic this time. It appears as if the electric bilge pump is totally non-functional. Man and woman the pumps! Mary and I both pump frantically in a hurried attempt to keep Zillah afloat. The water slowly recedes, and then the electric pump finally kicks in again, for reasons I don't understand, and in half an hour we are dry again. But as soon as the pump is turned off, water gushes back in. Ah ha! I reason, it's the vented loop. No problem. "Elementary, Watson," as Sherlock Holmes would have told his understudy. Just turn off the seacock when the bilge is pumped dry, open it again when pumping, and thank the gods for the new seacocks installed earlier this year in Italy. There's some confusion as to which lights mark the harbor entrance, but at 0200 hours we motor beneath the towering seacliffs at the entrance to the bay, eiry in the light of the full moon. The lights of the town come into view, and we manouver among the yachts in the harbor and drop the anchor. Another episode in the Zillah saga.

BALEARICS—MENORCA, MEJORCA AND IBIZA

Five weeks in the Balearics redeemed the summer. There are gales, but they lack the ferocity of the mistral. We kept anchor watch as boats dragged their anchors one night in Fornells. In Mahon, a magnificent harbor that sheltered Nelson's fleet, a shift in the wind, a middle of the night blow, and boats begin to drag their anchors; a night of anchor watch, horns blaring, lights flashing, motors revving. For several days there was relaxed gentle sailing in SW winds, blowing 15-20 knots, winds Zillah handled comfortably. We poked into rocky coves beneath limestone sea cliffs, studded with caves, some inhabited in neolithic times. We escaped the cities, and even there they have avoided the worst excesses of tourist development that plague the southern coast of Spain. At Polenca on Majorca we meet up with "Navarro" again, our New Zealand friends. Rob, a professional boatbuilder advises me on the stuffing box and packing gland, potential sources of the boat leaks. The head pump is still non functional, in spite of numerous attempts at repair. In Palma we find replacement parts. Michael and Susan, Americans on "Trilogy" are at anchor in Porto Colon when we sail in. We know them from Marmaris, but met them first four years ago, crossing from Sardinia to Sicily in a horrendous gale, our worst experience at sea. Garth and Beryl on "At Last" are there and we have a Marmaris reunion picnic on the beach.

And clear clean warm water for swimming, though I find my sciatic nerve is easily triggered by my awkward floundering movements in the water. While I delight in the cool freshness, and the chance to exchange sweat for salt, I don't enjoy swimming much for the exercise. But Mary is in her element, and goes splashing off like a torpedo leaving a white streak of bubbles in her wake. We had a guest for a week, Benjamin, a nephew of Mary's from Winnetka, who goes to North Shore Country Day School, where Andy and I both taught in the early 60's. He was born in the same hospital, as my daughters in Evanston. A large, laconic 13 year old in the body of a 17 year old. He had been at sailing camp earlier in the summer and handled the helm with confidence. He came laden with books we had requested. So Mary immersed herself in "The Lexus and the Olive Tree," by Thomas Freidman; and I bury my head in Barbara Tuchman's "The Guns of August." Our read aloud is a new John Le Carre thriller. Michael on "Trilogy" swapped us Richard Russo," Straight Man"—a hilarious account of academic life and mid-life marital confusion.

Our most extraordinary encounter was with John and Laurie Ridsdel on "Dany II" anchored off Las Illetas, near Palma. Fellow Canadians, they came over to admire the classical lines of "Zillah" and John told us his father once owned "Zillah." Chatting over a bottle of wine, we learn that we went to the same elementary school, in a remote town in Saskatchewan, and that he was an exchange student at Gordonstoun School in Scotland, where I had been a master for a year. We went to rival prep schools. An uncanny intertwining of life paths, albeit a generation apart.

We anchor in Cala Portales, a fascinating small cove surrounded by limestone cliffs and pagan cliff tombs, but poor holding. At 0130 hours the wind shifts and we begin to drag. So we raise anchor and run downwind through the night to Ibiza, the Balearic Island to the northwest. We round Punta del Serra at the northern end, and sail down the spectacular west coast, dramatic, multi-colored, conglomerate cliff bands, a jumble of geological nonconformities. It is one of the great days of sailing this summer. Entering the Bay of San Antonio we find a place to anchor amidst an international flotilla yachts. Among them is "Vitrain," with Leo and Ann-Marie, we met in Trinidad, six years previous.

SOUTH COAST OF SPAIN

Still dark, we raise the anchor at 0630 and motor on a hot, windless day, 50 miles across the shipping lanes back to mainland Spain. We anchor behind the headland at Moraya, on the Costa del Sol, a beautiful mountainous desert dry coastline, like Baja California,

Moving on next day, at noon the GPS reads 38 degrees 32 minutes North, 000degrees 01 minutes EAST and then ticked over to 000 degrees and 01 minutes WEST, as we crossed the Greenwich Meridian line. We entered the Western half of the world. The sense of "heading west" that we have had all summer was suddenly reinforced with mathematical certainty, going home.

The Alicante marina is part of a huge resort complex, classy glassy, their modern facilites satisfying our primitive needs. Mary put 3 loads of salt and sweat impregnated clothes and bedding through the dockside laundromat. We recharge the computer batteries, top up with fuel and water, stock up food in town at the local market.

The weather report from Gary on the cruiser's net is not too promising, 30 knot winds out of the SW, right on the nose. We head out with a weather eye on the horizon, and a lookout for the next harbor of refuge. We motorsail to Torreviejo along the Costa Blanca, miles of plastic shrouded prairie, greenhouses, the hydroponic vegetable garden of southern Europe. We shelter in the harbor, protected from the rising swell. The winds shift to the east, and next day we have a boistrous sail in 25-30 knot winds running downwind with 8-10 ft seas, and duck into the sheltered bay behind the rocky headland at Cala Bardina, amidst a holiday throng on paddle boats, kayaks, jet skis and power launches. A 75 mile run in 12 hours, near record speed for us. Another 50 miles day of downwind sailing brings us to San Jose, the smallest marina we had been in and the most expensive, $35/night. The front moves through and winds abate, and a day of motoring and sailing brings us to Almerimar, the least expensive marina, $9/night. We meet up with Peter and Jennika, Australians we knew from Marmaris and dine out together.

At Almerimar we luck on with Jerry, on "We Two," a jolly, red faced Brit, with great skill and energy, who in five days brings Zillah back to seaworthy condition, tightens the stuffing box to stop the persistent leak, remounts the wind steering vane we dismantled four years ago on entering the Mediterranean, repairs the head pump, installs a new head sink hand pump, and a dozen other minor jobs. Kevin on "Orion" goes up the mast, inspects the rigging and tightens the shrouds. Ian, with the lean, slim body of a jockey squirrels under the cockpit hatch, and greases the steering cables. They are Brits, escaping the miserable climate of England, financing their cruising kitty by their skill and wit.

We rent a car on Sunday, and with Jerry and his wife, drive to Grenada to visit the Alhambra. The formidable, hilltop fortress surrounds a magnificent palace, which is light, airy, a lacework of stone, delicate arches framed by arches, set among flowering gardens, mirrored in reflecting pools, fountains guarded by stone lions. The sound of water everywhere, dripping, trickling, gurgling, murmuring, an Arab's vision of paradise. A poem of stone, light and water . A three year old toddler stoops by the edge of a still pool which is mirror smooth, sticks his finger in the water and watches with delight the widening concentric ripples, ecstatic in the magic of his creation. Columbus was here when the Moors surrendered their last stonghold in mainland Spain, in January, 1492. Victorious Ferdinand and Isabella, freed of the burden of expensive war, gambled on a far fetched scheme to sail west to get east. And the rest is history.

Gibralter is an overnight run, seas calm, motoring. As we round Cape Europe, leaving the fickle Mediterranean behind, the wind picks up from the NW and we sail the last three hours into the huge harbor and pick up a berth at Queensway Maina. "The Rock" looms above, an ominous presence, inscrutable, like the monstrous warlord it is, gray, battered, gloomy, making its own weather, ringed by cloud, white spumes of mist blowing off the summit. Gibralter is all business. The narrow streets are crowded with a polyglot community of Brits and Spaniards, Arabs and Hindus, and a smorgosbord of varied Europeans and Americans off the cruise ships. We have the life raft inspected, flares and emergency food and water renewed, a routine safety procedure, replace a malfunctioning stern running light, Mary does massive laundry at the dockside laundromat, lay in stores from the local supermarket, Safeways, globalization's reach across the seas. Then wait for a weather window.

The wind blows NW all night and into the next day. We sit tight, haunted by stories of boats being weatherbound in Gib for weeks, unable to pass through the straits in a westerly. Winds can funnel through the narrow gap creating turbulent seas that are dangerous in a small boat. Then the wind abates and we hasten to check last minute items off our list. Pay the bill, the last round of telephone calls and e-mail, top up with water, take on fuel and wait for slack tide. There's no wind, but a heavy fog drifts into the bay, visibility 400 yards. The first fog we've been in, in five years! Do we risk it? "Let's go for it, " Mary suggests. She is the impatient one. Her suggestion is a good nudge. We pass beneath the grim bastion of the seawall, the fog horn at the harbor entrance moaning balefully. Not exactly a send-off with bells and whistles. A gray, bleak curtain draws closed and Gibralter disappears astern.

We launch out into the void. A world without sight and only sound. A freighter's fog horn blares a mile away, but it sounds as if it is just off the bow. I reply with a bronchial croak on my hand held tinny trumpet type horn, then scuttle below to radio our position on the VHF. No reply Back on deck, I repeat my feeble warning anxiously, immensely relieved to hear the ship's warning grow more distant. The darkening gray of the coastline begins to shade and fade in and out of view. Mid-way down the straits the fog lifts and clears to a bright, sunny day. We pass through the Pillars of Hercules of ancient myth and beyond the mountains where Atlas held up the end of the world. The grey green expanse of the brooding Atlantic opens up before us.

Tarifa is the south-western tip of Europe, and we are swept out into the expanse of the Atlantic on the outgoing tide. The levanter, the east wind that was predicted, picks up, 25 knots and gusting. Off shore the seas build up, 8 to 10 ft waves There are gusts to 35-40 knots and the growing swell 12-15 ft pushes the stern broadside to. Fighting the helm downwind we have an exhilerating race down the Atlantic Coast of Spain, to Barbate, the nearest harbor of refuge. It blows for two days and we sit out the gale beneath the gigantic seawall with the fishermen. It seems like an unnecessarily abrupt reintroduction to ocean sailing. "Lord hear us when we pray to Thee; For those in peril on the sea," we ponder the old Navy hymn.

We round Cape Trafalgar where Nelson met glory and a hero's death, scan the shoreline for the harbor entrance markers, and enter the magnificent Bay of Cadiz. The bay is huge, reminiscent of Boston Harbor or San Francisco Bay, several harbors in one bay, container ships moving in and out, cruise ships hovering at the docks, half a dozen yacht harbors, Rota, the American built NATO base across the bay. The city of Cadiz is built on a long slender neck that juts out to sea, water on all sides. There is a tradition of the sea that goes back far beyond Columbus, who sailed from here, to the Phoenicians who founded the city in the 6th century BC. It breaths old world charm, a city of sea wells, espalanades, open plazas, narrow alleys, ornate 19th century Victorian buildings, window boxes, flowering trees We thread our way through the maze of narrow streets to the busy market and wait for the arrival of crew.

Jennifer, sailor daughter and Johan, spelunker son-in-law, arrive to join us for the first leg of the crossing .

With the first break in the weather, we set out, optimistically, but an hour out of the bay, storm clouds gather in the north , rain showers and confused seas, so we turn back. There is a certain reluctance to leave the shelter and security of terra ferma. We have a lovely sunset through the rain clouds.

Chapter 115: Atlantic Crossing – Cadiz to Madeira

Early accounts of the voyages of discovery said little about the sea, Jonathon Raban writes in The Oxford Book of the Sea. The ocean was merely something to get across; the action began when you reached land on the other side. After our crossing from Cadiz in Spain to Porto Santo in the Madeira Islands, 550 nautical miles, no insignificant passage, I get the point. I'm hard put to describe much. Checking back to the ship's log, I see that we had an uncomfortable first night, light winds and a rolling beam sea, sails collapsing, boom banging. Three of us on seasickness pills, Johann too late, only "Iron Guts" Jennifer daring to go below to brew tea and see to the feeding of the rest of the crew. We motor over half the way, but with a wind shift to the NW we have a beautiful night of sailing. We appreciate the change, less for the romance of ocean cruising than for the comfort of being able to sleep without being tossed out of the bunk. One retreats into one's private space, catching sleep between watches, snacking when no longer worried about holding food down, scanning the skyline for passing ships, trying to stay awake on watch between 4am and dawn. Four days out, Porto Santo appears a darkened line on the SW horizon, and emerges miraculously from the sea.

One night at Porto Santo, where Columbus lived as a shipowner and merchant, before his day of fame. We resupply and assure family by e-mail of a safe arrival and we push on. Madeira, the main island, 40 miles to the west, is a 19,000 ft mountain, 14,000 feet of it under the sea. "The green island", madiera is the Portugese for woods, the terraced mountainside dissolves into the cloud cap shrouding the skyline ridge.

Twenty to thirty yachts roll at anchor in the outer harbor ar Funchal, the main town. There are another twenty inside, rafted up five deep, "like sardines," Mary says. We go in, an obliging gentleman on "Triton" British flag, takes our lines. We've arrived.

Funchal is where the action is, dancing in the streets, "Tourist Day!" young and old in peasant costumes, traditional slow stepping dances to accordian and varied percussives, roses given to visitors, samples of the famous wines---"Have some Madeira m'dear/ It made her feel so queer." The Friday market, more authentic, ablaze in color from tomatoes to bananas, cabbage to beans, and plants never seen before, amid the cacaphony of shouting, hailing, bargaining. Spotted as tourists, who else would wear shorts to market? We're overcharged for our mango, imported from Brazil, the downside of Tourist Day. The fish market displays octopus and squid, sardines and tuna, a particularly vicious looking black creature, eel like in shape with the jagged grinning teeth of a barricuda. Jennifer delights in the photo opportunity. Mary retreats to the flower stalls and buys a bouquet of lilies.

"I'm willing to rent the car, if you'll drive it," I tell Johan. We are eager to do a quick tour of the island. One look at the road map convinces me that the driving is best left to younger hands. Johann handles the sharp curves of the steep winding mountain roads like a Monte Carlo rally racer. Climbing through narrow gorges with steep terraced hillsides, we top out at Encumeada, the pass to the north coast. Here we get out and hike the Levada del Norte, a 3 ft wide irrigation ditches that brings water from the north slope, which gets of 70 inches of rainfall a year, to the populated south coast. Built early in the 16th century, when Madeira catered to Europe's sweet tooth and prospered with the cultivation of sugar. We follow the narrow path bordering the ditch a couple miles, turn back where it disappears into a tunnel. I forgot my flashlight. There are over 1000 miles of ditches and Levada trekking becomes our way of exploring the island. We climb from the banana groves and vineyards of the narrow coastal plain, to pine and gum tree eucalyptus above, laurel forest, the indigenous forest in wet, remote isolated pockets, and open heath on the upper plateau and the rounded mountain tops like a Scottish Highland landscape. Another trek on the Levada do Risco brings us to the spectacular waterfall, cascading 500 ft down the rocky wall, a green, dripping carpet of moss, lichen, ferns and tenacious hanging grass tendrils. Wild flowers edge the paths, hydrangeas in abundance, impatiens, fuschias, pale pink-purple resurrection lilies that spring directly from the ground on a tall slender stock without leaves, like Christ risen, bird of paradise, a brilliant orange yellow flower, like an exotic tropical bird startled into flight, and innumerable flowering trees and vines I haven't identified. The Levada do Torno, on the eastern end of the island is carved into the cliffside, tunneled in many sections, 300 hundred feet above the jungle floor, "vertiginous" a word I have never used, the walking guide warns, "danger of vertigo...for the sure footed only."

We see Jennifer and Johann off on the airport bus. They've been a good crew, competent and caring. It's been a great journey with them, and we feel sad that it should end. So it's back to deck boy for me, hauling anchor, raising sails, Mary competent at the helm.

But Madeira festivities go on. Reading the Herald Tribune (Milosovic loses the election) in the shade of a gigantic figus australienses tree in , I'm interrupted by a band playing a slow march to waltze tempo. It could be a scene out of Snow White, 12 beautiful young women in flowing white gowns being escorted down the tree lined boulevard of Avenida do Infanta to the flower strewn Cathedral, where a crowd gathers to witness a collective wedding. "Here Comes the Bride," the band plays on. Another band, another day, another crowd, the lowering of the flag outside the fortress, guarding the President's offices. From a bus window Mary spots a little boy sitting proudly on a stone lion guarding the gateway to his house, defending and defiant with a pacifier in his mouth. "Have some Madeira, m'dear."

FUNCHAL—MADEIRA—LIKE SARDINES.

The title refers to the marina araangements here at Funchal, Madeira. We are rafted up along the seawall -- 6 deep, we're the 4th boat out, which means that only the folks from 2 other boats tromp over our decks to get ashore and back. It could be worse—we could be the one alongside the wall. But we're a pretty cheery, friendly group of international sardines, the majority from Scandinavia. We escape from the madness with almost daily hikes up in the lush mountains of the interior, often accompanied by a nice young Australian woman from the next boat. Plenty of quiet, serenity, and beauty up there as we stroll along the levadas. The levadas are small canals, part of a 1350-mile-long network which distributes the rainfall, which is plentiful in the mountains, throughout the island. They all have paths alongside them, and we meander along with them as they wind their way through incredibly beautiful mountains and valleys. Flowers, trees, ferns, and mosses of many kinds are abundant, as are spectacular views out to the sea and down on villages below. Terraced fields cut into some of the steep hills add to the interest. Not a lot of wildlife, but some pretty finches and lots of lizards. And the odd goats and sheep who stop their browsing and gaze at us as we pass by.

The town of Funchal is likeable too, with many trees, flowers, squares with fountains, a large and colorful market on Fridays where they sell fruits and veggies, fish, flowers, baskets, etc. We'll stay here a few more weeks before sailing on down to the Canaries. Haven't figured out how far it is to our next destination, but we'll get out the charts and look at that one of these days.....

MADEIRA—HIKE LEVADAS

Two more boats outside us now, one Finnish and one Norwegian, so lots of stomping overhead. But we get away from it all most days by going out hiking. We've done several more nice ones, including a really spectacular one 2 days ago through a laurel forest. Wish we'd found it when you were still with us—you'd have loved it! Miles and miles through the lush forest, no buildings, ferns and mosses draping the walls next to the levadas, stone arches to pass through, tiny finches to share our lunch and a couple of fat sheep who stopped browsing to gaze at us as we passed, a variety of wildflowers in addition to the hydrangea and agapanthus, some darting fish (trout?) in a levada.

Yesterday we did the hike from Encumeada back along the ridge on the opposite side of the valley the highway is on. It is the old mountain trail developed in the 18th century to connect the north coast. And purely by chance one of the pictures picks up most of the route. A spectacular hike, high above the valley, climbing up and down along the skyline ridge, but a gruelling day, 10 miles, 1600 ft of climbing (the guide book recommends doing it the other way) and 1000 ft descent, with another 500 ft on the highway to catch a bus back to Funchall. Mary was a real trooper, in spite of aching back and creeking knees, and I went through most of my repetoire of hiking war stories, and humming every melody from John Brown's body to Beethoven' shepherds song in the 6th symphony to give her a rhythm to walk to. But we made it with two hours to spare, before the last bus at 8pm. We began the day catching a 7:30

bus still in the dark. Another great day. Today we nurture our aches and pains. Tomorrow we opt for a more tranquil levada hike with the soothing sound of gurgling water. So great to experience land again.

Joe is out hiking to the lighthouse at the eastern tip of the island. We started on that hike the other day but ran out of time, unfortunately. The very spectacular scenery out there is so different from all of our other hikes. Severe, rocky, dry, with colors of rust, brown, black, grey instead of "shades of green."

We're still on the waterfront in Madeira, resting up from a spectacular mountain hike yesterday, 10 miles along an old trail built in the 18th century, connecting the north side of the island, following a high ridge with expansive 2000 ft down to the valley below. More of a slog than we had bargained for, 1600 ft uphill climbing, 1000 ft descent, hard on the knees and back, but great to be in the high country again. Mary opts for a levada walk on the path along a gently sloping irrigation ditch tomorrow. Lush, semi-tropical trees, shrubs and flowers instead of the prickly gorse and blackberry bushes of yesterday, and the sound of gurgling water, visions of paradise.

LANZAROTTE TO TENERIFE

Things have been busy since we last wrote from La Graciosa. We made our way down, with jury-rigged sea water pump, to Lanzarote, where we were able to get the parts needed and repairs accomplished in good time. Then we explored that fascinating, stark, volcanic island for a couple of days in a rental car. An intriguing place—much of it like a moonscape, or perhaps what the earth looked like millions of years ago, before the plants were able to soften the landscape. Hard to describe; we'll show you pictures. On Monday morning, we left Lanzarote and sailed the 145 miles or so over here in 15- to 25-knot beam winds, making 7+ knots much of the time. A fast, exhilarating sail, and we covered the distance in 22 ½ hours. Now we're on the hard at a boatyard for a few days. We were concerned about some water seepage and decided to check the seams under the water line. Most are fine, but we're recaulking some of them. A capable boat carpenter (the yard men call him "Maestro" or something like that) is supervising and lending tools for the job, and it's going well. We're hoping to get back in the water soon, after doing the seams, fairing the hull, and applying bottom paint.

SANTA CRUZ—TENERIFE

We plan to leave Santa Cruz de Tenerife tomorrow morning and go down to Los Cristianos on the south coast for one night and then on over to La Gomera, the next island to the west, on Friday. We're getting tired of this place, a poorly run marina in a touristic big town without much charm, and we've heard and read very good things about La Gomera and the marina there. The boat work and provisioning (except for last minute fresh stuff) are pretty well completed, and so perhaps we'll be able to explore and enjoy La Gomera. We'll come back to Tenerife next Wednesday via ferry to meet you at the airport.

LA GOMERA

We had vegetable soup for Thanksgiving dinner at anchor at Los Cristianos at the SW end of Tenerife. A quiet evening, just the 2 of us, but nice.

We came over here to La Gomera the next day. An interesting trip—motoring for the first half or so on glassy seas, enjoying watching 3 small (pilot?) whales off our port side. Then a whisper of a breeze made a lovely herringbone pattern on the sea. This increased to a wind and we unfurled the genoa and turned off the motor. Soon we were doing 7 knots with the genoa alone. The wind kept increasing, we furled the sail in about 1/3 and kept zooming along. Made it here in very good time and moored in the marina in the strong wind without mishap.

As expected, we are loving it here. The marina is an excellent one, especially in contrast with the one at Santa Cruz de Tenerife. And the island is magnificent. We've been exploring it by buses and on foot, impressed by the spectacular scenery and variety of terrain and vegetation. Development has not run riot here, and the towns are pretty and clean.

There was a folk music/dance festival (free) at the plaza a few hundred yards from the marina last night. Rhythmic, sometimes haunting music and very lively dancing by groups from this island and Tenerife and Lanzarote. A real treat.

I checked out the produce market in a nearby square yesterday morning (it's there Wed and Sat mornings); it will be fine for our provisioning of fresh stuff for the trip. Our thought is to do that next Sat morning and then take off. This will allow 2 days for you to see some of this island before we leave. If you want to stay longer, that will be fine with us too.

ATLANTIC CROSSING—CANARIES TO CARIBBEAN REFLECTION

Dear Jennifer and Johan Jan 12, 2991 Pointe a Pitre, Guadeloupe

The Atlantic Crossing? Well, we're still trying to put it together in our heads. Reflecting on experience, you would say in the adventure education trade. In a sense we're still dealing with the aftermath of the crossing, having had a new Profurl roller furler installed only yesterday here in Guadeloupe. The focused attentiveness and the concerns that go along with all that, the cost, trying to figure out what preventive maintainance might have prevented the old one from failing, how to make necessary adjustments along the way, etc. I read the installation manual scrupulously—nothing on maintenance, blithely told it's maintenance free, wash the salt off with fresh water if you wish. Bug the rigger with questions, whose replies I only half understand in French and broken English.

But the crossing itself. Not easy. For at least two weeks Herb, the weather guru on Southbound Two, talked of a "high level trough" (which seems like a contradiction in terms) stretching from the Caribbean to Africa, bringing 20-25 knot winds, overcast skies, squalls and occassional rain and 6 to 8ft seas, combined with a deep north ocean swell, coming from a series of mid-Atlantic gales, often giving us 10-15 ft seas and a cross swell. And we were in the middle of it. So it was not the conventional south seas cruise that many people talk about, including "Abien Tot" that left the week before us.

Then Zillah also began to feel her age. We left Cadiz with you two, feeling the old girl was in pretty good shape for the crossing, having done a good job of maintenance at Almerimar in Mediterranean Spain, but after Madeira the gremlins came out of the woodwork. At Graciosa, the first of the Canary Islands, the seawater cooling pump to the engine gave out and had to be repaired at Lanzarote, involving lots of help and advice from other yachties, a quest for parts, a good deal of anxiety and no little expense. Then the leak where the hull abutts the keel, en route to Tenerife, involving a real emergency—my gawd, the boat is sinking, hauling out, a major recaulking of the starboard side and major expense. Leaving Gomera, where Columbus set sail on a couple of his expeditions, there was the nagging anxiety—what next?

Margaret and Olaf arrived with the new cruising spinnaker—a magnificent billowing cloud of a sail in blue, white and a big slash of purple, like the pope ascending to the skies, really a thrill. But they also brought their anxieties to add to mine. Will there be enough water? Then a question of enough food, the right sort of food. Protein? We questioned whether to stop in at the Cape Verde Islands to restock, another 500 miles out of the way, but it did shorten the distance between landfalls by a similar distance. But the answer was taken out of our hands. Little wind the first couple days, we motored, using up over half our fuel reserve. Ideal weather though for experimenting with flying the new spinnaker. We had to improvise a halyard, the one I had being too short, but once it took to the skies we could move along at 4 knots in wind that would barely flutter the flag. Glorious. Olaf was great at sail trim drawing on his windsurfing exertise. Bring the sail down at dusk, we raise it the second day with similar euphoria, then a sharp crack like a rifle shot breaks the tranquility, and a sudden deflation, our magical sail sloshing around in the water along side the boat. My improvised halyard had frayed on the genoa upper swivel rigging and snapped. The next day unfurling the genoa we also discovered the upper fitting on the roller furler had parted and the sail could only be run out under great pressure. Not good with 2000 miles of ocean still to cross, so we alter course for Sao Vicente in the Cape Verde Islands.

Within a couple hours of dropping the anchor, three guys came by in a dingy, asked if we had any mechanical problems, seemed to know what they were doing. One fellow asked for a #5 Allen key, his buddies hoisted him up the mast on the main halyard, in half an hour had the foil connected, suggested lowering the jib halyard several inches, a fatal error we learned later, but it did free up the furler, and we felt we got off easy. Two days later we launched out into the broad expanse of the Atlantic under an overcast sky, in 25 knots of wind out of the NE, the northern swell, Herb's upper level trough.

The days blur into each other as you know. The weather, sea state and food dominate one's waking thoughts. Food is a matter of ingestion, retention (helped by

Stugeron, the new miraculous motion sickness drug), and ejection. Sooner or later we all found "A Smooth Move", a senna herbal derivative tea, helpful at that end. We picked up Herb's daily report to other boats—we didn't try to contact him ourselves. He expects more radio discipline, being there every day punctually, than we are capable of, but he had little to offer other than stiff trades, heavy seas, regular squalls, his persistent "trough". We joined a cruisers' net with six other boats, and were able to pick up friends now 10 days downwind and there were regular reports of torn sails, broken autopilots and wind steering vanes. One yacht, a 37 ft trimaran, actually lost their rudder and sailed the last 800 miles into the British Virgin Islands steering with sails and drogues. Everyone complained of being tossed about, falling out of bunks, sleep a wrestling match clutching to hang on to anything solid.

So I wasn't too surprised when our steering system broke. Out with the emergency tiller. This was now old stuff, happened to us in the Balearics, earlier in the year. This time the steering cable itself had broken. Olaf, always the do-it, repair-it man is too big and bulky to fit in the narrow crawl hole, beneath the cockpit sole. Margaret, slim and trim, would have fit nicely. One of you spelunkers would have been in your element but it fell to you-know-who to wallow below. We hove-to in what seemed like a huge rolling sea, 12-15 foot waves, but the boat was amazingly stable, just bobbing up and down, making about one knot to leeward, but I took a Stugeron pill, just in case, and went below with tools and spare cable. Olaf extracted me from the bilge, otherwise I could never have gotten out. In five hours we were underway again, feeling very resourceful and competent problem solvers.

"Monty" the fifth member of the crew, the Monitor wind steering vane—we can't praise him enough. What a tireless performer, and no complaining. Or at least very little. A couple days later we noticed he was not as responsive at usual. Looking over the stern I noticed the stanchion from the transom to the bottom of the main frame was dangling loose, and the whole frame slightly askew. In an hour Olaf had that one put together again, involving an upside down manouver dangling over the stern, bolting together the two separated parts. In the process the main frame supports have been stressed and cracks began to appear in the steel tubing, but since we have not brought our aluminum welding kit with us, Olaf improvises a clamp system using conventional hose clamps. Resourceful. A good man to have on board.

Five days out of Antigua, there is a break in the weather. The genoa flops around. Good spinnaker day. But in the two weeks since departing Cape Verde Islands, the improvised spinnaker halyard had parted. The square knot I used to secure two lines has come undone, and the unsecured end caught in the wind, and collapsed on deck. Another trip up the mast, Olaf cranking, Margaret belaying on the security line, Mary steadying the boat downwind, the masthead swaying through a 12 ft arc, and a new better knotted improvised spinnaker halyard in place. Spinnaker aloft, feeling the elation of this marvellous spectacle, we make 5-6 knots in light SE winds and left over rolling seas.

There's an art to Being There (remember the Peter Seller movie?) as opposed to Getting There. The talk of the last week is of getting there. Margaret and Olaf are eager to split and get on to their vacation in Baja. Mary is eager to contact her children.

I have misgivings about returning to America and the trip has not dispelled them. Part of me would just like to keep sailing on. I'm still not sure what to make of the crossing. The objective conditions were certainly arduous, and we had our share of mishaps, and we made it safely. So that is no mean accomplishment and we all deserve credit. But it wasn't the sort of voyage that brought us together, and that makes me sad, confused. Margaret seems very anxious, which is not surprising perhaps, Olaf's close call only a year ago, they work very hard to make a go of their business and real estate investment; she seemed tired and drawn when she arrived and brought much of her shore side anxiety with her. She seems worried about her health. And neither Mary nor I were able to help her with this and may even have made the situation worse. Frankly, we worry about her. So there is a lot to sort out still. Perhaps the trip will improve with time and the telling. It was certainly a significant event, and I have yet to write my heroic epic. I've kept a good journal of the crossing, but deliberately have written this letter without reference to it, to see what would come out, what stands out, to share with you.

So thanks for your e-mail from Singapore and your prod to write. I apologize for the silence, but I really needed time to sort things through. Not only the trip, but the tender love and care that Zillah needs, and for me to make the transition to Caribbean Cruising and eventually to suburban life in America with Mary. By coincidence today Mary ran into two boats here in Pointe a Pitre that we know, an Australian we talked with by radio in Spain about a spinnaker, another American from Florida we met in Lanzarotte. And as I am writing another Australian boat, Discovery III came in that we know from Marmaris three years ago. A small world. We all plan dinner together. Wine and war stories, another side of yachting.

Time to go. Thanks for listening. Love you both. Dad, and Mary joins in sending love.

ATLANTIC CROSSING—CADIZ TO MADEIRA

In early accounts of the voyages of discovery little was said about the sea, Jonathon Raban writes (The Oxford Book of the Sea). The ocean was merely something to get across; the action began when you reached land on the other side. After our crossing from Cadiz in Spain to Porto Santo in the Madeira Islands, 550 nautical miles, no insignificant passage, I get the point. I'm hard put to describe much. Checking back to the ship's log, I see that we had an uncomfortable first night, light winds and a rolling beam sea, sails collapsing, boom banging. Three of us on seasickness pills, Johann too late, only "Iron Guts" Jennifer daring to go below to brew tea and see to the feeding of the rest of the crew. We motor over half the way, but with a wind shift to the NW we have a beautiful night of sailing. We appreciate the change, less for the romance of ocean cruising than for the comfort of being able to sleep without being tossed out of the bunk. One retreats into one's private space, catching sleep between watches, snacking when no longer worried about holding food down, scanning the skyline for passing ships, trying to stay awake on watch between 4am and dawn. Four days out, Porto Santo appears a darkened line on the SW horizon, and emerges miraculously from the sea.

One night at Porto Santo, where Columbus lived as a merchant seafaring trader, before his day of fame, to resupply and assure family by e-mail of a safe arrival and we push on. Madeira, the main island, 40 miles to the west, is a 19,000 ft mountain, 14,000 feet of it under the sea. "The green island", madiera is the Portugese for woods, the terraced mountainside dissolves into the cloud cap shrouding the skyline ridge.

Twenty to thirty yachts roll at anchor in the outer harbor of Funchal, the main town, another twenty inside, rafted up five deep, "like sardines," Mary says. We go in, an obliging gentleman on TRITON, British flag, takes our lines. We've arrived.

Funchal is where the action is, dancing in the streets, "Tourist Day!" young and old in peasant costumes, traditional slow stepping dances to accordian and varied percussives, roses given to visitors, samples of the famous wines---"Have some Madeira m'dear/ It made her feel so queer." The Friday market, more authentic, less contrived, ablaze in color from tomatoes to bananas, cabbage to beans, and plants never seen before, amid the cacaphony of shouting, hailing, bargaining. Spotted as tourists, who else would wear shorts to market? We're overcharged for our mango, imported from Brazil, the downside of Tourist Day. The fish market displays octopus and squid, sardines and tuna, a particularly vicious looking black creature, eel like in shape with the jagged grinning teeth of a barricuda. Jennifer delights in the photo opportunity. Mary retreats to the flower stalls and buys a bouquet of lilies.

"I'm willing to rent the car, if you are willing to drive." We are eager to do a quick tour of the island. One look at the road map convinces me that this is better left to younger hands. Johann handles the sharp curves of the steep winding mountain roads like a Monte Carlo rally racer. Climbing through narrow gorges with steep terraced hillsides, we top out at Encumeada, the pass to the north coast. We hike the Levada del Norte, a 3 ft wide irrigation ditches that brings water from the north slope, which gets of 70 inches of rainfall a year, to the populated south coast. Built early in the 16th century, when Madeira catered to Europe's sweet tooth and prospered with the cultivation of sugar. We follow the narrow path bordering the ditch a couple miles, turn back where it disappears into a tunnel. I forgot my flashlight. There are over 1000 miles of ditches and Levada trekking becomes our way of exploring the island. We climb from the banana groves and vineyards of the narrow coastal plain, to pine and gum tree eucalyptus above, laurel forest, the indigenous forest in wet, remote isolated pockets, and open heath on the upper plateau and the rounded mountain tops like a Scottish Highland landscape. Another trek on the Levada do Risco brings us to the spectacular waterfall, cascading 500 ft down the rocky wall, a green, dripping carpet of moss, lichen, ferns and tenacious hanging grass tendrils. Wild flowers edge the paths, hydrangeas in abundance, impatiens, fuschias, pale pink-purple resurrection lilies that spring directly from the ground on a tall slender stock without leaves, like Christ risen, bird of paradise, a brilliant orange yellow flower, like an exotic tropical bird startled into flight, and innumerable flowering trees and vines I haven't identified. The Levada do Torno, on the eastern end of the island is carved into the cliffside, tunneled in many

559

sections, 300 hundred feet above the jungle floor, "vertiginous" a word I have never used, the walking guide warns, "danger of vertigo...for the sure footed only."

We see Jennifer and Johann off on the airport bus. They've been a good crew, competent and caring. It's been a great journey with them, and we feel sad that it should end. So it's back to deck boy for me, hauling anchor, raising sails, Mary competent at the helm.

But Madeira festivities go on. Reading the Herald Tribune (Milosovic loses the election) in the shade of a gigantic figus australienses tree in , I'm interrupted by a band playing a slow march to waltze tempo. It could be a scene out of Snow White, 12 beautiful young women in flowing white gowns being escorted down the tree lined boulevard of Avenida do Infanta to the flower strewn Cathedral, where a crowd gathers to witness a collective wedding. "Here Comes the Bride," the band plays on. Another band, another day, another crowd, the lowering of the flag outside the fortress, guarding the President's offices. From a bus window Mary spots a little boy sitting proudly on a stone lion guarding the gateway to his house, a pacifier in his mouth. "Have some Madeira, m'dear."

CANARY ISLAND INTERLUDE

We motor from Tenerife to La Gomera on a windless morning, the mirror sea gently heaving on a six foot swell out of the northwest, a school of spouting whales breaking the tranquil surface. The first hint of wind, a peculiar cross hatch rippled herringbone effect on the water, and then the dark wind line appproaching rapidly tossing up waves. With a sudden gust the Canadian flag astern tugs and flaps. "There's probably enough wind to sail," I suggest to Mary. "Only seven miles to go. I don't think we need the main. Let's just run out the genoa." For non sailors, this is the large sail on a roller furler around the forestay that can be pulled out and furled back in without leaving the cockpit, labor saving, convenient. We cut the motor and Zillah continues to glide along at four and a half knots. A lovely sail, water slapping the hull, a peaceful hush after the throbbing of the motor. Within minutes waves begin to break, white caps form, the sail taughtens, rigging strains, the boat heels and we are making 7 knots, near hull speed for Zillah. We're in an acceleration zone between the mountains on the two islands, where the winds can pick up suddenly and gust to gale force. "We'd better reef down. Don't want to blow out the sail!" With shortened sail we settle to a comfortable five knots, pick up the harbor markers at Gomera and motor into the marina.

The Canaries, 150 miles off the west coast of Africa, are a cluster of six major islands, extinct volcanoes emerging from the sea, settled by the Spanish in the 15th century, the last bastion of European culture before launching out to cross the Atlantic. It is from Gomera, on the southwest of the archepelago, that Columbus sailed on his famous voyages. Legend has it that his mistress owned the island and he would stop off for one last call. Ships have followed his lead for 500 years.

We made the 250 mile crossing from Madeira a month earlier. Making landfall in a sheltered bay on La Graciosa, a tiny island at the northeast corner of the Canaries, we anchored among cruising friends we had met two years ago in Turkey. The sense of community was strong, potluck on the beach, exchanged war stories of torn sails and battering seas. Bronwyn, an attractive young Australian woman who had joined us in Madeira and is a professional sailmaker, offered her services to a couple of boats needing sail repairs. "Synergy," an American yacht with a broken steering cable, had to be towed in by the Spanish Coast Guard. As we motored through the narrow channel between La Graciosa and her much bigger sister island to the south, Lanzarote, Mary at the helm said, "Joe, the engine doesn't sound right." Soon the engine overheat alarm confirmed her suspicions. We turned around and sailed back into the anchorage. Kiwi friend Rob, a boatbulder on sabbatical, came over and diagnosed the problem. The raw water pump that brings cold sea water in to cool the deisel engine had broken, causing the engine to overheat. The repair was a long fascinating saga that I will spare you, no shortage of advice from other cruisers, an alternate pump improvised with a borrowed bilge pump, parts located at a Perkins dealer on Gran Canaria and flown in by DHL, and pump reassembled. Acts of spontaneous helpfulness, generosity and good humor that are overwhelming.

Lanzarote, "the dry island," appears like a gigantic volcanic cinder, pyramidal peaks, encrusted lava flows, black rock, brown, grey, yellow, russet, somber, dessicated colors, grotesque, phantasmagoric shapes. The brilliant Lanzarote architect, artist, sculptor, Cesare Manrique had a rare genius for combining the clean functional lines of modern architecture with the dynamic titanic forces of volcanic erupted nature. We visit his home and studio, now a museum, built into a series of connecting volcanic vents, spaces blown out by gases and hardened in lava, where elegant living space is created in the midst of the chaos of natural forces, the plain white of painted walls contrasted to the black of the scorched rock, stunning. At Jameos del Agua, Manrique turned a huge underground cavern into a spacious auditorium with perfect acoustics, a restaurant and bar surrounding a subterranean pool where white blind crabs survive, an art and photography gallery, and a volcano research center, impressive. At the Visitors Center at the Timanfaya National Park, another Manrique creation, built high on a volcanic outcrop with a view over a lunar lndscape, a wasteland, the malpais, of frozen lava, jagged, contorted, distorted, the restaurant grills its chicken over a hot air vent, the heat rising from inner antediluvian depths, a reminder that all below is not yet passive and cool.

The sea is our element. We have a glorious sail to Tenerife, 145 miles on a beam reach, wind NE 20-25 knots. We cover the distance in 23 hours, the best sail of the year. At night there is a brilliant full moon, clouds catching the silver light scudding cross the sky, the bloom of lights on Gran Canaria 30 miles to the south off to port, passing ships in the dark, freighters clearly altering course to go around us, a single yacht on a converging course coming so close, Bronwin on watch alters course. A darkenening cloud line ahead, the night turns a deep black, the world closes in. Wrapped in a dark gloom we sail through the squall. With dawn the cloud covered mountains of Tenerife emerge through the mist and the light falling rain.

Two hours out of Santa Cruz de Tenerife I am alerted to the automatic bilge pump running more frequently than usual. Instead of every two hours, every 20 minutes. Why? I check the pump for back syphoning, the stuffing box for a leak. Nada. Then lift the floor boards forward by the mast and detect a steady oozing of water from beside the keel. No immediate alarm, but something to be tended to before crossing the Atlantic. We have the boat lifted in Tenerife. An old fellow whom the yard men call affectionately "maestro," master carpenter, grey hair, yellow tobacco stained teeth, an alcoholic's red veined nose, who keeps himself fueled on dixie cups of high octane coffee, recaulks a 9ft by 3 ft section of the hull over the next week.

We use the time in Tenerife to lay in a month's supply of food, dry and tinned rations, top up the water tanks, squirrel extra bottles of water into every nook and cranny on the boat, fill fuel tanks and the eight 5-gallon cans lashed down on deck, refill camper gas bottles for cooking. We bid a fond farewell to Bronwyn as she joins an American singlehander to cross to the Caribbean. "Fair winds, see you over there!"

From 10 miles at sea La Gomera looks like a gigantic Homberg hat, battered and crushed, heavily creased and indented, with big chunks chewed out of it,a rounded volcanic dome shoved about by titanic forces, deeply grooved and eroded. To cross from San Sebastian, on the east end of the island, to Valle Gran Rey on the west, the road climbs 4000 ft up the ridge of Lomada del Camello over the top of the Garajonay plateau and back down the canyon of Barranco de Arure to sea level. We ride the buses as a child would a roller coaster, sitting up front next to the driver, thrilled. An afternoon hike takes us from the summit at 4500 feet, shrouded in cloud and perpetual mist among pine trees, laurel forest and heath trees (a species of huge heather), down through abandoned terraces high on the mountainside, past deserted homesteads in rubbled ruin, three lone houses in what was once a remote mountain hamlet.

Now is the moment of waiting, of anticipation, caught between the excitement of a major adventure, and the anxiety of the risks, real and imagined. As a boy I used to box; it is like that moment before stepping into the ring. A 2700 mile ocean, a 43 foot aged boat skippered by an aged captain. The owl and the pussey cat and Mary and Joe in a pea green boat. Yet only last Sunday nearly 200 yachts took off from Gran Canaria with the ARC, the Atlantic Rally for Cruisers, heading for St. Lucia in the Caribbean. Another 40 boats are here in La Gomera doing their last minute shopping, topping up with fuel and water, waiting for the next weather window before running south down to the trade wind latitudes, 20 degrees north. So why not Zillah too? We listen to weather reports twice a day and talk to our friends on A Beintot by short wave radio, already 700 miles out there, only 1800 miles to go to Barbados. Margaret and Olaf arrive tomorrow, and a couple of days later we too will be on the high seas.

ATLANTIC CROSSING—CANARIES TO ANTIGUA

Wednesday, December 20, 2000. 0200 hours. Latitude 16 degrees 32' North, Longitude 43 degrees 25' West. Distance to Antigua 1056 nautical miles at 292 degress. Distance from Cape Verde Islands 1061 nm.

"We're over half way there, " I tell Mary when she comes up on watch. We are eight days out from the Cape Verdes, eight rough days. There are following winds ENE 20-25 knots with 8 to 10 foot waves, and a NNE swell that combines with those to give 12-15 foot waves every two to three minutes, making for exhilarating, but very uncomfortable sailing. Occasionally a monster wave 20 feet high catches the boat, lifting the stern high and we look down into the deep trough as it slides by. The days have been grey, overcast, the sea a sheen of shattered glass, in the filtered sunlight, a dull platinum blue. Nights an eerie gloom until the moon breaks through the racing clouds and glows over the tossing wastes of the sea. Below we clutch to stay on our bunks, held in by lee cloths, bolstered in by pillows, and sleep fitfully. We sail with only genoa jib flying, the large sail that billows to port from the forestay. At night, concerned about sudden squalls that are hard to see in the dark, we roll the genoa half way in and still make five to six knots. Herb, the weather guru we listen to on SSB radio, reports an "upper level trough" (which sounds like a contradiction in terms) stretching from the Caribbean to the coast of Africa, and so unsettled conditions will prevail. It is not turning into the South Sea cruise we had anticipated.

Yesterday, Tuesday 19th I stand the mid morning watch. For exercise I stand, rather than sit, and detach the Monitor wind steering vane, nick-named "Monty," who does most of the steering work on this trip. The seas are running high, 10-12 feet, when a big swell rolls in, catches the stern and swings us beam to the sea. Trying to avoid being hit on the beam by the next swell, I push down hard on the wheel. I hear a loud "SNAP" much like my Achilles tendon made when it severed while I was deep powder skiing in Austria 30 years ago, and the wheel spins loosely in my hand. "On deck everybody!" I shout. "The steering's gone." Olaf, Margaret, and Mary are out in a flash. "No panic," I say, my own panic now under control, "we aren't going anywhere." I pull the emergency tiller from the bosun's locker, hand it to Olaf. He clamps it over the rudder post and in less than five minutes we are headed downwind again at 6 knots. A cockpit conference to assess what has happened and what to do about it. "The situation is not life threatening," I say, trying to make my voice sound as reassuring as I can. "The worst case scenario is that we hand steer with the emergency tiller the rest of the way. It's 1000 miles to the Caribbean. If it's something we can repair, let's repair it and sail on."

Turning around into the wind, we heave to by shortening and backwinding the genoa. The boat rocks in the swell, gently rising and falling, drifting slowly to leeward. Not the violent crashing of seas I had expected. Olaf lifts the cockpit hatch and puts his head below. "The steering cable is broken. I can see the frayed end." The broken cable will need to be replaced for us to steer with the wheel again and, even more important, for Monty to be able to steer. Someone will need to crawl under the cockpit floor to do the repairs. Olaf, our mechanical genius and Mister-Fix-It, is the logical choice, but he's a big man and can't fit into the tiny space. So the job falls to the back up team, and mine is clearly the body of choice. "I need a light. Pliers." In 20 minutes I have detached the broken cable, and Olaf extracts me from the ship's bowels, lifting and pulling me out feet first. "There's cable in the bosun's locker. A bolt cutter in the cockpit locker." We measure the length, 7ft 9inches. "Cut it 8 ft. Just to be on the safe side." "Measure twice and cut once," the old carpenter's contribution to philosophic thought. Descending into the depths once more, I tackle the more tedious job of reattaching the cable. I squirm and twist myself into the right position to thread it through the wheels and blocks, adjust the length. "Finished," I call out with relief. Olaf, the great extractor, pulls while I push, like a Lemas natural childbirth exercise, and I emerge from the womb of Zillah, scuffed and greasy, very much needing a good bath and scrub. Five hours after the sickening "snap," we are on our way again.

Back to the beginning of this final leg...

My daughter Margaret and her husband Olaf joined us at the Canary Islands. They arrive exhausted from travel, excited by the prospect of the great adventure, but anxious too. "Do we have enough water? Olaf and I each drink 4 liters a day." "That's a bit excessive by cruising standards. Some boats ration one liter per person per day," I reply. We have augmented our usual 60 gallons by squirrelling away plastic bottles full of water in every available nook and cranny., and we show them to her, trying to allay her fears. Food—the same anxious scrutiny. I'm concerned there's enough carbohydrates; Margaret that there's sufficient protein. Mary, who has been diligently stockpiling rations for the last month, is annoyed at our anxiety, confident we have enough of both. We make a last swing through the little supermarket at La Gomera and stock up on fresh fruit, vegetables, and bread at the Saturday market. The last few days at La Gomera are busy, but with four persons things get done. We warp out of our narrow berth and motor out the harbor entrance, feeling elated, exhilarated, but with also a gnawing uneasiness at the prospect of being out for three weeks or more, in an old boat, crossing an immense ocean. It's December 2, 1500 hours. The GPS gives us a reading of 2551 miles to Antigua on a bearing of 272 degrees, due west. But first we must go 500 miles south to pick up the trade winds.

Columbus left from La Gomera on his glorious second voyage in 1493 with a flotilla of 18 ships, all eagerly in search of the riches of the Orient. We follow in his wake. As we head south to pick up the trade winds, the winds are light and variable. A NW swell causes us to roll uncomfortably. We try various sail combinations and the motor. La Gomera fades, disappears behind us.

The next day the wind seems steadier at about 10 knots. "Let's try out the spinnaker!" Mary suggests. Our new toy, which Margaret and Olaf have brought over for us. A team effort to rig and raise the sail. Once it is aloft, Mary pulls up the sock that encloses the sail, and it bursts open, filling the heavens. It's a glorious moment. A huge, dazzling sail, blue and wine purple with a great white three cornered star centerpiece, it would do proud on the Pope's private yacht, if he has one.

For the rest of the week, the lack of wind continues to taunt us. We have to motor much of the time, using up almost half of our diesel fuel. When the fickle wind comes alive, we try to coax the most out of it with the genoa, the spinnaker, or the mainsail. One day as we attempt to raise the spinnaker, the halyard jams in the block at the head of the mast, so we crank Olaf up to change the block. The sail then twists on the halyard, and so we add a swivel. Fuel becomes our main concern. The Cape Verde Islands are 350 miles away, and we could go in to refuel, but that would take us 400 miles out of our way. What would we gain?

Then the decision is made for us. The roller furler for the genoa begins to jam, making a disturbing grating sound as we furl the sail in or let it out. This time it is my turn to go to the top of the mast, a sensation like doing a high rappell in reverse, both up and down. I can see the problem and I doubt if it is a repair we can do at sea. We alter course for Sao Vicente, on the Cape Verde Islands, 250 miles to the SSW. On our way there next morning a good 15 knot wind blowing, our beautiful spinnaker billowing out and pulling Zillah along at 7 knots. Now this is what an Atlantic crossing should be. Then "POW!" an explosion like a shotgun blast, and the spinnaker collapses, falls into the sea, and trails along beside the boat. "Is this what it sounds like when you blow out a sail?" I think, startled. But it is only the halyard that has chafed through at the head of the mast. All four of us lean overboard and quickly pull the sail in. We bag and stow it on the cabin top, raise the main, and sail on. "Well, that confirms our decision to put into the Cape Verdes," Margaret comments.

At Sao Vicente we are able to effect a hasty repair to the roller furler thanks to three fellows who row out in a dingy offering their services as mechanics. In half an hour it is done. They charge a reasonable fee, reasonable by yacht repair standards anyway, and we have a furling genoa again. We restock the larder with fresh fruit and vegetables from the local market, very expensive since everything has to be imported, and they spot us as tourists. Rice comes from Vietnam, carrots from Holland, apples from France, avocados from the Canaries. But diesel is a real bargain, US 40 cents a liter, rather than $1 a liter in most of Europe. And we top up with water. Two days after arrival at Sao Vicente, we are off again.

Antigua, our destination in the Caribbean is 2110 miles downwind from the Cape Verde Islands on a course of 288 degrees. Onward. Westward. Conditions as I mentioned above, with prevailing winds ENE 20 to 25 knots, often gusting to 35 or more in squalls. We make very good time, over 150 miles some days. But it is boisterous sailing, uncomfortable and exhausting, cooking below in the galley is a juggler's act, sleeping a wrestler's sprawl gripping the mat.

Night watch is magical. Through a break in the clouds we follow an evening star on the horizon. Venus? Jupiter? Bright enough to cast its own reflection on the sea. The Christmas star that led the Three Kings? Orion stalks across the sky tracked by his faithful dog Sirius. The moon three days past the full, glows behind the clouds casting an eerie sheen, breaking through spasmotically to illuminate sails, deck, the surrounding sea with almost daylight brilliance. Bright enough to read by, big print that is and with my reading glasses. Breaking waves roar from out the glowing gloom, froth and foam on the leading edge. The stern lifts, 10 feet? Fifteen? I look down into the yawning gap of the trough passing beneath the boat, the bow tilts down , and I brace like that moment taking off a steep mogul on skis, and Zillah slides down the wave.

Then the steering cable breaks. Aware of our vulnerability, we reduce sail even more. We're pleased to have made repair, but anxious too. And that triggers other anxieties. Water. Food. Fresh vegetables dwindle, we turn to cans. Fresh fruit almost gone, there are dates, figs, raisons and dried apricots. All according to schedule, but there is a general unease, nagging irritation. It's been too uncomfortable and too long.

"Thar she blows!" The first sign is a long arching leap out of the water. It must be 12 to 15 feet long. No dorsal fin like a porpoise. Could it be a whale? Then there is a mighty leap 10 feet straight up. "Whale breaching!" I shout. "There it is at 10 o'clock." It vents, water vapor and breath, a jet of steaming fog, and then the leviathon surfaces, water spilling off its black back, blunt head and beady eye, two boat lengths off. It follows us briefly, snorting and venting, then moves on to the watery depths.

This is probably a good place to stop. We have Christmas at sea. For our last few days approaching Antigua the wind eases and allows us a little respite, some lovely smooth spinnaker flying. We pick up the harbor lights of Antigua and make landfall on December 28, twenty six days from La Gomera, including the two days at the Cape Verde Islands. Now what?

CARIBBEAN CRUISING FEB 2001

Hard to believe 5 weeks have slipped by since we tied up to the slip at Antigua. Where has the time gone? We've beem slow making the transition to Island Time and even slower pulling together conflicting thoughts on the Atlantic Crossing. But here it is.It will seem like a very long time ago by the time you get to read it Margaret.

There's a lovely scene in Amadeus, the movie based on Mozart's life, where the Emperor yawns as he listens to one of Mozart's more elaborate piano sonatas, bored, "Too many notes, Mozart," he says. "Only as many as required," Mozart replies. I've been struggling with too many words. Hope you enjoy it.

"This is the first time we've sailed to windward in a long time," I told Mary the other day as we beat our way into 8 ft seas that washed right over the deck and into the cockpit. "I've changed my clothes three times today," Mary said, as we came into Antigua. We've working our way south. The trade winds are meant to be NE this time of year. Perversely they have been SE, and when we are between the islands, the seas are open to the full Atlantic swell. The "upper level trough" persists, days overcast withrain squall passing through, hot, humid and muggy when the sun comes out. But the sailing is exciting, particularly knowing that we can come into a sheltered cove at the end of the day, swim in warm, clear, clean water, pick up a cold beer and Mary an ice cream on shore, buy mangos and avocados at the mini-market, called a supermarket, and walk on dry land without the sensation of being on a heaving deck. The islands have a sameness about them, the main difference here being between the French speaking, Guadeloupe and Martinique, and the former English colonies, now independent little island nation states, with populations of less than 100,000--Antigua, Domenica, now St. Lucia, and the rest down the island chain will be English. We meet a wide variety of cruising couples, interesting,eccentric people (like ourselves?). The last couple days we share tea and rum punch with Vincent and Shiela, a wonderful Irish couple on a real tank of a boat, 40 ft, steel, built himself, painted black. He's a commercial diver, has that same boyish grin you see on so many of the Outward Bound adventure types, a jest for life, for stretching the limits. A couple days before, a Dutch couple heading for Panama, considering resettling in Australia, enthralled with the open space and the economic freedom. I should really start to describe people in my journal, they're far the most interesting in this part of the world. And then there are always books. Our current read aloud is Jane Austen, Sense and Sensibility, wonderful, subtle, characterisation a the slow moving pace of the pre-industrial age, the world confined to the front parlour.

"Have a good watch", as Herb says on Southbound

MORE CARIBBEAN CRUISING—TOBAGO CAYS

March 2, 2001. We sit at anchor on our 3rd day in a sheltered bay between two islands, the boundary line between two countries, Petit St Vincent to the NE, the southernmost island of the Commonwealth of St Vincent and the Grenadines, population 80,000,where by the way Margaret, jet skis are specifically prohibited by law, clearly stated on the ship's entrance papers. A mile across is Petit Martinique, not a part of Martinique at all which is 100 mi to the north, but the northernmost island of the Commonwealth of Grenada, population 120,000, another guess. A barrier reef a mile offshore gives protection from the Atlantic swell we know so well. Water a brilliant turquoise blue where it shallows up over sand, palm trees fringe the shoreline, scrubby jungly trees and shrubs behind, grass patches on the rocky hillside, cactus on barren slopes. Not exactly Shangri-la, but people do pay $1000 a day for secluded cottages with sunset views and a hammock under a thatched lean-to on the beach. We anchor for free, and walk a mile and a half around the island, sometimes twice a day, along the beach.

Two months since we made the crossing to Antigua. The weeks blend into each other with a benign sameness, as do the islands. None of the high drama we have come to expect, no heroics, no stories. Another day in paradise, ho hum. It would be easy to be bored, but there always seems something interesting to do, if not, another good book to read. We currently read Laurie Lee, Cider with Rosie, Jennifer. What a beautiful piece of writing. Yes, one theme per chapter would be a good way to write up Fife Lake memoires. We're eager to read more of his work.

For the first couple weeks we were preoccupied with making Zillah seaworthy again. The shive (block) for the starboard steering cable was realigned to reduce wear, though I suspect that was really a case of make-work, rather than necessity. But the roller furler was clearly beyond repair. Profurl is a French product, and Mary found a dealer in Guadeloupe, a French island, where we had it replaced for $800 less than it would have cost in Antigua, where it would have had to be shipped in FedExp from the States. We were still in an Atlantic Crossing mind set until this was done.

Sailing to Marie Galante, off Guadeloupe and Domenica, where Columbus made landfall on a Sunday on his spectacular second voyage, 1493, brought mythic closure to the crossing, having completed the loop following in his wake from Cadiz, to Madeira, the Canaries, Verdes and across. The trade winds still held up— "reinforced trade winds" according to Dave, our new weather guru on the Caribbean weather net, NE20-25, so the crossings between the islands, Antigua to Guadeloupe and on to Domenica, Martinique, and St Lucia, were brisk sailing, like some of the exhilarating days on the crossing. We were on a beam reach making hull speed 7 to 8 knots, waves crashing on the bow and spraying over the deck. "Some of the best sailing we've ever had," one boat reported over the radio net. We agreed, and the beauty of it was that it did not go on night and day, day after day, week after week. Twenty five miles south on a beam reach we would be in the lee of the next island, winds still gusty, but seas moderate, pulling into a sheltered harbor of refuge for the night, to try out and cook supper with only a gentle roll to the gimbles on the stove. A glass of wine with dinner on the French islands with Brie. Rum punch on the British islands. Now that's cruising!

I have to check the ship's log to recall where we have been. There is a benign similarity to the islands. The French islands, Guadeloupe and Martinique stand out because of their prosperity. They are a part of France, send representatives to the National Assembly, and benefit from the largesse of the European Community. Better roads, telephones. It is cheaper to e-mail with Tele-France through Marseilles than through ATT in Miami, a third of the cost. Largely self-sufficient in food, the countryside pastoral, cattle grazing rather than encroaching second growth jungle; French bread fresh every morning, get there early, even whole grain baguettes, goat cheese, Beaujolais $2.50 US a bottle. They are favored cruising locations, with large charter fleets, the 45 ft catamaran the popular boat of choice.

The French islands also have more advanced medical services and while in Martinique I had a wart like growth on my upper right leg surgically removed by a lady doctor, whose speciality was: Dermatology, Leprosy and Venerial Complications. Surely that would cover warts, I reasoned. I also had my shoulder x-rayed, as I had had an argument with the dingy coming ashore at Deshaies in a 3 ft swell that caught the dingy just as I was unsuspectingly stepping ashore. It tackled me, pinned me to the beach, with a blow to the shoulder. Reminiscent of a lifetime of skiing mishaps. But not breaks, only bruises, and Mary gradually massages it back to flex and bend.

Tobago Cays—a week back, also in the St Vincent group, is probably the most beautiful spot on the Caribbean chain. The other 50 yachts that were in the basin when we arrived seemed to agree. A cluster of five islands you tack your way into and around between coral reefs is sheltered from the west, and protected from the east by a wide encircling barrier reef, replendent in tropical fish. Hunting reef fish with mask and flippers was our most popular activity when we came through 6 years ago. We spotted 95 different species that year. This year has been a great disappointment. A couple years ago a freak hurricane, Lennie, hit from the west—they always come from the east—and wiped out the beaches, broke up the coral reefs and took out docks and jetties that are only now being rebuilt, and the reef fish. Tobago Cays with its unique configuration is sheltered from the west and was spared. We saw adult Stop Light Parrot fish, red and green, with yellow square dots on the flared tail, the beauty queen of the reefs, as well as yellow stripped grunts and bearded goat fish, comical box like trunk fish,spotted white and grey, blue tangs, black damsel fish, blue and yellow in the juvenile phase... and you name it. Great sport, though I find the water just chilling enough to make my joints stiff and ache. So I hover in the dingy while Mary and Helen frolic like porpoises, marvelling at the coral, rounded brain coral the size of a refrigerator, forked antler coral, others small, delicate, like fragile flowers, purpilish blue, swaying in the surge.

Helen Fouhey joined us for the week, the big event of our winter season. She brought a freshness of vision, a sense of enthusiasm and wonder that we needed to jolt us out of our jaded familiarity and sensory overload. "Snorkelling anyone?" "Anyone for a hike?" And I'd put down my book and trundle off. She even got us dancing one night at Union Island to a Rasta band, steel drums, I guess the locals would call it a "Jump Up!" for everybody was certainly jumping, particularly the drummers--15% melody—repetitive, 85% rhythm—monotonous if it were not so contagious. We twisted and wobbled and writhed with the locals, other yachties, and a platoon of young marines, detailed to the island to build a coast guard station—part of out drug interdiction program and renovate the community medical centre. Great goodwill ambassadors in their loose fitting T-shirts and baggy knee length shorts, available women in short supply they danced among themselves and we all joined in. Not exactly an evening of Mozart in Vienna but a memorable evening of music nevertheless.

We now cross over into Grenada waters and will head south over the next week or so to Prickly Bay and Hog Island, on the south end, where we have made arrangements to leave Zillah afloat under a caretaker's watchful eye, and in sheltered waters. If it works out we'll be back in Annapolis by the end of the month. And the beginning of a new chapter in our lives.

A sleek, graceful frigate bird circles overhead, black slender wings, soaring effortlessly, white underbelly, black head and a vicious white piercing beak, a wary eye. Better go now.

Chapter 116: Zillah Returns – Grenada to the Chesapeake

From Prickley Bay, Grenada Lat 12 N Long 61W to Annapolis, Chesapeake Bay Lat. 39 N Long.76.W. is 1806 nautical miles by GPS satellite reckoning. Given the curvature of the earth, the shifting of tectonic plates, the lay of the Caribbean islands , we travel more than 2500 miles. It takes awhile to cover a distance like that at five miles an hour.

In the 18th century, ships under sail plied the North Atlantic Triangle Route—cloth and cheap manufactured goods to Africa, slaves to the West Indies, sugar, molasses and rum to Europe or the United States. We have followed a similar route; Bermuda to Lisbon in 1996, Cadiz to Cape Verde and Antigua in 2000, and now the northern leg to the Chesapeake in 2002. Vestiges of this past abound in the Caribbean. The islands are former colonies of European nations. Most people are descendents of slaves, the mechanic and the electrician who work on "Zillah" in Grenada are both Black. The supervisor is White. St. George's, the patron saint of England, is the eponemous capital and main market town, where Christmas music blares fortissimo over the loudspeaker," Come All Ye Faithful", " The First Nowell", and "Rudolph the Red Nosed Raindeer", to an African rhythm calypso beat. Two hundred years of slavery has left an aversion for field work, so the island is not self-sufficient in food. I buy tomatoes from Florida, carrots from Canada, grapes from California. "Are these potatoes grown locally?" I ask the market lady. "No, we don't have the technology," she replies. I buy low tech bananas and plantains.

This is the year Mary and I are to play host to guests. Scheduled airlines provide easy access to most Caribbean islands from both the United States and Europe. The sailing distance between islands are short, easy one day hops, so it will be easy to rendezvous. Or so we thought. David, an old school mate, whom I have not seen in 50 years, surfaces through the connecting links of the internet. He travels widely, spending winters in Bali. "Why don't you come sailing with me?" Evenings over rum cocktails—the rum in Grenada costs less than the mixer—we reminisce with the nostalgia of two old men, the stories of our lives unfolding like the long drawn out plot of a Victorian novel. But then he becomes very ill and is hospitalized, a hospital established by Cubans during Grenada's short honeymoon with Castro communism, where he is very well looked after, recovering in time to catch his return flight home to Calgary. Not exactly the holiday either of us had imagined.

A week later, Tom, a mountain rescue colleague from New Mexico, whose sailing experience consists of one afternoon on a 14ft Sunfish, is at the helm. Cheryl is at the winch handling the jib sheet. Her first day at sea, she is understandably confused why a rope should be called a sheet. The day is a cloudy, overcast, the wind gusting. I go forward to tighten the jib halyard winch, an unreliable antiquated contraption with a clutch that slips, when a gust hits with full sails up. I rush aft to release the sheet, but before I reach the winch there is a loud burst, like a balloon popping, and the genoa sail rips, 45 ft from top to bottom, 15 ft across, and the tattered edges flap like laundry on the wash line on a windy day. I find a sailmaker at Prickley Bay who can repair it. "Be ready Saturday." Motoring out of St. George's Harbor three days later, on the way to pick up the sail, there is a piercing screech from the engine overheating alarm system, the red flashes of the oil and battery warning system, a faint whiff oc smoke. "Turn the key off, quick!" The raw water pump, which brings in sea water to cool the engine, has failed—again; it happened fifteen months ago at Lanzarote, in the Canary Islands before our Atlantic Crossing. Since then, I have carried a backup water pump that is electrically driven that can be connected in an emergency. Next day we motor on, pick up the repaired sail, and sail on.

The prevailing winds in the eastern Caribbean are the trade winds, named for the Triangle Trade, blowing from the East—ENE to ESE. On a passage north, we shelter in the lee, on the western side of the islands. Mountains covered in dense green tropical rain forest are capped by billowing clouds. It is a short leg, 30 miles to Carriacou, a day sail, we pass over an active subsurface volcano, appropriately named, "Kick em Jenny." In the gap between islands we face the full fetch of the open sea, the Atlantic stretching all the way from Africa. We are swept 10 miles to the west before I realize the strength of the current and we turn on the engine. But still make only 3 knots against the current. Dark descends suddenly, dropping like a curtain; there is little twilight in the tropics. The shore lights in Tyrell Bay are confusing and only with the GPS, Global Positioning System by satellite, are we able to find our way into harbor. Without GPS most amateur navigators like me would be hopelessly lost at sea.

The rhetoric of independence is another vestige of colonialism. When war weary Britain not longer had to will, nor the resources, to impose its hegemony over a colonial empire, it responded readily to the colonies demands for independence. Today the Caribbean is dotted with small English speaking island nations. The hope was for a West Indian Federation, but when the two major players, Trinidad and Jamaica could not agree on the location of the capital, it fell apart and the islands went their independent ways. Few have a population larger than a small city. With limited economic resources that are often mismanaged, the islands struggle to raise themselves above third world poverty, to the relative prosperity of a second world economy. Tourism has proven the economic boon, though suffering this year as a result of the post September 11 reluctance of Americans to travel.

Some islands fare better than others, St. Vincent and the Grenadines for instance. We anchor in Clifton Harbor on Union Island, as a succession of small aircraft, skim over the hilltop, roar past and land at small airport built on a spit overlooking the bay. I check in with Customs here, and read the plaque commemorating the building of the airport built by China—Taiwan China, while I wait. Clifton is the centre for a small charter fleet, has well stocked stores with impressive wine lists at even more impressive prices, fresh fruit and vegetable stalls run by cheerful entrepreneurial market ladies, with a healthy supply of home grown products. I read that the Prime Minister Mitchell was formerly Minister of Agriculture—with a Masters Degree in Agriculture from a Canadian university, as a Canadian I proudly note. He stressed the development of self-sufficiency, small businesses locally owned. At a political rally at Bequi last year, we heard the Minister of Fisheries advocating cleaner sanitation practices in the fish market to meet European Union standards to sell their lobsters to the wealthier French islands. We have an outstanding meal at Joella's, French cuisine, where the salad is crisp, the carrots taste like carrots, potatoes like potatoes and the fish fresh from the sea. At the Tobago Cays, one of the beauty spots of the eastern Caribbean, we anchor behind the protective coral reef in the hue lagoon. There are over fifty other boats widely spaced out. We snorkel among the scraggly elkhorn coral, huge round dome brain coral, resplendent in shades of aquamarine, leather buff and lemon yellow, tracking parrot fish, sargeant majors, blue tangs, and a dozen other colorful species we can identify. Returning to Grenada, I pick up Mary at the airport. Shearrives on New Year's Eve, her luggage, a bag of books, and Celia, our 10 lb pocket sized poodle, in her little Sherpa dog carry on kennel under her arm.

Engine repairs tie us down the full month of January, a frustrating month of waiting, procrastination and delays, waiting for partsfor the raw water pump. Later we discover the electrical wiring on the engine is so badly corroded that it needs to be replaced. We order an electical a loom, or harness that connects the electrical outlets through a local agent, from a dealer in the British Virgin Islands, to be shipped from England. While we wait and flinch at the expense. But there could be worse places then Hog Island Bay to wait. We swim, walk Celia on shore. When the boat drags in a rain squalland we begin to drift down on to a reef, we are unable to start the engine, but other yachtsmen come to our aid and help us reset the anchor. There is a fellowship of the sea. At the Sunday barbacue on the beach, we meet a gentleman who as a young apprentice helped build "Zillah" in 1955 at Newman and Sons yard in Poole, England.

We become part of the community of eccentrics who have fled the strictures of the office, or the factory, or the military, and "hang out" on boats where metal rusts and the bottom becomes fowl. "Zillah" too suffers the ravages of tropical heat and humidity.

"I know you," I tell big Geoff over a second rum.

"Where from?"he asks.

"The Wizard of Oz,"I reply.

"Give me courage," he growls.

Sure enough, he is the image of Dorothy's lion, bald head with long blond sidelocks, bare forehead, beefy Dutchman's face, rosy cheeks, broad jowls and a beaming smile.

Another compensation for being at anchor, with nowhere to go, is there is plenty of time for reading. Mary races through Barbara Kingsolver and others she has brought. I plod through Karen Armstrong, "The Fight for God," on fundamentalism,

Islamic, Jewish and Christian. We read Laurie Lee, "Cider with Rosie"aloud—Mary cooks, while I read, for sheer delight, and Agatha Christie for diversion. But the clock is ticking, we have miles to go and appointments to keep. On January 30 we raise anchor and point the bow into the wind and head north.

There is a fine line between cruising and passage making. Our journey north was a compromise. We stop at favorite places such as Bequi, with its French bread bakery and market stalls run by marajuana high Rastas. Others we pass by, Dominica with its beach boys. At Marigot, St.Lucia, we rendezvous with a SOS (Singles on Sailboats) charter group from Annapolis and party with friends of Mary. In Martinique I was able to find a backup raw water pump, and a part of the electrical harness for the engine I was missing, and we stand on a hilltop above St. Ann's Bay, are enchanted by the setting of the sun with a resplendant green flash.

At Rodney Bay, St.Lucia, I climb Lookout Point to see where the English spied the French fleet setting sail from Martinique in April 1782. Rodney took off in hot A week later we anchor off Isle de Saintes, where they engaged. Rodney scored a devastating defeat on the French, by "breaking the line", a new naval tactic, decimating the French fleet and capturing the "Villle de Paris", the biggest ship afloat and the French Admiral de Grasse. It is one of the great ironies of the fortunes of war, for the year before de Grasse became a great hero when he successfully blockaded the British fleet in the lower Chesapeake Bay, preventing them from either reinforcing or evacuating the British general Cornwallis who was trapped at Yorktown, Virginia. Cornwallis surrendered his army, thereby effectively ending the War of the American Revolution. A year later, de Grasse, taken prisoner of war, returned to France in disgrace, was stripped of his command, and exiled to his country estate.

In Guadeloupe we meet Jennifer, my daughter, and her Belgian husband, Johann. They flew direct from Paris. A craving, a European sweet tooth was the source of Guadeloupe's wealth. Immense fortunes were made in sugar,like oil fortunes today, coveted, a cause of international conflict. After the Seven Years War in 1763, sugar rich Guadeloupe was traded for empty wilderness of Canada. It was widely felt that the French got the better deal. We meet other Canadians—French Canadians, and they seemed to agree. "They speak our language," they joked,"and where else can you get such wine and cheese?"

The French islands, Guadeloupe and Martinique are indeed markedly different than the former British Islands. Where the British divested themselves of their former Caribbean colonies after WWII—all but Monserrat and the British Virgin Islands chose independence, with such rapidity that many felt they were abandoned, the French declared their islands a part of France, and the inhabitants citizens of France. They were granted representation in the French parliament, subsidies for their agriculture, a ready market for their produce, and all the benefits of the French welfare system. The result is a distinctly higher standard of living, and a higher standard of civility if excellent restaurants, superabundant hypermarkets, schools, hospitals, paved roads, garbage collection are any indices. We drive high into the mountains to the spectacular 350 foot Carbet Waterfalls on a well paved narrow, winding, and hike, and hike in a steady line of Sunday strolling families on a well groomed trail. There aree concrete steps on the steeper inclines, and a suspension footbridge over the ravine, all built and maintained by the government parks service. Off Pain de Sucre (Sugar Loaf) Bay we snorkel among the colorful assortment of parrot fish, yellow heads, banded butterfly fish. Jennifer surfaces with a broad grin, "Dad, come see this one." It looks like a huge bat, wings outspread 10 inches across the ocean floor, a purple grey color in the subsurface light, short legs like a birds claws scratching for grubs where the anchor chain drags in the sand. It's a flying gurnard, an evolutionary freak, one of the mysteries of the deep.

Sailing north we follow in the route of the 18th century Triangle Trade—cheap goods to Africa, slaves to the West Indies, sugar, molasses and rum to the newly independent United States and Europe. Europeans had developed an insatiable and ever growing sweet tooth, and fortunes were made in sugar. Sugar was then what oil is today, a financial bonanza. After the Seven Years War in 1763, sugar rich Guadeloupe was swapped for empty wilderness Canada, and the French felt they got the better deal. Flying the Canadian flag, we clear in with customs at Guadeloupe I find a competent mechanic for engine repairs and we pick up Jennifer and Johann, who have a direct flight from Charles de Gaulle in Paris. We meet other Canadians, French Canadians who prefer Guadeloupe, because its language, and they love the food, fabulous cheeses, inexpensive wine, excellent restaurants. Besides the French islands have an infrastructure and a civility, not found in the rest of the Caribbean, paved roads without potholes, garbage is collected. They have been incorporated into France, are French districts, sending their represenatives to the French Senate and General Assembly, and now are a part of the European Union, with all its trade benefits, markets for their sugar, bananas, and fish. The French Guadeloupians still think they got the better deal.

From Guadeloupe north and west we sail in the wake of Columbus, all the way to Cuba. On his second voyage of discovery, 1493, he landed at Maria Galante, naming the island after his trusty flagship. He landed on a Sunday, domingo in Spanish, and sighting an island on the southern horizon, named it Dominica. Columbus had a deep mystical religious faith, and before sailing, went on a pilgrimage to the famous shrine in Spain, Santa Maria de Guadeloupe, and dedicated the island to her.

He commenorated innumeralbe manifestations of the Holy Mother and his favored saints, Santa Maria de Nieves, Saint Mary of the Snows, now Neves; St. Christopher, St. Kitts: St. Barts—Bartholomew, and through the Christian pantheon, John, Thomas, Eustatia.

Winds hold fast to the NE 15-20 knots, often 25 knots, making for heavy sailing as we beat to windward. The trade winds normally shift to the east, and even south east this time of year, but to no avail. David Jones, the weather guru we listen to each morning, commiserates."It's very unusual weather for this time of year." He sounds apologetic that he can't give us better weather.

We wait out a weather front in Antigua, undecided as to whether we should push on. Jennifer and Johann have to take a feeder line flight back to Guadeloupe, to catch their flight back to France. A break in the weather is predicted. The question is when? We're undecided. "My option would be to go for it," Jennifer says,"we can always turn back if it gets too bad." Running downwind before a storm is more comfortable that trying to beat into it. We set off and as so often happens, immediately our spirits lift. St. Barts is 130 miles on a course of 327 WNW, an overnight passage, our first overnighter this year. It is glorious sail. I relieve Johann on the midnight watch. "Give me a tall ship/ And a star to steer her by," the poet Masefield rhapsodizes. The Big Dipper hangs suspended from its handle, as if nailed to the wall of the sky. Sighting it just inside the starboard shrouds, I have a point of reference. Polaris sparkles dimly to the north. "Follow the drinking gourd," the abolitionist song encouraged runaway Negro slaves escaping north, guided by the North Star. We too live out our fantasies of freedom, the romance and freedom of the seas. In St. Barts we rent a car, tour the island, chic European, where the rich and the famous like to be seen, and see our crew off on their plane.

The passage from St. Martin to Virgin Gorda (the fat virgin) is the perfect sail. The islands of the Caribbean chain begin to curve the west, and on a course of 308 degress WNW, we sail further off the wind. ENE 15-20 knots, it is ideal for a small boat. Seas running 6 to 8 feet, the deck tilts and rolls as the boat heels in the gusts, as if alive, a magical convergence of wind and wave. The moon nearly full, the world is aglow, electric. The Monitor wind steering vane, an ingenious device that uses the force of the wind to keep the boat on course, so a crew of only two, Mary and I can easily handle the boat through longer passages, particularly the long hours of night. "Zillah" literally steers herself.

"Joe, you ski just like your live," an Outward Bound instructor told me years ago, after a day at Vail, "always slightly out of control." Some days it applied to sailing as well. We departed the Virgin Islands in a light wind, NE 10-12 knots, off the starboard quarter. "An ideal a spinnaker run," Mary suggested. The spinnaker is a sail that billows out before the boat like a hovering cloud, a spectacular sensation, designed for light winds, down wind sailing. With a crew of only two, hoisting it is a complex process, Mary at the helm keeping the boat on course steadily down wind. I'm on the foredeck, wading knee deep through yards of sail. I attach the tack, the lower leading edge of the sail, to a block secured at the bow; then lift the clew, the following edge of the sail over the life line and outboard of the shrouds, (the cables that hold the mast upright); and finally pull up on the halyard, the line that hoists the sail to the top of the mast. Finally I tug on the downhaul that pulls down the sleeve or sock that encloses the sail. It billows out resplendent and magnificent, like the bursting glory of a sunrise, a marvellous moment. Mary pulls in on the spinnaker sheet and the boat sways and lifts to the new thrust of energy. We've carried the sail for a year and a half, but rarely use it, so each time the sail billows out we feel our spirits inflating as well.

Preoccupied with the dramatics of the spinnaker, we are slow to notice the aircraft carrier off Charlotte Amalie, the main port of St. Thomas. "How could you not notice an aircraft carrier?" you might be ask. At first glamce it appeared to be at anchor and we sail on."But isn't it moving?"Mary asks. "Hail it on the radio," as it gains speed, cutting straight across our bow. Technically, as a sailboat under sail, we have the right of way, but who is to argue rules of the road with an aircraft carrier? We scamble to give way, to get out of the way, slackening the spinnaker sheet, turning on the engine, powering into the wind. The grey monster, a huge wall of steel glides by less than 100 yards in front of us, lilliputian seamen on the deck, waving furiously. And we duck under the stern and slide by. On the radio I apologize for getting in the way. The deck officer apologizes for not noticing us. All very cordial. There had been a warning weeks before that any unaurthised vessels approaching with 400 yards of an American warship would be regarded as a hostile act. Had we been terrorists, we had the perfect opportunity we later speculate. So much for the Navy's state of alert.

Culebra, the easternmost island of Puerto Rico, 18 miles to the buoy marking the reef off the south shore, course of 282 degrees, almost due West. We reset the spinnaker and cruise on. Charged with adrenalin, intoxicated with the beauty and exhileration of the glorious sail, purple on white, a four armed star in the center, the wind picking up from 12 knots to 15, we move along downwind at 7 knots, then 8, hull speed. Clouds gather to the east behind us, white caps begin to break on the waves. "Better bring the spinnaker down," I suggest reluctantly. It is such a great sail. Mary agrees. I go forward to the mast. Mary slacks the spinnaker sheet from the cockpit cleat, while I pull on the downhaul that slides the sleeve down , snuffing the wind out of the sail. But it won't snuff. I call to Mary to slack the sheet more, to spill the wind. But the wind does not want to spill. "Let the sheet go!" The sail flaps and flutters out before the boat, flying high off the top of the mast like one of those gigantic flags that have burgeoned in recent shows of patriotism. I cling to the downhaul valiantly as I'm dragged out on to the foredeck, feeling I'm going to be lifted out into space, hang gliding, and surf sailing, like Dorothy being whisked off to Oz. I let the downhaul go. Now the sail is really free. The only way to get it down is to release the halyard and drop the whole sail into the sea. There is a sickening blowout, a sudden hush as the unruly sail collapses, doused, deflated, a huge wet soggy rag lying in the sea, along the full length of the boat—from flag to rag in five seconds. Slowly we retrieve the wet sail from the sea, pulling it onto the deck, roll it up, bag it. We unfurl the genoa, a more manageable sail and cruise on. A dark line of rain clouds move in, grey and gloomy, driven by gusty winds. We reef in the jib, and easy task given roller furling, and are hit by a squall driving rain pellets horizontally cross the sea, blowing off the top of the waves, Culebra disappears from sight and we are enveloped in the storm. Then as suddenly as it came, as suddenly it passes through, and we sail into Dewey in bright sunshine with a gently following breeze. I tell Mary of a day skiing at Vail years ago with Outward Bound instructors. "You ski just like you live, Joe, always slightly out of control," one told me.

Mary and Celia approaching Annapolis aborad Zillah in
the summer of 2002.

Chapter 117: Cuba – The Land of the Possible

"Is it possible?" I asked. "Isn't it prohibited?"

"It is prohibited," the Captain agreed," but it's possible."

We had landed at Cayo Paradona Chico, on the north coast of Cuba where the prominent lighthouse overlooks the busy shipping channel where the Old Bahama Channel narrows. Though our cruising permit was valid for this stretch of coast, we didn't have permission to land. Celia, our ten-pound poodle, was our main reason for coming ashore. In a dire emergency she would perform on the coconut mat aft, but she preferred terra firma. For the soldier who confronted us on the beach, even that was prohibited. The lighthouse was a military installation to be defended to the last man, even against poodles.

The soldier sent his comrade for advice. The young lieutenant, tall, elegant, clearly of the officer class even in a classless society, came to check us out. He was equally assertive.

"Over there," he pointed to the jagged coral reef a short distance offshore. We had tried to land there, unsuccessfully, not wanting to shred our inflatable dinghy on the abrasive rock. But Celia had avoided the diplomatic crisis without formality, squatted and did her bit, narrowly missing the lieutenant's boots.

We were stepping back into the dinghy when the Captain appeared. Curious about what was going on, and clearly in charge, he assumed the role of ambassador rather than guardsman. We chatted amiably, he in fractured English, myself in mangled Spanish. It's intriguing to see how well people can communicate in spite of language. "Would you like to visit the lighthouse?" he asked. It took me awhile to understand, "Es prohibite, pero possible," he assured me.

With the naivety of a spontaneous child showing off his favorite toy, the lighthouse keeper escorted us up the winding steps to the commanding heights. We were learning that the seeming paradox of prohibitions and possibilities was a fact of life in Communist Cuba.

"It must have been a great adventure," Janet commented when we resettled in Annapolis months later. Cuba always made entertaining cocktail party chatter.

"Yes, an adventure and a misadventure," I replied.

Cuba was our last port of call before returning to the United States. Mary and I had spent the last eight years cruising on "Zillah", a forty-three foot classic wooden sloop. We felt there was something special about Cuba. Because of its Communist regime it seemed more exotic than other developing Caribbean islands. We had visited post-Communist Eastern Europe and we wondered how Cuba compared. The fact that it was off limits—but not quite off limits—was part of the appeal too.

Recently the Bush administration had declared Cuba a rogue state, harboring terrorists. A hint of the clandestine was heightened when an unmarked helicopter circled us as we crossed the Windward Passage from Haiti, and an hour later the US Coast Guard Cutter "Sitkinak" hailed us. They requested permission to come aboard for "a courtesy safety inspection." Finding no Haitians, Cubans, drugs, nor contraband, and only outdated flares, a minor safety violation, they allowed us to sail on.

As a Canadian I was not restricted from traveling to Cuba. Mary, an American, was allowed to visit, but prohibited from trading. She could not spend any money. So we negotiated our own private North American trade agreement and I paid the bills.

Approaching Cuba from the east, Bahia de Vita was the first port of entry. We entered the serpentine harbor channel between low coral cliffs. Were we approaching an idyllic Communist paradise, or entering the heart of darkness? I wondered. The marina had been built only recently, since Simon Charles's 2nd edition, "Cruising Guide to Cuba" was printed. So we had no chart, took a wrong turn and promptly ran aground. In the process of trying to get off, our diesel engine, which had been giving us difficulty all the way from Grenada, gasped and died. Dante has sinners serving time in purgatory before entering paradise. Was this our lot? Pulled off the bar and towed in, we entered the Marina de Bahia de Vita.

"Welcome to Cuba," we were greeted at the dock by a tall robust woman, a commanding eminence in a blue suit. Ernestina, in her early forties, spoke good English and combined the qualities of an official hostess, dock master and a mother superior. She was the one who assigned us our dock slip, took our passports, conducted the phalanx of officials on board, the guardia frontera, harbor master, customs, immigration, agriculture, veterinary. She billed us for marina charges, sold us Cuban maritime charts, arranged for two mechanics to resuscitate our engine, booked a car rental. "You see me if you need any help," she said. As much as I appreciated her help, I also had the uneasy feeling that she was not a woman to be crossed.

There were twenty-five yachts in the marina, mostly European, British, French, German, four Americans, another Canadian, two Cuban catamarans, owned by a Cuban tourist company. The marina hosted a party for us. A six-piece band from a nearby resort hotel played compelling music with a lively rhythm that made it difficult to sit still. Communism with a smile. "Salsa Communism," the Frenchman said. If they were oppressed, they certainly did a good job hiding it. Ernestina pulled me onto the dance floor and deftly maneuvered me around the floor. What gave her her status? I couldn't help wondering. Party membership, where party hierarchy pre-empted bureaucratic rank? Given her command of English, her ability to insinuate herself into a group, she'd be an ideal informer for the security network. A mystery lady. Or had I been reading too much John LeCarre?

We spent a week playing tourist ashore. Though severely limited by our lack of Spanish, we did find Cubans, friendly, polite—with one exception near Guatanamo— and curious. We saw few pictures of Castro, who is not apparently the megalomaniac most Communist leaders are or were. Che Guevera was the photogenic star. We stayed at family guest houses, bed and breakfasts, and ate at small restaurants, which had been authorized by the government, in their effort to nurture an embryonic market economy.

The first night we banqueted at Elena's small bungalow, down the street from the marina security gate. She served us fresh grouper, boiled rice, beans, and a magnificent salad of lettuce, cucumber, tomatoes, simple, delicious, filling.

"Quanta costa?" How much does it cost?, we asked on getting up from the table.

"Nada." she said, nothing. "You are my guests. It is a gift," she waved us off. Elena, we were later told did not have a government permit, she could not charge. Like Mary, she was prohibited from trading with foreigners. So we in turn proffered our gift as well, six dollars a person, the recognized fee. Prohibited but possible.

Barracoa, on the NE coast of Cuba, was discovered by Columbus on his second voyage in 1493. We stayed at the home of "El Poeta," an officially approved private residence, $20 a night for two, plus $6 each for the standard fish and salad dinner. The three young daughters vied with each other to walk Celia. We found Cubans genuinely fond of dogs.

Alfredo, the oldest son, worked in the local chocolate factory, which produced a sickeningly sweet concoction of 80% sugar, 20% chocolate. Tomas, his younger brother, studied animal husbandry at the agricultural college, three weeks on, three off. There were too many students, too few places, so he could go only half time.

Father, "El Poeta," a radio script writer, was not at home. An official framed certificate hung on the wall, which I deciphered. It recognized him for service to the country, commending him for a hundred hours of voluntary work cutting sugar cane.

"Donde esta el padre?" Where's your father? I asked Tomas.

"He's working in the sugar cane fields." he replied. What was this all about? I wondered, annoyed that I could not pursue the question further. Was it a form of discipline? Or a Castro-Maoist continuing education program for intellectuals and bureaucrats? Or merely a work vacation, a way of gaining favor with the regime? Not required, but expected? Another Cuban Communist paradox?

"Do you ever work in the cane fields?" I asked the boy. After all, he was studying animal husbandry.

"Oh no!" he answered emphatically. This was clearly something from which he was exempt, as a son of the privileged. Or so I inferred.

Cuba was poor by capitalist standards, we learned, but several steps above a third world country. It has the lowest child mortality rate of any Latin American country. Illiteracy has been virtually wiped out, and every child goes to school. A house may be crudely constructed of overlapping planking with a tin roof, but everyone has a roof over his head. There were no homeless people. The government provided basic rations for those who cannot provide for themselves, and while few Cubans were fat, no one starves.

"For the poor, it's been a good deal," we agreed with our yachting friends.

Cruising the north coast of Cuba we were wary for an extensive reef system lies off shore. We followed the Cuban charts carefully, frequently checking our position with the GPS, the Global Positioning System, constantly worrying about our erratic engine. At Porto Manati, 48 miles to the west, two American yachts were at anchor. After clearing in with Cuban officials, we went ashore looking for them. Their table was already stacked with beer bottles when we found them at a sidewalk bar. They were negotiating with a local fisherman for lobsters. "A dollar a piece," Frank told me. "Non prohibito?" I asked. He grinned. They bought twenty. We took two. They ordered another round of beer.

Negotiating the process was an attractive woman in her thirties, big-boned, tall, long black hair. She spoke good English and was clearly someone to whom the locals were deferential. Another mystery woman. The ubiquitous security network? Or the emerging mafia? In some post-Communist countries we had visited they were one and the same.

The run down to Cayo Guillermo was a glorious day of sailing. Our best yet, we thought, prematurely. This was where Hemingway had fished and wrote "The Old Man and The Sea," which was based on a local story. The chart showed forty feet of water, a clear passage inside the barrier reef. Mary thought we should risk it. I put waypoints in the GPS to alert us to a couple shallow places indicated on the chart.. The wind was on the starboard quarter, that's on the right ear, NE 15 knots. With reefed main and full genoa, we made seven knots, great speed for vintage "Zillah." When the wind dropped to 10 knots we raised the spinnaker, a spectacular balloon-like sail that billows like a low hanging cloud soaring above the boat. Raising the spinnaker is one of the sensational moments of sailing, feeling ten tons of boat lift in the wind. As we approached the bay, the wind freshened. We dropped the spinnaker, unfurled the genoa again and sailed on.

There was a protected anchorage nestled behind Cayo Guillermita Este, Little William East, indicated on both the chart and Simon's cruising guide. We saw another yacht heading there, less than a mile off, and set our course to join them, We were well inside the reef indicated on the chart, or so we thought.

Then there was a sickening crunch of lead on rock, as we had hit the coral reef. I had a moment of disbelief. This can't be. There's no reef on the chart. But reality spoke louder than the chart's symbolism. Quickly Mary slackened the sails, I started the engine, and miracle of miracles, we were able to back off, and bump our way over the rock into deeper water. Thank God for five tons of lead and the full length keel. Checking the chart it looked as if we had miscalculated the position of the reef, but now we were clear of it. So we tightened sails and headed on. Ten minutes later we hit again, now firmly grounded in gravel and sand. This time there to stay.

We furled the sails, started the engine, tried to back off. Mary gave it full revs, but we didn't budge. She tried again, but we still stuck fast. Then smoke began to belch from below. "Quick, turn off the engine." Mary called from the helm. Now, not only were we aground. We were also without power. Again.

A quarter mile away, Rudi, an Austrian on "Anne Marie" hailed us on the VHF radio. He came over to help in his dinghy with extra line and anchor. We tried to kedge off, running an anchor out to the full length of the rope, dropping it and then cranking in on the windlass. Slowly we pivoted the boat around, turning it back in the direction we had come, but we were not able to move off the bar. Even running a second anchor out we could move no further. The tide was running out and "Zillah" began to heel, and by nightfall the boat was canted at a twenty degree angle. There we stayed for the night, the boat thudding on the hard gravel as it heaved in the persistent waves.

"Not our best day," Mary noted in the ship's log.

"Marina Cayo Guillermo. Marina Cayo Guillermo." I hailed them on the VHF radio at eight next morning. No reply. I persisted every 15 minutes.

"This is *Papageno*. They don't monitor their radio. Can we help you?" A voice responded.

"*Papagano*? I know a boat by that name. Are you the *Papageno* that was at Gibraltar six years ago?"

"Why yes."

"This is *Zillah*. Another Canadian yacht. We met you there." Disasters at sea have made a true believer of many a skeptic. How can you not believe in fate? Or at least in what Jung called synchronicity, seeming coincidence that has the element of intentionality. What Divine Hand had preordained "*Papageno*" to be in Cayo Guillermo on that morning?

"*Papageno*" went ashore and organized a rescue operation. The marina sent out a powerful deep sea sport fishing boat to tow us off. Eventually it took two boats, one pulling full throttle ahead, the other abeam pulling on a halyard coming off the masthead. This tilted the boat sideways until the deck rail was down to the water, angling the 7 foot keel up off the bottom until it came free. Then they towed us toward shore. The bar at the harbor entrance had only six feet of water over it, too shallow for us to cross, so we dropped the anchor, still half a mile from shore.

Lunch with Mike and Bet off "*Papageno*" was a heart warming reunion, relief, gratitude, sharing other epics of the sea. They showed us Nigel Calder's "Cruising Guide to Cuba," the other popular cruising guide, and it clearly indicated the reef. I saw the deep irony. Four year before in Gibraltar, we had swapped Calder with "*Papageno*" for Heikel's "Cruising Guide to Greece."

"Oh well, if you haven't been aground, you ain't been around," Mike consoled us.

"What about the engine?" I asked Sergio, a blond Cuban, the marina manager. "It's a fifty-five horsepower Perkins diesel."

"No problem. Manuel is a good mechanic," he said And manuel was. He diagnosed the problem quickly. A U-shaped bracket that fit over the head of the fuel injector and clamped it in place had bent out of shape. When the engine turned over, fuel sprayed from the injector head.

"Where do you get Perkins parts in Cuba?" I asked.

"No problema," Manuel affirmed.

He removed the faulty bracket, and returned to his workshop on shore. This was a rough plank table with a vise bolted to one end, which was braced against the outside wall of a shed under a corrugated sheet metal lean-to. He cannibalized a defunct Volvo diesel engine for parts, found a bracket that nearly matched and began to shape it to size, trimming length, width and thickness, by hand with a hacksaw. It took most of the morning, but the finished product fit with precision, and by noon the engine was running again.

"How much does it cost?" I asked Sergio, the manager.

"Sixty dollars," he said.

"Sixty dollars an hour?" I asked, surprised at the somewhat exorbitant charge.

"No. Sixty dollars is the charge, if it takes one hour, or takes all day." Modern cost accounting procedures do not seem to have kept pace with the modern economy. But we didn't complain.

"And the tow? How much does that cost?" I expected highway robbery. (Later in Florida, TowBoat US charged $200 to pull us off a sand bar, and another $200 to tow us ashore when the engine suffered chronic failure. Waterway robbery.)

"Twenty dollars," Sergio said, with not even a smile. Whoever fixed prices in the central planning office was certainly charitable to us that day.

Our original plan had been to continue on to Havana, another 150 miles to the west. But we were unnerved. I had lost all confidence in the charts and the cruising guide. The engine, which had given us a bad time all the way from Grenada, had become a nightmare. We were eager to head home, and take our problems with us.

"At least we'll be able to speak the language," Mary concurred.

But leaving was not so simple. There were three problems: the weather, the officials and locating the channel through the reef, so we could find our way out of the harbor. A weather front was predicted, adding to our sense of urgency, as we were still anchored half a mile off shore in exposed waters.

"You can follow our fishing boat out," Sergio told us, "We leave at 2:30." He would guide us over the reef.

The Guardia Frontera said that customs and immigration would not be there until late morning. We thought we had arranged for an early morning clearance the day before. By 11a.m. they still had not arrived. When they finally came after lunch there was clearly some difficulty. I couldn't follow the debate among the officials, but I could interpret the worried looks, the shaking heads. They spoke on the phone with backs turned to us, careful not to divulge state secrets. More delays.

They wouldn't clear us to leave the country. Our cruising permit was for Veradero, the yacht harbor for Havana. To clear out for the United States, we had to go to Veradero.

"OK. Clear us for Veradero then." More phone calls. Finally papers were signed and we cleared.

Sergio's boat that would guide us out of the harbor was already across the bay when we got the anchor up. I took a compass bearing and we followed as best we could. As the depth dropped from 20 feet, to 15, then 12, we slowed. We crept forward, our eyes glued to the depth sounder, expecting the fatal crunch. The depth held at 12 feet and we slipped across the reef. Then the depth sounder read 20 feet, 30 feet. At 40 feet we unfurled the genoa, hoisted the mainsail and headed for the openness of the sea.

"Free at last, free at last, Lord God, free at last," I exulted in the words of the gospel preacher.

The course for Veradero was 270 degrees, due west. The wind NE 12 knots, three foot seas. Five miles offshore, in international waters, Mary suggested, "Shouldn't we head for Florida?"

"Es prohibito," I said with a grin.

"Si, but possible," she beamed, and we set a course of 310 degrees, northwest up the Old Bahama Channel.

"Celia, go to the coco mat. It's a long way to Miami."

Cuba, 2002: Joe with new ship's dog, Celia.

Chapter 118: Crossing the Bar

"If you were to ask me if you should buy this boat, I'd say—don't," the yacht surveyor was emphatic. That wasn't what I wanted to hear. I was trying to sell the boat.

After eight years of cruising on *Zillah*, Mary and I returned to shore and advertised in Wooden Boat Magazine, "Classic 43-foot teak sloop. Built in England 1955. Cruising ready. $55,000. Call or e-mail."

"Rot!" Fred Hecklinger said authoritatively. Even his name resonated authority. A renowned Annapolis surveyor who had restored several wooden boats himself. A larger than life character, formidable, tall, with a full head of wavy white hair, flushed ruddy cheeks and jowls, "Rot," he repeated and thrust his knife into the mealy wood of the decayed ribs. "And the forged iron floors," he resumed with a long discourse on corrosion and incompatible metals. "You won't know how far the keel bolts are gone until you pull one," he paused, "or the keel falls off."

An accomplished raconteur, now with a captive audience, he continued with the story of a fifty-year-old *Alden* that, "Just came apart at sea. Split right down the middle. They fastened the ribs of old wooden boats to the keel and when they go, there's nothing to hold them together."

Hecklinger paused for dramatic effect and looked about *Zillah*. "She's a beautiful boat," he acknowledged. "Two feet above the keel."

"She should be sold only to somebody who knows what he's getting into, and who has either the skill or the money to restore her. She's not seaworthy in her present condition." It had not been one of my more felicitous days.

But one never crossed an ocean in a small craft without the belief, no matter how vague, in a Divine Providence, the suspicion that there is a Someone or a Something out there, up there, wherever, that was looking out for one. The ancients called it Fate. You can call it naïve optimism. Jung, the psychoanalyst, wrote of synchronicity, meaningful coincidence, the purposeful convergence of life altering events.

Two days later the phone rang. "Is she still for sale?" Chris Schollar was a boat carpenter, English, living in Spain. He'd seen our ad in a back issue of Wooden Boat Magazine. "Just what I'm looking for," he said.

How could that be? I wondered. He had only seen the postage stamp-sized photo that appeared in the ad.

"Have you sailed her much?"

"Two years in the Caribbean, two Atlantic Crossings, and four years in the Mediterranean," I extolled *Zillah's* sailing virtues and ventures, by-passing the misadventures, and expounded on the numerous upgrades, the new Perkins 55-hp diesel engine, a Profurl roller- furled genoa, Lighthouse anchor windlass, Monitor wind steering vane, all seacocks and thruhull fittings replaced, new stainless steel chainplates and rigging. And safety systems, a six- person Plastimo life raft, EPIRB (Emergency Positioning Intermittent Radio Beacon), SSB (Single Side Band) radio.

"The bad news is…" and I discussed the recent inspection. "Rot in the wooden ribs, possibly corroded keel bolts, leaking deck. But there's still life left in her," I added. "If it were not that Mary was eager to return home, we'd be living aboard and cruising on her still."

"The good news is, I'm reducing the price to $20,000." That's what I had paid for her nine years previously.

"I'll come over and have a look at her. If she's what I think she is, I'll sail her back to Spain," Mr. Schollar responded, a man of quick decision.

"During hurricane season?" I asked, taken aback.

"Oh? You have hurricanes there?"

Ten days later I picked him up at Reagan National Airport. Of medium height, he was built like a professional boxer, heavily muscled, thick arms and shoulders. A sun-scorched face, thinning red hair, and dark Mediterranean blue eyes flashing impatience. He hoisted his huge bulging sea-bag effortlessly and strode out to the car.

His sailing companion, Nigel, tall, heavy set, slightly overweight, bright sky blue eyes and a boyish smile, followed, dragging his duffle on wheels. He hurried to keep up with Chris, as I limped to keep up with the two of them.

"I'd like to see the boat tonight," Chris said once we were in the car, "if it's not too far out of the way." It had been twenty-two hours since he left Malaga on the Costa del Sol. He seemed determined to make the boat his. Their return airline tickets were for the following Friday. He had less than a week to decide.

The next four days Chris took the boat apart systematically and made his own survey. He lifted the forward cabin sole and floorboards, checking the iron floors and wooden ribs. "Yes, there's rot, but it's not as bad as he said." He'd called Hecklinger and the surveyor had given him the doomsday scenario.

The deepest bilge was beneath the main cabin. To get at it we had to unbolt the oak salon table and raise the teak floorboards, exposing the two 60-gallon cast iron water tanks. Chris tapped a suspicious rust spot on the aft tank, and flakes of corroded metal fell into the tank, leaving an inauspicious hole.

"That's no problem," Chris declared. "We can fiberglass a temporary patch over that. We should replace these tanks with fiberglass tanks anyway," and he explained how he would mold them using the shape of the old tanks. A true craftsman, he delighted in problems. Problems gave him the opportunity to devise solutions. He and Nigel manhandled the two 150- pound tanks out of the bilge and onto the deck. Nigel wrenched his back in the process.

The bilges were filthy, with the slime and grime of grit, spilled oil, food particles that had accumulated for nearly a decade. They hosed water in, pumped the sludge out, Nigel carrying buckets and jerry cans of slurry to the marina waste oil disposal drums. Chris worked below, cleaning and scraping the detritus and old paint. Wood rot was even worse in this section. Chris jammed a finger under one rib and his hand went right through.

I looked on in dismay. I felt the ghost of Hecklinger peering over my shoulder and adumbrating, "I told you so." I was certain that the deal was off. What charity would take the boat off my hands, "as is," in its present derelict condition? I began to wonder.

But again Chris had a solution, "We'll have to dry her out and get epoxy under there. That'll hold her 'til I get her home." Already he was talking as if he owned her. So I bought a Black and Decker electric heat gun at Ace Hardware, and a Makita mechanical grinder, and Chris began to clean the bilge down to bare wood and metal.

Rotting ribs were nothing new. Eight years previously in Trinidad, I had 40 ribs "sistered," duplicate ribs laid alongside the old ribs, which had cracked or rotted. As a part of the job, the workmen had covered the floors in tar, to prevent water from pooling along the ribs. "This has to come out," Chris said when he saw it, and he began the arduous job of chipping tar with hammer and chisel, then softening it with the heat gun and scraping.

"It's not as bad as the surveyor said," Chris announced over dinner that night. "The keel bolts are bronze as I thought. I doubt if there's much corrosion."

"It looks like we have a deal," I said tentatively, still uncertain of *Zillah's* seaworthiness.

"Yes." He phoned Linda, his wife, that night to arrange a wire transfer of funds from their bank in Kendall, England.

The commissioning of *Zillah* became a family affair. Mary housed and fed the crew. I became chauffeur on the many trips to the hardware store, West Marine and Boat US, chandlers, Oceanis Marine Supplies, where we bought bulk epoxy and fiberglass.

"What do you think need replacing?" Chris asked.

"I'd get another mainsail before doing an Atlantic crossing," I replied. "The old one was second hand when I bought it nine years ago. It's already blown out once, off Grenada, and we had to mend it by hand." I drove him to Bacon's with their inventory of 10,000 used sails.

He looked at the canvas again and said, "It just needs stitching." So he heaved it on his shoulders and we hauled it down to UK Sails for repair.

Over the next two weeks we set to making *Zillah* seaworthy. After cleaning and drying the bilge, Chris injected epoxy into the decayed wood, and then lay down a two-inch bed of fiberglass over wood ribs and iron floors, in effect creating a hull within the hull. He sweated over heat gun and grinder, chipped away with hammer and chisel, emerging every hour above deck, coated in sweat, dust and fiberglass residue, to revive in the fresh air, consuming a gallon of diluted orange juice each day from twelve-ounce bottles he froze each night. "That's how I manage the heat in Spain."

Nigel in a previous career had been a sound engineer for a touring music group. He grappled with the electrical system, a conundrum of tangled wires, corroded switches and faulty connections. The instrument panel was the master puzzle, a spaghetti of crossed wires, many of them obsolescent remnants of past electrical systems. To rewire the stern running light, he burrowed through the claustrophobic confines of the narrow stern, dragging his large torso through a space designed for a midget.

Between bouts in the bilge, Chris probed and discovered wires, "Corroded to dust," he winced, "could cause an electrical fire."

Less arduous tasks fell to me, installing the wind steering vane, the Life-sling, the mounting board for the dinghy outboard motor, and lashing the life raft to the fore-deck and extra fuel cans to the shrouds. I ran the engine an hour every day to charge the batteries, and when it began to cough and splutter, I changed the fuel filter which was clogged with sludge from the fuel that had sat idle in the tanks over the winter.

With each day the question of *Zillah's* seaworthiness became less problematic.

Mary continued to provide sustenance for the crew, fruit and granola breakfasts and pasta dinners. In the evenings Nigel read Walt Whitman's *Leaves of Grass*, from our bookshelf. Chris read the West Marine catalogue.

Once the bilge was glassed over, the water tanks dropped in and the salon table bolted down, Chris and Nigel moved on board. This gave them a longer working day and they began to develop a routine of shipboard living. "We're ready to sail in a couple days," Chris announced.

But two problems remained that even Chris could not solve. We expected the money transfer to be executed without delay, in this age of rapid communications. But Friday was Bank Holiday in England. Monday was Labor Day in America, so that put it back a week, and we waited impatiently for yet another week. Chris ran through the cash he had brought with him and began running up bills.

The other potential problem was the weather. Hurricane Fabian blew up from the tropics, missing the Caribbean islands, then swung north 500 miles off the East Coast of the United States and passed over Bermuda, wreaking havoc with 140-knot winds. Then it curved northeast over the North Atlantic shipping lanes, right across the route they planned to take. At the same time, Tropical Storm Henri blew up in the Gulf of Mexico, crossed over northern Florida with 60-knot winds, and worked its way up the coast before dissipating out to sea. Meanwhile another cyclonic disturbance formed off the coast of Africa, gathered force to become Hurricane Isabel, and rampaged across the southern Atlantic with 160-knot winds, a Category 5 Hurricane. I tracked the weather each night on internet, printing out a daily report. Where would Isabel hit? Would it veer north and come in on the coast, or blow out to sea. Either way it was not auspicious.

The money transfer finally came. We sprung to action stations with a flurry of last day preparations. At the bank, I withdrew funds, signed a bill of sale that was notarized by the bank officer, and made copies for each party at Office Depot.

Clearing Customs came next, an hour drive to Baltimore where I was informed that I would have to pay 1.5% duty on the sale of a foreign registered yacht and post a $125 bond. They issued a cruising permit for the yacht to leave the dock and sail in

U.S. waters and Coast Guard clearance to leave the country. Chris and Nigel checked out with the U.S. Immigration office, five blocks away.

Back in Annapolis we provisioned at Sam's Club. Two men for 30 days, 60 man-days of food. Their $313.94 bought 50 pounds of potatoes, 20 pounds of rice, 15 pounds of spaghetti, plus supplementary instant rice and pre-cooked spaghetti meals in cans. More tins of ham, tuna, chicken, Spam and corned beef, beef stew, stewed tomatoes, peas, baked beans, soup mixes; 12 pounds of Gouda cheese in waxed balls. Gravy mix, a 32-ounce bottle of minced garlic and Italian seasoning were thrown in for flavoring, and 2 liters of olive oil. A 5-pound box of Bisquick was added and another 5 pounds of long-life bread dough, found at Safeway, that had only to be heated. Fresh food was limited to 6 pounds of apples, 5 pounds of onions, 2 pounds of green peppers. Chris and Nigel debated each item, considering the ratio of cost to caloric value, durability, how long it would keep and how well it would store. It wasn't gourmet but there was no shortage of carbohydrates and protein. They topped off with 8 quarts of orange juice.

"To prevent scurvy?" I asked.

Dusk had settled over Forked Creek by the time the stores were stowed and we pulled in our docking lines. "You take the helm," Chris said, and I realized that he was now owner captain. I had agreed to pilot the boat down the Severn River. As we backed out of the slip at Sappington's Marina for the last time, there was a feeling of finality, the umbilical cord being severed. Motoring through the serpentine inlet, I kept left of the shoal, and *Zillah* crossed the bar.

We picked up the channel markers, green to starboard, red to port going out to sea." The opposite to Europe," I reminded Chris and Nigel, and recited the American mariner's mantra, "Red. Right. Returning." This further confused my instructions for it was opposite outward bound.

"There's enough wind to sail." Chris said, raised the main and unfurled the genoa. He shut down the engine. There was that moment of magic when the drumming of pistons dissolves into the laughter of the water against the hull, the boat lifting as if air born as the sails fill. I leaned into the cockpit as the boat heeled and gripped the helm more firmly.

"It must be hard to give this up," Chris said with unaccustomed sensitivity.

"Yah." What more could I say?

Where the river widened into Round Bay the breeze picked up to fifteen knots. Tightening the sails, I edged closer to the wind. We sailed that night with the full main, which I rarely did. *Zillah* carried too much sail and had a heavy weather helm, so Mary and I had always reefed the main. In the shelter of the bay there were no heading seas and we surged forward with a burst of power. "We're making 6.9 knots," Nigel shouted exuberantly from the navigation table below. *Zillah* shrugged off the lethargy from lying at dock for a year, and came alive again. With her deep keel and narrow beam, classic wooden boat lines, this was what she had been designed for.

An orange glow silhouetted the trees above the river bank to the east. The rising moon, the full moon of September, beamed across the bay in a flood of light. It was a visual poem of the moment that evoked the poetry of memory, thoughts of moonlight passages off Sicily and Guadeloupe and Atlantic high seas.

The realities of the moment interrupted; the depth sounder alarm blared. "Ten feet!" Nigel shouted. "Eight feet!" I headed into the wind, we furled the jib, and motored toward the channel marker off the end of the Sherwood Forest shoal, blinking four seconds each minute. More memories, the thud of lead on coral the time we ran aground in Cuba. "Twelve feet. Fifteen." Nigel affirmed and we glided through moonbeams to the reassuring throb of Perkins power.

"All experience is an arch where through gleams the untraveled world," Tennyson's *Ulysses* said, *"whose margin fades forever and forever when I move."* We passed through the arches of the Severn River bridges, turned at the green beacon on Naval Academy Point, and threaded our way through the yachts anchored in the bay.

I had arranged for Mary to pick me up at the Annapolis Marina fuel dock. I recognized the Shell sign with its own yellow moonlight glow, but my night vision was poor and the dock and pilings were a blur. Chris had to guide me in. Nigel jumped ashore with the bow line. I shook hands with Chris, turned over the helm for the last time, and went forward. I stepped across to the dock, pushed off the bow and *Zillah* slipped into the night and was gone.

Another dramatic discontinuity in my fragmented life, I thought. More than a boat was gone. I stood for a long moment looking into the void.

About The Author

Joe Nold was born and spent his early boyhood in a prairie village in Saskatchewan, Canada. After boarding school near Toronto, he attended the University of British Columbia (UBC). Between his first and second years there, he took his "first sabbatical," cycling down to Los Angeles with friend Rod Nixon, hitch-hiking to Miami, Florida, and sailing on an old cargo ketch through the Panama Canal to Costa Rica.

After earning his law degree from UBC, Joe decided to travel for a year before settling down to a law practice. Teaching in London to finance his travels, he was hooked! Teaching, traveling, and mountain climbing banished all thoughts of a law career. In following years Joe taught in England, Scotland, India, Canada, and the USA. He climbed mountains on five continents.

In 1956 Joe met a lovely American mountain climber, Andrea Lynd, while at the Austrian border helping Hungarian refugees who were escaping the Iron Curtain. Later he and Andy made their way to India, where they were married. Joe taught school, and they trekked the Himalayas together.

Joe and Andy returned to North America and settled near Chicago, where they taught at North Shore Country Day School and rejoiced at the birth of two beautiful daughters, Jennifer and Margaret.

They were lured back to the mountains when Joe was recruited by the fledgling Colorado Outward Bound School (COBS). Joe started as an instructor and then became Director of COBS. After leaving Outward Bound, Joe went to the United World College in New Mexico, where he was Director of the Mountain Search and Rescue Group and coordinated community service projects for the college.

As he approached the age of 65, he thought he could extend his adventuring lifestyle for another decade or so by trading in his mountain boots and heavy backpack for a sailboat. Aboard his lovely old wooden sloop, Zillah, Joe and his wife, Mary, sailed the Caribbean, Atlantic, and Mediterranean for nine years. While in Europe, they also land-cruised in a small camper van during the non-sailing seasons.

After moving ashore near Annapolis, Maryland, Joe began turning his journals and stories into these memoirs, his "shreds and patches" of a peripatetic life. Joe now resides in California with Mary, between the mountains and the sea.

Made in the USA
San Bernardino, CA
27 September 2017